2574

Survey
of Accounting

Survey
of Accounting

Joseph G. Louderback
Clemson University

G. Thomas Friedlob
Clemson University

Franklin J. Plewa
Idaho State University

West Publishing Company
Minneapolis/St. Paul   New York   Los Angeles   San Francisco

WEST'S COMMITMENT TO THE ENVIRONMENT

In 1906, West Publishing Company began recycling materials left over from the production of books. This began a tradition of efficient and responsible use of resources. Today, up to 95 percent of our legal books and 70 percent of our college and school texts are printed on recycled, acid-free stock. West also recycles nearly 22 million pounds of scrap paper annually—the equivalent of 181,717 trees. Since the 1960s, West has devised ways to capture and recycle waste inks, solvents, oils, and vapors created in the printing process. We also recycle plastics of all kinds, wood, glass, corrugated cardboard, and batteries, and have eliminated the use of styrofoam book packaging. We at West are proud of the longevity and the scope of our commitment to our environment.

Cover: East Building, National Gallery of Art, Washington D.C. © Steve Gottlieb
Problem Checking: Marie Archambault
Copyediting: Maggie Jarpey
Text and Cover Design: Peter Thiel/Peter Thiel Design
Illustrations: Precision Graphics
Composition: Carlisle Communications, Ltd.
Production, Prepress, Printing and Binding by West Publishing Company.

Insight 5–1, 168, Reprinted by permission of FORBES magazine. © Forbes Inc., 1988. Insight 5–3 and 5–4, 178–179, Reprinted by permission of FORBES magazine. © Forbes Inc., 1989. Insight 6–1, 206, Reprinted by permission of FORBES magazine, © Forbes, Inc., 1988.

Library of Congress Cataloging in Publication Data

Louderback, Joseph G.
    Survey of accounting / Joseph G. Louderback, G. Thomas Friedlob,
Franklin J. Plewa.
       p.   cm.
    Includes index.
    ISBN 0-314-01041-6
    1. Accounting. 2. Corporations—Accounting. I. Friedlob, G.
Thomas. II. Plewa, Franklin J. III. Title.
HF5635.L887   1993
657—dc20   92-24023
                                                   CIP ∞

CONTENTS IN BRIEF

CONTENTS

Chapter 1   Introduction to Accounting   2

Chapter 4   **Inventories and Cost of Goods
                            Sold   126**

Chapter 7   **Noncurrent Notes, Mortgages, Bonds,
                            and Deferred Taxes   238**

Chapter 8   Corporations: Stockholders' Equity   278

Chapter 9   Statement of Cash Flows   320

Chapter 10   Introduction to Managerial Accounting   354

Chapter 13   Budgeting   456

Chapter 17   Business Combinations: Acquisitions and Consolidated Financial Statements   576

Chapter 18   Auditors, Audit Reports, and Internal Control   608

PREFACE

This book is intended for undergraduate courses offered to non-accounting majors, especially non-business majors. For that reason, we assume nothing about the educational background of students, although, unavoidably, those who have had some exposure to business topics will see more quickly the relevance of some of the material. Nonetheless, we believe that the material is comprehensible by students of any background.

The book emphasizes the uses of accounting information, particularly in the managerial accounting chapters. We did not wish to make the book exhaustive, nor to delve into great detail in most topics. The book is not appropriate for use in a principles of accounting course by students who will go on to intermediate and advanced accounting.

There is ample material for a one-semester course that focuses on either financial or managerial accounting. With supplements, the book can be used for a two-term sequence. Besides the undergraduate survey course, it is useful for an MBA prerequisite, to fulfill the Common Body of Knowledge requirement.

Our objectives in writing this book are:

1. to present as clearly as possible the general principles that govern financial and managerial accounting so that students will be able to read and understand external and internal financial statements and reports.
2. to show how accounting data are used by managers and such outside parties as current and potential stockholders, bondholders, suppliers, and other creditors.
3. to show the relationships and relevance of accounting to other disciplines.
4. to illustrate how accounting operates in everyday economic affairs and influences economic decisions.
5. to show that accounting is not a static field, with every principle already known and every nuance worked out, but rather is evolving and improving.
6. to show that accounting is not cut-and-dried, and that choices abound in methods and techniques used for annual reports as well as for internal reports.
7. to offer flexible coverage to accomodate a variety of needs.

Assignment Material

The book contains ample assignment material ranging from discussion questions to decision cases. Very few questions require only that a student look up a specific term on a particular page. We have tried to order assignments by difficulty and to cover all points in the chapter. Earlier assignments tend to be straightforward and to focus on one or a few major points. Nonetheless, even these can be expanded in class. Later assignments are less straightforward, often contain extraneous information to alert students to that inconvenient characteristic of life, and require some qualitative response in addition to a numerical solution. Assignments can also be used for short examination problems. Some assignments can be solved by computer, using the Lotus 1-2-3 templates available from the publisher; these are designated with logos.

Features

Each chapter (but one) has at least one Demonstration Problem that covers the major analytical points of the chapter. Each chapter has a set of learning objectives so that students can gain some idea of their mastery of the material.

We use the annual reports of Boise Cascade and Wal-Mart extensively. Boise Cascade serves as a continuing example and, in addition to the entire report in the back of the book, selected sections appear in relevant places throughout the text. We use the Wal-Mart annual report for assignment material. Several late assignments in each chapter require that students use the report to answer questions or calculate ratios. Not only do these annual reports impart more realism to examples, illustrations, and assignments, but also afford instructors the opportunity to take up items appearing in them that are not specifically covered in the text.

We introduce financial ratios in appropriate chapters throughout the book (for example, accounts receivable turnover in Chapter 3). Our purpose is to get students thinking about how and why managers and outsiders use financial information, and for what types of decisions. We integrate the material in Chapter 19, which covers financial statement analysis.

Coverage

The first nine chapters are devoted to financial accounting, the next seven to managerial accounting. Chapter 17 covers consolidations, Chapter 18 examines auditing, both internal and external, and Chapter 19 treats the analysis of financial statements. We recommend covering the chapters at least roughly in sequence, though some skipping is possible. Instructors wishing more coverage of managerial accounting may move to Chapter 10 without completing the financial accounting chapters. Chapters 6, 7, or 8 can be omitted without interrupting continuity into the managerial section. Chapter 18 can be covered almost anytime after Chapter 2, and Chapter 19 can be covered after Chapter 7.

Within the managerial section, Chapter 12 can be covered before Chapter 11, but Chapter 14 requires Chapter 11. Chapter 15 requires Appendix B on the time value of money, as do some assignments in Chapter 7 on long-term debt.

Supplements

The solutions manual, prepared by the authors, contains solutions to all assignments, comments on effective use of assignments, and suggestions for taking assignments beyond the stated requirements.

The Test Bank contains multiple choice, matching, true-false, and problem items. It is available both in hard copy and in computerized form (West Test 3.0).

The Study Guide, prepared by the authors, helps students to gain the most from the text. It contains chapter outlines, objective questions, and problems. Solutions to all items are given.

Acknowledgments

We gratefully acknowledge the permission of the Institute of Management Accountants to excerpt from *Management Accounting*. We also wish to acknowledge the following reviewers.

Jan Grasman
Broward Community College

Krishnagopal Menon
Boston University

Raymond T. Holmes, Jr.
Virginia Commonwealth University

Kenneth R. Ferris
Southern Methodist University

Robert C. Elmore
Tennessee Technological Univ.

Jackie G. Williams
Virginia Commonwealth Univ.

Wagih G. Dafashy
College of William and Mary

Linda Nelsestuen
   Northern Illinois University

James P. Trebby
   Marquette University

Allan Drebin
   Northwestern University

Gloria Halpern
   Montgomery College

V. Gopalakrishnan
   George Mason University

Marie Archambault
   Michigan State University

John H. Overton
   University of New Hampshire

Rosalind Cranor
   Virginia Polytechnic Institute and State University

John A. Beegle
   Western Carolina University

Clifford D. Brown
   Bentley College

Peter B. Kenyon
   Humboldt State University

Ted R. Compton
   Ohio University

Abraham J. Simon
   CUNY - Queens College

Special thanks are due to Marie Archambault who made many useful suggestions.

Survey
of Accounting

1

Introduction to Accounting

LEARNING OBJECTIVES

After studying Chapter 1, you should be able to:
1. Describe the purpose of accounting and the difference between financial and managerial accounting.
2. Know what generally accepted accounting principles (GAAP) are and where they come from.
3. Use double-entry accounting to develop an income statement and balance sheet.
4. Explain how the entity concept and the cost, going concern, and realization principles affect modern accounting.
5. Identify the types of assets and equities in the balance sheet.

This book is about accounting. Accounting has been practiced for thousands of years. Accounting records found in Sumeria are among the earliest written documents, dating back to 3000 B.C. Modern accounting can be traced to the Renaissance during the fifteenth century. The first book to describe modern accounting methods was published two years after Columbus discovered America. In fact, Queen Isabella of Spain commissioned an accountant to accompany Columbus on his voyage. Accounting has evolved and improved greatly since its earliest days and is now a well-developed and rational discipline. Accountants have had 5,000 years to refine the system—to make it useful and easy to understand. Most of what you will have to do in accounting will make perfect sense once you learn the fundamental concepts and develop the ability to apply them in new situations. Despite some of the seeming complexities you will encounter in this book, the underlying logic is relatively consistent and reasonable: accounting makes sense. The author of the first modern accounting book is discussed in Insight 1–1.

An accountant accompanied Columbus to the New World.

Accounting has been called the language of business. It has been defined in dozens of ways by various writers, professional organizations,

INSIGHT 1–1
Leonardo da Vinci, Accounting, and the Renaissance

In 1494, Luca Bartolomes Pacioli documented the first modern, double-entry accounting system in his book, *Summa de Arithmetica, Geometria, Proportioni et Proportionalita* (often called, simply, *Summa*). The system was derived from Arabic algebra and was called the Venetian method, because Venetian merchants used it to record their business transactions. Because of this book, Pacioli is known as the "father of accounting," and many accountants picture him as a sort of primitive bookkeeper/author in the drab mold of Ebenezer Scrooge's poor Bob Cratchit.

But only one chapter of Pacioli's book actually dealt with accounting. The remainder was about mathematics, geometry, and proportionality. Pacioli was, in fact, a true Renaissance man, who kept company with artists and scholars and lectured on mathematics, geometry, chess, and military strategy. His work so impressed Leonardo da Vinci that da Vinci became Pacioli's student in mathematics and illustrated Pacioli's second major book on mathematics.

Pacioli's *Summa* was translated into many languages and was responsible for the acceptance of double-entry accounting throughout Europe. The accounting method used by accountants today is essentially Pacioli's Venetian method.*

*Peter Monaghan, "3 Seattle Business Professors Want You to Meet Luca Bartolomes Pacioli, 'Father of Accounting'," *The Chronicle of Higher Education*, 30 January 1991, A3.

and others. Accounting has been referred to as the incompetent explaining the incomprehensible to the uninterested; it also has been called the most important factor in the development of modern economies. Defining accounting is not critical to our needs. Roughly speaking, **accounting** has to do with recording, processing, and reporting financial information to interested parties.

TYPES OF ACCOUNTING

In this book, we will study two types of accounting: managerial accounting and financial accounting. Both have to do with providing information to interested parties.

Managerial Accounting

Managerial accounting is concerned with persons inside the company—its managers. Managers use accounting information to control day-to-day operations and to make decisions about such things as product pricing and equipment replacement. Managerial accounting is used only to satisfy the needs of a company's managers and, as a result, has few rules. The second part of this book deals with managerial accounting.

Financial Accounting

Financial accounting is principally used by businesses. In this book, we are concerned primarily with corporations, which are the most important type of business today. When you work, it will probably be for a corporation. If you consider investing, it might well be in the stock of a corporation. We recognize, of course, that many businesses are owned by one person (proprietorships) or by several people (partnerships) and that these businesses are important. However, we will concentrate on corporations.

Corporations can be owned by many people. To become a part owner of a corporation, you simply buy shares of its stock. In the United States, as in many other countries, there are organized stock exchanges where anyone can buy or sell shares in companies.

The first part of this book deals primarily with financial accounting. Financial accounting is concerned with reporting information about the business to outside parties, such as owners and potential owners (stockholders); creditors, such as banks and suppliers; and governmental agencies. Financial accounting also is used, with some significant modifications, to determine income taxes. Because financial accounting is used to report information to many types of users who have differing needs, many rules govern the presentation of financial accounting information. For an interesting perspective on the rigors of preparing accounting and tax documents, read Insight 1–2.

Just as there are different kinds of accounting, there are different kinds of accountants. Insight 1–3 discusses the credentials of the different types of accounting professionals.

INSIGHT 1–2
Was Murphy an Accountant?

Murphy's Law states that "if something can go wrong, it will." Captain Ed Murphy was a pilot in the U.S. Air Force during World War II, and when he uttered the statement that long since has passed into folklore, he was referring to the problems encountered in the increasingly complicated technology of aviation. But Murphy's Law seems to apply to all facets of life and summarizes a phenomenon currently recognized (more or less seriously) as "the revenge effect" or "revenge theory." Revenge theory holds that the solutions to many problems create unintended effects every bit as troublesome as the original problems themselves. Or, as defined in *Harvard Magazine,* "The world we have created seems to be getting even, twisting our cleverness against us."*

This, of course, is as true in accounting as elsewhere. Take, for example, accounting spreadsheets. When done by hand, they are extremely time-consuming. Before computers, accountants created spreadsheets with great care and only when necessary. Today, computerized packages have made spreadsheets much more easy to prepare—but at the cost to accountants of, first, having to learn the computer software and, second (because they are so easy), having to do many, many more spreadsheets than ever before. And because everyone has a spreadsheet package, the extra effort gives an advantage to no one.

The Business Council on the Reduction of Paperwork estimated that in 1988, following the 1986 congressional effort to simplify the tax code, the average time to complete Internal Revenue Service Form 1040 (the basic tax form) rose to 18.6 hours. The cost of preparing a tax return for a small company may be as much as 2% of total sales revenue—and no wonder: the rules on passive activity, for example, take 196 pages simply to define "activity!" Simplification?

*Edward Turner, "Revenge Theory," *Harvard Magazine,* March/April 1991, 27–30.

INSIGHT 1–3
CIA, CMA, CPA: Accounting's Alphabet Soup

Three certifications are available to accountants who satisfy the requirements. Two are credentials in auditing. Accountants who choose to work in industry or government, such as for Coca-Cola Company or the city of Boston, may strive to become Certified Internal Auditors (CIAs) or Certified Management Accountants (CMAs). Accountants who choose to work for public accounting firms, such as Ernest & Young or Price Waterhouse, eventually must become Certified Public Accountants (CPAs). All three certifications require the candidate to pass a rigorous, multipart examination and to meet experience requirements. Due to the expanding body of accounting knowledge, many colleges and universities are developing five-year programs to better prepare their graduates. Many states already require five years of college preparation before graduates are eligible to take the CPA examination. Each of the certifications and the areas covered in the certification examination are listed below.

- **CIA** Theory and Practice of Internal Auditing (two parts, 3½ hours each)
  Management, Quantitative Methods, and Information Systems (3½ hours)
  Accounting, Finance, and Economics (3½ hours)

- **CMA** Economics, Finance, and Management (4 hours)
  Financial Accounting (4 hours)
  Management Accounting I: Internal Reporting and Analysis (4 hours)
  Management Accounting II: Decision Analysis, Including Modeling and Information Systems (4 hours)

- **CPA** Auditing (3½ hours)
  Business Law (3½ hours)
  Accounting Theory (3½ hours)
  Accounting Practice (9 hours)

FINANCIAL ACCOUNTING REPORTS

Financial accounting is governed by **generally accepted accounting principles** (GAAP), which are rules, criteria, and guidelines for practice designed to give structure to the vocabulary of accounting to give the language of business meaning. These principles are necessary because many financial accounting reports are widely distributed. Anyone can obtain the annual reports of most large companies. The annual report contains the company's financial statements, which are the basis of many decisions.

Financial accounting is governed by generally accepted accounting principles (GAAP).

People decide whether to buy, sell, or hold the stock of a company based partly on the information contained in its financial statements. They decide whether to extend credit to it, or whether to sign long-term contracts with it based on the company's financial statements. There is, accordingly, a public trust in accounting because so many people use it for these important purposes.

In addition, many people use financial accounting information to advise others who make decisions. Major stock brokerage firms maintain research departments staffed by analysts who carefully monitor groups of companies. Analysts recommend buying, selling, and holding stock, and the brokerage firm passes along these recommendations to its customers. Other firms specialize in research and sell their findings, often through periodic reports, to subscribers. GAAP originate from several sources. One very powerful source is custom and tradition. More formal sources are the **Financial Accounting Standards Board (FASB)** and the **Securities and Exchange Commission** (SEC). The FASB is a private, independent body sponsored by the accounting profession. The SEC is the agency of the U.S. government charged with overseeing the operations of securities exchanges such as the New York Stock Exchange. We shall have more to say about these standard-setting bodies in later chapters.

GENERAL-PURPOSE FINANCIAL STATEMENTS

Three fundamental financial statements, called **general purpose financial statements,** are included in annual reports to shareholders:

1. The **balance sheet.**
2. The **income statement.**
3. The **statement of cash flows.**

Other statements are sometimes included but are not mandatory. Governmental agencies, such as the Internal Revenue Service, require some but usually not all of these statements. Other interested parties, such as creditors, might require different combinations of statements, based on their specific needs. Chapter 1 introduces you to the basic financial statements, illustrates them, and briefly describes how they are constructed.

The Entity Concept

Financial statements are prepared for a particular economic entity that is accounted for separately from all other entities. Although this might seem to be an obvious concept, it is sometimes not. The most common difficulties with the **entity concept** arise when events take place that affect the owners of a business but do not affect the business itself. For example, if you bought 100 shares of stock in General Motors Corporation (GMC) on the New York Stock Exchange, you would, in all likelihood, buy these shares through a broker from another person. You would probably never meet that person or even find out who he or she was. That person is affected by the transaction and so are you, but GMC is not. GMC does not care who owns its shares, except that it has to know to whom to send dividend checks and annual reports.

Financial statements are for an economic entity accounted for separately from all other entities.

GMC, you, and the person from whom you bought the stock are all accounting entities. Each of you accounts for your activities as entities separate from all others. GMC notes the change in ownership but does not make an accounting entry for the sale of its stock. The person who sold the stock accounts for the sale and any gain or loss on the sale. You record your purchase. Be sure you understand what *entity* is being accounted for in any given situation.

The Balance Sheet Equation

Accounting is based on a simple relationship that can be explained in two different ways. We present both views of the accounting relationship because some transactions can be understood better using the logic of one view or the other.

Resources and Their Sources

All the economic resources that a company owns came from somewhere. The dollar amount of resources must equal the dollar amount of sources. The basic accounting equation can be stated as:

Resources = Their Sources

$$\text{Resources} = \text{Their Sources}$$

The accounting term for the resources owned by the company is **assets.** (This and the following terms are explained more completely later.) The two sources of a company's assets are borrowing (debt) and owners' investment. The dollar amount of assets must be equal to the dollar amount of debts and owners' investment:

$$\text{Assets} = \text{Debts} + \text{Owners' Investment}$$

The accounting term for debts is **liabilities.** Another name for owners' investments is **owners' equity.** Owners' equity includes both the owners' initial investment and reinvestments of company earnings not distributed to owners. The **accounting equation,** or **balance sheet equation,** in its final form, is thus:

$$\text{Assets} = \text{Liabilities} + \text{Owners' Equities}$$

Properties and Property Rights

Another way to explain the logic of the accounting equation is to think in terms of properties and property rights. Following this logic, since all properties are owned by someone, the dollar amount of properties must equal the dollar amount of property rights:

Properties = Property Rights

$$\text{Properties} = \text{Property Rights}$$

Properties are assets; the accounting term for property rights is **equities.** Because all properties are owned by someone, the dollar amount of assets must equal the dollar amount of equities:

$$\text{Assets} = \text{Equities}$$

Equities are interests in the assets or claims on them. A homeowner has equity in a house but the mortgage holder also has an interest, or claim, on the house. The equation simply states that *someone* has equity interests in all assets shown on a company's balance sheet. The interests represented include those of creditors (such as suppliers, employees, and debtholders) and those of owners. Still expressed in terms of property rights, the equation can be:

Assets = Liabilities + Owners' Equity

$$\text{Assets} = \text{Creditors' Equity} + \text{Owners' Equity}$$

The equity interests of creditors are liabilities, and the balance sheet equation, once again, is:

$$\text{Assets} = \text{Liabilities} + \text{Owners' Equity}$$

The balance sheet equation is fundamental to accounting. It provides a system of checks on the accuracy of the accounting system. This system of checks is called the **double-entry accounting system,** because each economic event must affect the balance sheet equation in two ways if the equation is to be kept in balance. For instance, if a company is formed by a $10,000 investment in stock, two components of the equation must be increased to show the effect of this transaction: assets (cash) and owners' equity. If either assets or owners' equity is not increased, then the equation will not balance:

$$\begin{array}{rcl} \text{Assets} & = & \text{Liabilities} + \text{Owners' Equity} \\ +\$10,000 = & 0 & + \quad \$10,000 \end{array}$$

If the company then borrows another $20,000 from a bank, two more effects must be recorded. Assets are increased by the cash received and the property rights of the bank are recorded:

	Assets	=	Liabilities	+	Owners' Equity
	+$10,000 =		0	+	$10,000
	+20,000 =		+20,000	+	0
Total	$30,000 =		$20,000	+	$10,000

The treatment of other transactions is illustrated later in the section on developing the balance sheet.

BALANCE SHEET

The **balance sheet** shows, subject to GAAP, the assets, liabilities, and owners' equity of a company or other entity at a particular point in time. The balance sheet is often called the Statement of Financial Position, because it shows the *financial condition,* or *position,* of the company at a particular point in time. Balance sheets are typically prepared quarterly as well as annually for financial reporting purposes. For internal reporting purposes, they are usually prepared monthly. The balance sheet is based on the accounting equation and has two sections: the asset section and the equity section. As with the accounting equation, assets must equal equities.

Assets

Assets are resources.

The term "asset" has been defined in various ways by various authors and by authoritative bodies such as the FASB and its predecessor, the Accounting Principles Board. A good working definition is that an **asset** is an economic resource under the control of the entity. Let us examine this definition for a moment. First, an economic resource must have some value to the entity: it must be something that the entity can use in conducting its business. Assets include such obviously valuable items as cash, inventories of product, buildings, and machinery. Second, the

INSIGHT 1–4
Valuing Corporate Image

In the 1990s, car manufacturers are finding customer tastes in sporty cars to be fickle and elusive. Such models as the Ford Probe, the Nissan 240SX, and the Geo Storm give their manufacturers a first-year sales boost, but decline by 20–50% in the second year. The buyers of hot, sporty, new cars are young (in their twenties and early thirties), are often women, and do not have the automobile brand loyalty that their parents have. Still, automobile manufacturers invest hundreds of millions of dollars in sporty car models that may have a shelf life of only a year or two. In *The Wall Street Journal*, Bradley Stertz says: "[F]addish cars are worth the risk, the companies believe, because they can lend their youthful, sporty image to an entire model lineup—and thus draw curious shoppers into showrooms."* For example, sales of all Mazda models benefited when the Miata convertible was introduced in 1989.

"The gray area called image is one thing on every company's balance sheet that's hard to quantify but essential to go after," says Richard N. Beattie, Marketing Plans Manager for Ford Motor Company's Ford Division.*

Where is "image" in a company's balance sheet? The answer: it isn't there. Ford Motor Company's 1990 annual report shows no such asset. Image is not on the balance sheet because all assets are shown at their historical costs and "image" is not purchased directly. The Ford balance sheet shows inventories of finished products at their cost of $3.6 million. These inventories doubtlessly contain many of the cars that give Ford its "image." The cars have an historical purchase cost, but the image they project does not. As a result, the cars are shown as assets in the balance sheet; image isn't.

*Bradley A. Stertz, "Even Successful Sporty Cars Die Young, but Auto Makers Still Take the Gamble," *The Wall Street Journal* (April 23, 1991): B1, B6. Reprinted with permission of The Wall Street Journal. © 1991 Dow Jones & Company, Inc. All Rights Reserved WORLDWIDE.

not necessarily) means that the entity owns the asset. For example, a leased building or piece of equipment may be an asset to the company that uses it, even though this company does not own the item. Generally speaking, however, entities do own their assets.[1] Assets can be physical, such as buildings, machinery, and land. They also can be intangible, such as patents and copyrights. Insight 1–4 describes one type of intangible asset that accountants are unable to value.

[1] Some would say that the example of a leased asset is incorrect—that the company leasing it owns the *right* to use the asset and that this right (not the physical item) is the asset. In this text, we do not wish to enter into such theoretical arguments.

As we have said, GAAP give structure to the language of business. Two very important generally accepted accounting principles that relate to assets are the cost principle and the going concern principle.

The Cost Principle

For the most part, assets appear on the balance sheet at cost—the amount that the company spent to acquire them. In accounting terminology, this is referred to as the **cost principle.** As a general rule, assets are not shown at their "values" in the sense of what they would bring on the open market. Goods on hand that cost $2 million and will be sold for $6 million appear at $2 million. Land bought 20 years ago for $1 million will appear at $1 million today, whether it could now be sold for $1 million, $20 million, or $0.4 million. This use of cost might seem counter-intuitive, but there is a good deal of justification for it, as we will show throughout the book.

Going Concern Principle

One reason for the use of costs, as opposed to market values, in balance sheets, is the principle that financial statements should reflect the business as a going concern, not as if it is to be liquidated. According to this **going concern principle,** using market prices for assets reflects the sale price of the business, not its value as a continuing entity. Market value can mean two things: resale value or replacement cost. *Resale value* is the amount that the company could sell the asset for; *replacement cost* is what the company would have to pay to acquire the asset. In many cases, the two amounts will be close, but in some cases, they will be far apart. We must therefore be careful about using the term "market value" without specifying which definition is meant. To illustrate the importance of the going concern concept as support for valuing assets at cost, we turn to an example.

Suppose that General Motors Corporation spends several million dollars for equipment designed especially to manufacture one model Chevrolet. What is the resale value of the equipment? Probably very little, because the equipment has only one purpose; it cannot be used by anyone except General Motors because no one else makes Chevrolets. No one would buy it unless it could be used for the specific purpose for which it was built. So if it were shown at market resale price, it would be shown at zero, yet it is obviously a valuable asset. After the design of the model changes, the machine will carry no value on the balance sheet because it will then have no value either as part of a going concern or as an asset to be sold.

The point is that many assets have value only as they fit into an integrated whole, not as separate pieces. What about the replacement cost of the equipment referred to above? That could be much higher than the amount GM spent for it. The replacement cost could be valuable information for some purposes, but it is not especially helpful unless there is some reason to suspect that the company will have to replace the equipment.

Equities

Equities are of two general types: liabilities and owners' equity. The equities of a company are the sources of its assets—its financing. Equities also represent the claims on a company's assets that arise because the equity holders have financed the company in one way or another. Owners invest in a company by buying its stock, banks invest in a company by lending it money, suppliers extend credit, employees work for a week or two before being paid, and so on. All of these claims are represented on the equity side of the balance sheet.

Liabilities

Liabilities are amounts owed to suppliers, employees, taxing authorities, banks, and so on. For the most part, liabilities are payable in cash, but there are exceptions. For instance, the balance sheet of a magazine publisher usually shows a liability with a title such as Advance Deposits on Subscriptions. The title indicates that the magazine is obligated to deliver copies to people who have paid for their subscriptions in advance. The liability is satisfied by the delivery of magazines, rather than by the payment of cash.

Liabilities are debts.

Owners' Equity

Owners' equity represents the interests of the owners of the company. For the most part in this book, we deal with corporations and owners' equity is referred to as **stockholders' equity** or **shareholders' equity.** In a sole proprietorship or partnership, terms such as *owner's equity* or *partners' equity* would appear instead. Stockholders' equity is a residual amount, representing what is left over when liabilities are subtracted from assets. This is an intuitive notion, much as we speak of someone's equity, or ownership right, in a house or car as the value of the house or car less any amount owed on it.

In a corporation, stockholders' equity consists of two basic parts: paid-in-capital and retained earnings. **Paid-in-capital** represents the amounts paid to the corporation by stockholders—the amounts that the corporation received when the stock was issued. Subsequent sales of stock by owners (stockholders) do not change this initial amount. Thus, if all shares of stock were originally issued at $30 and the stock now trades on an exchange at $100, the amount shown for the shares in the balance sheet is still $30.

Retained earnings is not cash.

Retained earnings is a tricky concept. **Retained earnings** represents the total income (or loss) that the company has earned since its inception less the total dividends it has paid to stockholders. Essentially, retained earnings is the total of all earnings reinvested in the company over the years. Retained earnings is not cash, it is a source of assets, not an asset. The earnings retained are reinvested in inventory, equipment, and all the other assets the company uses in its operations. This concept will become clearer as we go on.

INCOME STATEMENT AND STATEMENT OF CASH FLOWS

The **income statement,** generally thought to be the most important financial statement, reports on the operations of the company for a period, such as a year, quarter, or month. The income statement shows the revenues and expenses that the company generated during the period. Briefly, revenues and expenses are increases and decreases, respectively, in owners' equity from operations. Sales of stock are increases and distributions of dividends are decreases that do not result from operations. Thus, changes in owners' equity can occur from four items.

Owners' equity is increased by:

■ Revenues earned
■ Investment by owners

Owners' equity is decreased by:

■ Expenses incurred
■ Dividends paid to owners

Revenues and expenses are categories of accounts, just like assets, liabilities, and owners' equity. The expanded accounting equation, including revenues and expenses, follows.

$$\text{Assets} = \text{Liabilities} + \text{Owners' Equity} + \text{Revenues} - \text{Expenses}$$

This equation contains all the categories of accounts that accountants use. There are no others.

Revenues

Revenues are increases in owners' equity produced by inflows of assets as a result of doing business. As properties increase, owners' property rights also increase. Revenues are amounts paid or promised to be paid by customers or clients. The revenues of a law firm, for example, are the fees it charges clients; the revenues of a retail store are its sales.

The Realization Principle

One important point about revenue is that it is not necessary to receive cash to generate revenue. Assets must be increased, but cash need not be received. If the business sells on credit to a customer, it still recognizes revenue, provided there is reasonable evidence that the customer will pay. The amount receivable from the customer is recorded as an asset. Recording revenue at the point of sale is known as the **realization principle.** This principle states that revenue is recorded when the earnings process is substantially complete. This, in turn, means that revenues usually are recognized when a service is performed or when goods are sold. Again, reasonable likelihood of payment is assumed.

It is not necessary to receive cash to generate revenue.

Expenses

Expenses are decreases in owners' equity resulting from outflows of assets (or inflows of liabilities) from doing business. Expenses result when the company consumes the benefit vested in its assets. This concept is a bit abstract, so let us look at two examples. A retail store keeps an inventory of merchandise. Merchandise is an asset because it can provide future benefits in the form of potential sales. When goods are sold, the cost of the goods sold becomes an expense. The outflow of inventory consumes the benefit and results in an expense. Both properties and owners' property rights decrease. (Of course, the sale also generates revenue, usually in amounts greater than the expense.)

An inflow of a liability perhaps is best illustrated by salaries. People usually are paid once a week or once every other week. But as they work, the employer becomes liable to pay the salaries its employees have already earned. Thus, a liability is increasing, as is an expense. Owners' property rights are decreased by the increasing property rights of the employees. There is an increase in a liability and a decrease in owners' equity (shown as an increase in an expense)—two effects that keep the accounting equation in balance. If salaries are $3,000, the effect is

$$\text{Assets} = \text{Liabilities} + \text{Owners' Equity} + \text{Revenues} - \text{Expenses}$$
$$+\$3,000 \qquad\qquad\qquad\qquad -\$3,000$$

The difficulty with expenses comes when a payment is made that has some future benefit, such as an insurance premium. Suppose that we pay our premium for the calendar year 19X2 on January 1, 19X2. On January 31, we have used only one-twelfth of the insurance coverage, so one-twelfth of the premium is an expense. (The benefit has been consumed in the form of protection received.) Eleven-twelfths of the premium is still an asset, providing benefit for the rest of the year. As each month goes by, we recognize another one-twelfth as an expense.

Everyone recognizes income in their personal lives, but it is not quite such a simple procedure in business. The following section discusses some of the major points of accounting for income, and much of the early part of the book is devoted to elaborating the determination of income. The recognition of revenues and expenses regardless of when cash flows is called **accrual accounting,** which is the basis of financial reporting under GAAP. We do not discuss the statement of cash flows until Chapter 9. This statement is a required part of general-purpose financial statements but is quite specialized. Although simple in concept, the statement of cash flows can be complicated to develop and to understand. This is, however, a good time to clear up the common misconception that income and cash flow are the same. They are not! Cash flow is very important (for instance, a company can go bankrupt if it cannot pay its creditors), but in accounting, the relationship between income and cash flow is far from direct.

The **matching principle,** which states that costs should be matched against the revenues they generate, is important in determining expenses. Thus, the cost of merchandise is not recorded as an expense when it is bought, but when it is sold. The cost of insurance is expensed as the coverage expires, not when the company pays for the policy.

ILLUSTRATIVE FINANCIAL STATEMENTS

Exhibit 1−1 presents income statements and balance sheets for Xest Company for the years ended December 31, 19X5 and December 31, 19X6. Let us look at these statements in some detail.

The balance sheet shows the name of the company, the title of the financial statement, and the date for which the balance sheet was prepared. The balance sheet is prepared "as of" a point in time. The income statement, in contrast, shows income for a specified period, such as "for the years ended. . . ." Presenting financial statements for two years side-by-side is common practice because it facilitates comparisons. Notice that the dollar amounts are in thousands of dollars. Financial statement numbers are rounded off, not shown to the last cent. The balance sheet is called a **classified balance sheet** because assets and liabilities are separated into two useful categories: current and noncurrent.

The balance sheet is prepared "as of" a point in time.

Exhibit 1–1
Financial Statements of Xest Company

Xest Company
Balance Sheets as of December 31 (millions of dollars)

	19X6	19X5
Assets		
Current assets:		
Cash	$ 62.2	$ 33.7
Accounts receivable, net	180.2	120.2
Inventory	190.1	230.6
Prepayments	18.2	16.3
Total current assets	450.7	400.8
Plant and equipment, cost	1,290.0	1,150.0
Accumulated depreciation	(280.0)	(250.0)
Net plant and equipment	1,010.0	900.0
Other assets	90.0	80.0
Total assets	$1,550.7	$1,380.8
Equities		
Current liabilities:		
Accounts payable	$ 110.0	$ 105.2
Bank loan	21.2	18.9
Accrued expenses	40.0	15.0
Total current liabilities	171.2	139.1
Long-term bonds, 9%, due 19X9	510.0	490.0
Total liabilities	681.2	629.1
Common stock	639.4	551.7
Retained earnings	230.1	200.0
Total stockholders' equity	$ 869.5	$ 751.7
Total equities	$1,550.7	$1,380.8

Continued

Current Assets

Virtually all balance sheets classify assets as either current or noncurrent. A **current asset** will be either converted into cash or used in the course of business within one operating cycle or one year, whichever

**Exhibit 1–1
Continued**

Xest Company
Income Statements and Statements of Retained Earnings
for the years ended December 31

	19X6	19X5
Sales	$1,330.3	$1,085.8
Cost of goods sold	812.1	672.3
Gross profit	518.2	413.5
Operating expenses:		
Salaries, wages, and commissions	180.0	160.1
Depreciation	40.4	33.2
Interest	48.6	42.8
Other	59.6	16.7
Total operating expenses	328.6	252.8
Income before taxes	189.6	160.7
Income taxes	84.8	73.2
Net income	$ 104.8	$ 87.5
Retained earnings, beginning of year	200.0	156.1
Less dividends	74.7	43.6
Retained earnings, end of year	$ 230.1	$ 200.0

Current assets are short-term assets.

is longer. Most current assets will be converted into cash. Accounts receivable will be collected in cash (for the most part); inventory will be sold and cash ultimately will be collected. The exception is assets such as prepayments. A good example of a prepayment is for insurance coverage. Businesses, like all of us, typically pay for insurance coverage in advance, creating an asset—the right to have insurance coverage for some future period. The value of the right (the amount of the asset) declines as time passes. The point is that the asset will not be converted into cash; instead, it will be used up, or consumed, in the course of business.

The other defining point—that the benefit of the asset will be used up within one year or one operating cycle, whichever is greater—is not usually troublesome. An operating cycle is the period of time that it takes a business to go from cash to cash: to use cash to acquire goods (by purchase or manufacture), sell them, and collect the cash for the sale. The cycle can be very short, as it is for a supermarket where goods turn over very rapidly and customers normally pay cash. But the cycle also can be very long; tobacco products and some alcoholic beverages are examples. A cigarette manufacturer buys tobacco and cures it for some time, often three years. Thus, the operating cycle is over three years. A distiller might age liquor in inventory for ten or more years.

The point of the operating cycle, vis a vis the year, should not be overemphasized. Inventory is the asset most affected by the "whichever is longer" clause. The one-year rule covers the vast majority of companies.

Xest's current assets are cash, accounts receivable, inventory, and prepayments. We shall cover each of these in greater detail later in the text, but for now the following basic descriptions are adequate. **Cash** consists of money on hand and on deposit. **Accounts receivable** are amounts owed by customers. The word "net" used with accounts receivable means that the amount shown is what the company expects to receive, which is less than the total amount it is owed. The difference is accounts that managers do not expect to collect. **Inventory** consists of goods held for resale—the stock in trade of the business. **Prepayments** are items paid in advance, such as insurance.

Noncurrent Assets

All assets that are not classified as current are noncurrent. **Noncurrent assets** have lives longer than one year or one operating cycle and, for the most part, are used in the business and are not converted into cash. Noncurrent assets are of several types. The most common long-lived assets are the property, plant, and equipment used to manufacture products.

Property, Plant, and Equipment

Most companies, especially manufacturers, own property, plant, and equipment. Land, buildings, machinery, office equipment, and all other long-lived physical assets used in the business appear in this category. **Accumulated depreciation** is the amount of depreciation that the company has taken on its assets since they were purchased. This is the amount of the asset cost that is charged off as an expense as the asset is used and its benefit is consumed. Accumulated depreciation does not represent, contrary to popular belief, an amount of cash that the company sets aside to replace its assets. Nor is it the change in the market value of an asset from the beginning to the end of the period. This confusion and others associated with depreciation will receive considerable attention later in the book.

Other Noncurrent Assets

As the term suggests, this category is used to show assets that do not fit neatly into any of the enumerated categories. Examples of other assets depend on the company and on the types of business that it conducts. Some intangible assets, such as patents and copyrights, might appear in this category.

Equities

Liabilities also can be classified as current and noncurrent, paralleling the distinction on the asset side of the balance sheet. **Current liabilities** are due within one year or one operating cycle; **noncurrent liabilities** are due after one year.

Xest has current liabilities consisting of accounts payable, accrued expenses, and a bank loan (see Exhibit 1–1). **Accounts payable** are amounts due to trade creditors (the companies from which Xest buys goods). Accrued expenses are the opposite of prepayments and usually represent amounts owed for services. A good example is the salaries and wages that are earned by workers but are unpaid as of the balance sheet date. Another is estimated amounts owed for utilities not yet billed.

The bank loan, shown as a current liability, also is due within one year. Long-term liabilities for Xest are bonds payable. The balance sheet in Exhibit 1–1 shows the year the bonds are due and the interest rate they bear.

Xest's stockholders' equity section contains two items. At this stage, we are going to ignore distinctions in types of stock and simply show (1) the retained earnings accumulated over the life of the company and (2) the amount paid to Xest by the people who purchased the stock.

INCOME STATEMENT

Xest Company earns revenues by selling products. The first expense is **cost of goods sold.** Other expenses consist of more or less self-explanatory items common to most companies. Salaries, commissions, utilities, and miscellaneous expenses are just what they seem to be. Depreciation is different. **Depreciation** represents an allocation of the cost of long-lived, productive assets over their useful lives. For now, consider an example. The company has fixed assets that cost $100,000 and have an estimated useful life of ten years. Each year, then, the company recognizes $10,000 depreciation expense ($100,000/10 years). As previously emphasized, depreciation is not the decline in the market value of the company's assets.

Revenue − Expenses = Income

The income statement also incorporates a **Statement of Retained Earnings,** which details the activity in retained earnings during a period. This statement typically shows net income and dividends for the period. We see from the statement in Exhibit 1–1 that Xest paid $74,700 in dividends in 19X6 and $43,600 in 19X5.

This completes our brief introduction to the basic financial statements. We now turn to an example of how the values on financial statements are developed.

DEVELOPING FINANCIAL STATEMENTS

TechHi Company was incorporated by Jim and Carol Watson on December 31, 19X0 for the purpose of buying and selling computer peripheral equipment. At that time, the Watsons paid $20,000 total into the corporation's bank account, receiving 1,000 shares each (2,000 shares total) of the company's common stock.

Investment in New Corporation

After this transaction, the amounts on the balance sheet of TechHi appeared as follows:

TechHi Company
Balance Sheet
As of December 31, 19X0

Assets		Owners' Equity	
Cash	$20,000	Common stock	$20,000
Total assets	$20,000	Total equities	$20,000

Note one very important point at the outset: the Watsons themselves are no better or worse off than they were before they made the investment in the corporation. They now have $20,000 less cash in their own personal accounts, but they own $20,000 of stock (equity) in the corporation, a new economic entity, which has the $20,000 cash. An *economic entity* is an activity for which separate accounting records can be created. In accounting, we focus on the entity that we are accounting for, and that entity is now TechHi (not the Watsons). Accordingly, we do not worry about how much each of the Watsons has invested in the company; we only record that the total investment was $20,000. (For some purposes not related to accounting, the corporation must keep records indicating how many shares of stock each stockholder owns. Determining what amount each shareholder should receive in dividends is one reason; another is counting absentee ballots that stockholders send in for annual meetings.)

Rent of Store

TechHi rented a store on a six-month lease at $1,000 per month, paying $6,000 in advance for the entire period. Note that the company now has an asset—the right to use the store premises for six months (for which it has paid)—although part of the asset will be used up each month. After this transaction, the balance sheet shows the following.

TechHi Company
Balance Sheet
As of January 1, 19X1

Assets		Equities	
Cash ($20,000 − $6,000)	$14,000		
Prepaid rent	6,000	Common stock	$20,000
Total assets	$20,000	Total equities	$20,000

As the company uses the premises, the asset Prepaid Rent will decline until, at the end of six months, it will show a zero balance. Although the asset is being used up every day, we usually wait until the end of each month to account for the use.

Purchase of Merchandise

TechHi bought $28,000 worth of merchandise from a manufacturer, agreeing to pay for the goods in 30 days. This type of purchase is called a *purchase on account* or *on open account*. In addition to purchasing for cash or on open account, companies sometimes give promissory notes when they make a purchase. A purchase on account is not paid for but is not secured by a formal note. A formal note accrues interest and is a stronger legal claim than an open account. The company now has a new asset, Inventory, and a liability, called Accounts Payable. After this transaction, the balance sheet shows the following.

TechHi Company
Balance Sheet
As of January 5, 19X1

Assets		Equities	
Cash	$14,000	Accounts payable	$28,000
Inventory	28,000		
Prepaid rent	6,000	Common stock	20,000
Total assets	$48,000	Total equities	$48,000

Sale of Merchandise

During January, TechHi sold merchandise for $29,000, all on open account. The merchandise had cost TechHi $17,000. This transaction is a bit more complicated than the previous ones, because it affects the income statement as well as the balance sheet. A new asset, Accounts Receivable, is created, and another asset, Inventory, declines. But the increase of $29,000 and the decrease of $17,000 leaves $12,000, which is the profit on the sale. (We are showing only the balance sheet here. Remember from our discussion of revenues and expenses that the $29,000 is also revenue, increasing owners' equity, and the $17,000 is also an expense, decreasing owners' equity. The net effect is an increase of $12,000 in owners' equity—the same increase we determined by considering only the balance sheet.)

TechHi Company
Balance Sheet
As of January 20, 19X1

Assets		Equities	
Cash	$14,000	Accounts payable	$28,000
Accounts receivable	29,000		
Inventory ($28,000 −			
$17,000)	11,000	Common stock	20,000
Prepaid rent	6,000	Retained earnings	12,000
Total assets	$60,000	Total equities	$60,000

Payment of Salaries and Other Expenses

TechHi paid its clerks and the Watsons $4,700 in salaries, all in cash. It also paid $800 for utilities and $2,500 for other expenses. Total payments were $8,000. The salaries were paid after work was performed, so that the salaries are an expense, not an asset (as TechHi would have if it paid salaries in advance). These transactions reduce income for the period and therefore reduce Retained Earnings.

TechHi Company
Balance Sheet
As of January 31, 19X1

Assets		Equities	
Cash ($14,000 − $8,000)	$ 6,000	Accounts payable	$28,000
Accounts receivable	29,000		
Inventory	11,000	Common stock	20,000
Prepaid rent	6,000	Retained earnings	4,000*
Total assets	$52,000	Total equities	$52,000

*$12,000 − $4,700 − $800 − $2,500 = $4,000

Payment of Dividends

Dividends are distributions of earnings and are not expenses.

As stockholders, the Watsons are entitled to dividends. Dividends are distributions of company earnings and are not expenses. Assume that TechHi paid $1,000 in dividends on the stock. The dividends reduce cash and the earnings retained in the business.

TechHi Company
Balance Sheet
As of January 31, 19X1

Assets		Equities	
Cash ($6,000 − $1,000)	$ 5,000	Accounts payable	$28,000
Accounts receivable	29,000		
Inventory	11,000	Common stock	20,000
Prepaid rent	6,000	Retained earnings	3,000*
Total assets	$51,000	Total equities	$51,000

*$4,000 − $1,000 = $3,000

End of Month

The end of the month is not a transaction in the sense in which we have dealt with transactions so far. But it is an event that requires our attention. Can you think why? Remember that the company paid $6,000 for six months rent at the beginning of the month, creating the asset Prepaid Rent. The month is over and the company has used up one month's worth of rent, so we must take care of the expiration of some of the Prepaid Rent. We do this by reducing the asset by $1,000 (to $5,000) and reducing Retained Earnings by $1,000. The $1,000 benefit is now used up, or consumed: it is an expense; it is no longer an asset. The final balance sheet follows.

TechHi Company
Balance Sheet
As of January 31, 19X1

Assets		Equities	
Cash	$ 5,000	Accounts payable	$28,000
Accounts receivable	29,000		
Inventory	11,000		
Prepaid rent ($6,000 − $1,000)	5,000	Common stock	20,000
		Retained earnings	2,000*
Total assets	$50,000	Total equities	$50,000

*$3,000 − $1,000

Accounting for the expiration of the prepaid rent is an example of a class of transactions, or events, called *adjustments*. An **adjustment** is a change that is made in the financial records to keep them up-to-date. In our example, we have been keeping the balance sheet up-to-date and accurate, except that throughout the month we did not periodically adjust the amount of prepaid rent. Having made this adjustment, we now can prepare an income statement for TechHi for January.

An adjustment is a change to the records to create up-to-date financial statements.

TechHi Company
Income Statement
For the month ended January, 31, 19X1

Sales		$29,000
Cost of goods sold		17,000
Gross profit		12,000
Operating expenses:		
Salaries	$4,700	
Utilities	800	
Rent	1,000	
Other	2,500	
Total operating expenses		9,000
Income		$ 3,000

We also can prepare a Statement of Retained Earnings for January. The Statement of Retained Earnings, like the Income Statement, shows activity for a period of time rather than balances as of a certain date.

TechHi Company
Statement of Retained Earnings
For the month ended January 31, 19X1

Retained earnings, January 1, 19X1	$ 0
Income for January	3,000
Subtotal	$3,000
Less dividends for January	1,000
Retained earnings, January 31, 19X1	$2,000

Preparing a new balance sheet after each transaction is tedious and, fortunately, unnecessary. The Appendix to Chapter 1 shows a much simpler and much more efficient way to keep track of accounts.

PRACTICAL APPLICATION

As we introduce you to the principles that govern accounting and financial reporting, we will provide real-world examples by continually using the annual reports of two actual companies: Boise Cascade and Wal-Mart. These annual reports are located at the back of the book. In each chapter on accounting basics and financial reporting, we discuss Boise Cascade, but we leave Wal-Mart for you to explore on your own in response to the end-of-chapter questions or in whatever alternative way your professor thinks appropriate. This chapter introduces you to the balance sheet and income statement. We encourage you to turn to the Boise Cascade annual report and locate the financial statements within it. In 1990, Boise Cascade had assets totaling $4,784,770,000 and shareholders' (owners') equity of $1,575,531,000. The balance sheet equation (in thousands) for Boise Cascade in 1990 follows.

The annual reports of Boise Cascade and Wal-Mart provide real-world examples of accounting practices.

$$\textbf{Assets} = \textbf{Liabilities} + \textbf{Owners' Equity}$$
$$\$4,784,770 = \$3,209,239 + \$1,575,531$$

At this point, after studying Chapter 1, we only want you to locate individual accounts and their balances in the Boise Cascade and Wal-Mart statements and to see that real companies do accounting just as it is explained in this book. In Chapter 2, we will introduce you to ratio analysis. If you work earnestly with the material in this book and relate the topics in each of the financial reporting chapters to the annual reports at the back of the book, you will learn to read and analyze the financial information published each year by thousands of companies.

Study the Boise Cascade annual report. On December 31, 1990, Boise Cascade had current assets totaling $997,583,000 and cash of $19,781,000. Current liabilities totaled $758,372,000, including current notes payable of $40,000,000. Profit in 1990 was $75,270,000. Can you locate these amounts? If you thumb through the Boise Cascade annual report, you will find that the company is an integrated forest products company that operates primarily in the United States and Canada. Its net income has fallen the last three years, and management is concerned. Pages 4–10 present management's plan, called "Blueprint for the '90s," to increase earnings and cash flows. There is a great deal of information in the Boise Cascade annual report. We will continue to explore its contents in the chapters to come.

SUMMARY

Companies prepare three fundamental financial statements: the balance sheet, income statement, and statement of cash flows. The balance sheet shows the assets and equities of the company as of a particular point in time. The income statement shows the results of operations of the company for a period of time. The income statement is often combined with a statement of retained earnings that shows the effects on retained earnings of income and dividends for the period.

Assets are generally shown at cost on the balance sheet, not at market value. Equities are of two principal types: liabilities and stockholders' (owners') equity. Liabilities usually require cash payments. Stockholders' equity is a residual amount that represents two types of investment by owners: (1) the amounts originally paid to the company to acquire its shares and (2) the earnings retained in the business.

APPENDIX—USING ACCOUNTING SYSTEMS

In Chapter 1, we constructed a new balance sheet each time we wished to show the effect of the business activity of the TechHi Company. We can also show the impact of TechHi's business activity by calculating the direct effect of each transaction on the balance sheet equation: Assets = Liabilities + Owners' Equity. In the example that follows, we have added titles for the individual assets, liabilities, and owners' equity accounts affected and recorded each transaction of TechHi Company directly in the expanded balance sheet equation. A summary of TechHi's transactions is repeated before each change is made in the expanded balance sheet equation. The results are the same, of course, as those achieved by preparing a new balance sheet after each event.

1. TechHi is incorporated, and the Watsons invest $20,000 in TechHi stock. This transaction results in an increase in the asset Cash and in the owners' equity account Common Stock. All amounts are given in thousands.

Assets				=	Liabilities +		Owners' Equity	
Cash +	Accounts +	Inventory +	Prepaid =		Accounts +		Common +	Retained
	Receivable		Rent		Payable		Stock	Earnings
+$20							+$20	

2. TechHi paid rent in advance (an asset with a future benefit) using $6,000 cash. This transaction decreases one asset, Cash, and increases another asset, Prepaid Rent. This is a common transaction, paying cash for other assets (inventory, trucks, buildings, and so forth).

Cash	+	Accounts Receivable	+	Inventory	+	Prepaid Rent	=	Accounts Payable	+	Common Stock	+	Retained Earnings
		Assets					=	**Liabilities** +		**Owners' Equity**		
+$20										+$20		
−6						+$6						
$14						+$6	=			$20		

3. TechHi bought $28,000 of merchandise on credit. This is another common transaction. The asset Inventory is increased, and the source of this asset, the liability Accounts Payable, also is increased. Notice that after each transaction, the balance sheet equation is still in balance. Each transaction must be recorded so that the equation remains in balance. If we make no errors, assets will always equal liabilities plus owners' equity.

Cash	+	Accounts Receivable	+	Inventory	+	Prepaid Rent	=	Accounts Payable	+	Common Stock	+	Retained Earnings
		Assets					=	**Liabilities** +		**Owners' Equity**		
+$20										+$20		
−6						+$6						
				+$28				+$28				
$14				+$28		+$6	=	$28		+$20		

4. TechHi sold merchandise for $29,000 on credit. The merchandise cost the company $17,000. One asset, Inventory, is exchanged for another asset, Accounts Receivable. The asset received is larger than the asset given up. The increase in properties ($12,000) is shown as an increase in owners' property rights, or owners' equity, by increasing the account Retained Earnings. The balance sheet is still in balance: $60,000 in assets equal $60,000 in liabilities and owners' equity.

Cash	+	Accounts Receivable	+	Inventory	+	Prepaid Rent	=	Accounts Payable	+	Common Stock	+	Retained Earnings
		Assets					=	**Liabilities** +		**Owners' Equity**		
+$20										+$20		
−6						+$6						
				+$28				+$28				
		+$29		−17								+$12
$14		+$29		+$11		+$6	=	+$28		+$20		+$12

5. TechHi paid salaries of $4,700, utilities of $800, and other expenses of $2,500 (total payments of $8,000). Cash is reduced by $8,000 and so are total assets. This decrease in properties results in a decrease in owners' property rights: Retained Earnings is reduced by $8,000.

Cash	+ Accounts Receivable	+ Inventory	+ Prepaid Rent	= Accounts Payable	+ Common Stock	+ Retained Earnings
Assets				**= Liabilities +**	**Owners' Equity**	
+$20					+$20	
−6						
			+$6			
		+$28		+$28		
	+$29	−17				+$12
−8						−8
$ 6	+$29	+$11	+$6 =	+$28	+$20	+$ 4

6. TechHi distributed dividends of $1,000. Part of the owners' properties are distributed to them. Dividends are a return to owners on their investment. Dividends are not expenses, but they do reduce both Cash and Retained Earnings.

Cash	+ Accounts Receivable	+ Inventory	+ Prepaid Rent	= Accounts Payable	+ Common Stock	+ Retained Earnings
Assets				**= Liabilities +**	**Owners' Equity**	
+$20					+$20	
−6						
			+$6			
		+$28		+$28		
	+$29	−17				+$12
−8						−8
−1						−1
$ 5	+$29	+$11	+$6 =	+$28	+$20	+$ 3

7. At the end of the month, TechHi must adjust its accounts to show that one month of Prepaid Rent has been used up. The $1,000 of Prepaid Rent consumed during the month is an expense of doing business: Prepaid Rent must be reduced, and the decrease in total assets must be balanced by a reduction in Retained Earnings.

Cash	+ Accounts Receivable	+ Inventory	+ Prepaid Rent	= Accounts Payable	+ Common Stock	+ Retained Earnings
Assets				**= Liabilities +**	**Owners' Equity**	
+$20					+$20	
−6						
			+$6			
		+$28		+$28		
	+$29	−17				+$12
−8						−8
−1						−1
			−1			−1
$ 5	+$29	+$11	+$5 =	+$28	+$20	+$ 2

Notice that each transaction recorded in the balance sheet equation is structured so that assets remain equal to liabilities plus owners' equity. If, for instance, an asset decreases (perhaps by a cash payment), then there must be either (1) an equal increase in another asset (such as inventory), (2) a decrease in a liability (such as accounts payable), or (3) a decrease in owners' equity (due to either an expense incurred or a dividend paid to owners). After all transactions and adjustments are recorded, TechHi has $50,000 in assets and $50,000 in liabilities plus owners' equity. The balance sheet is still balanced.

DEMONSTRATION PROBLEM

Major Company was incorporated on June 30, 19X1. Major Company sells garden tools. Stockholders paid $30,000 for 3,000 shares of Major Company's common stock. The company also borrowed $40,000 on a note payable in one year to City Bank. After both transactions, Major has $70,000 in cash. A balance sheet constructed after these transactions follows.

After reading the transaction, try to decide how the balance sheet should appear before you look at it.

Major Company
Balance Sheet
As of June 30, 19X1

Assets		Equities	
Cash	$70,000	Note payable	$40,000
		Common stock	30,000
Total assets	$70,000	Total equities	$70,000

On July 1, Major rented a store on a one-year lease at $2,000 per month, paying three months rent in advance. After this transaction, the balance sheet is as follows.

Major Company
Balance Sheet
As of July 1, 19X1

Assets		Equities	
Cash	$64,000	Note payable	$40,000
Prepaid rent	6,000	Common stock	30,000
Total assets	$70,000	Total equities	$70,000

On July 2, Major bought $40,000 inventory of merchandise from Garden Supply Company on account. Garden Supply requires payment in 30 days. After this transaction, the balance sheet is as follows.

**Major Company
Balance Sheet
As of July 2, 19X1**

Assets		Equities	
Cash	$ 64,000	Accounts payable	$ 40,000
Inventory	40,000	Note payable	40,000
Prepaid rent	6,000	Common stock	30,000
Total assets	$110,000	Total equities	$110,000

During July, Major sold merchandise for $50,000 on open account. The merchandise cost Major $26,000. An asset, Accounts Receivable, is created, and another asset, Inventory, declines. The increase of $50,000 and the decrease of $26,000 result in a $24,000 profit on the sale, because the $50,000 is also a revenue, increasing owners' equity, and the $26,000 is also an expense, decreasing owners' equity.

**Major Company
Balance Sheet
As of July 31, 19X1**

Assets		Equities	
Cash	$ 64,000	Accounts payable	$ 40,000
Accounts receivable	50,000	Note payable	40,000
Inventory ($40,000 − $26,000)	14,000	Common stock	30,000
Prepaid rent	6,000	Retained earnings	24,000
Total assets	$134,000	Total equities	$134,000

During July, Major paid employee salaries totaling $6,000, all in cash. The cost of electricity was $2,000, and the cost of newspaper advertising was $4,000. These costs were paid in cash. The payments for salaries, electricity, and advertising all reduce Major's income for the month and therefore reduce Retained Earnings.

Major Company
Balance Sheet
As of July 31, 19X1

Assets		Equities	
Cash ($64,000 − $12,000)	$ 52,000	Accounts payable	$ 40,000
Accounts receivable	50,000	Note payable	40,000
Inventory	14,000	Common stock	30,000
Prepaid rent	6,000	Retained earnings	12,000
Total assets	$122,000	Total equities	$122,000

On July 31, Major repaid the $40,000 note payable to City Bank. Major also paid $4,000 in interest due on the note. Cash was reduced by $44,000, and Note Payable by $40,000 (to zero). The $4,000 is an expense and is a reduction in retained earnings.

Major Company
Balance Sheet
As of July 31, 19X1

Assets		Equities	
Cash ($52,000 − $44,000)	$ 8,000	Accounts payable	$40,000
Accounts receivable	50,000		
Inventory	14,000	Common stock	30,000
Prepaid rent	6,000	Retained earnings	8,000
Total assets	$78,000	Total equities	$78,000

By July 31, the company also has used up one month's worth of rent. Prepaid rent must be reduced and, because properties are reduced, owners' property rights (retained earnings) must also be reduced in turn.

Major Company
Balance Sheet
As of July 31 19X1

Assets		Equities	
Cash	$ 8,000	Accounts payable	$40,000
Accounts receivable	50,000		
Inventory	14,000	Common stock	30,000
Prepaid rent ($6,000 −		Retained earnings	6,000
$2,000)	4,000		
Total assets	$76,000	Total equities	$76,000

At the end of the month, we can also prepare an income statement to show the increases and decreases in owners' equity (revenues and expenses) from doing business in July.

Major Company
Income Statement
For the month ended July 31, 19X1

Sales		$50,000
Cost of goods sold		26,000
Gross profit		24,000
Operating expenses:		
Salaries	$6,000	
Interest	4,000	
Advertising	4,000	
Electricity	2,000	
Rent	2,000	
Total operating expenses		18,000
Income		$ 6,000

We can also prepare a statement of retained earnings that shows the change in retained earnings during July.

Major Company
Statement of Retained Earnings
For the month ended July 31, 19X1

Retained earnings, July 1, 19X1	$ 0
Income for July	6,000
Subtotal	6,000
Less dividends for July	0
Retained earnings, July 31	$6,000

Key Terms

accounting (balance sheet)
    equation

accrual accounting

asset

balance sheet

cost principle

current assets

current liabilities

depreciation

entity concept

equities

expenses

financial accounting

Financial Accounting Standards
    Board (FASB)

generally accepted accounting
    principles (GAAP)

general-purpose financial
    statements

going concern principle

income statement

liabilities

managerial accounting

matching principle

noncurrent assets

noncurrent liabilities

owners' equity

paid-in capital

realization principle

retained earnings

revenues

Securities and Exchange
   Commission (SEC)

statement of cash flows

statement of retained earnings

stockholders' (shareholders')
   equity

ASSIGNMENTS

I-I   Market Values and Costs
A company bought land ten years ago for $13 million, planning to build a factory. The land is now worth $56 million and the company is seriously considering selling it and building the factory somewhere else. At what amount will the land be shown on the balance sheet? Why?

I-2   Continuity
Why don't balance sheets show the amounts for which assets could be sold? When is such information useful?

I-3   Cash and Accrual Accounting
One of your classmates just said, "Net income is the difference between cash receipts and cash disbursements." Is he right? Why or why not?

I-4   Asset and Liability Categories
Why do balance sheets show current assets and liabilities separately from noncurrent items?

I-5   Depreciation
A classmate states, "Depreciation is the amount of money you set aside to replace assets." Is he correct? Why or why not?

I-6   Retained earnings
Can a company with $10 million in retained earnings necessarily pay a $10 million dividend to its stockholders? Why or why not?

I-7   Classification
Indicate where each of the following items will be found on a balance sheet, using the codes provided.

CA = current asset   NCA = noncurrent asset   CL = current liability
LTL = long-term liability   OE = owners' equity

a. Amounts owed to suppliers _____

b. Cash _____

c. Amount paid for next year's insurance coverage _____

d. Amount originally paid for shares of the company's stock _____

e. Bank loan, payable in six months _____

f. Bank loan, payable in six years _____

g. Amounts owed to company by customers _____

h. Total income a company has earned *less* dividends it has paid since it began _____

i. Unpaid utility bill _____

j. Amounts paid for goods on hand _____

k. Amount paid for buildings and equipment _____

l. Amount paid for trademarks and copyrights _____

m. Amounts owed to workers for work done before balance sheet date _____

1–8 Classification

Classify each of the following items using the codes provided.

CA = current asset   NCA = non-current asset   CL = current liability
LTL = long-term liability   OE = owners' equity

a. Common stock   _OE_
b. Accounts receivable .   _CA_
c. Plant and equipment, cost   _NCA_
d. Long-term bonds, 9%, due 19X9   _LTL_
e. Accumulated depreciation   _NCA_
f. Cash   _CA_
g. Short-term bank loan   _CL_
h. Accrued expenses   _CL_
i. Accounts payable   _CL_
j. Prepayments and other current assets   _CA_
k. Retained earnings   _OE_
l. Inventory   _CA_

1–9 Effects of Transactions

Give the effect of each of the following transactions (I = increase, D = decrease, N = no effect) on the indicated amounts.

	Total Assets	Total Liabilities	Total Owners' Equity
Sold goods at a profit, on account	_____	_____	_____
Customers paid for goods already bought	_____	_____	_____
Borrowed money from a bank, to be repaid in six months	_____	_____	_____
Issued ▬ common stock to investors for cash	_____	_____	_____
Purchased merchandise on account	_____	_____	_____
Paid for merchandise already bought	_____	_____	_____
Paid wages and salaries earned by employees	_____	_____	_____
Paid rent six months in advance	_____	_____	_____
Occupied rented premises (above) for one month	_____	_____	_____
Received but did not pay a utility bill	_____	_____	_____

1–10   Effects of Transactions

Indicate the effect of each of the following transactions (I = increase, D = decrease, N = no effect) on the indicated amounts.

	Total Current Assets	Total Current Liabilities	Total Owners' Equity
Sold goods at a profit, on account	_____	_____	_____
Customers paid for goods already bought	_____	_____	_____
Borrowed money from a bank, to be repaid in six months	_____	_____	_____
Sold common stock to investors for cash	_____	_____	_____
Purchased merchandise on account	_____	_____	_____
Paid for merchandise already bought	_____	_____	_____
Paid wages and salaries earned by employees	_____	_____	_____
Paid six months rent in advance	_____	_____	_____
Occupied rented premises (above) for one month	_____	_____	_____
Received but did not pay a utility bill	_____	_____	_____

1–11   Classifications

Classify each of the following items using the codes provided.

A = asset   L = liability   R = revenue   E = expense

1	Accounts receivable	R̷	A
2	Salaries	L̷	E
3	Plant and equipment, cost	E̷	A
4	Long-term bonds, 9%, due 19X9	L	
5	Cash	A	
6	Accumulated depreciation	A	
7	Cost of goods sold	E	
8	Short-term bank loan	L	
9	Depreciation on building	E	Income Sheet
10	Accounts payable	L	BAL
11	Sales	R	
12	Prepayment of rent	A	
13	Inventory	A	Bal

1–12   Effects of Transactions

Indicate the effect of each of the following transactions (I = increase, D = decrease, N = no effect) on the indicated amounts.

	Revenues	Expenses
Sold goods at a profit, on account		
Customers paid for goods already bought		
Borrowed money from a bank, to be repaid in six months		
Sold common stock to investors for cash		
Bought merchandise on account		
Paid for merchandise already bought		
Paid wages and salaries		
Paid wages and salaries owed from last year		
Paid six months' rent in advance		
Occupied rented premises (above) for one month		
Received, but did not pay, a utility bill		
Paid utility bill received and recorded last month		

1–13   Analyzing Transactions

Roberts Realty began business on January 1, 19X5. During January, the company had the following transactions.

1. Owners invested $50,000 cash in the business.
2. Signed a lease on a building, agreeing to pay $2,000 per month. Paid first month's rent in advance.
3. Hired salespeople and a clerk/receptionist.
4. Paid $600 for insurance coverage for the year beginning January 1.
5. Sold houses, earning $60,000 in total commissions, all paid to Roberts in cash. The salesperson receives 40% of each commission; Roberts gets 60%.
6. Paid share of commissions from transaction 5 to salespersons.
7. Paid $2,000 in salaries, utilities, and other operating expenses related to January.
8. Paid $2,000 rent for February in advance.

REQUIRED:

1. Prepare a balance sheet after each transaction. Use the format illustrated in the Appendix to this chapter.
2. Prepare an income statement for Roberts Realty for January.

1–14   Understanding Financial Statements

A balance sheet and income statement for Margo Inc. appear below. Use them to answer as many of the following questions as you can. (Some of these questions cannot be answered with the information available.)

1. How much do customers owe to Margo?
2. How much did Margo pay for the plant and equipment it currently owns?
3. What was the cost to Margo of the goods it sold during the year?
4. What is the difference between Margo's total net income since it began business and the total dividends it has paid to shareholders?
5. How much is Margo's plant and equipment worth today?
6. What is the market value of Margo's common stock today?
7. What is the cost of the merchandise that Margo currently has on hand?
8. How much has Margo paid in advance for such items as rent and insurance?
9. How much does Margo owe in total to its creditors?

10. How much did Margo receive when it first sold common stock to shareholders?

11. Are the people who first bought Margo's common stock the same ones who own it now?

12. Does Margo have cash of $236.1 million set aside to replace its plant and equipment?

13. What is the selling price of the merchandise that Margo currently has on hand?

14. How much cash did Margo collect from its customers?

Financial Statements of Margo Company
Margo Company
Balance Sheet as of December 31, 19X6

Assets

Current assets:	
Cash	$ 23.4
Accounts receivable, net	229.1
Inventory	187.2
Prepayments and other current assets	16.8
Total current assets	456.5
Plant and equipment, cost	1,198.1
Accumulated depreciation	(236.1)
Net plant and equipment	962.0
Other assets	61.0
Total assets	$1,479.5

Equities

Current liabilities:	
Accounts payable	$ 117.2
Short-term bank loan	45.6
Accrued expenses	38.9
Total current liabilities	201.7
Long-term bonds, 9%, due 19X9	770.7
Total liabilities	972.4
Common stock	234.1
Retained earnings	273.0
Total stockholders' equity	507.1
Total equities	$1,479.5

Margo Company
Income Statement and Statement of Retained Earnings
for the Years Ended December 31, 19X6

Sales	$1,330.3
Cost of goods sold	925.7
Gross profit	404.6
Expenses:	
Salaries, wages, and commissions	180.0
Depreciation	40.4
Interest	48.6
Other	59.6
Total expenses	328.6
Income before taxes	76.0
Income taxes	28.1
Net income	$ 47.9
Retained earnings, beginning of year	235.9
Less dividends	10.8
Retained earnings, end of year	$ 273.0

1–15   Analyzing Transactions

Barton Products began business on January 1, 19X5. During January, it had the following transactions.

1. Issued common stock for $100,000 cash.
2. Bought a building and fixtures for $60,000, paying $20,000 cash and assuming a $40,000 loan due in five years.
3. Bought $25,000 in merchandise on credit.
4. Hired various employees.
5. Paid $600 for an insurance policy covering the year beginning January 1.
6. Sold merchandise that cost $18,000 for $30,000, all on credit.
7. Paid $8,000 in salaries, utilities, and other operating expenses related to January.
8. Paid suppliers of merchandise $22,000 for goods bought in item 3.
9. Received $19,000 from customers for sales made in item 5.
10. Depreciation for the month was $800.
11. January's interest on the five-year loan of $400 will be paid in early February.

REQUIRED:

1. Prepare a balance sheet after each transaction. Use the format illustrated in the Appendix at the end of this chapter.
2. Prepare an income statement for January.

1–16 Balance Sheet

Use whatever relevant information that follows to prepare a balance sheet as of December 31, 19X6, for Kroll Company. All amounts are in millions of dollars.

Cash in bank at December 31	$ 46.2
Prepayments and other current assets	19.2
Cash paid by customers during year	2,396.3
Cost of goods sold for the year	1,609.2
Operating expenses for the year	555.2
Cost of plant and equipment	2,071.2
Amounts owed to suppliers	98.2
Retained earnings, beginning of year	87.7
Amounts owed to bondholders, due in five years	590.0
Common stock	399.6
Other current liabilities	262.1
Amounts owed by customers	198.2
Inventory	167.3
Cash paid for operating expenses	435.4
Accumulated depreciation	992.2
Sales	2,387.2
Retained earnings, end of year	206.0
Dividends declared and paid	22.1
Other assets	46.0
Income tax expense	82.4

1–17 Income Statement (continuation of assignment 1–16)

Use the data from assignment 1–16 to prepare an income statement and a statement of retained earnings 19X6 for Kroll Company.

1–18 Balance Sheet

Data (in millions of dollars) for KRM Company as of December 31, 19X8, follow.

Cash in bank	$ 90.2
Plant and equipment, cost	1,982.3

c(L)	Accounts payable	98.2
c(A)	Accounts receivable	264.8
OE	Common stock	777.0
NC (A)	Accumulated depreciation	1,086.3
OE	Retained earnings, end of year	643.0
Income Stmt	Sales - Revenue	2,387.2
Income Stmt	Cost of goods sold Expense	1,398.2
Income Stmt	Salaries, wages, and commissions expense	331.3
c(A)	Inventory	267.2
Income Stmt	Depreciation Expense	99.3
	Other operating expenses	135.2
Income Stmt	Net income	423.2
Stmt of Retained earning	Retained earnings, beginning of year	535.1
	Cash collected from customers N/A Statement	2,337.7
	Cash paid to suppliers N/A of cash flow	1,453.4

REQUIRED:

Prepare a balance sheet for KRM Company as of December 31, 19X8.

1–19   Income Statement—Continuation of Assignment 1–18

Use the data from Assignment 1–18 to prepare an income statement and a statement of retained earnings for 19X6 for KRM Company.

1–20   Wal-Mart Annual Report

Study the Wal-Mart annual report at the back of the book.

REQUIRED:

Use the Wal-Mart annual report to answer the following questions.

1. What kind of company is Wal-Mart?

2. What is Wal-Mart's profit for its fiscal year ended January 31, 1991? Is Wal-Mart's profit increasing or decreasing?

3. Find Wal-Mart's total assets, liabilities, and owners' equity. Place these figures in the balance sheet equation.

1–21 DECISION CASE: ANALYZING PROFITABILITY

The most recent income statement for ST Company, a store owned by Yves and Marie St. Tropez, follows. The St. Tropezes started the store several years ago and have built it up to its present state. They both work long hours in the store.

ST Company
Income Statement
For the Year Ended December 31, 19X6

Sales	$987.3
Cost of goods sold	609.2
Gross profit	378.1
Operating expenses	219.4
Net income	$158.7

Some friends have suggested that the St. Tropezes sell the store and go to work for someone else as managers. The friends believe that Yves and Marie work much too hard for their money and might be endangering their health. Yves and Marie have received an offer of $700,000 for the store and believe that they could earn a 10% return by investing that money. They also believe that they could earn $120,000 ($60,000 each) working for others.

REQUIRED:

Make a recommendation to Yves and Marie regarding their store.

2

Recording Accounting Transactions

LEARNING OBJECTIVES

After studying Chapter 2, you should be able to:
1. Understand how different kinds of accounting systems work.
2. Know what a ledger account is and how it is used to record a transaction.
3. Use T-accounts to represent ledger accounts when recording transactions.
4. Remember the increase and decrease sides of each of the five types of accounts.
5. Analyze transactions to determine the accounts that are affected.
6. Record transactions and post them to the proper accounts.
7. Create a balance sheet and an income statement from information in accounts.

In Chapter 1, we kept a record that resulted in a new balance sheet after each transaction—an extremely cumbersome procedure. Companies actually keep records in much more efficient ways, which we illustrate in this chapter. Our objective here is not to teach you how to keep a set of books; it is to show you how to record economic events in an accounting framework, efficiently and effectively, so that your study of accounting will go smoothly. As we proceed through the book, you will see that the recordkeeping framework provides a simple way to record and display the effects of a company's financial activities. Accounting systems have evolved over thousands of years. Insight 2−1 discusses the very beginning of accounting recordkeeping.

Insight 2−2 discusses Dow Jones & Company, the major supplier of financial information used by bankers and stockholders in the United States. Recordkeeping is necessary not only for preparing financial statements for banks and stockholders but also for providing information for managers to use in making decisions. For example, managers often need to know how much was spent on each particular cost in the most recent month so that they can budget costs for the next month and provide a basis for price quotes on products. Such information must be available and accessible inexpensively and quickly if managers are to be able to perform their tasks efficiently.

Most companies today use computers to keep records. Once data are entered, computers make short work of classifying and accumulating accounting information and of recasting the information in financial statements or reports to management. Our descriptions of the process are not to be taken as literal representations of how companies actually keep their records. Rather, we are describing the basic manual process and its results. If you understand the basic process, you can understand more complex and efficient accounting methods, such as computerized systems. The Appendix at the back of the chapter describes one improved way of keeping some accounting records. This method, using **special journals,** improves the efficiency of manual systems and is easier to computerize than the basic system.

Today, many companies use computers to keep their accounting records.

ACCOUNTS

It is perhaps easiest to understand the accounting process if we work backward from financial statements to their underlying **transactions.** Each dollar amount that appears on an income statement or balance sheet comes from one or more accounts. An **account,** sometimes called a **ledger account,** is simply a place to accumulate information about a particular asset, liability, or element of owners' equity. An

A ledger account is used to accumulate information about an asset, liability, or element of owners' equity.

INSIGHT 2–1
Babylonian: The Language of Business

Most people in the ancient world were illiterate. For those who were not, writing materials were expensive and the writing process was cumbersome, especially the creation of numerals. In most cases, the process was further complicated because money was not used as a common measure of value. Despite these problems, the oldest known business records were produced more than 7,000 years ago in Babylon, Assyria, and Sumeria. Babylonian was the language of commerce in the ancient world, much as English is the language of commerce today, and the cities of Babylon and Ninevah became known as the "queens of commerce."

The incentive to develop an accounting system came from both government and private business. Governments needed accurate records of receipts and disbursements. It was (and still is) particularly important for governments to record and control tax collection. As business and land owners accumulated private wealth, these individuals demanded that the servants who conducted their business affairs and managed their wealth account for the assets and the earnings produced.

Scribes were the predecessors of today's accountants. Truly, they were a combination of accountant and lawyer. Scribes recorded business transactions and saw to it that business agreements complied with all laws. Public scribes sat outside city gates. Persons conducting business explained their agreement or transaction to the scribe, who recorded it in moist clay using a wooden rod. The clay was inscribed with the names of the parties, any promises made, and descriptions of items to be paid or received. Each person, generally illiterate, "signed" the clay record using a stone signature amulet. Stone amulets, engraved with a person's signature or mark, were worn around the neck and buried with the owner at death. To ensure that the original record was not altered, the scribe wrapped the tablet in a clay envelope imprinted with the seal or mark of the scribe. Both the tablet and the envelope were dried. To alter the original record, a forger had to break the clay envelope. Sometimes, if the agreement was not secret, the contents of the original clay tablet were also inscribed on the envelope and functioned as sort of a carbon copy.*

*Michael Chatfield, *A History of Accounting Thought* (Hinsdale, IL: Dryden Press, 1974), 4–6.

account can be a written record, such as a piece of paper or a page in a book, or it can be a file on a computer-readable medium, such as a disk or a tape. An account can be as simple as the following example of an account for cash. (Note that parentheses are used instead of a minus sign to show when an amount should be subtracted. Because accoun-

INSIGHT 2–2
Dow Jones & Company, Inc.

Probably no other company has as much effect on the opinions and decisions of business leaders and investors in the United States as Dow Jones does. The Dow Jones Industrial Average (of 30 stocks picked by Dow Jones) is the most widely used measure of stock-market performance. Dow Jones publishes *The Wall Street Journal,* a daily business newspaper, *Barron's,* a weekly business newspaper, and 23 other daily newspapers in nine states. *The Wall Street Journal* has the highest circulation of any newspaper in the United States and provides about 70% of the company's revenues. Both *The Wall Street Journal* and *Barron's* give readers information that helps them to make investment decisions. The Dow Jones news and data services, Broadtape, News/Retrieval, and Telerate, supply financial and stock-market information to banks, insurance companies, pension funds, and others.

The company was started in the late 1800s by Charles H. Dow and Edward D. Jones. These two young men began by collecting and selling the daily news of Wall Street in a hand-written publication called the *Customer's Afternoon Letter.* They operated from a small office located behind a basement soda fountain on Wall Street. *The Wall Street Journal* began officially in 1889 when the two men purchased a printing press. Clarence Barron bought the business in 1902 and started *Barron's Weekly* in 1921. *The Wall Street Journal* and *Barron's* have been successful because they present business and financial news in language nonbankers can understand *and* they make their stories interesting.

Dow Jones has benefited the stock market and the stock market has benefited Dow Jones. Between 1980 and 1990, the market value of an investment in Dow Jones stock increased over 600%.*

*See the discussion of Dow Jones & Company in Milton Moskowitz, Robert Levering, and Michael Katz, *Everybody's Business* (New York: Doubleday, 1990), 367–68.

tants deal with many numbers, they feel parentheses are easier to see— and far less likely to be mistaken for a spot of dust!)

Cash	
Jan. 1 balance	$12,450
Jan. receipts	35,240
Jan. disbursements	(28,660)
Jan. 31 balance	$19,030

This account tells us the following: on January 1, the company had $12,450 in cash; it collected $35,240 during January and paid out

$28,660. These transactions resulted in a cash balance of $19,030 at the end of January. For illustrative purposes, this form of account will be replaced by a more explicit form of account, called the **T-account.** An example is given here.

Cash

Jan. 1 Balance	$12,450		
Jan. Receipts	35,240	$28,660	Disbursements
Jan. 31 Balance	$19,030		

The structure of this account resembles a "T" (hence, the name T-account). T-accounts are the traditional way of setting up accounts. These accounts are very efficient: they clearly show what is increasing and decreasing the account; the increases and decreases appear on different sides of the T. This simple form of account is used in accounting education to show the increases and decreases in an account. However, businesses do not use T-accounts in their formal accounting systems. Insight 2–3 explains how Luca Bartolomes Pacioli's work in 1494 introduced the concept of negative numbers and enabled accounting to develop as it has.

T-accounts are used to represent ledger accounts.

Debits and Credits

To simplify references to account entries and balances, accountants use the terms *debit* and *credit*. A **debit** is simply an entry to the left-hand side of an account; a **credit** is an entry to the right-hand side. Debit and credit are conventional terms; **charge** is a frequently used synonym for debit.[1] The use of debits and credits allows us to avoid referring to "increases" and "decreases," which can become confusing. At this point, note that in the preceding T-account for cash, the balance appears on the left-hand side (a debit balance). Also recall that Cash, an asset, appears on the left-hand side of the balance sheet. This orientation of debits and credits to the balance sheet is constant: items that appear on the asset side of the balance sheet normally have debit balances; items that appear on the equity side of the balance sheet normally have credit balances.[2]

---

[1] When a bank teller says, "I will charge your account for the new checks" or a department store clerk says, "I am crediting the returned merchandise to your account," these statements refer to the accounting entries that will be made. The bank teller debits, or charges, your account for new checks; the teller is reducing (with a left side entry) the bank's liability to you. When the department store clerk credits your account for a return, the clerk is decreasing (with a right side entry) the store's amount receivable from you, an asset.

[2] There are some exceptions to this principle, such as Accumulated Depreciation, which appears on the asset side of the balance sheet but has a credit balance because it is a negative item on the asset side.

INSIGHT 2–3
Arithmetic and Accounting

As we study T-accounts and journal entries, it is interesting to note just how important the work of Pacioli was in the development of modern accounting, and how innovative it was at the time he published his book, *Summa* (see Insight 1–1). Another Italian, 'Filippo Calandri, published *Arithmetica* in 1491, three years before the publication of *Summa*; another author, whose name is not known, published *Treviso Arithmetic* in Florence in 1478. These two manuscripts were the first arithmetic books ever published. Both books used business transactions, such as buying and selling merchandise, to explain and illustrate the four rules of arithmetic: addition, subtraction, multiplication, and division.

Both of these books were similar to Pacioli's *Summa*. But *Summa* was different in one very important way: in *Summa*, Pacioli introduced the concept of negative numbers. Always before, authors simply put the biggest number over the smallest and subtracted. The concept of negative numbers was new to Europe, and authors avoided it. But Pacioli did not. Pacioli provided the first printed explanation of negative numbers and used this new concept in recording the results of business activities.

In this chapter, the two sides of a T-account separate positive numbers from negative numbers. The concept of negative numbers allows us to keep accounting records as we do today. As simple as this sounds to us now, negative numbers were a giant leap forward for people who were trying to record the results of their commercial activities in the fifteenth century.*

*Michael E. Scorgie, "Early Arithmetics and Accounting Histories: A Comment," *Abacus* 27 (March 1991): 78–79.

The basic accounting equation with T-accounts for assets, liabilities, and owners' equity follows. The increase and decrease sides are marked for each T-account. Also note that the normal balance side of the account is the same as the side that indicates an increase or positive (+) amount.

Assets are debits.

$$\begin{array}{ccccc} \text{Assets} & = & \text{Liabilities} & + & \text{Owners' Equity} \\ +\qquad- & & -\qquad+ & & -\qquad+ \end{array}$$

Cash is an example of an asset account that shows increases on the left side. An example of two equity accounts—a liability and an owners' equity account—with the increases shown on the right side follows.

Accounts Payable

		$21,670	Balance Jan. 1
Jan. payments	$58,990	$67,220	Jan. purchases
		$29,900	Balance Jan. 31

Common Stock

		$124,700	Balance Jan. 1
		44,100	Stock issued Jan. 15
		$168,800	Balance Jan. 31

But what about revenues and expenses? These accounts are not on the balance sheet. We cannot determine the increase side of these accounts by noting on which side of the balance sheet they appear. But can we use logic to determine which side of these two account types is the increase side? Yes, we can. We already know that because owners' equity is on the right side of the balance sheet, its right side is the increase side. An entry on the right side of an owners' equity account increases the account; an entry on the left side decreases it. Because revenues increase owners' equity (through Retained Earnings), increases in revenues are shown on the right side of the T-account—the side that causes an increase in owners' equity. More revenues result in more owners' equity. Similarly, because expenses decrease owners' equity, increases in expenses are shown on the left side of the T-account—the side that causes a decrease in owners' equity. More expenses result in less owners' equity. The normal balance side of a revenue account is a credit; of an expense account, a debit.

Revenue increases owners' equity.

The expanded balance sheet equation with T-accounts for all five account types, including revenues and expenses, follows.

Assets   =   Liabilities   +   Owners' Equity   −   Expenses   +   Revenues
  +   −   −   +   −   +   −   +
or
Assets   =   Liabilities   +   Owners' Equity   +   Revenues   −   Expenses
  +   −   −   +   −   +   +   −

Students sometimes forget which side is debit, left or right. To avoid this minor but annoying problem, you can use the "Washington, D.C. rule": debits and credits are left and right, just as the D and C are left and right in Washington, D.C.

Real Accounts and Nominal Accounts

Accounts that represent assets and equities are called **real accounts.** In contrast, accounts that represent income statement items are called

nominal accounts. The difference between real and nominal accounts parallels a difference between the balance sheet and the income statement: the balance sheet is prepared as of a given point *in* time; the income statement covers a period *of* time. Real accounts are balance sheet accounts and show balances as of a particular time. Nominal accounts are income statement accounts and show the results of activity for a period of time. Real accounts carry balances that continue from period to period. Thus, the balance in the real account Cash shows the cumulative effects of cash receipts and disbursements, beginning when the company received its first cash (just as your checkbook balance shows the cumulative effect of all your deposits and checks).

Nominal accounts are temporary accounts.

Nominal accounts cover a period of time and do not carry balances from one period to the next. For example, the nominal account Sales only records sales made in the current year, not the cumulative amount sold since the company started operations. The Sales account is used in every period, but its *balance* is not carried forward and accumulated from period to period. At the beginning of each year, the balance of this account starts at zero. Examples of nominal accounts after the first quarter of a new year follow.

Remember: Real accounts are balance sheet accounts; Nominal accounts are income statement accounts.

Sales

	$44,320	Jan.
	62,180	Feb.
	58,650	Mar.

Cost of Goods Sold

Jan.	$22,450	
Feb.	31,334	
Mar.	29,030	

Unlike Cash, Accounts Payable, or Common Stock, these accounts did not have balances to start the year. They are used to collect data on income statement items, which usually are updated monthly (as shown here). A real account, because it is a balance sheet item, almost always has a balance and accumulates a balance from year to year. (Of course, this balance can be zero. The point is that balance sheet accounts continue; they do not originate each and every year.)

ANALYZING TRANSACTIONS WITH JOURNAL ENTRIES

How does information get into accounts? Where did the $58,650 in the sales T-account in the preceding example come from? The accounting process starts with an examination of each transaction to determine its effect on the business. Information about each transaction is then recorded in a **journal,** and later is transferred to individual accounts. The journal used by a business is somewhat like the journal or logbook kept by the captain of a ship: entries are in chronological order and describe activities day by day as they occur. Transferring information to accounts from journals is called **posting.** Journal entries typically are recorded daily or even immediately as transactions occur; however, these entries may be posted to accounts only once a month. In our examples of accounts, only one posting was made each month, although the company surely made many sales during each month. Daily sales are recorded in a journal; then, at the end of the month, total sales are determined from the journal and recorded in the Sales account.

The key to accurate recording—and, therefore, to accurate financial statements—is to analyze the transaction into its debit and credit components. In Chapter 1, recall that when we prepared a new balance sheet after each transaction, we were careful to maintain the equality of assets and equities. Recording transactions so that the debits equal the credits ensures that we maintain this critical equality. Examples of some common journal entries follow. After each entry, we describe the transaction and explain how the entry affects the balance sheet equation by showing what T-accounts are involved. For simplicity, each T-account shows the entry for *only the transaction being analyzed.* Other transactions that must have taken place (the purchase of goods before their sale, for instance) are omitted. The convention for journal entries is that debits appear first, followed by credits. Credits are indented for easy identification. The entries are numbered for convenience. It is customary to include explanations with journal entries.

(1) Accounts Receivable	$15,654	
Sales		$15,654
Sale of goods on account.		

This transaction increases the asset account Accounts Receivable and the revenue account Sales.

Assets	=	Liabilities	+	Owners' Equity	+	Revenues	−	Expenses
+ −		− +		− +		− +		+ −
Accounts Receivable $15,654						Sales $15,654		

(2) Cost of Sales	$9,876	
Inventory		$9,876
Recording cost of goods sold.		

This entry decreases the asset Inventory and keeps the equation in balance by also decreasing owners' equity. Owners' equity is decreased by the entry to the expense Cost of Sales. Remember that expenses are the decreases in owners' equity caused by doing business.

Assets = Liabilities + Owners' Equity + Revenues − Expenses

+   −   −   +   −   +   −   +   +   −

−Inventory   Cost of Sales

$9,876 $9,876

(3) Cash $12,568

     Accounts Receivable $12,568

     Recording payment on accounts receivable.

Payment on accounts receivable is not necessarily from the sales recorded in journal entry (1). Some portion of the payment could be related to sales made earlier than those recorded in entry (1). This entry increases the asset Cash and decreases the asset Accounts Receivable. The company has exchanged one asset for another.

Assets = Liabilities + Owners' Equity + Revenues − Expenses

+   −   −   +   −   +   −   +   +   −

Cash

$12,568

    Accounts

    Receivable

    $12,568

(4) Inventory $17,455

     Accounts Payable $17,455

     Purchase of goods on account.

This entry increases the asset Inventory and increases the liability Accounts Payable.

Assets = Liabilities + Owners' Equity + Revenues − Expenses

+   −   −   +   −   +   −   +   +   −

Inventory   Accounts

              Payable

$17,455 $17,455

(5) Accounts Payable $13,390

     Cash $13,390

     Payment for goods previously purchased.

Payments to suppliers of goods are not necessarily made for the goods purchased in journal entry (4). These payments may have been made for goods purchased earlier than those recorded in entry (4). This entry decreases the asset Cash and the liability Accounts Payable.

Assets	=	Liabilities	+	Owners' Equity	+	Revenues	−	Expenses
+	−	−	+	−	+	−	+	+	−
Cash		Accounts Payable						
$13,390		$13,390						

We have shown the effect on the accounts after each journal entry so that you can understand the debit and credit orientation of the entries. In reality, a company generally does not post the entries so quickly. At the end of the accounting period (say, one month), company accountants transfer information from the journal to the accounts. Thus, the entry to Sales in our example and all other entries to Sales during the month are posted to the Sales account. Similar treatment is given to all other journal entries.

Accountants generally do not post journal entries daily.

EXAMPLE

Let us look at a series of transactions to see how the whole structure works, from start to finish. We shall use the example from Chapter 1. The transactions are reproduced in Exhibit 2−1 for your convenience. You might wish to try to record the transactions yourself before looking at the solution. Also note that the transactions we are working with are summaries of many similar transactions. Almost any company would have many more individual transactions in a month—probably hundreds of individual sales, purchases, and payments. But we have shown only one figure for each type of transaction for the whole period. This is to simplify the work you have to do. If we showed 500 different sales transactions, with correspondingly higher numbers of purchases, payments by customers, payments to suppliers, and so on, the example would be tedious and very time-consuming.

The journal entries follow. We have omitted explanations here because the entries are self-explanatory.

(1) Cash	$20,000	
Common Stock		$20,000
(2) Prepaid Rent	$ 6,000	
Cash		$ 6,000

Example   55

> **Exhibit 2–1**
> **January Transactions for TechHi Company**
>
> **(1)** Company started with an investment of $20,000. Issued 2,000 shares of common stock.
>
> **(2)** Rented a building for $1,000 per month. Paid $6,000 in advance rent for six months.
>
> **(3)** Purchased merchandise for resale costing $28,000 from one vendor. Payment to be made in February.
>
> **(4)** Sold merchandise costing $17,000 for $29,000. Payment to be made by customers in February.
>
> **(5)** On January 31, company paid various expenses for January: salaries of $4,700, utilities of $2,500, and miscellaneous office expenses of $800. These expenses were not previously recorded as accounts payable.

(3) Inventory	$28,000	
Accounts Payable		$28,000
(4a) Accounts Receivable	$29,000	
Sales		$29,000
(4b) Cost of Goods Sold	$17,000	
Inventory		$17,000

To record sales, we use the nominal revenue account Sales, instead of the owners' equity account Retained Earnings, as we did in Chapter 1. We also recognize the $17,000 cost of goods sold using a nominal expense account instead of Retained Earnings. Remember that revenues and expenses are increases and decreases in owners' equity.

Sales are recorded in a nominal account.

(5) Salaries Expense	$4,700	
Utilities Expense	2,500	
Miscellaneous Expense	800	
Cash		$8,000

To recognize payments of expenses, again note that we use nominal accounts, instead of Retained Earnings, as we did in Chapter 1. Also note that we do not need to show each payment separately: we use a compound journal entry and show the total expenditure of $8,000 as the credit, with the debits distributed among the affected accounts.

(6) Rent Expense	$1,000	
Prepaid Rent		$1,000

This entry adjusts Prepaid Rent (for rent that is no longer prepaid) and recognizes rent expense, using the nominal account Rent Expense instead of Retained Earnings. This is an example of an **adjusting entry.** Adjusting entries are made to reflect the use of the accrual method of accounting (discussed in Chapter 1), where revenues are recorded when earned and expenses are recorded when incurred, regardless of whether cash has been received or paid. Adjustments, such as Rent Expense, result in revenues and expenses being recorded in the proper period.

There generally are two types of adjustments, the first of which is accruals. **Accruals** are adjusting entries for transactions in which cash has not yet been received or paid. To reflect a proper matching of revenues and expenses in the financial statements, these transactions must be recorded. Accruals generally are related to unrecorded revenues and expenses. An example is salaries of employees who have worked in the current accounting period but who will not be paid until the subsequent accounting period. For example, assume that Troy Company pays its workers $25,000 per week and that payday is always on Friday. If the end of the accounting period falls on Thursday, June 30, Troy will make the following adjusting entry.

Salaries Expense (4 days/5 days $\times$ $25,000)	$20,000	
Salaries Payable		$20,000

The other type of adjusting entry relates to reclassifications. **Reclassifications** result because the existing balance of, say, an asset such as prepaid rent (although correctly recorded initially) does not reflect the proper apportioning of the cost of the asset to the periods of benefit. The preceding adjusting entry relating to rent expense is an example of a reclassification.

We are now ready to post these entries to T-accounts, from which we will be able to prepare financial statements. The numbers next to the entries are the journal entry numbers. When several events affect an account, we show the totals of the debits and credits as well as the final balance in the account.

Cash					Accounts Receivable		
(1)	$20,000	$6,000	(2)	(4a)	$29,000		
		8,000	(5)	Bal.	$29,000		
Bal.	$ 6,000						

Sales					Prepaid Rent		
		$29,000	(4a)	(5)	$ 6,000	$1,000	(6)
		$29,000	Bal.	Bal.	$ 5,000		

Salaries Expense		
(5)	$ 4,700	
Bal.	$ 4,700	

Utilities Expense		
(5)	$ 2,500	
Bal.	$ 2,500	

Miscellaneous Expense		
(5)	$ 800	
Bal.	$ 800	

Rent Expense		
(6)	$ 1,000	
Bal.	$ 1,000	

Common Stock		
	$20,000	(1)
	$20,000	Bal.

Accounts Payable		
	$28,000	(3)
	$28,000	Bal.

Inventory			
(3)	$28,000	$17,000	(4b)
Bal.	$11,000		

Cost of Goods Sold		
(4b)	$17,000	
Bal.	$17,000	

At the end of an accounting period, clerks close the nominal accounts to zero and go through other procedures to help smooth the recordkeeping process. This process, known as **closing the books**, brings the balances in the nominal accounts to zero so that the accounts will be ready for recording revenues and expenses during the next period. The net difference between revenues and expenses is closed to the Retained Earnings account and, assuming that revenues are greater than expenses, reflects the net increase in Retained Earnings for the period. We shall omit further discussion of these matters; a simple understanding of how to reflect economic events in entry-account form is sufficient for this course.

Nominal accounts are closed to zero at the end of the accounting period.

EXTENSION OF BASIC EXAMPLE

Let us now extend our example through February to show how some other transactions affect the accounts and financial statements. Exhibit 2–2 summarizes the transactions for TechHi Company for February. The journal entries for these transactions appear in Exhibit 2–3.

Let us look at these entries and their effects on TechHi's financial statements. Journal entry (1) reduces an asset and a liability. The company simply paid an amount that it had already recorded as owed in January. Entry (2) is a repeat of an entry from January, recording the

Exhibit 2–2
TechHi Company
Transactions for February

(1) Paid $28,000 on accounts payable to suppliers.

(2) Bought $30,000 additional merchandise on account.

(3) Collected all accounts receivable from January sales.

(4) Sold goods costing $24,000 for $37,000. Collected $14,000 of the balance; remainder of payment to be made by customers in March.

(5) Paid the following expenses: salaries $5,200; utilities $2,100; miscellaneous $1,300. These expenses were not previously recorded as accounts payable.

(6) At the end of February, the company owes employees $900 for their work in the last week of February. Money will be paid to the employees in the first week of March.

(7) At the end of February the company had used up another month's prepaid rent.

Attempt to analyze and journalize these transactions. At a minimum, try to decide what balance sheet and income statement accounts are affected by each transaction. In addition, try to think of what else is required to prepare financial statements.

purchase of inventory and the company's liability to pay. Entry (3) is the exchange of one asset for another (cash is received; accounts receivable is reduced). Note that this entry does not affect the income statement: the sales were recorded in January and recognized on the January income statement, according to the realization principle.

Entry (4a) records the sale of goods. The only difference between this entry and the similar entry from January is that some of the February sales were paid for in cash and some were on credit but all of the January sales were on credit. Entry (4b) is just like its January counterpart, except for the amounts. The same is true of entry (5).

Entry (6) is different: here, the company recognizes an expense when it has not yet paid cash. This is an application of the accrual principle, recognizing that an expense has arisen and that a corresponding liability must be paid. The company owes the salaries because the work was done in February. The company has benefited from the work and must recog-

**Exhibit 2–3
TechHi Company
Journal Entries for February**

(1)	Accounts Payable	$28,000	
	Cash		$28,000
(2)	Inventory	30,000	
	Accounts Payable		30,000
(3)	Cash	29,000	
	Accounts Receivable		29,000
(4a)	Cash	14,000	
	Accounts Receivable	23,000	
	Sales		37,000
(4b)	Cost of Goods Sold	24,000	
	Inventory		24,000
(5)	Salaries Expense	5,200	
	Utilities Expense	2,100	
	Miscellaneous Expense	1,300	
	Cash		8,600
(6)	Salaries Expense	900	
	Accrued Salaries Payable		900
(7)	Rent Expense	1,000	
	Prepaid Rent		1,000

nize the expense. Note that this is just the reverse of a prepayment like prepaid rent. Entry (7) is the same as its January counterpart.

As a review exercise, post the February entries to T-accounts, determine the balances in these accounts, and prepare a balance sheet, income statement, and statement of retained earnings for TechHi for February. Remember that the revenue and expense accounts now reflect *two* months of activity, not just activity for February. The T-accounts at the end of February appear in Exhibit 2–4. The balance sheet as of the end of February and the income statement for February appear in Exhibit 2–5. Note that the income statement amounts for February are only the February entries to the accounts. If we wanted to prepare an income statement for January and February cumulatively, we would use the whole set of entries affecting each of the accounts. The Salaries Expense account contains two entries for February: one for the cash payments, and one for the accrual adjustment. The other expense accounts show a single entry for February.

Exhibit 2–4
TechHi Company
Accounts as of February 28

Cash					Accounts Receivable			
(1)	$20,000	$ 6,000	(2)	(4a)		$29,000		
		8,000	(5)	Jan. Bal.		$29,000		
Jan. Bal.	$ 6,000			(4a)		23,000	$29,000	(3)
(3)	29,000	28,000	(1)	Feb. Bal.		$23,000		
(4a)	14,000	8,600	(5)					
Feb. Bal.	$12,400							

Sales					Prepaid Rent			
		$29,000	(4a)	(5)		$6,000	$1,000	(6)
		37,000	(4a)	Jan. Bal.		$5,000		
							1,000	(7)
				Feb. Bal.		$4,000		

Salaries Expense				Utilities Expense	
(5)	$4,700		(5)	$2,500	
(5)	5,200		(5)	2,100	
(6)	900				

Miscellaneous Expense				Rent Expense	
(5)	$ 800		(6)	$1,000	
(5)	1,300		(7)	1,000	

Common Stock				Accounts Payable			
		$20,000	(1)			$28,000	(3)
				(1)	$28,000	30,000	(2)
						$30,000	Feb. Bal.

Inventory					Accrued Salaries Payable		
(3)	$28,000	$17,000	(4b)			$900	(6)
Jan. Bal.	$11,000						
(2)	30,000	$24,000	(4b)				
Feb. Bal.	$17,000						

Cost of Goods Sold		
(4b)	$17,000	
(4b)	24,000	

Exhibit 2-5

TechHi Company Financial Statements
Balance Sheet as of February 28

Assets		Equities	
Cash	$12,400	Accounts payable	$30,000
Accounts receivable	23,000	Accrued salaries payable	900
Inventory	17,000	Common stock	20,000
Prepaid rent	4,000	Retained earnings	5,500
Total assets	$56,400	Total equities	$56,400

TechHi Company
Income Statement
For the Month Ended February 28

Sales		$37,000
Cost of goods sold		24,000
Gross profit		13,000
Operating expenses:		
Salaries	$6,100	
Utilities	2,100	
Rent	1,000	
Miscellaneous	1,300	
Total operating expenses		10,500
Income		$ 2,500

Statement of Retained Earnings for February

Retained Earnings, February 1, 19X1	$3,000
Income for February	2,500
Retained Earnings, February 28, 19X1	$5,500

BOISE CASCADE CORPORATION

This chapter shows that the nominal accounts in the income statement are used to gather information for one year and then are closed to zero and used to collect information for another year. Boise Cascade labels its income statement "Year Ended December 31." The annual report for Boise Cascade shows income statements for three years: 1988, 1989, and 1990. Boise Cascade's report also displays two other statements

Income statements are for a period of time.

that reflect the results of activity for a period of time: the **statements of cash flows** and the **statements of shareholders' equity.** Boise's balance sheets, in contrast, show the balances in the real accounts as of December 31. Balances are shown at the end of each of the three years for which income statements are provided. Financial statements that present data for several years, side by side, as Boise Cascade's do, are called **comparative statements.**

SUMMARY

Understanding the recordkeeping process is helpful in studying accounting. Journal entries and T-accounts are efficient tools for analyzing transactions and indicating how an economic event affects a company's financial statements. Business transactions and other economic events (such as the expiration of prepaid insurance) are recorded in journals and then posted to individual accounts. In the journal, events are recorded chronologically. Accounts summarize journal information about particular assets, equities, revenues, and expenses.

APPENDIX—SPECIAL JOURNALS

Recording each transaction using the process illustrated in the chapter is often tedious and inefficient. In our example, we assumed that TechHi Company was recording transactions in summary each month. In reality, the company would deal with hundreds of sales, purchases, cash receipts, and cash disbursements. If TechHi recorded each of these transactions individually, it would have to post each entry separately or sort through hundreds of journal entries to add up the debits to cash, credits to sales, and all of the other highly repetitive items. To avoid all of this, virtually all organizations use **special journals,** in which they record only repetitive transactions. Companies usually have special journals for sales, purchases, cash receipts, and cash disbursements. A **general journal** is used to record transactions that do not fit in one of the special journals. This limits the use of the general journal to unusual items, adjustments, and a few other purposes.

To illustrate, we examine the journal entries recording sales for The Desk Top, an office supply company open six days a week. Desk Top sells to customers on account and records credit sales to individual customers. Desk Top has over 100 regular customers, many of whom make multiple purchases each month. Sample journal entries from Monday's sales follow.

Accounts Receivable—Able Construction	$3,407	
Sales		$3,407
Accounts Receivable—Baker Travel	2,789	
Sales		2,789

And so on . . .

If Desk Top uses a special journal to record credit sales, then the entries are simpler. One column is used to record both the debit and credit entry. Only the total is posted to the sales account each month, instead of a dozen entries each day. Separate records must be kept for individual customers using either method.

Credit Sales Journal

Account	Debit to Accounts Receivable Credit to Sales
Able Construction	$ 3,407
Baker Travel	2,789
And so on . . .	
Total for month	$67,652

This is a lot simpler and more efficient than just using a general journal.

There are several advantages to recording financial data in special journals. In addition to saving time, special journals allow a division of labor that is not possible when a single general journal is used. One person can be in charge of the credit sales journal; another person, in another office, can be in charge of recording cash receipts; another, of recording cash payments; and so on. The use of special journals also makes it much easier to computerize the records.

DEMONSTRATION PROBLEM

The Haigen Corporation was formed on April 1 of the current year. The company is involved in the excavating business. Journalize the following transactions for the month of April for Haigen Corporation, and prepare a balance sheet and an income statement for Haigen for the month of April.

Apr. 1   The corporation is organized by selling stock for $50,000.

Apr. 1   Purchased a parcel of land for $8,000; paid $1,000 in cash, and issued a promissory note for the balance.

Apr. 1   Purchased excavating equipment for $10,000.

Apr. 1   Purchased a two-year liability insurance premium for $3,264.

Apr. 10   Purchased office supplies for $1,240 on account.

Apr. 12   Purchased a used bulldozer for $3,700 cash.

Apr. 14   Paid $2,400 to rent a warehouse for one year.

Apr. 15   Paid Jones Construction Company $5,000 for a building to be used as an office. Paid additional costs of $2,000 to move the building to the company's site.

Apr. 16   Paid employee salaries of $4,000.

Apr. 17   Billed Powers Construction $8,000 for excavating work performed in April.

Apr. 18   Received $13,000 from Settle Contractors, Inc., for excavating work performed earlier in the month.

Apr. 19   Paid $2,000 on the note payable signed on April 1.

Apr. 21   Paid $750 for advertising incurred during April.

Apr. 22   Received a check from Powers Construction for $1,800 for work completed in April.

Apr. 23   Received a bill for utilities from Bonneville Power Company for $200; bill to be paid in May.

Apr. 25   Paid Amoco Oil Company bill for $1,200 for gasoline used during April.

Apr. 26   Billed Toronto Contractors, Inc., $7,500 for work performed in April.

Apr. 27   Paid $1,300 for repairs made on the bulldozer.

Apr. 30   Recognized insurance expense for the month of April.

Apr. 30   Recognized salary expense of $3,800; salaries to be paid in May.

Apr. 30   Remaining office supplies amount to $400.

Apr. 30   Recognized a portion of the prepaid rent on the warehouse.

Solution to Demonstration Problem 2–1

Apr. 1	Cash	$50,000	
	Common Stock		$50,000

Apr. 1	Land	$ 8,000	
	Cash		$ 1,000
	Note Payable		7,000
Apr. 1	Equipment	$10,000	
	Cash		$10,000
Apr. 1	Prepaid Insurance	$ 3,264	
	Cash		$ 3,264
Apr. 10	Office Supplies	$ 1,240	
	Accounts Payable		$ 1,240
Apr. 12	Equipment	$ 3,700	
	Cash		$ 3,700
Apr. 14	Prepaid Rent	$ 2,400	
	Cash		$ 2,400
Apr. 15	Building	$ 7,000	
	Cash		$ 7,000
Apr. 16	Salaries Expense	$ 4,000	
	Cash		$ 4,000
Apr. 17	Accounts Receivable	$ 8,000	
	Excavating Revenues		$ 8,000
Apr. 18	Cash	$13,000	
	Excavating Revenues		$13,000
Apr. 19	Note Payable	$ 2,000	
	Cash		$ 2,000
Apr. 21	Advertising Expense	$ 750	
	Cash		$ 750
Apr. 22	Cash	$ 1,800	
	Accounts Receivable		$ 1,800
Apr. 23	Utilities Expense	$ 200	
	Accounts Payable		$ 200
Apr. 25	Gasoline Expense	$ 1,200	
	Cash		$ 1,200
Apr. 26	Accounts Receivable	$ 7,500	
	Excavating Revenues		$ 7,500
Apr. 27	Repairs Expense	$ 1,300	
	Cash		$ 1,300
Apr. 30	Insurance Expense ($3,264/24 months)	$ 136	
	Prepaid Insurance		$ 136
Apr. 30	Salaries Expense	$ 3,800	
	Salaries Payable		$ 3,800
Apr. 30	Office Supplies Expense ($1,240 − $400)	$ 840	
	Office Supplies		$ 840
Apr. 30	Rent Expense	$ 100	
	Prepaid Rent		$ 100

**Haigen Corporation
Income Statement
For the Month Ended April 30**

Revenues:		
Excavating revenues		$28,500
Expenses:		
Salaries expense	$7,800	
Utilities expense	200	
Office supplies expense	840	
Advertising expense	750	
Rent expense	100	
Gasoline expense	1,200	
Insurance expense	136	
Repairs expense	1,300	12,326
Net income		$16,174

**Haigen Corporation
Balance Sheet as of April 30**

Assets	
Cash	$28,186
Accounts receivable	13,700
Prepaid insurance	3,128
Prepaid rent	2,300
Office supplies	400
Land	8,000
Building	7,000
Equipment	13,700
Total assets	$76,414
Liabilities and Stockholders' Equity	
Accounts payable	$ 1,440
Note payable	5,000
Salaries payable	3,800
Total liabilities	10,240
Common stock	50,000
Retained earnings	16,174
Total stockholders' equity	66,174
Total liabilities and stockholders' equity	$76,414

Key Terms

account (ledger account)

accrual

adjusting entry

closing the books

comparative statement

credit

debit (charge)

general journal

journal

journal entry

nominal account

posting

real account

reclassification

special journal

statement of cash flows

statement of shareholders'
   equity

T-account

transaction

ASSIGNMENTS

2–1 Basic Accounting Equation

Determine the missing amounts.

	Assets	= Liabilities	+ Owners' Equity
1.	$345,789	?	$198,709
2.	145,876	$98,030	?
3.	?	78,345	204,116

2–2 Basic Accounting Equation

Information is given here for four separate companies. Determine the missing amounts.

1. If Able Company has liabilities of $98,765 and total owners' equity of $56,000, what are Able Company's total assets?

2. Jones, Inc., has total assets of $789,021 and total liabilities of $576,008. What is the amount of owners' equity for Jones?

3. The total assets of Winnemuka Company are $785,000 and the company's owners' equity is $578,008 at year end. What is the amount of the company's total liabilities?

4. At the beginning of the year, France Company has assets of $585,000 and total owners' equity of $345,000. Liabilities increase by $125,000 during the year. If total assets are $567,000 at year end, what is the amount of total owners' equity at year end?

2–3   Nominal and Real Accounts

Indicate whether each of the following accounts are nominal (income statement) or real (balance sheet) accounts.

1. Cash
2. Depreciation expense
3. Accounts payable
4. Retained earnings
5. Sales
6. Salaries expense
7. Accounts receivable
8. Inventory
9. Common stock
10. Accrued salaries payable
11. Prepaid rent
12. Advertising expense
13. Cost of goods sold
14. Utilities expense

2–4   Posting to T-Accounts

Record the following transactions for Wrathall Corporation by posting directly to the appropriate T-account, and determine the ending balance in each account. The following accounts will be needed: Cash, Common Stock, Office Supplies, Inventory, Accounts Payable, Building, Office Equipment, Cost of Goods Sold, Sales, Accounts Receivable, Utilities Expense, Advertising Expense, Salary Expense, and Retained Earnings.

1. The company was started by Brian Wrathall, who invested $125,000 cash for 5,000 shares of stock.
2. A building was purchased for $30,000 cash.
3. Merchandise inventory was purchased for resale by paying a vendor $5,000.
4. Office supplies were purchased for $1,257 cash.
5. The company purchased a copy machine for $1,000 and agreed to pay the balance in ten days.
6. The company sold merchandise inventory costing $3,000 for $6,000 on credit.
7. Wrathall purchased merchandise inventory for $2,500 on account.

8. A customer paid $2,000 on his account.

9. Monthly utility bill for $300 was paid.

10. The copy machine purchased in (5) was paid for.

11. A bill for $180 was received from Bell Advertising Company for ads placed the previous month. The bill was paid immediately.

12. Additional merchandise inventory was purchased on credit for $2,670.

13. Salaries paid during the month amounted to $1,250.

2–5 Preparing Financial Statements—Continuation of Assignment 2–4

Use the information in Assignment 2–4 to prepare a balance sheet and an income statement for Wrathall Corporation.

2–6 Journalizing Transactions—Continuation of Assignment 2–4

Use the data in Assignment 2–4 to journalize the transactions for Wrathall Corporation.

2–7 Journal Entries and Accounts—Continuation of Assignment 1–13

Use the information in Assignment 1–13 and your solution to prepare journal entries to record the transactions of Roberts Realty for January.

2–8 Journal Entries and Accounts—Continuation of Assignment 1–15

Use the information in Assignment 1–15 and your solution to prepare journal entries to record the transactions of Barton Products for January.

2–9 Journalizing Transactions

Sleepy Breeze Motel had the following activity during August.

Aug. 1   Interest accrued on a bank loan for three months amounted to $1,200.

Aug. 3   Purchased an automobile for $10,460 to be used in the business. The company issued a note for the full amount.

Aug. 7   Customer receipts to date amounted to $12,400.

Aug. 10 Salaries paid to motel employees amounted to $6,700.

Aug. 13 Purchased fire and liability insurance for the next two years at a cost of $1,400.

Aug. 20   Additional customer receipts amounted to $9,300.

Aug. 24   Purchased office supplies costing $750 on account.

Aug. 26   Issued a check for $100 for advertising.

Aug. 29   Paid for the office supplies purchased on August 24.

Aug. 30   Several customers staying at the motel will not check out until next week and will not pay their bills until September. However, revenues of $1,200 have been earned for the month of August.

REQUIRED:

Make the journal entries for August.

2–10   Account Analysis

Compute the unknown amount in each of the following five independent situations.

Account	Beginning Balance	Ending Balance	Additional Information
Cash	$10,000	$ 7,800	Cash disbursed: $6,200
Accounts Receivable	15,000	30,600	Sales on account: $32,400
Accounts Payable	7,800	17,000	Purchases on account: $12,200
Prepaid Rent	3,400	2,900	Rent expense: $3,200
Retained Earnings	16,000	19,000	Dividends paid: $12,000

1. Cash received. $ _____
2. Amount received from credit customers.   _____
3. Amount paid on accounts payable.   _____
4. Amount paid for prepaid rent.   _____
5. Net income.   _____

2–11   Normal Balance

Indicate the normal balance (debit or credit) for the following accounts.

1. Cash   _____
2. Depreciation Expense   _____
3. Accounts Payable   _____
4. Retained Earnings   _____
5. Sales   _____
6. Salaries Expense   _____
7. Accounts Receivable   _____
8. Inventory   _____
9. Common Stock   _____

10. Accrued Salaries Payable   ———————
11. Prepaid Rent   ———————
12. Advertising Expense   ———————
13. Cost of Goods Sold   ———————
14. Utilities Expense   ———————
15. Rent Expense   ———————
16. Miscellaneous Expense   ———————

2–12 Proper Financial Statement—Continuation of Assignment 2–11

Using the data from Assignment 2–11, indicate whether each account can be found on the balance sheet or on the income statement.

2–13 Journalizing Transactions

Entries in ten T-accounts are shown here.

Cash					Inventory	
(1)	$10,000	$17,000	(4)	(2)	$6,000	
		6,200	(5)			

Land			Equipment	
(4)	$13,000	(5)	$6,200	

Accounts Payable			Common Stock	
	$6,000	(2)	$10,000	(1)

Accounts Receivable			Note Payable	
(3)	$7,000		$8,000	(4)

Building			Sales	
(4)	$12,000		$7,000	(3)

REQUIRED:

Analyze the T-accounts, and prepare the journal entries that served as the basis for the five transactions.

2–14 Analyzing the Effects on the Balance Sheet and the Income Statement

Analyze the effects of the following transactions on the balance sheet and the income statement of XYZ Company for the month of October.

1. Purchased equipment costing $5,600 on October 1 for cash.
2. Purchased a liability insurance policy for $3,600 on October 1. The policy is for three years.
3. Paid an installment of $4,000 on an existing note payable.
4. Purchased supplies for $5,300.
5. Billed customers $17,000 for services rendered during October.
6. Received an invoice for $880 for advertising in October; bill to be paid in November.
7. Received $13,590 from customers for services rendered in October.
8. Paid $1,100 utilities expense for October.
9. An October 31 inventory of supplies indicated that $2,700 was still on hand.
10. Purchased inventory for resale at a cost of $6,500 and agreed to pay the balance within ten days.
11. Collected $7,300 on account from customers.
12. Paid for the inventory purchased in (10).
13. Paid employee salaries of $3,800 for the month of October.
14. Recorded insurance expense related to policy purchased in (2) for the month of October.
15. Sold common stock for $15,000.

REQUIRED:

Use the following format and indicate + for an increase, − for a decrease, and NE for no effect.

Balance Sheet			Income Statement	
		Owners'		
Assets =	Liabilities +	Equity	+ Revenues	− Expenses

2–15 Journalizing Transactions—Continuation of Assignment 2–14

Using the data from Assignment 2–14, journalize the transactions relating to XYZ Company.

2–16 Journalizing Transactions

Caccia Company pays its employees $75,000 per week. The company always pays this amount on Fridays. Caccia's year end is December 31; this year, December 31 falls on a Thursday.

REQUIRED:

1. Prepare the entry at December 31 to record salary expense for Caccia.

2. Prepare the entry on Friday January 1 to record the payment of weekly salaries.

2–17   Journalizing Transactions

Brassington & Brassington law firm pays its legal staff on Fridays. Weekly salaries amount to $25,000. This year, the firm's year end, July 31, falls on a Tuesday. The company also is defending a client, Joe Bologna, in a civil suit. The fee is $1,500 per day; at year end, the firm has been defending Bologna for 13 days. The fee will not be paid until the suit is settled sometime in August.

REQUIRED:

1. Record the salary expense for Brassington & Brassington at July 31.

2. Record the accrual of the fees earned from the Bologna suit.

3. Record the payment of the weekly salaries on Friday, August 3.

2–18   Wal-Mart Nominal Accounts

Examine the Wal-Mart income statement at the back of the book.

REQUIRED:

1. What period is covered by Wal-Mart's income statement for the current year?

2. How many years are shown?

3. Does the Wal-Mart annual report contain any other statements that show the results of activity for a period of time?

2–19   Wal-Mart Real Accounts

Examine the Wal-Mart balance sheet.

REQUIRED:

1. The Wal-Mart balance sheets show account balances as of what dates?

2. Why does the Wal-Mart annual report show comparative statements?

2–20   Wal-Mart Journal Entries

Each year, Wal-Mart is involved in millions of transactions. Examine the Wal-Mart financial statements.

REQUIRED:

Prepare five journal entries that Wal-Mart might have made during the year. You may make up the amounts that you use. For example, a store might make an entry to record daily sales as shown here.

Cash	$30,000	
Sales Revenue		$30,000

2-21 DECISION CASE:
ANALYZING STATEMENTS AND TRANSACTIONS

The following balance sheet and income statement were prepared after the first month of business of Titan Corporation.

Titan Corporation
Balance Sheet

Assets

Cash	$12,250
Prepaid rent	1,100
Inventory	1,000
Office supplies	1,500
Office equipment	1,000
Total assets	$16,850

Liabilities and Stockholders' Equity

Accounts payable	$ 1,000
Common stock	12,000
Retained earnings	3,850
Total liabilities and stockholders' equity	$16,850

Titan Corporation
Income Statement

Revenues:		
Sales		$10,000
Expenses:		
Cost of goods sold	$5,000	
Telephone expense	450	
Advertising expense	700	6150
Net income		$ 3,850

REQUIRED:

Analyze the balance sheet and income statement of Titan Corporation, and list the nine transactions that occurred during the first month of operations. *Hint:* The first transaction, a purchase of merchandise, resulted in the following journal entry.

Inventory	$6,000	
Cash		$6,000

3

Current Assets and Revenue Recognition

LEARNING OBJECTIVES

After studying Chapter 3, you should be able to:
1. Describe the internal control procedures over cash receipts and cash disbursements.
2. Explain how the cash bank balance and book balance are reconciled, and prepare the journal entries necessary to adjust the book balance to the adjusted ledger balance.
3. Account for the purchase and valuation of short-term investments.
4. Prepare entries to record sales, sales returns and allowances, and sales discounts.
5. Record entries to account for credit customer transactions, uncollectible accounts expense, the allowance for uncollectible accounts, and the write-off of accounts receivable.
6. Prepare entries to account for short-term notes receivable.
7. Account for prepaid expenses.
8. Explain the point of sale, collection basis, and the production bases of revenue recognition.
9. Explain the procedures associated with the operation of a petty cash fund.

Cash is the most active account in a company's ledger. Almost everything a company does affects cash in some way. Building a plant, employing workers, buying and selling merchandise or services—all ultimately affect the cash account. Cash is also the most desirable asset that most companies possess; it is small, easy to transport, and readily converted or exchanged for goods or services. As a result, accounting for cash requires great care, and it is subject to many business controls. This chapter covers accounting for cash and the other most common current assets that a company holds—short-term investments, accounts and short-term notes receivable arising from credit sales, and prepaid expenses. The discussion of accounts receivable includes the treatment of uncollectible accounts arising from credit sales. Additionally, the chapter discusses revenue recognition in special situations, including the collection basis, and the production basis of revenue recognition.

CASH

The account Cash appears in the current asset section of the balance sheet. Cash is one of a company's most important assets because it is the most liquid asset. The accounting cycle is a cash-to-cash cycle: a company spends cash to purchase or manufacture goods or services, then sells the goods or services, and ultimately collects cash from the sale. Operating expenses, dividend payments, and purchases of assets (such as inventory, supplies, or plant and equipment) all eventually consume cash. Debts must be paid; stockholders must be rewarded. A business cannot survive unless it generates enough cash to make its payments.

The amount of cash reported on the balance sheet is the amount of cash available to the company as of the balance sheet date. **Cash on hand** includes currency, coins, and undeposited customer checks. **Cash in bank** includes checking accounts and savings or time deposit accounts. These amounts are generally shown as a single amount on the balance sheet. Because cash is the most liquid asset, it is listed first in the current asset section of the balance sheet.

Because a company engages in a large number of cash transactions, the opportunity for theft or negligence is great. Cash is easier to misappropriate than a company's other assets, such as machinery or equipment. It is very important that a company safeguard its cash and establish a system of internal control over cash and cash transactions.

INTERNAL CONTROL

A system of **internal control** is a company's plan of organization and the procedures it uses to accomplish the following four basic objectives:

1. Protect the company's assets against loss by theft and/or waste.
2. Ensure accuracy and reliability in its accounting data and reports.
3. Encourage and measure conformance with company policies established by management.
4. Maintain and evaluate the efficiency of operations of the company.

The first two objectives are financial or accounting controls; the last two are administrative controls. In this chapter we are concerned with accounting internal controls that affect the safety of a company's cash, and the accuracy and reliability of the Cash account.

Internal Control over Cash Transactions

Internal control over cash follows three primary rules:

A. A company should maintain separation of duties so that the individual responsible for handling and custody of cash is not the same individual who is responsible for maintaining the cash records. This separation or division of duties means that collusion between two or more employees must take place for a theft to be concealed in the accounting records.
B. All cash should be deposited intact in the bank, each day. Employees will be unable to use the company's cash for their own personal use if deposits are made daily. The bank statement can then be used to corroborate the validity of the company's accounting records.
C. All disbursements should be made by check. (The exception is the use of a petty cash fund, where insignificant payments are made in cash. The petty cash fund is discussed in the appendix to this chapter.) If all disbursements are made by check, the bank statement can also be used to check the accuracy of the company's accounting records.

The following list of internal control procedures are illustrative of those that might be applied to cash. Be aware, though, that internal control procedures vary from company to company based on such factors as company size and number of employees.

1. A list of all cash receipts and checks received in the mail should be made as soon as they are received. A copy of the list should be kept by the employee who opened the mail for later comparison and

copies sent to the cashier (with the cash and checks) and bookkeeper. Cash sales should be recorded by means of cash registers and/or prenumbered sales receipts. Copies of the cash register tape, or of sales receipts, are removed each day and sent to the cashier (along with the cash) and the bookkeeper. The cashier is responsible for depositing the cash and the bookkeeper for maintaining the cash records. This procedure essentially separates the accounting and custody functions in that the cashier never has access to the accounting records and the bookkeeper never has control of the cash.

2. Cash receipts should be recorded and deposited on a daily basis so that an employee cannot use the cash for his or her personal use.

3. The list, cash register, or sales receipts should be compared to the daily deposit slip and the bank account reconciled. In this manner the cash deposited must agree with the records of three people, so errors or irregularities will be discovered. The cashier must deposit all receipts, because the bank balance must agree with the bookkeeper's cash balance in the accounting records. The mail clerk or salesperson must report all cash receipts, or customers will question their account balances or the amount that was rung up on the cash register.

Most thefts of cash occur not from embezzlement of cash receipts but from the payment of fictitious invoices. Therefore, control over cash disbursements is thought to be more important than control over cash receipts.

For controlling cash disbursements the following rules should be followed.

1. All disbursements should be made by check or from the petty cash fund.

2. All checks should be serially numbered and access limited to those responsible for writing checks.

3. All disbursements should be properly authorized and supported by appropriate documentation. The documentation should then be marked or stamped "paid."

4. The individual responsible for authorization should not be the individual who signs the check.

5. Signed checks should be mailed promptly by persons other than those having access to cash and the cash records.

6. The person who signs the checks should not have access to canceled checks, nor should this person reconcile the bank account (reconciliation will be discussed shortly).

7. The bank reconciliation should be prepared promptly. Normally it is prepared on a monthly basis.

The first three steps ensure that only properly authorized invoices are paid. These last four steps separate the functions of recordkeeping and custody.

The Bank Account

A company may have any number of checking accounts. Each month the bank furnishes the company a statement of each of its accounts. A bank statement shows (1) the beginning cash balance, (2) deposits and other additions to the account, (3) checks and other deductions to the account, and (4) the account balance at the end of the month. Normally, a bank statement includes the canceled (paid) checks processed during the month and advice slips showing any other charges or credits to the account. Some banks, however, do not return canceled checks but instead maintain microfilm copies of them. In these instances, if a firm desires a copy of a check, the bank will provide a photocopy for a small fee. When checks are not returned, the bank lists the paid checks in numerical sequence on the statement.

Reconciling the Bank Statement

Monthly the company needs to reconcile its bank statement to its cash balance in order to have the proper balance at the end of the accounting period.

Rarely does the ending cash balance on the bank statement agree with the balance in the company's Cash account. For this reason, the two must be **reconciled.** One or more of the following causes of the difference in balance may be found.

1. **Outstanding checks**—these are checks that have been written by the company and recorded in the cash account, but have not been presented to the bank for payment.

2. **Deposits in transit**—these are deposits that the bank has not yet credited to the company's account as of the date of the statement. Normally, they are made at the end of the business day after the bank has closed. They are recorded by the company on the date the deposit is made but are not recorded by the bank until the next day—the day after the statement—so they will appear on next month's bank statement.

3. **Charges made by the bank**—these are charges not yet entered on the company's books. Examples include bank service charges and collection fees and NSF ("not sufficient funds") checks. The bank notifies the company of the deduction to its account by sending a **debit memo.** The company's checking account is debited (decreased) because a checking account is a liability on the bank's books.

Banks generally send you debit and credit memos to alert you to the fact that they have decreased or increased your account.

4. **Credits made by the bank**—these are credits made by the bank to the company's checking account and not yet recorded in the com-

pany's books. Examples include collection of notes receivable by the bank and interest earned on the checking account. The bank notifies the company that it is increasing its account by sending a **credit memo.**

5. **Errors**—these are errors made by the bank or the company that are not discovered until the cash balance is reconciled.

To illustrate a bank reconciliation, assume that Mike Bunce Construction Company found the following in its December 31 bank statement:

1. The bank statement balance was $3,615, but Bunce Construction Company showed a cash balance of $1,894 on its books.

2. A $360 deposit, placed in the bank's night depository on December 31 did not appear on the bank statement.

3. Check #1012 was returned in the bank statements and was determined to have been incorrectly recorded as being for $489 instead of $498. The check was a payment for supplies.

4. After comparing the checks that had been written by Bunce to those that had been paid by the bank, the company found the following checks to be still outstanding:

#1016	$ 66
#1017	1,572
#1018	943
	$2,581

5. Among the returned checks in the statement was a credit memo indicating the bank had collected a note receivable (discussed later in this chapter under "Receivables") for the company on December 20, crediting the proceeds of $300 less a $20 collection fee to the company's account.

6. Also returned with the bank statement was an NSF check for $555. This check had been received from Stan Vogt, a customer, on December 28 and was included in that day's deposit.

7. Examination of the bank statement revealed a $200 charge for a check that could not be accounted for. After discussion with the bank, it was discovered that the bank had incorrectly charged the company's account for a check drawn on the account of Bance Construction Company. The bank indicated that it would properly credit Bunce Company's account.

8. Bank service charges made to Bunce Company's account amounted to $16.

Exhibit 3–1
Bunce Construction Company
Bank Reconciliation at December 31

Balance per bank		$3,615	Balance per ledger	$1,894
Add: Deposit in transit		360	Add: Note receivable	300
Bank error		200		2,194
		4,175		
Less: Outstanding checks			Less: Service chg. $ 16	
#1016	$ 66		NSF check 555	
#1017	1,572		Bank fee 20	
#1018	943	2,581	Error 9	600
Adjusted ledger balance		$1,594	Adjusted ledger balance	$1,594

Preparation of the bank balance tells you what the balance should be; it is still necessary to adjust the book balance to that figure.

Bunce Construction Company's bank reconciliation is shown in Exhibit 3–1. After the reconciliation is completed, Bunce must adjust its cash ledger account to the actual cash balance of $1,594. The following four journal entries are made:

1. The collection of the note receivable and payment of the bank collection fee is recorded:

Cash	$280	
Collection Fee Expense	20	
Note Receivable		$300

2. The NSF check from Stan Vogt is recorded as a receivable because Vogt still owes the $555:

Accounts Receivable—Stan Vogt	$555	
Cash		$555

3. The error in recording check #1012 is corrected:

Supplies Expense	$ 9	
Cash		$ 9

4. The bank service charge is recorded:

Bank Service Charge Expense	$ 16	
Cash		$ 16

As we noted, the bank agreed to credit Bunce Company's account for its error. No adjustment on Bunce's books is necessary for the bank's error.

Internal Controls for Small Companies

But what about internal controls for small firms? How can a small firm or even a one-person firm develop a cost-effective system of internal control?

Many small businesses cannot justify an elaborate system of internal control simply because they are cost-prohibitive. Hiring a staff of accountants and clerical personnel just to establish an effective system of internal control is absurd! However, small companies cannot afford to completely overlook internal controls because of cost. In fact, to do so could lead to bankruptcy because of employee misuse of funds. An example of an appropriate system of internal control over cash transactions for a small company is discussed in Insight 3–1.

SHORT-TERM INVESTMENTS

Idle cash is not a productive asset and therefore companies invest this cash in **short-term investments** which include treasury bills, certificates of deposit, bonds, and common and preferred stock. Management invests in short-term investments all cash not needed for day-to-day operations or to increase return on investment. These short-term investments are classified as current assets on the balance sheet if they are readily marketable and if management intends to convert them into cash in a short period of time (usually one year). Exhibit 3–2 shows the current asset section of the Boise Cascade Corporation's balance sheet from its 1990 annual report, along with the related note disclosure.

Short-term investments are (1) readily marketable and (2) intended to be disposed of within one operating cycle.

All short-term investments are recorded at their acquisition cost, which includes additional costs such as brokerage fees. Assume that Faye Company acquired short-term investments in common stock for a total cost of $36,620 cash on June 1 of the current year. The following entry is made:

Short-Term Investments	$36,620	
Cash		$36,620

If Faye sells the short-term investments on November 1 and receives $38,200, the following entry is made:

Cash	$38,200	
Short-Term Investments		$36,620
Gain on Sale of Short-Term Investments		1,580

INSIGHT 3–1
Internal Control Over Cash Transactions for Small Companies

For a small-company owner, the rules of internal control are, to some extent, "thrown out the window." That is, the basic principles of internal control such as separation of duties, "must give way to a 'jerry-rigged' system built on illusion, subterfuge and sometimes outright deception."

For example, in a company run by an owner with one employee, the employee who does the bank reconciliation more than likely has access to the bank statement, blank checks, and the accounts receivable records. This situation becomes more prevalent as the owner comes to trust the employee more. One method used to control cash is to involve the spouse of the owner (especially if the spouse is of the opposite sex) in accounting for cash. The spouse many times does not trust the employee nearly as much as the owner and therefore will monitor the employee more carefully. The involvement of the spouse can be announced at a meeting with the employee, who will now be aware of the likelihood of additional monitoring.

To assist in controlling cash the owner can have all bank statements sent to his or her home. The owner or spouse opens the envelope and shuffles all the checks even if the documents are not examined. When the statement is given to the employee, the opened envelope will alert the employee "to the existence of some form of real or imagined monitoring" by the owner.

Blank signed checks are usually left with the employee in order to meet unforeseen events that may arise when the owner is not in the office. As a control device, these checks could bear a handwritten inscription (perhaps in a bright color) across the top of the check stating "NOT GOOD FOR MORE THAN $XXX.XX." This inscription controls the use of checks and also makes them stand out when the bank statement is opened by the owner or his or her spouse.*

*David P. Kirch, "Internal Controls for Very Small Firms," *The Practical Accountant,* November 1990, 104–108. Reprinted with permission from *The Practical Accountant* Volume 23 Number 11. Copyright Warren Gorham & Lamont a division of Research Institute of America, 210 South Street, Boston, MA 02111. All rights reserved.

The account Gain on Sale of Short-Term Investments appears on the income statement. If instead, the investments had been sold for $35,420, the company would have recognized a loss of $1,200, which also would have appeared on the income statement.

If Faye invested in bonds as a short-term investment there is *accrual* of interest on the bonds, meaning that as time expires, the company earns interest on its investment. Faye earns interest because it has

Exhibit 3–2
Boise Cascade Corporation
Portion of Balance Sheet

Balance Sheets
Boise Cascade Corporation and Subsidiaries

	December 31		
Assets	1990	1989	1988
	(expressed in thousands)		
Current			
Cash and cash items (Note 1)	$ 19,781	$ 19,715	$ 12,103
Short-term investments at cost, which approximates market (Note 1)	6,165	5,526	11,157
	25,946	25,241	23,260
Receivables, less allowances of $4,315,000, $3,800,000, and $3,405,000	412,558	421,568	393,371
Inventories (Note 1)	484,972	424,439	398,749
Deferred income tax benefits	55,115	48,716	40,404
Other	18,992	12,353	10,819
	997,583	932,317	866,603

■ **Cash and Short-Term Investments.** Short-term investments consist of investments that have a maturity of three months or less. At December 31, 1990, $9,712,000 of cash and short-term investments of a wholly owned insurance subsidiary was committed for use in maintaining statutory liquidity requirements of that subsidiary.

loaned money to the seller of the bonds, who in turn has the use of that money over time. Assume that Faye purchased bonds for $25,700 on November 1 of the current year. If interest is paid on October 31 and April 30 of each year, then an entry will be needed at December 31 (assuming this is Faye's fiscal year-end) to accrue the interest earned on the bonds from the date of purchase. If the semiannual interest payment is $6,000, then two months, or $2,000 (2/6 × $6,000) of interest must be accrued. The entry is:

Interest Receivable	$2,000	
Interest Revenue		$2,000

The account Interest Receivable appears in the current asset section of the balance sheet, and the account Interest Revenue appears on the income statement for the current period.

The market price of many short-term investments is subject to constant fluctuation due to changes in market conditions. Generally accepted accounting principles (GAAP) do not call for the recognition of changes in the market values of such short-term investments as certificates of deposit, bonds, or treasury bills; however, they do call for the recognition of changes on marketable equity securities (common and preferred stocks). The concept behind this accounting treatment is the **lower of cost or market** rule. That is, the short-term investment in marketable equity securities is carried on the balance sheet at the portfolio's aggregate cost or market, whichever is lower. To illustrate, assume that Faye Company purchased short-term marketable equity securities on September 1 for $35,000 cash. The entry to record this event is:

Short-Term Investment in Marketable Equity	$35,000	
Securities		
Cash		$35,000

If we assume that the market value of this investment is $33,000 on December 31, Faye makes the following entry on December 31:

Loss on Decline of Short-Term Investment in	$2,000	
Marketable Equity Securities		
Allowance to Reduce Short-Term Investment		$2,000
in Marketable Equity Securities to Market		

The account Loss on Decline of Short-Term Investment in Marketable Equity Securities appears on Faye's income statement. The allowance account is a contra account to the Short-Term Investment in Marketable Equity Securities account. It is called a **contra asset account** because it is reported as a subtraction from an asset account in the balance sheet. The balance sheet presentation of short-term investments is:

Short-Term Investment in Marketable Equity Securities	$35,000
Less: Allowance to Reduce Short-Term Investment in	
Marketable Equity Securities to Market	(2,000)
	$33,000

In this case, the short-term investments are carried on the balance sheet at the lower of cost ($35,000) or market ($33,000), which is the $33,000 figure.

Refer back to Exhibit 3–2: Boise Cascade carries its short-term investments at cost, which approximates market. Therefore, no allowance account is needed.

SALES AND ACCOUNTS RECEIVABLE

One part of determining net income involves deciding when revenue is earned and recorded in the accounts, a process called *revenue recognition*. The **realization principle** requires that revenue be recorded when it is realized, and stipulates that revenue is recognized only when (1) the earnings process is complete, and (2) there is a reliable measure of the worth of the goods or services provided. Completion of the earnings process means that the company has completed the major economic activities involved in the production and sale of the completed product to a customer. The proceeds from the sale must be objectively measurable. The selling price must be known with certainty and any remaining events that might affect that price must be reasonably estimable. For example, adjustments to the proceeds of a sale occur when customers return goods for a refund or credit, or seek a reduction in the purchase price of a good because it is slightly damaged or defective. Also, some customers might not pay their bills, reducing the proceeds actually received from the initial credit sales. In anticipation of this, accountants estimate uncollectible accounts based on the company's experience and reduce earnings by that amount.

As a general rule, accountants recognize revenue at the point of sale, when goods are sold or services are rendered. At this point, (1) the earnings process is usually complete, and (2) the sales price provides objective evidence of the amount of revenue to be recognized, and both sales returns and allowances and uncollectible accounts can be reasonably estimated. Exceptions to the general rule are discussed in the last section of this chapter.

Sales

Sales Revenue (often called simply **Sales**) is revenue a company earns by selling a product it has manufactured or purchased. An example of a sales transaction is a company selling merchandise to a customer for $16,000. The customer either pays cash at the time of the sale, or agrees to pay cash at a later date, creating an account receivable for the selling company:

Cash (or Accounts Receivable)	$16,000	
Sales		$16,000

Sales Returns and Allowances

To maintain good customer relations, companies often allow their customers to return unsatisfactory merchandise (called a sales return) or keep the merchandise in exchange for a reduction in the sales price (called a sales allowance). **Sales returns and allowances** are subtracted from the recorded amount of sales to determine the net sales for the period. When a return is accepted or an allowance made, the company makes either a cash refund or a credit reducing the customer's account receivable. A **credit memo** is issued informing the customer of the credit made on the company's books.

Sales returns and allowances are recorded in a separate account to allow management to monitor the amount of these items in relation to total sales. The amount of sales returns and allowances may have an important effect on customer relations and future sales. The account Sales Returns and Allowances has a debit balance and is a contra account to Sales. If a customer returns $200 of unsatisfactory merchandise purchased on account, or receives an allowance for that amount, the entry is:

Sales Returns and Allowances	$200	
Accounts Receivable		$200

(The credit is to Cash if the customer originally paid cash.)

Cash Discounts

Many firms grant **cash discounts** for prompt payment of trade accounts. A cash discount allows the customer to deduct a specific percentage of the amount owed if payment is made within a stipulated time period, called the **discount period.** If the payment is not made within this period, the amount owed must be paid in full. For example, suppose that on May 1, Jolly Fabricating Company sells merchandise to Stratton Amusement Corporation for $20,000. The invoice states that Stratton can deduct 2% of the price if payment is received within 10 days; otherwise, full payment is due 30 days from the date of the invoice. These credit terms are abbreviated as 2/10, n30. The 2/10 refers to the discount terms, and the n30 means that the net amount of invoice is due within 30 days.[1] In this example, Stratton has two options. It can pay $19,600 [$20,000 − ($20,000 × 2%)] by May 11, or it can pay the full $20,000 by May 31.

The entries that follow would be made by Jolly to record the sale and ultimate receipt of payment from Stratton if payment were received on May 8. The initial entry records both sales and accounts receivable

---

[1] In this situation, the term *net* really means the "gross" amount of the invoice.

at the gross invoice price of $20,000. Sales discounts are not recorded until the customer takes advantage of the cash discount.

May 1	Accounts Receivable	$20,000	
	Sales		$20,000
	Sale of the merchandise.		
May 8	Cash	$19,600	
	Sales Discounts	400	
	Accounts Receivable		$20,000
	Payment of the invoice.		

Sales discounts are accounted for separately so that management can monitor the amount of sales discounts taken by customers and adjust credit terms if necessary. The Sales Discounts account has a debit balance and is a contra Sales account. Sales, sales discounts, and sales returns and allowances are all used in the income statement to determine net income, but in practice it is unusual to see either sales discounts or sales returns and allowances on the face of the income statement. Instead, the income statement usually shows only net sales, which is actually the gross, total sales less sales returns and allowances and less sales discounts.

If payment is received from Stratton after the discount period, the entry to record the receipt of cash is:

Cash	$20,000	
Accounts Receivable		$20,000

As stated, the seller's purpose in offering a discount is to encourage the customer to pay quickly so the company will have cash available for other uses. The customer must decide whether to take advantage of the discount by paying within the discount period. Most companies will benefit from taking the discount because the annual cost of not taking discounts is frequently high. For example, assume that an item sells for $200, with credit terms of 2/10, n30. The buyer should make payment by the tenth day to obtain the $4 cash discount. If the buyer does not take advantage of the discount, he or she has the use of the $196 for 20 more days and essentially incurs an interest charge of $4 over that period, which is a rate of 2.04% ($4/$196). Since there are eighteen 20-day interest periods during the year (360 days divided by 20-day interest period), the effective annual rate is 36.7% (18 × 2.04%), which is quite high. A company is usually wise to borrow, if necessary, to pay within the discount period. Most sources of funds are cheaper than not paying suppliers during the discount period.

Receivables

A company's receivables are generally of three types: accounts receivable, notes receivable, and nontrade receivables. **Accounts receivable** (sometimes called *trade receivables* or *trade accounts receivable*) are amounts due from customers arising from the sale of goods or services.

Up to this point, when recording a credit sale we debited a single account called Accounts Receivable. In reality, a company normally has many credit customers and so maintains a separate account for each credit customer to show the amount of customer purchases, amounts collected, and the amount owed. The amount appearing in the general ledger for accounts receivable represents the total amount due from all the individual customers. This single amount appearing in the general ledger is called an **accounts receivable controlling account,** and the individual accounts are maintained in what is called the **accounts receivable subsidiary ledger.** At any time, the amount appearing in the general ledger (controlling account) must equal the sum of all the customers' accounts in the subsidiary ledger. To preserve this relationship, every posting of a credit sale or cash receipts on account to the control account must also be posted to the proper customer account in the subsidiary ledger.

Notes receivable are a more formal type of receivable and involve a legal negotiable instrument, such as a promissory note. The note is negotiable because it can be transferred to a third party. Notes receivable generally are interest-bearing while accounts receivable are not. Notes receivable are discussed later in the chapter.

Nontrade receivables are receivables that are not amounts due from customers arising from the sale of goods or services. Examples include those arising from advances to officers or employees; from claims for losses, damages, or tax refunds; from dividends or interest to be received; or from deposits with creditors such as a utility.

Accounting for Uncollectible Accounts

Companies sell on credit (rather than strictly on a cash basis) to generate additional sales; however, along with the additional sales come increased costs in terms of uncollectible accounts.

No matter how strict a company's credit-granting policies, some customers that receive credit will not pay. Managers know this and, based upon experience and the state of the economy, can usually estimate the total amount of uncollectible accounts quite accurately. **Uncollectible accounts expense** is a part of doing business on credit. In measuring the periodic income of a business, we match or offset the expenses incurred, in generating sales revenue. Because there is no way to predict which accounts will not be collected, the expense must be estimated, either by using a percentage of sales or a percentage of accounts receivable that normally involves an aging of the accounts. Each of these methods will be discussed.

At the end of the accounting period, when the amount of accounts receivable estimated to be uncollectible has been determined, an adjusting entry is made with a debit to Uncollectible Accounts Expense (or Bad Debt Expense), and a credit to the **Allowance for Uncollectible Accounts** (or Allowance for Doubtful Accounts).

The matching concept requires that the expense resulting from uncollectible accounts be matched against the related sale in the same period.

For example, if in its first year of operations Gallagher Company determines after reviewing customer accounts, that $4,000 of its accounts receivable will likely not be collected, the following adjusting entry is made:

Uncollectible Accounts Expense	$4,000	
Allowance for Uncollectible Accounts		$4,000

The Allowance for Uncollectible Accounts account normally has a credit balance and is a contra Accounts Receivable account. Notice that the Allowance is credited and not Accounts Receivable. If we credited Accounts Receivable, we would also have to reduce specific customer accounts and, at the time of the adjusting entry, Gallagher does not know which accounts will prove to be uncollectible.

If the balance in the Accounts Receivable account was $100,000 at year end, the current asset section of the balance sheet would show one of the following forms of presentation:

Accounts Receivable	$100,000
Less: Allowance for Uncollectible Accounts	(4,000)
	96,000

or

Accounts Receivable (less Allowance for Uncollectible Accounts of $4,000)	$ 96,000

The $100,000 is the gross amount of accounts receivable, and $96,000 is the amount expected to ultimately be collected. This amount is also called the **realizable value** of the accounts receivable.

There are two procedures for determining the estimate of uncollectible accounts. One bases the estimate on a **percentage of credit sales** and the other on a **percentage of accounts receivable.**

The percentage of credit sales is often referred to as an *income statement approach* because the estimate is based on a percentage of an income statement amount and determines the bad debt expense associated with a certain sales activity. To illustrate the percentage of credit sales method, assume that Orofino Company had a year-end balance in its Allowance for Uncollectible Accounts account of $1,000. Sales for the period amounted to $125,000 and the balance in Accounts Receivable is $50,000. Based on past experience the company believes

Income Statement Approach: Historical percentage of uncollectible accounts from sales × net credit sales = Adjustment.

that 1.5% of this period's sales will be uncollectible. The following adjusting entry is made:

Uncollectible Accounts Expense (.015 × $125,000)	$1,875	
Allowance for Uncollectible Accounts		$1,875

Note that the unadjusted balance of $1,000 was not considered in this estimate of uncollectible accounts expense. Under the percentage of credit sales method, any existing balance in the allowance account does not influence the adjusting entry. The balance in the allowance account is now $2,875 ($1,000 + $1,875). The estimate of collectible accounts receivable is $47,125 ($50,000 − $2,875).

The second method of estimating uncollectible accounts is to find the amount of accounts receivable that will prove to be uncollectible. The amount of collectible accounts receivable (or realizable value) is estimated, and the allowance is increased or decreased so that net *Balance Sheet Approach:* accounts receivable equals the estimate. This method is called a *bal-* *Historical percentage of* *ance sheet approach* because it results in a more accurate estimate of *uncollectible accounts in* collectible accounts receivable in the balance sheet than the result *accounts receivable ×* produced by the percentage of credit sales method. Suppose the *Balance in accounts* Orofino Company has an unadjusted balance in the Allowance for *receivable = Required* Uncollectible Accounts account of $1,000. Sales for the period were *balance in allowance for* $125,000, and the balance in the Accounts Receivable account was *doubtful accounts. The* $50,000. On the basis of experience, Orofino estimates that 6% of its *difference between the* outstanding accounts receivable of $50,000 will not be collected. After *required balance and* the adjusting entry for uncollectible accounts expense is made, the *the existing balance* balance in the allowance account should be $3,000 ($50,000 × .06). *equals the adjustment.* Since the unadjusted balance is $1,000, the year-end adjusting entry should be for $2,000 ($3,000 − $1,000). The entry required to bring the balance in the allowance account to $3,000 is:

Uncollectible Accounts Expense	$2,000	
Allowance for Uncollectible Accounts		$2,000

It is possible that the unadjusted balance in the allowance account could be a debit instead of a credit. If the balance in the allowance had been a debit of $1,000 instead of a credit of $1,000, the adjusting entry would have been:

Uncollectible Accounts Expense	$4,000	
Allowance for Uncollectible Accounts		$4,000

The balance in the allowance account after adjustment is now $3,000 ($4,000 credit minus the $1,000 debit balance), which is 6% of the balance of accounts receivable of $50,000.

Instead of using one overall historical percentage to compute uncollectible accounts expense, most companies prepare an **aging schedule** that arranges customer accounts into categories according to how many days each has been outstanding. Then different historical percentages are applied to each category to determine the approximate percentage of each age group that will be uncollectible. The older an account receivable is, the greater the probability that it will not be collected.

Exhibit 3–3 presents an aging schedule for Bear River Manufacturing Company. Note that $14,953 is the desired balance in the Allowance for Uncollectible Accounts account. If Bear River had a $1,000 unadjusted credit balance in its allowance account, the year-end adjusting entry would be:

Uncollectible Accounts Expense ($14,953 − $1,000) $13,953
     Allowance for Uncollectible Accounts $13,953

The balance in the allowance account is now $14,953.

A company tries to collect its past due accounts receivable by contacting the debtor orally and in writing, and eventually turning the

---

Exhibit 3–3
Aging Schedule

Bear River Manufacturing Company
Accounts Receivable Aging Schedule
December 31, 19X1

Customer	Balance	Not Yet Due	1–30	31–60	61–90	Over 180
				Number of Days Past Due		
S. Jones	$ 25,000		$25,000			
B. Jackson	76,000	$ 70,000	1,000	$ 5,000		
B. Hartman	3,000				$3,000	
T. Frank	35,000		26,000	5,000	3,000	$ 1,000
T. Buttross	8,000					8,000
K. Soto	74,000	63,000	2,000	4,000	1,500	3,500
R. LeBlanc	52,300	52,300				
Totals	$273,300	$185,300	$54,000	$14,000	$7,500	$12,500
Estimated Uncollectible Percentage		1%	5%	10%	20%	60%
Amount Uncollectible	$ 14,953	$ 1,853	$ 2,700	$ 1,400	$1,500	$ 7,500

receivable over to a collection agent. If the company decides that an uncollected account is not collectible, it makes an entry to remove, or *write off,* the account by debiting the allowance account and crediting the account receivable. For example, if after repeated attempts to collect, the $8,000 account of Tom Buttross is determined to be uncollectible, the following entry is made.

Allowance for Uncollectible Accounts	$8,000	
Accounts Receivable—Tom Buttross		$8,000

Notice that this entry has no effect on uncollectible accounts expense. That expense was previously recorded as a year-end adjusting entry. At that time no one knew which accounts would not be collected, making it necessary to credit the Allowance for Uncollectible Accounts rather than Accounts Receivable. But now one uncollectible account has been identified, and $8,000 of the credit can be removed from the allowance account and used to write off (zero out) the uncollectible receivable from Tom Buttross. In this case the uncollectible account reduces the control account Accounts Receivable and also the subsidiary ledger account for Tom Buttross.

If after the account is written off, Tom Buttross eventually does pay his account, the account receivable will be reestablished in the accounts in order to preserve the credit history of the customer. The following entries are made to recognize the *collection* of the $8,000 previously written off:

Accounts Receivable—Tom Buttross	$8,000	
Allowance for Uncollectible Accounts		$8,000
Cash	$8,000	
Accounts Receivable—Tom Buttross		$8,000

The first entry restores the customer account by reversing the entry made to write off the account, and the second entry records the receipt of the cash and the reduction in accounts receivable. Note that for each entry the control account and the subsidiary ledger accounts are adjusted.

Disclosure of Receivables

A company may sell its accounts receivable or may be required to pledge or assign them as security for a loan. The sale, pledge, or assignment of accounts receivable is disclosed in the footnotes to the financial statements. Exhibit 3–4 is from the footnotes in the 1988 annual report of CSX Corporation, a company in the transportation industry. Note that the CSX receivables were sold "with recourse." This means that

---

Exhibit 3–4
CSX Corporation
Accounts Receivable Footnote Disclosure

NOTE 1. Significant Accounting Policies
Accounts Receivable

In December 1987, the company entered into an agreement to sell, on a revolving basis, an undivided percentage ownership interest in a designated pool of accounts receivable with recourse. The agreement, which allows for the sale of accounts receivable up to a maximum of $300 million, expires not later than December 31, 1992. Average monthly proceeds from the sale of accounts receivable were $300 million representing receivables sold.

The company maintains an allowance for doubtful accounts based upon the expected collectibility of all trade accounts receivable, including receivables sold with recourse. Allowances for doubtful accounts of $62 million, $58 million and $76 million have been applied as a reduction of accounts receivable at December 31, 1988, 1987 and 1986, respectively.

CSX guarantees payment to the purchaser of the receivables in the event the debtor does not pay. The sale of receivables with recourse does not transfer the risk of ownership of the receivables. The question thus arises as to whether the transaction should be viewed as a sale or a loan. The Financial Accounting Standards Board (FASB) requires certain conditions for the transaction to be treated as a sale. Readers should carefully analyze the footnotes and be alert for these types of transactions to distinguish between a sale of receivables and the creation of a liability. For CSX Corporation, the conditions for a sale have been met because the company indicated in another footnote that the FASB criteria had been met and therefore the accounts receivable account was reduced by the amount of the accounts sold.

Companies also generally disclose significant receivables from officers or employees and from related parties, such as an unconsolidated subsidiary.

Management of Accounts Receivable

Many believe that the best management technique associated with accounts receivable is to maintain a tight credit policy resulting in minimal bad debt losses. However, net income and return on investment (ROI) can often be improved by taking another strategy, discussed in Insight 3–2.

INSIGHT 3–2
Accounts Receivable Management

Assume a company has the following monthly sales levels, variable costs, and fixed costs. Variable costs are those that fluctuate with activity (such as the cost of goods sold), and fixed costs are those that do not (such as rent on the factory facilities).

Sales (10,000 units @ $10)	$100,000
Variable costs (10,000 @ $3)	30,000
Fixed costs	50,000
Net income	$ 20,000

Now suppose that the company determines that a new market exists where an additional 1,000 units can be sold each month on credit. The company can produce these 1,000 units using its existing production facilities; however, bad debt losses are expected to be 35%. The company's credit manager says, "Forget it! The bad debt losses are too high." But let's analyze the impact on profits of entering this market. Additional sales of $10,000 (1,000 units × $10) will yield only $6,500 in collectible sales revenue. But how much will costs increase? Because the company can manufacture the product in its existing facilities, there is no increase in monthly fixed costs. Variable costs will increase by $3,000 (1,000 × $3) and the impact on net income is:

Additional collectible sales revenue	6,500
Additional variable costs	3,000
Additional fixed costs	-0-
Additional net income per month	$3,500

If the company enters the new market, net income will increase from $20,000 to $23,500 per month, or an annual increase of $42,000. This results even with bad debt losses of 35% from the new sales. In this case, conventional wisdom (tight credit, low bad debt losses) does not hold; each new marketing opportunity must be analyzed by considering its total effect on net income.

Short-Term Notes Receivable

Notes receivable normally arise through transactions with customers, creditors, and suppliers. In general, notes receivable bear interest while accounts receivable do not. Notes receivable also differ from accounts receivable in that a note is a formal document that specifies the due date of the note, the amount borrowed, and the interest rate used to compute the interest that must be paid at the due date. Notes also state the penalties for nonpayment. If the note is *secured,* it also includes a description of the collateral used to back the note.

Sometimes a company will lend money to another company and request that company to sign a note. A common example is where a company lends money to one of its suppliers. Other times a note receivable results when a customer has an overdue account receivable and seeks more time to pay for a purchase. For example, assume that on March 1, 19X1, Beesley Company receives from Bannock Company a 60-day note for $12,000 at an annual interest rate of 10%. The note replaces an open accounts receivable resulting from a sale made in the previous month. The initial sales resulted in a debit to Accounts Receivable and a credit to Sales. The entry on March 1, 19X1 is:

Notes Receivable	$12,000	
Accounts Receivable		$12,000

Note that one asset is exchanged for another. Notes Receivable replaces Accounts Receivable as a current asset. Interest Revenue is earned over the 60-day period and is not recorded until the note is paid at maturity. When the note is paid by Bannock Company on April 30, 19X1, Beesley Company makes the following entry:

Cash [$12,000 + ($12,000 × .10 × 60/360)]	$12,200	
Notes Receivable		$12,000
Interest Revenue		200

The general formula for computing interest on a note receivable is:

$$\text{Interest} = \text{Principal} \times \text{Rate} \times \text{Time}$$

where:

- Interest = the revenue to be earned from lending cash.
- Principal = the initial amount lended.
- Rate = the interest rate expressed as an annual rate.
- Time = the time period (or fraction of the year) that the principal amount will be outstanding.

Dishonored Notes Receivable

If, on the other hand, Bannock Company failed to pay (defaulted) the note at maturity, Beesley Company would have made the following entry:

Dishonored Notes Receivable	$12,200	
Notes Receivable		$12,000
Interest Revenue		200

Dishonored notes receivable are presented in the current asset section of the balance sheet directly below notes receivable. Beesley then would make every effort to collect the balance of $12,200.

Discounted Notes Receivable

Sometimes a company will **discount a note receivable** at a bank. This means that the company is in effect selling the note to the bank—in order to obtain cash earlier than the maturity date. However, you should note that the company is still contingently liable. That is, if the note is not paid to the bank at maturity, the company that sold the note must pay the bank the principal of the note plus interest.

The process of discounting a note generally involves four basic steps:

Remember the four-step approach:
1. Calculate maturity value.
2. Calculate discount period.
3. Compute discount charged by bank.
4. Subtract discount from maturity value to determine proceeds.

1. Calculate the **maturity value** of the note, which is the principal plus interest that will be paid at maturity.

2. Calculate the number of days from the date of the sale to the bank to the maturity date. This period is known as the discount period (discussed earlier) and excludes the date of sale but includes the maturity date.

3. Using the bank's **discount rate** (which might differ from the rate used to compute the maturity value), compute the discount charged by the bank for the discount period.

4. Subtract the discount charged by the bank from the maturity value to arrive at the **proceeds** to be received by the company discounting the note receivable.

Example

Returning to our fictitious Beesley Company, let us assume that on March 16, 19X1, it discounted Bannock Company's 60-day note at the Fifth National Bank at a discount rate of 12%. The calculation of the bank discount and the proceeds to Beesley are as follows:

1. Maturity value [$12,000 + ($12,000 × .10 × 60/360)	$12,200.00
2. Deduct: Bank discount ($12,200 × .12 × 45/360)	(183.00)
3. Proceeds to Beesley	$12,017.00

Beesley Company would make the following entry on March 16, 19X1:

Cash	$12,017.00	
Notes Receivable		$12,000.00
Interest Revenue		17.00

In the financial statements the footnotes would disclose the fact that Beesley Company is contingently liable for the $12,000 discounted note if the note is not paid by Bannock at the maturity date.

Dishonored Discounted Notes Receivable

If Bannock does not pay the note at the maturity date, the note is paid by Beesley. In this case Beesley makes the following entry:

Dishonored Notes Receivable	$12,200	
Cash		$12,200

Alternatively, some companies debit Accounts Receivable instead of Dishonored Notes Receivable. Beesley Company will then make every effort to collect the account from Bannock. If Beesley is unable to collect the account, one option is to debit Uncollectible Accounts Expense and credit Dishonored Notes Receivable.

PREPAID EXPENSES

Companies frequently make payments in advance for a number of expenses including insurance and rent. These payments benefit and are therefore chargeable to future periods as expenses. They are called **prepaid expenses.** On the balance sheet, items chargeable to the next accounting period are classified as current assets, while those that will expire after that time period are appropriately classified as noncurrent assets. Assume that Warbonnet Company purchased a three-year insurance policy for $3,600 cash on August 1. Warbonnet makes the following entry on August 1:

Prepaid Insurance	$3,600	
Cash		$3,600

If we assume that Warbonnet's fiscal year ends on December 31, an adjusting entry will be necessary to recognize the portion of the asset Prepaid Insurance that has expired. In this instance 5 months has expired. Since the policy is for 36 months (3 years × 12 months), $100 expires each month ($3,600/36 months). Therefore, the following entry is made by Warbonnet:

Insurance Expense (5 months × $100)	$ 500	
Prepaid Insurance		$ 500

The balance in the Prepaid Insurance account is now $3,100 ($3,600 − $500) and this is the amount that appears on the December 31 balance sheet. The income statement will show $500 of Insurance Expense for the year ended December 31.

TIMING OF REVENUE RECOGNITION

Throughout the operating cycle a company works toward the sale of the product and collection of the sales price of the product. Because each step in producing and distributing a product is essential to earning revenue, some accountants argue that the recognition of revenue should be continuous rather than being linked to a single critical event, such as the point of sale. Theoretically, they claim, we should allocate earned revenue to each part of the process. But this could be done only on an arbitrary basis, because in general, revenue can be objectively measured only at the point of sale. The critical event for revenue recognition may not be the point of sale, however, in the following three instances: (1) when collection is not reasonably assured, (2) in accounting for long-term construction contracts, and (3) in accounting in the extractive and agricultural industries.

Collection Basis

The **collection basis** of revenue recognition is used in accounting for transactions where a low down payment is made and the risk of default is high. Because the risk is high, the collection basis delays revenue recognition until cash is collected. There are two methods of collection basis revenue accounting: (1) the cost recovery method and (2) the installment sales method.

Under the **cost recovery method,** all collections are first assumed to be recoveries of the cost of the product sold. After the total cost is recovered, additional collections are considered to be gross profit. The FASB requires the use of the cost recovery method for franchise and real estate transactions because a high degree of uncertainty frequently exists regarding the collectibility of the related receivables. The FASB has mandated this requirement because in the past, some firms recognized revenue prematurely in accounting for franchise and real estate transactions where a nominal down payment was made and there was no reasonable basis for estimating collectibility. This practice was called *front-end loading.*

The **installment method** treats each dollar collected as part *return of cost* of the product and part *gross profit.* As an example, assume that a freezer with a cost of $800 is sold for $1,000 with payment over 10 months at $100 per month. Each dollar received from the buyer is viewed by the seller as a return of cost of 80% ($800/$1,000) and realization of gross profit of 20% ($200/$1,000). Therefore, a monthly payment of $100 results in a recovery of cost of $80 and the recognition of $20 of gross profit. The installment method should be used when a firm cannot reasonably estimate the extent of collectibility of the installment receivable.

Retailers like J.C. Penney, Sears, and Neiman-Marcus sell merchandise on the installment basis.

The choice between the cost recovery method or the installment method hinges on the degree of uncertainty surrounding the collectibility of the receivable. The cost recovery method is used when there is a greater degree of uncertainty regarding collectibility.

Revenue Recognized During Production

Some projects, such as the construction of ships, roads, dams, or large buildings, may take several years to complete. A **production basis of revenue recognition** is usually most appropriate in these cases. The **completed contract method,** where revenue is recognized after all production is complete, recognizes no revenue (nor expense) before completion of the project (in other words, the point of sale). This can result in a misleading income statement if the project spans several periods because prior to completion no revenue is recognized. In contrast, the **percentage of completion method** allows recognition of revenue during production. The justification for the percentage of completion method is that a continuous sale occurs as the work progresses. This method is preferred when the contract price and costs incurred are known and reliable estimates of future costs can be made.

Use of the completed contract method would result in no profit being reported until the project was completed resulting in a distorted earnings picture.

Under the percentage of completion method, a portion of the *gross profit* (revenue minus expense) from the total project is recognized each fiscal period. This is the portion estimated to have been completed during the period. A popular method of measuring the extent of progress toward completion and calculating the percentage of completion is to take the current period's actual costs and divide them by the estimated total cost of the project.

For example, assume that Hoge Construction Company has contracted to construct a large dam for $90,000,000 for which the estimated cost is $75,000,000. The estimated gross profit is therefore

$15,000,000. Construction costs consisting of materials, labor and overhead are charged to the job as incurred. If $25,000,000, or one-third ($25,000,000/$75,000,000 = 1/3), of the construction costs are incurred in the current period, then $30,000,000, or one-third (1/3 × $90,000,000), of the revenue is recognized in the current period. Since the construction costs were $25,000,000, gross profit recognized during the period is $5,000,000. (The estimated total gross profit of $15,000,000 multiplied by the percentage of completion of 33⅓% is equal to $5,000,000). Assuming a three-year construction period, revenues, costs incurred, and gross profit are calculated as follows:

Year	Cost Incurred	Percentage of Completion	
1	$25,000,000	$25,000,000/$75,000,000 =	33⅓%
2	$35,000,000	$35,000,000/$75,000,000 =	46⅔%
3	$15,000,000	$15,000,000/$75,000,000 =	20 %

Revenue Contract Price × Percent of Completion	−	Expense	=	Gross Profit Year Recognized
Year 1 $90,000,000 × 33⅓% = $30,000,000	−	$25,000,000	=	$ 5,000,000
Year 2 $90,000,000 × 46⅔% = $42,000,000	−	$35,000,000	=	$ 7,000,000
Year 3 $90,000,000 × 20 % = $18,000,000	−	$15,000,000	=	$ 3,000,000

At times actual construction costs will vary from initial estimates. When this occurs, and the variation is material, an adjustment of the amount of revenue (and profit) taken into the accounts may be necessary. Also, if at the end of any fiscal period it becomes likely that a loss will occur on the project (because of unforeseen cost changes or faulty cost estimates), the loss is recognized immediately.

Revenue Recognized at Conclusion of Production

Revenue may be recognized when production is complete, as in the mining and refining of precious metals such as gold and silver, or the production of certain agricultural products, such as corn or soybeans, where production results in a product that has a ready market at stable or assured prices. If the items are homogeneous, and there are no significant marketing costs yet to be incurred, the completion of production may be viewed as the culmination of the earnings process and revenue recognized. This is called the **completed production basis** of revenue recognition. The rationale behind this method is that revenue is realized prior to delivery to a customer because the selling price and additional costs are known with certainty and because performance (by the miner or the farmer, for example), has been substantially completed. The only remaining uncertainties relate to recovery of the selling price and delivery expenses; and these costs can be estimated as accurately as they are when revenue is recognized at the point of sale. Because of recent volatility in the market price of some precious metals and certain agricultural products, the production method is not as widely used as it once was.

In summary, the general rule is that revenue is recognized at the point of sale, but accountants have established rules dictating when it is acceptable or necessary to depart from that general rule. First, revenue can be recognized earlier than the point of sale if there is a high degree of certainty as to the amount of revenue earned and its collectibility. This means that there are no significant uncertainties regarding the remaining events in the earnings process, and the sales price and its collection are certain. Second, revenue recognition can be deferred beyond the point of sale if there is a high degree of uncertainty as to the amount of revenue, the additional costs related to the sale, or the collection of the sales price through cash payments.

The footnotes accompanying the financial statements should disclose the use of any revenue recognition methods differing from the point of sale general rule. The reader of financial statements should be aware of these alternate methods and understand their effects on net income.

Controversy over Timing of Revenue Recognition—An Example

Although accountants have developed guidelines for determining when revenue should be recognized, these guidelines do not apply to all circumstances that arise as business practices change.

For example, two exposure drafts have been issued stating the FASB's position on revenue recognition for frequent flier plans. At this writing, the Board has not finalized a position on the accounting treatment for these plans. Frequent flier plans started out in 1981 as a way for airlines to retain their most valued customers. The way the plans work is that after you travel a minimum number of miles on a particular airline, you become eligible for free trips and/or upgrades to first class. Because of competition, some airlines have awarded triple the number of actual miles traveled to a frequent flier's account. The result is that frequent fliers are amassing so many miles of free travel and tickets (some estimates are as high as 30 billion miles of free travel!) that they are often replacing paying passengers at peak hours on heavily traveled routes.

The airlines account for the revenue derived from the sale of a ticket at the date the transportation is provided with no provision for the liability associated with the frequent flier awards. The costs associated with the free travel are recognized when the free travel award is earned. This practice was acceptable when the use of these travel awards was insignificant, because (it was argued) free flight passengers filled only the airplane seats that would have been empty anyway. However, with the increasing amount of free travel awarded, it is obvious that travelers are purchasing tickets with the expectation of using the free flights when they are earned. As a result, some accountants suggest that when the ticket is sold and the ticketed travel provided, the earnings process is not complete. They believe that a part of the revenue derived from the original sale of the ticket should be deferred and reported as a liability. Other accountants feel that, additionally, airlines should be required to recognize a liability to cover the full value of free tickets and the upgrading of economy class tickets. To date, this issue is still unresolved, and any of the methods discussed may be used.[2] How significant is the problem? See Insight 3–3 for a discussion of the information airlines recently disclosed regarding their frequent flier programs.

RATIO ANALYSIS

Current Ratio =

$\dfrac{\text{Current Assets}}{\text{Current Liabilities}}$

Liquidity refers to the company's ability to pay its short-term obligations. Liquidity can be measured by several ratios, of which two are especially important and relate to current assets. Both ratios are affected by a company's balances in its current asset accounts. The first is the **current ratio,** a measure of the relationship between current assets and current liabilities.

$$\text{Current Ratio} = \frac{\text{Current Assets}}{\text{Current Liabilities}}$$

Current assets are short-term assets that either are cash, or will become cash, or will be used in operations in one year. Examples are receivables that will be collected in 90 days, or inventory on hand that will be sold in the next quarter. Current liabilities are debts that must be paid in one year or less. Any part of a long-term debt that comes due in the next year is also a current liability. Accounts payable or next year's install-

---

[2] In 1988 the Accounting Standards Executive Committee of the American Institute of Certified Public Accountants issued a Statement of Position (SOP) regarding frequent flier programs. The SOP recommended that a part of the revenue obtained from the sale of tickets to frequent fliers be deferred and recognized when the frequent flier tickets were used. The SOP is only a recommendation and does not have the same effect as a FASB pronouncement.

INSIGHT 3–3
Frequent Flier Liabilities

At the request of the federal government, U.S. airlines are divulging information on their frequent flier programs in filings with the Securities and Exchange Commission (SEC). The airlines include Alaska, American, American West, Continental, Pan Am, Southwest, TWA, United and USAir. The disclosures could ease worries regarding the airlines giving away too many free seats and not leaving enough seats for paying passengers—free trips by frequent fliers amounted only to a little less than 6% of the miles flown by paying customers. The reports showed that:

1. The nine airlines "collectively gave 4.5 million free trips to members of their frequent flier programs last year (up from 3.6 million trips the year before).

2. Free travel appears to be up from 1988.

3. The airlines believe many frequent fliers will not use all the free trips to which they are entitled. American puts this figure at 20% and United at 25%.

4. When the free trips that will not be claimed are taken into consideration, the dollar amount of the free flights is small compared to total expenses.

The disclosures were mandated by the SEC because of investor concern over the amount of liabilities relating to these programs. Since then, several airlines have reduced these liabilities by setting deadlines to redeem miles for free trips and raising the number of miles needed to claim trips.

The requirement by the SEC followed three years of debate within the accounting profession as to how airlines should account for the liability for providing for these free trips. The FASB ultimately decided not to take a position on the issue.*

* "Accounting For Frequent Fliers," *USA Today*, May 22, 1991, 9B. Copyright 1991, USA TODAY. Reprinted with permission.

ment on a 40-year mortgage are examples of current liabilities. Exhibit 3–5 shows the current asset and current liability sections of the 1990 Boise Cascade Corporation's annual report. We can compute the current ratios for the years 1990, 1989, and 1988 by dividing the current assets for each year by the current liabilities for that year. In this case, the current ratios are 1.32:1, 1.37:1, and 1.27:1 for the years 1990, 1989, and 1988, respectively.

Exhibit 3–5
Boise Cascade Corporation
Portions of Balance Sheet

Balance Sheets
Boise Cascade Corporation and Subsidiaries

	December 31		
Assets	**1990**	**1989**	**1988**
	(expressed in thousands)		
Current			
Cash and cash items (Note 1)	$ 19,781	$ 19,715	$ 12,103
Short-term investments at cost, which approximates market (Note 1)	6,165	5,526	11,157
	25,946	25,241	23,260
Receivables, less allowances of $4,315,000, $3,800,000, and $3,405,000	412,558	421,568	393,371
Inventories (Note 1)	484,972	424,439	398,749
Deferred income tax benefits	55,115	48,716	40,404
Other	18,992	12,353	10,819
	997,583	932,317	866,603

	December 31		
Liabilities and Shareholders' Equity	**1990**	**1989**	**1988**
	(expressed in thousands)		
Current			
Notes payable	$ 40,000	$ —	$ —
Current portion of long-term debt	136,731	30,390	73,320
Income taxes payable	140	4,273	4,558
Accounts payable	344,384	391,542	354,827
Accrued liabilities			
Compensation and benefits	99,530	114,082	111,508
Interest payable	38,460	40,071	37,194
Other	99,127	97,866	99,208
	758,372	678,224	680,615

Quick Ratio =

Cash
+ Short-Term
Investments
+ Receivables
Current Liabilities

The second important liquidity ratio is called the **quick,** or **acid-test, ratio.** The quick ratio refers to the quick assets of cash, short-term investments, and receivables divided by current liabilities. This ratio is a more short-term measure of liquidity because inventories and prepaids are excluded from the calculation. Generally, inventory is sold to create an account receivable, and the receivable must then be collected before cash is available to pay short-term creditors. Prepaids are not sold but their benefit expires over time. Because prepaids and inventory are further removed from conversion into cash, only the highly liquid current assets of cash, short-term investments and receivables, are used in the numerator. The quick ratio therefore provides a worst-case scenario. That is, can the firm meet its current obligations even if the inventory is not sold. From Exhibit 3–5 we can calculate the quick ratios for 1990, 1989, and 1988 by adding cash, short-term investments, and accounts receivable and dividing this sum by the current liabilities for each of the three years. The quick ratios for 1990, 1989, and 1988 are .58:1, .66:1, and .61:1, respectively.

As a general rule, companies strive to maintain current ratios of 2:1 and quick ratios of 1:1. In looking at the Boise Cascade ratios you might think that a problem exists because the ratios are less than the rule of thumb. However, in reality these rules of thumb are relatively useless. To have any meaning these ratios must be compared to ratios of other companies in the same industry or viewed as part of a trend for that company. Primarily, ratios serve only to signal the need for further analysis. We are interested in them when they show an increase or decrease or fall below an industry average. Ratios that are less than the rules of thumb may nevertheless be appropriate for the changing economic climate of a particular company's industry.

SUMMARY

Internal control is extremely important, particularly in conjunction with the cash account. Good internal controls over cash include the prompt deposit of cash receipts as well as the use of checks for disbursements of cash. The bank reconciliation is another example of the use of internal control over cash transactions. The use of a petty cash fund for small expenditures is demonstrated in the appendix.

Companies periodically make use of idle cash by investing in short-term investments such as treasury bills, certificates of deposit, bonds, and common and preferred stocks. These short-term investments are recorded at their acquisition cost and carried on the balance sheet as current assets.

Sales revenue is earned when companies sell products that have been purchased or manufactured. Adjustments to sales revenue include discounts for prompt payment and sales returns and allowances.

Accounts receivable is an amount owed to the company resulting from sales made on credit. The allowance method is used in accounting for uncollectible accounts.

Notes receivable result from transactions with creditors, customers, and suppliers. Sometimes customers exchange notes receivable for their overdue accounts receivable. Unlike accounts receivable, notes receivable customarily bear interest. Notes receivable that are not paid on their maturity date are reclassified as dishonored notes receivable, also a current asset.

A company might not want to wait until the maturity date to collect the proceeds of a note receivable. In this case, the company would discount the note receivable at a financial institution, normally a bank. The bank would charge the company a discount based on the time period that the bank holds the note.

Prepaid expenses are current assets that a company pays for currently with the expectation that the benefit to be received from the payment will occur in a future period or periods. Prepaid expenses, such as insurance, are evaluated at year end and adjusted for the expired portion of the asset.

The current ratio and the quick ratio are two important measures of a company's liquidity. Liquidity ratios are designed to measure a company's ability to meet its short-term obligations.

The most common point of revenue recognition is the point of sale. Other possible points of revenue recognition exist too. Specifically, the installment or cost recovery method on a cash basis for revenue recognition is appropriate if no reasonable basis for estimating collectibility exists. Revenue can be recognized on a production basis for long-term construction contracts if reliable estimates of the extent of completion and the cost to completion can be made, and if reasonable assurance as to collectibility can be ascertained. If current marketability at a stated price exists for a homogeneous product, revenue can be recognized at the end of production.

APPENDIX—THE PETTY CASH FUND

In this chapter we noted that companies should deposit cash receipts daily and should make payments using serially numbered checks to have proper control over cash receipts and disbursements. However, many times it is convenient to have small amounts of cash on hand to pay for small expenditures such as postage, freight, supplies, or stamps. For this reason, companies establish **petty cash funds.**

The fund is established by writing a check for a small amount, perhaps $150. This amount should be enough to cover expenditures for a short period of time such as a month. A petty cash custodian cashes the check and is responsible for maintaining the fund. The journal entry to establish the fund is:

Petty Cash Fund	$150	
Cash		$150

Exhibit 3–6
Petty Cash Voucher

Petty Cash Voucher

No. _____343_____ Amount _____$26.75_____

Date _____10/26/90_____

Explanation _____Payment to Great Western Trucking_____

_____for freight on office furniture_____

Approved by _____ Received _____

A petty cash voucher, such as that shown in Exhibit 3–6, is prepared by the custodian each time cash is disbursed from the fund. (It is possible that a company may not use a voucher system but instead use an invoice or some other type of receipt as support for expenditures from the fund.) The voucher shows the date, amount, and reason for the expenditure. Approval for the expenditure is evidenced by the signature of the custodian and the voucher is signed by the person receiving the cash. Note that the custodian is responsible for seeing that the sum of the remaining cash in the fund and vouchers are equal to the total amount initially put into the fund.

From time to time, the petty cash fund must be replenished. Assume that on September 30 the fund contains:

Cash	$ 27.38
Voucher #16 Supplies	13.27
Voucher #17 Postage	17.88
Voucher #18 Freight	37.29
Voucher #19 Employee Advance (Loan)	54.18
Total of Petty Cash Fund	$150.00

After the vouchers have been inspected for completeness, a check is drawn for $122.62 (the amount of the four vouchers). The fund is now restored to the $150 balance. The following journal entry is made to record the reimbursement and the as yet unrecorded loan and expenditures:

Supplies Expense	$ 13.27	
Postage Expense	17.88	
Freight Expense	37.29	
Employee Advance Receivable	54.18	
Cash		$122.62

Petty Cash Vouchers + Amount in Petty Cash should always equal the established petty cash amount.

Notice that the account Petty Cash Fund was not affected by the reimbursement entry, and the expenditures are recorded only when the fund is replenished. The account Petty Cash Fund is debited only when the fund is established or enlarged. Similarly the fund is credited only when it is reduced (and the excess is deposited in another company bank account) or abolished.

What happens if a company discovers upon replenishment that the total of the cash and the vouchers in the fund does not equal the established fund balance? The implication is that an error has been made in making change from the petty cash fund. If the total of the vouchers plus the cash on hand is less than the fund balance, the fund is "short." On the other hand, if the total of the vouchers and the cash on hand exceeds the established fund balance, the fund is "over." These shortages and overages are debited or credited to an account called Cash Short or Over. Assume in our preceding example that instead of cash on hand of $27.38, the cash on hand was $25.00. The following entry would have been made to replenish the fund:

Supplies Expense	$13.27	
Postage Expense	17.88	
Freight Expense	37.29	
Employee Advance Receivable	54.18	
Cash Short or Over	2.38	
Cash		$125.00

The cash on hand of $25.00, and the replenishment with $125.00 now totals the established fund balance of $150.00. A debit balance in the Cash Short or Over account signifies a miscellaneous expense, and a credit balance is treated as miscellaneous revenue for income statement purposes.

DEMONSTRATION PROBLEMS

Demonstration Problem 3–1
The bank statement of Crouse Company's checking account was received from the Bank of Rhode Island for the month ended November

30, 19X1. The ending balance on that day per the bank statement was $10,341.29. Crouse Company's accountant noted that the bank's service charge for the month was $21.26 and two customer NSF checks were returned with the statement. One was for $626.00 from F. Poole and the other was for $910.25 from L. Floyed. The following disbursement checks had not cleared the bank and were outstanding on November 30: #2103 for $1,046.90, #2105 for $623.22, and #2167 for $89.11. Additionally, the bank collected a note receivable for Crouse Company of $1,100, including interest of $90. A deposit made by Crouse Company's accountant on the night of November 30 (not reflected on the bank statement) was for $2,200.00. The accountant noted that check #2101 for supplies still on hand was incorrectly recorded on the company's books at $302.00 and was properly deducted by the bank for $203.00. The company's balance per books on November 30, 19X1 was $11,140.57.

a. Prepare a bank reconciliation as of November 30, 19X1.

b. Prepare any adjusting entries to properly reflect the cash balance on the books of Crouse Company as of November 30, 19X1.

Solution to Demonstration Problem 3–1

Balance per bank statement as of November 30, 19X1		$10,341.29
Add: deposit in transit		2,200.00
		12,541.29
Deduct: outstanding checks		
#2102	$1,046.90	
#2105	623.22	
#2167	89.11	1,759.23
Adjusted balance as of November 30, 19X1		$10,782.06
Balance per books as of November 30, 19X1		$11,140.57
Add: Note receivable collected by bank	$1,010.00	
Interest revenue	90.00	1,100.00
Error ($302.00 – $203.00) by company		99.00
		12,339.57
Less: bank service charge	$ 21.26	
NSF check—F. Poole	626.00	
NSF check—L. Floyed	910.25	1,557.51
Adjusted balance as of November 30, 19X1		$10,782.06

Demonstration Problem 3–2

The Koster Company had the following transactions for the month of May 19X1 relating to its investments in short-term marketable equity securities. Prepare journal entries to record these transactions.

May 2   Purchased 25,000 shares of Bortz Company stock at $3.50 per share.

May 3   Purchased 9,100 shares of Cable Company when the stock was trading for $7.00 per share.

May 7   Purchased 7,350 shares of Aztec Corporation stock at a market value of $26.00 per share.

May 19 Sold 10,000 shares of Bortz Company stock for $3.75 per share.

May 21 Sold 2,300 shares of Aztec for $21.00 per share.

May 31 To prepare its quarterly financial statements, Koster valued its portfolio of short-term marketable equity securities at the lower of cost or market. Market prices for its investments were:

Aztec Corporation	$27.30 per share
Bortz Company	1.25 per share
Cable Company	5.00 per share

Solution to Demonstration Problem 3–2

May 2	Investment in Short-Term Marketable Equity Securities	$87,500	
	Cash (25,000 × $3.50)		$87,500
May 3	Investment in Short-Term Marketable Equity Securities	$63,700	
	Cash (9,100 × $7.00)		$63,700
May 7	Investment in Short-Term Marketable Equity Securities	$191,100	
	Cash (7,350 × $26.00)		$191,100
May 19	Cash (10,000 × $3.75)	$37,500	
	Investment in Short-Term Marketable Equity Securities (10,000 × $3.50)		$35,000
	Gain on Sale of Investment in Short-Term Marketable Equity Securities		2,500

May 21	Cash (2,300 × $21.00)	$48,300	
	Loss on Sale of Investment in Short-Term Marketable Equity Securities	11,500	
	Investment in Short-Term Marketable Equity Securities (2,300 × $26.00)		$59,800
May 31	Unrealized Loss on Investment in Short-Term Marketable Equity Securities	$45,385	
	Allowance to Reduce Investment in Short-Term Marketable Equity Securities to Market ($247,500 − $202,115)		$45,385

	Cost
Aztec Corporation (5,050 × $26.00)	$131,300
Bortz Company (15,000 × $3.50)	52,500
Cable Company (9,100 × $7.00)	63,700
	$247,500

	Market
Aztec Corporation (5,050 × $27.30)	$137,865
Bortz Company (15,000 × $1.25)	18,750
Cable Company (9,100 × $5.00)	45,500
	$202,115

Demonstration Problem 3-3

Journalize transactions for Peyron Company for the month of April 19X1. Its fiscal year-end is April 30.

April 1   Purchased a three-year property insurance policy for $5,400 cash.

April 3   Sold merchandise to Wall Company for $7,800, terms 2/10, n30.

April 4   Sold merchandise to Small Company for $10,000, terms 3/10, n30.

April 5   Wall Company returned $500 of the merchandise purchased on April 3, and Small Company returned $550 of the merchandise purchased on April 4.

April 10   Wall Company paid the balance of its account.

April 15   Ball Company exchanged its $4,000 90-day, 12% note receivable for its overdue account receivable.

April 17   Small Company paid the balance of its account.

April 25   Discounted the Ball Company note receivable at Bob's Bank. The bank's discount rate is 14%.

April 30   The company made its year-end adjusting entry to record uncollectible accounts expense. The company records uncollectible accounts expense under the percentage of credit sales method. Past experience indicates that 4% of credit sales made in 19X1 will not be collected. Credit sales for the current year were $345,600.

April 30   The company prepared its year-end adjusting entry to reflect the expired portion of prepaid insurance.

Solution to Demonstration Problem 3–3

April 1	Prepaid Insurance	$5,400	
	Cash		$5,400
April 3	Accounts Receivable	$7,800	
	Sales		$7,800
April 4	Accounts Receivable	$10,000	
	Sales		$10,000
April 5	Sales Returns & Allowances	$ 500	
	Accounts Receivable		$ 500
April 5	Sales Returns & Allowances	$ 550	
	Accounts Receivable		$ 550
April 10	Cash ($7,800 − $500).98	$7,154	
	Sales Discounts	146	
	Accounts Receivable		$7,300
April 15	Notes Receivable	$4,000	
	Accounts Receivable		$4,000
April 17	Cash ($10,000 − $550)	$9,450	
	Accounts Receivable		$9,450

April 25	Maturity value [$4,000 + ($4,000 × .12		
	× 90/360)]		$4,120.00
	Less: discount ($4,120 × .14 × 80/360)		128.18
	Proceeds to Peyron Company		$3,991.82
	Cash	$3,991.82	
	Interest Expense	8.18	
	Notes Receivable		$4,000.00
April 30	Uncollectible Accounts Expense		
	($345,600 × .04)	$13,824	
	Allowance for Uncollectible		
	Accounts		$13,824
April 30	Insurance Expense (1/36 × $5,400)	$150	
	Prepaid Insurance		$150

Demonstration Problem 3-4

During the current year Allen Company sold 150 refrigerators to customers on credit. The sales price of each refrigerator was $800 and the cost of each refrigerator was $600. Cash payments received by Allen Company totaled $42,000 for the year. Because of the risk associated with the collectibility of the total sales price of the refrigerators, the company decided to use the installment method of gross profit recognition in accounting for these sales. What was the total amount of gross profit recognized by Allen Company from the sales of the refrigerators?

Solution to Demonstration Problem 3-4

Gross Profit = $800 − $600 = $200
Gross Profit Percent = $200/$800 = 25%
Cash Collections × Gross Profit Percent = Gross Profit Recognized
$42,000 × 25% = $10,500

Demonstration Problem 3-5

Crash Construction Company has contracted with Kalivas Shipping Company to build a 200,000-ton freighter for a contract price of $32,000,000. Crash estimates the freighter will cost $26,000,000 and will take approximately three years to construct. For this reason, Crash will use the percentage of completion method to account for the revenue derived from the construction of the freighter. Total costs incurred in the first two years of construction were $6,500,000 and $10,400,000, respectively. What was the amount of gross profit recognized by Crash Construction Company in each of the two years?

Solution to Demonstration Problem 3–5

Total contract price	$32,000,000
Estimated construction costs	26,000,000
Estimated gross profit	$ 6,000,000

Year 1

$$\text{Percent of completion} = \frac{\$6,500,000}{\$26,000,000} = .25$$

$6,000,000 × .25 = $1,500,000 gross profit recognized in current year

Year 2

$$\text{Percent of completion} = \frac{\$6,500,000 + \$10,400,000}{26,000,000} = .65$$

$6,000,000 × .65 =	$3,900,000
Less gross profit recognized in previous year	1,500,000
Gross profit recognized in current year	$2,400,000*

*Alternatively, the calculation could have been made by:

$$\frac{\$10,400,000}{\$26,000,000} = .4$$

$6,000,000 × .4 = $2,400,000

The gross profit could also have been calculated by taking the contract price of $32,000,000 and multiplying it by the percentage of completion (.25), resulting in gross revenue of $8,000,000. If we subtract the cost incurred in year 1 of $6,500,000 from the $8,000,000, the result is gross profit of $1,500,000. This process could be repeated for the second year to arrive at the gross profit of $2,400,000.

Key Terms

accounts receivable

allowance for uncollectible
    accounts

bad (uncollectible) debt

cash discounts

collection basis

completed contract method

completed production basis

contra asset account

cost recovery method

current ratio

discounted notes receivable

discount rate

installment method

internal control

liquidity

lower of cost or market

maturity value

notes receivable

percentage of completion
    method

petty cash fund

prepaid expenses

production basis of revenue
    recognition

quick (or acid-test) ratio

realizable value

realization principle

sales

sales returns and allowances

short-term investments

uncollectible accounts expense

ASSIGNMENTS

3-1   Bank Reconciliation

The bank statement for Moore Company's checking account with the
Third National Bank showed an ending balance of $6,345 on November
22, 19X1. The statement also indicated that service charges were
$22.50, an NSF check was returned amounting to $610, and the bank
collected a note of $1,300 plus interest of $15.75. A deposit of $700
made late on November 22 by Moore Company is included in the
general ledger balance but did not appear on the bank statement from
Third National Bank. The general ledger balance on November 22,
19X1 was $1,031, and after a review of the checks returned by the
bank, the amount of outstanding checks totaled $5,330.75.

REQUIRED:

1. Prepare a bank reconciliation as of November 22, 19X1.

2. Prepare any adjusting entries to properly reflect the cash balance in
    the account of Moore Company on November 22, 19X1.

3-2   Calculation of Outstanding Checks

As of December 1, 19X1, Reynolds Company had outstanding checks of $12,500 per its bank reconciliation. During that same month, the company issued $49,300 in checks. The bank statement as of December 31, 19X1 indicated that $42,800 in checks had cleared during the month. What was the amount of outstanding checks as of December 31, 19X1?

3-3   Calculation of Deposits in Transit

Russky Company's March 31 bank statement shows total deposits into its checking account of $29,870 for the month of March. On February 28 deposits in transit per books totaled $4,456. Cash receipts per books totaled $38,778 for the month of March. What were the total amount of deposits in transit at March 31?

3-4   Bank Reconciliation

Prepare a bank reconciliation as of January 31 from the following information:

1. The balance shown on the bank statement on January 31 is $1,690.
2. Outstanding checks totaled $613.
3. A deposit in-transit was made for $340.
4. Interest earned on the account but not reflected on the books was $17.
5. The bank statement showed a service charge of $8 that was not reflected on the books.
6. In reviewing the canceled checks returned with the bank statement, it was determined that check #307 was correctly issued for $96 but was erroneously recorded at $69.
7. The balance per books on January 31 was $1,435.

3-5   Accounting for Short-Term Investments—Common Stock

Kell Company purchased 2,000 shares of Sybex Corporation common stock on September 25 when its market value was $25 per share. Brokerage fees were $185. On December 15 of the current year Kell Company sold the shares.

REQUIRED:

1. Record the purchase of the shares on September 25.
2. Record the sale of the shares on December 15 assuming they were sold for $23 per share.
3. Record the sale of the shares on December 15 assuming they were sold for $30 per share.

3–6 Accounting for Short-Term Investments—Bonds

On August 1, 19X1, Dos Corporation purchased bonds for $12,250 including brokerage fees. The semiannual interest payment dates are January 1 and July 1, and the semiannual interest paid to the bondholder is $840. The company has a calendar year-end.

REQUIRED:

1. Record the purchase of the bonds on August 1, 19X1.
2. Record the necessary adjusting entry on December 31, 19X1 for the accrued interest on the bonds.

3–7 Accounting for Short-Term Investments—Marketable Equity Securities

Nickerson Company has the following portfolio of marketable equity securities at December 31, the company's fiscal year-end:

- Janus Company—cost 1,000 shares @ $11 per share
- Twentieth Century Company—cost 1,700 shares @ $17 per share
- Financial Company—cost 1,350 shares @ $13 per share

On December 31, the market values of the company's investment in marketable equity securities was:

Janus Company	$12.00 per share
Twentieth Century Company	$16.50 per share
Financial Company	$11.00 per share

REQUIRED:

1. Provide the journal entry that is needed to value the portfolio at the lower of cost or market on December 31.
2. Provide the financial statement presentation at December 31 of the marketable equity securities.

3–8 Accounting for Sales

Journalize the following transactions for the Shirley Corporation assuming all accounts receivable are recorded at gross:

1. January 12, 19X1 Alpha Company purchased on account $7,500 of merchandise from Shirley at terms 3/10, n30.
2. January 21, 19X1 Alpha returned $600 of the merchandise purchased on January 12 to Shirley for credit.

3. January 29, 19X1 Beta Company purchased on account $12,489 of merchandise from Shirley at terms 2/12, n20.

4. February 5, 19X1 Alpha paid the balance in full on its account.

5. February 6, 19X1 Beta paid the balance in full on its account.

3–9   Cash Discounts—Effective Rate of Interest

Based on the following terms, calculate the effective rate of interest assuming that the merchandise was purchased for $100, and payment was not made within the discount period.

1. 1/10, n30

2. 2/10, n30

3. 3/15, n30

4. 1/5, n60

3–10   Cash Discounts

Butler Manufacturing Company sold merchandise to LeBlond Company for $25,000 with terms of 2/10, n30 on April 1.

REQUIRED:

1. Record the sale of the merchandise by Butler on April 1.

2. Record the payment by LeBlond Company for the merchandise on April 8 on Butler's books.

3. Record the payment by LeBlond Company for the merchandise assuming instead that the payment was made on April 16 on Butler's books.

3–11   Accounting for Accounts Receivable

On September 30, 19X2, Cleboe Company had an accounts receivable net realizable value of $68,625. The balance in accounts receivable on October 1, 19X1, was $6,458, while the balance in the Allowance for Uncollectible Accounts account on the same day was a debit balance of $1,200. Uncollectible accounts expense was estimated to be $5,260 based on fiscal year 19X1-X2 sales of $160,000 (of which $44,351 was for cash). The balance in the Allowance for Uncollectible Accounts account on September 30, 19X2 was $2,540.

REQUIRED:

1. What were cash collections on account for 19X1–X2?

2. Record the journal entry for uncollectible accounts expense for 19X1–X2.

3. If one-half of the total accounts receivable written off in 19X1-X2 were subsequently collected in December 19X2, what would the entry be?

3–12 Calculation of Uncollectible Accounts Expense

Richmond Corporation had the following information for calendar year 19X1:

Sales (including $117,000 for cash)	$387,000	
Allowance for Uncollectible Accounts, January 1, 19X1	2,700	50,000
Accounts Receivable balance, December 31, 19X1	116,000	
Write-offs of accounts receivable for the year	1,850	

REQUIRED:

Calculate and record the amount of uncollectible accounts expense under each of the following assumptions:

1. The company records uncollectible accounts expense using the percentage of credit sales method. Past experience indicates that 3% of credit sales made in 19X1 will not be collected.

2. The company records uncollectible accounts expense under the percentage of accounts receivable method. Past experience indicates that 4% of the existing balance of accounts receivable will not be collected.

3–13 Accounting for Uncollectible Accounts Receivable— Aging Method

Big Breath Company uses the percentage of accounts receivable method to calculate uncollectible accounts expense. Big Breath furnishes you with the following information:

Balance in Receivables	Not Yet Due	Number of Days Past Due			
		1–30	31–60	61–90	Over 90
$425,000	$275,000	$87,000	$26,780	$19,546	$16,674

Past experience indicates that 1.2% of those accounts not yet due will prove to be uncollectible. For 1–30 days past due, 4.9% will be uncollectible; 31–60 days past due, 6.7% will be uncollectible; 61–90 days past due, 8.3% will be uncollectible, and over 90 days past due, 55.0% will be uncollectible. The beginning balance in the allowance for uncollectible accounts account was $1,256.

REQUIRED:

Calculate the uncollectible accounts expense using the information provided.

3–14   Management of Accounts Receivable

Harvey Company has monthly sales of 15,000 units at $12 per unit. The company has variable costs of $4 per units and fixed costs of $45,000. The sales manager feels that a new market segment will generate additional sales of 2,000 units; however, the sales will be on account, and the estimate of bad debt losses is 45%. The credit manager emphatically states that "this is too high a risk and the company should not make the sale." What do you think?

3–15   Accounting for Notes Receivable

Record the following transactions for the Delta Company:

1. June 1   The Delta Company sold $5,000 of merchandise to XYZ Company, terms, 2/10, n 30.

2. July 15   XYZ Company exchanged a $5,000 90-day, 13% note receivable for its overdue account receivable.

3. July 31   Delta sold $7,000 of merchandise to ABC Company. Because of previous credit problems with ABC, Delta required ABC to sign a 60-day, 15% note receivable.

4. September 29   The ABC Company informed Delta Company that it would be unable to pay the note receivable at the maturity date.

5. October 13   The XYZ Company paid the note receivable in full.

3–16   Discounting of Notes Receivable

Reese Company issued a $21,000 note receivable in exchange for merchandise purchased from Weeks Company on March 15 of the current year. The note receivable was for 120 days at an annual interest rate of 11%. On June 13, Weeks Company discounted the note at the Valley Bank at a discount rate of 9%. Provide the journal entry to record the receipt of the proceeds by Weeks Company on June 13.

3–17   Accounting for Prepayments

Soto Corporation purchased casualty insurance on September 1 of the current year for $2,400. The policy is for two years. The company's fiscal year-end is December 31.

REQUIRED:

1. Provide the entry to record the purchase of the policy.

2. Provide the year-end adjusting entry to recognize the expired portion of the insurance.

3–18 Ratio Analysis

Refer to the balance sheet for Wal-Mart Stores, Inc., for the years ended January 31, 1991, and 1990:

REQUIRED:

1. Calculate the current ratio for Wal-Mart Stores, Inc., for the years ended January 31, 1991, and 1990.

2. Calculate the quick ratio for Wal-Mart Stores, Inc. for the years ended January 31, 1991, and 1990.

3–19 Wal-Mart Stores, Inc., Annual Report

Refer again to the annual report of Wal-Mart Stores, Inc., and answer the following questions:

1. What types of receivables did Wal-Mart hold on January 31, 1991?

2. What types of current liabilities did Wal-Mart owe on January 31, 1991?

3. What were the amounts of prepaid expenses for Wal-Mart as January 31, 1991, and 1990, respectively?

4. What do you think accounted for the significant increase in accounts receivable from 1990 to 1991?

3–20 Ratio Analysis

The following information is presented for Lycra Company:

Cash	$ 3,000
Short-Term Investments	5,000
Accounts Receivable (net)	5,000
Inventory	10,000
Prepaid Insurance	2,000
Total Current Assets	$25,000

REQUIRED:

1. If the company's current ratio is 1.95:1, what are total current liabilities?

2. What is the company's quick ratio?

3–21 Revenue Recognition

Bonneville Power Company has contracted to construct a power station next to the Island Park Dam on Henry's Fork of the Snake River. The contract price was $44,000,000. Initial total cost estimates of Bonneville Power were $40,000,000 to complete the project. At the end of

124

the current year $10,000,000 had been incurred on the project with the projected total cost estimate still at $40,000,000.

REQUIRED:

1. Assuming Bonneville Power uses the percentage-of-completion method for recognizing revenue, how much revenue should be recognized in the current period?

2. What is the amount of gross profit that Bonneville Power should recognize for the current year?

3–22   Revenue Recognition

LJP Company is deciding whether to use the installment method or the cost recovery method to account for its 19X0 and 19X1 sales. The following information is taken from LJP's accounting records:

	19X0	19X1
Installment Sales	$60,000	$200,000
Cost of Installment Sales	30,000	150,000
Cash Collected on 19X0 Sales	25,000	30,000
Cash Collected on 19X1 Sales	-0-	40,000

REQUIRED:

1. Compute the gross profit recognized by LJP under the installment method for 19X0 and 19X1 and explain when this method should be used.

2. Compute the income recognized by LJP under the cost recovery method for 19X0 and 19X1 and explain when this method should be used.

3–23   Petty Cash Fund

Gary Rhoades Company uses a petty cash fund totaling $250 to account for small expenditures. At June 30, a count of the fund disclosed the followed information:

Voucher for employee advance	$102.20
Voucher for payment of supplies	23.78
Voucher for stamps	16.89
Voucher for freight	38.92
Currency	54.67
Coins	6.38

REQUIRED:

Provide the proper entry to replenish the fund.

3–24 DECISION CASE: CREDIT POLICY AND PRODUCT LINE EXPANSION

Jimmy's All-Season's Angler is a retail store selling top-of-the-line fly fishing rods. These graphite and bamboo fly rods are normally sold to upper-income professionals. Because of the high selling prices, he makes very few credit sales. In fact, over the past five years Jimmy has averaged credit sales of approximately 12% of total sales. However, in the past several years, a significant number of his competitors have begun to sell their fishing rods on credit. He is concerned about his strict credit policy and has asked you to advise him as to whether he should ease his credit policy and perhaps expand his line of rods. Jimmy tells you that total sales have been averaging approximately $115,000 a year with uncollectible accounts averaging 2%, gross margin of 25%, and selling expenses of $13,000. Jimmy estimates that he can sell two additional lines of fishing rods that are less expensive and would appeal to two other groups of customers, if credit were extended. These customers are spinner fishermen and bait fishermen. He tells you that if he sells these fishing rods on credit terms, his sales will increase but so will his uncollectible accounts. The estimate of the increase in credit sales for spinning rods is $25,000 with 7% uncollectible and additional selling expenses of $1,100. The estimated increase in credit sales of bait-casting rods is $17,000 with 5% uncollectible and additional selling expenses of $1,300. The gross margin on spinning and bait-casting rods is the same as that on fly rods. Finally, Jimmy tells you that if he decides to carry the additional lines, he will have to ease his credit policy and this would result in additional credit sales from existing lines of $20,000, uncollectible accounts of approximately 5% of that amount and additional selling expenses of $900. What would you advise Jimmy to do? Are there any additional factors that Jimmy should consider in making his decision regarding his credit policy and whether to expand his product line?

4

Inventories and Cost of Goods Sold

LEARNING OBJECTIVES

After studying Chapter 4, you should be able to:
1. Discuss the importance of accounting for inventory properly.
2. Account for inventories using either the periodic or perpetual method, and know when each should be used.
3. Record purchases using either the gross or net price method, and describe how each method might affect the behavior of the company's financial officer.
4. Record inventory using each of the cost-flow assumptions and describe how each method affects the income statement and balance sheet.
5. Estimate inventories using the gross margin and retail inventory methods.

The largest single expense for many companies is the **cost of goods sold** and the largest current asset is the **inventory** of merchandise awaiting sale. Accountants can choose from among several methods of accounting for inventory. Each method is appropriate for some business conditions and results from making an assumption about the flow of goods through the company or costs through the accounting system.

We begin by examining the basic principles of calculating and recording cost of goods sold and investment in inventory. In the second part of the chapter we discuss and illustrate several cost-flow assumptions, and in the last section we deal with several popular methods of estimating cost of goods sold and inventory.

PERIODIC METHOD

The most basic method of accounting for merchandise inventory is the **periodic method.** Using this procedure we simply count the inventory at the end of a period and determine its cost to find the balance sheet figure for merchandise inventory. Insight 4−1 describes one cost-effective way of counting inventory. We then subtract that inventory cost from the sum of the beginning inventory and purchases to determine cost of goods sold. For example, suppose that a company begins a month with $120,000 inventory and purchases $670,000 during the month. At the end of the month employees count the inventory and determine its cost to be $90,000. What is cost of goods sold? The answer is $700,000 ($120,000 + $670,000 − $90,000).

The most basic method of accounting for merchandise inventory is the periodic method.

Purchases

Most companies that use the periodic inventory method use a temporary account for purchases of inventory, usually called Purchases. If the Inventory account had a beginning balance of $1,000, and $5,000 of merchandise was purchased during the period, the Purchases account would have a balance of $5,000 and the Inventory account would still have its beginning balance of $1,000. If a count of merchandise in the storeroom at the end of the period found $2,000 still on hand, the accounts would be adjusted to show a current asset, Inventory, of $2,000 and an expense, Cost of Goods Sold, of $4,000 ($1,000 + $5,000 − $2,000). The adjusting entry (below) brings the balance in the Purchases account to zero, and the account would be ready to accumulate the cost of purchases made during the next period. If the revenue from sales of inventory totaled $8,000, journal entries for these events as follows during the period.

INSIGHT 4–1
Counting Inventory Takes Time

Inventory must be counted for control purposes, but a company's periodic count of inventory often requires a great deal of time and involvement by company personnel. As a result, many companies use *inventory cycle counts* that involve rotating inventory counts from location to location during the year. Following is the experience of a company in Philadelphia.

One of our company's inventory control devices is the semiannual verification and reconciliation of the product inventory in the storage tanks of its several thousand retail outlets.

This 100 percent verification and reconciliation has been performed each May and November. This scheduling placed unusually heavy manpower [drains] on both field and headquarters stock personnel during May/June and November/December, resulting in severe overtime peaks and disruption of regular stock work.

During our recent audit of the headquarters stock section, we recommended that the verification and reconciliation be scheduled throughout the year on a regular cycle basis. The stock section management agreed to eliminate two work weeks, thus saving substantial overtime costs by providing for a more even distribution of work.*

*E. Theodore Keys, Jr., ed., *How to Save Millions* (Altamonte Springs, FL: Institute of Internal Auditors, 1988), 65.

Purchases	$5,000	
Cash or Accounts Payable		$5,000
To record purchases.		

Accounts Receivable	8,000	
Sales Revenue		8,000
To record sales to customers.		

At the end of the period, after inventory has been counted, entries are:

Cost of Goods Sold	$4,000	
Inventory	2,000	
Inventory		$1,000
Purchases		5,000

To: (1) record the cost of goods sold,
(2) update the inventory account balance (the credit removes the old balance, and the debit puts in the new), and
(3) zero out the balance in the temporary purchases account.

As we have seen before, the entries above are summary entries. During the accounting period, companies make separate entries for each purchase and each sale. But only one entry is necessary to record the cost of goods sold during the period. No record is made for the cost of goods sold for individual sales.

Three types of events may cause the periodic method of accounting for inventory to differ from our description.

1. A company might pay a separate bill for the cost of having inventory shipped to it.

2. A company might return inventory to a supplier for credit, or it might receive a rebate of a portion of the purchase cost because the goods are damaged or unsuitable for some other reason.

3. A company might receive a discount for paying a supplier promptly.

Freight-in

The cost of shipping inventory from the supplier to the buyer has a future benefit and is therefore an asset. **Freight-in** is an ordinary and necessary cost of getting the inventory to a place where it can be sold. Thus, the cost of freight-in is properly included as an addition to the purchase cost of inventory. It is recorded in a separate account called Freight-in or Transportation-in and is added to the Purchases account balance to calculate the delivered cost of purchases.

The cost of shipping inventory to the buyer has a future benefit and is therefore an asset.

Purchase Returns and Allowances

In a **purchase return,** a company returns inventory to a supplier and receives a credit for the full cost. In a **purchase allowance,** a company receives a rebate of a portion of the purchase cost because the inventory received is damaged or unsuitable for some reason. In either case, the amount is recorded in a separate account called Purchase Returns and Allowances. This is a **contra account** and is subtracted from the Purchases account balance to calculate the net cost of purchases.

Purchase Discounts

Many companies offer **purchase discounts** for prompt payment. One common discount agreement is expressed as 2/10, n/30. These terms are read "the buyer may take a 2% discount if the bill is paid within ten days of the invoice date; otherwise, the entire (net) amount is due 30 days from the date of the invoice." Suppliers offer a wide variety of credit terms, such as 1/15, n/60 (a 1% discount if paid in 15 days; otherwise, the net amount is due in 60 days) and n/60 (no discount; the entire amount is due in 60 days).

A discount for prompt payment could be recorded in an account called Purchase Discounts Taken, or Purchase Discounts. Like Purchase

---

Exhibit 4–1
Expanded Schedule of Cost of Goods Sold Using Periodic Inventory

Inventory, beginning balance		$1,000
Plus: Purchases for the period	$5,000	
Plus Freight-In	700	
Less Purchase Returns and Allowances	(300)	
Less Purchase Discounts Taken	(94)	
Net delivered cost of purchases		5,306
Total cost of goods available for sale		6,306
Less Inventory, ending balance by count		2,000
Cost of Goods Sold (for the period)		$4,306

Returns and Allowances, this is a contra account and is subtracted from the Purchases account balance to calculate the net cost of purchases. The measure of the asset (inventory) obtained is its cost. Since purchase discounts reduce the cost of the inventory, they must be subtracted so that the cash price is shown as the cost of the inventory purchased.

An expansion of the example begun above will help show how freight-in, purchase returns and allowances, and purchase discounts are included in calculating Cost of Goods Sold using periodic inventory. First, let's assume the following costs and terms:

Freight-in	$700
Purchase returns and allowances	$300
Terms (assume the buyer pays within the discount period)	2/10, n/30

Exhibit 4−1 shows the expanded schedule.
Journal entries during the period are as follows:

Purchases	$5,000	
Accounts Payable or Cash		$5,000
To record purchases.		
Freight-in	700	
Cash		700
To record the cost of freight-in.		
Accounts Payable	300	
Purchase Returns and Allowances		300
To record the return or allowance allowed by the supplier.		

Accounts Payable ($5,000 − $300)	4,700	
Purchase Discounts Taken ($4,700 × .02)		94
Cash		4,606
To pay the supplier during the discount period.		

Accounts Receivable	8,000	
Sales Revenue		8,000
To record sales to customers.		

At the end of the period after inventory was counted, entries are:

Cost of Goods Sold	$4,306	
Inventory	2,000	
Purchase Returns and Allowances	300	
Purchase Discounts Taken	94	
Inventory		$1,000
Purchases		5,000
Freight-in		700

To: (1) record the cost of goods sold,
   (2) update the inventory account balance, and
   (3) zero out the balance in the temporary purchasing accounts
       (Purchases, Freight-in, Purchase Returns and Allowances, and
       Purchase Discounts Taken).

Treatment in Financial Statements

Exhibit 4−2 shows how inventory appears in the current assets section of the balance sheet of Boise Cascade Corporation in 1990. Exhibit 4−3 shows how cost of goods sold appears in its income statement. As these examples show, the periodic inventory method is simple and requires a minimum of bookkeeping because no effort is made to track individual units or maintain the current amounts for inventory or cost of goods sold. No entry is made to the inventory account when goods are sold. Inventory is adjusted only periodically, when financial statements are prepared and the units on hand are counted.

The periodic inventory method is simple and requires a minimum of bookkeeping.

While the periodic method has the advantage of simplicity, it has the disadvantage of providing the company with only minimal information about inventory flows. Between financial statement dates, managers have no record of the cost of inventory on hand or of the cost of goods sold since the last inventory count. The periodic method also gives no information about inventory shrinkage, that does not result from sales to customers or returns to suppliers. Losses from theft or spoilage are treated as part of cost of goods sold because there is no way to identify them separately.

Exhibit 4-2
Boise Cascade Corporation Portion of Balance Sheet

Balance Sheets
Boise Cascade Corporation and Subsidiaries

Assets	December 31		
	1990	1989	1988
	(expressed in thousands)		
Current			
Cash and cash items (Note 1)	$ 19,781	$ 19,715	$ 12,103
Short-term investments at cost, which approximates market (Note 1)	6,165	5,526	11,157
	25,946	25,241	23,260
Receivables, less allowances of $4,315,000, $3,800,000, and $3,405,000	412,558	421,568	393,371
Inventories (Note 1)	484,972	424,439	398,749
Deferred income tax benefits	55,115	48,716	40,404
Other	18,992	12,353	10,819
	997,583	932,317	866,603

Consequently, the periodic method is satisfactory when the benefit of more informative inventory accounting methods is outweighed by the cost of maintaining the additional records. This method is best suited to products that are inexpensive and not unique (such as identical, inexpensive toothbrushes in a large display in a pharmacy). A company whose managers want more information can use the perpetual method, discussed next. Insight 4-2 describes one way companies decide how much to spend on inventory control and thus which method to use for various types of inventory.

PERPETUAL METHOD

The perpetual method is used when units are expensive or unique.

The **perpetual method** is best used when units are either expensive or unique (such as television sets in a department store or prescription drugs in a pharmacy). In this method, each increase and decrease in inventory (purchase, sale, or return to supplier) is recorded as it occurs.

Companies using the perpetual method still do periodic physical counts of inventory. They then compare the results of the count to the balance in the inventory account. Managers can therefore investigate discrepancies. (Managers will be quite concerned about shortages in television sets or prescription drugs.) It is not necessarily as expensive to keep perpetual inventory records as it might appear. Computer tech-

Exhibit 4–3
Boise Cascade Corporation Portion of Income Statement

Statements of Income
Boise Cascade Corporation and Subsidiaries

| | Year Ended December 31 | | |
	1990	1989	1988
	(expressed in thousands)		
Revenues			
Sales	$4,185,920	$4,338,030	$4,094,630
Other income (expense), net (Note 1)	(1,360)	15,020	4,710
	4,184,560	4,353,050	4,099,340
Costs and expenses			
Materials, labor, and other operating expenses	3,318,350	3,218,120	2,974,370
Depreciation and cost of company timber harvested	212,890	202,060	187,600
Selling and administrative expenses	419,430	406,400	362,480
	3,950,670	3,826,580	3,524,450
Income from operations	233,890	526,470	574,890
Interest expense	(116,620)	(95,810)	(100,460)
Interest income	3,610	6,370	3,540
Foreign exchange gain (loss)	520	(160)	(90)
	(112,490)	(89,600)	(97,010)
Income before income taxes	121,400	436,870	477,880
Income tax provision (Note 2)	46,130	169,290	188,760
Net income	$ 75,270	$ 267,580	$ 289,120
Net income per common share (Note 1)			
Primary	$1.62	$6.19	$6.34
Fully diluted	$1.62	$5.70	$6.15

The accompanying notes are an integral part of these Financial Statements.

nology has reduced the amount of work. The exotic cash registers in many stores, called *point-of-sale terminals,* keep perpetual records up to date and generate reports for managers that show what products need restocking.

Journal Entries

The following journal entries illustrate the perpetual inventory method using the same information that was given for the periodic method earlier in the chapter. During the period, entries are:

Inventory	$5,000	
Accounts Payable		$5,000
To record purchases.		

INSIGHT 4–2
ABC Inventory Method

Many companies use a method of inventory control called the ABC method in which they classify product lines as either A, B, or C according to the attention that is to be paid to inventory control of each one. Type A receives the most attention and type C the least.

This approach is practical because companies often find that most of the dollar investment in inventories is in only a few product lines. For example, 80% of the investment in inventories might be in only 10% of product lines inventoried. The remaining 20% of the investment in inventory might be distributed such that the least valuable items in inventory, perhaps half of the product lines, account for as little as 5% of the total investment in inventory. An ABC inventory classification for a hypothetical equipment retailer with 100 product lines is shown below.

Class of inventory	Number of product lines	Total dollar value	Level of inventory control
A	12	$ 82,000	High
B	33	13,000	Moderate
C	55	5,000	Low
Total	100	$100,000	

Managers in the company illustrated would direct employees to pay closer attention to equipment product lines classified A or B, particularly A, since those 12 product lines account for 82% ($82,000 of the total $100,000 value) of the company's investment in inventory. Employees would monitor inventory levels of class A product lines to prevent both stockouts (resulting in lost sales) and excess inventory investment. The rationale for this treatment is that 10% excess inventory in class A product lines requires an investment of $8,200, but management can maintain a buffer of 20% extra inventory above that needed to support sales of class C product lines for only $1,000. With this buffer of extra inventory, employees spend less time monitoring the 55 class C product lines and focus on the 12 in class A. Without this ABC classification, employees might spend so much time monitoring inventory levels in each of 100 product lines that they would neglect the 12 most important to the company.

Inventory	700	
Cash		700
To record the cost of freight-in.		

Accounts payable	300	
Inventory		300
To record the return or allowance allowed by the supplier.		

Accounts Payable ($5,000 − $300)	4,700	
Inventory ($4,700 × .02)		94
Cash		4,606
To pay the supplier during the discount period.		

Cost of Goods Sold	4,306	
Accounts Receivable	8,000	
Sales Revenue		8,000
Inventory		4,306
To record sales to customers and the related cost of goods sold.		

At the end of the period, the inventory account appears as follows:

	Inventory	
Beg. Bal.	$1,000	
	5,000	$ 300
	700	94
		4,306
End. Bal.	$2,000	

Again, the entries illustrated are summaries. As in the periodic method, separate entries are made for each sale. But, unlike the periodic method, cost of goods sold is recorded for each sale. The $4,306 cost of goods sold (and decrease in inventory) is determined from the inventory records and recorded as each sale is made. When inventory is counted, no entry to cost of goods sold is necessary. The only entries necessary at the end of the accounting period are to account for inventory shrinkage.

Inventory Losses

One of the benefits of the perpetual method is that it highlights losses. Let us compare it with the periodic method, where we assume that all goods not on hand were sold. The periodic calculation takes the be-

One benefit of the perpetual method is that it highlights inventory losses.

ginning inventory, adds purchases, and subtracts ending inventory to find cost of goods sold. But actually what is found is the cost of goods not on hand. There is no guarantee that everything was sold. The perpetual method, on the other hand, allows us to determine how much was actually sold and how much was lost to other causes, such as theft, shrinkage, evaporation, and so forth. We identify losses when we count the physical inventory. There are two possibilities:

1. If the physical count of inventory agrees with the balance in the Inventory account, no additional entry is necessary. The balance in the Inventory account is correct.
2. If the physical count determined that, say, only $1,800 of inventory was on hand at the end of the period, implying a loss of $200, a loss account is debited and the balance in the Inventory account corrected.

Loss from Inventory Shrinkage	$200	
Inventory		$200

RECORDING PURCHASES

In the examples so far, purchases have been recorded at gross price, before subtracting any discounts. This method is called the **gross price method.** An alternative to recording purchases at gross price is to record them at the price net of discounts available, the **net price method.** Both methods can be used with either the periodic or perpetual inventory methods. The illustration below shows how a $5,000 purchase using the periodic method is recorded, first, at the gross amount, and second then at the net amount. The supplier allows terms of 2/10, n/30.

Gross Method

In this example, the purchase is recorded at gross amount and paid during the discount period.

Purchases	$5,000	
Accounts Payable		$5,000
Accounts Payable	5,000	
Purchase Discounts Taken ($5,000 × .02)		100
Cash		4,900

In this example, the purchase is recorded at gross amount and paid after the discount period.

Purchases	$5,000	
Accounts Payable		$5,000
Accounts Payable	5,000	
Cash		5,000

Net Method

In this example, the purchase is recorded at net amount and paid during the discount period.

Purchases ($5,000 × .98)	$4,900	
Accounts Payable		$4,900
Accounts Payable	4,900	
Cash		4,900

In this example, the purchase is recorded at net amount and paid after the discount period.

Purchases	$4,900	
Accounts Payable		$4,900
Accounts Payable	4,900	
Purchase Discounts Lost (an expense)	100	
Cash		5,000

Gross and Net Methods Compared

Recording purchases gross or net is an excellent example of the effect of accounting methods on the behavior of employees. Suppose the company managers want the financial officer to pay suppliers during the discount period. When the gross method is used, no record is made of discounts lost. Managers cannot determine how much money was lost when discounts were *not* taken. But the net method highlights the financial officer's failure to pay. Any balance in the Purchase Discounts Lost account indicates that the financial officer did not pay invoices during the discount period. In this case, therefore, a financial officer is more motivated to pay invoices during the discount period, knowing that failure to do so will be brought to the attention of upper management by the accounting system.

Recording purchases gross or net shows how accounting methods affect behavior.

The net method is also superior to the gross method in the way costs are classified as assets or expenses. When the gross method is used, the cost of paying late (the amount of the discount lost) is recorded as an increase in inventory. In our example, the company records an asset of only $4,900 when the financial officer pays during the discount period and the gross method is used. But if the financial officer pays the supplier after the discount period, the same inventory is recorded at $5,000. In contrast, the net method records the inventory at $4,900, the cash cost of the inventory acquired, regardless of when the financial officer pays the supplier.

Generally speaking, assets should be recorded at their cash costs, the amounts required to pay for them at the time of purchase. Any cost of paying later is interest expense. (Such cost is often called *implicit interest* because there is no stated interest. But anytime you must pay more if you pay later there is an interest component.) If the discount period is missed, the cost of paying late is incurred for waiting to pay, which is similar to interest expense. The value of inventory (future benefit) does not increase when the supplier is paid after the discount period.

To summarize, the advantages of the net method are that (1) it motivates employees to pay during the discount period, and (2) inventory is stated at its cash cost.

COST-FLOW ASSUMPTIONS

So far, we have avoided one of the major problems accountants face in determining inventory on hand and cost of goods sold. When identical units are purchased during a period at different prices, accountants often do not know the cost of the specific units in inventory. When inventory is counted using the periodic method, or when items are sold using the perpetual method, accountants must assign a cost to the units counted or sold even if they do not know the cost of each specific unit. Let us illustrate this problem on a small scale.

Assume a company had a beginning inventory of one unit on January 1 and purchased three more units during the month. The company also sold one unit for $10 during January, leaving an ending inventory of three units. If all the units are identical, what are the dollar amounts of ending inventory and cost of goods sold? The calculation poses no problem if all the identical units were purchased for five dollars each: inventory is $15 (3 × $5) and cost of goods sold is $5 (1 × $5). But assume the units, though identical, were not purchased for the same price. Assume inflation caused the purchase cost of the units to be as follows:

Beginning inventory	1 unit @ $4/unit	$ 4
Purchases:		
January 8	2 units @ $5/unit	10
January 20	1 unit @ $6/unit	6
Totals	4 units	$20

When units are not purchased at the same price, the accountant may choose among several methods of accounting for inventory and cost of goods sold:

1. Specific identification
2. First in, first out (FIFO)
3. Last in, first out (LIFO)
4. Weighted average

Since inventory was purchased at three different prices, the accountant has three choices for cost of goods sold and ending inventory.

	Choice		
	One	**Two**	**Three**
Sales	$10	$10	$10
Cost of Goods Sold	4	5	6
Gross Profit	6	5	4
Inventory	$16	$15	$14
	($5 + $5 + $6)	($4 + $5 + $6)	($4 + $5 + $5)

Specific Identification

Under the **specific identification** method, a merchant can affect income by choosing the unit to be sold. In our example, the merchant can choose to report a gross profit (as illustrated) of $4, $5, or $6. Accountants do not like specific identification because it allows managers to manipulate earnings. Problems with managers falsifying inventory records often arise. Insight 4–3 describes one historic case of fraud involving phony inventories. Few companies use specific identification because it is appropriate only for high-value, unique items such as diamonds or automobiles.

With specific identification, income is changed by changing the unit sold.

INSIGHT 4-3
McKesson & Robbins Fraud

Today a company's independent auditors observe and verify its inventory count each year. This was not always the case. The McKesson & Robbins fraud in the late 1930s is credited with spurring this requirement. Perpetrating the fraud were the company's president and his three brothers, one who was assistant treasurer, one who was head of shipping, receiving, and warehousing, and one who managed dummy companies with which the other brothers pretended to conduct business. The brothers pretended to purchase inventories from Canadian suppliers who then held the inventory in their warehouses for McKesson. The fictitious company, W. W. Smith and Company, acted as a sales agent for McKesson, selling the nonexistent inventory to nonexistent customers. All fictitious cash payments to suppliers and collections from customers were supposedly made to a McKesson account by a Montreal banking firm. The only real cash flow—and the money the brothers embezzled—was the payment of sales commissions by McKesson's real headquarters to the dummy W. W. Smith and Company. All fictitious activities were supported by extensive false documentation: invoices, receipts, contracts, and so forth.

The fraud was discovered when the McKesson controller went to Montreal and found no inventories. McKesson's audited financial statements at December 31, 1937, contained $20 million in fictitious inventories and receivables out of $87 million in total assets. The fraud investigation took 146,000 man-hours and cost $3 million. The scheme involved 91 bank accounts, 57 brokerage accounts and 10 loan accounts. Approximately $3,200,000 was stolen. The president of McKesson turned out to be an ex-convict using an alias and forged credentials. (The auditors were not the only ones fooled. In 1942, the editors of Who's Who referring to their 1938–39 edition declared the president of McKesson to be "the only instance . . . of a fictitious biographee foisting himself on the editors.") The president ultimately killed himself. As a result of the publicity this fraud received, auditors must now verify the inventory count each year before they can certify financial statements.*

*For an intriguing discussion of the McKesson & Robbins Fraud, see "Annals of Crime: The Metamorphosis of Philip Musica," parts I and II, in The New Yorker, October 22 and 29, 1955, 49–81 and 39–79, respectively.

First-in, First-out (FIFO)

Choice One in the preceding illustration charges the cost of the oldest unit (from beginning inventory) as the cost of goods sold and places the most current costs (of the most recent purchases) in ending inventory.

This method, **first-in, first-out,** or **FIFO,** flows costs through the accounting system the way most merchants flow units of inventory through their stores: the oldest units are sold first to keep the stock fresh. FIFO is a very popular method, partly because it reflects the usual flow of goods.

FIFO flows costs the way most merchants flow units of inventory.

Last-in, First-out (LIFO)

Choice Three in our example is the **last-in, first-out,** or **LIFO,** method. It charges the cost of the most recently purchased unit as the cost of goods sold, and leaves the oldest costs in ending inventory. It is difficult to find situations where goods flow through the company in LIFO fashion. A hardware store that keeps bolts in a wooden box might flow units in a LIFO manner. As new bolts are purchased, they might be poured into the box on top of the old bolts. New bolts are thus sold first.

LIFO leaves the oldest costs in ending inventory.

Weighted Average

Choice Two is a compromise that charges the **weighted average** cost of all units to both the cost of goods sold and ending inventory. The weighted average cost per unit is calculated by dividing the total cost of units available for sale by the number of units available to be sold.

Total cost of units available for sale	$20
Total units available for sale	4
Weighted average cost per unit	$ 5

Which Method to Use?

Which choice is correct? All three methods are acceptable for determining cost of goods sold and ending inventory. We cannot say that one is best. We must think about the effects of each method on the financial statements. How much better off are we after selling one unit in the previous example? Should gross profit be $4, $5, or $6? Students and theorists may argue this point. For example, let us think about what happens next. If the company is to continue in business, the unit sold must be replaced. If costs are rising and the replacement cost of these units is increasing rapidly (as in our example), the next unit will be purchased for $6 (the cost of the most recent purchase) or perhaps even more. If we sell a unit for $10 and must pay $6 (or more) to replace it, we are only better off by $4 (or less). In fact, if we must pay taxes on the profit created, we are not $4 better off. LIFO gives results that best reflect the extent to which a company is better off each period. FIFO gives deceptively high profits when costs are rising and the units sold must be replaced. Weighted average gives results that fall between LIFO and FIFO.

But what about the balance sheet? Under LIFO the cost of the oldest units is shown as the cost of ending inventory. FIFO provides better information about the cost of units in ending inventory. FIFO shows the most recent costs as the cost of ending inventory and the oldest costs as the cost of units sold. Again, weighted average gives results between those achieved with LIFO or FIFO.

Many investors and other financial statement readers believe that the income statement is more important than the balance sheet. A weak financial position may be overcome by a strong earnings record, but a strong financial position will seldom outweigh poor earnings. Many accountants prefer that the income statement reflect the best available information, so it is usually the balance sheet that is sacrificed. As a result, accountants generally prefer LIFO inventory because, under LIFO, the most current costs are charged against earnings as cost of goods sold.

Accountants generally prefer LIFO.

Tax Effects

When costs are rising, LIFO gives lower income than FIFO or weighted average because LIFO charges the most current, higher costs against earnings. As a result, companies that use LIFO pay lower taxes when costs are rising. But if costs are falling, the results are reversed: LIFO charges the most current, lower prices against earnings, increasing income and reporting higher earnings than would be obtained using FIFO or weighted average. Because there has been much more inflation (rising prices) than deflation (falling prices) over the years, companies using LIFO tend to pay lower taxes than those using FIFO.

Companies that use LIFO pay lower taxes when costs are rising.

It is important to note that companies can use LIFO, FIFO, or weighted average to flow costs through the accounting system, regardless of the way individual units flow through the company. The choice of an inventory accounting method is an accounting decision. The choice of a policy for rotating stock and flowing units is a marketing decision. A firm can have a FIFO flow of actual units, selling the old units first, and still use the LIFO method to prepare financial statements and pay taxes.

International Restrictions on LIFO

Boise Cascade uses LIFO in its domestic operations but uses weighted average or FIFO for inventories outside the United States. LIFO inventory method is not allowed in Canada and many other foreign countries.

Exhibit 4–4
Boise Cascade's Inventory Accounting Method

Notes to Financial Statements
Boise Cascade Corporation and Subsidiaries

■ **Inventory Valuation.** The Company uses the last-in, first-out (LIFO) method of inventory valuation for raw materials and finished goods inventories at substantially all of its domestic wood products and paper manufacturing facilities. All other inventories are valued at the lower of cost or market, with cost based on the average or first-in, first-out (FIFO) valuation method. Manufactured inventories include costs for materials, labor, and factory overhead. The cost of inventories, valued at the lower of average cost or market, exceeded the LIFO inventory valuation by $52,608,000 in 1990, $58,618,000 in 1989, and $42,583,000 in 1988.

Inventories include the following:

	December 31		
	1990	1989	1988
	(expressed in thousands)		
Finished goods and work in process	$ 261,312	$ 235,627	$ 221,516
Logs	45,502	39,516	35,675
Other raw materials and supplies	178,158	149,296	141,558
	$ 484,972	$ 424,439	$ 398,749

(Many of Boise Cascade's plants are in Canada.) Boise Cascade's inventory accounting policies are described in a note to its financial statements (see Exhibit 4–4).

LIFO Reserve

The difference between LIFO cost and the replacement cost of the inventory is called the *LIFO reserve*. This difference occurs because LIFO shows inventories at older costs, which are generally less than replacement costs. Some companies show the LIFO reserve in the balance sheet, as follows:

Inventories at replacement cost	$90,000
Less LIFO reserve	16,000
Inventories at LIFO	$74,000

When the LIFO reserve is shown, financial statement readers know the current replacement cost of the inventories, and the company receives the tax and other benefits of using LIFO.

INVENTORY ESTIMATING METHODS

There is often a predictable, continuing relationship between sales revenue and cost of goods sold. Such a relationship occurs because many companies mark up merchandise by the same percentage each period. Even a company that sells many types of products and marks each product up by a different percentage might still have a relatively constant markup on all its products as a whole. For example, assume that the Brooks Clothing Company sells suits, shoes, and sport clothes, and marks up each type of merchandise by a different percentage. Cost and markup calculations for the first quarter are given below.

Merchandise	Cost of Items	×	Markup on Cost	=	Gross Profit	Selling Price (Cost + Gross Profit)
Suits	$20,000		100%		$20,000	$ 40,000
Shoes	10,000		20		2,000	12,000
Sport clothes	30,000		60		18,000	48,000
Total	$60,000				$40,000	$100,000

The weighted average markup on all sales is gross profit/cost ($40,000/$60,000), or 66.7 percent. The gross profit percentage is gross profit/selling price ($40,000/$100,000), or 40 percent. A partial income statement shows the relationship between sales revenue, cost of goods sold, and gross profit.

Sales	$100,000	
Cost of Goods Sold	60,000	60% of sales
Gross Profit	$ 40,000	40% of sales

Sales mix is the set of percentages in which merchandise is sold. The mix of suits, shoes, and sports clothes at Brooks Clothing is 40% suits, 12% shoes, and 48% sport clothes. As long as Brooks Clothing maintains the same sales dollar mix, and marks up each product line at the same rate, it will continue to have a 66.7 percent weighted average markup on total sales.

The presumption of a continuing relationship between sales, cost of goods sold, and gross margin allows accountants to estimate cost of goods sold and inventories from incomplete information. Two estimating techniques are used: the gross margin method and the retail inventory method.

Gross Margin Method

Assume that Brooks Clothing has prepared financial statements for the first quarter. Inventory at the beginning and end of the first quarter was $25,000 at cost. Sales and cost of goods sold were $100,000 and $60,000, respectively, as shown earlier. Assume further that two months into the second quarter, the store and its contents are destroyed by fire. The company needs an estimate of the cost of the inventory destroyed for its insurance claim and an estimate of cost of goods sold for its income tax return.

All accounting records are lost. The president of Brooks has a copy of the first-quarter financial statements, and the sales manager has records documenting sales of $80,000 for the second quarter to the date of the fire. Second-quarter purchases, determined from supplier records, were $70,000.

If it is reasonable to assume that Brooks purchased and sold merchandise during the second quarter in the same mix and at the same markup as during the previous quarter, the **gross margin method** can be used to estimate cost of goods sold by multiplying sales from the sales manager's record by the weighted-average percentage of cost of goods sold (calculated from goods sold during the first quarter).

Accountants can estimate cost of goods sold and inventories from incomplete information.

Second-quarter sales (from manager's records)	$80,000
Times first-quarter percentage of cost of goods sold	.60
Estimated second-quarter cost of goods sold	$48,000

Inventory lost in the fire can be estimated by subtracting the estimated cost of goods sold from the total goods available for sale. The total goods available for sale is the sum of the beginning inventory (contained in the first-quarter balance sheet) and the second-quarter purchases (from supplier records). Note that the ending inventory for the first quarter is the beginning inventory for the second quarter.

Beginning inventory (from first-quarter balance sheet)	$25,000
Plus second-quarter purchases (from supplier records)	70,000
Total goods available for sale	95,000
Less estimated cost of goods sold	48,000
Estimated ending inventory (lost in the fire)	$47,000

The advantage of the gross margin method is that it can be used to make estimates quickly and easily from historical data. The disadvantage is that the method assumes that the sales mix and markup percentages have remained constant. If they have not, results from the gross margin method will be inaccurate.

Retail Inventory Method

As discussed in the first part of this chapter, a company using the periodic inventory method must count its inventory to calculate cost of goods sold and ending inventory. When a business sells many different inventory items at many different prices, it can be difficult and time-consuming to determine each item's original cost because the manager must refer to purchasing records to find that cost. However, a manager can use the premise of the gross margin method to estimate ending inventory and cost of goods sold with the retail inventory method. The retail inventory method is a modification of the gross margin method and provides more accurate estimates. Its estimates can be used for interim (monthly or quarterly) financial statements. Inventory must still be counted to prepare annual financial statements.

The retail inventory method provides more accurate estimates than the gross margin method.

To reduce the loss in accuracy of the gross margin method caused by changes in the sales mix and markup percentages, the retail inventory method requires managers to maintain a record of goods purchased and available for sale at both (1) original purchase cost and (2) retail price after markup.

To illustrate, Now Girl Fashion Shop stocks over 100 different fashions purchased from over 40 manufacturers. As a result, counting inventory and looking up the cost of each item each month would be very expensive. On January 1, Now Girl has an inventory with a purchase cost of $300,000 and a retail value of $450,000. During January, Now Girl purchases additional merchandise costing $400,000 that is marked to sell for $550,000. Sales for January total $600,000. Total goods available for sale are thus $300,000 + $400,000 = $700,000 at cost, and $450,000 + $550,000 = $1,000,000 at retail. The cost to retail ratio for all merchandise available for sale during January is thus $700,000/$1,000,000 = 70 percent. Cost of goods sold and ending inventory can now be estimated. A schedule of estimated cost of goods sold and ending inventory for Now Girl is shown below.

	At Cost	At Retail
Beginning inventory	$300,000	$ 450,000
Plus purchases	400,000	550,000
Total available for sale	$700,000	$1,000,000
Cost-to-retail ratio ($700,000/$1,000,000)		.70
Sales at retail prices		$ 600,000
Cost-to-retail ratio		.70
Estimated cost of sales ($600,000 × .70)	$420,000	
Estimated ending inventory	$280,000	

The cost-to-retail ratio reflects the relationship of current costs to current retail (sales) prices. Calculated using the retail method, it provides more accurate estimates of cost of goods sold and ending inventory than does a ratio based on prior-period costs and sales, as in the gross margin method.

Ending inventory estimated using the retail method can provide management an estimate of losses from theft or other sources. Assume that Now Girl employees count inventory on January 31 and determine its retail value by adding up the selling prices on the tags of all items. If the count of inventory totaled $375,000 at retail, the cost of ending inventory could be estimated to be $375,000 × .70 = $262,500. The difference between the cost of inventory estimated from sales records and from a physical count provides an estimate of loss.

Inventory estimated from sales	$280,000
Inventory estimated from retail count	262,500
Estimated loss	$ 17,500

LOWER OF COST OR MARKET

So far we have concerned ourselves only with the cost of inventory. But the principle of conservatism requires that we recognize declines in the *value* (service potential) of assets. Accordingly, accountants show inventories in balance sheets at the **lower of cost or market.** *Market* generally means replacement cost, although it has other meanings that we will not cover. Thus, if a company has inventory that cost $1,000,000 but can be replaced for $800,000 at the balance sheet date, there is reason to believe that the market for these goods is deteriorating. The company's selling prices will probably fall also. The inventory will appear on the balance sheet at $800,000, the lower of its historical cost or replacement cost (market). The $200,000 loss in value will be shown in the income statement as a loss.

ACTIVITY RATIOS

Activity ratios measure management's effectiveness in using assets. The ratio is generally a measure of the relationship between some asset, such as inventory, and some surrogate for management's ability to employ the investment in the asset effectively. The general form of an activity ratio is the asset (for which you want an activity measure) divided into the best measure of that asset's activity.

$$\text{Activity Ratio} = \frac{\text{Best Measure of Asset Activity}}{\text{Asset}}$$

For inventory, the best measure of the asset activity is cost of goods sold. The less management is forced to invest in inventories for a given volume of sales, the better. For an annual cost of goods sold of $1 million, management might have $500,000 invested in inventories during the year. Management's performance would be improved if the same level of sales could be supported with only $100,000 in inventory.

The best measure of the inventory activity is cost of goods sold.

Activity ratios are often referred to as **turnover ratios.** An inventory balance of $100,000 is said to have turned over ten times if annual cost of goods sold is $1 million. All merchandise sold passes through inventory to become part of the cost of goods sold, like water through a water wheel. The activity ratio is:

$$\text{Inventory Turnover} = \frac{\text{Cost of Goods Sold}}{\text{Average Inventory}}$$

In this example, the ratio is calculated as $1 million divided by $100,000 equals 10 times. When the turnover of inventory is known, the average number of days funds are tied up in inventory can be calculated. If inventory turns over 10 times in a 360 day year (a banker's year), the average turnover period is 360 divided by 10 equals 36 days.

$$\text{Average Turnover Period} = \frac{360}{\text{Asset Turnover}}$$

This relationship can also be used to calculate the number of days funds are tied up in any other asset once the asset turnover is known. The number of days funds are invested in accounts receivable is of interest to financial analysts, for example. The best measure of activity of the asset accounts receivable is sales, or, preferably, credit sales (though credit sales are generally not available in financial statements). The equation for accounts receivable (AR) turnover is:

$$\text{AR Turnover} = \frac{\text{Sales}}{\text{Average AR}}$$

The inventory and accounts receivable turnovers for Boise Cascade are:

$$\text{Inventory Turnover} = \frac{\text{Cost of Goods Sold}}{\text{Average Inventory}}$$

$$= \frac{\$3,318,350}{(\$484,972 + \$424,439)/2} = 7.3 \text{ times}$$

Average turnover period for inventory is 360 days/7.3 = 49 days.

$$\text{AR turnover} = \frac{\text{Sales}}{\text{Average AR}}$$

$$= \frac{\$4,185,920}{(\$412,558 + \$421,568)/2} = 10 \text{ times}$$

Average turnover period for accounts receivable is 360 days/10 = 36 days.

SUMMARY

For retailers, the largest single expense is often the cost of goods sold, and the largest current asset is the inventory of merchandise on hand awaiting sale. Accounting for the activities of companies that sell merchandise to customers has several facets. There are two principal ways to keep track of inventory, the periodic and perpetual methods. There are several assumptions about the flow of costs, FIFO, LIFO, and weighted average. Each method might be appropriate for a certain set of business conditions, or might result from making a particular assumption about the flow of goods through the company or costs through the accounting system.

In cases where it is not possible, or is extremely costly to take a physical inventory, we can use one of several popular methods to estimate inventory and cost of goods sold. When the value of inventory declines, accountants recognize the decline by invoking the lower-of-cost or market rule.

DEMONSTRATION PROBLEM

Blazer Company uses LIFO inventory but is examining the effect of its inventory accounting method on the profit reported in its income statement. Blazer has sales of $80,000 and general and administrative expenses of $10,000 during the first quarter of the year. The following inventory and purchases data are for the Blazer Company for the first quarter.

Beginning inventory	100 units @ $120 each
Purchases:	
1/7	150 units @ $110 each
2/10	150 units @ $120 each
2/26	100 units @ $130 each
3/15	200 units @ $140 each

There are 300 units in inventory at the end of the quarter.

REQUIRED:

Determine ending inventory and cost of goods sold using LIFO, FIFO, and weighted average inventory. Use the cost of goods sold figure to prepare an income statement for each inventory method.

Solution

LIFO Inventory Calculation

LIFO inventory and cost of sales are calculated as follows. The total goods available for sale is calculated by determining the dollar amount of beginning inventory and each purchase, and then adding these totals. Total units in inventory are determined by summing the units in beginning inventory and in each purchase.

Beginning inventory	100 units @ $120 each =	$12,000
Purchases:		
1/7	150 units @ $110 each =	16,500
2/10	150 units @ $120 each =	18,000
2/26	100 units @ $130 each =	13,000
3/15	200 units @ $140 each =	28,000
Total available	700 units	$87,500

There are 700 units at a total cost of $87,500 available for sale. There were 400 units sold, as calculated below.

Total available	700 units
Ending inventory	300 units
Units sold	400 units

To calculate the cost of the 300 units remaining in inventory using LIFO, find the cost of the 300 oldest units:

Beginning inventory	100 units @ $120 each =	$12,000
Purchases:		
1/7	150 units @ $110 each =	16,500
2/10	50 units @ $120 each =	6,000
Total	300 units	$34,500

Therefore:

Total available	$87,500
Ending inventory	34,500
Cost of goods sold	$53,000

Using LIFO, inventory in the balance sheet is $34,500 and cost of goods sold is $53,000. If LIFO is used, Blazer Company's income statement for the first quarter is as follows.

Blazer Company
Income Statement (using LIFO)
First Quarter

Sales	$80,000
Cost of goods sold	53,000
Gross profit	27,000
General and administrative expenses	10,000
Net income	$17,000

FIFO Inventory Calculation

FIFO inventory contains the cost of the 300 units most recently purchased. Cost of goods sold contains the cost of the oldest 400 units. The 300 units most recently purchased are the units purchased on 2/26 and 3/15. FIFO inventory is calculated as shown.

2/26	100 units @ $130 each =	$13,000
3/15	200 units @ $140 each =	28,000
Total available	300 units	$41,000

Therefore:

Total available	$87,500
Ending inventory	41,000
Cost of goods sold	$46,500

Using FIFO, inventory in the balance sheet is $41,000, and cost of goods sold is $46,500. If FIFO is used, Blazer Company's income statement for the first quarter is as follows.

Blazer Company
Income Statement (using FIFO)
First Quarter

Sales revenue	$80,000
Cost of goods sold	46,500
Gross profit	33,500
General and administrative expenses	10,000
Net income	$23,500

Weighted Average Inventory Calculation

The weighted-average cost per unit is calculated by dividing the total number of units available for sale (700) into the total cost of those units ($87,500). Total cost/number of units = $87,500/700 units = $125 weighted average cost per unit. The weighted average cost of the 300 units in ending inventory is calculated as follows:

Ending inventory = 300 units × $125 wt. avg. cost/unit = $37,500

Therefore:

Total available	$87,500
Ending inventory	37,500
Cost of units sold	$50,000

Using weighted average, inventory in the balance sheet is $37,500, and cost of goods sold is $50,000. Thus, if weighted average is used, Blazer Company's income statement for the first quarter is as follows.

**Blazer Company
Income Statement (using weighted average)
First Quarter**

Sales revenue	$80,000
Cost of goods sold	50,000
Gross profit	30,000
General and administrative expenses	10,000
Net income	$20,000

Key Terms

activity ratios

contra account

cost of goods sold

first in, first out (FIFO)

freight-in

gross profit

gross margin method

gross price method

inventory

last in, first out (LIFO)

lower of cost or market

net price method

periodic method

perpetual method

purchase returns and allowances

purchase discounts

purchases

retail inventory method

sales mix

specific identification

turnover ratios

weighted average

ASSIGNMENTS

4–1 Calculating Basic Cost of Goods Sold

Simple Inventory Company uses the periodic inventory method and wishes to prepare financial statements for the year. On examining the books, the accountant finds a beginning inventory of $34,000 and purchases of $256,000. A count of inventory on hand in the storeroom revealed only $18,500 in goods still on hand.

REQUIRED:

1. Prepare a schedule of cost of goods sold for the year.
2. Write the journal entry or entries to record cost of goods sold and update the balance in the inventory account.

4–2 Periodic Inventory Cost of Goods Sold and Journal Entries

The following summary information relates to Simmons Company for the first quarter. Simmons uses a periodic inventory method and records purchases at the gross amount.

1/1	Beginning inventory is $10,000.
1/1–3/31	Total purchases of $40,000 were made.
1/1–3/31	Purchase discounts taken totaled $500.
1/1–3/31	The cost of freight-in on merchandise purchased was $6,000.
2/17	Merchandise costing $3,000 was returned to vendors.
1/1–3/31	Merchandise costing $38,000 was sold on account for $63,000.

Simmons paid all but $5,000 of the balance in Accounts Payable. (There was no beginning balance.)

REQUIRED:

1. Prepare a schedule of cost of goods sold for the first quarter.
2. Make summary journal entries for Simmons Company.

4–3 Perpetual Inventory Cost of Goods Sold and Journal Entries

The following summary information relates to Jackson Company for the first quarter. Jackson records purchases at the gross amount and uses the perpetual inventory method.

1/1	Beginning inventory is $15,000.
1/1–3/31	Total purchases of $60,000 were made.

1/1–3/31   Purchase discounts taken totaled $1,000.

1/1–3/31   The cost of freight-in on merchandise purchased was $5,000.

2/17   Merchandise costing $8,000 was returned to vendors.

1/1–3/31   Merchandise costing $65,000 was sold on account for $80,000.

Jackson paid all but $10,000 of the balance in accounts payable. (There was no beginning balance.)

REQUIRED:

1. Prepare a schedule of cost of goods sold for the first quarter.
2. Make summary journal entries for Jackson Company.

4–4   Periodic Inventory Journal Entries

Expanded Inventory Company uses the periodic inventory method and wishes to prepare financial statements for the year. On examining the books, the accountant finds a beginning inventory of $88,000 and purchases of $796,000. A count of inventory on hand in the storeroom revealed $76,500 in goods still on hand. Discounts taken during the period total $13,000, and $28,000 in merchandise was returned to suppliers. Freight-in was $17,500. Sales, all on credit, were $1,307,000. All accounts payable were paid.

REQUIRED:

Prepare journal entries to summarize the activity of Expanded Company during the year. Purchases are recorded at their gross amount.

4–5   Schedule of Cost of Goods Sold—Continuation of Assignment 4–4

REQUIRED:

Prepare a schedule of cost of goods sold for Expanded Company for the year.

4–6   Financial Statement Presentation—Continuation of Assignments 4–4 and 4–5

Other expenses for Expanded Company total $400,000. Cash and accounts receivable at the end of the period were $40,500 and $80,000, respectively.

REQUIRED:

Prepare an income statement and the current asset section of the balance sheet for Expanded Company.

4–7   Perpetual Inventory Journal Entries

Perpetual Inventory Company uses the perpetual inventory method. Beginning inventory for the first quarter was $45,000 and purchases, all on credit, were $290,000. A count of inventory in the warehouse revealed $57,000 on hand at the end of the quarter. Discounts taken during the first quarter totaled $23,000, and $8,000 in merchandise was returned to suppliers. Freight-in was $17,500. Sales, all on credit, were $990,000. Purchases were recorded at their gross amount.

REQUIRED:

1. Prepare all the journal entries to summarize the activity of the Perpetual Company during the year.

2. Using a T-account, post the entries to the inventory account.

4–8   Inventory Shrinkage Using Perpetual Method

Rayman Company uses a perpetual inventory system. A count of inventory at year-end has revealed an inventory shortage of $66,500. "Great Scott!" the company president exclaims, "Our stockholders are going to hit the ceiling if we book the discrepancy as a loss. We should be using the periodic inventory method. We wouldn't have to expense this shrinkage if we used periodic inventory. It's a crying shame!"

REQUIRED:

1. Make the journal entry to account for the shrinkage. What is the effect of the shrinkage on the balance sheet and income statement?

2. Would Rayman's income be different if it used periodic inventory? Why or why not?

3. What kinds of companies use perpetual inventory? What kind use periodic? Why?

4–9   Recording Purchases Gross

Blossom Company uses a periodic inventory system and records purchases at their gross amount. Blossom purchased $10,000 in merchandise from Gross Company on account with terms of 2/10, n/30.

REQUIRED:

1. Prepare the journal entries that would result if Blossom pays during the discount period.

2. Prepare the journal entries that would result if Blossom pays on day 20, after the discount period has expired.

3. What annual interest rate is Blossom paying if it fails to pay during the discount period?

4–10   Recording Purchases Net

Campbell Company uses a periodic inventory system. Campbell purchased $40,000 in merchandise from the Net Company on account with terms of 1/10, n/60. Campbell records purchases at their net amount.

REQUIRED:

1. Prepare the journal entries that would result if Campbell paid during the discount period.
2. Prepare the journal entries that would result if Campbell paid on day 60, after the discount period has expired.
3. What annual interest rate is Campbell paying if it fails to pay during the discount period?

4–11   Basic Inventory Methods

Wigito Products has the following inventory and purchases data for the first quarter. At the end of the quarter, 150 units were still on hand.

Beginning inventory	50 units @ $300 each
Purchases:	
2/12	100 units @ 400 each
3/25	100 units @ 500 each

REQUIRED:

Calculate ending inventory and cost of goods sold using LIFO, FIFO, and weighted average

4–12   LIFO Inventory

The following inventory and purchases data are for Kelly Co. for March.

Beginning inventory	220 units @ $7.50 each
Purchases:	
3/6	150 units @ $8.00 each
3/18	150 units @ $8.25 each
3/21	300 units @ $9.00 each
3/29	300 units @ $8.90 each

There are 450 units in inventory at the end of March.

REQUIRED:

Determine ending inventory and cost of goods sold using LIFO.

4–13   FIFO Inventory—Continuation of Assignment 4–12

Use the information for Kelly Co.

REQUIRED:

Determine ending inventory and cost of goods sold using FIFO.

4–14 Weighted Average Inventory—Continuation of Assignment 4–12

Use the information for Kelly Co.

REQUIRED:

Determine ending inventory and cost of goods sold using weighted average inventory.

4–15 Retail Method of Estimating Inventories

Mind Game stocks 20 lines of hobby products. On January 1, Mind Game had inventory with a purchase cost of $130,000 and a total retail value of $200,000. During the first quarter, Mind Game purchased additional merchandise for $350,000 and marked it to sell for $600,000. Sales for the first quarter total $700,000.

REQUIRED:

Use the retail method to estimate ending inventory and cost of goods sold.

4–16 Estimating Theft Loss—Continuation of Assignment 4–15

A count of Mind Game's ending inventory for the first quarter finds hobby merchandise totaling $80,000 at retail.

REQUIRED:

Use your answer to Assignment 4–15 to estimate theft loss for the first quarter.

4–17 Estimating Inventories

Suzy Spirit Clothing Company sells three lines of women's fashions, Simply Style, Fantasy, and Executette. Suzy Spirit marks up each line by a different percentage. Cost and markup calculations for the first quarter are as follows:

Line	Cost of Goods	×	Markup on Cost	=	Gross Profit	Selling Price (Cost + Gross Profit)
Simply Style	$ 50,000		100%		$50,000	$100,000
Fantasy	30,000		33⅓		10,000	40,000
Executette	30,000		60		18,000	48,000
Total	$110,000				$78,000	$188,000

REQUIRED:

1. Calculate the weighted average markup on all sales and the gross margin percentage.
2. Prepare a partial income statement showing the relationship between sales revenue, cost of goods sold, and gross profit.

3. Suzy Spirit's actual first-quarter sales totaled $150,000. Use the relationships examined in Requirements 1 and 2 to estimate Suzy Spirit's cost of goods sold.

4–18   Gross Margin Method of Estimating Inventories

Mighty Mite Clothing has prepared financial statements for the first quarter. Inventory at the end of the first quarter was $50,000 at cost. Sales and cost of goods sold were $90,000 and $49,500, respectively. Just after midnight on June 23, the store and its contents were destroyed by fire. All accounting records were lost. The accountant has a copy of the first-quarter financial statements, and the sales manager has a record documenting sales of $85,000 for the second quarter to the date of the fire. Second-quarter purchases, calculated from supplier records, were $40,000 at cost. An estimate of inventory destroyed in the fire is needed to process Mighty Mite's insurance claim. An estimate of cost of goods sold is needed to file income taxes.

REQUIRED:

Use the gross margin method to estimate cost of goods sold for the second quarter and the cost of goods lost in the fire from the fragments of data available.

4–19   Wal-Mart Inventory and Cost of Goods Sold Accounts

Study the financial statements in the Wal-Mart annual report.

REQUIRED:

1. How much was Wal-Mart's cost of goods sold in 1991?
2. What inventory method did Wal-Mart use in 1991? (Hint: Read note 1.)
3. How much inventory did Wal-Mart have at the end of 1991?
4. How much did inventory increase between 1990 and 1991?

4–20   Wal-Mart's Inventory Turnover Ratio

Study the financial statements in the Wal-Mart annual report.

REQUIRED:

1. What was Wal-Mart's inventory turnover in 1991?
2. What was Wal-Mart's average turnover period for inventory in 1991?
3. Did Wal-Mart's inventory turnover period change between 1990 to 1991?

4–21   Wal-Mart's Accounts Receivable Turnover Ratio

Study the financial statements in the Wal-Mart annual report.

REQUIRED:

1. What was Wal-Mart's accounts receivable turnover in 1991?

2. What was Wal-Mart's average turnover period for accounts receivable in 1991?

3. Did Wal-Mart's accounts receivable turnover period change from 1990 to 1991?

4—22 DECISION CASE:
RECORDING PURCHASES GROSS OR NET

Nettle Grossman, the president of Ramstock Industries, is concerned about the golf game of Ramstock's treasurer. "I'm stuck at the office til after five *every* day," Nettle groaned, "while that darned treasurer hits the links three, maybe four afternoons a week. Still, I just received this report that shows she has taken over $50,000 in purchase discounts so far this year. So I guess she's right on top of things. She sure makes me feel slow!"

Nettle's assistant shook her head. "I don't want to rock anyone's boat, but you might get better information if we recorded purchases net, rather than gross."

The president was puzzled. "I think you'd best just make the coffee, Mrs. Oleson," he said. "I'll tend to the performance measures."

REQUIRED:

Comment on the effectiveness of discounts taken as a measure of the treasurer's performance. Could discounts lost offer a better measure?

4—23 DECISION CASE:
LIFO VERSUS FIFO INVENTORY

Apple Company buys merchandise to meet seasonal demand and tries to keep about a one-month supply of inventory on hand. Dave Apple has always used FIFO inventory. "When I restock," Dave explains, "I always move the old merchandise to the front of the shelf and put the new stuff in the back. Unless, of course, I think the customers are going to try to take their merchandise from the back. In that case, I put the new stuff in the front. I use FIFO because it flows the cost of inventory the same way I flow the actual units through my business."

"But Dad," laments Dave, Jr., "here is a can of Kisgrow that you have marked to sell for $10.95. It's from a batch we bought back in the spring for $8.50 each. The Kisgrow we received in last month's shipment cost us $9.49, and I see the price has just gone up to $11.50. When we sell this can for $10.95, we will show a profit of $2.45 using FIFO. But if you consider that we've got to buy another order of Kisgrow to replace the merchandise we sell—well, gosh, Dad—we'll have to use all the money we received for the old Kisgrow, plus fifty-five cents more to buy replacement merchandise. And that's not counting taxes on the profit we report. Even LIFO would have us earning $1.46. I think we should use NIFO—Next-In, First-Out. That would give us a better picture of our profit!"

"Davie, Davie, Davie," responded Dave, Sr., "why don't you go help Mama?"

REQUIRED:

Discuss the arguments advanced by Dave and his son.

5

Long-Lived Productive Assets: Acquisition and Depreciation

LEARNING OBJECTIVES

After studying Chapter 5, you should be able to:
1. Determine the initial cost of plant assets.
2. Understand the accounting for self-constructed assets, basket purchases, noncash exchanges, and donated assets.
3. Understand the concept of allocating the cost of plant assets to the periods of benefit—the process of depreciation.
4. Understand and compute periodic depreciation under various methods.
5. Describe the group and composite depreciation methods.
6. Discuss the limitations of depreciation methods.
7. Understand the relationship between depreciation and income taxes.
8. Describe the accounting for changes in calculating periodic depreciation expense.
9. Discuss partial-year depreciation.
10. Describe the disclosures relating to plant assets in the financial statements.

For many companies, the largest dollar category of assets on the balance sheet is for long-lived tangible productive assets, called **plant, property, and equipment,** or **fixed assets.** For example, these assets were 77% of total assets of Anheuser-Busch Companies, Inc., in 1988. This chapter first discusses how to determine the cost of plant, property and equipment, then moves to determining the depreciation on them. Accounting for the addition to and disposal of these assets and the methods used to account for natural resources, intangible assets, and "other assets" are contained in Chapter 6.

Accountants group long-lived assets into three general categories: (1) plant assets (property, plant, and equipment); (2) natural resources (such as oil or gas deposits, mines); and (3) intangible assets (including copyrights, trademarks, and goodwill). Allocating the costs of natural resources to the periods benefited is called *depletion* and is similar to depreciation. Allocating the costs associated with intangibles to the periods benefited is called *amortization.* Natural resources and intangibles are discussed in Chapter 6.

COST OF PLANT ASSETS

The cost of a long-lived asset is determined by totaling all the costs of getting the asset in place and/ready for its intended use. All such costs have future benefits, and are therefore assets. These costs are expensed over the lives of the assets as the benefits are consumed. (This is the process of depreciation, which will be discussed later in the chapter.) Thus, the cost of a machine includes its purchase price, transportation costs, insurance in transit, installation, testing, and electrical connections. In other words, all costs necessary to make the asset ready for its intended use are **capitalized,** or debited to the machinery asset account, rather than expensed. The rationale behind this approach stems from the **matching principle,** where, in measuring periodic net income, revenue is offset or matched against all expenses incurred in producing that revenue. For a company, the benefits of owning a machine accrue over a period of time, say five years. The expenditures relating to the acquisition of the machine are included in its cost, because they will be matched against revenue derived from the operation of the asset over that five-year period. That is, the total costs of the machine are recorded in the asset account Machine and allocated against the earned revenue from the machine over the five-year period.

The cost of plant assets are all costs necessary to make the asset ready for its intended use.

Cost of Machinery

Injection Molding Company (IMC) purchases a piece of injection molding equipment for an invoice price of $90,000. The cost of having the equipment delivered is $10,000, and the cost of installing it is $6,000. IMC's production managers determine that $5,000 in materials and $9,000 in labor were consumed in set-up trial runs, calibration testing and adjustments to the equipment before it produced good units.

What is the cost of the equipment? The company could not use the equipment if it were not delivered to the plant. The company could not produce salable units if the machine were not installed, calibrated, and adjusted. Exhibit 5–1 shows the cost of the equipment.

Capitalized expenditures should only include those that are reasonable and essential. If, in our example, the equipment were damaged during installation by a negligent forklift operator, repair costs would not be capitalized but rather expensed, because these costs are not reasonable and essential.

Cost of Buildings

The cost of a building includes its purchase price, closing costs, commissions, and other costs necessary to prepare it for its intended use. Other costs might include materials, labor, and overhead costs incurred during construction. All costs incurred from site excavation to completion of the building are included in the cost of the building.

Cost of Land

The cost of land includes the purchase price, title search and other closing costs, commissions, accrued property taxes, and other liens. Grading and drainage are examples of costs that might be necessary to make land ready for some intended use. Some companies buy land that has an existing structure, such as a building. If the structure must be removed to make the land suitable for a new building, the net costs of

---

Exhibit 5–1
Cost of Equipment for IMC

Purchase price	$ 90,000
Delivery cost	10,000
Installation cost	6,000
Set-up (material and labor) cost	14,000
Total cost	$120,000

Exhibit 5–2
Cost of Land for PPC

Purchase price	$275,000
Net removal costs ($8,300 − $2,000)	6,300
Unpaid property taxes	5,000
Attorney's fees	1,500
Real estate broker's commissions	10,000
Other closing costs	2,000
	$299,800

removal (cost to remove minus any proceeds from sale of scrap), are costs of the land, not of the new building. Because it does not deteriorate with use and therefore has an unlimited life, land is not depreciated.[1]

As an example, suppose Pacioli Pacific Company (PPC) spends $275,000 for a piece of land that has an abandoned warehouse on it. The property is subject to a $5,000 lien for unpaid property taxes, which PPC assumes. The company incurs attorney's fees of $1,500, real estate broker's commissions of $10,000, and other closing costs of $2,000. The cost of razing the existing building is $8,300 and the salvaged materials are sold for $2,000. The cost of the land is computed in Exhibit 5–2.

The transaction is recorded as follows, assuming all items are paid in cash:

Land	$299,800	
Cash		$299,800

Improvements to Land

Although land lasts indefinitely, some land improvements have limited lives. Paving, fencing, and sprinkler systems are examples. Because of their limited lives, their costs are debited to a land improvement account and depreciated over their useful lives.

---

[1] The treatment of removal costs as part of the cost of the land and not as part of the cost of the building is consistent with current tax law. This treatment discourages attempts to "load" these costs onto the building instead of the land.

Complexities in Determining Cost of Long-Lived Assets

Special problems in determining cost can arise when a company builds its own plant, purchases a group of assets, acquires plant assets for noncash consideration, or receives assets as a donation.

Self-Constructed Assets

Companies often build their own assets because of lower costs, the special nature of their needs for a machine, or other reasons. Many companies routinely construct assets such as garages or loading docks for their own use. The cost of such **self-constructed assets** includes the materials and labor cost plus other costs such as power, heat, light, and depreciation on plant assets (such as trucks) used in construction.

Basket Purchases

Land, buildings, and machinery are sometimes purchased in a group for one price. These transactions are called **basket** or **lump-sum purchases** and can pose problems. For example, the cost of a basket purchase of land and building must be allocated to land and building because land is not depreciated. As another example, a basket purchase of several machines might require allocating some cost to each because they have different useful lives and therefore different depreciation. A popular method of determining how much to allocate to each asset is to obtain the **appraised value** of each and allocate the total purchase price to each asset based on that. For example, assume that in a basket purchase of three assets, land represented 50% of the total appraised value of the three assets, and the building and machinery, 30% and 20%, respectively. Then 50% of the total cost of the assets would be allocated to the land, 30% to the building, and 20% to the machinery.

Noncash Exchanges

Companies sometimes acquire assets by issuing securities or paying with nonmonetary assets instead of cash. These types of transactions are called **noncash exchanges.** For example, a company could issue its own common stock to buy a plant. Generally accepted accounting principles (GAAP) provide that in this type of transaction the recorded value of the asset acquired should be either the fair market value of the securities or the asset given up, or of the asset received, whichever is more objectively determinable. That is, we want to record the asset at a value as close to its cash price as possible. For example, a new company decides to purchase land for a fabrication plant by issuing 10,000 shares of its stock. If the stock has a market value of $15, the following entry is recorded:

Land	$150,000	
Common Stock (10,000 × $15)		$150,000

If the market value of the stock is not known, the market value of the land should be used to record the acquisition. For example, if the land was appraised at $140,000 while the value of the stock was in doubt (because the company is new and the stock is not traded on an organized exchange), the following entry would be made:

Land	$140,000	
Common Stock		$140,000

Donated Assets

Cities and counties sometimes donate land and perhaps buildings to companies to attract them to the area and provide jobs for residents. The company records such a donation at its appraisal or fair market value as **donated capital.** The donation of land valued at $225,000 to Ida-Ore Company by the city of Pecos to build a potato processing plant is recorded as:

Land	$225,000	
Donated Capital		$225,000

The account Donated Capital appears in the stockholders' equity section of the balance sheet.

DEPRECIATING PLANT ASSETS

Much of accounting involves recording assets and then expensing those costs against revenues as the assets' benefits are consumed. With an insurance policy that expires continuously, or inventory that is sold in a particular period, there is no difficulty matching the expense (insurance expense or cost of goods sold) and the period benefited. For plant and equipment, matching the cost of the asset to the periods benefited (and in the correct amounts) is not so easy.

Depreciation can be defined as the process of allocating the costs of long-lived productive assets to the periods that benefit from their use in producing revenue. In other words, the cost of a plant asset is expensed over its useful service life in a rational and systematic manner.

Depreciation is the process of expensing the cost of a plant asset over its useful service life in a rational and systematic manner.

Our discussion in this chapter focuses on depreciating the plant assets of private businesses. But what of not-for-profit entities? Should the fixed assets (excluding land) of all entities be depreciated? See Insight 5–1 for a discussion of the controversy surrounding the depreciation of fixed assets of private colleges and universities.

Depreciation is an estimate because it is impossible to know in advance an asset's service life and the pattern of its benefits. The key to understanding the concept of depreciation is that, to the accountant, depreciation is the assignment of a part of the asset's cost to the appropriate accounting period so as to match that cost with the revenues or services produced by that asset during that period. Note that *accounting depreciation is not the decline in economic value* during the period. Some assets that are depreciated by companies might surprise

INSIGHT 5–1
Should All Fixed Assets Be Depreciated?

Effective May 15, 1988, the Financial Accounting Standards Board (FASB) No. 93 required not-for-profit groups (such as private colleges and universities), to depreciate their fixed assets, just as private businesses do. Many college presidents and administrators were stunned. Dartmouth College treasurer Robert Field notes that "The FASB has completely missed the mark on this one." David Alexander, president of Pomona College, agrees: "The traditional (accounting) system has worked well for years."

The controversy? The FASB feels that like factories and corporate headquarters buildings, lecture halls and chapels wear out over time. The failure to recognize depreciation results in cheating future students by undercharging today's students.

But many disagree, seeing no sense in writing down the value of fixed assets. Robert Anthony, chairman of the audit committee at Colby College notes that most academic buildings are acquired with contributions, making a college different from a business. "The only reason to depreciate is to figure out whether you broke even," says Anthony. "Who needs to know the depreciation expense of a cathedral?"

Many college administrators feel that it will be too costly to comply and that by writing down the fixed assets they will look like incompetent managers to the alumni and trustees. Additionally, they are especially concerned about being compared unfavorably with their counterparts at public colleges and universities, who are not required to depreciate fixed assets, and with whom they compete for students and funding.

SOURCE: Penelope Wang, "High Dungeon in the Ivory Tower," *Forbes*, 4 April 1988, 78.

INSIGHT 5–2
Depreciation and Professional Sports Franchises

Early in this text in our discussion of a company's assets, we mentioned that one of its most important assets was not reflected in the balance sheet—its employees! It is almost impossible to place a dollar value on a company's employees. For this reason only salaries and wages expense appear in the financial statements. These expenses are reflected in the income statement and are deducted in arriving at periodic net income.

However, some companies do depreciate their employees as if they were tangible assets. Professional sports franchises, such as football, basketball, and baseball teams, ascribe a large proportion of the franchise's value to the players they employ. Many players have employment contracts that provide for guaranteed payments if the employee is injured or released. These required contract amounts are capitalized and appear on the franchise's balance sheet. These amounts are subsequently depreciated over the useful life of the asset, that is, the player's estimated useful life to the team. The resulting depreciation expense is deducted in arriving at the franchise's net income and also deducted for income tax purposes on its annual income tax return.

you. See Insight 5–2 for a discussion of professional sports franchises. This does not imply that accountants are unconcerned with declines in the economic values of assets. The usefulness and value of an asset falls because of physical wear and tear, obsolescence, and inadequacy. These factors influence accounting estimates of the asset's useful life and its salvage value at the end of its life.

Inadequacy refers to the inability of the asset to meet the existing and increasing demands for its product or service because of growth. Inadequacy is difficult to predict. It occurs when a firm or business grows more rapidly than anticipated.

Obsolescence occurs when technological advances create new assets that make older models relatively less efficient and therefore of lesser value. Virtually all types of assets have improved over time. Some, such as microcomputers, have improved enormously in only a few years.

Determining Periodic Depreciation

Determining the pattern of depreciation expense involves three steps:

1. The periods benefited—that is, the **useful life**—must be estimated.
2. The salvage value must be estimated.
3. The pattern of consumption of the benefit must be determined, and an appropriate depreciation method chosen.

It is important to note that the periods benefited (useful life) and the salvage value are both estimates. Annual depreciation expense is thus an estimate, and the balance of plant and equipment in the balance sheet is an estimate. The whole process is very exact mathematically, but very inexact from a practical standpoint, as will become apparent in the discussion that follows.

Period Benefited

The asset's estimated economic life is not necessarily the same as its physical life. The estimated economic life is affected by physical wear and tear, obsolescence, and inadequacy, making it generally shorter than the physical life.

Suppose a company purchases, for $14,000, a piece of equipment that is capable of producing 20,000 units of product per year for ten years. Managers believe, however, that due to changing market conditions, they will be able to use the equipment for only five years, producing an average of 15,000 units of product per year. After five years, they predict, the equipment will be obsolete.

The physical life of the equipment is thus ten years or 200,000 units, while its economic life is only five years or 75,000 units. The $14,000 cost of the equipment must be expensed as it is consumed over the five-year useful life.

Cost Consumed

The residual value is the amount that management expects to recover at the end of the asset's useful life. The residual value is not depreciated.

The **salvage value** (or **residual value**) of a plant asset is the amount that the firm expects to receive from selling it at the end of its economic life. This value might be as low as zero or it might be quite high in relation to the original cost. The **depreciable base** is the cost of the asset less its residual value. This is the total amount to be depreciated over the asset's economic life.

Let us continue with our example of the $14,000 equipment. We must determine its depreciable base by estimating its salvage value. Suppose management estimates that the equipment can be sold for scrap for $2,000 at the end of its useful life. The depreciable base is:

Cost of equipment	$14,000
Less salvage value	2,000
Depreciable base	$12,000

Regardless of the pattern of benefits of the equipment, the amount to be expensed is $12,000 over its useful life.

Depreciation Patterns

The pattern of depreciation expense over the useful life of the asset should reflect the pattern of its benefits. In general, accountants use depreciation methods that assume the benefit is consumed in one of the following three ways:

1. When benefit consumption is even over the useful life of the asset, use **straight-line depreciation.**

2. When benefit consumption is in the same pattern that utility is provided (as units produced, kilowatts generated, or miles traveled) use **units-of-activity depreciation** (sometimes called *production-units depreciation*).

3. When benefit consumption is greatest in the early years of the life of the asset and less in later years, use either **sum-of-the-years'-digits depreciation,** or **double-declining-balance depreciation** (also called *double-rate depreciation*). These are referred to as **accelerated depreciation methods.**

Straight-Line Method

Under the straight-line method of depreciation an equal amount of the depreciable base is charged to expense each period of the asset's useful life. The calculation is:

The use of the straight-line method results in equal amounts of depreciation expense each period.

$$\text{Annual Depreciation Expense} = \frac{\text{Cost of Asset} - \text{Salvage Value}}{\text{Useful Life}}$$

For example, if a piece of machinery cost $65,000, has a ten-year useful life, and a salvage value of $5,000, depreciation expense is $6,000 per year [($65,000 − $5,000)/10].

The entry for recording the annual charge for depreciation expense is:

Depreciation Expense	$6,000	
Accumulated Depreciation—Machinery		$6,000

The account Depreciation Expense appears on the income statement as an expense and is deducted in determining periodic net income. The account Accumulated Depreciation—Machinery appears in the balance sheet. Note that the credit was to the Accumulated Depreciation—Machinery account and not to the Machinery account. The account, Accumulated Depreciation—Machinery, is a contra asset account, just as the Allowance for Doubtful Accounts is a contra asset to Accounts Receivable. Accumulated Depreciation *accumulates* charges to depreciation expense over the life of the asset. The difference between the historical cost of the machinery and its related accumulated depreciation is its **book value.** Remember that because of the use of historical cost and the fact that salvage values and useful lives are estimates, the book value of a plant asset does not necessarily indicate its market value. This is one reason the balance sheet shows the historical cost and accumulated depreciation of the machinery rather than just its book value. This is done for several reasons. First, this form of presentation allows the reader to gain some understanding of the condition of a company's plant assets. For example, a building costing $2,500,000 with $2,000,000 accumulated depreciation is probably quite different from one recently purchased for $500,000, even though both of their book values are $500,000. Second, the reader might be able to approximate the average age of the company's assets from this information on the balance sheet. Third, ratios might assist the reader in evaluating the company. For example, gross plant and equipment cost divided by the current year's depreciation expense yields the approximate average total life span of plant and equipment if straight-line depreciation is used. Similarly, total accumulated depreciation balance divided by the current year's depreciation expense gives us the average age of plant assets. Finally, the average remaining life of plant assets is the book value of plant assets divided by the current year's depreciation expense.

Please note carefully that accumulated depreciation does not represent amounts of cash set aside to pay for the replacement of old assets. The purchase of a plant asset is a prepayment for services. The recognition of depreciation expense is merely an allocation of that prepayment to the periods in which the services are consumed. Cash (or some other form of financing) is used to replace old equipment, and there is no cash in the accumulated depreciation account.

Units-of-Activity Method

The units-of-activity method results in a fixed amount of depreciation being assigned to each unit of output produced; thus depreciation per period fluctuates.

The units-of-activity method assumes that the benefit provided by the asset is closely related to some activity (such as the number of units manufactured or services rendered), rather than to the passage of time. Therefore, the annual charge to depreciation expense is the depreciation per unit multiplied by the number of units produced or services rendered during the period.

To illustrate, assume that the depreciable base of a piece of machinery is $60,000 and that management estimates that the machinery will manufacture 100,000 units. Depreciation per unit is then $0.60 ($60,000/100,000). If production in 19X0, 19X1, and 19X2 is 20,000, 30,000 and 15,000 units, respectively, depreciation expense is $12,000, $18,000, and $9,000 for those years.

This method is particularly appropriate for assets whose benefits are easily measured. Automobiles and trucks are good examples. Depreciating them based on miles driven makes sense because the use of a car or truck is the benefit received. One warning, however. If an asset being depreciated using a units-of-production method is idle for an extended period, say, a year, it still must be depreciated even though it produced no benefits. This is because some depreciation follows time, rather than use. Obviously, a 20-year old truck that has never been driven is not as useful as a new one.

Accelerated Depreciation Methods

Accelerated methods are used when the benefits received from the use of the asset are greater in the early years of the asset's life and less in the later years. Such a pattern might occur because of technological developments, wear and tear, or increases in repairs and maintenance costs as the asset becomes older. In addition, an asset might generate less revenue in later years than in earlier years. For example, a hotel might not be as appealing in its thirtieth year of operation as it was in the first year. This results in charges to depreciation expense that begin high and decline over the useful life. Following are two accelerated depreciation methods.

Sum-of-the-Years'-Digits Method

The sum-of-the-years'-digits method depreciates a different fraction of cost in each year. The numerator of the fraction is the number of years remaining in the asset's useful life at the beginning of the year. The denominator is the sum of the years' digits and is calculated as follows for a five-year life.

$$\text{Sum of years' digits} = 1 + 2 + 3 + 4 + 5 = 15$$

Depreciation in year 1 is $5/15$ times the depreciable base and in year 4 is $2/15$ times the depreciable base. Recall that the machinery in our example had a depreciable base of $60,000 and a useful life of ten years. We first sum the number of years' digits in the asset's life ($1 + 2 + 3 + 4 + 5 + 6 + 7 + 8 + 9 + 10 = 55$). Next, use the number of years remaining in the asset's life at the beginning of the period as the numerator. Multiply that fraction by the depreciable base. Annual depreciation charges, accumulated depreciation, and book values for the asset appear in Exhibit 5–3. Total depreciation expense for the ten-year period is $60,000, leaving a salvage value of $5,000.

Both double-declining-balance and sum-of-the-years'-digits methods are accelerated methods and result in higher depreciation charges in the earlier years of an asset's life because the asset is assumed to be more productive in those years.

Because the sum-of-the-years'-digits method results in higher depreciation in the early years of the asset's life, remember to use the last year of the asset's life as the numerator, for example 3/6, not 1/6 for an asset with a three-year life.

Book Value
Salvage Value
Depr Cost

Exhibit 5–3
**Computation of Periodic Depreciation Expense Using
Sum-of-the-Years'-Digits Depreciation**

Year		Depreciation Expense	Accumulated Depreciation	Book Value
				$65,000
1	10/55 × $60,000	$10,909	$10,909	54,091
2	9/55 × $60,000	9,818	20,727	44,273
3	8/55 × $60,000	8,727	29,454	35,546
4	7/55 × $60,000	7,636	37,090	27,910
5	6/55 × $60,000	6,545	43,635	21,365
6	5/55 × $60,000	5,455	49,090	15,910
7	4/55 × $60,000	4,364	53,454	11,546
8	3/55 × $60,000	3,273	56,727	8,273
9	2/55 × $60,000	2,182	58,909	6,091
10	1/55 × $60,000	1,091	60,000	5,000
		$60,000		

A simple mathematical formula can be used to determine the denominator under the sum-of-the-years'-digits depreciation method. The formula is

$$S = \frac{n(n + 1)}{2}$$

where S is the sum-of-the-years'-digits and n is the useful life of the asset. In our example

$$\frac{10(10 + 1)}{2} = 55$$

Under the double-declining-balance method you ignore salvage or residual value in computing depreciation expense for the period (Depreciation Expense = Cost × DDB Percent).

Double-Declining-Balance Method

The double-declining-balance method begins with the straight-line rate (in our example ¹⁄₁₀ or 10%). Using this method, you double the straight-line rate. Thus, an asset with a ten-year life has a straight-line rate of 10% and a double-declining-balance rate of 20%. That rate is applied to the book value of the asset, not to the depreciable base. You ignore salvage value when computing double-declining-balance depre-

Exhibit 5–4
Computation of Periodic Depreciation Expense Using
Double-Declining-Balance Depreciation

Period	Depreciation Expense	Accumulated Depreciation	Book Value
			$65,000
1 (.20 × $65,000)	$13,000	$13,000	52,000
2 (.20 × $52,000)	10,400	23,400	41,600
3 (.20 × $41,600)	8,320	31,720	33,280
4 (.20 × $33,280)	6,656	38,376	26,624
5 (.20 × $26,624)	5,325	43,701	21,299
6 (.20 × $21,299)	4,260	47,961	17,039
7 (.20 × $17,039)	3,408	51,369	13,631
8 (.20 × $13,631)	2,726	54,095	10,905
9 (.20 × $10,905)	2,181	56,276	8,724
10 (.20 × $ 8,724)	1,745*	58,021	6,979

*The amount would be $3,724 if the expected salvage value were still $5,000. This is the amount necessary to reduce the book value to $5,000.

ciation. However, you depreciate the asset only down to salvage value. Exhibit 5–4 illustrates the calculations for our $65,000 machine.

A quick way to calculate the double-declining-balance rate is to divide 2 by the estimate of the asset's useful life; for example, an asset with a ten-year life has a rate of 20% (2/10).

Group and Composite Depreciation

Most large companies do not depreciate each and every asset separately because of the enormous number they own. Instead, they combine assets into classes and depreciate them at an average rate. **Group depreciation** is used for collections of similar assets (for example, a fleet of automobiles). This method assumes that the assets have approximately the same useful lives. **Composite depreciation** is used for collections of dissimilar assets that are used together. For example, this method is appropriate for equipment on a manufacturing production line or for different types of delivery vehicles.

The computation for depreciation expense is the same for both methods. That is, an average rate is determined and applied each period. Exhibit 5–5 illustrates composite depreciation for a fleet of delivery trucks, assuming straight-line depreciation. The composite rate is 17.4%, determined by dividing total depreciation expense per year by the total depreciable base ($27,000/$155,000). Annual depreciation

Exhibit 5-5
Computation of Composite Depreciation
Assuming Straight-Line Depreciation

Asset	Original Cost	Residual Value	Depreciable Base	Estimated Life (Years)	Depreciation Per Year
Vans	$ 30,000	$ 3,000	$ 27,000	3	$ 9,000
Trucks	90,000	10,000	80,000	8	10,000
Cars	60,000	12,000	48,000	6	8,000
	$180,000	$25,000	$155,000		$27,000

expense is 17.4% of depreciable cost or $27,000 per year. The composite life is 5.74 years ($155,000/$27,000). Depreciation Expense is debited and Accumulated Depreciation for the collection of assets is credited.

The major advantage of the composite and group methods is the time and cost saved by not maintaining separate asset and accumulated depreciation accounts for every individual asset.

Exhibit 5-6 is an excerpt from the "Summary of Significant Accounting Policies" section from the 1988 annual report of Georgia-Pacific Corporation.

Limitations of Depreciation Methods

Comparability of financial statements is hindered by allowing companies a choice of depreciation methods. In our examples, the first year's depreciation expense was as follows: straight-line, $6,000; units-of-

Exhibit 5-6
Notes to the Financial Statements
Georgia Pacific Corporation

Note 1. Summary of Significant Accounting Policies
Property, Plant and Equipment (excerpt)

Depreciation expense is computed using the straight-line method with composite rates based upon estimated service lives. The ranges of composite rates for the principal classes are: land improvements— 5% to 7%; buildings— 3% to 5%; and machinery and equipment—5% to 20%.

activity, $12,000; sum-of-the-years'-digits, $10,909; and double-declining-balance, $13,000. If four otherwise identical companies used each one of these depreciation methods, their book values and net incomes would be different.

However, it should be noted that for financial accounting purposes a particular depreciation method should be chosen on the basis of the pattern of service benefits expected to be received from the asset involved. That is, given a choice of methods, a company should match the method to the pattern of service benefits provided by the asset. Thus, one airline might depreciate a 747 airplane used only for domestic flights over a useful life of eight years using an accelerated method. The airline might do so because of the many flights the airplane makes and resulting hours of flying time. Another airline that uses the same type of airplane only for international flights might choose a different method and a useful life of 12 years because of the airplane suffering less physical deterioration due to fewer hours of flight time. Some individuals are critical of this practice by the airlines. See the discussion in Insight 5–3.

Depreciation and Income Taxes

Depreciation is a tax-deductible expense for federal and state income tax returns. For income tax purposes, assets acquired before 1981 are depreciated over their useful lives using straight-line, units-of-activity, or one of the accelerated methods. The method used on the tax return need not be the same as the method used for financial reporting purposes, and many times a company employs an accelerated method for income tax purposes and the straight-line method for financial reporting purposes. The company pays less income tax in the early years of an asset's life and more in the later years. Therefore, the income taxes are postponed or deferred, and the firm has these postponed funds available for other uses.

Assets purchased between January 1, 1981 and December 31, 1985, are depreciated using the **Accelerated Cost Recovery System (ACRS)** for tax purposes. ACRS uses a 150% declining-balance method. After 1985 companies must use the **Modified Accelerated Cost Recovery System (MACRS)** for tax purposes on new assets placed in service. Both ACRS and MACRS establish classes of property with established lives and subject to a certain depreciation method. For example, with MACRS, cars and light trucks with a life of more than four years and less than ten are in the five-year classification, and subject to 200% declining-balance depreciation with a switch to straight-line at an appropriate point in the asset's useful life. Residential rental property is in the 27.5-year class and is depreciated using the straight-line method.

In general, both ACRS and MACRS permit a faster recovery of an asset's cost and larger tax benefits during the early years of an asset's

INSIGHT 5–3
Different Periods of Benefit, Different Consequences

Comparing the earnings of two different companies is very difficult for an investor without direct knowledge of the companies' accounting principles. In the case of airlines the same kind of equipment is written off over very different periods, resulting in significant differences in net income figures. For example, Delta Air Lines depreciates its planes over 15 years and figures on a 10% residual value. Pan Am estimates a life of 25 years for the same 727s that Delta writes off in 15 —and assumes a 15% residual value. Texas Air also writes off its planes over up to 25 years.

Are Pan Am and Texas Air being too aggressive, or is Delta too conservative? "There is a justification for lives well beyond 20 years, if the planes are properly maintained," says Robert Fenimore (a partner and airline specialist at the accounting firm of KPMG Peat Marwick). "But in reality, it's obvious that the airlines with less financial strength are the ones with longer depreciation lives."

Critics suggest that the American Institute of CPAs and the Securities and Exchange Commission should insist upon more conformity in companies' depreciation policies. The accounting profession responds that when reviewing depreciation, auditors look at engineering reports, industry practices, and the company's historical use of its assets. Even so, "it is difficult to pass judgment on how much value can be squeezed from the assets" and therefore determine their depreciable lives. Fenimore goes on to say, "You can count fixed assets and make sure they're there," but determining depreciable lives and salvage values are difficult to determine accurately. Says Fenimore, "There could be numerous studies done, all of which could give you reasonable answers with different conclusions."

SOURCE: Dana Wechsler, "Earnings Helper," *Forbes*, 12 June 1989, 150, 153.

life. The intent of Congress in enacting legislation creating ACRS and MACRS was to encourage and stimulate capital investment.

Depreciation is an estimate. When management discovers more precise information on the estimated life and residual value of an asset, a revision is made in the calculation.

Changes in Calculating Depreciation Expense

As we previously stated, depreciation is an estimate based on such factors as useful life and salvage value. Estimation is, in fact, an inherent part of the accounting process. Therefore, at times it is necessary to revise various types of computations when new information or developments arise. Depreciation calculations may change accordingly. See Insight 5–4 for further discussion of this subject.

INSIGHT 5–4
Depreciation Estimates and Their Impact on Earnings

No one has ever accused accounting of being an exact science. However, some companies have been accused of minimizing the depreciation charges on fixed assets to increase reported earnings. Although generally accepted accounting principles allow management to estimate the useful life, some observers feel that management is allowed too much discretion and that some investors might therefore be misled. Examples by critics include:

• Cineplex Odeon, a movie theater circuit depreciates its leasehold improvements (seats, carpet, and equipment) over an average useful life of 27 years, even though these assets will almost be scrapped long before that period elapses.

• Blockbuster Entertainment, a videotape rental store chain, spread the depreciation period of its tapes from a "fast writeoff over 9 months to a slow one over 36 months. That bookkeeping gimmick added $3 million, or nearly 20%, to Blockbuster's reported 1988 income."

• Until 1987 General Motors (GM) wrote off its tools and dies at the fastest rate in the auto industry. In that year GM slowed the depreciation of its tools and dies down to a level similar to that of Ford and Chrysler. "GM was in no way cooking the books, but the move did increase GM's reported earnings by $2.55 per share; total earnings came to $10.06 per share that year."

• In 1984 IBM shifted from accelerated depreciation to the straight-line method for its rental machines, plant, and other property. The change increased IBM's reported earnings by $375 million, or 37 cents per share.

SOURCE: Dana Wechsler, "Earnings Helper," *Forbes*, 12 June 1989, 150, 153.

The procedure for changing a depreciation calculation is to spread the book value remaining at the date of revision over the remaining useful life. The rationale for not going back and adjusting for previously recorded depreciation expense and accumulated depreciation is that our original estimates for salvage value and useful life were not wrong but were based on the most current information available at that time. When new information regarding a plant asset becomes available, we simply revise our initial estimate.

To illustrate, assume that we purchase a machine costing $86,000, with a salvage value of $6,000 and a useful life of eight years. Annual depreciation expense is $10,000 per year. At the beginning of the fourth year the book value of the machine is $56,000 [$86,000 − ($10,000 × 3 years)]. If because of improved maintenance procedures, the machine has a remaining useful life of ten years, and the salvage value remains the same, and the annual charge to depreciation expense for the current and each of the next nine years is $5,000.

Partial-Year Depreciation

Throughout our previous examples we have assumed that depreciable assets were purchased at the beginning of an accounting period. In actuality companies purchase and dispose of assets throughout the year. Theoretically, depreciation expense should be recorded for each asset based on the number of days in each year that the asset is held. Many times this is impractical or not worthwhile, and in these cases **half-year averaging convention** is used. The procedure involves taking one-half year's depreciation in the year of acquisition and one-half year's depreciation in the year of disposal, regardless of the actual date of acquisition or disposal. The convention can be justified on the grounds that the additional recordkeeping cost is not worth the benefit of increased accuracy. In practice, this method is generally acceptable as long as it does not result in a material distortion of income.

Disclosures Relating to Plant Assets

The following disclosures of depreciable assets and depreciation should be made in the financial statements or the related footnotes:

1. Depreciation expense for the period.
2. Balances of major classes of depreciable assets by nature or function.
3. Accumulated depreciation by classes or in total.
4. The methods used, by major classes of assets, in computing depreciation.

Exhibit 5–7 shows the disclosures relating to plant assets from the 1990 annual report of Boise Cascade Corporation and Subsidiaries for the years 1990, 1989, and 1988, respectively.

SUMMARY

All plant assets are recorded at acquisition cost, which includes all reasonable expenditures necessary to make the asset ready for its intended use. These costs are included as part of the cost of the plant asset because they are expected to have future benefit to the firm.

Exhibit 5–7
Boise Cascade Corporation and Subsidiaries
Balance Sheets (excerpt)

	December 31		
	1990	1989	1988
	(expressed in thousands)		
Property (Note 1)			
Property and equipment	$4,881,672	$4,211,786	$3,649,164
Accumulated depreciation	(1,726,794)	(1,583,210)	(1,473,079)
	3,154,878	2,628,576	2,176,085

The company indicated on its income statement that depreciation expense was (in thousands) $212,890, $202,060, and $187,600 for the years 1990, 1989, and 1988, respectively.

The footnotes to the Boise Cascade financial statements indicate that the company records its property and equipment at cost. Additionally, substantially all of the company's paper and wood products manufacturing facilities determine depreciation by the units-of-production method, and other operations use the straight-line and composite depreciation methods.

Complexities can arise in determining the acquisition cost of some long-lived assets. For example, firms may construct their own assets or acquire assets in basket purchases or in noncash exchanges.

With the exception of land, the cost of plant assets is allocated to the periods benefited through depreciation. The depreciation method should reflect the pattern of benefits to be received from the particular asset and should be consistently applied from period to period.

DEMONSTRATION PROBLEMS

Demonstration Problem 5–1

Armstrong Company purchased an assembly machine for use in its manufacturing facility on November 15 of the current year. The machine had an invoice price of $21,000 and was purchased on credit with terms of 1/20, n60. The company paid freight charges of $1,230. Armstrong paid for the machine on November 29 of the current year. Labor charges incurred in setting up the machine totaled $1,950, and repair costs of $750 were necessary because of damage to the machine caused by the negligence of company personnel. Raw materials used in calibrating the machine had a cost of $1,378. The company also had to pay for special power connections totaling $3,456. Prepare a schedule showing the cost of the new machine.

Solution to Demonstration Problem 5–1

Invoice price less discount ($21,000 × .99)		$20,790
Add:		
Freight charges	$1,230	
Labor set-up charges	1,950	
Raw materials for calibration	1,378	
Power connections	3,456	8,014
Cost of new machine		$28,804

Demonstration Problem 5–2

The Miggs Company purchased a five-acre tract of land for construction of a new factory facility for $178,500. The company also paid $4,200 of unpaid property taxes on the land. Survey costs totaled $950, and a title search was done costing $400. The land also had an old barn on the property that had to be removed at a cost of $3,100. The scrap lumber from the barn was sold for $700. The real estate broker was paid a commission of 5% of the purchase price. The company also had the land graded at a cost of $1,200. Prepare a schedule showing the cost of the land.

Solution to Demonstration Problem 5–2

Initial cost of the land		$178,500
Add:		
Payment of unpaid property taxes	$4,200	
Survey costs	950	
Title search	400	
Broker's commission ($178,500 × 5%)	8,925	
Removal of barn less scrap proceeds ($3,100 − $700)	2,400	
Cost of grading	1,200	18,075
Cost of land		$196,575

Demonstration Problem 5–3

On January 1, 19X2, Bellows Company purchased a tract of land, a building, and a machine for a total cash purchase price of $450,000. Since the purchase of the three assets was for one lump sum, an appraisal was necessary so that an allocation of the purchase price could be made. The appraisal resulted in the following fair market values:

	Fair Market Value
Land	$250,000
Machine	100,000
Building	150,000
Total fair market value	$500,000

The building has an estimated useful life of 25 years, and the machine has an estimated useful life of ten years. The salvage value for the building is estimated to be $10,000, and the salvage value for the machine is estimated to be $2,000. Both the building and the machine will be depreciated using the straight-line method. The company's fiscal year-end is December 31.

1. Provide the journal entry to record the purchase of the land, building, and machine on January 1, 19X2.

2. Provide the year-end adjusting entry to record depreciation on the building and the machine.

3. If, on January 1, 19X5, the company discovers new information indicating that the machine has a remaining useful life of nine years and an estimated salvage value of $600, what would be the adjusting entry that the company would make on December 31, 19X5, relating to depreciation expense?

Solution to Demonstration Problem 5-3

1.

	FMV	%	
Land	$250,000	50	$450,000 × 50% = $225,000
Machine	100,000	20	450,000 × 20% = 90,000
Building	150,000	30	450,000 × 30% = 135,000
	$500,000	100	$450,000

Land	$225,000	
Machine	90,000	
Building	135,000	
Cash		$450,000

2. Depreciation Expense ($135,000 − $10,000)/25 ... $5,000

Accumulated Depreciation—Building ... $5,000

Depreciation Expense ($90,000 − $2,000)/10 ... $8,800

Accumulated Depreciation—Machine ... $8,800

3.

Original cost of machine	$90,000
Accumulated depreciation (3 years × $8,800)	26,400
Remaining book value at January 1, 1995	63,600
Less: estimated salvage value	600
Depreciable base	$63,000
Divided by remaining useful life	9 years
Depreciation expense	$ 7,000

Depreciation Expense	$7,000	
Accumulated Depreciation—Machine		$7,000

Demonstration Problem 5–4

Apache Corporation purchased a new assembly machine on January 1 of the current year. The machine had a cost of $45,000, an estimated salvage value of $5,000, and an estimated useful life of five years. Prepare a schedule showing depreciation expense and the book value of the machine for each of the five years under:

1. Straight-line method of depreciation.
2. Units-of-activity method of depreciation, assuming that the estimated number of units to be produced over the life of the machine is 100,000 and the number units produced is, respectively, 30,000, 27,000, 16,000, 15,000, and 12,000, over each year of the five-year life of the machine.
3. Double-declining-balance method of depreciation.
4. Sum-of-the-years'-digits method of depreciation.

Solution to Demonstration Problem 5–4

1. Straight-line method

$$\frac{\$45,000 - \$5,000}{5} = \$8,000$$

Year	Depreciation Expense	Book Value
		$45,000
1	$8,000	37,000
2	8,000	29,000
3	8,000	21,000
4	8,000	13,000
5	8,000	5,000

2. Units-of-activity method

$$\frac{\$45,000 - \$5,000}{100,000 \text{ units}} = \$0.40/\text{unit}$$

Year		Depreciation Expense	Book Value
			$45,000
1	30,000 units × $0.40 =	$12,000	33,000
2	27,000 units × $0.40 =	10,800	22,200
3	16,000 units × $0.40 =	6,400	15,800
4	15,000 units × $0.40 =	6,000	9,800
5	12,000 units × $0.40 =	4,800	5,000

3. Double-declining-balance method

$$2/5 = 40\%$$

Year		Depreciation Expense	Book Value
			$45,000
1	$45,000 × .40 =	$18,000	27,000
2	$31,667 × .40 =	10,800	16,200
3	$16,200 × .40 =	6,480	9,720
4	$ 9,720 × .40 =	3,888	5,832
5	$ 5,832 × .40 =	2,333*	3,499

*The amount would be $832 if the salvage value at the end of year 5 was $5,000.

4. Sum-of-the-years'-digits method

$$5 + 4 + 3 + 2 + 1 = 15$$

Year		Depreciation Expense	Book Value
			$45,000
1	($45,000 − $5,000) 5/15	$13,333	31,667
2	($45,000 − $5,000) 4/15	10,667	21,000
3	($45,000 − $5,000) 3/15	8,000	13,000
4	($45,000 − $5,000) 2/15	5,333	7,667
5	($45,000 − $5,000) 1/15	2,667	5,000

Demonstration Problem 5–5

Mavis Rent-a-Car Company has a fleet of rental cars and vans. This is the first year of depreciation for Mavis. All of the vehicles were purchased on January 1 of the current year. Because of the large number of cars and vans, the company uses the composite method of computing depreciation rather than depreciating each individual vehicle separately. The company's year-end is December 31. The estimated useful life of the vans is five years, and the estimated useful life of the cars is four years. The estimated residual value of vans is $20,000; of cars, $32,000. The total cost of the vans was $140,000, and the total cost of the cars was $220,000. Provide a schedule showing the depreciation expense for the year for Mavis Rent-a-Car Company.

Solution to Demonstration Problem 5–5

Computation of Composite Depreciation
Assuming Straight-Line Depreciation

Asset	Original Cost	Residual Value	Depreciable Base	Estimated Life (Years)	Depreciation per Year
Vans	$140,000	$20,000	$120,000	5	$24,000
Cars	220,000	32,000	188,000	4	47,000
	$360,000	$52,000	$308,000		$71,000

Key Terms

ACRS

accelerated depreciation methods

appraised value

basket (lump-sum) purchase

book value

capitalized

composite depreciation

depreciable base

depreciation

donated capital

double-declining-balance depreciation

group depreciation

MACRS

noncash exchanges

salvage value (residual value)

self-constructed asset

straight-line depreciation

sum-of-the-years'-digits depreciation

units-of-activity (production) depreciation

ASSIGNMENTS

5–1   Recording Assets at Historical Cost

Over pizza, you and two friends are discussing the merits of the use of historical cost for recording assets. You explain to your friends that historical cost is the basis used to record long-lived productive assets principally because it is conservative and can be objectively determined as opposed to other measures (e.g., market values). One friend counters that historical cost may indeed be objective but in many cases is irrelevant. He states that "after the initial purchase of a long-lived productive asset, its market value is much more relevant than its historical cost for purposes of decision-making." Your other friend remarks, "I would much rather have a number that is subjective and relevant than one that is objective but irrelevant."

REQUIRED:

Discuss your reply to your friend.

5–2 Calculating Cost of Machinery

On September 23, 19X0. CanCo International purchased a canning machine for $10,000, terms 2/10, n/30. Transportation charges of $1,100 were included in the invoice. The invoice was paid on September 30, 19X0. Because of the special nature of this machine it required a concrete base and special power connections costing $2,345. The canning machine was assembled by CanCo personnel who were paid wages of $950. Operating personnel charged 20 hours at $12.50 an hour to calibrate the machine. Additionally, they spent another 4 hours at the same hourly rate adjusting the machine and wasted $325 of aluminum.

REQUIRED:

Prepare a schedule to show the cost of the machine.

5–3 Determining Cost of a Building

Shelton Company purchased a piece of land for $350,000 on February 1 of the current year. An old maintenance building on the land had to be razed at a cost of $7,500. Proceeds from the sale of lumber and bricks from the building amounted to $3,000. Survey and title costs cost the company a total of $1,700. An architect was paid $3,300 for drawing the building plans. A new building was completed on April 30 at a cost of $225,500. During construction of the building a liability insurance premium for $1,100 was purchased.

REQUIRED:

Prepare a schedule to show the cost of the building.

5–4 Determining Cost of Land

Green Highlander Company purchased a tract of land on June 1, 19X1, for the purpose of constructing a plastics plant. The initial cost was $263,500. Unpaid property taxes on the land at the date of purchase amounted to $6,000. Estimated property taxes for 19X1 are $7,000.

Additionally, survey costs were $400, a title search was $300, and the company spent $3,200 for options that were acquired in 19X0. Regarding the options, Green Highlander spent $1,000 for the option relating to the purchased property and the remainder for two parcels that were considered as possible sites for the plant but were not acquired. The land had an existing structure on it that was removed at a cost of $11,945. Materials salvaged from the removal operation were sold for $1,800. Real estate broker's commissions amounted to 3% of the purchase price.

REQUIRED:

Determine the cost of the land on the accounting records for Green Highlander Company.

 5–5   Lump Sum Purchase

Melvin, Inc., agrees to purchase the following assets from Douglas Company, which is going out of business:

	Book Value
Inventory (FIFO basis)	$ 20,000
Land	110,000
Building	83,000
Assembly machine	44,000
Total book value	$257,000

Melvin pays $450,000 for the assets and obtains the following appraisal from Dewey & Howe, an appraisal firm: inventory, $50,000; land, $250,000; building, $125,000; and assembly machine, $75,000.

REQUIRED:

Assign the $450,000 to the assets purchased by Melvin from Douglas, and prepare the journal entry to record the transaction.

5–6   Determining Recorded Value of Land and Building

Jumonville Company has decided to build its new factory on a heavily timbered piece of land. The land has an existing building that the company will use; however, the structure will have to be remodeled and expanded. An independent appraisal resulted in the following market values: land, $500,000; building, $300,000. The company agreed to a purchase price of $700,000 for both the land and the building. The company will also pay the $3,400 of unpaid property taxes on the land. Additionally, the company incurred a broker's commission of 2% of the purchase price of $700,000 and attorney's fees of $2,750. After the purchase, the company cut down the timber and sold it for $27,460.

The cost of cutting was $32,000. A wing was added to the building at a cost of $43,000, and other remodeling costs totaled $13,400.

REQUIRED:

Determine the recorded cost of the land and the building.

5–7 Recording Noncash Exchanges and Donated Assets

The city of Bone, New Mexico, is interested in enticing a large manufacturing firm, M. F. Young, Inc., into locating in New Mexico. On February 16, the city donated ten acres of land to the company. An appraisal indicated that the land had a fair market value of $26,000. M. F. Young, Inc., accepted the land and agreed to relocate to Bone, New Mexico; however, the company felt it would be necessary to acquire an additional five acres for its site and therefore issued 1,000 shares of its common stock with a market value of $14 in exchange for the additional five acres on March 17.

REQUIRED:

Record the transaction relating to the donated land and the noncash exchange on the books of M. F. Young, Inc.

5–8 Compute Depreciation for Two Years

LMA Company purchased a new machine for its fabrication process at a cost of $14,400. The company estimated that the machine would have a trade-in value of $1,200 at the end of its useful life, which is estimated to be eight years. The machine is estimated to produce 110,000 units over its useful life, with 32,000 units being produced in the first year of operations and 26,000 in the second year.

REQUIRED:

Calculate depreciation expense for years 1 and 2 using the following:

1. Straight-line method
2. Units-of-activity method
3. Double-declining-balance method
4. Sum-of-the-years'-digits method

5–9 Calculation of Annual Depreciation Expense

Schonberger International Inc. purchased a large industrial machine for $255,000 on January 1, 19X0. Based on past experience, the controller, M. Bezzler, CPA, estimates that the life of the machine will be five years, at which time the machine will have a trade-in value of $5,000. Bezzler also feels that the machine will produce 100,000 units of product during its life. Assume that it actually produced the following number of units: year 1, 12,000; year 2, 18,000; year 3, 40,000; year 4, 20,000; and year 5, 10,000.

REQUIRED:

Compute the annual depreciation expense for the estimated life of the machine using the following:

1. Straight-line method
2. Units-of-activity method
3. Sum-of-the-years'-digits method
4. Double-declining-balance method

 ### 5–10   Determining Depreciation Expense

On January 1 of the current year a company purchased a machine with a ten-year life. Salvage value is estimated to be $5,000 at the end of its useful life. The cost of the machine is $65,000. The company has decided to use the double-declining-balance method to record periodic depreciation charges. The company's fiscal year ends on December 31.

REQUIRED:

In what year of the asset's life will the charge to depreciation expense for this asset total $2,726? (Round to whole dollars.)

5–11   Calculation of Acquisition Cost

On January 1, 19X7, Abscond Company purchased equipment to be used in its assembly operations. The equipment has an estimated useful life of ten years and an estimated salvage value of $5,000. The depreciation applicable to this equipment was $24,000 for 19X9, computed under the sum-of-the-years'-digits method.

REQUIRED:

What was the acquisition cost of the equipment?

5–12   Journal Entries for Plant Assets

Harrop Corporation had the following transactions:

(1) Purchased land for $75,000 cash in 19X0.

(2) On January 1, 19X1, completed construction of a building at a cost of $50,000. The contractor was paid in cash. The estimated useful life of the building is 25 years with no salvage value. The building was depreciated using the straight-line method.

(3) Purchased a machine for $10,000 cash on April 1, 19X1. The machine has a useful life of ten years and a salvage value of $1,200. The straight-line method of depreciation is used.

(4) On July 1, 19X2, Harrop purchased equipment for $25,000. The equipment had a useful life of six years and an estimated salvage

value of $1,000. The sum-of-the-years'-digits method was used to depreciate the equipment.

(5) On July 1, 19X2, Harrop Corporation also purchased a computer system for $32,000. The computer has a useful life of four years with no estimated salvage value and will be depreciated using the double-declining-balance method.

REQUIRED:

1. Prepare the appropriate journal entries to record these events in 19X0–19X2.

2. Prepare the year-end adjusting entries for depreciation expense for 19X1 and 19X2 assuming Harrop Corporation has a calendar year-end.

5–13 Calculate Salvage (Residual) Value

George Company has an assembly machine that cost $105,000. The machine has an estimated useful life of five years. The company uses the sum-of-the-years'-digits method to compute periodic depreciation expense.

REQUIRED:

If depreciation expense is $12,000 in the third year of the machine's useful life, what is the estimated salvage value of the machine?

5–14 Solving for Book Value

Checko, Inc., has equipment that has an original cost of $10,000 with a residual value estimated to be $750. If straight-line depreciation were used, the annual charge to depreciation expense would be $1,850; however, the company has elected to use the double-declining method.

REQUIRED:

If depreciation expense is $1,440 in year three, what was the book value of the machine at the end of year two?

5–15 Individual and Group Depreciation Methods

The certified public accountant is frequently called upon by management for advice regarding methods of computing depreciation. Although it arises less frequently, the question can be whether the depreciation method should be based on consideration of the assets as individual units, as a group, or as a composite.

REQUIRED:

Describe the depreciation methods that treat assets as (a) individual units, or as (b) combined (as in group or composite depreciation). State the advantages and disadvantages of using each of the two methods.

5–16   Compute Depreciation Expense Using the Composite Method

Wulff Company makes integrated circuits and has an assembly machine consisting of three major components. These components are listed below:

Component	Cost	Salvage Value	Life in Years
A	$220,000	$20,000	10
B	80,000	10,000	7
C	95,000	5,000	5

Wulff Company depreciates the machine using the composite straight-line method.

REQUIRED:

1. Compute the composite life and rate for the assembly machine.
2. Compute depreciation expense using the composite method.

5–17   Acquisition of Machinery and Revision of Estimated Useful Life

The Trout Corporation acquired a packaging machine on August 1, 19X1. The machine had an invoice price of $11,400 subject to a 2% cash discount for paying within the discount period. Trout paid within the discount period. Transportation was paid by Trout amounting to $900. Installation costs were $1,300 paid in cash. Additionally, the machine was slightly damaged during installation. Repairs amounted to $200. The machine has a useful life of five years, a salvage value of $1,400, and will be depreciated using the double-declining-balance method. Trout Corporation's fiscal year ends on December 31.

REQUIRED:

1. Prepare the entry to record the acquisition of the packaging machine.
2. Prepare the journal entry to record depreciation expense for 19X1.
3. On January 1, 19X5, Trout Corporation estimated that the machine's remaining useful life is four years and the salvage value is $1,000. Prepare the journal entry to record depreciation expense for 19X5.

5–18   Revision of Estimated Useful Life

On July 1, of 19X1, Bass, Inc., purchased equipment for $25,000. The company estimated that the trade-in value would be $3,000 at the end of the equipment's useful life. The equipment is estimated to have a useful life of 11 years based on similar machines the company has used in the past. Bass has a fiscal year-end of December 31. During 19X4 the Bass Company accountant reported that the original estimate of the equipment's life should have been 13 years and the trade-in value should be $4,250.

REQUIRED:

1. Record the acquisition of the equipment by Bass, Inc. on July 1, 19X1.

2. Record the annual adjusting entry to record depreciation expense on December 31, 19X1, 19X2, and 19X3, respectively, assuming Bass uses the straight-line method.

3. Record the annual adjusting entry to record depreciation expense on December 31, 19X4 assuming Bass revises the useful life of the equipment and the trade-in value.

5–19 Wal-Mart Stores, Inc., and Subsidiaries Annual Report

Refer to the Wal-Mart Stores, Inc., annual report and answer the following questions:

1. What was the cost of property, plant, and equipment for Wal-Mart at the end of 1991 and 1990?

2. What was the book value of property, plant, and equipment for Wal-Mart at the end of 1991 and 1990?

3. What accounts for the difference between your answers to 1 and 2 above for the years 1991 and 1990?

4. What depreciation method does Wal-Mart use for depreciating its long-lived assets for financial reporting purposes?

5. What was the depreciation and amortization expense for Wal-Mart for 1991 and 1990?

5–20 DECISION CASE
PURCHASE OF A COMPANY

On January 1, 19X5, a client asks you to assist him in determining which of two companies he should purchase. He tells you that Jenson Company and Janson Company both started operations on January 1, 19X1. On that date each company purchased the following assets: land costing $300,000; a building costing $150,000 with a salvage value of $30,000 and a useful life of 20 years; and machinery costing $70,000 with a salvage value of $10,000 and a useful life of 12 years. Jenson Company reported net income figures of $126,000, $120,000, $118,500, and $106,700 for the years 19X4, 19X3, 19X2, and 19X1, respectively. Janson Company reported net income figures of $122,425, $116,050, $115,500, and $98,000 for the years 19X4, 19X3, 19X2, and 19X1, respectively. The client also tells you that he feels that he should purchase Jenson Company because Jenson has a higher net income in total and in each of the four years. He says though, that he is confused, because in looking at the companies' respective balance sheets he noticed that Janson has more cash each year and a higher current ratio (current assets/current liabilities) and resulting higher working capital position. The only other difference that you can ascertain from the information given to you is that Jenson uses the straight-line method to depreciate its building and machinery while Janson uses the sum-of-the-years'-digits method. (Income taxes are ignored.)

REQUIRED:

What should you advise your client?

6

Long-Lived Productive Assets: Additions and Disposals, Natural Resources, Intangibles, and Other Assets

LEARNING OBJECTIVES

After studying Chapter 6, you should be able to:
1. Distinguish between revenue and capital expenditures.
2. Account for the disposal of plant assets through sale, retirement, destruction, or exchange.
3. Understand accounting for asset disposals when the composite or group depreciation method is used.
4. Account for the impairment in value of plant assets.
5. Understand the accounting for natural resources and the expensing of the costs of these assets through depletion.
6. Describe the accounting for intangible assets and the expensing of the costs of these assets through amortization.
7. Discuss the balance sheet classification, other-assets, consisting of assets not properly classified as current assets, investments, plant, property and equipment, natural resources, or intangibles.

Chapter 5 introduced accounting for long-lived productive assets. That chapter discussed the elements of acquisition cost and how these costs are charged against earnings through depreciation. Chapter 6 now discusses the accounting treatment for additions to and disposals of plant, property and equipment. Here we introduce accounting for other long-lived productive assets: natural resources, intangibles, and other assets.

EXPENDITURES FOR PLANT ASSETS SUBSEQUENT TO ACQUISITION

Companies often spend money on existing assets. It is then necessary to distinguish between revenue expenditures and capital expenditures. The accounting policy for revenue and capital expenditures of American Brands, Inc., is displayed in Exhibit 6–1. The company's products include tobacco, life insurance, distilled spirits, office products, hardware and home improvements products, and golf and leisure products.

Revenue Expenditures

Revenue expenditures are for ordinary maintenance (such as machine lubrication) and repairs (replacing a broken part). These expenditures are incurred to maintain the asset in its *current operating condition* and do not increase the economic benefit or service quality obtained from it. For example, lubricating a packaging machine does not extend its useful life nor help it to increase output.

Exhibit 6–1
Plant Asset Policy Disclosure
American Brands, Inc.

Significant Accounting Policies (excerpt)
Property, Plant and Equipment

Property, plant and equipment are carried at cost. Depreciation and amortization are provided, principally on a straight-line basis, over the estimated useful lives of the assets. Profits or losses resulting from dispositions are included in income. Betterments and renewals which improve and extend the life of an asset are capitalized; maintenance and repair costs are expensed.

These expenditures are assumed to benefit only the current period, so they are expensed as incurred. If the cost of lubricating and oiling an assembly machine is $200 cash, the entry to record this event is:

Maintenance and Repairs Expense	$200	
Cash		$200

Capital Expenditures

Capital expenditures are costs incurred to increase service quality, expected useful life, or productive capacity.

If the capital expenditure increases the asset's service quality or quantity of output, the debit is to the asset account.

If the capital expenditure extends the asset's useful life, the debit is to accumulated depreciation account.

Capital expenditures either (1) increase the service quality to be received from the asset, (2) extend the useful life, or (3) increase the quantity of output produced by the asset. To record a capital expenditure, we debit the asset account or the related accumulated depreciation account and credit cash or accounts payable. We refer to this process as **capitalization,** hence the term capital expenditure.

An example of a situation where the service quality is increased is installing air conditioning in company automobiles. The useful lives of the cars are not extended nor their quantity of output improved. The amount of the expenditure is debited to the asset account, and depreciation expense is increased over the remaining useful life of the asset. The same entry would be made if an expenditure increased the operating capabilities of an asset. For example, a wing might be added to a hospital, resulting in a larger physical unit and increased capacity. This type of expenditure is called a **betterment** or **improvement.**

Some expenditures extend an asset's expected useful life and/or increase the quantity of output expected beyond the original estimate. These capital expenditures are debited to the accumulated depreciation account, not to the asset account. The same entry would be made for an expenditure that increased the operating capabilities of an asset—for example, a company might replace a motor in a machine with one of a new design that increases the capacity of the machine. The rationale for this approach is that some of the previous years' depreciation has been recovered through the expenditure.

To illustrate, Ace Corporation has a three-year-old machine that cost $60,000. The machine originally had an 11-year life and a salvage value of $5,000. At the beginning of the fifth year the machine was reconditioned at a cost of $10,000. The reconditioning extended the machine's useful life another 10 years, to a total of 14 years. Computations for depreciation expense for the remainder of the life of the machine are shown in Exhibit 6−2 (assuming straight-line depreciation).

Many times in practice it is difficult to distinguish among expenditures that increase an asset's service quality, extend its useful life, or increase its quantity of output. An expenditure might both improve an

Exhibit 6-2
Revision of Depreciation Caused by Capital Expenditure

Original cost	$60,000
Depreciation to date ($5,000 × 4 years)	20,000
Undepreciated amount	40,000
Plus capital expenditure	10,000
Balance	50,000
Less salvage value	5,000
Revised depreciation base	$45,000
Divided by remaining useful life of 10 years =	$ 4,500 per year

asset's service quality and extend its useful life. It is important that in recording these events that we concentrate on the primary reason for making the expenditure.

The proper classification of revenue and capital expenditures is important because misclassification leads to inaccurate financial statements covering several accounting periods. The effect is the over/understatement of net income on the income statement and the balance sheet accounts relating to plant assets and accumulated depreciation, as well as total assets and stockholders' equity.[1]

Capital expenditures always increase the book value of the asset and therefore necessitate a revision in future depreciation expense.

DISPOSAL OF PLANT ASSETS

With the possible exception of land, all plant assets are eventually disposed of in some manner. They might be sold, retired, destroyed, or exchanged for other assets. At such time, depreciation expense is recognized up to the date of disposition, and the asset and its related accumulated depreciation amounts are eliminated from the accounts.

Because depreciation is an estimate, the book value of a plant asset rarely corresponds to its fair market value. Therefore, the disposition generally gives rise to a gain or loss. The gain or loss is the difference between the book value of the asset and any proceeds received. These gains and losses are aggregated and included in the operating section of the income statement. If the amounts are not a material component of

Compare book value and proceeds to determine gain or loss. If book value is more than proceeds, you have a loss; if book value is less than proceeds, you have a gain.
(BV > Proceeds = Loss)
(BV < Proceeds = Gain)

---

[1] Capital expenditures are often a significant outflow of resources for a firm. For example, in 1988, American Brands, Inc., reported capital expenditures of $235 million, about 41% of its net income of $580 million. In contrast, in 1990 Boise Cascade Corporation had capital expenditures of $824 million and reported net income of $75 million.

Exhibit 6–3
Disclosure of Disposal of Plant Assets
Champion International Corporation

Note 11 Other (Income) Expense—Net

Years Ended December 31 (in thousands of dollars)	1988	1987	1986
Interest income	$(25,589)	$ (19,847)	$(13,362)
Foreign currency (gains) losses—net	(15,123)	392	935
Minority interest in income of subsidiaries	9,114	11,353	6,801
Equity in net income of unconsolidated affiliates	(2,294)	(2,009)	(1,548)
Royalty, rental, and commission income	(12,033)	(11,578)	(12,563)
Net gain on disposal of fixed assets, timberlands, and investments	(3,279)	(12,930)	(9,731)
Gain on sale of investments in Stone Container Corporation and U.S. Plywood Corporation	–	(142,763)	
1988 St. Regis merger related—net	23,300	–	–
Miscellaneous—net	(4,052)	(20,574)	(16,005)
	$(29,956)	$(197,956)	$(45,473)

net income, they are not disclosed in the body of the financial statements or the footnotes. However, Exhibit 6–3 is an excerpt from the 1988 annual report of Champion International Corporation disclosing the disposal of fixed assets as a component of other income. This company markets paper and wood products.

Sales of Plant Assets

Ace Concrete purchased a cement mixer on January 1, 19X4, for $40,000. The useful life was seven years, and salvage value was $5,000. On August 1, 19X9 the mixer was sold for $13,000. The calculation of the gain and the journal entry to record the sale are as follows.

Cost of the mixer	$ 40,000
Depreciation expense 19X4 through 19X8 (5 years × $5,000)	(25,000)
Partial year's depreciation 19X9 ($7/12$ × $5,000)	(2,917)
Book value of mixer at August 1, 19X9	12,083
Gain on sale of mixer	$ 13,000

Accumulated Depreciation—Mixer ($25,000 + $2,917)	$27,917	
Cash	13,000	
Mixer		$40,000
Gain on Sale of Mixer		917

If instead the mixer had been sold for $11,000, the entry would have been this way.

Accumulated Depreciation—Mixer	$27,917	
Cash	11,000	
Loss on Sale of Mixer	1,083	
Mixer		$40,000

Retirement of Plant Assets

At some point it may be necessary to retire or scrap a plant asset. This could be caused by technological changes or other events that render the asset obsolete. The asset and its related accumulated depreciation accounts are removed from the records, and any gain or loss is recognized.

For example, the entry to record the retirement of a crane costing $27,000 with accumulated depreciation of $20,000 is:

Accumulated Depreciation—Crane	$20,000	
Loss on Retirement of Crane	7,000	
Crane		$27,000

If the asset had been scrapped and $3,000 received as salvage, the loss would have been reduced to $4,000.

Destroyed plant assets are handled in a similar manner. That is, the asset and related accumulated depreciation are removed from the accounts. The difference between the book value and any insurance proceeds is treated as a net gain or loss.

Exchanges of Plant Assets

Plant assets are often exchanged for other plant assets. For example, a construction company might exchange an old dump truck and cash for a new dump truck. Or, the same company might exchange cash and the old dump truck for an automobile. In these cases (also referred to as *trade-ins*), we use the value of the old asset to determine the cost of the new asset. Additionally, we must determine whether the assets involved are similar or dissimilar.

Similar assets are alike or perform the same function (dump truck traded for a dump truck or a computer for a computer). **Dissimilar**

assets are not the same type or are not used for the same purpose (dump truck exchanged for an automobile or a building for a road grader).

Similar Assets

Similar assets: if a gain, record the new asset at the BV of the old asset plus cash paid; if a loss, record the new asset at the FMV of the old asset plus cash paid.

If the exchange is of similar assets, and the exchange involves a gain, the new asset is recorded at the book value of the old asset plus any additional consideration given (usually cash). For example, assume our old dump truck has an original cost of $40,000 and accumulated depreciation of $35,000. If the truck is traded for a new truck with a list price of $70,000 by exchanging the old truck and $60,000 cash, the following entry would be recorded:

Dump Truck (new) ($5,000 book value + $60,000 cash)	$65,000	
Accumulated Depreciation—Dump Truck (old)	35,000	
Dump Truck (old)		$40,000
Cash		60,000

The new truck is recorded at the book value of the old truck plus the cash paid. The cost of the old truck and its related accumulated depreciation is removed from the accounts, and the Cash account is credited. The list price is not used to record the exchange. This is because the list price is usually inflated and concessions are made to arrive at a cash equivalent price. For example, most people do not pay list price for a new car. Trade-in allowances make actual selling prices below list prices.

Suppose also that the fair market value (FMV) of the old dump truck is $6,500. Even though a $1,500 gain exists ($6,500 fair market value versus a book value of $5,000), it is not recognized. The reason for nonrecognition is that accountants do not view these transactions as a completion of the earnings process. That is, one productive asset has replaced another productive asset. Income should not be recognized from substituting one productive asset for a similar one.

Recall that the fair market value of the old dump truck was $1,500 greater than its book value. If we now assume that the fair market value of the old dump truck is $2,000, the entry to record the exchange for the new dump truck is as follows.

Dump Truck (new) ($2,000 FMV + $60,000 cash)	$62,000	
Accumulated Depreciation—Dump Truck (old)	35,000	
Loss on Exchange of Dump Trucks	3,000	
Dump Truck (old)		$40,000
Cash		60,000

Because of the principle of **conservatism,** we recognize the loss. The cost assigned to the new truck is the fair market value of the old truck plus the cash paid or the value of the asset acquired, whichever is easier to determine. The cost of the old truck and its accumulated depreciation is removed from the accounts, and cash is credited. Failure to record the loss or overstatement of the new dump truck would result in a journal entry where the debits do not equal the credits or overstatement of the new dump truck.

Dissimilar Assets

In the case of exchanges of dissimilar assets, the earnings process is considered to be complete. Gains and losses on exchanges of dissimilar assets are recognized and recorded.

Dissimilar assets: new asset is recorded at the FMV of the old asset plus cash paid.

Assume that the same dump truck (original cost of $40,000, accumulated depreciation of $35,000, and fair market value of $6,500) and $10,000 were exchanged for a parcel of land. The entry to record the exchange is:

Land ($6,500 FMV + $10,000 cash paid)	$16,500	
Accumulated Depreciation—Dump Truck (old)	35,000	
Dump Truck (old)		$40,000
Cash		10,000
Gain on Exchange of Dump Truck for Land		1,500

Note that we recorded the new asset, land, at its fair market value of $6,500, plus the cash paid of $10,000, or $16,500.

Asset Disposals When Using Group or Composite Depreciation

Recall from Chapter 5 that group or composite depreciation is used for a whole collection of assets. *Group depreciation* is used where the assets are similar in nature (for example, a fleet of automobiles) and the assets are homogeneous and have approximately the same useful lives. *Composite depreciation* is used when the collection of assets is dissimilar and have different useful lives but have some similar characteristics. For example, this method could be used for equipment components on a manufacturing production line.

In group or composite depreciation, gains and losses are not recognized on disposals.

The calculation of depreciation expense is the same for both methods. An average rate is determined and applied each period. Depreciation Expense is debited, and Accumulated Depreciation is credited for the collection of assets. Upon disposal of any asset, gain or loss is not recognized since the Accumulated Depreciation account does not

---

Exhibit 6–4
Notes to the Financial Statements
Georgia-Pacific Corporation

Note 1. Summary of Significant Accounting Policies
Property, Plant and Equipment (excerpt)

Depreciation expense is computed using the straight-line method with composite rates based upon estimated service lives. The ranges of composite rates for the principal classes are: land improvements—5% to 7%; buildings—3% to 5%; and machinery and equipment—5% to 20%.

Under the composite method of depreciation, no gain or loss is recognized on normal property dispositions because the property cost is credited to the property accounts and charged to the accumulated depreciation accounts and any proceeds are credited to the accumulated depreciation accounts. However, when there are abnormal dispositions of property, the cost and related depreciation amounts are removed from the accounts and any gain or loss is reflected in income.

---

relate to any one asset but to all assets in the group. The difference between the proceeds from the disposal of an asset and its cost is simply debited or credited to Accumulated Depreciation. When the components of the group change materially, the depreciation rate should be revised.

As an example, assume that a company disposes of a van with an original cost of $4,000 for $650 cash. Assuming group depreciation is used, the following entry would be made.

Accumulated Depreciation—Vans	$3,350	
Cash	650	
Vans		$4,000

As we stated in Chapter 5, the major advantage of the composite and group methods is the time and cost saved by not maintaining separate asset and accumulated depreciation accounts for individual assets. A disadvantage is that gains and losses are not recognized as individual assets within the group are disposed of, and as a result, incorrect estimates of useful lives are not revealed.

Exhibit 6–4 is an excerpt from the "Summary of Significant Accounting Policies" section of the 1988 annual report of Georgia-Pacific Corporation.

Impairment in Value of Plant Assets

If an asset becomes permanently impaired, the company recognizes a loss and reduces the book value of the asset. The impairment might be total or partial. In some cases the company continues to use the impaired asset, and in others the asset is written down to its salvage value or zero. A partial permanent impairment in the value of a plant asset is recorded by recognizing a loss and reducing the book value of the asset through a credit to accumulated depreciation. For example, assume a company purchased computer-operated equipment for $2,000,000. The estimated life of the equipment was 10 years with no salvage value. Therefore, depreciation expense is $200,000 per year ($2,000,000/10). Two years later, when the book value of the equipment was $1,600,000 [$2,000,000 − ($200,000 × 2)], the company learned that a new, faster machine was now on the market. The company's management thus believed the equipment's value had been reduced to only $400,000. The entry to record the partial impairment in value is:

Loss Due to Impairment in Value of Equipment	$1,200,000	
Accumulated Depreciation—Equipment		$1,200,000
($1,600,000 − $400,000)		

The loss is reported in the income statement.

Asset impairment can be significant. In 1987 the Pillsbury Company reported a $113 million loss in its annual financial statements on the sale or shutdown of several of its restaurant operations, including Godfather's Pizza chain. In examining Pillsbury's financial statements, it was impossible (as it is in almost any other case) to determine how Pillsbury came up with the $113 million figure.

When does an asset become impaired? Current accounting rules leave that decision to management, and some question whether this is wise. See Insight 6−1 for a discussion of the controversy.

NATURAL RESOURCES

Many companies own assets such as stands of timber, oil fields, and coal, mineral, or other ore deposits. These assets are called **natural resources** or **wasting assets.** As of December 31, 1990, 8.2% of Boise Cascade Corporation's total assets consisted of timber, timberlands, and timber deposits. As with other long-lived productive assets, the basis for recording them is the cost of acquiring the property and placing it in service—including costs of exploration and development. That is, there

INSIGHT 6–1
Determining Asset Impairment

Accounting for impaired assets is controversial. This is because management must resolve two issues: (1) when should the impairment be recognized and (2) how should the impairment be measured? Deciding whether the impairment is permanent is difficult. Current accounting principles state that an asset is impaired when there is no hope of recovering its book value. Of course, hope, or lack of it, is in the eye of the beholder. Comments Wayne Kolins, partner at accounting firm Seidman & Seidman/BDO: "In these situations, it's often a case of people saying, 'You know it when you see it.'"

To complicate matters, once a company has judged an asset to be impaired, a balance sheet value has to be assigned to the asset. Among the acceptable methods are (1) net realizable value (the sales price of the asset), (2) the total projected cash flows over the life of the asset, and (3) present value of the cash flows (discounting the cash flows based on a given rate of return).

Many feel that the subjective criteria gives management too much latitude in reporting asset impairments. A study by the National Association of Accountants concluded that behind the numbers lurks, "a climate of vague accounting standards" that give companies too much leeway in choosing when and how to write down assets.

SOURCE: Penelope Wang, "You Know It When You See It," *Forbes*, 25 July 1988, 84.

are three categories of costs related to natural resources: (1) acquisition cost, (2) exploration costs, and (3) development costs. There is some controversy surrounding the treatment of exploration costs, especially for international oil companies. See Insight 6–2 for a discussion of the treatment of these costs. These assets are consumed through extraction or production. The expensing of the costs of natural resources is called **depletion** and is similar to depreciation. For financial accounting purposes, depletion means **cost depletion** and should not be confused with **percentage of revenue depletion** as found in the tax code.

Computing Depletion

Depletion is calculated in the same manner as units-of-production depreciation.

Depletion is computed in the same manner as units-of-activity depreciation and requires estimates of the salvage or residual value of the property and of the total resource available (such as tons of ore or barrels of oil). For example, assume that a coal deposit is purchased for

INSIGHT 6–2
Exploration Costs in the Oil Industry

After acquiring a piece of property, a firm must spend a substantial amount of money on exploration costs to find the oil. The accounting treatment for these costs varies. A few firms expense all exploration costs; however, most use either the successful-efforts approach or the full-cost approach. Under the *successful-efforts approach,* only those costs that are directly related to the successful effort (finding oil) are capitalized. Proponents of this approach contend that in the short run, unsuccessful companies who capitalize all exploration costs will look as profitable as a successful company that uses the successful efforts approach. The *full-cost approach* capitalizes all costs whether related to successful or unsuccessful efforts (finding oil). Proponents of this approach argue that the cost associated with unsuccessful efforts (dry holes) are necessary and a part of successful efforts (finding oil). They feel that the cost of drilling dry holes is part of eventually finding where the oil is located. Current accounting principles allow the use of either method, and the difference in using one method versus another can be significant. Full-costing can increase profits, because the costs accumulate on the balance sheet and are depleted, whereas under the successful-efforts approach, the costs not associated with finding oil are expensed on the income statement.

a total cost of $5,000,000. Exploration and development costs total $1,500,000, so the total cost is $6,500,000. We estimate that after the deposit is exhausted and the land reclaimed, we can sell the property as a recreation site for $250,000. The company's geologist estimates that the deposit contains 3,125,000 tons of coal resulting in depletion per ton of $2.00 [($6,500,000 − $250,000)/3,125,000]. Assume that 250,000 tons are extracted in 1990, 200,000 tons are sold for $800,000, and other mining costs are $100,000. These other costs are part of the cost of the inventory of coal and are expensed when the coal is sold. Journal entries to record these events are as follows.

Per Unit Depletion =

$$\frac{(Cost - Salvage\ Value)}{Estimated\ Resource\ Available}$$

To record the purchase of the land:

Coal Deposits	$5,000,000	
Cash		$5,000,000

To record the exploration and development costs:

Coal Deposits	$1,500,000	
Cash		$1,500,000

To recognize that 250,000 tons of coal were extracted during the year plus mining costs of $100,000:

Inventory of Coal (250,000 × $2.00)	$500,000	
Accumulated Depletion—Coal Deposits		$500,000
Inventory of Coal	100,000	
Cash		100,000

The total cost per ton is $2.40 [($500,000 + $100,000)/250,000]. The entry to record the sale of 200,000 tons of coal for $800,000 and the cost of the units sold is as follows.

Cash	$800,000	
Sales		$800,000
Cost of Coal Sold ($2.40 × 200,000)	480,000	
Inventory of Coal		480,000

Similar to accumulated depreciation, sometimes a contra asset account called Accumulated Depletion is credited when recording depletion.

There is no depletion expense account because the charge for depletion goes to Inventory of Coal and is included in the debit to Cost of Coal Sold (an expense) when the coal is sold. The depletion that is expensed for the period is a function of the number of units sold, not produced. The Cost of Coal Sold account appears in the income statement.

The Inventory of Coal account appears in the current asset section of the balance sheet. The presentation of the natural resource appears in the noncurrent asset section of the balance sheet this way.

Coal Deposits	$6,500,000
Less Accumulated Depletion	500,000
Net Coal Deposits	$6,000,000

It is permissible to credit the natural resource (in our example, Coal Deposits), account directly instead of Accumulated Depletion. As with plant assets, retention of the historical cost of the asset may assist financial statement readers in determining the percentage of the cost of the resource that has been removed. However, this form of presentation does not assist the reader in ascertaining the value of the natural resource, which may be greatly in excess of its recorded value.

If assets such as buildings, equipment, or improvements, are constructed or purchased in connection with the removal of natural resources, they should be depreciated over the shorter of (1) physical life of the asset, or (2) the life of the natural resource. In such cases, it is reasonable to use the units-of-activity method to compute periodic depreciation.

Exhibit 6–5
Natural Resource Policy Disclosure

Phillips Petroleum Company—Accounting Policies (excerpt)

Depletion and Amortization—Leasehold costs of producing properties are depleted using the unit-of-production method based on estimated proved oil and gas reserves. Amortization of intangible development costs is based on the unit-of-production method using the estimated proved developed oil and gas reserves.

International Paper Company—Summary of Significant Accounting Policies (excerpt)
Timberlands

Timberlands are stated at cost, less accumulated depletion representing the cost of timber harvested. Timberlands include owned timberlands as well as timber harvesting rights with terms of one or more years and having a fixed total price. Costs are allocated to either standing timber or the underlying. Those costs attributable to standing timber are charged against income as the timber is cut. The depletion rate charged is determined annually, based on the relationship of remaining timber costs to the estimated volume of recoverable timber. The costs of roads and land improvements are capitalized and amortized over their economic lives.

Periodically, the estimates of recoverable resources and residual value should be reevaluated and adjusted if necessary. To revise the depletion rate, the remaining undepleted balance, less any salvage value, is divided by the estimate of the remaining recoverable units.

Exhibit 6–5 presents the disclosure from two 1988 annual reports relating to natural resources.

INTANGIBLES

Intangible assets are long-lived productive resources that generally (but not always) have no physical existence. They derive their value from the rights and privileges granted to the firm owning them. Examples include patents, copyrights, trademarks and tradenames, franchises, organization costs, leases, leaseholds, leasehold improvements, and goodwill.

Intangible assets are recorded at historical cost. The allocation of the cost of the intangible asset to the periods of benefit is called **am-**

The process of amortizing intangibles is the same allocation process as depreciating plant assets and depleting natural resources.

ortization. With the exception of certain leases, leaseholds, and lease-hold improvements, generally accepted accounting principles (GAAP) require straight-line amortization unless a company can demonstrate that another method is more appropriate in the circumstances. Amortization is recorded in the accounts by debiting the account Amortization Expense and crediting the specific intangible asset account. An Accumulated Amortization account is generally not used.

An Accumulated Amortization account is not used in recording amortization expense, unlike depreciation and depletion.

Some accountants believe that many intangibles have an unlimited life and consequently should not be amortized. However, current GAAP requires that these assets be amortized over the shorter of their (1) legal lives, (2) their economic (useful) lives, or (3) 40 years.

Patents

A **patent** is an exclusive right to use, produce, and sell a particular product or process for 17 years. The cost of a patent that is purchased is easily valued. Companies also put millions of dollars into the development of patents;[2] however, the costs of internally developed patents are much more difficult to determine because it is difficult to allocate the costs associated with on-going research to individual patents. Before 1975, some companies charged research and development costs to expense as they were incurred, while others treated these costs as assets and amortized them over future periods. To eliminate this inconsistent treatment the Financial Accounting Standards Board (FASB) decided that all research and development costs should be expensed as incurred. This means that the costs associated with internally developed patents are expensed rather than capitalized. Only legal fees paid to defend the patent are properly capitalized as assets. The FASB position eliminates the subjectivity in evaluating whether a research and development expenditure is an asset or an expense, even though this treatment can result in removing from the balance sheet what might be a company's most valuable asset. This treatment can be especially troublesome in an industry such as bio-technology, where significant research and development expenditures are necessary for product development.

Even though the legal life of a patent is 17 years, its economic life might be shorter. This is apparent in areas of rapidly changing technology such as the computer industry.

---

[2] Expenditures for research and development are significant for most major companies. For example, EG&G, Inc., is a technologically diversified *Fortune* 500 company providing advanced scientific and technical products and services worldwide. During 1988, 1987, and 1986, it had research expenditures of approximately $20.2 million, $18.6 million and $17.2 million, respectively. Net income for 1988, 1987, and 1986 was $68.6 million, $57.5 million and $47.9 million, respectively.

Copyrights

A **copyright** protects the author of a literary or artistic work by giving only the owner, or heirs, the right to reproduce and sell that work. A copyright is not renewable and is granted for the life of the author plus 50 years. Books currently under copyright include *Misery* by Stephen King (1987) and *Dances With Wolves* by Michael Blake (1988). On the other hand, *Tom Sawyer* (1876) and *Huckleberry Finn* (1884) by Samuel L. Clemens (alias Mark Twain) are off copyright since Clemens died in 1910.

Trademarks and Tradenames

Trademarks and **tradenames** entitle the owner to exclusive use of certain names, logos, labels, and symbols, which companies use to create product identification in the minds of consumers in order to improve the marketability of products. Examples of tradenames include Coca-Cola, General Motors Corporation, Kellogg's Corn Flakes, Wheaties, Lotus 1-2-3, and the Chicago Bulls. Trademarks include the golden arches of McDonald's Corporation, Philip Morris Corporation's Marlboro cowboy, the unique pocket stitching and patch of Levi's jeans, and the Roll's Royce emblem. The right to use these names, logos, labels and symbols is granted by the U.S. government, and the legal life is usually unlimited. However, sometimes they become so widely used that they lose their legal protection, because the government deems them to be already in public use. Kleenex is an example of a tradename that has become a generic term.

Franchises

Franchises are rights granted to an individual or company to sell a product or service. Examples include Wendy's and Burger King restaurants and Nutri-System weight control centers. See Insight 6–3 for a discussion of Wendy's International, Inc.

Organization Costs

Organization costs are the initial costs of creating a business. They include attorneys' and accountants' fees, monies paid to state agencies for incorporation fees, and other start-up costs. In most instances, companies choose an amortization period ranging from five to ten years.

INSIGHT 6–3
Old-Fashioned Hamburgers

R. David Thomas opened his first Wendy's in Columbus, Ohio, in 1969. He named the restaurant after his eight-year-old daughter. At that time, McDonald's already had 1,200 restaurants but Thomas felt there was a place for Wendy's. He decided to create a restaurant that was a "folksy place that emphasized old-fashioned values," cooked hamburgers to order, had carpets, Tiffany-style lamps, and bentwood chairs. When Wendy's celebrated its twentieth anniversary in 1989, it had 3,700 restaurants as compared to the 10,000 of McDonald's. However, the average McDonald's had sales of $1.6 million annually, while Wendy's sales averaged $759,000, lagging behind Burger King, Hardee's, and Jack in the Box. Wendy's enjoyed a brief moment of glory in the mid-1980s with the advertising campaign that asked "Where's the beef?" and in 1989, commercials appeared with founder Thomas stating, "Our hamburgers are the best in the business, or I wouldn't have named the place after my daughter." Wendy herself was an off-screen voice in some of these commercials. In the 1990s, Wendy's menu has expanded from the hamburger to include all-you-can-eat salads, Mexican food, and pasta. The company has restaurants in all 50 states, with the biggest concentration in Ohio (289 stores).

SOURCE: "Wendy's," Milton Moskowitz, Robert Levering, and Michael Katz, *Everybody's Business* (New York: Doubleday, 1990), 72–73.

Leases

The owner of the property is the lessor.

The person or company acquiring the property is the lessee.

A **lease** is a contract to rent property. Examples include machinery, buildings, land, and vehicles. The owner of the property is the **lessor,** and the person or company acquiring the property is the **lessee.** The property rights stated in the contract and transferred to the lessee are called a **leasehold.** In general, the leasehold agreement provides for the right of the lessee to use the property of the lessor for a certain period of time.

Accounting for leases depends on whether the lease is an operating or capital lease. The rules for classifying leases as operating and capital are complex and beyond the scope of this book. Generally speaking, though, an **operating lease** is one that either party can terminate on notice of a year or so. In these cases the rent appears as an expense on the books of the lessee and as revenue on the books of the lessor. **Capital leases** are for longer periods, typically for nearly the entire useful life of the asset. The party that agrees to lease an asset for virtually all of its useful life is, in essence, buying the asset. Capital leases are in substance purchases whereby the lessee is essentially acquiring the asset on an installment basis. The lessee is taking on virtually all of the risks and rewards of owning the asset. Operating leases, in contrast, do not transfer the risks and rewards of ownership from the lessor to the lessee.

Capital leases transfer the risks and rewards of ownership to the lessee while operating leases do not.

While a discussion of the accounting procedures relating to capital leases is beyond the scope of this text, some observations are in order. If a lease is classified as a capital lease, the leased asset is recorded as an asset and the lease obligation as a liability at the present value of the lease payments. Present value is the value today of the future payments discounted by an appropriate interest rate. (The present value concept is discussed in Chapter 7.) The leased asset is depreciated over its useful life just as if it were owned, and a portion of each lease payment is recorded as interest expense, just as if the payments were payments on a mortgage.

Leasing is important in the analysis of financial statements because not only is a company receiving benefits from the leased asset, but it has also incurred an obligation. Exhibit 6–6 is an example of disclosure relating to leasing activities from the 1988 annual report of Figgie International Inc.

Leasehold Improvements

Leasehold improvements are expenditures made by a lessee to improve leased property. An example is building interior walls in a retail store or office building to suit the premises for the lessee's use. These improvements become the property of the lessor at the termination of the lease. Their expected period of benefit is longer than one year, and they are therefore capitalized by debiting the account Leasehold Improvements. The improvements are amortized over the shorter of (1) the useful life of the improvement or (2) the lease term. Under current practice, leasehold improvements are normally presented in the tangible plant asset section of the balance sheet, although some accountants classify them as intangible assets.

Goodwill

Goodwill is probably the least understood intangible asset. Conceptually, the goodwill of a company is a function of many factors, including the reputation of its products or services, superior management or personnel, location, or monopoly status. Goodwill generally leads to an above average return on funds invested in the company.

Goodwill generally leads to an above average return on funds invested in the company.

Because measuring the dollar effects of the aforementioned factors is difficult, or impossible, and because goodwill cannot be bought or

Exhibit 6–6
Figgie International, Inc.
Leasing Activities

Figgie International Inc. and Subsidiaries
Consolidated Balance Sheets With Selected Consolidating Data
December 31, 1988 and 1987
(in thousands of dollars)

Selected Consolidating Data

	Manufacturing and Service Companies 1988	Insurance and Finance Companies 1988	Consolidated 1988	Consolidated 1987
Property under capital leases, less accumulated amortization of $6,073 in 1988 and $7,213 in 1987	$18,966	–	$18,966	$4,716

Notes to Consolidated Financial Statements (excerpt)
(5) Property Under Capital Leases:

The Company operates various facilities and equipment under lease arrangements which are classified as capital leases. The following is a summary of assets under capital leases:

(in thousands of dollars)	December 31	
Classes of Property	1988	1987
Buildings	$ 2,637	$ 2,668
Machinery and equipment	22,402	9,261
	25,039	11,929
Less accumulated amortization	6,073	7,213
	$18,966	$ 4,716

Continued

sold separately, accountants record goodwill in the accounts only when it is purchased. This occurs when one firm purchases another for a price that exceeds the fair market value of the identifiable net assets of the firm acquired.

To illustrate, assume that Teddy Manufacturing Company purchased Bear, Inc., for $1,700,000. Teddy will also assume a $200,000 note

Exhibit 6–6
Continued

The following is a schedule by year of future minimum lease payments under capital lease payments together with the present value of the net minimum lease payments as of December 31, 1988:

(in thousands of dollars)

Year Ending December 31

1989	$ 4,910
1990	4,347
1991	4,237
1992	4,043
1993	3,986
Total minimum lease payments	$21,523
Less amount representing interest	4,452
Present value of net minimum lease payments	$17,071

(8) Commitments:

The Company leases various facilities and equipment under operating lease arrangements. Rental commitments under noncancellable operating leases as of December 31, 1988 were as follows:

(in thousands of dollars)

Year Ending December 31

1989	$10,977
1990	7,486
1991	5,702
1992	4,622
1993	3,261
Later years	13,138
Total minimum payments required	$45,186

Total operating lease expense was approximately $14,476,000 in 1988, $15,847,000 in 1987 and $12,710,000 in 1986.

payable. Additionally, the fair market values (not book values) of the assets are: accounts receivable $40,000; inventory $50,000; machinery $400,000; land $700,000; building $500,000; patents $60,000. The $150,000 excess of the amount paid ($1,700,000) over the identifiable net assets ($1,550,000) is goodwill. Exhibit 6–7 shows the calculation.

> **Exhibit 6–7**
> **Computation of Goodwill**
>
> | | | |
> |---|---:|---:|
> | Amount paid | | $1,700,000 |
> | Less fair market value of identifiable net assets: | | |
> | Accounts receivable | $ 40,000 | |
> | Inventory | 50,000 | |
> | Machinery | 400,000 | |
> | Land | 700,000 | |
> | Building | 500,000 | |
> | Patents | 60,000 | |
> | Note payable | (200,000) | 1,550,000 |
> | Goodwill | | $ 150,000 |

The journal entry to record the purchase of Bear, Inc., by Teddy Manufacturing Company is:

Accounts Receivable	$ 40,000	
Inventory	50,000	
Machinery	400,000	
Land	700,000	
Building	500,000	
Patents	60,000	
Goodwill	150,000	
Note Payable		$ 200,000
Cash		1,700,000

Like other intangible assets, goodwill is amortized to expense over a period not to exceed 40 years. Assuming a 40-year amortization period, Teddy Manufacturing would make the following periodic entry:

Amortization Expense ($150,000/40 years)	$3,750	
Goodwill		$3,750

Successful companies continually make expenditures to develop and preserve goodwill, but because of the difficulty of measuring the effects of these expenditures, they are expensed. Thus, firms that internally generate goodwill will not see it reflected in their financial records. The account Goodwill arises only from a purchase transaction.

INSIGHT 6-4
Goodwill is Making People Upset

Some people are angry over the accounting treatment of goodwill. They feel that "would-be U.S. purchasers of U.S. firms are being burdened by accounting rules that favor foreign bidders." The rules require U.S. companies to write off or amortize goodwill against earnings but not to deduct the amortization for tax purposes. In most European countries goodwill remains on the balance sheet and is not amortized; hence, no affect on earnings. U.S. companies bidding for other U.S. companies would be at a disadvantage because a successful bid would result in "lower incremental reported earnings," which is "no slight disadvantage, since U.S. companies are valued to a significant degree on a multiple of reported earnings."

Canada, Japan, and West Germany require goodwill to be amortized but allow a tax deduction giving "companies from these countries a cash-flow advantage over a U.S. purchaser." The enhanced after-tax cash flows resulting from goodwill tax deductions allow these foreign companies to bid higher than U.S. companies and has made it very difficult for U.S. companies to compete in the bidding for leading U.S. companies.

To solve the problem, some accountants suggest that international rules be changed "so that similar standards are used world-wide." Other possible remedies include suspending the current U.S. rule requiring amortization of goodwill, placing tariffs on U.S. operations of foreign companies, and making changes in the U.S. tax law regarding the deductibility of goodwill amortization.

SOURCE: Sanford Pensler, "Accounting Rules Favor Foreign Bidders," *The Wall Street Journal*, 24 March 1988, A18. Reprinted with permission of The Wall Street Journal. © 1988 Dow Jones & Company, Inc. All Rights Reserved.

(Chapter 17 presents a more in-depth discussion of goodwill relating to business acquisitions.) Because of this inconsistency and the problems associated with the measurement of goodwill, some companies call the Goodwill account Excess of Cost Over Net Assets of Acquired Businesses. In fact, there is even some disagreement over the process of amortizing goodwill as discussed in Insight 6-4.

Exhibits 6-8 and 6-9 detail the disclosure for intangible assets from the 1988 annual reports of the Brunswick Corporation and the Colgate-Palmolive Company.

Exhibit 6–8
Intangible Asset Disclosure
Brunswick Corporation

Balance Sheet (excerpt)

	1988	1987
Other assets (in millions)		
Dealer networks	$ 330.7	$ 362.5
Trademarks and other	102.2	112.1
Excess of cost over net assets of businesses acquired	184.1	177.1
Investments	57.7	47.4
Other assets	674.7	699.1
Total assets	$2,092.0	$1,896.3

Significant Accounting Policies

Intangibles. The costs of dealer networks, trademarks and other intangible assets are amortized over their expected useful lives using the straight-line method. Accumulated amortization was $125.3 million and $68.6 million at December 31, 1988 and 1987, respectively. The excess of cost over net assets of businesses acquired is being amortized using the straight-line method, principally over 40 years. Accumulated amortization was $17.3 million and $24.3 million at December 31, 1988 and 1987, respectively.

Exhibit 6–9
Intangible Asset Disclosure
Colgate-Palmolive Company

Summary of Significant Accounting Policies
Goodwill and Other Intangibles

Goodwill represents the excess of purchase price over the fair value of identifiable net assets of businesses acquired. Goodwill and other intangibles are amortized on a straight-line basis over periods not exceeding 40 years. Goodwill, net of accumulated amortization totaled $276,985 and $149,008 at December 31, 1988 and 1987, respectively. During 1988, goodwill of $28,864, net of accumulated amortization, was written off in connection with the sale of The Kendall Company. Amortization expense totaled $3,980, $1,633 and $1,483 in 1988, 1987 and 1986, respectively.

Exhibit 6–10
Disclosure of Other Assets
ERC International Inc.

5. Supplemental Balance Sheet Information

Other assets consist of:	December 31	
	1988	1987
Acquired intangible assets, primarily contract rights, less accumulated amortization of $427 and $203	$1,787	$2,011
Deposits	345	795
Investments	1,163	739
Notes receivable	1,730	981
Software	853	230
Other	626	508
	$6,504	$5,264

OTHER ASSETS

The items classified in this section vary widely in practice. This category includes all other assets not classified as current assets, long-term investments, property, plant and equipment, natural resources, or intangibles. Some commonly included items are **deferred charges** (for example, debt issuance and software costs), intangibles, advances to subsidiaries, and long-lived assets held for resale. Classifying land that is held for resale as property, plant, and equipment implies that the land is currently in use. Ideally, the other asset section should be restricted to assets that are different from those included in the aforementioned categories.

Exhibit 6–10 is an excerpt from the notes to the 1988 financial statements of ERC International Inc. detailing the company's other asset balance sheet category.

DISCLOSURE OF LONG-LIVED PRODUCTIVE ASSETS

Plant assets, natural resources, intangible assets, and other assets are normally presented in the balance sheet below the current asset section. Exhibit 6–11 is an excerpt of the consolidated balance sheet from the 1988 annual report of International Paper Company.

Exhibit 6–11
International Paper Company
Consolidated Balance Sheet

in millions at December 31	1988	1987
Current Assets		
Cash and temporary investments, at cost, which approximates market	$ 122	$ 233
Accounts and notes receivable, less allowances of $41 million in 1988 and $39 million in 1987	1,153	998
Inventories	971	852
Other current assets	97	80
Total Current Assets	$2,343	$2,163
Plants, Properties and Equipment, Net	5,456	5,125
Timberlands	772	780
Investments	88	109
Goodwill	304	170
Deferred Charges and Other Assets	499	363
Total Assets	$9,462	$8,710

RATIO ANALYSIS

Two common activity ratios are the fixed asset turnover ratio and the total asset turnover ratio. Like other turnover ratios, these ratios involve a measure of the relationship between fixed assets and total assets and a surrogate for management's ability to employ the investment in those assets effectively. In this case the surrogate is sales. Both of the ratios indicate how efficiently a company utilizes its assets. High turnover indicates that a company is using its assets efficiently to generate sales, while low turnover either might mean that asset utilization is inefficient or that disposal of some of the assets is warranted.

The fixed asset turnover ratio is calculated as:

$$\frac{\text{Sales}}{\text{Average Fixed Assets}}$$

For Boise Cascade Corporation the fixed asset turnover ratios for 1990 and 1989 are calculated as:

1990		1989	
$\dfrac{\$4,185,920}{(\$3,546,863 + \$3,016,870)/2}$	$= 1.28{:}1$	$\dfrac{\$4,338,030}{(\$3,016,870 + \$2,565,286)/2}$	$= 1.55{:}1$

You can see that the ratio has decreased from 1989 to 1990; however, it is not possible to tell whether this is good or bad without some basis of comparison. The comparison must be made to other similarly sized companies engaged in the same line of business. The decrease is cause for concern; however, the trend of recent years for Boise Cascade Corporation should be evaluated.

Total asset turnover is calculated as:

$$\frac{\text{Sales}}{\text{Average Total Assets}}$$

Total asset turnover ratios for 1990 and 1989 for Boise Cascade Corporation follow.

$$\frac{\$4,185,920}{(\$4,784,770 + \$4,142,625)/2} = .94{:}1 \qquad \frac{\$4,338,030}{(\$4,142,625 + \$3,610,243)/2} = 1.12{:}1$$

Again the ratio has decreased from 1989 to 1990 and is a cause for concern; however, comparisons must be made with other firms in the industry, over time, in order to interpret the decrease.

SUMMARY

Companies spend money to maintain or improve plant assets, and these expenditures are categorized as either revenue or capital expenditures. Revenue expenditures are routine and recurring and benefit only the current period. Capital expenditures increase service quality, quantity of units produced, and/or extend the life of the asset. Revenue expenditures are expensed when incurred, whereas capital expenditures are capitalized and depreciated over the asset's remaining useful life.

Plant asset disposals are accounted for by recording any proceeds from the sale and removing the asset and its accumulated depreciation from the accounts. Any resulting gain or loss is recognized, unless group or composite depreciation is used.

Natural resources, or wasting assets, are recorded at acquisition cost and expensed to subsequent periods through depletion. Depletion is computed in the same manner as the units-of-activity method of depreciation.

Intangible assets are recorded at historical costs and amortized to expense over the expected period of benefit, not to exceed 40 years. The straight-line method is used to amortize intangibles. Intangible assets may include the account Goodwill, which is only found in the financial statements of a company that has purchased the identifiable net assets of another company.

Conceptually, the other asset classification should include only those assets not classified as a current asset, investment, plant, property and equipment, natural resource, or intangible. In practice, however, many items, such as intangibles, are incorrectly classified in this section. These assets are properly amortized to expense over the period of expected future benefit.

DEMONSTRATION PROBLEMS

Demonstration Problem 6–1

Jamestown Company is involved in the construction business and has a fiscal year-end of December 31. The company purchased a crane on January 1, 19X1, for $35,000. The crane had an estimated useful life of seven years with no salvage value. The straight-line method was used to depreciate the asset. On January 1, 19X2, the company purchased a bulldozer for $47,000. The sum-of-the-years'-digits method was used to depreciate the bulldozer, which had an estimated useful life of five years and a $2,000 salvage value. The company also purchased two pick-up trucks on July 1, 19X2, for $13,000 each. The trucks are estimated to have useful lives of four years each and a salvage value of $1,000 each. The straight-line method was used to depreciate the trucks. On January 1, 19X3, the company purchased used equipment costing $53,000. The company depreciates the equipment using the double-declining-balance method and estimates that the equipment has a useful life of five years and a $4,000 salvage value.

On January 1, 19X5, the company overhauled and reconditioned the crane for $10,000. The expenditure extended the crane's useful life an additional three years from the company's original estimate, and the salvage value was estimated to be $1,000. On January 1, 19X5, the bulldozer was sold for $25,000.

On July 1, 19X5, one of the trucks was involved in an accident. The truck was completely destroyed and insurance proceeds totaled $3,500. The remaining truck was traded for a similar truck with a list price of $12,000 by exchanging the old truck and $7,000 on December 31, 19X5. The old truck had a fair market value of $4,000. The equipment was retired on December 31, 19X5.

Provide journal entries (including year-end adjusting entries for depreciation expense) relating to Jamestown's five plant assets for the year 19X5.

Solution to Demonstration Problem 6–1

Crane

$$\$35,000/7 \text{ years} = \$5,000/\text{year}$$

Original cost	$35,000
Depreciation to date ($5,000 × 4 years)	20,000
Undepreciated amount	15,000
Plus capital expenditure	10,000
Balance	25,000
Less salvage value	1,000
Revised depreciation base	$24,000
Divided by remaining useful life of 6 years =	$ 4,000 per year

1/1/X5	Accumulated Depreciation—Crane	$10,000	
	Cash		$10,000
12/31/X5	Depreciation Expense	$ 4,000	
	Accumulated Depreciation—Crane		$4,000

Bulldozer

$$5 + 4 + 3 + 2 + 1 = 15$$

Year	Depreciation Expense
19X2 5/15 × ($47,000 − $2,000) =	$15,000
19X3 4/15 × ($47,000 − $2,000) =	12,000
19X4 3/15 × ($47,000 − $2,000) =	9,000
Accumulated depreciation to 12/31/X4	36,000

Cost of Bulldozer	$47,000
Less accumulated depreciation	36,000
Book value	11,000
Proceeds	25,000
Gain on sale of Bulldozer	$14,000

1/1/X5	Cash	$25,000	
	Accumulated Depreciation—Bulldozer	36,000	
	Bulldozer		$47,000
	Gain on Sale of Bulldozer		14,000

Destroyed Truck

$$(\$13,000 - \$1,000)/4 = \$3,000/\text{year}$$

Year	Depreciation Expense
19X2 $3,000 × 6/12 =	$ 1,500
19X3	3,000
19X4	3,000
19X5 $3,000 × 6/12 =	1,500
Accumulated depreciation to 7/1/X5	$ 9,000

Cost of Truck	$13,000
Less accumulated depreciation	9,000
Book value	4,000
Insurance proceeds	3,500
Loss on destruction of truck	$ 500

7/1/X5	Depreciation Expense	$1,500	
	Accumulated Depreciation—Truck		$1,500
7/1/X5	Cash	$3,500	
	Loss on Destruction of Truck	500	
	Accumulated Depreciation—Truck	9,000	
	Truck		$13,000

Truck

$$(\$13,000 - \$1,000)/4 = \$3,000/\text{year}$$

Year	Depreciation Expense
19X2 $3,000 × 6/12 =	$ 1,500
19X3	3,000
19X4	3,000
19X5	3,000
Accumulated depreciation to 12/31/X5	$10,500

Cost of truck	$13,000
Accumulated depreciation	10,500
Book value at 12/31/X5	$ 2,500

12/31/X5	Depreciation Expense	$3,000	
	Accumulated Depreciation—Truck		$3,000
12/31/X5	Truck (new) ($2,500 + $7,000)	$ 9,500	
	Accumulated Depreciation—Truck	10,500	
	Truck (old)		$13,000
	Cash		7,000

Equipment

DDB rate = 2/5 = 40%

Year		Depreciation Expense	Book Value
			$53,000
19X3	$53,000 × .40 =	$21,200	31,800
19X4	$31,800 × .40 =	12,720	19,080
19X5	$19,080 × .40 =	7,632	11,448
Accumulated depreciation to 12/31/X5		$41,552	

12/31/X5	Depreciation Expense		$7,632	
	Accumulated Depreciation—Equipment			$7,632
12/31/X5	Accumulated Depreciation—Equipment		$41,552	
	Loss on Retirement of Equipment		11,448	
	Equipment			$53,000

Demonstration Problem 6–2

Yosemite Mining Company purchased a parcel of land on January 1, 19X2 for $5,000,000. The company estimates that 1,000,000 tons of ore can be extracted over the life of the mine. After extracting the ore, the company believes the property can be sold for $300,000. Exploration and development costs totaled $2,500,000. For 19X2, mining labor costs amount to $900,000, and other mining costs were $550,000. A total of 200,000 tons of ore were extracted during 19X2, and 40,000 tons were sold at $25 per ton. The company has a calendar year-end. Record journal entries resulting from the 19X2 transactions. Also indicate the balance sheet presentation relating to the mineral deposits for 19X2.

Solution to Demonstration Problem 6–2

To record the purchase of the land:

Mineral Deposits	$5,000,000	
Cash		$5,000,000

To record the exploration and development costs:

Mineral Deposits	$2,500,000	
Cash		$2,500,000

The depletion per ton is calculated as:

[($5,000,000 + $2,500,000) − $300,000]/1,000,000 tons = $7.20/ton

To recognize that 200,000 ton of ore were extracted during the year and mining labor costs of $900,000 and other mining costs of $550,000 were incurred:

Inventory of Ore ($7.20 × 200,000 tons)	$1,440,000	
Accumulated Depletion—Mineral Deposits		$1,440,000

Inventory of Ore ($900,000 + $550,000)	$1,450,000	
Cash		$1,450,000

The cost per ton of ore is $14.45 −($1,440,000 + $1,450,000)/ 200,000 tons.

    To record the sale of 40,000 tons of ore:

Cash (40,000 tons × $25.00)	$1,000,000	
Sales of Ore		$1,000,000

Cost of Ore Sold (40,000 tons × $14.45)	$ 578,000	
Inventory of Ore		$ 578,000

Balance Sheet Presentation

Mineral Deposits	$7,500,000
Less Accumulated Depletion	1,440,000
Net Mineral Deposits	$6,060,000
Inventory of Ore ($1,440,000 + $1,450,000 − $578,000)	$2,312,000

Demonstration Problem 6–3

On January 1 of the current year, Pepper Company purchased the net assets of Salt, Inc., for $1,600,000 and also assumed a note payable for $100,000. On that date the following book and fair market values were determined for the assets and the liability of Salt:

	Book Value	Fair Market Value
Accounts receivable	$ 30,000	$ 30,000
Inventory	50,000	62,000
Machinery	250,000	300,000
Land	550,000	600,000
Building	400,000	490,000
Patents	68,000	70,000
Note payable	100,000	100,000

1. Prepare an analysis to determine if any goodwill exists.
2. Prepare the journal entry to record the acquisition of Salt by Pepper.
3. Assuming Pepper decides to amortize any goodwill over the maximum allowable period, record the year-end adjusting entry to recognize amortization expense.

Solution to Demonstration Problem 6–3

1. Computation of Goodwill

Amount paid		$1,600,000
Less fair market value of identifiable net assets:		
Accounts receivable	$ 30,000	
Inventory	62,000	
Machinery	300,000	
Land	600,000	
Building	490,000	
Patents	70,000	
Note payable	(100,000)	1,452,000
Goodwill		$ 148,000

2. Journal Entry

Accounts Receivable	$ 30,000	
Inventory	62,000	
Machinery	300,000	
Land	600,000	
Building	490,000	
Patents	70,000	
Goodwill	148,000	
Note Payable		$ 100,000
Cash		1,600,000

3. Adjusting Journal Entry

The maximum allowable period to amortize goodwill over is 40 years. Assuming a 40-year amortization period, Pepper Company would make the following periodic entry:

Amortization Expense ($148,000/40 years)	$3,700	
Goodwill		$3,700

Key Terms

amortization

betterment

capital expenditure

capitalization

capital lease

copyright

cost depletion

deferred charge

depletion

franchise

goodwill

improvement

intangibles

lease

leasehold improvement

natural resources

operating lease

organization costs

patent

revenue expenditure

trademark

tradename

wasting assets

ASSIGNMENTS

6–1   Accounting for Property, Plant and Equipment

Phillips Company purchased land in for use as its corporate headquarters. A factory that was on the land when it was purchased was razed before construction of the headquarters building began. A substantial amount of rock blasting and removal had to be done to the site before construction of the building began. Because the building site was far removed from the public road, Phillips Company had the contractor construct a paved road from the public road to the parking lot of the building.

Three years after the building was occupied, the company added a warehouse to the building. The building had an estimated useful life of six years more than the remaining estimated useful life of the original building. Seven years later the land and building were sold at an amount more than their book value, and Phillips Company had a new building constructed in another state for use as its corporate headquarters.

REQUIRED:

1. Which of the above expenditures should be capitalized and how should each be depreciated or amortized?

2. How would you account for the sale of the land and building?

6–2   Revenue and Capital Expenditures

Many significant expenditures for plant assets are made subsequent to their purchase.

REQUIRED:

Identify each of the following items as either a revenue or capital expenditure.

1. Addition of a wing to a plant. *cap*
2. Replacement of an electric heating system with a gas heating system. *cap*
3. Lubricating and cleaning factory machinery and equipment. *REV*
4. Repainting the company fleet of delivery trucks. *REV*
5. Maintenance on the company fleet of delivery trucks. *REV*
6. Major overhaul of a large assembly line resulting in an increase in its estimated useful life. *cap*
7. Replacement of a stairway in the company showroom with an escalator. *cap*
8. Replacement of a wooden floor in the factory with a concrete one. *cap*
9. Annual painting of the corporate administrative offices. *REV*

6–3   Accounting for Capital Expenditures

Melrose Corporation purchased an assembly machine on April 1, 19X1, for $225,000. At that time Melrose estimated the useful life of the machine to be eight years, with a salvage value of $1,400. The company decided to use the straight-line method to determine periodic depreciation expense. On January 1, 19X5, the company completely reconditioned the machine at a cost of $21,000. The reconditioning extended the asset's useful life for seven more years from January 1, 19X5 and increased its salvage value to $2,000.

REQUIRED:

1. Provide the entry to record the expenditure and the journal entry necessary to record depreciation expense for the year-ended 19X5 for Melrose Corporation.
2. Suppose that the expenditure did not extend the life of the assembly machine but instead improved the service quality of the machine. Would your entries change from those in part (1)?

6–4   Disposal of Machinery

On September 1, 19X1, Zane Company sold a machine for $8,500. The machine originally cost $14,000 and was being depreciated using the straight-line method over ten years with no salvage value. As of December 31, 19X0 the machine had a balance in its accumulated depreciation account of $4,200.

REQUIRED:

1. Provide the entry necessary to record depreciation expense up to the date of disposal.
2. Provide the entry necessary to record the disposal of the machine.

6–5 Retirement and Exchange of Equipment

Traver Company has equipment with a cost of $75,000, accumulated depreciation of $55,000, and a fair market value of $21,000.

REQUIRED:

Prepare journal entries to record the disposal of the equipment under each of the following independent events:

1. The equipment is scrapped for $2,000.
2. The equipment is retired.
3. The equipment is traded for similar equipment, and cash of $2,000 is paid.
4. The equipment is exchanged for a press (dissimilar), and $3,500 is paid.

6–6 Exchange of Machinery

On January 1, 19X1 Moe Company purchased an adding machine for $500 cash. The adding machine had a useful life of ten years and no salvage value. On July 1, 19X7 Moe exchanged the adding machine and $200 cash for a new one from Curly. On that date, Curly indicated that the selling price of the new adding machine without a trade-in was $400.

REQUIRED:

Record the journal entry(ies) for the exchange on the books of Moe.

6–7 Recording a Trade-in

The V. Price Wax Museum purchased a red, white, and blue electric wax melter on 6/30/X1 by trading in its old basic black one and paying the balance in cash. The following information relates to the purchase.

List price of new melter	$10,000
Cash paid	5,800
Cost of old melter (eight-year life, no residual value)	8,000
Accumulated Depreciation -old melter (straight-line)	
to December 31, 19X0	4,000
Second-hand market value of old melter	3,600

REQUIRED:

The company's year-end is December 31. Give the entry(ies) necessary to record this transaction.

6–8   Impairment in Value of an Asset

Hinthorne, Inc., completed a brewery at a cost of $22,000,000 on January 1, 19X2. Salvage value was estimated to be $3,000,000, the estimated useful life of the brewery was 20 years, and the company computed depreciation using the sum-of-the-years'-digits method. The brewery operated unsuccessfully for three years in a significantly deteriorating market for its product. On December 31, 19X4, management of the company decided to close the brewery because it felt there was no market for its product and concluded that the brewery had suffered an impairment in value. The company felt that it could sell the brewery and its equipment for $7,500,000.

REQUIRED:

Prepare the journal entry to record the impairment in value of the brewery on December 31, 19X4.

6–9   Natural Resources and Depletion

The income derived from the use of natural resources often bears no relationship to the amount at which the asset is presented on the balance sheet.

REQUIRED:

Do you feel that it is reasonable in these situations to record periodic depletion and the resulting write-down of the natural resource?

6–10   Use of Discovery Value of Assets

On April 1, 19X2, Bumpkin Company purchased a parcel of land for $200,000, which included closing costs. The very next day Bumpkin engineers discovered an oilfield on the property. The engineers estimate that the field is worth at least $10,000,000. Bumpkin's president, Argyle Finsterwald, argues that the land should be written up. The controller, Maud Lynn, states that plant assets should not be written up to reflect appraisal, market, or current values, which are above cost to the entity. Finsterwald contends that the oil is an asset that existed but was unknown at the date of purchase. Therefore, it is a different situation from one in which an asset appreciates in value resulting from changing market conditions, consumer tastes, or other factors occurring after acquisition.

REQUIRED:

Discuss the situation relating to the discovery value of the oilfield.

6–11   Accounting for Natural Resources

On July 1, 19X0, Boa Constrictor, Inc., a calendar year corporation, purchased the rights to a copper mine. Of the total purchase price of $2,800,000, 85% was appropriately allocable to the copper and the remainder to the land. Estimated reserves were 800,000 tons of copper. Production began immediately. Boa extracted 60,000 tons of copper and sold 50,000 in 19X0. The selling price of copper is $25 per ton.

To aid production, Boa also purchased some new equipment on July 1, 19X0. The equipment cost $76,000 and had an estimated useful life of eight years. However, after all the copper is removed from this mine, the equipment will be of no use to Boa and will be sold for an estimated $4,000.

At the start of 19X1, as a result of expenditures of $100,000 for development costs, the estimate of remaining resources was now appropriately raised to 1,000,000 tons. During 19X1, 70,000 tons were removed and 55,000 tons were sold on a first-in, first-out basis. The selling price was still $25 per ton.

REQUIRED:

1. What amounts will appear in Boa Constrictor's December 31, 19X0, financial statements relating to the mine?

2. What amounts will appear on Boa Constrictor's December 31, 19X1, financial statements relating to the mine?

6–12   Goodwill

You closely examine the balance sheet of Hay Company and notice the account Goodwill. The company has had an excellent earnings record over the last ten years, and the financial press is very positive about the firm's future. This puzzles you because you also observe that in the income statement the firm has a significant amount of Amortization Expense that relates to the write-off of Goodwill. You ask yourself, "If a firm is doing well from a financial standpoint, it makes sense that its goodwill must be increasing. Then how can a supposedly healthy firm be recognizing an expense by writing down the asset Goodwill?"

Additionally, you have obtained the annual report from a close competitor of the Hay Company, Ray Company. Your analysis indicates that, financially, Ray seems to be doing as well as Hay but does not have a recorded amount for Goodwill.

REQUIRED:

1. Comment on the write-off of the account Goodwill by Hay Company.

2. Discuss the implications of some companies having a Goodwill account in their financial statements while other companies do not.

6–13 Research and Development Expenditures

Generally accepted accounting principles indicate that, with few exceptions, research and development costs must be expensed as incurred.

REQUIRED:

Do you agree with this policy? Give arguments for and against it.

6–14 Journalizing Net Asset Acquisitions

The identifiable assets and liabilities of Corvallis Company as of December 31, 19X1, are as follows:

	Book Value	Fair Value
Accounts receivable	$ 50,000	$ 50,000
Inventory	85,000	90,000
Building (net of accumulated depreciation)	190,000	300,000
Land	110,000	130,000
Patent	50,000	50,000
	485,000	620,000
Liabilities	75,000	75,000
	$410,000	$545,000

On January 1, 19X2, Eugene Company purchased all the assets and assumed the liabilities of Corvallis Company for $610,000.

REQUIRED:

Prepare the entry necessary on the books of Eugene to record the assets acquired and the liabilities assumed.

6–15 Determining Costs Relating to Patents

Durham Ranger, Inc., developed a new process to be used in its manufacturing operations. The following costs were incurred in January 19X0 relating to that process: (1) cost of materials used in development of the new process, $83,000; (2) testing of the new process (including $62,000 of labor), $100,000; (3) laboratory research related to development of the new process, $155,000; and (4) attorneys' fees relating to the filing for a patent for the new process, $51,000.

REQUIRED:

1. Describe the effect of each of the items on the balance sheet and/or the income statement.
2. What is the overall effect on the income statement for 19X0?

6–16   Computing Periodic Amortization Expense

On January 1, 19X1, Noodle Company purchased a patent relating to its new process for making pasta. The patent cost $60,000. Based on past experience, Mack A. Roni, the company accountant, estimated that the useful life of the patent was ten years. On January 1, 19X4, the company successfully prosecuted a competitor for patent infringement. Legal fees were $23,000, and Noodle was awarded $15,000 in settlement of the lawsuit. On January 1, 19X6, Noodle purchased for $10,000 a patent expected to protect and prolong the life of the original patent by four years.

REQUIRED:

What is the amount of amortization expense that will appear in the income statement for Noodle Company for the years 19X1 through 19X6?

6–17   Deferred Charges

Deferred charges are often listed in the other asset category of the balance sheet.

REQUIRED:

1.   Describe and give an example of a deferred charge asset.

2.   What are some possible problems in accounting for these assets?

6–18   Wal-Mart Stores, Inc., and Subsidiaries Annual Report

Refer to the Wal-Mart Stores, Inc., annual report.

REQUIRED:

1.   What were the dollar amounts of Wal-Mart's capital leases at the end of 1991 and 1990?

2.   What were the dollar amounts of Wal-Mart's other assets and deferred charges at the end of 1991 and 1990?

3.   What is the present value of the minimum lease payments for capital leases at the end of 1991?

4.   What are the total minimum rentals for operating leases at the end of 1991?

5.   What were Wal-Mart's capital expenditures for the year ended January 31, 1991?

6–19   Wal-Mart Stores, Inc., and Subsidiaries Annual Report Ratio Analysis

Refer to the Wal-Mart Stores, Inc., annual report.

REQUIRED:

1.   Calculate the fixed asset turnover ratio for the year ended 1991.

2.   Calculate the total asset turnover ratio for the year ended 1991.

6–20 DECISION CASE:
FIND CORRECT NET INCOME

Greg Gorious, your new and inexperienced accountant, has just prepared annual financial statements for your small business. Your purpose
in requesting the preparation of the financial statements is to obtain a
bank loan for your business. The financial statements are for calendar
year 19X9. You carefully scrutinize the financial statements and note
the following problems:

1. There was no depreciation expense recorded on the facsimile machine. The machine was purchased on January 1, 19X6 for $2,500
   and has a useful life of five years with no salvage value. The double-
   declining-balance method of computing depreciation is being used.

2. A noncancelable lease agreement was entered into on January 1,
   19X9, to lease a machine. The lease called for payments of $12,000
   a year for five years, payable at the end of each year. Based on your
   earlier discussion with Greg, you understood that the lease should
   be capitalized and depreciated over the useful life of the machine,
   which was five years, using the straight-line method. Your records
   indicate that the present value of the lease payments is $45,490,
   which is also the fair market value of the machine. You receive title
   to the machine at the termination of the lease. Greg has incorrectly
   classified the lease as an operating lease and expensed the payment
   during 19X9. The lease obligation should also have been recorded
   at $45,490, and the interest expense for 19X9 should be $4,549,
   calculated at a rate of 10%.

3. You updated the company computer on January 1, 19X9, at a cost
   of $1,200. However, you notice in looking at the balance sheet that
   this amount was not added to the original cost of $6,000. The
   $1,200 was expensed instead of capitalized. The expenditure in-
   creased the original estimate of the useful life of the computer from
   four years to six years. The computer was purchased on January 1,
   19X8, and the straight-line method has been used to compute depreciation expense.

4. You also notice that the balance sheet does not contain the account
   Organizational Costs. These costs totaled $10,000 on January 1,
   19X7, when you started your business. The income statement indicates that Amortization Expense—Organizational Costs is $3,333.
   You know for certain that the amortization period should be five
   years.

5. A copy machine purchased on March 31, 19X9 for $5,000 has been
   expensed instead of capitalized. The useful life of the machine is

four years, and its salvage value is estimated to be $600. The sum-of-the-years'-digits method of depreciation should be used to reflect the pattern of benefits to be received from the machine.

6. On November 1, 19X9, the company acquired a new delivery truck in exchange for an old delivery truck that it had acquired in 19X6. The old truck was purchased for $7,000 and had a book value of $2,800. On the date of the exchange the old truck had a market value of $3,000. In addition, the company paid $3,500 cash for the new truck, which had a list price of $8,000. The new truck has an estimated useful life of four years, a salvage value of $2,500, and will be depreciated using the straight-line method. Greg incorrectly recorded the exchange as that of dissimilar assets, when in fact the exchange was that of similar productive assets. Greg also did not record depreciation expense on the new truck.

7. The unadjusted income statement shows net income for 19X9 as $143,750.

You are very concerned about these items and their possible impact on the net income figure for 19X9 as well as your chances of obtaining the loan.

REQUIRED:

Prepare a corrected net income figure for 19X9.

7

Noncurrent Notes, Mortgages, Bonds, and Deferred Taxes

LEARNING OBJECTIVES

After studying Chapter 7, you should be able to:
1. Distinguish between long-term and current liabilities.
2. Account for long-term notes and mortgages payable.
3. Use the straight-line or effective interest rate methods to account for bonds issued at a discount or premium.
4. Explain how convertible and zero coupon bonds work.
5. Account for bonds as either the debtor or creditor.
6. Make the calculations relating to deferred tax liabilities and explain the rollover effect.

Some of the material in this chapter is based on the concepts of the *Time Value of Money,* which are covered in the Appendix at the back of the book. Read this appendix at this time if you are not familiar with the time value of money.

In dollar amounts, noncurrent liabilities, those due after one year, are usually much greater than current liabilities. Companies use such noncurrent liabilities as bonds and notes to finance significant portions of their assets and operations. The accounting for noncurrent liabilities by debtors is mirrored by the accounting for creditors. Some companies invest significant amounts in the noncurrent liabilities of other companies.

While much of the accounting for noncurrent liabilities accords easily with what you already know about liabilities, some areas are not so straightforward. We discuss one such area, deferred taxes, a subject on which relevant authorities have issued several pronouncements. Most recently, the Financial Accounting Standards Board has formulated new rules.

NONCURRENT LIABILITIES

A **noncurrent** (long-term) **liability** is a debt that will not be paid for at least one year or one operating cycle, whichever is longer. Such liabilities are not properly classified as current. There are many kinds of noncurrent liabilities: long-term notes, mortgages, bonds, and obligations that arise from pensions, leases, and deferred taxes. Noncurrent liabilities appear in balance sheets at their present values. The **present value** of a noncurrent liability is the amount required to pay off the debt on the date of the balance sheet, excluding all future interest not yet due. For instance, a company that has borrowed $100,000 and is scheduled to pay this amount off in one year at 10% interest will pay $110,000 at the end of the year—$100,000 in principal and $10,000 in interest. However, the present value of the obligation is $100,000, because the $10,000 interest has not been accrued yet; if the company were to pay the debt today, it would pay $100,000. (There could be penalties associated with early repayment, but we shall ignore such possibilities.)

Many noncurrent liabilities call for periodic payments of principal and interest. Any portion of the principal of a long-term liability that will be paid within the next year or operating cycle is classified as a **current liability.** The first sections of this chapter describe the accounting for long-term notes and mortgages.

Noncurrent debts will not be paid for one year or one operating cycle, whichever is longer.

Payments to be made on long-term debt within one year are current liabilities.

LONG-TERM NOTES PAYABLE

A long-term or noncurrent note is a note that will not be paid for at least one year or one operating cycle, whichever is longer. The present value of a long-term note (or any other debt) is the amount required to pay it off today. The amount that actually will be paid at some future date is called the **future value** of a debt. If on December 31, 19X1, a company borrows $5,000 on a note payable at 12% interest, compounded annually, that is due in two years, then the amount that ultimately will be paid—the future value of the note—is calculated as follows.

Future Value

Present value at balance sheet date (principal of note)	$5,000
× 1 + the interest rate	× 1.12
Due in one year (principal and interest)	5,600
× 1 + the interest rate	× 1.12
Future value due in two years (principal and interest)	$6,272

When the note is paid in two years, the $6,272 payment consists of $1,272 in interest and $5,000 in principal. The liability will be shown in the balance sheet as the amount owed at the end of each year.

Balance Sheet Disclosure

The note will be paid on December 31, 19X3, and will not appear on the balance sheet as of that date.

Balance Sheet Disclosure
December 31, 19X1

Noncurrent Liabilities:	
Note Payable (due in two years)	$5,000

December 31, 19X2

Current Liabilities:	
Note Payable (due in one year)	$5,000
Interest Payable (on note due in one year)	600

Journal Entries

The journal entries to record the loan creating the note payable, the accrual of interest payable, and the payment of the debt follow. There is no journal entry to change the note from a noncurrent to a current liability. Each entry is made on a balance sheet date anniversary of the note.

December 31, 19X1

Cash	$5,000	
Note Payable		$5,000

December 31, 19X2

Interest Expense	$ 600	
Interest Payable		$ 600

December 31, 19X3

Interest Expense ($6,272 − $5,600)	$ 672	
Interest Payable	600	
Note Payable	5,000	
Cash		$6,272

Discounted Notes Payable

A note can be recorded for the total future amount due (principal and interest). In this case, the $5,000 borrowed is recorded as a note for $6,272. The liability still is presented in the balance sheet at its present value plus the amount of any interest accrued. The total liability (principal and interest) is the same using either method. The discount represents interest charges applicable to future periods.

Liabilities are shown at their present values.

December 31, 19X1

Noncurrent Liabilities:		
Note Payable (due in two years)	$6,272	
Less Discount on Note Payable	1,272	$5,000

December 31, 19X2

Current Liabilities:		
Note Payable (due in one year)	$6,272	
Less Discount on Note Payable	672	$5,600

The journal entries for a note recorded at its future value follow. Again, each entry is made on a balance sheet date anniversary of the note.

December 31, 19X1

Cash	$5,000	
Discount on Note Payable	1,272	
Note Payable		$6,272

December 31, 19X2

Interest Expense	$ 600	
Discount on Note Payable		$ 600

December 31, 19X3

Interest Expense	$ 672	
Note Payable	6,272	
Cash		$6,272
Discount on Note Payable		672

The note payable is recorded as a credit of $6,272. The discount account appears as follows:

Discount on Note Payable

$1,272		(19X1)
	$600	(19X2)
	672	(19X3)
0	0	(balance at end of 19X3)

We have illustrated two alternative methods of accounting for a $5,000 bank loan, based on the form of the note payable. Both methods result in recognizing the same amount of interest expense each period and the same liability on the balance sheet.

MORTGAGES

A **mortgage loan** is a long-term installment note. The unpaid principal plus any accrued interest is the amount required to pay off the mortgage debt at any time and is therefore the present value of the debt.

Payments on a mortgage are often made monthly but can be made quarterly, semiannually, or annually. Each payment reduces the principal of the loan and pays the interest for the period. A **loan-amortization schedule** shows how each payment is split between principal and interest. Such a schedule for a $500,000, 10%, eight-year mortgage with annual payments follows. (The annual payment of $93,722 is $500,000 divided by 5.335, which is the present value factor for an eight-year, 10% annuity.)

Year	Principal Amount p	Interest Rate r	Interest Expense $i = pr$	Annual Payment a	Applied to Principal $a - i$
1	$500,000	.10	$50,000	$93,722	$43,722
2	456,278	.10	45,628	93,722	48,094
3	408,184	.10	40,818	93,722	52,904
4	355,280	.10	35,528	93,722	58,194
5	297,086	.10	29,709	93,722	64,013
6	233,073	.10	23,307	93,722	70,415
7	162,658	.10	16,266	93,722	77,456
8	85,202	.10	8,520	93,722	85,202

Once a loan amortization schedule has been prepared, it is simple to make the journal entries for a mortgage payment. Cash is credited for the amount of the payment, and debits are made to interest expense and to the mortgage principal for the amounts in the schedule. For example, the journal entry to record the payment for the sixth year is

A loan-amortization schedule shows the principal and interest for each payment.

Interest Expense	$23,307	
Mortgage Payable	70,415	
Cash		$93,722

BONDS

A **bond** is a form of long-term debt that is usually repaid in 10–20 years. Each bond is typically a debt agreement for $1,000. A $50,000,000 debt is divided into 50,000 bonds, each of which is a contract for a debt of $1,000. An investor (lender) who "buys" $100,000 in bonds has agreed to lend the debtor $100,000. The debt is supported by 100 bonds of $1,000 each. The **contract** or **nominal interest rate,** which determines the amount of the periodic interest payments, the interest payment schedule (usually semiannual), and the bond **maturity date** (when the principal, or **face amount,** is to be paid

A bond may be secured or unsecured.

in a single payment) are all contained in the bond contract, called an **indenture.**

The bond debt may be **secured** by a pledge of property or it may be **unsecured.** A mortgage bond is secured by property. Bonds for unsecured debt are called **debentures.** All the bonds may be **retired** (repaid) at the same time or may mature (come due) over several years. Bonds that mature in increments are called **serial bonds.** The schedule of long-term debt that appears in note 3 of the Boise Cascade financial statements is shown in Exhibit 7–1. The schedule discloses the interest rates and maturity dates of all Boise Cascade's long-term debt.

Issuing Bonds and Interest Expense

Suppose that a company issues a bond for a face amount of $1,000 for ten years, with nominal interest of 10% per year to be paid annually. The face amount is paid at the end of year 10. When the company issues this bond, it is making two promises:

1. To pay the lender $1,000 in ten years.
2. To pay interest of $100 ($1,000 × .10) each year.

Suppose that the market rate of interest—the rate that investors are willing to accept for bonds of the same general characteristics—is 10%. The relevant characteristics include whether the bonds are secured or unsecured, their maturity date (ten years in this example), and the general credit standing of the company, which is a function of its profitability and debt load, among other things. The company can then issue the bond for $1,000. If the bond is issued on December 31, the journal entries are as follows.

When the bonds are issued:

Cash	$1,000	
Bond Payable		$1,000

For each interest payment:

Interest Expense	100	
Cash		100

The market interest rate determines the amount received when bonds are issued.

Bonds Issued at Premiums and Discounts

Now suppose that the **effective** or **market interest rate** goes higher than the 10% nominal rate prior to the issue. A lender will then no

Exhibit 7–1
Schedule of Long-Term Debt from Boise Cascade Note 3

	December 31		
	1990	1989	1988
	(expressed in thousands)		
7.75% notes, due in 1991	$ 100,000	$ 99,966	$ 99,863
11.875% notes, due in 1993, net of unamortized discount of $161,000 (1)	99,839	99,760	99,681
13.125% notes, due in 1994, callable in 1991	58,145	58,145	58,145
8.375% notes, due in 1994, callable in 1992, net of unamortized discount of $118,000 (1)	99,882	99,810	99,737
10.25% notes, due in 1996, callable in 1993	100,000	100,000	100,000
10.125% notes, due in 1997, net of unamortized discount of $306,000 (1) (2)	99,694	—	—
9.625% notes, due in 1998, callable in 1995, net of unamortized discount of $260,000 (1)	99,740	99,683	99,626
9.9% notes, due in 2000, net of unamortized discount of $506,000 (1)	99,494	—	—
9.875% notes, due in 2001, callable in 1999	100,000	100,000	—
9.85% notes, due in 2002	125,000	—	—
9.45% debentures, due in 2009, net of unamortized discount of $424,000 (1)	149,576	149,554	—
7% convertible subordinated debentures, due in 2016, net of unamortized discount of $1,862,000 (1)	96,026	95,677	95,328
Medium-term notes, Series A, with interest rates averaging 9.5% in 1990, due in varying amounts through 2000	79,000	—	—
Notes payable and other indebtedness, with interest rates averaging 8.9%, 10.7%, and 11%, due in varying amounts annually through 2012	69,528	58,508	114,410
Revenue bonds, with interest rates averaging 7.9%, 7.8%, and 7.7%, due in varying amounts annually through 2014, net of unamortized discount of $2,222,000 (1)	166,149	141,201	142,995
American & Foreign Power Company Inc. 5% debentures, due in 2030, net of unamortized discount of $2,055,000 (1)	32,510	35,144	38,647
Commercial paper, with interest rates averaging 8.2% in 1990 and 9.4% in 1989, net of unamortized discount of $416,000 (1)	160,974	47,920	—
Revolving credit borrowings, with interest rates averaging 8.2% in 1990	50,000	—	—
12% notes, due in 1992, called in 1990	—	50,000	50,000
	1,785,557	1,235,368	998,432
Less current portion	136,731	30,390	73,320
	1,648,826	1,204,978	925,112
Guarantee of 8.5% ESOP debt, due in installments through 2004	285,678	292,581	—
	$1,934,504	$1,497,559	$ 925,112

(1) The amount of net unamortized discount disclosed applies to long-term debt outstanding at December 31, 1990.

(2) In January 1991, the Company drew an additional $20,000,000 of 10.125% notes pursuant to a delayed delivery contract.

longer purchase a $1,000 bond for 10% interest. The lender will demand a higher return, which can be obtained by investing less than $1,000 to receive the payments (principal and interest). It is too late and much too expensive to print new bonds with the new interest rate. In any case, interest rates change every day, so it is almost impossible to match the nominal and effective (market) rates. Suppose that at the higher effective rate of interest, the lender agrees to lend only $900 for the bonds. The company would then pay:

1. At the end of ten years	$1,000
2. In equal annual payments ($100 × 10)	1,000
Total amount paid	$2,000
Less amount received from lender	900
Excess paid over amount received	$1,100

The excess paid over the amount received is the true interest cost of the funds. The company pays $100 cash in interest per year, but the average annual cost of the money borrowed is $110 ($1,100/10) per year. The excess of the issue price over the face value is **premium**. The excess of face value over issue price is **discount**.

Amortization of Discount and Premium

Using **straight-line amortization,** the company records the $100 cash outflow each year and the $110 average annual interest expense. The extra $10 interest expense ($110 − $100) in excess of the actual cash paid is the **amortization** of the excess paid over the amount received. The difference between the cash paid and the interest expense is recorded as an equal amount each year. The journal entries are as follows.

When the bonds are issued:

Cash	$900	
Discount on Bond Payable	100	
Bond Payable		$1,000

For each interest payment (done once each year):

Interest Expense	$110	
Discount on Bond Payable		$ 10
Cash		100

Suppose that instead of rising, the interest rate falls before the bond is issued. A lender then will be willing to purchase a $1,000 bond at less than 10% interest. The lender will invest more than $1,000 to receive the payments (principal and interest) described in the bond agreement. At the lower market rate of interest, the lender may agree to lend

$1,080 in exchange for the payments described on the bond. The company then would pay:

1. At the end of ten years	$1,000
2. In equal annual payments ($100 × 10)	1,000
Total amount paid	$2,000
Less amount received from lender	1,080
Excess paid over amount received	$ 920

The excess paid over the amount received is again the true interest cost of the funds. The company pays $100 cash in interest per year, but the average annual cost of the money borrowed is $92 ($920/10) per year. Using straight-line amortization, the company records the $100 cash outflow each year and the $92 average annual interest expense. The $8 cash paid in excess of the interest expense is the amortization of the bond premium. The difference between the cash paid and the interest expense is recorded as an equal amount each year. The journal entries are as follows.

Interest is the excess paid over the amount received.

When the bonds are issued:

Cash	$1,080	
Premium on Bond Payable		$ 80
Bond Payable		1,000

For each annual interest payment:

Interest Expense	$ 92	
Premium on Bond Payable	8	
Cash		$ 100

Describing Bond Issues

Bonds that are issued at face value are said to be issued at 100, meaning 100% of face value. If, as in the previous example, the bonds were issued for only $900, they are described as issuing at 90, meaning 90% of face value. Likewise, bonds issued for $1,080 are described as issuing at 108.

Presentation in Annual Report

When bonds are presented in an annual report, details of the security · agreement, maturity dates, and interest rates appear in the notes to the financial statements, as shown in Exhibit 7–2. The bonds are shown in

Exhibit 7–2
Details on Debt in the Financial Statement Notes of Boise Cascade

Notes to Financial Statements
Boise Cascade Corporation and Subsidiaries

3. Debt

At December 31, 1990, the Company had an unsecured revolving credit agreement that permitted it to borrow up to $750,000,000, of which $161,390,000 of borrowing rights had been allocated by the Company to support outstanding commercial paper. During 1990, a $110,000,000 unsecured revolving credit agreement was completed for one of the Company's Canadian subsidiaries that permitted borrowing in either U.S. or Canadian dollars. Amounts drawn under this revolver are guaranteed by the Company and are consolidated with borrowings of the Company for reporting purposes. On December 31, 1990, borrowings of US$50,000,000 were outstanding under the Canadian revolver. In addition, the Company had entered into an "interest rate swap," resulting in an effective fixed interest rate of 8.9% with respect to that borrowing. The difference between the variable and fixed interest rates is accrued as either a payable or receivable as interest rates change during the life of the swap agreement. The Company will resume payments of interest based on one of the pricing formulas available under the credit agreement upon termination of the swap agreement.

The revolving credit agreements provide the Company with a choice of several pricing formulas. At December 31, 1990, the effective interest rates would have ranged from 7.6% to 10.3% for borrowings in U.S. dollars and from 11.2% to 12.6% for borrowings in Canadian dollars. Commitment fees are required on the unused portion of the credits. The revolving period on the $750,000,000 lending commitment expires in May 1994, and any borrowings outstanding at that time

are payable in quarterly installments ending in May 1997. The revolving period on the $110,000,000 lending commitment expires in May 1995, and any amounts outstanding at that time are payable in quarterly installments ending in June 1996. Compensating balances are not required.

In December 1990, the Company filed a new shelf registration with the Securities and Exchange Commission for additional debt securities. After incorporating the remaining $26,000,000 from a prior shelf registration, the Company had $426,000,000 of shelf capacity for new publicly registered debt.

In 1989, the Company guaranteed debt used to fund an employee stock ownership plan that is part of the Savings and Supplemental Retirement Plan for the Company's U.S. salaried employees (see Note 5). The Company has recorded the debt on its Balance Sheets, along with an offset in the shareholders' equity section that is entitled "Deferred ESOP benefit." The Company has guaranteed certain tax indemnities on the ESOP debt, and the interest rate on the guaranteed debt is subject to adjustment for events that are described in the loan agreement.

The Company may redeem all or part of the 7% unsecured convertible subordinated debentures at specified amounts that decline to $50 par value per debenture on May 1, 1996. Sinking fund payments are required after May 1, 1996. Each debenture is convertible into 1.1415 shares of the Company's common stock.

Long-term debt, most of which is unsecured, consists of the following:

Continued

Exhibit 7–2
Continued

	December 31		
	1990	1989	1988
	(expressed in thousands)		
7.75% notes, due in 1991	$ 100,000	$ 99,966	$ 99,863
11.875% notes, due in 1993, net of unamortized discount of $161,000 [1]	99,839	99,760	99,681
13.125% notes, due in 1994, callable in 1991	58,145	58,145	58,145
8.375% notes, due in 1994, callable in 1992, net of unamortized discount of $118,000 [1]	99,882	99,810	99,737
10.25% notes, due in 1996, callable in 1993	100,000	100,000	100,000
10.125% notes, due in 1997, net of unamortized discount of $306,000 [1] [2]	99,694	—	—
9.625% notes, due in 1998, callable in 1995, net of unamortized discount of $260,000 [1]	99,740	99,683	99,626
9.9% notes, due in 2000, net of unamortized discount of $506,000 [1]	99,494	—	—
9.875% notes, due in 2001, callable in 1999	100,000	100,000	—
9.85% notes, due in 2002	125,000	—	—
9.45% debentures, due in 2009, net of unamortized discount of $424,000 [1]	149,576	149,554	—
7% convertible subordinated debentures, due in 2016, net of unamortized discount of $1,862,000 [1]	96,026	95,677	95,328
Medium-term notes, Series A, with interest rates averaging 9.5% in 1990, due in varying amounts through 2000	79,000	—	—
Notes payable and other indebtedness, with interest rates averaging 8.9%, 10.7%, and 11%, due in varying amounts annually through 2012	69,528	58,508	114,410
Revenue bonds, with interest rates averaging 7.9%, 7.8%, and 7.7%, due in varying amounts annually through 2014, net of unamortized discount of $2,222,000 [1]	166,149	141,201	142,995
American & Foreign Power Company Inc. 5% debentures, due in 2030, net of unamortized discount of $2,055,000 [1]	32,510	35,144	38,647
Commercial paper, with interest rates averaging 8.2% in 1990 and 9.4% in 1989, net of unamortized discount of $416,000 [1]	160,974	47,920	—
Revolving credit borrowings, with interest rates averaging 8.2% in 1990	50,000	—	—
12% notes, due in 1992, called in 1990	—	50,000	50,000
	1,785,557	1,235,368	998,432
Less current portion	136,731	30,390	73,320
	1,648,826	1,204,978	925,112
Guarantee of 8.5% ESOP debt, due in installments through 2004	285,678	292,581	—
	$1,934,504	$1,497,559	$ 925,112

[1] The amount of net unamortized discount disclosed applies to long-term debt outstanding at December 31, 1990.

[2] In January 1991, the Company drew an additional $20,000,000 of 10.125% notes pursuant to a delayed delivery contract.

The scheduled payments of long-term debt are $136,731,000 in 1991, $49,022,000 in 1992, $159,964,000 in 1993, $159,741,000 in 1994, and $25,757,000 in 1995. Cash payments for interest, net of interest capitalized, were $118,231,000 in 1990, $92,928,000 in 1989, and $93,012,000 in 1988.

The Company's loan agreements contain covenants and restrictions, none of which are expected to affect its operations significantly. At December 31, 1990, $275,814,000 of retained earnings was available for dividends.

the long-term liabilities section of the financial statements. When bonds are sold at a discount or a premium, they are shown in the balance sheet at their face amount, minus or plus the discount or the premium. The balance sheet of Boise Cascade shows its long-term debt (in thousands) at December 31, 1990 as:

Debt (Note 3)

Long-term debt (less current portion)	$1,648,826
Guarantee of 8.5% ESOP debt	285,678

Bonds and noncurrent notes are included in the total long-term debt. Interestingly, there is a negative stockholders' equity item of $285,678 called Deferred ESOP benefit. The company guaranteed debt used to fund an Employee Stock Ownership Plan (ESOP) and recorded the debt and an offsetting entry to stockholders' equity for the same amount.

Effective Interest Amortization of Premium and Discount

The effective interest rate method is required for financial reporting.

The straight-line method of amortization is simple but only can be used in published financial statements when the discount or premium is immaterial. Otherwise, the effective interest rate method must be used. When the straight-line method is used, interest expense is the same in each period. This is misleading, because the effective interest rate is set when the bond is issued and all parties know how much has been borrowed (received by the company) and how much will be paid (as specified in the bond agreement).

If we return to the example of the bond issued at a premium described previously, we know that $1,080 has been borrowed and $2,000 is to be paid over ten years. Total interest expense is calculated to be $920. Total interest expense will be the same, regardless of the method used to amortize the bond premium. When the effective interest rate is used, each annual payment is still $100, which is calculated by multiplying the face amount of the bond ($1,000) by the nominal interest rate (10%). However, the interest expense changes each period, just as it does in the loan-amortization schedule for a mortgage payable. Using present values in an electronic spreadsheet, we can determine that the effective interest rate for the bond just described is 8.77%. An amortization schedule for this bond, using the effective interest rate method, follows. (This example is of bonds issued at a premium. Bonds issued at a discount are dealt with in the Demonstration Problem at the end of this chapter.)

Year	(1) Bond Face f	(2) Premium p	(3) Total Debt $p + f$	(4) Effective Rate e	(5) Interest Expense $E = e(p + f)$	(6) Nominal Rate r	(7) Interest Payment $P = rf$	(7)–(5) Applied to Debt $P - E$
1	$1,000	$80.00	$1,080.00	.0877	$94.72	.10	$100.00	$ 5.28
2	1,000	74.72	1,074.72	.0877	94.25	.10	100.00	5.75
3	1,000	68.97	1,068.97	.0877	93.75	.10	100.00	6.25
4	1,000	62.72	1,062.72	.0877	93.20	.10	100.00	6.80
5	1,000	55.92	1,055.92	.0877	92.60	.10	100.00	7.40
6	1,000	48.52	1,048.52	.0877	91.96	.10	100.00	8.04
7	1,000	40.48	1,040.48	.0877	91.25	.10	100.00	8.75
8	1,000	31.73	1,031.73	.0877	90.48	.10	100.00	9.52
9	1,000	22.21	1,022.21	.0877	89.65	.10	100.00	10.35
10	1,000	11.86	1,011.86	.0877	88.74	.10	100.00	11.86*

*Increased $.60 to correct for cumulative rounding error.

Just as we were able to make journal entries for payments on a mortgage using the loan-amortization table, we can make entries for bond interest payments using the effective interest rate bond-amortization table. To illustrate, the journal entries to record the bond issuance and for the first and third interest payments follow.

Journal entries contain the amounts in the amortization schedule.

When the bonds are issued:

Cash	$1,080	
Premium on Bond Payable		$ 80
Bond Payable		1,000

For the first interest payment:

Interest Expense	$94.72	
Premium on Bond Payable	5.28	
Cash		$100.00

For the third interest payment:

Interest Expense	$93.75	
Premium on Bond Payable	6.25	
Cash		$100.00

Determining the Amount to be Received

A company can use the market interest rate to determine the amount that will be received when a bond is issued. Suppose that a company intends to issue 20-year bonds with a total face value of $20,000,000. The bonds have a nominal interest rate of 12%, but at the time of issue, the effective interest rate is 15%. Again, for simplicity, we use annual interest payments. Taking PV factors from present value tables, we can determine the present value of the two promises contained in the bond contract. In the following calculation, .061 is the present value of $1 and 6.259 is the present value of an annuity, both at 15% for 20 years.

Promise	× (15% PV factor)	= Present value
To pay $20,000,000 in 20 years	× .061	= $ 1,220,000
To pay 12% interest on the face amount of the bonds each year for 20 years:		
$20,000,000 × .12 = $2,400,000	× 6.259	= 15,021,600
Present value of total bond liability		$16,241,600

The company will receive $16,241,600, leaving a discount of $3,758,400 ($20,000,000 − $16,241,600) to be amortized over the 20-year life of the bonds.

Convertible Debt

Some bonds, when issued, have a contractual provision that allows the bondholders the option of exchanging their bonds for common stock—of changing their status from creditors to owners of the company. Such bonds are called **convertible bonds.** Generally, creditors can be expected to accept a slightly lower interest rate on convertible bonds because they have the option of converting them to common stock if the stock increases in value.

Suppose that the Duffer Company issues $50,000,000 in 20-year bonds. Each bond has a face value of $1,000, pays 12% interest, and can be converted to 25 shares of Duffer's stock. At the time the bonds are issued, the stock is selling for $30 per share. Because the market value of 25 shares at $30 per share is only $750, none of the bondholders want to convert their bonds to common stock at that time.

Over time, however, the market price of the stock may rise. At $40 per share, 25 shares are worth $1,000, or the face value of the bonds. If the market value of the stock continues to rise, at some point above $40 per share, the bondholders can be expected to exercise their option and exchange their $50,000,000 in bonds for shares of common stock. When they do, Duffer's debt will be satisfied. The convertible bonds essentially will be self-retiring. If all the bonds are converted, Duffer will make the following journal entry to retire the bonds and issue stock:

Bonds Payable	$50,000,000	
Common Stock		$50,000,000

The note 3 schedule of long term debt for Boise Cascade shows 7% convertible debentures of $96,026,000 (see Exhibit 7–2). Two other interesting forms of debt—zero coupon bonds and paid-in-kind bonds—are discussed in Insights 7–1 and 7–2, respectively. The accounting for bonds from the issuer's (debtor's) point of view is mirrored on the purchaser's (creditor's) side. We now turn to the creditor's accounting.

DEBT PAYABLE IN A FOREIGN CURRENCY

When a company operates in the international arena, either to do business or to raise capital, its debt may be payable in a specified amount of a foreign currency rather than in U.S. dollars. This may cause problems because the foreign currency needed to pay the debt must be purchased with U.S. dollars but the cost of the foreign currency, or the **foreign currency exchange rate,** at the date the debt is to be repaid will not be known at the time the debt is incurred. Assume, for example, that a U.S. company purchases equipment on a one-year note payable from a company in Taiwan for NT$1,000,000 (NT$ means New Taiwan dollar) when the exchange rate is NT$25 = US$1, or .04 US$ per NT$. The transaction requires NT$1,000,000 to pay the note when it becomes due. The transaction is measured and recorded on the books of the U.S. company in U.S. dollars. At the time of the purchase, NT$1,000,000 is worth US$40,000, calculated as NT$1,000,000 × .04 US$ per NT$ = $40,000 (or, alternatively, NT$1,000,000/25 = US$40,000).

Some debts are payable in foreign currency.

| Equipment | $40,000 | |
| Note payable | | $40,000 |

Let's assume that the note is paid when the exchange rate is NT$20 = US$1. Remember that the note is for NT$1,000,000, not the US$40,000 recorded! Now NT$1,000,000 is worth US$50,000, calculated as NT$1,000,000 × .20 US$ per NT$ = $50,000 (or, alternately, NT$1,000,000/20 = US$50,000). The $10,000 increased amount of cash paid is a loss due to changes in the exchange rate. (Because foreign currency transactions are complicated, consideration of the interest on the note is omitted here.)

Note Payable	40,000	
Exchange Rate Loss	10,000	
Cash		50,000

When a company has a foreign currency transaction, the risk of exchange rate losses can be **hedged** by a **forward exchange contract.**

INSIGHT 7–1
Zero Coupon Bonds

Many companies have issued bonds that do not pay periodic interest. They are called zero coupon bonds, or simply zeros. They are issued at considerable discounts and pay their face value at maturity. For instance, Xerox Corporation issued $250 million in zero coupon bonds due in 1992. The effective interest rate on these bonds, given in the company's 1990 annual report, is 14.64%. The value of those bonds in 1990 is $190,225,030, as we can see by multiplying the $250 million face value due in two years by the present value factor for two years and 14.64%. Alternatively, we can simply solve for the present value factor (PV), using the equation $190,225,030 = $250,000,000 × PV. PV = .761. (A full explanation of present value is given in Appendix B at the back of the book.)

Each year, the issuer debits interest expense and credits discount on bonds payable to show the accumulation of interest. The issuer should use the **effective interest rate method of amortization,** as shown in the following example. CBC Company issued zero coupon bonds with a face value of $10 million due in ten years. The issue price of $3,860,000 yields a 10% interest rate. The journal entries to record the issue and the interest expenses at the end of the first and third years follow.

Cash	$3,860,000	
Discount on Bonds Payable	6,140,000	
Bonds Payable		$10,000,000

End of first year:

Interest Expense (10% × $3,860,000)	$386,000	
Discount on Bonds Payable		$386,000

End of third year:

Interest Expense	$467,060	
Discount on Bonds Payable		$467,060

At the end of year 1, book value of Bonds Payable is $4,246,000 ($3,860,000 + $386,000, the interest for year 1). At the end of year 2, Bonds Payable is $4,670,600 ($4,246,000 + $424,600, interest for year 2). So the interest for year 3 is 10% of $4,670,600.

Zero coupon bonds are especially desirable to investors who want a given sum of money at some future date but do not need periodic interest payments. Individual Retirement Accounts (IRAs) often invest in zeros that mature after the IRA holders retire.

INSIGHT 7–2
PIK Bond: The Ultimate Junk Bond

A **junk bond** is a bond with a low credit rating by Standard and Poor or Moody's. Junk bonds have speculative overtones. Perhaps the ultimate junk bond is a PIK (paid-in-kind) bond. The holder of a PIK bond does not receive cash payments of interest. Instead, when interest is due to be paid, the bond-holder·is simply given another PIK bond for the amount of the interest. A holder of $10,000 of PIK bonds might, for example, receive another $1,000 PIK bond as an interest payment. Cash payments are made only when the bonds mature. PIKs are often used in a leveraged buyout (LBO). In an LBO, a company is acquired by a second company, which leverages its buying power by issuing debt to be paid off by selling parts of the acquired company.

The largest LBO in history was the takeover of RJR Nabisco by the invest-ment firm of Kohlberg Kravis Roberts for $25 billion. To fund the takeover, KKR floated several issues of bonds, yielding up to 17%. However, some bonds issued in the takeover were PIKs. No cash will flow to these bondholders until the bonds mature or are retired.

A forward exchange contract is an agreement to buy or to sell foreign currency at some specified date at a specified rate. For example, at the time of the purchase, the company in our illustration might enter a contract to purchase NT$1,000,000 on the due date of the note for US$42,000. This removes the company's risk of exchange rate loss by *Hedging limits loss.* fixing the cost of the equipment plus the cost of the NT$ necessary to pay the note at US$42,000.

Note 1 in the Boise Cascade 1990 annual report states that the company's foreign currency exchange rate gains and losses result from transactions with Boise's Canadian subsidiaries and that "The company has entered into forward contracts to purchase 100,000,000 Canadian dollars at various dates in 1992."

INVESTMENTS IN BONDS

The owner of bonds, the creditor, shows them in the balance sheet as a noncurrent asset called **investments.** Investments are assets because the creditor company expects to receive interest payments and to collect the face amount of the bonds on their maturity date. If the interest and principal will not be collected as expected, the debt must be either written off (if nothing will be received) or reclassified to reflect the failure of the debtor to honor the terms on the original debt agreement. Insight 7–3 discusses the problems encountered when some banks reclassify loans.

INSIGHT 7–3
Hiding Bad Debt With Accounting Techniques

When banks have problems with bad loans—loans that do not pay interest to the bank—the banks must reclassify the bad loans as nonperforming assets. The banks lose whatever profit the loans might have produced, and the banks' assets appear less favorable to investors when loans are reclassified as nonperforming.

Many banks have had problems with bad real estate loans. Some banks have found a way to "restructure" bad loans so that they can be shown as performing loans. The restructuring involves granting more favorable terms to borrowers, such as reduced interest rates and write-offs of portions of the debt. If a bank has a nonperforming loan of $3,000,000, for example, the bank may negotiate with the debtor to write off $1,000,000 of the debt and reduce the interest rate by two percentage points. The debtor may be able to meet the new terms and begin paying interest. Sometimes banks accept part ownership of the real estate in payment for granting more favorable terms.

The problem is how to treat the renegotiated loan. Robert Storch, head of a task force that oversees how federal regulators conduct examinations, wants to restrict the way banks treat restructured loans. "Just changing the terms of the loan doesn't change the fact that the borrower didn't comply with the original terms," he maintains. "Just by paper shuffling, you can't make problems go away." But some bankers disagree. Peter Manning, Chief Financial Officer of Bank of Boston argues: "A renegotiated loan is really a new loan. And, under those new terms, it is performing fine. The old loan doesn't exist anymore."

Still, restructured loans may carry interest rates that are below the effective (market) rate. The Bank of Boston, for example, reclassified $76 million of restructured loans from nonperforming to performing loans, even though the interest rates on these loans average 1.5% below what those funds cost the bank. Are these loans truly performing assets? Or are they simply drains on future profits that should not be shown favorably? According to a banking specialist at one accounting firm: "You have some banks that are finally facing problem loans and handling them creatively, and then you have banks with desperate people doing desperate things. The problem is that it's impossible to tell them apart."

SOURCE: This information is taken from Ron Suskind, "Some Banks Use Accounting Techniques That Conceal Loan Woes, Regulators Say," The Wall Street Journal (November 29, 1990). Reprinted with permission of the Wall Street Journal. © 1990 Dow Jones & Company, Inc. All Rights Reserved WORLDWIDE.

The amount of the bond investment is determined in exactly the same way as the amount of the bond liability, except that the face amount of the bond and any discount or premium are shown as a single amount. The entries appearing previously to illustrate the effective interest rate method are repeated here as they would appear on the creditor's books. The credit entries to the investments account are the amounts required to amortize the bond premium each time interest is paid.

When the bonds are purchased:

Investments	$1,080	
Cash		$1,080

For the first interest payment:

Cash	100.00	
Investments		5.28
Interest Revenue		94.72

For the third interest payment:

Cash	100.00	
Investments		6.25
Interest Revenue		93.75

The creditor's entries and reporting are the mirror images of those of the debtor, even to the amounts, as long as both use the same method of amortization.

DEFERRED TAXES

The accounting methods required for income tax reporting frequently differ from generally accepted accounting principles (GAAP). The objectives of tax law include raising revenue and promoting social goals through the redistribution of income. They do not include accurately measuring accrual net income. As a result, there are often differences between income for financial reporting and income for tax reporting. These differences can be permanent—as, for example, when revenue is included in accounting income but not in taxable income, as is the case with municipal bonds. These bonds, issued by state and local governments, generally are free from federal income tax.

Tax law and accounting have different goals.

More often, however, differences are temporary, resulting from rules that require a revenue or an expense to be recognized in one year for tax purposes and in another year for financial reporting. For example, in December 19X2, a company receives a rental payment for the entire year of 19X3. The company must include the entire receipt in 19X2 taxable income, but it reports the income in 19X3 in its financial statements. (Of course, it does not report the 19X2 receipt in its 19X3 taxable income.) Similarly, a company recognizes the expected costs to service products under warranties in the year in which the products are sold, but the company can claim no tax deduction until it actually pays for the services. Many other cases create the same problem.

If companies simply reported income taxes as they were paid, the results could be as follows. RST Company has sales of $100,000 in both 19X3 and 19X4. For simplicity, we assume the following expenses.

Year	For Income Tax Reporting	For Financial Reporting
19X3	$70,000	$50,000
19X4	$30,000	$50,000

Note that the total expenses are the same over the two years. The differences between the income tax and financial reporting expenses are temporary. Further suppose that the income tax rate is 40%. The tax returns for the two years show the following.

	19X3	19X4
Revenue	$100,000	$100,000
Expenses	70,000	30,000
Income before taxes	30,000	70,000
Income taxes at 40%	$ 12,000	$ 28,000

If we report the amounts actually owed for each year as income tax expense, we have the following income statements for financial reporting.

	19X3	19X4
Revenue	$100,000	$100,000
Expenses	50,000	50,000
Income before taxes	50,000	50,000
Income taxes (above)	12,000	28,000
Net income	$ 38,000	$ 22,000

However, this report could be confusing to readers. The income tax rate appears to have gone from 24% ($12,000/$50,000) in 19X3 to

56% ($28,000/$50,000) in 19X4. To overcome this problem, GAAP require that we ignore the timing of tax effects and act as if the income taxes relate to particular transactions and occur in the same period in which we recognize the transactions for financial reporting.

The rules governing deferred taxes are quite complex, but this introductory treatment should permit you to understand the basics of this common balance sheet item. Essentially, we report as if the income taxes are levied on the income reported in the financial statements of the company, not on its taxable income. In our example:

	19X3	19X4
Revenue	$100,000	$100,000
Expenses	50,000	50,000
Income before taxes	50,000	50,000
Income taxes	20,000	20,000
Net income	$ 30,000	$ 30,000

Notice that total income taxes over the two years are still $40,000, which is the amount paid. Also notice that the tax rate is a constant 40%. But what happens to the difference between the amount the company pays in income taxes and the amount the company reports on its income statement? The cumulative effects of these differences appear on the balance sheet as **deferred taxes** on either the asset side or the equity side.

In our example, the journal entry for 19X3 is:

Income Tax Expense	$20,000	
Cash, or Accrued Taxes Payable		$12,000
Deferred Income Taxes		8,000

The $8,000 appears on the equity side of the balance sheet as Deferred Income Taxes. The 19X4 entry is:

Income Tax Expense	$20,000	
Deferred Income Taxes	8,000	
Cash, or Accrued Taxes Payable		$28,000

It is unusual for deferred income taxes to reverse exactly in two years. Many companies have considerable balances in deferred tax liabilities because they use straight-line depreciation for book purposes and an accelerated method for tax purposes. Income tax law permits

Different depreciation methods for tax and financial reporting cause deferred taxes.

much faster depreciation than the straight-line method does and allows an item to be depreciated over a shorter period than its expected useful life.

The same total depreciation is deducted over the life of the item for tax and reporting purposes, but taxes are postponed when an accelerated depreciation method is used to report them. The taxpayer receives, in effect, an interest-free loan in the amount of the taxes deferred. For example, suppose that Interstate Shipping, Inc., purchases a piece of equipment for $3,000 that has a three-year life. Interstate uses straight-line depreciation for financial reporting and an accelerated method for reporting taxes. In each year of the life of the equipment, revenues are $10,000 and all other expenses are $5,000. Interstate pays taxes of 40% of taxable income.

For Financial Reporting

	Year 1	Year 2	Year 3	Total
Revenue	$10,000	$10,000	$10,000	$ 30,000
Depreciation	(1,000)	(1,000)	(1,000)	(3,000)
Other Expenses	(5,000)	(5,000)	(5,000)	(15,000)
Taxable Income	4,000	4,000	4,000	12,000
Taxes (40%)	(1,600)	(1,600)	(1,600)	(4,800)
Net Income	$ 2,400	$ 2,400	$ 2,400	$ 7,200

For Tax Reporting

	Year 1	Year 2	Year 3	Total
Revenue	$10,000	$10,000	$10,000	$ 30,000
Depreciation	(1,500)	(1,000)	(500)	(3,000)
Other Expenses	(5,000)	(5,000)	(5,000)	(15,000)
Taxable Income	3,500	4,000	4,500	12,000
Taxes (40%)	(1,400)	(1,600)	(1,800)	(4,800)
Net Income	$ 2,100	$ 2,400	$ 2,700	$ 7,200
Tax Deferred (difference)	$ 200	0	($ 200)*	0

*A negative difference in this example means that less depreciation is recorded on the tax return than in the financial statements, increasing the amount of tax due.

In year 1, Interstate defers $200 in taxes. In year 2, the tax on income reported for both tax and financial statement purposes is the same. In year 3, the depreciation for tax purposes is less than the depreciation for financial reporting and the $200 deferred in year 1 is paid.

Interestingly, if Interstate purchased another $3,000 asset in year 3, the accelerated depreciation on the second asset would defer the $200 for two more years. This is called the **rollover effect.** If Interstate continued to purchase new assets, the initially deferred $200 would never come due. When companies are growing, larger and larger amounts of tax are deferred each year because firms acquire replacement assets at costs higher than the costs of the assets replaced. As a result, the **deferred tax liability** grows each period because the accelerated depreciation and, hence, the amount of tax deferred is greater on the new asset than it was on the old one.

The example that follows shows the annual tax deferrals over nine years as a company purchases five machines, one every third year. For simplicity, replacement cost does not increase and each machine yields a pattern of tax deferral identical to the previous example: $200 deferred in the first year and paid in the third year. In this example, as the $200 comes due in year 3 of the machine's life, the $200 tax deferral from accelerated depreciation in year 1 of a new machine "rolls over" the liability for another three years.

The rollover effect may defer payment indefinately.

Year

Machine	1	2	3	4	5	6	7	8	9	etc.
1	$200	0	($200)							
2			$200	0	($200)					
3					$200	0	($200)			
4							$200	0	($200)	
5									$200	etc.
Total Tax Deferred	$200	0	0	0	0	0	0	0	0	etc.

The tax liabilities in this example roll over very quickly. For actual companies, the time required for tax liabilities to roll over is often quite long; as a result, the deferred income tax liabilities of many companies represent more than 20% of their total shareholders' equity. For Boise Cascade, 1990 deferred taxes were 25% of total stockholders' equity. This means that if the tax expenses that created the deferred tax liability had not been recorded, the stockholders' equity in Boise Cascade would be 25% larger (an arguable position; due to the rollover effect, that amount probably will never be paid!).

Deferred Tax Assets

Far less common than deferred tax liabilities are **deferred tax assets,** which arise when earnings are recognized for tax purposes before they are recognized for accounting purposes. A deferred tax asset is, in effect, a prepayment of taxes. A company that receives 19X2 rent on a building in advance on December 31, 19X1, records the payment as a liability (to furnish space to the renter in the next year). Tax law, however, recognizes a rent receipt as taxable in the year in which it is received, so the company must pay the tax on the rent payment in 19X1. The rent receipt and the related tax payment are recorded as follows, at a 30% tax rate. The deferred tax is an asset in the balance sheet.

December 31, 19X1

Cash	$10,000	
Rent Received in Advance		$10,000
Rent is received for 19X2.		

19X2

Deferred Tax Asset	3,000	
Cash		3,000
Taxes are paid on 19X1 taxable income, including tax on the unearned rent received in advance in 19X1.		

Rent Received in Advance	10,000	
Rent Revenue		10,000
The rent received in advance in 19X1 is earned.		

Tax Expense	3,000	
Deferred Tax Asset		3,000
Tax expense is recognized on the 19X2 accounting earnings, including the rent received in advance in 19X1 and earned in 19X2.		

Exhibit 7–3 shows selected deferred tax information from note 2 of Boise Cascade's 1990 annual report. Boise Cascade showed a tax expense of $46,130,000 on its income statement and a total deferred tax liability (for the current and all past years) of $394,162,000 on its balance sheet. Note 2 shows how the tax expense was calculated and how the difference between accounting and tax depreciation, and other items created the 1990 addition to Boise Cascade's deferred tax liability.

SOLVENCY RATIOS

Too much debt increases risk.

Solvency ratios are sometimes called overall ratios or debt and equity ratios because they are used to evaluate a company's capital structure. Liquidity ratios (discussed in chapter 4) assist analysts in examining a

Exhibit 7–3
Deferred Tax

The deferred income tax provision results from timing differences in recognition of revenue and expense for tax and financial reporting purposes. The nature of these differences and the tax effect of each are as follows:

	Year Ended December 31		
	1990	1989	1988
	(expressed in thousands)		
Book depreciation less than tax depreciation	$ 52,325	$ 37,834	$ 24,712
Expenses deferred for book purposes	6,293	—	—
Investment and other tax credits used	—	—	19,631
Other	(4,172)	(1,808)	3,218
Deferred income tax provision	$ 54,446	$ 36,026	$ 47,561

company's ability to pay its short-term debts. Solvency ratios assist the analyst in assessing the relative size of the claims of long-term creditors, compared to the claims or property rights of owners.

Too much long-term debt places restrictions on management and increases risk to stockholders. Large amounts of long-term debt increase the fixed charges against income each period. The times interest earned ratio assists analysts in evaluating the burden of fixed interest charges. This ratio is similar to the rules of thumb that say a consumer's house payment or house and car payments should only be a certain percent of the consumer's income. The proportion of company income that should be consumed by interest, however, varies from industry to industry.

Another effect of high levels of long-term debt is added risk to creditors. As levels of long-term debt rise, creditors are reluctant to continue to loan money to a company. Eventually, funds will not be available or will be available only at very high interest rates.

The more common ratios used to evaluate a company's solvency or overall debt and equity position, with calculations of the same measures for Boise Cascade for 1990, follow. We have used total debt where debt is specified. (Some analysts prefer to use only noncurrent debt.)

$$Times\ Interest\ Earned\ Ratio = \frac{Earnings\ before\ Interest\ and\ Taxes^*}{Interest\ Expense}$$

*Often calculated by adding interest and taxes to net income.

$$= \frac{\$75,270 + \$46,130 + \$116,620}{\$116,620} = 2.04\ times$$

$$\text{Debt to Total Assets} = \frac{Debt}{Total\ Assets}$$

$$= \frac{\$758,372 + \$1,934,504 + \$516,363}{\$4,784,770} = 67.07\%$$

$$\text{Debt to Stockholders' Equity} = \frac{Debt}{Stockholders'\ Equity}$$

$$= \frac{\$758,372 + \$1,934,504 + \$516,363}{\$1,575,531} = 2.037\%$$

Too much debt can be bad, but debt, in itself, is not bad—no more than using a mortgage to purchase a home is bad. In both instances, the danger is in the level of total indebtedness and the burden of the resulting fixed payments.

SUMMARY

Notes, mortgages, and bonds are the most common forms of long term debt. These obligations are reported at the present values of their future payments. Bonds are issued at a premium when the effective interest rate is less than the nominal interest rate and at a discount when the effective rate is higher than the nominal rate. The resulting discount or premium is amortized as an adjustment to interest expense. Unamortized premium or discount are shown separately from the face value of the debt.

Most companies experience some differences in the timing of revenues or expenses for tax and financial reporting purposes. Such companies must show deferred tax assets or liabilities. The income statement shows the income tax that the company would have paid if it had used the same method for tax purposes that it used for accounting purposes.

DEMONSTRATION PROBLEM

Barker Company has two loans: a five-year mortgage on a plant for $300,000 at 8% interest, and $500,000 in five-year bonds at 10% interest. The bonds were issued for $463,000 when the effective (market) interest rate was 12%. (Note that these bonds were issued at a $37,000 discount because the effective rate of 12% means investors are demanding a higher interest rate than the bond's nominal rate of 10%. The text of the chapter illustrates bonds issued at a premium.) The mortgage was issued when the effective (market) interest rate was 8%.

The mortgage is paid annually; the bonds, semiannually. Both loans were made on December 31. Because the bonds pay interest twice a year, each interest payment is one-half the annual payment and interest expense for each six-month period is one-half the effective rate times the book value of the debt. Most bonds pay interest semiannually.

REQUIRED:

Create loan-amortization schedules for both loans. Use the effective interest rate method. Make the journal entries for each loan and for the first two payments on each loan.

Solution to Demonstration Problem

When Barker received the $300,000 from the mortgage loan, the company recorded the receipt as follows.

Cash	$300,000	
Mortgage Payable		$300,000

A loan-amortization schedule for Barker's mortgage, showing how each payment is split between principal and interest, follows. Annual payment is computed to be $75,131.48 ($300,000/3.993).

Year	Principal Amount p	Rate r	Interest Expense $i = pr$	Annual Payment a	Applied to Principal $(a) - (i)$
1	$300,000.00	.08	$24,000.00	$75,131.48	$51,131.48
2	248,868.52	.08	19,909.48	75,131.48	55,222.00
3	193,646.52	.08	15,491.72	75,131.48	59,639.76
4	134,006.77	.08	10,720.54	75,131.48	64,410.94
5	69,595.84	.08	5,567.67	75,131.48	69,563.81*

*Difference due to rounding.

Now it is simple to make the journal entries for each mortgage payment. Cash is credited for the amount of the payment, and debits are made to interest expense and to the mortgage principal for the amounts in the schedule. The first two payments on the mortgage are journalized.

Interest Expense	$24,000.00	
Mortgage Payable	51,131.48	
Cash		$75,131.48

Interest Expense	$19,909.48	
Mortgage Payable	55,222.00	
Cash		$75,131.48

When Barker issues the bonds, the company records the bonds at their face amount of $500,000, even though cash of only $463,000 is received.

Cash	$463,000	
Discount on Bonds Payable	$ 37,000	
Bonds Payable		$500,000

A loan-amortization table for Barker's bonds, using the effective interest rate method, follows.

Year	(1) Book Value of Debt D	(2) Effective Rate e	(3) Interest Expense E = .5eD	(4) Nominal Rate r	(5) Interest Payment P = .5rf*	(6) Applied to Debt (3) − (5) E − P
1	$463,000.00	.12	$27,780.00	.10	$25,000	$2,780.00
	465,780.00	.12	27,946.80	.10	25,000	2,946.80
2	468,726.80	.12	28,123.61	.10	25,000	3,123.61
	471,850.41	.12	28,311.02	.10	25,000	3,311.02
3	475,161.43	.12	28,509.69	.10	25,000	3,509.69
	478,671.12	.12	28,720.27	.10	25,000	3,720.27
4	482,391.39	.12	28,943.48	.10	25,000	3,943.48
	486,334.87	.12	29,180.09	.10	25,000	4,180.09
5	490,514.96	.12	29,430.90	.10	25,000	4,430.90
	494,945.86	.12	29,696.75	.10	25,000	4,696.75**

*f = $500,000 (the face amount of the bonds)
**Difference is due to cumulative rounding error ($357.39).

We can make entries for bond interest payments using the effective interest rate bond-amortization method:

For the first interest payment on June 30:

Interest Expense	$27,780.00	
Discount on Bond Payable		$ 2,780.00
Cash		25,000.00

For the second interest payment on December 31:

Interest Expense	$27,946.80	
Discount on Bond Payable		$ 2,946.80
Cash		25,000.00

Key Terms

amortization	investments
bond	junk bond
convertible bond	loan-amortization schedule
current liability	long-term note
debenture	mortgage loan
deferred tax	nominal interest rate
deferred tax asset	noncurrent liability
deferred tax liability	premium
discount	present value
effective interest rate method of amortization	rollover effect
	secured bond debt
effective (market) interest rate	serial bond
face amount	solvency (overall or debt and equity) ratio
foreign currency exchange rate	
forward exchange contract	straight-line amortization
future value	unsecured bond debt
hedge	zero coupon bond
indenture	

ASSIGNMENTS

7–1 Characteristics of Current and Noncurrent Liabilities

Several statements about liabilities follow.

a. Noncurrent liabilities are debts that will not be paid for at least one year or one operating cycle, whichever is longer.

b. The time standard for identifying current liabilities is the same as the time period for identifying current assets.

c. A noncurrent liability is a debt that is not paid during the period covered by the current balance sheet.

d. Current liabilities (such as accounts payable) are the short term debts incurred to acquire current assets (such as inventory, supplies, and prepayments).

REQUIRED:

Which of these statements are true?

7–2 Characteristics of Current and Noncurrent Liabilities

Several statements about liabilities follow.

a. Noncurrent liabilities are shown in the balance sheet at the amount that would be required to pay off the debt on the date of the balance sheet, excluding all future interest not yet due.

b. Current liabilities are debts that will not be paid during the period covered by the current balance sheet.

c. Any portion of the principal of a long-term liability that will be paid within the next year (or operating cycle) is classified as a current liability.

d. Noncurrent liabilities (such as notes or mortgage payable) are the debts incurred to acquire noncurrent assets (such as land, buildings, and equipment).

REQUIRED:

Which of these statements are false?

7–3 Accounting for Long-term Notes Payable

On balance sheet date, year 1, Bobby Del Fashions borrows $10,000 on a note payable at 10% interest, compounded annually, due in two years. Bobby Del Fashions pays the note when it comes due.

REQUIRED:

1. Calculate interest expense for each year.

2. What is the total amount Bobby Del Fashions will pay at the end of year 2?

3. Prepare the journal entries pertaining to the note for all years affected.

7–4 Balance Sheet Disclosure of Long-term Notes—Continuation of Assignment 7–3

REQUIRED:

How will Bobby Del Fashions present the note payable in the balance sheet at the end of each year?

7–5 Notes Recorded at the Future Amount Due

On balance sheet date, year 1, Kellogue Company borrows $20,000 on a long-term note at 15% interest. The note is due in three years and is recorded at the future amount due.

REQUIRED:

1. Calculate the interest for each year.

2. What is the total amount Kellogue will pay at the end of year 3?

3. Prepare the journal entries pertaining to the note for all years affected.

4. Prepare the T-account for the discount.

7–6 Balance Sheet Disclosure of Discounted Notes—Continuation of Assignment 7–5

REQUIRED:

How will Kellogue present the note payable in the balance sheet at the end of each of the three years?

7–7 Mortgage Amortization Schedule

Big Gear Company has a mortgage on its Chicago factory for $700,000 at 12% interest payable over five years. Payments of $194,186.60 are made annually.

REQUIRED:

1. Prepare a loan-amortization schedule showing how each payment is split between principal and interest.

2. Record the journal entry for the payment made in year 4.

7–8 Mortgage Payments

A loan-amortization schedule for a $200,000, 8%, six-year mortgage with annual payments follows.

Year	Principal Amount p	Interest Rate r	Interest Expense $i = pr$	Annual Payment a	Applied to Principal $(a) - (i)$
1	$200,000.00	0.08	$16,000.00	$43,263.07	$27,263.07
2	172,736.93	0.08	13,818.95	43,263.07	29,444.12
3	143,292.81	0.08	11,463.43	43,263.07	31,799.64
4	111,493.17	0.08	8,919.45	43,263.07	34,343.62
5	77,149.55	0.08	6,171.96	43,263.07	37,091.11
6	40,058.45	0.08	3,204.68	43,263.07	40,058.39*

*Difference due to rounding.

REQUIRED:

1. What is the annual payment?

2. Prepare journal entries for the first, second, and last annual payments.

7–9 Bond Issue Prices

Ingram Steel has financed the construction of three new plants with separate bond issues in years 1, 2, and 3. The amount of the bonds and their terms and issue prices are given here. All bonds pay 13% semi-annual interest.

Year	Total Bonds Issued	Issue Price	Term (in years)
I	$10,000,000	99	20
2	8,000,000	103	10
3	12,000,000	100	20

REQUIRED:

1. What is the nominal (contract) rate of interest for each bond issue?
2. In which year is the effective (market) interest rate below the nominal interest rate? Above the nominal rate? Equal to the nominal rate?

7–10   Bond Issue Prices—Continuation of Assignment 7–9

Three bond issues of Ingram Steel are described in the Assignment 7–9.

REQUIRED:

Give the journal entry for each of Ingram Steel's bond issues.

7–11   Bonds Issued at Face Value

On December 31, Faceco issues $1,000,000 in 20 year, 12% nominal interest rate bonds at face value.

REQUIRED:

1. Construct the first three years of a bond-amortization table for Faceco's bonds. Interest is paid semiannually.
2. Make the journal entries for the issuance and the second year interest payments.
3. Was the effective (market) interest rate greater than or less than the nominal rate when Faceco issued the bonds? How do you know?
4. Show how the bonds would appear in the Faceco balance sheet at the end of year 2.
5. Make the journal entry to record the last interest payment and retire the bonds.

7–12   Investment in Bonds Issued at Face Value—Continuation of Assignment 7–11

Assignment 7–11 describes bonds issued by Faceco. Backco Company purchases all the bonds issued by Faceco.

REQUIRED:

1. Make the journal entries for the investment by Backco and the second year interest payments. Interest is paid semiannually.
2. Show how the investment would appear in the Backco balance sheet at the end of year 2.

7–13 Straight-line Amortization; Bonds Issued at Less than Face Value

On December 31, KMG Company issues $10,000,000 in 20-year bonds at a 10% nominal interest rate bonds at 98.

REQUIRED:

1. Make the journal entries for the issuance and the first-year interest payments. Interest is paid semiannually.
2. Show how the bonds would appear in the KMG balance sheet at the end of year 1.
3. Make the journal entry to record the last interest payment and retire the bonds.

7–14 Straight-line Interest Rate Investment in Bonds Issued at Less than Face Value—Continuation of Assignment 7–13

Assignment 7–13 describes bonds issued by KMG Company. LPP Company buys all the bonds issued by KMG.

REQUIRED:

1. Make the journal entries to record the investment by LPP and the first-year interest payments. Interest is paid semiannually.
2. Show how the investment would appear in the LPP balance sheet at the end of year 1.

7–15 Straight-line Method; Bonds Issued at More than Face Value

On December 31, L. Smythe Limited issues $20,000,000 in 20-year, bonds at a nominal interest rate of 8% at 101.

REQUIRED:

1. Make the journal entries for the issuance and the third-year interest payments. Interest is paid semiannually.
2. Show how the bonds would appear in the L. Smythe balance sheet at the end of year 3.
3. Make the journal entry to record the last interest payment and retire the bonds.

7–16 Straight-line Amortization; Investment in Bonds Issued at More than Face Value—Continuation of Assignment 7–15

Assignment 7–15 describes bonds issued by L. Smythe Limited. Jones Company purchases all the bonds issued by L. Smythe.

REQUIRED:

1. Make the journal entries to record the investment by Jones and the receipt of the third year interest payments. Interest is paid semiannually.

2. Show how the investment would appear in Jones' balance sheet at the end of year 3.

7–17   International Debt Repayment

Overseas Company, headquartered in Nashville, Tennessee, borrows 1,000,000 pounds (£) from a banking firm in London. The exchange rate at the time of the loan is US$2 = 1 £. When the debt is repaid, the exchange rate is US$2.10 = 1 £.

REQUIRED:

1. Make the entry to record the loan in Overseas Company's accounting records.

2. What amount (in U.S. dollars) is required to repay the loan? Make the entry to record the repayment of the loan.

3. How can Overseas avoid the risk of exchange-rate losses on international transactions?

7–18   Deferred Tax Asset

Crayfish Company received a $45,000 cash payment in 19X4 that was not earned until year 19X5. Tax regulations hold that due to the nature of the receipt, Crayfish must pay taxes on the $45,000 in the year the payment is received, not in the year it is earned. Taxes due on the payment amount to $12,000.

REQUIRED:

1. Make the journal entry in 19X4 to record the receipt of the cash and the payment of the taxes.

2. How are the Crayfish financial statements impacted by the 19X4 transactions?

3. Make the journal entry in 19X5 to record the earning of the revenue and the expensing of the taxes.

4. How are the Crayfish financial statements impacted by the 19X5 transactions?

7–19   Effective Interest Rate Amortization; Bonds Issued Above Face Value

On December 31, Dalton Company issues $1,000,000 in 20-year bonds at a 13% nominal interest rate for $1,074,990. Interest is paid semiannually. The effective interest rate is 12%.

REQUIRED:

1. Construct a bond-amortization table for Dalton's bonds for the first three years. Interest is paid semiannually.

2. Make the journal entries to record the issuance and the first-year interest payments.

3. Show how the bonds would appear in the Dalton balance sheet at the end of year 1.

4. Make the journal entry to retire the bonds. Assume that the last interest payment has been made.

7–20 Effective Interest Rate Investment in Bonds Issued Above Face Value—Continuation of Assignment 7–19

Assignment 7–19 describes bonds issued by Dalton Company. Jesse Company purchases all the bonds issued by Dalton.

REQUIRED:

1. Make the journal entries to record the investment by Jesse and the first year interest payments. Interest is paid semiannually.

2. Show how the bonds would appear in the Jesse balance sheet at the end of year 1.

7–21 Effective Interest Rate Method; Bonds Issued at More than Face Value

On December 31, Green Company issues $20,000,000 in ten-year bonds at a 12% nominal interest rate for $22,457,768. The effective interest rate is 10%. Interest is paid annually.

REQUIRED:

1. Make the journal entries to record the issuance and the first year interest payment.

2. Show how the bonds would appear in the Green Company balance sheet at the end of year 1.

3. Make the journal entry to retire the bonds. Assume that the last interest payment has been made.

7–22 Effective Interest Rate Amortization; Financial Statement Presentation of Investment in Bonds Issued at More than Face Value—Continuation of Assignment 7–21

Assignment 7–21 describes bonds issued by Green Company. Jay Company purchases all the bonds issued by Green.

REQUIRED:

1. Make the journal entries to record the investment by Jay and the receipt of the first-year interest payments. Interest is paid annually.

2. Show how the bonds would appear in Jay's balance sheet at the end of year 1.

7–23   Deferred Tax Liability

Holsmith, Inc. purchases a piece of equipment for $10,000 that has a four-year life. Holsmith uses straight-line depreciation for financial reporting and sum-of-the-years digits for reporting taxes. Revenues are $10,000 in each year of the equipment's life, and all other expenses are $4,000. The tax rate is 40% of taxable income.

REQUIRED:

1. Calculate Holsmith's taxable income and tax expense for financial reporting.
2. Calculate Holsmith's taxable income and tax payable for reporting to the Internal Revenue Service.
3. By using an accelerated depreciation method for tax reporting, how much tax does Holsmith defer each year?

7–24   Wal-Mart Ratios

Ratios are frequently used to assess a company's solvency.

REQUIRED:

Calculate the following ratios for Wal-Mart for 1991:

1. Times interest earned ratio.
2. Debt to total assets.
3. Debt to total equity.
4. Debt to stockholders' equity.

7–25   Wal-Mart Long-Term Liabilities

Information about Wal-Mart's long-term liabilities is contained several places in the annual report.

REQUIRED:

1. What is the total of Wal-Mart's total long-term liabilities?
2. What financial statement note(s) gives additional details about Wal-Mart's long-term liabilities?
3. What kinds of long-term liabilities does Wal-Mart have? What interest rates is are being paid by Wal-Mart?

7–26   Present Value (Appendix)

The following problems provide a general review of the present value concepts discussed in the Appendix at the back of the book.

REQUIRED:

1. To accumulate $500,000 at the end of 20 years, how much must you invest today at an interest rate of 12%?

2. To accumulate $500,000 at the end of 20 years, how much must you invest today at an interest rate of 12% compounded semiannually?

3. What is the interest rate on a $5,000 investment that returns $7,000 at the end of five years?

4. A bond will pay $10,000 interest per year for ten years and $90,000 at the end of year 10. What will a lender pay for this investment if the effective rate is 10%?

7–27 Present Value and Bonds (Appendix)

Whitehall Company has issued the following ten-year bonds in each of the last three years.

Year	Face Value	Nominal Interest Rate	Effective Annual Interest Rate
19X1	$500,000	10%	12%
19X2	$100,000	12%	12% — 100,000 par
19X3	$400,000	12%	10% — 449,360 → premium

REQUIRED:

How much did Whitehall receive for each of the three issues?

7–28 Using Present Value to Calculate a Mortgage Payment

The Baby J Stores are considering purchasing a new plant. The cost of the plant is expected to be $2,000,000. The managers of Baby J have requested that City Bank make a $1,500,000 mortgage loan.

REQUIRED:

If City Bank loans Baby J $1,500,000 at 12% interest for six years, how much will the annual payments be?

7–29 DECISION CASE:
DEFERRED TAXES AND THE ROLLOVER EFFECT

The Milling Company is five years old and growing fast. Brenda Falco, Milling Company CFO, expects Milling to purchase a new $10,000 milling machine every third year. Machines have a 4-year life. "In fact,"

Brenda projects, "if we get that new contract and enter the California market, we could be buying two machines every three years."

F. B. Clary, Milling's treasurer, is delighted. "That's great, Brenda! With the tax break the government gives us when we buy those machines, we'll be able to defer a bundle in taxes. That will certainly help our cash position."

But Tom Brown, Brenda's administrative assistant, is disturbed. "I don't know, Brenda. If you acquire machines at that rate, we will build up millions in unpaid tax liabilities. Somehow that seems foolhardy to me. When might we have to pay all those taxes, anyway? Remember, we all own stock in this company."

Milling uses straight-line depreciation for financial reporting and sum-of-the-years digits for tax reporting. Taxes are of 40% of taxable income.

REQUIRED:

1. Show how Milling defers paying taxes by rolling over its tax liabilities. What amounts might be deferred each year?

2. Comment on Tom Brown's statement. When might Milling have to pay its deferred tax liabilities?

8

Corporations: Stockholders' Equity

LEARNING OBJECTIVES

After studying Chapter 8, you should be able to:
1. Describe the basic characteristics of a corporation.
2. Explain the major sources of stockholders' equity.
3. Record journal entries to record the issuance of common stock.
4. Discuss the characteristics of preferred stock.
5. Prepare journal entries to record the issuance of preferred stock.
6. Explain accounting for cash, stock dividends, and stock splits.
7. Record journal entries for the issuance of stock in exchange for noncash assets.
8. Understand accounting for treasury stock under the cost method.
9. Understand the statement of retained earnings.
10. Describe the concept of book value.
11. Explain the foreign-currency adjustment that might appear in the stockholders' equity section of a company's balance sheet.

This chapter discusses the corporate form of business organization and how corporations obtain funds. Our discussion of the stockholders' equity section of the balance sheet focuses on the accounts that constitute the sources of capital available to a corporation. We consider common and preferred stock, and stock reacquired by the corporation. Next, we direct our attention to the retained earnings account and the effects of dividends and appropriations. Finally, we discuss the foreign-currency adjustment account and the concept of book value per share.

CHARACTERISTICS OF A CORPORATION

The characteristics of a corporation include the following:

1. *A corporation is a separate legal entity.* Once created, it takes on a life of its own and operates as if it were an individual like you or me. A corporation can own property, lend and borrow money, enter contracts, conduct business, and sue or be sued in its own name, separately from its owners. A corporation can do essentially everything real people can do except vote and have babies (corporations can, nonetheless, influence legislation and create subsidiaries!). The other characteristics of a corporation come from its status as a separate legal entity.

2. *The owners of a corporation have limited liability for the debts of a corporation.* Proprietorships or partnerships are business arrangements and, as such, are not legal entities separate from their owners. Each owner of a proprietorship or partnership can act on behalf of the business and all the other owners. This can be dangerous: one partner can sign a contract on behalf of a partnership and, by signing, bind all the partners to the agreement. If one partner, acting for the business, borrows money or agrees to sell merchandise at a foolishly low price, all partners are bound by the agreement. They do not have to agree, or even know of the action. Each partner, individually, is liable for all debts and other obligations of the partnership. As a result, a plaintiff needs only to sue one partner (the richest!) to obtain relief. The plaintiff does not have to sue the partnership or each partner individually to obtain that partner's proportionate share of an obligation. Creditors can look to the personal assets of the owners to satisfy unpaid claims against the entity.

In contrast, stockholders (individual owners of a corporation) cannot bind the corporation or the other owners to a contract; the corporation (through its managers) must act on its own behalf. Each stockholder is not individually liable for the debts or other obligations of the corporation. Stockholders can lose only the amounts they invest (in stock) and thus can control their financial exposure. Creditors cannot look to the personal assets of the individual owners in the event of business failure.

The limited liability of corporate stockholders is very important. It allows large numbers of investors who do not know each other to become owners of a business, thus providing large amounts of capital. Investors who do not know each other are reluctant to become owners in a partnership because, as owners, they become liable for the foolish actions of the other partners and for all debts of the business if it fails. Large businesses such as General Motors Corporation or IBM could not exist if it were not for the limited liability of owners provided by the corporate form of business.

3. *A corporation has an unlimited life.* When a proprietor or partner dies, retires, or sells out, those wishing to continue the business must start a new one. Any change in ownership requires that a new business agreement be formed. Unlike proprietorships and partnerships, most corporations have unlimited lives, unaffected by changes in ownership. The death or withdrawal of one owner or the addition of another has no effect on the continuity of the corporation.

4. *Ownership in a corporation is easy to transfer.* Ownership changes in a proprietorship or partnership terminate the business arrangement and require that a new arrangement be formed: assets must be revalued and new capital accounts started for the new owners. In contrast, routine transfers of stock do not affect a corporation. Indeed, sales of shares among stockholders are not recognized in the accounts of the corporation. (Sales are noted only in the stockholder *book of record,* a listing used to determine who receives annual reports, dividend checks, and other correspondence.) Coupled with the limited liability of owners, this feature allows a corporation to raise more capital from a wider group of investors than can proprietorships or partnerships.

5. *Corporate ownership is separate from its management.* The owners of proprietorships and partnerships are usually involved in managing the business. Corporations, in contrast, are owned by stockholders, who elect a board of directors, and this board of directors establishes corporate policy and appoints the corporation's officers. Individual stockholders are not required to manage and attend to the day-to-day affairs of the corporation. A stockholder need know nothing about the business. Managers who are specialists can be hired.

6. *Corporations are taxed separately from their owners.* As separate legal entities, corporations are subject to state, local, and federal income taxes on their earnings. They are also subject to a variety of other taxes not ordinarily levied on proprietorships and partnerships. In addition, stockholders of the corporation pay income taxes on dividends received. This results in taxation at both the corporate and

individual levels and is called *double taxation.* Proprietorships and partnerships pay no taxes; their incomes are taxed only once, to the individual owners.

7. *Corporations are subject to many government regulations.* Because corporations are separate legal entities and their stockholders have limited liability against the claims of outsiders, corporations are subject to strong government regulation. Unlike proprietorships and partnerships, a corporation must adhere to a host of state, local, and federal regulations and restrictions. Adherence to these regulations is costly and a disadvantage of the corporate form of organization; however, these regulations are necessary to ensure that investors and creditors receive the information they need to make informed decisions.

Forming a Corporation

People form a corporation by applying for a *charter* from the state. The application includes the *articles of incorporation,* which contain (1) the name of the corporation, (2) the location of its offices, (3) the purpose for which the business is formed, (4) names and addresses of the incorporators, and (5) the dollar amount and number of shares of stock to be authorized. After approval by the state, the charter is granted and the incorporators elect a board of directors, who are responsible for the general management of the corporation.

Large corporations have the additional obligation of meeting certain filing requirements with the Securities and Exchange Commission, including an annual audit.

Corporations of a certain size must meet filing requirements (including an annual audit) with the Securities and Exchange Commission.

Corporations sell stock to obtain the funds necessary to commence operations. They incur various accounting, legal, and state fees in establishing themselves, called *organization costs.* These costs are carried as an asset on the balance sheet and are amortized to expense over their period of benefit. Many times the period of benefit is arbitrary because a corporation has an unlimited life; however, this period cannot exceed 40 years.

STOCKHOLDERS' EQUITY

In this section we examine the owners' equity section of the balance sheet. Remember from our discussion in Chapter 1 that *equity* is simply a term meaning "property right." Recall that in the basic accounting equation, $A = L + OE$, the property rights to the assets are held by the creditors and the owners. From the owners' perspective, the equation could be rewritten as $A - L = OE$. For a corporation, the owners'

$A - L = OE$, where OE is the residual amount accruing to the stockholders.

equity section of the balance sheet is referred to as *stockholders' equity* because the owners hold shares of stock representing their ownership interest.

The stockholders' equity section of the balance sheet shows the investment of the owners in the assets of a company and their equity interest (property rights) in those assets. The claims of stockholders are subordinate to the claims of creditors. They are a residual claim to the assets, honored only after creditor interests have been satisfied. (Remember, assets minus liabilities equal equity.) This is the key to understanding stockholders' equity: stockholders' equity contains no assets, but merely represents the owners' claim to those assets.

There are two basic components of stockholders' equity. They are invested or paid-in capital and retained earnings. **Paid-in capital** is the amount invested by the stockholders of the company, while **retained earnings** is the amount of profits that have been retained by the company since the company's inception. Exhibit 8–1 presents the stockholders' (sometimes called shareholders') equity for Gannett Company, Inc., an international diversified news and information company that operates newspapers, television and radio stations and outdoor advertising, research, marketing, printing and news subsidiaries. Notice that Gannett's balance sheet dates for year-end are December 25, 1988 and

Exhibit 8–1
Gannett Company, Inc.
Consolidated Balance Sheets

Shareholders' equity (excerpt)

	December 25, 1988	December 27, 1987
Preferred stock, par value $1:		
Authorized 2,000,000 shares: Issued None		
Common stock, par value $1:		
Authorized 400,000,000 shares: Issued 162,211,590 shares and 161,966,964 shares, respectively	$ 162,212,000	$ 161,967,000
Additional paid-in capital	37,233,000	28,329,000
Retained earnings	1,624,443,000	1,424,766,000
Foreign currency translation adjustment	(1,334,000)	(5,668,000)
Less treasury stock, 1,154,105 shares, at cost	(36,113,000)	
Total shareholders' equity	$1,786,441,000	$1,609,394,000

December 27, 1987. Some companies use a 52-week fiscal year while others end their fiscal year on a specific day of the week each year. This can result in some companies having a 52- or 53-week fiscal year, and therefore their year-end date may not be the same each year.

As you can see in the exhibit, the stockholder's equity section can become somewhat complex in a large corporation. We will examine in detail the stockholders' equity section of Gannett Company, Inc., and the procedures used in accounting for stockholders' equity transactions. Additionally, we discuss footnote disclosure associated with the equity section of the balance sheet.

SOURCES OF PAID-IN CAPITAL

Paid-in capital is the source of assets contributed to the company in several different transactions: the sale of stock, donations, stock dividends and other changes in capital structure. The primary source represented by paid-in capital is from the issuance of shares of stock. There are two basic types of stock: common and preferred. The corporation's charter indicates the maximum number of shares of stock that a corporation is **authorized** to issue for each class of stock. The number of shares **issued** is the total number sold by the corporation since its inception. The number of shares **outstanding** is the number of shares currently held by stockholders. In Exhibit 8–1, Gannett Company, Inc., has 400,000,000 shares authorized and 162,211,590 shares issued on December 25, 1988. The number of shares outstanding is 161,057,485. The difference between the number of shares issued and outstanding is the 1,154,105 shares held as treasury stock. There are 237,788,410 shares of stock **unissued** and not outstanding. The unissued shares and the shares of treasury stock do not carry any rights or privileges until they are issued or resold. The owners of the corporation are the stockholders owning the 161,057,485 shares.

The amount of stock initially authorized is generally quite large so that the corporation can raise additional capital by selling stock without having to request authorization from the state in which it is incorporated.

Common Stock

Common stock is the basic ownership equity of a corporation. A stock certificate is issued by the corporation as evidence of this ownership. The certificate contains information such as the name of the corporation, rights of the stockholder, and the number of shares owned by the stockholder. Common stockholders all have the same rights and privileges, including (1) the right to elect the members of the board of directors of the corporation, (2) the right to share in earnings, (3) the right to purchase additional shares of new issues of stock in the same proportion as they presently hold (called the *preemptive right*), and (4) the right to a proportionate share in assets upon liquidation of the corporation.

Occasionally, a firm issues more than one class of common stock. In such cases, classes are distinguished by differences in dividend preferences or voting rights.

Accounting for common stock is fairly simple. To illustrate, assume that Gannett Company, Inc., issued 200,000 shares of stock when the market value for its shares was $10 per share. Each share has a par value of $1. The following entry records the issuance.

Cash (200,000 shares × $10)	$2,000,000	
Common Stock (200,000 shares × $1)		$ 200,000
Paid-in Capital in Excess of Par		1,800,000

Note that any excess of the proceeds over the par value is credited to the Paid-in Capital in Excess of Par account. Sometimes this account is called Additional Paid-in Capital.

We should point out that most major corporations report the proceeds of the issuance of common stock in two accounts, the **par value** and the paid-in capital accounts. Beyond its use for financial reporting, *par* has little or no significance in accounting. Par value is sometimes called *legal capital*. It has a complex history difficult to summarize. Suffice to say it is the minimum contribution required by law from stockholders. Par value also establishes the maximum responsibility of a stockholder in the event of insolvency or dissolution.

What happens if a stockholder pays less than par value for his shares of stock? In this instance, we say the stock was sold at a **discount.** If a corporation suffers losses so severe that it cannot pay its creditors, the creditors can force the stockholders to pay to the corporation (and subsequently to the creditors) the amount of the discount on their shares of stock. This means that the *original* purchasers of stock issued at a price below par are contingently liable to creditors of the corporation. Because of this potential liability, many states have enacted laws that allow corporations to issue stock with no par value, avoiding the sale of stock at a discount. **No-par value** stock is recorded in the accounts at issue price without any Paid-in Capital in Excess of Par account.

To illustrate, assume that in our previous example the stock issued by Gannett Company, Inc., was no-par value stock. The entry to record the issuance is:

Cash (200,000 shares × $10)	$2,000,000	
Common Stock—No-Par Value		$2,000,000

Legal capital as it relates to par value protects creditors because it cannot be paid out to stockholders in the event of liquidation until the creditor's claims are satisfied.

If stock is sold at a discount, the original purchasers of the stock are contingently liable to creditors of the corporation in the event of liquidation.

Many states that allow the issuance of no-par stock still adhere to the concept of "legal capital" in that they require or permit the board of directors to designate a portion of the proceeds from a stock issuance to be stated, or "legal" capital. And, in effect, a stated value per share is identical to a par value per share. In most cases, the stated value per share is very low relative to the market value per share. This ensures against the stock being issued at a discount with a corresponding contingent liability. If, in our previous example, the 200,000 shares were no-par value stock with a $4 stated value, the entry to record the issuance would be as follows.

Cash (200,000 shares × $10)	$2,000,000	
Common Stock—No-Par, Stated Value		$ 800,000
(200,000 shares × $ 4)		
Paid-in Capital in Excess of Stated Value		1,200,000

Notice the similarity to the entry recording the issuance of stock with a par value. The only difference is that the paid-in capital account relates to a stated value rather than par value.

Preferred Stock

Corporations sometimes issue **preferred stock.** Normally, preferred stockholders are not entitled to vote; however, they are granted other rights or privileges not given to common stockholders. These preferences relate to dividends and claims on the net assets of the corporation and will be discussed in detail here. The characteristics or combinations of characteristics of preferred stock vary depending on market conditions and the target investor group of the corporation. Generally speaking, preferred stock appeals to investors who desire a fixed rate of return without the risk associated with common stock (for example, the risk of a fluctuating dividend rate). If, however, corporate earnings increase, the common stock may pay a higher dividend rate than the preferred stock.

In general, preferred stockholders do not vote but have other rights or preferences not given to common stockholders.

Preference as to Dividends

Dividends are distributions of assets by a corporation to its stockholders. The dividend on preferred stock is expressed as a percentage of par or, if no-par value preferred stock is issued, the dividend is stated as a set dollar amount. For example, if a 9%, $100 par value preferred stock is issued, the stockholder is entitled to a dividend of $9 per share of stock upon declaration of a preferred dividend. The preference entitles the holder to a dividend payment before any dividends are paid to the

INSIGHT 8–1
Preferred Stock Making a Comeback

Preferred stock is becoming an increasingly popular vehicle for companies attempting to raise money. This is especially true for banks attempting to raise their capital base. Just recently, Security Pacific Corporation (a West Coast banking giant) said it would issue $175 million of preferred stock to meet higher capital guidelines mandated by federal regulators. A day earlier, Citicorp said it was issuing $600 million in convertible preferred stock. The company had previously placed $590 million of convertible preferred stock with Prince al-Waleed bin Talal of Saudi Arabia. Barnett Banks of Jacksonville, Florida, raised $100 million from the sale of convertible preferred stock. Dick Still-inger, analyst at Keefe, Bruyette & Woods, said, "I wouldn't be surprised if there were more" issues because regulators have been prodding banks to raise cash to cushion their loan portfolios. The goal is to avert another financial crisis such as the one that necessitated the bailout of savings and loans. Cash raised through preferred stock sales helps satisfy capital requirements for banks.

What investors like about preferred stock is that at dividend time they are the first in line. Additionally, preferred stock often carries a higher dividend rate than common shares, which typically offer annual dividends of between 1% and 5% of the market value of a share. Finally, many issues of preferred stock are convertible to shares of common stock.

SOURCE: James Kim, "Capital Choice: Preferred Stock," *USA Today,* 8 March 1991, 3B. Copyright 1991, USA TODAY. Reprinted with permission.

common stockholders. Note that the preference does not ensure that a dividend will be declared—only that, if one is, the preferred stockholders will be paid first.

As you can see from Exhibit 8–1, although Gannett Company, Inc., has 2,000,000 shares of $1 preferred stock authorized, none is issued and outstanding. Preferred stock has become less important in recent years.[1] When one purchases preferred stock with a fixed rate of return with no voting privilege, the stock exhibits more of the features of debt than equity. When dividends are declared, the fixed payment on preferred shares is like interest on bonds but without the tax deduction to the corporation that bond interest affords. Preferred stock may be making a comeback, though, as discussed in Insight 8–1.

---

[1] In fact, of 600 firms surveyed in 1988, *Accounting Trends and Techniques* reported that only 165 had preferred stock outstanding.

A preferred stock may be **cumulative** with respect to dividends. In this case, the accumulated amount of any unpaid dividends from prior years must be paid before any dividends can be declared and paid to common stockholders. Undeclared cumulative dividends from prior periods are also referred to as **dividends in arrears.**

In rare cases, preferred stock is **participating.** This means that after the common stockholders have received a specified dividend, any remaining portion of the total dividend is distributed between common and preferred shareholders in some specified amount or formula. Thus, participating preferred stockholders can receive higher dividends when earnings and common dividends are high, participating with common shareholders in the company's success.

Dividends in arrears are disclosed in the notes to the financial statements. They are not liabilities until declared by the board of directors.

Preference as to Assets on Liquidation

Preferred stock normally has a **liquidation value.** This is an amount declared when the stock is issued and payable to the preferred stockholders upon liquidation of the company before any payment is made to the common stockholders.

Most preferred stock is outstanding for an indeterminate amount of time. However, some preferreds are **callable,** meaning the company can redeem them at a set price at its discretion. The call price is normally slightly higher than the issuance price so as not to discourage potential investors.

Convertible preferred stock entitles the holder to exchange preferred stock for common stock at a predetermined price or ratio (for example, four shares of common stock for each share of preferred). The advantage is that the stockholder is able to become a common stockholder and participate in the growth in market value or dividends of common stock if it appears advantageous to do so.

Redeemable preferred stock requires the corporation to redeem and retire the stock on a specified date at a specific price. It should not be confused with callable preferred stock, where repurchase by the company is not required. Occasionally, redemption is at the stockholder's discretion. Normally, the redemption price is considerably higher than the stock's par or stated value at the date of issuance and is also considerably higher than the issue price.

Accounting for the issuance of preferred stock parallels that of common stock: the proceeds are debited to the Cash account, the Preferred Stock account is credited for the par value, and any excess is credited to a Paid-in Capital in Excess of Par account. Frequently, for presentation in the financial statements, the preferred stock account and its related paid-in capital account are combined.

Dividends

As mentioned earlier, dividends are distributions of assets by a corporation to its stockholders. Normally, distributions are in cash, but sometimes other assets, such as marketable securities, are distributed. Corporations differ in their dividend policies, since to a large extent, dividends are a function of the amount and direction of earnings. Some firms believe in a stable or growing quarterly dividend payment. Others pay little or no dividend as they expand the company and increase earnings, choosing instead to allow the market value of shares outstanding to increase in response to increasing owners' equity.

Journal entries are made on the declaration and payment dates. No journal entry is made on the record date.

Three dates are important in accounting for dividends: (1) the declaration date, (2) the record date, and (3) the payment date. The **declaration date** is the date that a dividend is declared and its payment becomes a legal obligation of the corporation. It is set by the board of directors. On the declaration date, a record date and payment date are selected. Owners of stock on the **record date** receive the dividends paid on the **payment date.** Journal entries are required on the record date to record a liability, and on the payment date, when cash is paid. No entry is required on the date of record.

If shares are sold between the date of record and the payment date, who receives the dividend? Suppose on March 15 the board of directors of Sybex Company declare a 25-cent per share dividend on 10,000 shares of common stock outstanding, to be paid May 1, to stockholders of record on April 5. Stockholders who own the stock on April 5 receive the dividend even if they sell their shares before the payment date. This is because the corporation is unable to note the ownership change by the record date. Shares sold between the record date and the payment date are sold **ex-dividend,** which means without the right to receive the latest dividend. The seller reserves the right to receive the dividend. Sometimes shares are sold prior to the date of record. See Insight 8−2 for a discussion of this situation.

The following entries show the declaration and payment of the Sybex Company cash dividend. On the date of declaration the following entry is made.

Dividends Declared (10,000 shares × $.25)	$2,500	
Dividends Payable		$2,500

On the date of payment the following entry is made.

Dividends Payable	$2,500	
Cash		$2,500

INSIGHT 8–2
Ex-Dividend Date

But what about shares sold immediately prior to the date of record? In this instance, there may not be an adequate amount of time to notify the corporation of the transfer. Stock exchanges, such as the New York Stock Exchange, have a rule that new stockholders are entitled to receive dividends only if they buy the stock more than four business days before the date of record. If the stock is bought after this time, the stockholder is not entitled to the dividend. The date is known as the *ex-dividend date*. Assume the date of record was April 5. If this is a Friday, the ex-dividend date is April 1, or four business days before the record date. To receive the dividend, a new stockholder must purchase the stock on March 31 or before. If purchased on or after April 1, the stock trades without (ex) the right to the dividend.

If a balance sheet is prepared between the declaration date and the date of payment, Dividends Payable appears as a current liability. The Dividends Declared account is closed to (that is, reduces) the Retained Earnings account at the end of the accounting period.

Dividends Payable appears on the balance sheet as a current liability.

It is highly unusual for a corporation to rescind a dividend once declared. However, in March of 1988, a savings and loan association, Western Savings of Phoenix, Arizona, rescinded a 6-cent quarterly cash dividend and then declared a 5% stock dividend—"as if to let shareholders know that all was well." The cash dividend was rescinded because, based upon common stock repurchases, and a $1.9-million-dollar loss in the first quarter, the company was in violation of a loan agreement and could not pay the dividend.[2]

Stock Dividends

Frequently a company distributes shares of its own stock to its stockholders. These **stock dividends** are a proportional distribution of shares of stock issued to stockholders based on the number of shares held. For example, if a stockholder owns 100 shares of stock and a 10% stock dividend is declared, the holder receives ten additional shares. Although the total number of shares increases, the percentage of ownership of each stockholder is unchanged. Assume that the total number of shares of stock prior to a 10% stock dividend was 10,000 shares. The

[2] Sloan, Allan, "Phoenix' Wild West show," *Forbes*, May 30, 1988, 37–38.

stockholder owning 100 shares has an ownership interest of 1% (100 shares divided by 10,000 shares). After the 10% stock dividend, the number of shares outstanding is 11,000 and the number held by the stockholder is 110. The ownership interest is still 1% (110 shares divided by 11,000 shares). Logically, the total market value of all the company's stock does not change, but the market value per share should decrease to reflect the increased number of shares. If the market value per share was $110 before the dividend, it should decrease to $100 immediately afterward.

Before: 10,000 Shares × $110 = $1,100,000
After: 11,000 Shares × $100 = $1,100,000

The market value of the stock *should* fall in direct proportion to the number of shares issued; however, this is not always the case, as the market value of a share of stock is influenced by a myriad of factors.

Companies declare stock dividends for a variety of reasons. A corporation may want to conserve cash for expansion and so, instead of paying a cash dividend, issue a stock dividend. In this way management is able to "plow earnings back" into the business, meaning that the cash is used for operations. This is especially true for new companies attempting to grow. Companies may also desire to reduce the market price of their stock, and a stock dividend usually does that.

Accounting for Stock Dividends

As with cash dividends, the dates of declaration, record, and distribution (instead of payment), are important for stock dividends. Entries are made on the date of declaration and the date of distribution. However, unlike the case with a cash dividend, a liability is not created on the date of declaration, because a stock dividend is not a transfer of assets but merely a distribution of stock. To illustrate the accounting for a stock dividend, assume that Barron Corporation has the following stockholders' equity section prior to declaring a stock dividend:

Barron Corporation
Stockholders' Equity

Paid-in Capital:	
Common Stock, $50 par value, 10,000 shares authorized, 4,000 shares issued and outstanding	$200,000
Paid-in Capital in Excess of Par	100,000
Total Paid-in Capital	300,000
Retained Earnings	600,000
Total Stockholders' Equity	$900,000

The accounting for a stock dividend is dictated by the size of the dividend. Generally accepted accounting principles (GAAP) differentiate between a **small stock dividend** (additional shares are fewer than 20 to 25%) and a **large stock dividend** (those over 20 to 25%).[3] Let us first assume that Barron declares a 10% stock dividend on April 1 to the stockholders of record on April 15. The shares are to be distributed on April 30. The market value of Barron's stock on the date of declaration is $100. The following entry would be made on the date of declaration:

Retained Earnings (10% × 4,000 = 400) $100	$40,000	
Common Stock Dividend Distributable (400 × $50)		$20,000
Paid-in Capital in Excess of Par		20,000

GAAP requires that a small stock dividend be accounted for by using the market value of the stock at the date of declaration. When retained earnings is debited, we say we are **capitalizing** (reducing) retained earnings because a portion of retained earnings has been transferred to paid-in capital. The market value is used to capitalize retained earnings because the effect of a small stock dividend on the market value of the shares is likely to be insignificant—even though theoretically the market value should adjust proportionately. Some stockholders view the dividend as a distribution of earnings, and this reason is often used as justification for using market value. But is the stockholder any better off? A stock dividend is not a distribution of assets. Actually, total assets, total liabilities, and total stockholders' equity remain the same. Since the stockholder has not, in fact, realized income, the use of market value to capitalize retained earnings is of questionable validity.

The account Stock Dividend Payable is sometimes used instead of Common Stock Dividend Distributable; however, the account is not a liability but a stockholders' equity account.

Common Stock Dividend Distributable is a stockholders' equity account that is credited for the par (or stated) value of the shares to be distributed. If a balance sheet is prepared between the declaration date and the date of issuance of the shares, the account should be presented in the stockholders' equity section beneath the Common Stock account. On April 30, when the stock is issued, the following entry is made:

Common Stock Dividend Distributable	$20,000	
Common Stock		$20,000

If we review the stockholders' equity section of Barron Corporation's balance sheet after the issuance of the stock dividend, we find that

After the effects of a stock dividend are recorded, total stockholders' equity remains unchanged.

[3] The Securities and Exchange Commission has indicated that for purposes of filings with the commission, distributions of 25% or more should be considered large stock dividends and those of less than 25% small stock dividends.

the Retained Earnings account has decreased, and Common Stock and Paid-in Capital in Excess of Par accounts have increased. Total stockholders' equity remains the same.

Barron Corporation
Stockholders' Equity

Paid-in Capital:	
Common Stock, $50 par value, 10,000 shares	
authorized 4,400 shares issued and outstanding	
($200,000 + $20,000)	$220,000
Paid-in Capital in Excess of Par ($100,000 + $20,000)	120,000
Total Paid-in Capital	340,000
Retained Earnings ($600,000 − $40,000)	560,000
Total Stockholders' Equity	$900,000

Now let us assume that instead of a 10% stock dividend the company declares a 40% stock dividend. In this instance the distribution is deemed to be a large stock dividend, and GAAP requires that retained earnings be capitalized at the par or stated value of the stock rather than the market value.[4] A large stock dividend is more likely to significantly decrease the market value of shares outstanding, and will not likely be viewed as a distribution of earnings by investors. Therefore, the old market value of the stock should not be used to record the declaration of the stock dividend. The following entry records the declaration of the 40% stock dividend:

Retained Earnings (40% × 4,000 × $50)	$80,000	
Common Stock Dividend Distributable		$80,000

The following entry is made the date of the issuance of the stock:

Common Stock Dividend Distributable	$80,000	
Common Stock		$80,000

Notice that accounting for a large stock dividend causes the Retained Earnings account to decrease and the Common Stock account to increase by the same amount. The balance in total stockholders' equity is, again, unchanged.

---

[4] If a corporation declares a stock dividend on its no-par stock, the amount used to capitalize retained earnings is set by the state of incorporation.

Stock Splits

A **stock split** is an increase in the number of shares outstanding and a proportionate reduction in the par or stated value of each share. It is declared by the board of directors. For example, if a company splits its 1,000 outstanding shares of $10 par value stock 2 for 1, the number of outstanding shares is doubled to 2,000, and each share's par value is halved to $5. This type of transaction has no effect on stockholders' equity, and the total par value remains $10,000. After the stock split, each stockholder has twice the number of shares held prior to the split. No journal entry is made because a stock split does not affect any stockholders' equity account balances. The split is recorded in a memorandum entry noting the change in the par or stated value and the call and issuance of the new shares of stock.

The main reason for a stock split is to reduce the market price of the company's stock so it will be affordable to a wider range of investors.

The primary reason for a stock split is to reduce the market value of the stock to make the stock more attractive to a broader group of investors. Stock trading in a range of $30 to $50 per share is generally more favorably perceived than higher amounts would be, and many managers feel that a wider ownership base is desirable. Reducing the market value per share may also increase the rate of growth in market value as more investors trade the stock.

Less frequently, companies declare **reverse stock splits,** or *glue-ups,* accomplished by increasing the par or stated value and reducing the number of shares outstanding. The object here is to increase the market price of the stock. This technique is used when the market price of the stock is unusually low, although there may be other reasons for declaring a reverse stock split, as discussed in Insight 8–3.

Stock Dividends versus Stock Splits

A stock split results in an increase (a reverse stock split in a decrease) in the number of shares outstanding and a proportionate decrease (or increase in a reverse stock split) in the par or stated value per share of stock. Total par or stated value remains the same. On the other hand, even though a stock dividend results in an increase in the number of shares of stock outstanding, the par or stated value per share remains unchanged. The stock dividend does have the effect of increasing total par value.

Stock Issued for Noncash Assets

A corporation might issue stock in exchange for assets such as buildings, machinery, or land. In such instances, GAAP calls for recording the asset received at its fair market value or at the fair market value of the

INSIGHT 8–3
Reverse Stock Split

The nude "Playmate" on stock certificates for Playboy Enterprises, Inc., will not be there much longer. The "magazine for men" isn't changing its image; it is just trying to save money.

Since the company went public in 1971, the reclining nude has attracted thousands of "novelty" shareholders who bought one share just to get the stock certificate. Playboy has 14,000 "novelty" shareholders, and they cost the company $100,000 a year on administration and report mailing to service their accounts. Cutting that cost is part of the reason Playboy announced last week it will exchange one new share for every two old ones in a reverse stock split. Single-share owners get only a check and a facsimile of the old certificate.

"The new certificate will have no nude figure on it," company spokeswoman Terri Tomcisin said. It will have some figure, because the New York Stock Exchange requires human images on certificates to make forgery tougher. But Playboy has not decided whether to clothe its playmate or use another image.

Investor relations experts predict a number of one-share owners will forgo the check— 12 ⅞ at Friday's close—and keep their old certificates.

SOURCE: "Playboy Takes Stock of Nude on Shareholders' Certificates," *The Idaho Statesman*, 14 May 1990, 5A.

---

shares of stock, whichever is more clearly determinable. Assume a corporation acquired a building by issuing 1,000 shares of its $10 par value common stock. The corporation's stock is actively traded, and its market value on the date of the exchange was $25. The following entry is made to record this transaction:

Building (1,000 shares × $25)	$25,000	
Common Stock (1,000 × $10)		$10,000
Paid-in Capital in Excess of Par		15,000

Sometimes an established market for a company's stock does not exist. Typically, this is the case for a new company or for one whose shares are closely held and not traded actively. When there is no reliable measure of the value of the stock, the value of the asset received is used. For example, in anticipation of building a factory, the newly formed Rhoades Company acquired land by issuing 2,000 shares of its

$5 par value common stock. The land is appraised at $16,000. The following entry records the exchange:

Land	$16,000	
Common Stock (2,000 shares × $5)		$10,000
Paid-in Capital in Excess of Par		6,000

TREASURY STOCK

The balance sheet of Gannett, Company, Inc., in Exhibit 8−1 shows 1,154,105 shares of treasury stock in the amount of $36,113,000. **Treasury stock** is stock the company has reacquired but not retired. Corporations reacquire their stock for many reasons, including (1) for officer and employee stock bonus plans, (2) to increase earnings per share or the market value of the firm's stock, and (3) for use in mergers and acquisitions. Sometimes treasury stock is acquired to prevent a takeover attempt by another company. In each situation, the result is to reduce stockholders' equity. The corporation uses its assets (usually cash) to purchase the shares and reduces the number of shares outstanding.

Treasury stock is a contra stockholder's equity account, not an asset. This is why Gannett Company, Inc., has subtracted the cost of the treasury stock in arriving at total stockholders' equity. Treasury stock does not carry voting privileges or receive cash dividends.

Even though Treasury Stock has a debit balance, it is not an asset. It is a contra stockholders' equity account.

The method most generally used to account for the acquisition of treasury stock is called the **cost method.** Treasury stock is debited for the price paid by the corporation to reacquire the shares. When treasury shares are sold, if the sales price is greater than the cost to acquire the stock, the excess is credited to Paid-in Capital from Treasury Stock, and Treasury Stock is credited for the cost of the shares.

To illustrate the accounting for treasury stock, assume that Shoshoni Company acquires 500 shares of its previously issued shares for $20 a share. The entry to record the acquisition is:

Treasury Stock (500 shares × $20)	$10,000	
Cash		$10,000

If subsequently, Shoshoni sells 200 of the shares for $22, the entry to record the sale is:

Cash (200 shares × $22)	$ 4,400	
Treasury Stock (200 shares × $20)		$ 4,000
Paid-in Capital from Treasury Stock		400

Notice that even though Shoshoni sold the treasury stock for more than it cost, no "gain" is recognized. Instead, the difference of $400 is reflected as an addition to paid-in capital. The reason for this is that a corporation cannot legally create gains and losses by trading in its own stock. Consequently, it does not record the differences between the reacquisition and reissue price as gains or losses.

If the amount received from the sale of treasury stock is less than its cost, the difference is offset (debited) against previously recorded paid-in capital from treasury stock transactions. If there is no balance in this account, retained earnings is reduced (debited).

Shares of treasury stock are considered issued but not outstanding.

Shares of treasury stock are still shares of issued stock but are not outstanding. The proper form of balance sheet presentation is to list treasury stock as a reduction in stockholders' equity.

Donated Capital and Treasury Stock

Donated capital arises from donations to the company by shareholders or others of assets. For example, a city might donate a land site as an inducement to a company to locate in the city. If the land has a fair market value of $60,000, the company makes the following entry:

Land	$60,000	
Donated Capital		$60,000

The account Donated Capital appears in the stockholders' equity section of the balance sheet.

Sometimes a stockholder may donate shares of stock to the corporation, usually for the individual tax benefit he or she receives. Normally, only a memorandum entry is recorded when stock is reacquired through donation, noting the number and class of shares received. A formal journal entry is not required because the shares are acquired without cost. When these shares are subsequently sold, the proceeds are credited to the account Donated Capital.

RETAINED EARNINGS

Gannett Company, Inc., shows a balance in retained earnings of $1,624,443,000 at the end of 1988. Retained earnings, as discussed earlier, is the stockholders' equity (or property rights) arising from retaining assets in the corporation rather than distributing them to stockholders as dividends. Recall that retained earnings is increased at the end of the accounting period by closing out the income statement accounts and crediting the account for a firm's net income. Conversely, if a firm experiences a net loss for the period, the closing process results in a debit and a reduction in retained earnings. If the board of directors declares a dividend, the dividend reduces retained earnings. Retained earnings can also be affected by prior period adjustments and appropriations. These items are discussed later in the chapter. Remember that retained earnings is not *cash,* but is instead the source of assets not distributed to stockholders.

Statement of Retained Earnings

Because retained earnings is a significant part of the stockholders' equity section of a company's balance sheet, companies prepare statements of retained earnings that disclose the changes in the account during the period. Exhibit 8−2 is a statement of retained earnings for the Champion International Corporation from its 1988 annual report. (The term "Consolidated" as it appears in the title to this statement will be discussed later in this chapter.) Champion is in the forest products industry.

Some firms combine the reconciliation of beginning and ending retained earnings in a statement that reconciles all of the stockholder equity accounts. Exhibit 8−3 is such a statement for American Brands, Inc. from its 1988 annual report. American Brands is a multinational

Beginning Balance of Retained Earnings + Net Income (or − Net Loss) − Dividends = Ending Balance of Retained Earnings

---

Exhibit 8−2
Champion International Corporation and Subsidiaries
Consolidated Statement of Retained Earnings

	Champion International Corporation and Subsidiaries		
Years Ended December 31 *(in thousands of dollars)*	**1988**	1987	1986
Beginning Balance	$1,777,218	$1,463,795	$1,331,648
Net Income	456,445	382,012	200,832
Cash Dividends Declared:			
$1.20 Convertible preference—$.35 per share in 1986	—	—	(356)
$4.60 Convertible preference—$1.87 per share in 1986	—	—	(5,584)
Common—$.95 per share in 1988; $.72 per share in 1987; $.52 per share in 1986	(90,593)	(68,589)	(48,793)
Redemption of convertible preference shares (Note 9)	—	—	(13,952)
Ending Balance	$2,143,070	$1,777,218	$1,463,795

The accompanying notes are an integral part of this statement.

Exhibit 8–3
American Brands, Inc., and Subsidiaries
Consolidated Statement of Common Stockholders' Equity (in millions)

American Brands, Inc. and Subsidiaries

CONSOLIDATED STATEMENT OF
COMMON STOCKHOLDERS' EQUITY
(In millions)

	Common Stock	Paid-in Surplus	Unrealized Appreciation (Depreciation) on Marketable Equity Securities	Foreign Currency Adjustments	Retained Earnings	Treasury Stock, at Cost
Balance at January 1, 1986, as reported	$179.4	$63.4	$ 4.1	$(264.2)	$2,509.5	$(114.1)
Cumulative adjustment for change in accounting policy	—	—	—	—	(5.2)	—
Balance at January 1, 1986, as restated	179.4	63.4	4.1	(264.2)	2,504.3	(114.1)
Net income	—	—	—	—	364.1	—
Cash dividends	—	—	—	—	(240.2)	—
Two-for-one stock split, in form of a 100% stock dividend	179.3	—	—	—	(179.3)	—
Translation adjustments[1]	—	—	—	52.6	—	—
Net unrealized depreciation	—	—	(2.0)	—	—	—
Purchases	—	—	—	—	—	(34.0)
Conversions of preferred stock and exercise of options	—	(3.0)	—	—	—	24.8
Expenses incurred in connection with Plan of Reorganization	—	(0.8)	—	—	—	—
Balance at December 31, 1986	358.7	59.6	2.1	(211.6)	2,448.9	(123.3)
Net income	—	—	—	—	521.8	—
Cash dividends	—	—	—	—	(247.9)	—
Redemption of preferred stock purchase rights	—	—	—	—	(5.5)	—
Translation adjustments[1]	—	—	—	134.0	—	—
Net unrealized depreciation	—	—	(8.0)	—	—	—
Purchases	—	—	—	—	—	(17.3)
Conversions of preferred stock and exercise of options	—	(1.5)	—	—	—	15.7
Balance at December 31, 1987	358.7	58.1	(5.9)	(77.6)	2,717.3	(124.9)
Net income	—	—	—	—	580.0	—
Cash dividends	—	—	—	—	(237.1)	—
Translation adjustments[1]	—	—	—	(11.8)	—	—
Net unrealized depreciation	—	—	(0.1)	—	—	—
Purchases	—	—	—	—	—	(777.3)
Conversions of preferred stock and exercise of options	—	(6.9)	—	—	—	19.9
Balance at December 31, 1988	**$358.7**	**$51.2**	**$(6.0)**	**$ (89.4)**	**$3,060.2**	**$(882.3)**

(1) Includes exchange rate fluctuation related to pound sterling denominated debt which is a hedge of the Company's net investment in Gallaher Limited.
See Notes Accompanying Financial Statements.

firm in the tobacco, life insurance, distilled spirits, office products, and hardware businesses.

Restrictions and Appropriations of Retained Earnings

Companies sometimes show restrictions or **appropriations of retained earnings** in their financial statements. The effect of an appropriation is that a company cannot pay out dividends equal to its total balance in retained earnings. Because a decrease in assets, particularly cash, leaves less available for the payment of liabilities, creditors may restrict a company's dividend payments and treasury stock purchases before extending credit.

Exhibit 8–4 shows a debt restriction on retained earnings in the financial statements of Zenith Electronics Corporation's Company's 1988 annual report. Many states limit the amount of dividends that can be paid when a company holds treasury stock. That is, an amount of retained earnings equal to the balance in the treasury stock account is restricted and unavailable for the purpose of paying dividends to stock-

---

Exhibit 8–4
Zenith Electronics Corporation
Disclosure of Obligations to Maintain Working Capital and/or Restrict Dividends

Notes to Consolidated Financial Statements
Note 6: Long-Term Debt (excerpt)

The company's short- and long-term debt agreements contain certain restrictive covenants that, if not met, would cause acceleration of all the company's obligations under which it has borrowed money.

The principal restrictive covenants of the company's debt agreements are as follows: The company must maintain

- Tangible net worth of at least $440.0 million. The actual amount as of December 31, 1988, was approximately $498.0 million.
- A working capital ratio of at least 1.5 to 1. The actual ratio as of December 31, 1988, was 2.0 to 1.
- A ratio of adjusted income to net interest expense of at least 1.15 to 1. The actual ratio as of December 31, 1988, was 2.2 to 1.

In addition, there are restrictions concerning additional borrowings, and limitations on liens and retained earnings available for stock purchases or payment of dividends. As of December 31, 1988, approximately $18.2 million of retained earnings was available for the payment of dividends.

holders. Restrictions on retained earnings are normally disclosed in the notes to the financial statements.

Appropriations of retained earnings are one method of restricting dividend payments by reducing retained earnings to a certain level. (Remember that when dividends are paid, both the Retained Earnings account and the Cash account are reduced.) A company might wish to restrict dividends and thus appropriate part of retained earnings during such activities as (1) building a new plant, (2) purchasing other long-lived productive assets, or (3) paying off a large liability. Usually a company will record a formal journal entry to recognize an appropriation. For example, assume that instead of financing by selling stocks or bonds, a company intends to use internally generated funds to build a new plant. The company has $2,500,000 of retained earnings. To disclose its intentions, management might make the following entry:

Retained Earnings	$900,000	
Retained Earnings Appropriated for Plant Construction		$900,000

Entries to appropriate a portion of retained earnings do not involve cash.

Notice that the appropriation does not change the total balance in retained earnings, but only segregates total retained earnings into two components - the part that is appropriated ($900,000) and the part that is unappropriated ($2,500,000 − $900,000 = $1,600,000). Do not be confused into thinking that $900,000 of cash is set aside by an appropriation of retained earnings. Look at the journal entry recording the appropriation. No asset account is affected; the appropriation represents nothing more than a segregated portion of retained earnings. When the appropriation is no longer necessary, the journal entry is reversed. The Retained Earnings Appropriated for Plant Construction account is debited, and the Retained Earnings account is credited.

In practice, the use of formal journal entries to record appropriations is uncommon because most restrictions on dividends are best described by a note to the financial statements. However, this does not lessen the importance of restrictions on retained earnings. Disclosure of restrictions on retained earnings is important to stockholders and potential investors because the restricted amounts are not available for the payment of dividends.

Book Value

The book value of a share of stock is a measure of the stockholders' equity of that share of stock in the assets of a corporation. Many corporations regularly report **book value per share** in their annual financial statements. If a corporation has only common stock, book value per share is simply the total of paid-in capital and retained earnings divided by the total number of shares of common stock outstanding.

$$\text{Book Value per Share} =$$

$$\frac{(\text{Total Stockholders' Equity} - \text{Preferred Stockholders' Equity} - \text{Dividends in Arrears})}{\text{Number of Common Shares Outstanding.}}$$

The divisor does not include treasury stock or unissued stock. If Linda Loma Company has 1,000 shares of $20 par value common stock, additional paid-in capital of $10,000, and retained earnings of $22,100, then the book value per share is $52.10 ($20,000 + $10,000 + $22,100)/1,000 shares).

When a corporation issues both common and preferred stock, the calculation of book value per share is more complex. The book value of each class of stock is affected by the preferences attached to the preferred stock and we must determine the portion of total stockholders' equity attributable to each class. The book value of common stock is total owners' equity minus the property rights of preferred shareholders, divided by the number of common shares outstanding (for example, common stockholders' property rights divided by the number of common shares outstanding). The book value per share of preferred stock is the property rights of preferred stockholders divided by the number of preferred shares outstanding. We elaborate below.

If the preferred stock has a liquidation value, book value per preferred share is simply the liquidation value of the shares. If preferred stock does not have a liquidation value, its book value per share is simply the total of (1) the preferred stock par or stated value and (2) any paid-in capital in excess of par or stated value on the preferred stock, divided by the number of preferred shares outstanding. If the preferred stock dividends are cumulative, any dividends in arrears are added to the denominator. In cases where the preferred stock is cumulative and preferred dividends are in arrears, the book value per share is the liquidation value plus the dividends in arrears divided by the number of preferred shares outstanding.

To illustrate, assume that Best Company reports the following stockholders' equity in its latest balance sheet:

Paid-in Capital:

Preferred Stock, $100 par value, 7%, cumulative and nonparticipating, 1,000 shares authorized, 500 shares issued and outstanding. Liquidation value of $145 per share	$ 50,000
Paid-in Capital in Excess of Par - Preferred Stock	5,000
Common stock, $30 par value, 5,000 shares authorized, 4,000 shares issued	120,000
Paid-in Capital in Excess of Par - Common Stock	80,000
Total Paid-in Capital	255,000
Retained Earnings	97,000
Total Stockholders' Equity	$352,000

Assume that the liquidation value of the cumulative preferred stock is $145 and dividends are in arrears for two years. The current year's dividend has not been paid. The book value for the common and preferred stock are calculated as follows:

Preferred Stock

Cumulative dividends ($100 × 500 shares × 7%) for 2 years	$ 7,000
Current year's dividend not paid ($100 × 500 shares × 7%)	3,500
Liquidation value ($145 × 500 shares)	72,500
Total stockholders' equity allocated to preferred stockholders	$ 83,000

Common Stock

Amount allocated to preferred stockholders (as above)	$ 83,000
Amount allocated to common stockholders ($352,000 − $83,000)	269,000
Total stockholders' equity	$352,000

Book value per share is calculated by dividing the stockholders' equity allocated to each class of stock and dividing it by the number of shares outstanding for that class. The book value for preferred stock is $166.00 ($83,000/500 shares), and the book value for the common stock is $67.25 ($269,000/4,000).

Book value is not equivalent to either par or market value. Par value relates to common and preferred stock. Because of the use of the historical cost concept, the market value of a company's stock usually exceeds its book value. Book value, because of its dependence on GAAP and historical cost figures, is not a very valuable measure in assessing performance or predicting earnings or cash flows.

Other Items Affecting the Presentation of Stockholders' Equity

Theoretically, retained earnings represents the cumulative earnings less dividends paid over the life of the corporation. However, as we have seen, events such as stock dividends and certain treasury stock transactions may affect it. Additionally, retained earnings may be adjusted for errors made in recording revenues and expenses. When these errors are detected in the period in which they occur, an adjustment is made prior to preparing the financial statements. The errors might not be discovered by the company until a subsequent period. In this case, the company would have issued financial statements with incorrect amounts. Corrections of these types of errors are called **prior period**

Exhibit 8–5
Firecreek Company
Statement of Retained Earnings
For the Year Ended December 31, 19X3

Retained Earnings, December 31, 19X2, as reported	$ 265,000
Prior period adjustment—overstatement of depreciation expense	5,000
Retained Earnings, December 31, 19X2, as adjusted	270,000
Net income for 19X3	125,000
	395,000
Dividends for 19X3	(25,000)
Retained Earnings, December 31, 19X3	$ 370,000

---

adjustments. If an adjustment affects the income statement, it does not appear in the statement for the period in which the error was discovered. Instead, it is directly debited or credited to the Retained Earnings account and is reported as an adjustment to the beginning balance of retained earnings in the current year.

To illustrate, assume that the controller of Firecreek Company discovered in December of 19X3 that a mathematical error resulted in an overstatement of depreciation expense in 19X2 amounting to $5,000. The current period's depreciation expense is not affected. However, the depreciation expense for the prior period was $5,000 too high. That amount reduced the Retained Earnings account, leaving the account understated. Firecreek would make the following entry:

Accumulated Depreciation	$5,000	
Retained Earnings		$5,000

Exhibit 8–5 displays Firecreek's statement of retained earnings for 19X3:

Foreign Currency Adjustment

Consolidated financial statements discussed in Chapter 17, contain the financial statements of a parent company and its subsidiary companies, combined as if they were a single large company. Often consolidated statements include the financial results of subsidiaries located in other countries. Before the financial statements of a foreign subsidiary can be combined with those of a domestic parent, however, the financial statements of the subsidiary must be *translated* into U.S. dollars.

In the process of translation and consolidation, exchange rate fluctuations (that is, changes in the value of the foreign currency in U.S.
dollars), will cause a difference between the translated values of a
subsidiary's net assets and its stockholders' equity. This difference will,
of course, be either a debit or credit amount, and will require an
adjustment (a gain or loss) to make total debits equal total credits. The
cumulative **foreign-currency translation adjustment** (the debit or
credit amount accumulated over the years) is reported in the stockholders' equity section of the balance sheet.

Referring back to Exhibit 8–1, we see that Gannett Company, Inc.,
reported adjustments of $1,334,000 and $5,668,000 in years 1988 and
1987, respectively. Gannett discussed the adjustment in its notes to the
financial statements. The note is reproduced in Exhibit 8–6.

The translation adjustment arises because some of a company's
accounts are translated at current exchange rates and other accounts
are translated at different historical exchange rates. A foreign-currency
adjustment with a debit balance is a loss, decreasing the balance in
owners' equity; and a credit balance, using the same logic, is a gain.
These translation gains and losses are caused by a company's exposure
to exchange risk and are not included in determining net income.
Instead, they are accumulated and disclosed as a separate component of
stockholders' equity, normally reported between paid-in capital and
retained earnings until the parent company's investment in the foreign
subsidiary is sold or liquidated. At that time they are reported as part of
the gain or loss on sale or liquidation of the parent's investment. The
justification for reporting the gain or loss as a component of stockholders' equity and not as an item on the income statement, is that (1) the
gains or losses can have a significant impact on consolidated net income

---

Exhibit 8–6
Foreign Currency Translation Disclosure
Gannett Company, Inc.

Notes to Consolidated Financial Statements (excerpt)
Note 1: Summary of Significant Accounting Policies

Foreign currency translation—the income statement of Mediacom, the
Company's Canadian outdoor advertising operation, has been translated to
U.S. dollars using the average currency exchange rates in effect during the
year. Mediacom's balance sheet has been translated using the currency exchange rate as of the end of the accounting period. The impact of currency
exchange rate changes on the translation of Mediacom's balance sheet has been
charged directly to shareholders' equity.

because of large swings in exchange rates and (2) the gains and losses do not represent changes in asset values because they are unrealized and, in fact, may reverse in subsequent periods.

Unrealized Losses on Marketable Equity Securities

One other item might appear as a separate component in the stockholders' equity section: **unrealized losses.** This is the case when the total market value of long-term marketable equity securities is less than its total cost. In accounting for long-term marketable equity securities, unrealized losses are credited to a contra asset account and debited to a stockholders' equity contra account instead of being deducted in computing net income. The entry is:

Unrealized Loss on Long-Term Marketable Equity Securities	$10,000	
Allowance to Reduce Long-Term Marketable Equity Securities to Market		$10,000

Recoveries of unrealized losses recorded in earlier periods are handled by debiting the allowance account and crediting the account Unrealized Loss on Long-Term Marketable Equity Securities (the reverse of the entry just shown). Because of accountants' conservatism, recoveries can never exceed previously recognized unrealized losses (in other words, the investment cannot be recorded at an amount greater than its cost). The balance in the Unrealized Loss on Long-Term Marketable Equity Securities account will therefore always be a debit amount or zero. Exhibit 8–7 shows the disclosure of these unrealized losses on the-balance sheet of American Brand's 1988 annual report. The company refers to the unrealized loss on long-term marketable equity securities as "Unrealized depreciation on marketable equity securities."

RATIO ANALYSIS

Profitability ratios are expressed in a "return on" format - return on investment or return on sales, for example. Profitability ratios that relate the earnings reported by the company to the price of its stock or the dividend pattern established by management include:

$$\text{Price-Earnings Ratio} = \frac{\text{Common Stock Market Price}}{\text{Earnings per Common Share}}$$

$$\text{Dividend-Payout Ratio} = \frac{\text{Dividend per Common Share}}{\text{Earnings per Common Share}}$$

Exhibit 8–7
Disclosure of Unrealized Losses on Long-Term
Marketable Equity Securities
American Brands, Inc.

December 31	1988	1987
Liabilities and stockholders' equity		(Restated)
Consumer products and corporate		
Current liabilities		
Notes payable to banks	$ 433.9	$ 253.0
Commercial paper	289.2	492.0
Accounts payable	378.1	316.0
Accrued excise and other taxes	911.9	923.2
Accrued expenses and other liabilities	606.0	478.5
Current portion of long-term debt	106.2	6.4
Total consumer products and corporate current liabilities	2,725.3	2,469.1
Long-term debt	2,359.2	1,631.5
Deferred income taxes	160.4	138.6
Total consumer products and corporate liabilities	5,244.9	4,239.2
Life insurance		
Policy reserves and claims	2,448.0	2,365.9
Investment contract deposits	794.7	671.6
Other policyholders' funds	824.9	750.1
Other liabilities	227.4	181.2
Total life insurance liabilities	4,295.0	3,968.8
Redeemable preferred stock		
$2.75 Preferred stock, without par value, stated value and mandatory redemption price $30.50 per share	137.5	137.5
Convertible preferred stock—redeemable at Company's option		
$2.67 Convertible Preferred stock, without par value, stated value $30.50 per share	30.8	33.4
Common stockholders' equity		
Common stock, par value $3.125 per share, 114.8 shares issued	358.7	358.7
Paid-in surplus	51.2	58.1
Unrealized depreciation on marketable equity securities	(6.0)	(5.9)
Foreign currency adjustments	(89.4)	(77.6)
Retained earnings	3,060.2	2,717.3
Treasury stock, at cost	(882.3)	(124.9)
Total Common stockholders' equity	2,492.4	2,925.7
Total liabilities and stockholders' equity	$12,200.6	$11,304.6

The **price-earnings ratio** helps an analyst decide if the stock is overpriced or underpriced in the market for the income the company is reporting. The **dividend-payout ratio** helps an analyst determine what management is doing with the earnings produced by operations. Both ratios are important in establishing the price of the company's stock in the market.

The price-earnings ratio and the dividend-payout ratio for Boise Cascade are calculated below.

	1990	1989
Price-earnings ratio	$= \dfrac{\$26.00}{\$\ 1.62} = 16.0{:}1$	$\dfrac{\$44.38}{\$\ 6.19} = 7.2{:}1$
Dividend-payout ratio	$= \dfrac{\$\ 1.52}{\$\ 1.62} = .94$	$\dfrac{\$\ 1.52}{\$\ 6.19} = .25$

SUMMARY

A corporation is a legal entity characterized by ease of transferability of ownership, limited stockholder liability, unlimited life, double taxation, government regulation, and separation of ownership from management. Formation of a corporation starts with obtaining a corporate charter. Next, a board of directors is elected, bylaws are adopted, and equity securities, or stock, are issued.

Investments by stockholders are one source of capital for a corporation. Another is earnings retained or reinvested in the corporation. Holders of common stock are entitled to vote at stockholders' meetings, to receive dividend payments, to maintain their respective interest in the corporation if additional shares of stock are issued, and to share in the distribution of assets upon dissolution. Preferred stockholders do not normally have the right to vote but are first to receive dividends and distributions of assets in the event of dissolution.

Stock may or may not have a par value. Stock with no-par value might have a stated value set by the board of directors. Par and stated value are arbitrary amounts that historically are linked to protection of creditors and that are used as accounting values in the common and preferred stock accounts.

Corporations sometimes purchase and resell their own stock. The transaction is called a treasury stock transaction. Treasury stock is not an asset; its cost is deducted on the balance sheet in arriving at total stockholders' equity.

With minor exceptions, retained earnings is the accumulated net income and losses of the corporation, less dividend distributions, from the first day of company operations. While cash dividends are distributions of assets, stock dividends are not. Stock dividends require a transfer from the Retained Earnings account to the Common or Preferred Stock account and sometimes also to a Paid-in Capital account. A corporation might also issue additional shares in a stock split. Again, no distribution of assets occurs.

Appropriations of retained earnings are made by a corporation to inform readers that a portion of retained earnings is not available for the payment of dividends because of some special condition. Corrections of errors are treated as prior period adjustments in that they are direct adjustments to the beginning balance of retained earnings. Retained earnings might also be restricted as to dividend payments because of the provisions of loan agreements. Normally, a corporation presents a separate statement of retained earnings detailing the changes in the account for the period.

The book value per share of common stock, computed by dividing total stockholders' equity, less any preferred stockholder equity, by the number of shares of common stock outstanding, bears no relationship to par or stated value or market value.

DEMONSTRATION PROBLEMS

Demonstration Problem 8–1
On June 15 Challin Company issued 20,000 shares of its common stock with a market value of $20.

REQUIRED:

Record the issuance of the common stock under each of the following independent assumptions:

1. The common stock has a par value of $5.
2. The common stock has no par value, but a stated value of $15.
3. The common stock has no par or stated value.

Solution to Demonstration Problem 8–1

1. Cash (20,000 × $20)	$400,000	
Common Stock—Par Value (20,000 × $5)		$100,000
Paid-in Capital in Excess of Par—Common		300,000
Stock ($20 − $5) × 20,000		

2. Cash $400,000
　　　Common Stock—Stated Value (20,000 × $15) $300,000
　　　Paid-in Capital in Excess of Par Stated
　　　　Value—Common Stock ($20 − $15) × 20,000   100,000

3. Cash $400,000
　　　Common Stock—No Par Value $400,000

Demonstration Problem 8–2

REQUIRED:

Journalize the following transactions for the Mars Company.

Feb. 3　　Issued 3,000 shares of $5 par value common stock at a market value at $6.

Feb. 6　　Issued 2,000 shares of 8%, $25 par value preferred stock at $70.

Mar. 6　　The common stock split 4 for 1.

Mar. 17　A cash dividend of $.25 per share was declared on the common stock with a payment date of March 28. Also, a cash dividend was declared on the preferred stock with a payment date of April 1.

Mar. 28　The cash dividends were paid on the common stock.

Apr. 1　　The cash dividends on the preferred stock were paid.

Apr. 25　A 15% stock dividend was declared on the common stock to the holders of record on May 10. Distribution of the shares is to be made on May 15. The market value of Mars Company's stock was $26 per share.

May 15　Issued the additional shares from the stock dividend.

May 25　The company purchased 600 shares of its own common stock in the open market for $16 per share.

May 27　Sold 450 of the shares purchased on May 25 for $21 per share.

May 29　Sold the remaining shares of treasury stock for $15 per share.

Solution to Demonstration Problem 8–2

Feb. 3　　Cash (3,000 × $6) $18,000
　　　　　　Common Stock (3,000 × $5) $15,000
　　　　　　Paid-in Capital in Excess of Par -
　　　　　　　Common Stock ($6 − $5) × 3,000   3,000

Feb. 6	Cash (2,000 × $70)	$140,000	
	Preferred Stock (2,000 × $25)		$50,000
	Paid-in Capital in Excess of Par -		
	Preferred Stock ($70 − $25) × 2,000		90,000
Mar. 6	Stock split 4 for 1. Exchanged 12,000 shares of $1.25 par value of common stock for 3,000 shares of $5 par value common stock.		
Mar. 17	Dividends declared (12,000 × $.25)	$3,000	
	Dividend Payable - Common Stock		$3,000
	Dividends declared (2,000 × $25 × .08)	$4,000	
	Dividend Payable - Preferred Stock		$4,000
Mar. 28	Dividend Payable - Common Stock	$3,000	
	Cash		$3,000
Apr. 1	Dividend Payable - Preferred Stock	$4,000	
	Cash		$4,000
Apr. 25	Retained Earnings (12,000 × .15) × $26	$46,800	
	Common Stock Dividend		
	Distributable (1,800 × $1.25)		$2,250
	Paid-in Capital in Excess of Par -		
	Common Stock ($26.00 − $1.25) ×		
	1,800		44,550
May 15	Common Stock Dividend Distributable	$2,250	
	Common Stock		$2,250
May 25	Treasury Stock (600 × $16)	$9,600	
	Cash		$9,600
May 27	Cash (450 × $21)	$9,450	
	Treasury Stock (450 × $16)		$7,200
	Paid-in Capital from Treasury Stock		
	Transactions ($21 − $16) × 450		2,250
May 29	Paid-in Capital from Treasury Stock		
	Transactions ($16 − $15) × 150	$ 150	
	Cash (150 × $15)	2,250	
	Treasury Stock (150 × $16)		$2,400

Demonstration Problem 8–3

Lundem Company has the following stockholders' equity section on its current balance sheet

(handwritten in margin: par value of 200,000 shares issued)

(handwritten in margin: Book Val. Total Stkh. Eq. minus preferred)

Stockholders' Equity

Paid-in Capital		
Common stock, par value, 500,000 shares		
authorized, 200,000 shares issued	$600,000	
Paid-in Capital - Common Stock	400,000	$1,000,000
Preferred Stock, par value, cumulative, 5,000 shares		
authorized, 1,000 shares issued and outstanding		300,000
Total Paid-in Capital		1,300,000
Retained Earnings		2,300,000
Total Paid-in Capital and Retained Earnings		3,600,000
Less Treasury Stock - Common Stock (10,000 shares)		(50,000) .
Total Stockholders' Equity		$3,550,000

Answer the following questions by referring to Sundem's stockholders' equity section:

1. If the company had net income for the year of $75,000 and paid dividends of $12,000 on the common stock and $30,000 on the preferred stock what was the beginning balance in retained earnings?

2. What is the par value of Lundem's preferred stock?

3. Assuming that the company uses the cost method, what was the average price paid for treasury stock?

4. How many shares of the company's common stock are outstanding?

5. What is the dividend rate on preferred stock?

6. What is the book value per share of common stock for Lundem?

7. What is the par value of the company's common stock?

8. What was the average market price for which the company sold its common stock?

Solution to Demonstration Problem 8–3

1. Beginning Retained Earnings + Net Income − Dividends = Ending Retained Earnings
   ? + $75,000 − ($12,000 + $30,000) = $2,300,000
   ? + $75,000 − $42,000 = $2,300,000
   ? = $2,267,000

2. $300,000/1,000 shares = $300 per share

3. $50,000/10,000 shares = $5 per share
4. 200,000 − 10,000 = 190,000 shares outstanding
5. $30,000/$300,000 = 10.0%
6. Total stockholders' equity $3,550,000
   Less:
   Preferred stock equity (300,000)
   Common stockholders' equity $3,250,000/190,000 shares = $17.11 book value per share

7. $600,000/200,000 shares = $3 per share
8. $1,000,000/200,000 shares = $5 per share

Key Terms

appropriations of retained earnings

authorized shares

book value per share

callable preferred stock

convertible preferred stock

cumulative preferred stock

dividend-payout ratio

dividends

dividends in arrears

donated capital

foreign-currency translation adjustment

issued shares

liquidation value

no-par value

outstanding shares

paid-in capital

participating preferred stock

par value

preferred stock

price-earnings ratio

prior period adjustment

redeemable preferred stock

retained earnings

stock dividend

stock split

treasury stock

unissued shares

unrealized loss on marketable equity securities

ASSIGNMENTS

8–1 Characteristics of a Corporation

Discuss the characteristics of a corporation as distinguished from the partnership form of business.

8–2 Components of Stockholders' Equity
What are the two main components of the stockholders' equity section of the balance sheet?

8–3 Stock Dividends
Why would a corporation declare a stock dividend? Explain the difference in accounting for a small and a large stock dividend.

8–4 Stock Dividends versus Cash Dividends
Are stock dividends the same as cash dividends?

8–5 Stock Split
Explain a stock split.

8–6 Treasury Stock
Why would a corporation purchase treasury stock? Where does the account Treasury Stock appear in the balance sheet?

8–7 Appropriations of Retained Earnings
What is the purpose of an appropriation of retained earnings? What two methods are used in accounting for an appropriation of retained earnings?

8–8 Accounting for Issuance of Common Stock
On March 15 Celebrity Company issued 10,000 shares of its common stock with a market value of $25.

REQUIRED:

Record the issuance of the common stock under each of the following independent assumptions:

1. The common stock has a par value of $10.
2. The common stock has no par value, but a stated value of $12.
3. The common stock has no par or stated value.

8–9 Prepare Stockholders' Equity Section of Balance Sheet
O'Dhoul Corporation received its charter and was organized on April 25, 19X1. The charter provided that the company was authorized to sell 2,000,000 shares of $10 par value common stock and 300,000 shares of $50 par value, 8%, cumulative preferred stock. On the date that the company was organized, 1,400,000 shares of common stock were sold for $13.50, and 230,000 shares of preferred stock were sold for $55. There were no other sales of stock during the year. The company had net income of $2,345,000 for 19X1 and paid the required dividend to the preferred stockholders.

REQUIRED:

Prepare the stockholders' equity section of the balance sheet for O'Dhoul Corporation as of December 31, 19X1.

8–10   Terminology Relating to Common Stock

The stockholders' equity section of the balance sheet for Carlson Company on October 31, 19X1, shows common stock, $10 par, 100,000 shares authorized, 50,000 shares issued, 45,000 shares outstanding

REQUIRED:

1. Define the terms authorized, issued, and outstanding as they relate to common stock.

2. What is the dollar amount that would appear on the balance sheet next to the caption appearing above?

8–11   Accounting for Stock Issuances, Dividends, and Treasury Stock

REQUIRED:

Journalize the following transactions for the Juniper Company:

Jan. 2	Issued 2,000 shares of $5 common stock at a market value of $7.
Jan. 8	Issued 1,200 shares of 6 percent, $50 par value preferred stock at a market price of $60.
Feb. 15	The common stock split 2 for 1.
Feb. 18	A cash dividend of $.85 per share was declared on the common stock with a payment date of February 28. Also, a cash dividend was declared on the preferred stock with a payment date of March 1.
Feb. 28	The dividend was paid on the common stock.
Mar. 1	The cash dividends on the preferred stock were paid.
Mar. 25	A 10% stock dividend was declared on the common stock to the holders of record on April 10. Distribution of the shares is to be made on April 15. The market value of Juniper Company's stock was $17 per share.
Apr. 15	Issued the additional shares from the stock dividend.
Apr. 25	The company purchased 750 shares of its own common stock at $18 per share.
May 21	Sold 500 of the shares purchased on April 25 for $20 per share.
May 29	Sold the remaining shares of treasury stock for $13 per share.

8–12   Stock Dividends and Stockholders' Equity

Mackay Corporation showed the following stockholders' equity section on March 1:

Paid-in Capital:	
Common Stock, $50 par value, 10,000 shares authorized,	
5,400 shares issued and outstanding	$270,000
Paid-in Capital in Excess of Par	130,000
Total Paid-in Capital	400,000
Retained Earnings	530,000
Total Stockholders' Equity	$930,000

REQUIRED:

1. Assuming the company declared an 8% stock dividend on March 15, prepare the stockholders' equity section of the balance sheet after distribution of the stock dividend on April 15. The market value of the common stock was $63 on the date of declaration.

2. If you owned 600 shares of Mackay prior to the declaration of the dividend, how many shares would you own after distribution of the dividend? What was your percentage of ownership of Mackay Corporation before and after the stock dividend?

3. What would you expect the market value of Mackay Corporation's stock to do between March 15 and April 15? Why?

4. Prepare the stockholders' equity section of the balance sheet assuming instead that a 30% stock dividend was declared and distributed.

8–13   Calculation of Stockholders' Equity and Book Value

Esso Corporation had the following stockholders' equity accounts at November 30, 1991: Common Stock, $81,600,000; Paid-in Capital in Excess of Par Value - Common Stock, $29,000,000; Preferred Stock, $3,000,000; Treasury Stock - Common Stock, $4,700,000; and Retained Earnings, $293,500,000. The common stock has a par value of $25 with 10,000,000 shares authorized and 3,264,000 shares issued. The common stock purchased as treasury stock is accounted for by the cost method. There are 47,000 shares of treasury stock. The preferred stock is an 8% preferred, noncumulative and nonparticipating, with a par value of $100, 1,000,000 shares authorized and 30,000 shares issued and outstanding. The preferred stock has a liquidation value of $105 per share.

REQUIRED:

1. Prepare the stockholders' equity section of the Esso Corporation's balance sheet.

2. Calculate the book value per share of common stock for Esso Corporation.

8–14   Comprehensive Problem on Stockholders' Equity

Springstein Corporation shows the following information from the stockholders' equity section of its balance sheet.

Paid-in Capital

Issued in Excess of Par ——Common stock, par value, 700,000 shares
authorized, 300,000 shares issued $4,500,000

Paid-in Capital - Common Stock   1,500,000 $6,000,000

Issued at Par ——Preferred Stock, par value, cumulative, 15,000   *3,000,000*
shares authorized, 2,500 shares issued and
outstanding   400,000

Total Paid-in Capital   6,400,000

Retained Earnings   2,860,000

Total Paid-in Capital and Retained Earnings   9,260,000

Less Treasury Stock - Common Stock (24,000
shares)   (240,000)

Total Stockholders' Equity $9,020,000

REQUIRED:

Answer the following questions by referring to Springstein's stockholders' equity section:

1. If the company experienced a net loss for the year of $560,500 and paid dividends of $112,100 (including $26,000 on the preferred stock), what was the beginning balance in retained earnings?

2. What is the par value of Springstein's preferred stock?

3. Assuming that the company uses the cost method, what was the average price paid for treasury stock?

4. How many shares of the company's common stock are outstanding?

5. What is the dividend rate on preferred stock.

6. What is the book value per share of common stock for Springstein?

7. What is the par value of the company's common stock?

8. What was the average market price for which the company sold its common stock?

8–15   Comprehensive Problem on Balance Sheet Effects

Using the following headings, indicate the effects (+ for increase, − for decrease, or NE for no effect) of the following transactions on the accounts of ABC Company: Assets, Liabilities, Common Stock, Preferred Stock, Paid-in Capital (includes Paid-in Capital in Excess of Par and Donated Capital), Retained Earnings, and Treasury Stock.

1. A portion of retained earnings was appropriated for plant expansion by making a journal entry.
2. Treasury stock was purchased by the company at a price greater than its par value.
3. ABC declared and issued a 10% stock dividend on its common stock. The market price of the stock was in excess of its par value.
4. ABC declared and issued a 2 for 1 stock split.
5. The company declared and paid a cash dividend.
6. The treasury stock purchased in item (2) above was sold for an amount greater than the purchase price.
7. A cash dividend was declared on the company's preferred stock.
8. A 35% common stock dividend was declared and distributed.
9. A city donated land on which the company will construct a factory.
10. An additional 5,000 shares of preferred stock were sold for an amount in excess of par value.

8–16 Stock Issued for Noncash Assets

A new corporation issued 7,000 shares of $50 par value common stock to owners of a parcel of land that the corporation needs to begin operations. An independent appraiser estimated the fair market value of the land at $370,000.

REQUIRED:

At what amount should the land be recorded on the corporation's books? Why?

8–17 Wal-Mart Stores, Inc., and Subsidiaries Annual Report

Refer to the Wal-Mart Stores, Inc., annual report.

REQUIRED:

1. How many shares of Wal-Mart's common stock were outstanding at the end of 1991?
2. What was the total par value of Wal-Mart's common stock at the end of 1991?
3. What was the balance in Wal-Mart's Capital in excess of par value account at the end of 1991?
4. What was the balance in Wal-Mart's Retained earnings account at the end of 1991?
5. What was total shareholders' equity for Wal-Mart at the end of 1991?
6. What was the amount of dividends paid by Wal-Mart in 1991?
7. What was the book value per share at the end of 1991?

8–18   Wal-Mart Stores, Inc., and Subsidiaries Annual Report Ratio Analysis

Refer to the Wal-Mart Stores, Inc., annual report.

REQUIRED:

1. Calculate the price-earnings ratio for the year ended 1991.
2. Calculate the dividend-payout ratio for the year ended 1991.

8–19 DECISION CASE:
ANALYSIS OF STOCKHOLDERS' EQUITY

Ulbrich Corporation had a balance in Retained Earnings of $178,000 on December 31, 19X1. On the same date the company had a 10%, $40 par value preferred stock with 2,500 shares authorized, issued, and outstanding. The preferred stock is noncumulative and nonparticipating. The company had 1,800 shares of common stock, which it had purchased on the open market for $5,400. It also had common stock with a $2 par value, 200,000 shares authorized and a total par value of $360,000. Paid-in Capital in Excess of Par—Common Stock totaled $180,000. Net income for the year was $450,000.

REQUIRED:

1. What is the amount of total stockholders' equity?
2. What is the number of shares of common stock issued?
3. What is the number of shares of common stock outstanding?
4. What is the annual amount of dividends required to be paid on the preferred stock?
5. What is the total par value to be shown in the stockholders' equity section for the account Preferred Stock?
6. What is the book value per share of common stock?
7. Assuming that the common stockholders received a dividend of $30,000 and the required preferred dividend was paid, what was the beginning balance in the Retained Earnings account?

9.

Statement of Cash Flows

LEARNING OBJECTIVES:

After studying Chapter 9, you should be able to:
1. Recognize the importance of analyzing cash flows.
2. List the general sources and uses of cash.
3. Recognize the cash flows associated with the classes of activities found in a statement of cash flows.
4. Prepare a statement of cash flows using either the direct or indirect method.
5. Analyze a company's statement of cash flows.

$\mathbf{C}$ash flow is vitally important. It is so important, in fact, that one company, discussed in Insight 9–1, bases its managers' bonuses on cash flow rather than profit. Many small businesses that are able to generate net income using accrual accounting still fail because they are unable to generate sufficient cash to support operations. When a bank considers granting a loan or extending a line of credit, the lending officers want to examine the company's past and projected cash flows, not just accounting net income. The lending officers are more concerned about a company's ability to repay the debt than about its ability to generate accounting profits. Investors are interested in cash flows because they provide information about the company's ability to pay dividends. A profitable company might be unable to pay dividends if cash flows are poor—although sometimes a company with declining profits can pay larger dividends because of healthy cash flows.[1] This chapter discusses the statement of cash flows and shows how cash flows and accounting net income are very different measures of the same business activity.

[1] United Asset Management Corporation increased its dividend payment by 50%, from $2,672,000 in 1987 to $3,990,000 in 1988, even though net income decreased by 8% to $12,099,000 during the same period.

INSIGHT 9–1
Taking Cash Flow Seriously

"Put your money where your mouth is" is an idiom that challenges someone to risk money—to bet—on the truth of an assertion the person has made. In corporate circles, the management of Lifetime Products, Inc. does just that. In May of 1991, *The Wall Street Journal* made unfavorable comments about Lifetime. Jennifer P. Runyeon, president and CEO of Lifetime responded with a letter to the editor that asserted, among other things, that Lifetime's cash flow showed the company to be quite healthy. In the first quarter of 1991, Runyeon stated, Lifetime used cash flow from operations to pay off almost $3 million in debt. Additionally, the debt agreements for a recent leveraged purchase of Lifetime's principal subsidiary required only 25% of cash flow for debt service—compared to 90% to 100% of cash flow required to service debt in most leveraged buyouts.

In fact, Runyeon noted (presumably putting her money where her mouth is), Lifetime's management "gets paid a percentage of cash flow and gets no bonus if there is no positive cash flow." Lifetime apparently takes cash flow *very* seriously.*

*Ms. Runyeon's letter to the editor appeared in *The Wall Street Journal*, 21 May 1991, A23.

STATEMENT OF CASH FLOWS

For years, creditors and financial analysts have requested more information on cash flows. In 1987 the Financial Accounting Standards Board (FASB) issued Statement No. 95, "Statement of Cash Flows", which requires companies to prepare a **statement of cash flows** for inclusion in published financial statements. The general format of the statement is as follows.

Statement of Cash Flows
For the Year Ended December 31, 19X2

Cash provided by (or used in):	
Operating activities	$ 50,000
Investing activities	40,000
Financing activities	(10,000)
Increase (or decrease) in cash or cash equivalents	$ 80,000
Cash and cash equivalents, beginning of year	25,000
Cash and cash equivalents, end of year	$105,000

IMPORTANCE OF STATEMENT OF CASH FLOWS

The statement of cash flows assists financial statement users by:

1. Providing information about a company's liquidity, as shown in its short-term operating cash receipts and payments.
2. Providing information about a company's solvency, as affected by its investing and financing activities—including those activities not affecting cash flows.

Cash flows help assess solvency and liquidity.

  Liquidity refers to a company's ability to pay its short-term credit obligations. A company that is unable to pay its liabilities is not liquid. **Solvency** refers to the company's ability to meet all its credit obligations, short- and long-term. Solvency depends both on a company's ability to produce positive cash flows and its **capital structure** (proportion of debt to equity on the balance sheet).

  By determining and presenting the change in cash resulting from operating activities, the statement of cash flows helps analysts judge the **quality of earnings.** Analysts believe that the quality of a company's earnings is determined, in part, by the extent to which accrual net income represents increases in net distributable assets generated by

INSIGHT 9–2
The Quality of Earnings

Prominent financial publications such as *The Wall Street Journal* and *Forbes* as well as financial analysts have warned of decreases in the quality of reported earnings. "Earnings quality" is related to "paper gains" that are reported on income statements.

For example, companies using FIFO inventory during inflation charge old, and low, inventory costs to cost of goods sold. But they must spend much more to replace the inventory. The cash flow required to replenish inventory is not shown in cost of goods sold, so reported earnings are much greater than cash from operations.

Other practices that have created questionable profits are known as "front-end loading." Until the FASB stopped the practice, land companies reported sales on which they received miniscule down payments and for which default rates were extremely high. A company that sold a lot in Florida for $10,000, but got only a $200 down payment, would report the $10,000 as a sale. But the default rate on such sales was often over 50%.

Franchisers often used similar practices. A franchiser might require a one-time fee of $50,000 from someone opening a store. The fee might entitle the franchisee to services for some years to come, yet the franchisor might recognize the entire fee as income in the first year. Cash provided by operations helps analysts assess the quality of a company's reported earnings.

operations. Earnings of high quality ultimately generate increases in cash and cash equivalents (defined later in this section) that can be distributed to creditors and owners. Without the statement of cash flows it is difficult to judge the quality of a company's earnings. Additional discussion of the quality of earnings is contained in Insight 9–2.

The statement of cash flows also helps analysts determine the value of the firm and, hence, the value of its stock in the market. Many analysts believe that the present value of the firm is related to the amounts of its future cash flows (rather than to its prospective accrual earnings) and that the best basis for estimating future cash flows is a knowledge of present and past cash flows.

The statement of cash flows explains the change in cash and cash equivalents each period. **Cash** is all amounts that are available for withdrawal at any time without penalty or advance notice. **Cash equivalents** are short-term liquid investments. Treasury notes, commercial paper and money market funds can be cash equivalents. FASB No. 95 requires that securities be highly liquid, low risk, and within 90 days of maturity to be classified as cash equivalents.

The statement of cash flows explains the change in cash.

SOURCES AND USES OF CASH

Exhibit 9–1 contains a detailed listing of sources and uses of cash. It appears quite complicated. There appear to be many, many sources and uses of cash, but in fact, this is not true. Where can a company obtain cash? From operations, of course. But where else? A company can also issue stock, borrow, and sell assets. These are the four general types of sources of cash. All sources of cash listed in Exhibit 9–1 fall into one of these four general sources.

There are four general sources and five general uses of cash.

The general uses of cash are corollaries to the sources of cash, with one additional item. Operations can consume cash (instead of providing cash), the company may reacquire its stock, repay debt, buy assets and pay dividends. All the detailed uses of cash in Exhibit 9–1 are examples of these five general uses of cash, summarized in Exhibit 9–2.

As we saw in the general format for the statement of cash flows, Statement No. 95 requires a company to present its sources and uses of cash according to three classes of activities:

1. Operating activities
2. Investing activities
3. Financing activities

There are three classes of activities.

Let us now examine each class of activities and see which of the general sources and uses of cash apply to each activity.

Operating Activities

The FASB uses the phrase "associated with net income" to describe activities that should be classed as **operating activities.** Generally, all cash flows that do not result from investing or financing activities are presumed to result from operating activities.

Operating cash flows include all income statement items except gains and losses, as explained later. All financing expenses (such as interest paid) are income statement items and are included in operating cash flows. All investing costs (such as commissions) and income (such as dividends or interest received) are income statement items and are included in operating cash flows. All income taxes paid are operating cash flows. Other operating cash flows are shown in Exhibit 9–1.

Investing Activities

Making temporary, short-term investments is an operating activity. Making long-term, noncurrent investments is, for cash flow purposes, an

---

Exhibit 9–1
FASB Statement No. 95 Classification of Typical Cash Receipts and Payments

Investing Activities
Cash paid to:

- Acquire property, plant, and equipment and other productive assets (including capitalized interest) provided the cash is paid soon before, at the time of, or soon after the purchase.
- Acquire a business.
- Purchase debt (other than cash equivalents) or equity securities of other entities.
- Make loans to another entity.
- Purchase loans from another entity.

Cash received from:

- Sale of property, plant, and equipment and other productive assets.
- Sale of a business unit, such as a subsidiary or division.
- Sale of a debt (other than cash equivalents) or equity securities of other entities.
- Collection of principal on loans made to another entity.
- Sale of loans made by the entity.

Financing Activities
Cash paid to:

- Owners in the form of dividends or other distributions.
- Repay amounts borrowed—includes amounts related to short-term debt, long-term debt, capitalized lease obligations, and seller-financed debt.
- Reacquire treasury stock and other equity securities.

Cash received from:

- Issuing equity securities, such as common stock.
- Issuing bonds, mortgages, notes, and other short- or long-term borrowing.

Continued

---

investing activity. Investing activities consume cash when noncurrent investments are acquired, and provide cash when noncurrent investments are liquidated. (However, the *income* from a noncurrent investment—typically interest or dividends—is an income statement

Exhibit 9–1
Continued

Operating Activities
Cash received from:

■ Sale of goods or services, including receipts from collection or sale of trade accounts and short- and long-term notes receivable from customers arising from sales (including sales-type leases).

■ Returns on loans (interest) and on equity securities (dividends), including dividends from equity method investors.

■ All other transactions not defined as investing or financing activities, such as amounts received to settle lawsuits, proceeds of insurance settlements not pertaining directly to investing or financing activities, and cash refunds from suppliers.

Cash paid to:

■ Acquire materials for manufacture or goods for resale, including principal payments on trade accounts and both short- and long-term notes payable to suppliers for those materials or goods.

■ Employees for compensation.

■ Creditors for interest.

■ Governments for taxes, duties, fines, and other fees or penalties.

■ Other suppliers for other goods and services.

■ All other transactions not defined as investing or financing activities, such as payments to settle lawsuits, cash contributions to charities, and cash refunds to customers.

SOURCE: This exhibit was taken from Ernst & Young, *Financial Reporting Developments, Statement of Cash Flows, Understanding and Implementing FASB Statement No. 95*, January 1988.

Exhibit 9–2
General Sources and Uses of Cash

Sources	Uses
Operations	Operations
Issue stock	Reacquire stock
Borrow	Repay debt
Sell assets	Buy assets
	Pay dividends

item and hence is an operating cash flow.) The general sources of cash that are classified as investing activities are:

- Sale of long-term assets (inventory sales are operating activities)
- Sale or collection of loans (as a creditor)
- Sale of stock investment

The general uses of cash that are classified as investing activities are:

- Purchase of long-term assets (inventory purchases are operating activities)
- Becoming a creditor (lending money or purchasing a loan)
- Purchase of stock investment

Financing Activities

Financing activities include most of the transactions a company has with its stockholders and long-term creditors. (The major exception is interest, as explained shortly.) Financing activities provide the company its long-term capital. The two general sources of cash from financing activities are:

- Issuing stock
- Long-term borrowing (short-term borrowing is an operating activity)

There are only three general uses of cash classified as financing activities:

- Reacquiring a company's own stock
- Repaying loans
- Paying cash dividends

The cost of the capital provided by owners (stockholders) is paid as **dividends.** Dividends are distributions of income, not income statement items, and are shown as a financing use of cash. The cost of the capital provided by creditors is paid as interest. Interest is an income statement item and is an operating cash flow.

Dividends are not operating cash flows.

Noncash Investing and Financing Activities

Some investing and financing activities might not involve the payment or receipt of cash. A company might, for instance, issue shares of stock worth $500,000 in exchange for new equipment. Ordinarily, the issuance of stock is a financing activity providing an inflow of cash, and the purchase of a long-term asset is an investing activity, requiring an outflow of cash, so both activities appear in the statement of cash flows. But when the stock is exchanged for equipment, no cash actually flows, so neither activity is included in the body of the statement of cash flows. Examples of noncash investing and financing activities include the following (all asset, debt and equity items below are *noncurrent*):

■ Acquiring assets by issuing stock or debt (including capital leases)
■ Exchanging assets for debt or stock
■ Issuing stock in exchange for debt
■ Issuing debt in exchange for stock
■ Trading assets for other assets
■ Issuing debt to retire other debt
■ Issuing stock to retire other stock (common for preferred, or the reverse)

To avoid misleading financial-statement readers, Statement No. 95 requires that noncash investing and financing activities must be shown in a supplementary schedule to the statement of cash flows or in the notes to the financial statements.

PREPARING A STATEMENT OF CASH FLOWS FOR ABC COMPANY

Preparing a statement of cash flows is easier to understand in the context of an example. Data for ABC Company are given in Exhibit 9–3. We begin by examining the income statement in Exhibit 9–3.

Gains and Losses

Gains and losses are not cash flows.

As stated earlier, gains and losses are income statement items, but they do not always result from operating activities and the amount of a gain or loss is not directly representative of the amount (or even the direction!) of the related cash flow.

The income statement for ABC Company in Exhibit 9–3 shows the following item:

Loss on sale of equipment	$8,000

Exhibit 9-3

ABC Company
Income Statement
For the year ended December 31, 19X2

Sales revenue		$120,000
Less operating expenses:		
Cost of goods sold	$35,000	
Salaries	26,000	
Depreciation	15,000	
Loss on sale of equipment	8,000	
Other operating expenses (including income taxes)	12,000	96,000
Net Income		$ 24,000

ABC Company
Balance Sheets as of December 31

Assets	19X1	19X2	Increase (Decrease)
Cash	$ 25,000	$ 20,000	$ (5,000)
Accounts receivable	15,000	5,000	(10,000)
Inventories	10,000	25,000	15,000
Prepaid items	6,000	4,000	(2,000)
Property and equipment	400,000	250,000	(150,000)
Accumulated depreciation	(230,000)	(135,000)	95,000
Total assets	$ 226,000	$ 169,000	$ (57,000)
Liabilities			
Accounts payable	$ 7,000	$ 17,000	10,000
Salaries payable	10,000	6,000	(4,000)
Noncurrent note payable	63,000	0	(63,000)
Total liabilities	80,000	23,000	(57,000)
Shareholders' Equity			
Capital stock ($10 par)	90,000	80,000	(10,000)
Paid-In capital	21,000	17,000	(4,000)
Retained earnings	35,000	49,000	14,000
Total shareholders' equity	146,000	146,000	0
Total liabilities and shareholders' equity	$ 226,000	$ 169,000	$ (57,000)

The loss decreases earnings by $8,000. What is the effect on cash flow? Did ABC "lose" $8,000 in cash? No, it did not. The $8,000 loss resulted from selling equipment for $8,000 less than its book value. What then, was the cash flow? Was it an outflow or an inflow? Let us examine the journal entry for this specific sale.

Cash	$ 82,000	
Loss on sale of equipment	8,000	
Accumulated depreciation - equipment	110,000	
Equipment		$200,000

ABC sold equipment with a book value of $90,000 ($200,000 − $110,000) for $82,000 cash, resulting in a loss of $8,000 and a *cash inflow* of $82,000. The statement of cash flow will show an investing activity cash inflow of $82,000 from the sale of equipment.

Cash from Operating Activities

There are two methods for determining the cash flow from operating activities, the direct method and the indirect method. The only difference between cash flow statements prepared by the direct and indirect methods is the manner of calculating cash flow from operations. Everything else is the same. The direct method is more widely used than the indirect. The FASB encourages the use of the direct method but allows use of the indirect.

Direct Method

The direct method resembles a cash-basis income statement.

The **direct method** simply presents the major categories of operating cash receipts and payments. The amounts of these receipts and payments determine the net cash flow from operations. The direct method resembles a cash-basis income statement and might take the following form.

ABC Company
Schedule of Operating Cash Flows Using Direct Method
For the Year Ended December 31, 19X2

Cash collected from customers		$130,000
Less cash paid for expenses:		
For goods sold	$40,000	
For salaries	30,000	
For other operating costs	10,000	80,000
Net cash provided by operating activities		$ 50,000

In a statement of cash flows using the direct method, cash flows are generally determined from the revenue or expense accounts, adjusted for changes in the related asset and liability accounts during the period. Cash collected from customers, for example, is determined by adjusting sales for changes in accounts receivable. ABC Company (see Exhibit 9–3) had sales revenue of $120,000. Accounts receivable decreased from $15,000 at the beginning of the year to $5,000 at the end of the year. ABC must have collected cash for the entire $120,000 sold during the year, plus $10,000 from sales to customers in previous years, as shown.

Cash from customers equals sales plus or minus the change in accounts receivable.

Schedule of Cash Collected from Customers

Sales revenue	$120,000
Plus decrease in accounts receivable	10,000
Cash collected from customers	$130,000

Again referring to Exhibit 9–3, we can see how ABC determined the cash paid for inventories, salaries, and other operating costs. To determine the cash outflow for cost of goods sold, we must adjust the income statement amount for this expense for changes in both inventories and accounts payable. The logic is as follows: If the company sold only goods purchased for cash this period and sold all the goods that were purchased, the cash flow would be equal to the cost of goods sold expense: $35,000 for ABC Company in Exhibit 9–3. But when ABC Company increases inventories from $10,000 to $25,000 then an additional $15,000 in cash is consumed. However, ABC Company did not pay for all of its inventory purchases in cash. Accounts payable were $7,000 at the beginning of the year (representing inventory purchases from the previous year) and were $17,000 at year-end. ABC Company did not pay cash equal to its inventory purchases this year.

Schedule of Cash Paid for Goods Sold

Cost of goods sold expense	$35,000
Plus cash paid to increase inventory	15,000
Less payment postponed by increasing accounts payable	(10,000)
Cash paid for goods sold	$40,000

Cash flows for salaries and other operating costs can be calculated using similar logic. All figures are taken from Exhibit 9–3.

Schedule of Cash Paid for Salaries

Salaries expense	$26,000
Plus cash paid to decrease salaries payable	4,000
Cash paid for salaries	$30,000

Schedule of Cash Paid for Other Operating Costs

Other operating expense	$12,000
Less payment postponed by decreasing prepaid insurance	2,000
Cash paid for other operating costs	$10,000

Indirect Method

The **indirect method** does not determine the major categories of operating cash flows such as the cash cost of goods sold or cash paid for salaries. Instead, accrual net income as shown on the income statement is adjusted for changes in the related asset and liability accounts to determine cash flow from (or to) operations. For ABC Company, we have seen the effect on cash flow of the loss on the sale of equipment and of changes in Inventories, Accounts Receivable, Prepaid Items, Accounts Payable, and Salaries Payable. For ABC Company, cash from operations would be determined by the indirect method as shown in the statement of cash flows in Exhibit 9–4.

When the indirect method is used, cash provided by operations is calculated by (1) increasing net income for changes in the current asset and liability accounts that result in increases in cash from operations, and (2) decreasing net income for changes that result in decreases in cash from operations. If you examine the determination of cash flow using the direct method and the reconciliation of net income to cash flow using the indirect method, the following pattern emerges.

Change in Account	Effect on Cash from Operations	Add to (Subtract from) Net Income (NI) to Determine Cash from Operations
Increase in current asset	Decrease in cash	Subtract from NI
Decrease in current asset	Increase in cash	Add to NI
Increase in current liability	Increase in cash	Add to NI
Decrease in current liability	Decrease in cash	Subtract from NI
Items not consuming cash:		Add to NI

Some expenses do not consume cash.

When the indirect method is used, net income is adjusted for income statement items that do not consume or provide cash. We have

Exhibit 9–4

ABC Company
Statement of Cash Flows—Indirect Method
For the year ended December 31, 19X2

Operating Activities

Net income	$ 24,000	
Adjustments to reconcile net income to cash provided by operating activities:		
Depreciation	15,000	
Loss on sale of equipment	8,000	
Changes in operating assets and liabilities:		
Decrease in accounts receivable	10,000	
Increase in inventory	(15,000)	
Decrease in prepaid items	2,000	
Increase in accounts payable	10,000	
Decrease in salaries payable	(4,000)	
Cash provided by operating activities		$ 50,000

Investing Activities

Sale of equipment (book value of $90,000 — loss of $8,000)	82,000	
Purchase of equipment	(50,000)	
Cash provided by investing activities		32,000

Financing Activities

Repayment of note payable	(63,000)	
Repurchase of capital stock (capital stock $10,000 + paid-in capital of $4,000)	(14,000)	
Payment of dividends	(10,000)	
Cash used in financing activities		(87,000)
Decrease in cash or cash equivalents		(5,000)
Cash and cash equivalents, beginning of year		25,000
Cash and cash equivalents, end of year		$ 20,000

already seen that the $8,000 loss on the sale of equipment is not an operating cash flow. The $8,000 loss is added back to net income since the loss is not an operating cash outflow. (The $82,000 cash inflow resulting from the equipment sale—calculated earlier—is shown as an investing activity inflow.) Losses are added back to net income; gains are subtracted.

Depreciation and amortization are operating expenses that do not require operating cash outflows each year. Cash is used to purchase the asset being depreciated or amortized when it is acquired. In the following years, the depreciation or amortization expense deducted from earnings is only an allocation of the original cost to the period benefited. No additional cash is required. Because depreciation expense of $15,000 in ABC Company's income statement reduced earnings but did not consume cash, it is added back to net income in the reconciliation of net income to determine cash from operating activities in Exhibit 9–4.

Investing and Financing Cash Flows

Once we have determined cash from operating activities (by either the direct or indirect method), we examine the change in the period for the noncurrent account balances of the balance sheet items to identify other transactions that occurred. (We have already examined the current accounts.) When cash is increased or decreased, another account must be affected. For ABC Company, we see that—in addition to the changes in current accounts already analyzed—there were changes in Property and Equipment, Accumulated Depreciation, Notes Payable, Capital Stock, Paid-In Capital, and Retained Earnings. We can examine these changes in account balances to identify the investing and financing cash flows during the period. We must, ultimately, examine *all* accounts, for an account might have equal increases and decreases— such as the sale and purchase of land for equal amounts.

We know (as analyzed earlier) that ABC Company sold equipment for $82,000 cash. This cash inflow is shown as an investing activity in Exhibit 9–4. The changes in Property and Equipment and Accumulated Depreciation are analyzed as below.

	Property and Equipment	Accumulated Depreciation
Beginning account balance	$ 400,000	$ 230,000
Removed by equipment sale	(200,000)	(110,000)
Depreciation expense		15,000
	200,000	135,000
Ending account balance	250,000	135,000
To be explained	$ 50,000	$ 0

The $95,000 decrease in Accumulated Depreciation shown in Exhibit 9–3 is the result of the $110,000 in accumulated depreciation removed when the equipment was sold and the $15,000 depreciation expense of the year.

Property and equipment decreased $150,000 during the year as a result of the $200,000 in equipment sold and (we now discover) a purchase of equipment of $50,000. Both of these transactions are investing activities in Exhibit 9–4. The $200,000 equipment sale is shown in the statement at its cash proceeds of $82,000, increasing the Cash account. The purchase of equipment is shown as a $50,000 decrease in cash.

Notes payable decreased from $63,000 to zero. This repayment is a financing activity, as shown in Exhibit 9–4. The payment of notes payable requires cash and thus is shown as a decrease in cash on the statement.

Capital stock and paid-in capital decreased $10,000 and $4,000, respectively, when ABC Company repurchased and retired shares of its capital stock. This is a financing activity, consuming cash, and is subtracted on the statement.

Finally, retained earnings increased by $14,000. Since earnings were $24,000, we determine that ABC Company paid $10,000 in dividends during the year. The payment of dividends is a financing activity, using cash, and is subtracted on the statement.

ANALYZING ABC COMPANY

When we examine the cash flow statement for ABC Company in Exhibit 9–4, we can see that ABC Company had large cash inflows from both operations and the sale of equipment. These two items totaled $132,000. This cash was used primarily to purchase new equipment and retire debt. These two items totaled $113,000. Smaller amounts of cash were used to pay dividends ($10,000) and to reacquire shares of capital stock ($14,000).

ABC Company has a positive cash flow from operations.

How healthy are operations? Although we must also consider the changes made in the current asset and liability accounts (have we depleted our working capital?), earnings of $24,000 have resulted in an increase in net distributable assets (cash from operations) of $50,000, an indication of high quality earnings.

CASH FLOW RATIOS

Insight 9–3 describes how cash flows may change during a company's life. Analysts use ratios to assess the adequacy of a company's cash flow. Because the cash flow statement has only recently become a required

Cash flow ratios are useful in analyzing cash flows.

INSIGHT 9–3
Raising Cash Cows

Researchers at the Strategic Management Institute found that a third of companies they studied had negative cash flow from operations.* Many companies fail because of cash shortages, but shortages of cash are not necessarily associated with operating losses and business failure. The cash position of a company is strongly related to factors other than earnings and a negative cash flow might even be a sign of a successful operation.

The type of market in which a company operates and the company's growth rate often determine whether the company generates cash or consumes it. Companies in slow-growth markets tend to generate cash while companies in rapidly growing markets usually consume cash. The reason is that rapid sales growth requires large amounts of cash for increased investment in inventories, receivables, and fixed assets.

The highest positive cash flows occur in companies that have a large market share in a slow growth market. The Boston Consulting Group has called these companies "cash cows." Often companies will try to develop a "cash cow" segment or subsidiary. The cash generated by the cow can be used to finance a new venture where the company does not have an established market share and expects to consume cash through rapid growth.

*The work of the Strategic Planning Institute and the cash flow patterns described are discussed at length in Bradley T. Gale and Ben Branch, "Cash Flow Analysis: More Important Than Ever," *Harvard Business Review,* July–August 1981, 131–136.

statement, cash flow ratios are relatively new. Three ratios proposed by Brandt et al. appear particularly useful.[2]

$$\text{Overall Cash Flow Ratio} = \frac{\text{Cash Flow from Operations}}{\text{Financing} + \text{Investing Cash Outflows}}$$

$$\text{Cash Return on Sales} = \frac{\text{Cash Flow from Operations}}{\text{Sales}}$$

$$\text{Cash Flow to Net Income} = \frac{\text{Cash Flow from Operations}}{\text{Net Income}}$$

The overall cash flow ratio measures the extent to which internally generated cash flow from operations supplies the cash required for

[2] For a discussion of the ratios cited in this chapter, plus other ratios that can be used to analyze cash flows, see Lloyd Brandt, Jr., Joseph R. Danos, and J. Herman Brasseaux, "Financial Statement Analysis: Benefits and Pitfalls" (Part Two), *The Practical Accountant,* June 1989, 69–78.

investing and financing activities. Cash return on sales is a measure similar to the traditional return on sales (that is, net income/sales). This ratio and the ratio of cash flow to net income help analysts determine if the company's ability to generate sales and earnings is matched by appropriate cash flows.

The cash flow ratios for ABC follow.

$$\text{Overall Cash Flow Ratio} = \frac{\text{Cash Flow from Operations}}{\text{Financing} + \text{Investing Cash Outflows}}$$

$$\frac{\$50,000}{-\$32,000 + \$87,000} = .91$$

Notice that because financing activities resulted in positive cash flow, we must *subtract* that amount here. We want the *net* outflow from financing and investing activities.

$$\text{Cash Return on Sales} = \frac{\text{Cash Flow from Operations}}{\text{Sales}}$$

$$= \frac{\$50,000}{\$120,000} = .42$$

$$\text{Cash Flow to Net Income} = \frac{\text{Cash Flow from Operations}}{\text{Net Income}}$$

$$= \frac{\$50,000}{\$24,000} = 2.08$$

ABC has nearly enough cash flow from operations to supply the cash needed for investing and financing. Forty-two cents in cash flows from each sales dollar, and cash provided by operations is over twice net income. The new cash flow ratios provide structure to our analysis of the cash flow statement. We cannot draw conclusions about ABC's ratios without knowing more. For instance, how have these ratios been changing? It is better for them to have improved than deteriorated. How do they compare with other companies in the industry?

EXAMINING THE CASH FLOW STATEMENT OF BOISE CASCADE

Exhibit 9–5 contains the statement of cash flows from the 1990 annual report of Boise Cascade Corporation. The company uses the indirect method of preparing a statement of cash flows: net income is adjusted for changes in the current asset and liability accounts to convert accrual net income to cash flow from operations.

Exhibit 9–5
Cash Flow Statement

Boise Cascade Corporation

Statements of Cash Flows
Boise Cascade Corporation and Subsidiaries

	Year Ended December 31		
	1990	1989	1988
	(expressed in thousands)		
Cash provided by (used for) operations			
Net income	**$ 75,270**	$267,580	$289,120
Items in income not using cash			
Depreciation and cost of company timber harvested	**212,890**	202,060	187,600
Deferred income tax provision	**54,446**	36,026	47,561
Amortization and other	**6,779**	6,095	11,005
Receivables	**36,947**	(28,057)	(33,873)
Inventories	**(63,822)**	(43,550)	(27,393)
Accounts payable and accrued liabilities	**(60,525)**	50,876	119,635
Current and deferred income taxes	**(7,065)**	9,234	(22,062)
Other	**(3,034)**	(5,222)	(665)
Cash provided by operations	**251,886**	495,042	570,928
Cash provided by (used for) financing			
Cash dividends paid			
Common stock	**(57,671)**	(60,774)	(54,866)
Preferred stock	**(22,348)**	(11,192)	(3,500)
	(80,019)	(71,966)	(58,366)
Notes payable	**40,000**	—	(31,000)
Additions to long-term debt	**649,917**	304,923	99,737
Payments of long-term debt	**(91,978)**	(75,063)	(195,545)
Purchases of common stock (Note 6)	**(158)**	(316,476)	(12,753)
Issuance of preferred stock (Note 6)	**—**	303,541	—
Other	**782**	1,805	(64)
Cash provided by (used for) financing	**518,544**	146,764	(197,991)
Cash provided by (used for) investment			
Expenditures for property and equipment	**(744,020)**	(693,771)	(424,258)
Expenditures for timber and timberlands	**(13,681)**	(5,158)	(6,055)
Sales of operating assets (Note 1)	**14,359**	66,428	71,608
Other	**(26,383)**	(7,324)	(12,630)
Cash used for investment	**(769,725)**	(639,825)	(371,335)
Increase in cash and short-term investments	**705**	1,981	1,602
Balance at beginning of the year	**25,241**	23,260	21,658
Balance at end of the year	**$ 25,946**	$ 25,241	$ 23,260

The accompanying notes are an integral part of these Financial Statements.

The statement in Exhibit 9–5 separates Boise Cascade's cash flows into those resulting from operating, investing, and financing activities. Boise Cascade's operating cash flows are calculated by adjusting accrual net income following the sequence presented earlier for ABC Company.

Operating-Activity Cash Flows

To calculate operating cash flows from reported net income, several adjustments must be made. These adjustments are the same type of adjustments illustrated for ABC Company. First, noncash items for Boise Cascade are depreciation, amortization, deferred taxes, and the cost of timber harvested in 1990 but paid for during prior years. Noncash items are added to net earnings to reconcile accrual earnings to cash provided by operating activities. There are no gains or losses on the sale of noncurrent assets, as there were with ABC Company. There is, however, a foreign currency exchange rate gain in 1990. Some portion of this gain may be included in the "other" adjustments in net income necessary to arrive at cash from operations.

Depreciation is added to earnings.

Second, changes in current assets and current liabilities are added to or subtracted from net income to calculate cash flow from operations. As explained in the discussion of ABC Company, decreases in current assets yield increases in cash (inventory decreases, for example, are merchandise sold without spending cash for replacement, thus increasing cash balances) and so are added to net earnings in calculating (or reconciling to) cash from operations. This is shown in the decreases in inventories subtracted in 1990, 1989 and 1988. Conversely, increases in current assets result in decreases in cash (the increase in Boise's 1990 receivables, for example, results from more sales dollars not being collected, thus reducing cash balances), so the increase should be subtracted from net income in calculating (or reconciling to) cash from operations.

Similarly, increases in current liabilities allow cash to increase, so the increase must be added to net income in calculating (or reconciling to) cash from operations. This is shown in the increases in accounts payable and accrued expenses added to net income in 1989 and 1988. And decreases in current liabilities decrease cash (as paying off accounts payable requires cash), so they must be subtracted from net income in calculating (or reconciling to) cash from operations. This is shown in the decreases in accounts payable and accrued expenses subtracted from net income in 1990.

Investing-Activity Cash Flows

Boise Cascade invested cash to acquire property, equipment, timber, and timberlands. The only investing activity that provided cash was the sale of operating assets. (Note 1 to the financial statements states that in 1989 the company sold its Specialty Paperboard Division.)

Financing Activity Cash Flows

Boise Cascade used cash to pay dividends and make payments on long term debt. It obtained large amounts of cash from new notes payable ($40 million) and "additions to long-term debt" (almost $650 million). It raised relatively small amounts of cash from "other" sources.

Change in Cash During the Year

Boise Cascade generated cash with its operating and financing activities and used cash in its investing activities. The last several lines in the cash flow statement show the increase or decrease in cash during each year and the total cash and cash equivalents at the beginning and end of each year. The financial-statement reader can see the beginning and ending cash balances for the year and, by examining the cash flow statement, can analyze the sources and uses of cash during the period: where did Boise Cascade's cash come from, and where did it go? For Boise Cascade, the flow was from operations and financing activities to investments.

Overview of Boise Cascade Cash Flow
(in thousands)

Cash provided by:	
Operations	$ 251,886
Financing activities	518,544
Cash used by:	
Investing activities	(769,725)
Increase in cash	$ 705

Cash Flow Ratios

The cash flow ratios for Boise are:

$$\text{Overall Cash Flow Ratio} = \frac{\text{Cash Flow from Operations}}{\text{Financing} + \text{Investing Cash Outflows}}$$

$$= \frac{\$251,886}{-\$518,544 + \$769,725} = 1.00$$

$$\text{Cash Return on Sales} = \frac{\text{Cash Flow from Operations}}{\text{Sales}}$$

$$= \frac{\$251,886}{\$4,185,920} = .06$$

$$\text{Cash Flow to Net Income} = \frac{\text{Cash Flow from Operations}}{\text{Net Income}}$$

$$= \frac{\$251,886}{\$75,270} = 3.35$$

Boise's cash flow from operations is almost equal to the cash needed for investing and financing. Cash provided by operations is over three and one-third times net income, but only 6 cents in cash flows from each sales dollar. Again, we cannot conclude that these ratios are good or bad without comparing them with other companies and with Boise Cascade's historical results. We might note that the 1989 overall cash flow ratio was also just about 1.0 [$495,042/(− $146,764 + $639,825)], indicating no major change.

SUMMARY

The cash flow statement gives vital information about a company's liquidity and solvency by disclosing the cash flows that result from its operating, investing, and financing activities. The statement of cash flows also helps analysts judge the quality of a firm's earnings by disclosing the extent to which accrual net income represents increases in net distributable assets generated by operations. The operating activities section of the statement differs depending on whether we use the direct or indirect method. The direct method adjusts the individual accounts on the income statement to a cash basis. The indirect method makes these adjustments to net income in determining cash from operations. Both methods adjust or eliminate the effect of items not affecting cash (such as depreciation or gains and losses).

In general, only five kinds of events affect cash flows: operations, buying and selling noncurrent assets, borrowing and repaying debt, issuing and reacquiring stock, and paying dividends. Control of cash and cash flow is vitally important. The statement of cash flows assists managers and financial-statement users in analyzing a company's control over cash.

DEMONSTRATION PROBLEM

Beta Company's 19X2 income statement and balance sheet accounts on December 31, 19X1 and 19X2 are shown below. The differences between the 19X1 and 19X2 account balances (the increase or decrease in each account) are shown in a separate column. Beta paid $5,000 dividends in 19X2. It sold equipment that originally cost $20,000 for a $6,000 gain. The equipment had been used by Beta for several years.

REQUIRED:

Use the indirect method to prepare a cash flow statement for Beta for 19X2. Analyze Beta's cash flows for 19X2.

Beta Company
Income Statement
For the Year Ended December 31, 19X2

Sales revenue		$100,000
Less operating expenses:		
Cost of goods sold	$ 50,000	
Depreciation	20,000	
Gain on sale of equipment	(6,000)	
Other operating expenses (including income taxes)	25,000	89,000
Net Income		$ 11,000

Beta Company
Balance Sheet Data as of December 31

Assets	12/31/19X1	12/31/19X2	Increase (Decrease)
Cash	$ 15,000	$ 17,000	$ 2,000
Accounts receivable	8,000	14,000	6,000
Inventories	12,000	10,000	(2,000)
Prepaid items	15,000	25,000	10,000
Property and equipment	200,000	250,000	50,000
Accumulated depreciation	(96,000)	(100,000)	(4,000)
Total Assets	$154,000	$ 216,000	$62,000
Liabilities			
Current payables	$ 10,000	$ 6,000	$ (4,000)
Noncurrent note payable	0	40,000	40,000
Total liabilities	10,000	46,000	36,000
Shareholders' Equity			
Common stock (no par)	100,000	120,000	20,000
Retained earnings	44,000	50,000	6,000
Total shareholders' equity	144,000	170,000	26,000
Total liabilities and shareholders' equity	$154,000	$ 216,000	$62,000

Solution to Demonstration Problem

In this solution to the demonstration problem, each class of activity—operating, investing, and financing—is discussed separately. Cash flow ratios are calculated at the end of the analysis.

Operating Activities

We begin determining cash from operations by subtracting the gain from net income and adding depreciation expense to net income to remove the effect of these two noncash items. Next, the change in each current account is added or subtracted as is necessary to adjust the related expense to its cash flow effect, just as we did for ABC Company. For example, the decrease in Beta's current payables is subtracted from net income, because Beta not only paid the amount charged to its current payables during the year, but also paid an additional amount that reduced the balance in current payables.

Investing Activities

We are told that Beta sold equipment that had cost $20,000 for a $6,000 gain, but we are not told the amount of accumulated depreciation on the equipment sold. To understand the changes in property and equipment and the related accumulated depreciation account, we must analyze the changes in those accounts as we illustrated in the chapter.

	Property and Equipment	Accumulated Depreciation
Beginning account balance	$200,000	$ 96,000
Depreciation expense		20,000
Cost of equipment sold	(20,000)	
Subtotal	180,000	$116,000
Ending account balance	250,000	100,000
To be explained	$ 70,000	$(16,000)

The analysis shows that there is a decrease in accumulated depreciation of $16,000 that must, by deduction, be the accumulated depreciation on the equipment sold. If we make the entry for the sale of the equipment, and "plug" the amount of cash received to make debits equal credits, we find that Beta received $10,000 for the equipment, as shown below.

Cash	$10,000	
Accumulated Depreciation	16,000	
Equipment		$20,000
Gain on Sale		6,000

Interestingly, the analysis also discloses a $70,000 increase in property and equipment not mentioned in the problem. Beta must have purchased $70,000 in property and equipment. Both items, the sale for $10,000 and the purchase for $70,000 are shown as investing activities in the Beta statement of cash flows.

Financing Activities

Beta obtained cash by borrowing $40,000 on a note payable and by issuing additional common stock for $20,000. Beta's only financing outflow is the $5,000 paid in dividends. (Note that the beginning balance in retained earnings of $44,000 was increased by earnings of $11,000 and reduced by dividends of $5,000 to obtain the ending balance in retained earnings of $50,000.)

Beta Company
Statement of Cash Flows—Indirect Method
For the Year Ended December 31, 19X2

Operating Activities

Net income	$ 11,000	
Adjustments to reconcile net income to cash provided by operating activities:		
Depreciation	20,000	
Gain on sale of equipment	(6,000)	
Changes in operating assets and liabilities:		
Increase in accounts receivable	(6,000)	
Decrease in inventory	2,000	
Increase in prepaid items	(10,000)	
Decrease in current payables	(4,000)	
Cash provided by operating activities		$ 7,000
Investing Activities		
Sale of equipment	10,000	
Purchase of equipment	(70,000)	
Cash used in investing activities		(60,000)
Financing Activities		
Borrowing on note payable	40,000	
Sale of stock	20,000	
Payment of dividends	(5,000)	
Cash provided by financing activities		55,000
Increase in cash and cash equivalents		2,000
Cash and cash equivalents, beginning of year		15,000
Cash and cash equivalents, end of year		$ 17,000

Cash flow ratios
The cash flow ratios for Beta follow.

$$\text{Overall Cash Flow Ratio} = \frac{\text{Cash Flow from Operations}}{\text{Financing} + \text{Investing Cash Outflows}}$$

$$= \frac{\$7,000}{\$55,000 - \$60,000} = 1.40$$

$$\text{Cash Return on Sales} = \frac{\text{Cash Flow from Operations}}{\text{Sales}}$$

$$= \frac{\$7,000}{\$100,000} = .07$$

$$\text{Cash Flow to Net Income} = \frac{\text{Cash Flow from Operations}}{\text{Net Income}}$$

$$= \frac{\$7,000}{\$11,000} = .64$$

Beta's cash flow from operations is greater than the cash needed for investing and financing activities. However, cash provided by operations is much less than net income, and only seven cents in cash flows from each sales dollar.

Key Terms

cash flow

cash

cash equivalents

direct method

dividends

financing activities

indirect method

investing activities

liquidity

operating activities

quality of earnings

solvency

statement of cash flows

ASSIGNMENTS

9–1 Cash Flow and Depreciation

"Depreciation is the biggest source of cash for many companies," Ralph observed. "In fact, according to my accounting book, there are just two primary sources of cash: net income and depreciation. You can get a good estimate of the cash inflow of most companies just by adding these together."

REQUIRED:

Comment on Ralph's observation.

9–2   Cash Flow in Different Businesses

Bob's mother has her own accounting firm. Sally's father owns a factory that molds and machines parts for the automobile industry. Both businesses had the same net income last year.

REQUIRED:

Which business do you think had the most cash provided by operations last year? Why do you think that?

9–3   Ratios and Basic Statement of Cash Flows

Omega Company had $32,000 in cash on January 1. During the year, Omega used $27,000 in cash repaying a long-term debt and invested $10,000. Operating activities provided $44,000. Net income was $20,000 and sales were $160,000.

REQUIRED:

1. Prepare a statement of cash flows for Omega for the year.
2. Calculate the following cash flow ratios.
    a. Overall cash flow ratio
    b. Cash return on sales
    c. Cash flow to net income

9–4   Solvency and Liquidity

"C. J., you are solvent, but you are not liquid," C. J.'s accountant pronounced at the board meeting.

   "I'm *what?*" C. J. exclaimed. "That doesn't make sense!"

REQUIRED:

1. Respond to C. J. Include an explanation of the difference between solvency and liquidity.
2. How does the cash flow statement help assess solvency and liquidity?

9–5   Uses of the Statement of Cash Flows

Identify the statement below that is not true.

a. *Liquidity* refers to a company's ability to pay its short-term credit obligations.

b. *Solvency* refers to the company's ability to meet all its credit obligations, short- and long-term.

c. The statement of cash flows assists financial-statement users by providing information about a company's solvency, as shown in its short-term operating cash receipts and payments.

d. The quality of a company's earnings is determined, in part, by the extent to which accrual net income represents increases in net distributable assets generated by operations.

9–6 Characteristics of Cash Flow

Identify the statement below that is not true.

a. Earnings of high quality ultimately generate increases in cash and cash equivalents that can be distributed to creditors and owners.

b. The statement of cash flows helps analysts judge the quality of a company's earnings.

c. Companies with high cash returns are more profitable than other companies.

d. The statement of cash flows also helps analysts determine the value of the firm and, hence, the value of its stock in the market.

9–7 Cash Flow Multiple Choice

Identify the statement below that is not true.

a. The statement of cash flows reconciles the change in retained earnings during the year.

b. Many analysts feel that the present value of the firm is related to the amounts of its future cash flows rather than to its future accounting earnings.

c. The statement of cash flows explains the change in cash and cash equivalents each period.

d. Cash is all amounts that are available for withdrawal at any time without penalty or advance notice.

e. Cash equivalents are short-term liquid investments such as treasury notes, commercial paper, and money market funds.

9–8 Cash Flow from Operations—Classifying Activities

Acme Wholesalers is preparing a statement of cash flows using the indirect method. Which of the following items should appear in the operations section?

a. Increase in inventories

b. Cost of goods sold

c. Depreciation expense for the year

d. Accumulated depreciation

e. Decrease in accounts receivable

f. Amortization of patents for the year

g. Utilities expense

h. Increase in utilities payable

i. Increase in retained earnings caused by net income for the year

9–9   Sources and Uses of Cash—Classifying Activities

The accountant at Wilson Sports is preparing a statement of cash flows. Indicate whether each of the following items should appear in the statement, and if so, whether the item should appear in the operating, investing, or financing section.

a. Sale of machinery for cash

b. Declaration of cash dividends on stock

c. Sale of inventory for cash

d. Sale of inventory on account

e. Payment of interest on bonds

f. Payment of bond principal not due for two years

g. Payment of a cash dividend on stock

h. Write off of uncollectible accounts receivable

i. Cash purchase of additional stock in a subsidiary

j. Trade of land for additional stock in a subsidiary

k. Payment of rent

l. Prepayment of insurance for two years

9–10   General Sources and Uses of Cash

This chapter identifies four general sources and five general uses of cash. Identify the two items that are included incorrectly in the following list.

General Sources and Uses of Cash

Sources	Uses
Operations	Operations
Issue stock	Reacquire stock
Borrow	Repay debt
Sell assets	Buy assets
Receive dividends	Pay dividends
Depreciate assets	

9–11   Cash from Operations

Judy Company had net earnings of $50,000 in 19X5. The following information is available from the financial statements.

Accounts receivable increased	$ 8,000
Inventory decreased	12,000
Accrued payables decreased	10,000
Prepaid insurance increased	4,000
Depreciation expense	15,000
Dividends paid	10,000

REQUIRED:

Calculate cash flow from operations.

9–12 Cash from Operations with Asset Sold at Loss

Carne Company had net earnings of $120,000 in 19X9. Depreciation expense for the period was $30,000. During 19X9, land that had cost Carne $50,000 was sold for $40,000. The loss was included in the calculation of net income. Changes in current accounts during the period were as follows.

Accounts receivable decreased	$15,000
Inventory decreased	25,000
Accounts payable increased	20,000
Prepaid items increased	40,000

REQUIRED:

Calculate cash flow from operations.

9–13 Effect of Activities on Cash and Earnings

The transactions below might affect cash, net income, or both cash and net income. Determine the effect of each transaction on (1) cash and (2) net income. Show the amount of the effect and whether it is an increase or decrease.

a. Inventory is purchased for $34,000 cash.

b. Half the inventory is sold for $40,000 on account.

c. $30,000 of the accounts receivable in item b are collected.

d. An account receivable for $6,000 is written off as uncollectible.

e. A production line is shut down, and equipment with a book value of $75,000 is sold for cash at a loss of $15,000.

f. A truck worth $35,000 is acquired by trading land of equal value.

g. Depreciation of $5,000 is taken on the truck acquired in item f.

h. Dividends of $62,000 are declared when retained earnings total $200,000.

i. The dividends declared in item h are paid when cash in the bank is $104,000.

9–14   Gains and Losses

Gains and losses are income statement items but they do not always result from operating activities, and the amount of a gain or loss is not the amount of the related cash flow. Roberts Company shows one gain and one loss.

Loss on sale of equipment	$23,000
Gain on sale of land	40,000

Roberts sold equipment with a book value of $173,000 (cost of $300,000 and accumulated depreciation of $127,000) for cash, and sold land with a book value of $90,000 for $20,000 cash and the remainder on a two-year note receivable. Roberts' net income is $510,000.

REQUIRED:

1. How must the gain and loss be treated if a statement of cash flows is prepared using the indirect method?

2. Journalize each sale. What is the cash effect of each, and where will the effect be shown?

9–15   Statement of Cash Flows—Direct Method

Ableson Company has prepared the following cash flow information.

	Increases	Decreases
Collected from customers	$150,000	
For dividends		$12,000
For goods sold		60,000
For salaries		30,000
For other operating costs		30,000
For truck purchased		80,000

REQUIRED:

Prepare a schedule of cash flows from operations for Ableson using the direct method.

9–16   Cash Collected from Customers

Hyatt Company had sales revenue of $500,000. Accounts receivable decreased from $75,000 at the beginning of the year to $50,000 at the end of the year.

REQUIRED:

Calculate cash collected from customers.

9–17 Cash Flow for Cost of Goods Sold

McNalley and Flyson had cost of goods sold for 19X3 of $65,000. Accounts payable and merchandise inventory balances were as shown below.

	Balance, Beginning of Year	Balance, End of Year
Inventory	$22,000	$17,000
Accounts payable	14,000	18,000

REQUIRED:

Calculate the cash flow for cost of goods sold.

9–18 Cash Flows for Operating Expenses

TopDog Company had net income of $85,000. Except for rent, TopDog paid cash for all operating costs as they were incurred. Rent was paid in advance every six months. For the month of March, TopDog had rent expense of $3,000. Additionally, salaries for each month were paid on the first and fifteenth. Salary expense for March was $110,000. On March 31, prepaid rent and salaries payable balances were as shown below.

	Balance, February 28	Balance, March 31
Prepaid rent	$12,000	$ 9,000
Salaries payable	52,000	60,000

REQUIRED:

1. Calculate the cash flows for rent and salaries during March.

2. What was TopDog's cash flow from operations during March?

9–19 Noncash Investing and Financing Activities

Woodside Mills acquired three trucks from a local dealer in exchange for 1,000 shares of its $50 par value common stock. At the time of the exchange, Woodside's stock was trading at $75 per share.

REQUIRED:

What is the cash flow effect of the acquisition of the trucks? How is this transaction shown in the statement of cash flows?

9–20 Wal-Mart Cash Flows

Analyze the Wal-Mart 1991 statement of cash flows. Comment separately on each of the following:

a. What is cash provided by operating activities? What are the most significant items in the reconciliation of net income to cash flow from operations? What noncash items are included?

b. What is cash used in investing activities? What are the largest cash flows resulting from investing activities?

c. What is cash provided by financing activities? What are the largest cash flows resulting from financing activities?

9–21 Wal-Mart Cash Flow Ratios

Three cash flow ratios are discussed in the chapter. Calculate Wal-Mart's cash flow ratios and discuss the significance of your findings.

9–22 DECISION CASE: CHANGES IN LONG-LIVED ASSETS

Bolton Company is a metal fabricator. It leases land and buildings but owns equipment and several patents on equipment design. During the year, Bolton sold equipment for $35,000 that had originally cost $75,000, and on which Bolton had recorded accumulated depreciation of $50,000. Depreciation expense for the year was $40,000. The equipment and accumulated depreciation accounts contained the following.

	Equipment	Accumulated Depreciation
Beginning account balance	$660,000	$400,000
Ending account balance	690,000	390,000

Patents, net of amortization, were $95,000 at the first of the year but decreased to $55,000 during the year. The income statement shows amortization expense of $10,000 and a loss on the sale of patents of $4,000. The amortization and sale were the only activities in the patent account during the year.

REQUIRED:

1. How does the equipment sale affect cash flow? (What is the amount and nature of the cash flow?) Create the journal entry that shows the sale of the equipment, including the gain or loss on the sale and the related cash flow.

2. Was other equipment purchased or sold during the year? If so, what kind and amount of cash flow was involved?

3. How does the patent sale affect cash flow? (What is the amount and nature of the cash flow?) Create the journal entry that shows the sale of the patent, including the loss on the sale and the related cash flow.

4. The gain(s) and/or loss(es) on the sales of long lived assets have what effect on cash flow?

9–23 DECISION CASE: CHANGES IN EQUITIES

Houston Company has completed its sixth year of operations. Following a loss of $23,000 last year, earnings this year are $100,000. Houston issued bonds with a face value of $1,000,000 in exchange for a packaging plant (including property, plant and equipment). A financial analyst determined that identical bonds, issued in the market, would have sold at 98. This finding was consistent with an independent appraisal of the value of the packaging plant. Additional selected information follows.

	Beginning Balance	Ending Balance
Notes payable	$350,000	$420,000
Capital stock	960,000	900,000
Retained earnings	550,000	600,000

REQUIRED:

Comment on the amount and classification of the discussed items in the statement of cash flows.

9–24 DECISION CASE: ANALYSIS INCLUDING CASH FLOW RATIOS

In 19X3 Able Company had net earnings of $93,000 on sales of $777,000. Depreciation expense for the year was $35,000. During 19X3, land that had cost $87,000 five years ago was sold for $140,000. The gain was included in the calculation of net income. Able issued $200,000 in ten-year bonds payable and paid $41,000 in dividends. The proceeds of the bonds were used to finance the purchase of a new factory. The total cost of the factory was $350,000. Changes in current accounts during 19X3 were as follows.

Accounts receivable decreased	$10,000
Inventory increased	33,000
Accounts payable increased	24,000
Prepaid items increased	27,000

Naddy O'Leary is pleased with Able's earnings performance. "Earnings last year were less than $40,000. We have more than doubled that this year. Our new plant will give us 15% additional capacity. We should easily crack $100,000 in earnings next year. Maybe we should think of expanding production again!"

REQUIRED:

Prepare a cash flow statement and analyze Able's cash flows. Include a discussion of the ratios presented in the chapter.

10

Introduction to Managerial Accounting

LEARNING OBJECTIVES

After studying Chapter 10, you will be able to:
1. Describe the differences between financial accounting and managerial accounting.
2. Describe several classifications of costs, and state why each is important.
3. Isolate the fixed and variable components of a mixed cost.
4. Describe how managers use information to plan and control.
5. Prepare a statement of cost of goods manufactured and sold.

This chapter begins our study of managerial accounting, which deals with gathering, interpreting, and reporting information for use by managers within economic enterprises, rather than by outsiders. Managers use accounting information for various purposes, including planning operations. Managers use accounting information to answer such questions as, "How many units must we sell to earn $50,000"? "What will profits be if we increase our selling price and step up promotional efforts"? Decision making is an important part of planning and managerial accountants supply much of the information used for such decisions as whether to sell some of our products to a chain store at less-than-normal prices or expand productive capacity. Chapters 12, 13, and 15 cover these types of decisions.

Another major use of managerial accounting information is in controlling operations, discussed later in this chapter, where the concern is whether operations are going according to plan, and if not, what might be done. As part of the control process, managerial accounting information is also used to evaluate the performance of workers and managers. Chapters 14 and 16 treat these matters.

Managerial accounting encompasses **cost accounting,** determining costs of manufactured inventories. Chapters 11 and 14 cover product costing.

MANAGERIAL ACCOUNTING AND FINANCIAL ACCOUNTING

The first part of this book dealt with profit-seeking businesses. Managerial accounting applies to profit-seeking businesses, but also applies to not-for-profit entities such as colleges, churches, social organizations, and government units. Managerial accounting is directed toward people inside the organization—its managers—not toward the creditors, stockholders, economists, regulators, and other external users of published financial information. Because managers make daily decisions they need more information, and need it more frequently than do external users.

Managerial accounting information usually relates to a part, or segment, of an organization: a division of a business, a department in a factory, a product or product line. *Financial accounting* is usually concerned with the financial position and earnings of the entire organization: the big picture. This difference in focus is related to the difference in purpose: financial accounting serves diverse groups of outsiders who make many judgments about the enterprise as a whole, while managerial accounting serves individual managers charged with

Managerial accounting differs from financial accounting in audience, scope, and purpose.

Exhibit 10–1
Users of Accounting Reports

Users of financial accounting information:

User Group	Primary Concern

Long-term creditors:
  Bondholders
  Mortgage holders
  Lease holders
	Long-term creditworthiness and cash flows

Owners (stockholders)
  Common
  Preferred
	Income, dividend and stock safety and growth potential

Suppliers	Short-term cash flows and debt repayment
Customers	Product quality; stability
Financial analysts	Investment potential
Economists	Economic trends

Regulators
  federal
  state
  industry
	Compliance with regulations

Users of managerial accounting information:

Managers	Planning and controlling operations, making routine and nonroutine decisions, evaluating the efficiency and effectiveness of operations and managers, the ability to raise capital, and to sell products or services.

controlling individual parts of the organization. The principal concerns of some groups of users of accounting information appear in Exhibit 10–1.

Managerial accounting has developed in many directions, most recently to accommodate changes in manufacturing operations such as just-in-time manufacturing, flexible manufacturing, and computer-assisted manufacturing (all discussed in Chapter 11). These changes have caused managerial accountants to rethink many concepts and practices. Another area of continuing concern is the behavioral aspects of managerial accounting—such as determining how performance measures and reports influence the behavior of managers and workers and how they might be designed to avoid undesirable influences. For example, production managers who are evaluated primarily on meeting cost targets have little incentive to improve product quality if such efforts will increase costs.

There are no GAAP in managerial accounting: managerial accountants are concerned with what is relevant to a particular purpose. In providing information to managers, managerial accountants are less concerned with the form of a report than with its appropriateness for the intended purpose. Accordingly, managerial accounting reports often use future costs, market values, or replacement costs rather than the historical costs that are the principal bases for published financial statements. Such valuation methods are often more relevant than historical cost. For example, a manager deciding whether to continue manufacturing a particular product needs information about the cost to replace the machinery and equipment required to make the product, not the historical cost. Most of managerial accounting relates to the future, not to the past.

As we mentioned earlier, the entity concept of financial accounting is interpreted quite differently in managerial accounting. Managerial accounting reports deal with segments of an organization rather than the organization as a whole. These segments change depending on the purpose of the report, though some segments (such as departments in a factory) will receive many of the same necessary reports weekly. In contrast, financial accounting reports cover longer periods, such as quarters or years.

Although managerial accounting and financial accounting differ in many important respects, they are still closely related. Both rely on economic events and transactions. Both use the fundamental financial statements (though the balance sheet is less important in managerial accounting) and both are concerned with providing information to users.

CONTROLLER'S ROLE

The chief managerial accountant in most organizations is the controller, who also has responsibilities relating to financial accounting. In well-run companies, controllers are important managers. Daniel C. Ferguson, chief executive officer of Newell Corporation, has stated that controllers should control, not simply record and audit.[1] Insight 10–1 describes how one large company views the controller and how controllers have become more active in long-term planning.

---

[1] "A CEO's View of the Controller," *Management Accounting,* February 1987, 21–23.

INSIGHT 10–1
Controlling the Brewery

The controller at Coors, the brewer, is an important manager, a major participant, not a scorekeeper. Reports are called "management reports," not "accounting reports" because they are intended to help managers manage. The Coors controller is seen as the chief processor of information, is consulted on all major decisions, and participates in management meetings.*

Controllers are becoming more important in strategic planning, a preserve once denied them in many companies. Strategic planning includes developing the corporate mission, establishing corporate objectives, and other activities not normally associated with accounting. However, it is becoming widely recognized that controllers generally understand their companies very well. Consequently, chief executive officers in various fields have been supportive of more visible roles for controllers.**

*Kenton B. Walker, "Coors: Brewing a Better Controllership," *Management Accounting*, January 1988, 23–27.
**Richard H. Fern and Manuel A. Tipgos, "Controllers as Business Strategists: A Progress Report," *Management Accounting*, March 1988, 25–29.

ETHICS

The Institute of Management Accountants (formerly the National Association of Accountants), the principal organization of managerial accountants, has promulgated Standards of Ethical Conduct for Management Accountants, as well as established an Ethics Committee and an Ethics Counseling Service. Unlike the certified public accountants who audit companies, management accountants are not independent of the company they serve. Management accountants are, however, bound by the Standards. The Standards have four main sections: competence, confidentiality, integrity, and objectivity.

The **competence** provisions require management accountants to develop their knowledge and skills and to do their tasks in accordance with relevant laws, regulations, and standards. The **confidentiality** provisions forbid management accountants from acting on, or appearing to act on, confidential information they acquire in doing their work. This provision thus forbids "insider" actions such as selling the company's stock upon learning that it is very likely to lose a major customer. The **integrity** provisions cover avoidance of conflicts of interest, improprieties of acceptance of gifts or favors, and other items generally

associated with professional behavior. The **objectivity** provisions require management accountants to "communicate information fairly and
objectively" and to "disclose fully all relevant information."

Taken as a whole, the standards require professional behavior, especially in such areas as conflicts of interest. They require management
accountants to bring bad news, as well as good, to the attention of their
superiors, and to work competently. They also state that the management accountant faced with a serious ethical conflict might have to
resign and explain why to "an appropriate representative of the organization."

INTERNATIONAL ASPECTS OF MANAGERIAL ACCOUNTING

Controllers in today's global economy have important responsibilities
in managing and controlling foreign operations. Such issues as deciding
whether to borrow or issue stock in foreign countries or in the U.S.,
where to locate specific operations, and what product parts and components to make overseas are important to the profitability of the company. We consider some of these issues at various points later in the
text.

ACCOUNTING INFORMATION FOR MANAGEMENT

Managers spend a great deal of time and effort processing information
to help them carry out their responsibilities, especially planning and
controlling. **Planning** is the setting of goals and objectives (such as a
10 percent rate of growth in sales, or a profit of 12 percent of sales) and
the selecting of the strategies and tactics to achieve them (such as
introducing a new product at a $14 selling price, or reducing the costs
of a product by increasing automation). Managerial accounting information is thus essential for planning, especially in preparing **budgets**
—plans that describe objectives and the actions to be taken to achieve
them. Chapter 13 discusses budgets in detail.

Managers use managerial accounting information to operate economic organizations.

Decision making is part of planning because managers must decide
how to carry out plans—how to use resources (money, people, productive equipment, etc.) to achieve goals. Where should we build a
new factory? How much of this or that product should we make? Should
we buy more machinery?

Controlling is ensuring that operations are going according to
plan, and if not, deciding what to do. Control reports are the backbone

of accounting for this purpose. They tell managers how actual performance compares with planned (budgeted) performance and suggest ways to eliminate unfavorable differences. Control also includes evaluating the performance of managers—again, often by comparing their actual and expected (budgeted) results.

Anyone who uses economic resources needs accounting information for planning and controlling: you must plan both how to use resources, and how to determine whether you are using them wisely. It is, however, not always a simple matter to determine what information is relevant for a particular purpose. It is the managerial accountant's role to help managers decide what information to use, how to analyze the information, and how to apply it.

Large-capacity computers, networked personal computers, and enormous databases have contributed to *information overload,* a state of having so much information that you cannot use it all in any sensible way in the time available to make a decision. Indeed, as advertisements often show, managers drown in seas of data, bobbing up and down in computer printouts. Today it is possible, and easy, to get a slew of *data,* but data are not *information.* Information is data that are refined and tailored to a specific purpose.

The watchword, "different costs for different purposes," should govern much of what we study. However, sometimes the reason for not collecting more information is that the cost of doing so exceeds the benefits we are likely to reap. For instance, in deciding which car to buy, you will almost certainly not examine engine specifications such as cylinder displacement of *all* of the models that interest you. Similarly, a managerial accountant might prepare a report that includes results from only 80% of the company's sales territories, not waiting for results from the remaining 20% to come in because those results will probably not affect the decisions the managers will make.

COST CLASSIFICATIONS

One sharp difference between financial and managerial accounting is in classifying costs. As you know, in financial accounting, costs are classified by either object or function. Costs classified by object include salaries, interest, depreciation, utilities. *Salaries* includes salaries of production workers, salespersons, administrators, and so on. Those same costs classified by function are aggregated as cost of goods sold, selling expense, administrative expense, and financing expense. *Cost of goods sold* includes such costs as production salaries, depreciation, and utilities. Costs are more useful for some purposes classified by object (how much did we spend on utilities?), and for others classified by function (how much do we spend to sell our products?). Managerial accounting also uses cost classifications to serve different managerial purposes.

We earlier introduced the tenet that you cannot determine what information to collect, report, or interpret until you know the purpose for which the information is needed. Take the seemingly simple question, "How much does it cost us to manufacture chair model 15634?" There are at least two answers, depending on the questioner's purpose. If the questioner is considering making 5,000 units of that chair to sell to a discount store at a below- normal, one-time price, the answer is the additional or incremental cost of making the chairs—the additional labor, materials and other costs that the company will incur by making the 5,000 chairs for the special order. If the questioner wants instead to evaluate the profitability of that model chair to determine whether to keep making it, then other costs are also relevant, such as the salary of a supervisor who is primarily responsible for that model and all other costs that the company incurs to make it. (The salary of the supervisor is not relevant to the cost of the special order if it is not increased by the additional production.)

Behavioral Cost Classification

The first major cost classification in managerial accounting is behavioral. In other words, how do costs behave when activity changes? Accountants can measure *activity* by sales dollars, units of production, hours of labor time, hours of machine time, number of production runs, or any other way that will help managers to plan. (Managerial accountants often speak of *volume* as well as activity.) The activity that causes a particular cost is called a **cost driver.** The basis for classifying costs is whether *total* cost changes as activity changes or whether total cost remains constant. Costs that change in direct proportion to changes in activity are *variable costs.* Examples of variable costs are the cost of materials used to make a product (variable with the number of units produced) and commissions paid to salespeople (variable with sales dollars). Costs that remain constant despite changes in activity are *fixed costs.* Examples are salaries, depreciation, property taxes, rent, and interest on long-term debt. The fixed-variable distinction is sometimes difficult to make, and numerous costs have both fixed and variable components. Chapter 12 refines and uses this classification in profit planning. The cost-behavior classification is fundamental to much of managerial accounting. Figure 10−1 shows the behavior of fixed and variable costs and of total costs.

One use of information about cost behavior is in predicting costs. Managers are always concerned about what costs will be in the future.

Classifying costs by behavior is especially important in planning.

Figure 10–1
Cost Behavior

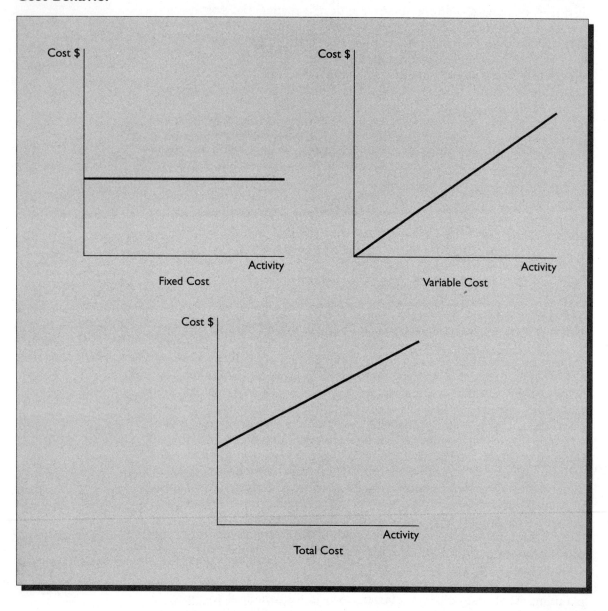

Predicting costs is critical to budgeting and to decision making. To predict total costs, we can use a simple formula:

Total Cost = Total Fixed Cost + (Variable Cost per Unit of
Activity × Amount of Activity)

For example, suppose that the following data relate to a product marketed by Gentry Company. The unit of activity is units of product sold. Again, depending on the organization, activity might be stated in labor hours worked, miles flown, or some other measure.

Fixed costs	$25,000 per month
Variable cost per unit of product	$ 6
Expected sales next month	12,000 units

We predict that total cost will be:

Total Cost = $25,000 + ($6 × 12,000) = $97,000

We can now use the $97,000 in our planning. If we sell the product for $10 per unit, we predict that revenue will be $120,000 and profit $23,000.

Understanding cost behavior is obviously very important for budgeting and decision making because in both endeavors we are concerned about what costs are likely to be at different levels of activity. We are also concerned with cost behavior because it is fundamental to **cost management.** Managers are always trying to find ways to reduce costs without sacrificing quality. Determining what drives a particular cost enables managers to judge whether to reduce particular activities, or even stop doing them entirely. For example, a company that adopts modern manufacturing principles has workers inspect products as the products go through the manufacturing process. This practice eliminates the need for inspection at the end of the process and therefore saves costs.

Figure 10-2 shows another type of cost behavior, the *step-variable cost.* As the figure shows, this type of cost remains constant over a range of activity, then jumps abruptly to a new level. Many costs reflect such a pattern because resources come in large chunks. As the activity that drives supervisory costs rises, the company cannot add $1,000 worth of supervision, but must hire a person full-time. Similarly, companies cannot add a few square feet to a factory when they get pinched for space, but rather must wait to make major additions. Step-variable costs do not present any conceptual difficulties. Planning for them is a matter of determining in what range of activity the company will operate. (You ignore the variable component of the cost.)

Figure 10–2
Step-Variable Cost

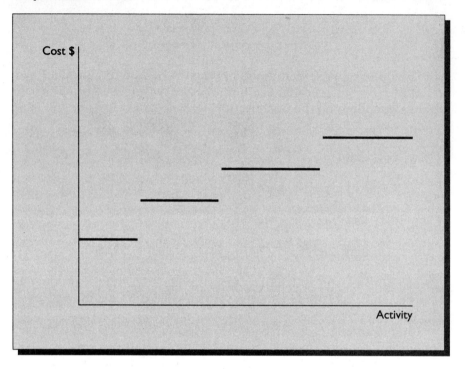

Determining Cost Behavior

To use fixed and variable costs for predicting, we must first determine whether costs are fixed, variable, or a mixture of the two. We can sometimes tell from the name of the account, but relying solely on names is unwise. For example, depreciation, salaries, and advertising are all fixed costs, but wages could be partly fixed, partly variable, depending on whether the company lays off or hires additional workers when production changes. Rent is usually fixed, but retail stores often pay a fixed monthly amount plus a percentage of sales. Costs that contain both fixed and variable components are called *mixed costs* or *semi-variable costs*. Mixed costs are very common, and it is important to determine their fixed and variable components. Graphically, a mixed cost appears just as total cost does in Figure 10–1, because it has both a fixed and a variable component. There are several approaches to analyzing mixed costs. The objective is to develop a formula such as we showed earlier,

Total Cost = Total Fixed Cost + (Variable Cost per Unit of Activity × Units of Activity)

Account Analysis

As just mentioned, you can often determine whether a cost is fixed or variable by its name. Accounts such as Depreciation, Salaries, and Property Taxes contain fixed costs, while Direct Labor, Commissions, and Royalties typically contain variable costs. Accounts such as Supplies and Power probably contain both fixed and variable components. While a useful first step, account analysis does not help in determining the amount by which a cost varies. For instance, you cannot tell the sales commission percentage simply by looking at the Commissions account.

High-Low Method

One way to estimate the fixed and variable components of a mixed cost is the *high-low method.* Using this method, we first find the variable component by dividing the change in cost between the high and low activity levels by the change in activity levels. (The high and low levels should be within the range where the company normally operates.) You should not use costs for a month that the factory was shut down by a strike, for example, because those costs are not representative of normal operations. The only costs that change when activity changes are variable costs, so once we know the variable cost per unit, we rely on the formula for total costs to determine the fixed-cost component. For example, suppose we have the following data related to wages and sales.

Month	Sales	Wages
April	15,000	$32,600
May	18,000	34,800
June	3,000	21,500
July	14,000	31,800

The high volume is 18,000, the low is 3,000. But the low volume is very low compared to the other operating levels, so we might decide that it comes from an abnormal month. Perhaps the company shut down for a significant part of June for remodeling. When either the high or low observation appears way out of line with the others, we usually regard it as not being representative of normal operations and leave it out of the analysis. In this case, therefore, we use the July data as the low point. The variable portion of wages is:

$$\frac{\$34{,}800 - \$31{,}800}{18{,}000 - 14{,}000} = \$3{,}000/4{,}000$$

$$= \$0.75$$

Notice that all we are doing here is dividing the change in cost by the change in volume to determine the rate of *change of total cost* (the slope of the line). The rate at which total cost changes as activity changes is the variable cost per unit. For the fixed portion, we rely on the formula, Total Cost = Total Fixed Cost + (Unit Variable Cost × Volume). Total variable cost equals unit variable cost times volume. We know total cost (at two levels of volume), unit variable cost, and volume. Therefore, we can use costs at either the 18,000 or 14,000 volumes to find total fixed costs.

$$\$34,800 = \text{Fixed Cost} + (\$0.75 \times 18,000)$$

Therefore, fixed cost is:

$$\$34,800 - (\$0.75 \times 18,000) = \$21,300$$

Solving with total cost at the 14,000 unit levels gives the same $21,300. The high-low method is crude and uses only two observations, so it is not the best method, but can be a starting point in analysis.

Scatter-Diagram Method

A better method is to plot the data on a **scatter-diagram,** then draw in a straight line that seems to fit the data as well as possible as in Figure 10–3. As with the high-low method, we ignore unusual observations, such as the one toward the upper left of the Figure, which is a clearly unusual high cost at low volume. The line goes through the middle of the observations, excluding the odd one, and no point is very far from the line.

The line should give us a good idea of how costs behave. The *intercept* of the line with the Y-axis is the fixed component, the *slope* of the line is the variable component. To find the variable component, find total cost at some volume other than zero. Then subtract total fixed cost, which is the Y-intercept. The result is total variable cost at the higher volume. Simply divide total variable cost by the higher volume to obtain unit variable cost.

Because no two people are likely to draw exactly the same line, the scatter-diagram method is not precise. It is nevertheless effective. Plotting the data also gives an idea about how well the line will predict future costs. If the observations are fairly close to the line, predictions will probably be good. If, however, they are spread in a circular, random pattern, as the left-hand side of Figure 10–4 shows, then predictions will be poor. In such a case, the cost might truly be random, with no discernible pattern. It might also be that the cost does have a pattern, but it does not vary with sales. Some other measure of activity might yield better results. The right-hand side of Figure 10–4 shows

**Figure 10–3
Plot of Cost Data**

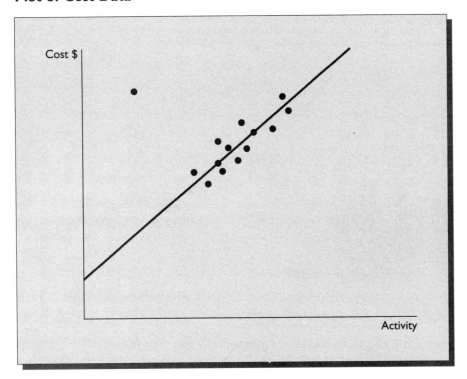

the same cost plotted against a different measure where the fit of a line would be much better.

A technique called *regression analysis* is often used to analyze mixed costs. This technique provides the line that minimizes the deviations between the line and the data points. Regression not only gives a mathematically precise fit of the line to the data, but also provides other helpful information about how good predictions are likely to be. Regression analysis is beyond the scope of this book, but you might study it in other courses.

We should note here that we do not expect costs to be perfectly fixed or perfectly variable from shutdown to 100% of capacity. We do expect cost relationships to hold up over a *relevant range.* For instance, utility costs might have a $3,500 per month fixed component related to heating and lighting a factory (and a variable component related to operating machinery). But if the company shut the factory down for a month, it would turn out the lights and cut off the heat, so that utility cost would be much less than $3,500. This $3,500 fixed component is

Figure 10–4
Dispersion of Costs

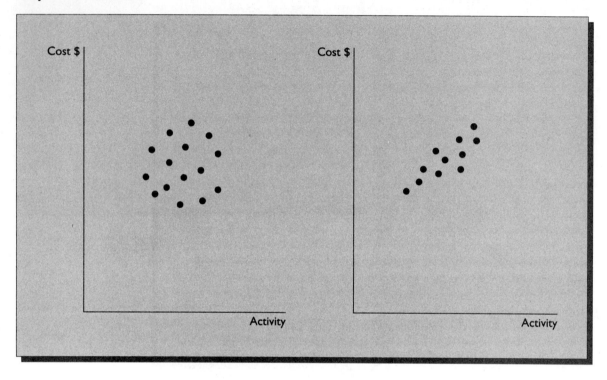

therefore best thought of as the fixed amount *within the relevant range.* The relevant range will vary from company to company. Some companies will find that costs behave as expected over a wide range of activity, while in other companies the range might be relatively narrow.

Responsibility Cost Classification

Classification by responsibility is important in controlling operations.

Another fundamental cost classification is by responsibility: which manager is reponsible for which cost? **Responsibility accounting** is concerned with reporting information for managers to use in controlling their operations and in evaluating the performance of their subordinates. The concern here is with **controllable costs.** Of course, all costs are, or should be, controllable by *some* manager, but the question is whether a particular cost is controllable by a *particular* manager. A manager should not be held responsible for costs that he or she cannot control.

Suppose you own a restaurant with a bar, all in one building, and have a manager for each. In trying to decide whether each is doing the job well, you have prepared the income statement shown in Exhibit 10–2. Because the restaurant occupies three fourths of the space and the bar one fourth, you have split up, or allocated, the heat, light, and rent expenses between the managers in the same ratios.

Do these statements clearly show the responsibilities of the managers? No, because the managers cannot control heat/light, the rent on the building, and perhaps some of the miscellaneous expenses. Just because they occupy particular amounts of space does not mean that they should "pay for" those amounts. You are interested in how they manage what they can control. These costs are *allocated*, meaning that they are apportioned among segments, such as departments. Here the restaurant and bar are departments. Cost allocation plays an important role in several areas that we consider in later chapters, but the important point here is that allocated costs are generally not controllable by the managers of segments. The heat/light and rent are controllable by the overall manager, but not by the manager of either segment of the business. A **performance report** using the principle of controllability appears in Exhibit 10–3.

This report shows only the controllable costs as the responsibility of each manager. The costs they do not control appear only in the total column because they are controllable only by the overall manager. The costs not controllable by the segment managers are not allocated to the segments.

Exhibit 10–2
Income Statement for Combined Restaurant and Bar

		Restaurant		Bar
Sales		$13,300		$8,400
Cost of sales		4,100		2,800
Gross profit		9,200		5,600
Operating expenses:				
Salaries	$2,200		$1,300	
Heat/light	1,200		400	
Rent on building	900		300	
Miscellaneous	2,000		1,200	
Totals		6,300		3,200
Income		$ 2,900		$2,400

Exhibit 10–3
Income Statement for Combined Restaurant and Bar

	Total	Restaurant	Bar
Sales	$21,700	$13,300	$8,400
Cost of sales	6,900	4,100	2,800
Gross profit	14,800	$ 9,200	$5,600
Operating expenses:			
Salaries	3,500		
Heat/light	1,600		
Rent on building	1,200		
Miscellaneous	3,200		
Totals	9,500		
Income	$ 5,300		

You also need budgets or some other indication of expectations to evaluate performance. Should the bar be doing better than it is? Is the gross profit percentage high enough? How do you know? You might consult trade journals. Some trade associations publish reports showing cost percentages for restaurant/bar combinations, and so forth. Most businesses can find information that will assist in controlling operations and evaluating performance.

Direct and Common Costs

The distinction between controllable and noncontrollable costs is often reflected in another distinction, that between direct costs and indirect costs. A **direct cost** relates only to one segment of the organization: the cost of food is direct to the restaurant segment in our example. An **indirect cost** (also called **common cost**) relates to more than one segment. Heat and light on the building in our example above are common to the restaurant and bar. The selection of segments is important in determining whether a cost is direct or common. In general, the smaller the segment, the less direct cost associated with it. For example, if salespeople sell all of the products in a single product line, their salaries and travel expenses are direct to the line, but not to any single product.

The direct-indirect classification has several important uses.

The direct-indirect distinction has many uses. Managers often use it to distinguish between controllable and noncontrollable costs—although this is not always a good use because some direct costs are not controllable, and some indirect costs are at least partially controllable. Depreciation on assets used only in a particular department is direct to the department, for example, but the department manager cannot control the cost because depreciation depends on equipment purchase decisions made in the past. If the maintenance staff works on machinery used in all departments, its costs are largely indirect to any one department. But the department managers partly control the cost because they order maintenance work and therefore determine the total workload of the maintenance staff, and certainly the workloads in their departments.

The direct-common distinction is perhaps most used in preparing income statements for segments of an organization, as we did earlier for the restaurant. A segment can be a product, product line, geographic area, class of customer, or other separation of the business that interests its managers. Such income statements are prepared to determine how each segment is doing and what it is contributing to the overall business. They also assist in evaluating the performance of the managers of the segments.

Avoidable (Differential) and Unavoidable Costs

For decision making, the relevant cost classification is *avoidability,* which relates to a proposed action, such as closing a sales office or dropping a product. An **avoidable cost** can be eliminated by a particular action, while an unavoidable cost cannot be eliminated by *that same action.* (It might be eliminated by another action.) The terms *incremental* and *differential* also refer to avoidability. A cost is incremental or differential if it will change as the result of taking an action. For example, if the decision were to expand a plant, we would use the terms *incremental* or *differential* to refer to the additional costs the company would incur. (We could say that the company could avoid the expansion costs by not expanding, and thus term the costs *avoidable,* but it probably makes more sense to say differential.) Many accountants use the term *relevant cost* to describe those costs that are differential to a particular decision.

Avoidability is a "how much" question. Consider again the example of the salaries and travel expenses of salespeople. If the company were considering dropping a single product from the line, it might be able to reduce the salesforce, or cut travel costs. The whole account, Sales Salaries Expense, is not avoidable, but some of it probably is. The name of the cost does not usually indicate whether it is avoidable, although names can give some strong hints. Unless a plant will be closed, depreciation is almost certainly unavoidable. The cost of materials to make a product is almost surely avoidable if the decision is to drop the product.

The avoidability of costs is critical for decision making.

For a different example, suppose that you want to take a 300-mile trip in your car. You make up the following analysis of costs for an average year of 10,000 miles.

Gas, oil, maintenance	$ 500
Insurance	600
Depreciation	1,800
Other	300
Total	$3,200/10,000 = $0.32 per mile

What costs are relevant (avoidable) to the trip? Insurance and depreciation are unavoidable: taking the trip does not affect those costs. Gas, oil, and maintenance will increase if you take the trip. (They are variable with the number of miles you drive.) The "other" costs might or might not be relevant: you have to investigate them further. If gas, oil, and maintenance are the only relevant costs, they should total about $15 for 300 miles, at $0.05 per mile ($500/10,000 miles). The $15 is avoidable: you do not incur it if you do not take the trip. It is also differential. You incur it if you go, you do not incur it if you do not go.

Product Costs and Period Costs

Up until now this book has treated merchandising companies—companies that buy goods, then sell them. Merchandisers do no manufacturing on the goods they buy. They sell essentially the same goods they buy. Manufacturers, in contrast, buy materials (wood, iron, fabric) and components (transistors, motors, handles), then fashion them into different products. Accounting for manufacturing operations is somewhat more complicated than it is for merchandisers, but the basic principles you already know remain relevant.

Manufacturers make a special distinction between costs. GAAP includes principles for calculating inventory costs for manufacturers that must be followed for published financial statements. The major principle relates to the distinction between product costs and period costs. A **product cost,** also called **inventoriable cost,** enters into the determination of inventory cost. The cost of inventory is recorded as an asset so long as the inventory is held and becomes an expense when the goods are sold. A **period cost** is expensed as incurred. For manufacturers, product costs consist of all manufacturing costs, and period costs are those associated with selling products and administering the overall company. Manufacturing costs consist of direct materials, direct labor, and manufacturing overhead. **Direct materials,** or simply *ma-*

The period-product classification relates to inventory determination for manufacturers.

terials, includes all raw materials, parts, and components traceable to units produced. **Direct labor** cost is the wages of people who work directly on the product. People who support production— maintaining machinery, moving materials and goods, storing and issuing materials are called *indirect laborers.* Salaries and wages of indirect laborers are part of **manufacturing overhead,** which consists of all costs reasonably associated with manufacturing products, except for materials and direct labor. Manufacturing overhead is also called *factory overhead, burden,* or often just *overhead.* Examples of manufacturing overhead costs in addition to indirect labor are depreciation on the factory building, depreciation on factory equipment, utilities used in the factory, salaries of factory supervisors, and manufacturing supplies. Groups of manufacturing overhead costs are driven by many activities, including labor hours and machine hours. Other activities that drive manufacturing overhead include the number of suppliers the company uses (some costs of the purchasing department) and the number of parts and components that products require (some storekeeping and recordkeeping costs).

It is not always a simple matter to distinguish product and period costs and some estimates are necessary. For instance, if a single building holds both the factory and a sales office, accountants must *allocate* such costs as building depreciation, real estate taxes, and utilities to manufacturing and nonmanufacturing activities. Some costs are treated as period costs by custom, even though they have something to do with manufacturing. The presidents of manufacturing companies are responsible for manufacturing (and everything else) and spend time on manufacturing questions, yet their salaries are considered period costs.

Manufacturers have special problems in determining inventory, partly because they have three kinds of inventory, in contrast to the one type that a merchandiser has. The three are materials, work-in-process, and finished goods. **Materials,** or **materials inventory,** consists of raw materials, purchased parts, and components used to make products. When workers begin transforming materials into finished product, we have **work-in-process inventory,** consisting of semi-finished goods, goods on which some, but not all work, has been done. **Finished goods inventory** corresponds to merchandise for a retailer or wholesaler. Such goods are ready for sale. When goods are finished, we have finished goods inventory, and when they are sold, we have cost of goods sold.

A merchandiser has a simple flow of costs: it buys goods, and the cost flows into Merchandise Inventory. When it sells the goods, the cost flows out of Inventory and into Cost of Goods Sold. A manufacturer has additional steps.

Exhibit 10–4
Product Costing Data

Inventories:	Beginning	End
Materials and components	$223,560	$ 198,239
Work-in-process	143,287	146,981
Finished goods	529,877	567,145
Other data:		
Purchases of materials and components		$2,456,320
Direct labor cost		721,568
Factory overhead cost		4,532,897

Manufacturers record costs in their object classifications (direct labor, utilities, etc.). As they buy materials and components, they debit Materials Inventory. As they pay direct laborers and incur overhead costs, they debit Direct Labor and various overhead accounts. All of these costs then flow to Work-in-Process Inventory, to Finished Goods Inventory, and ultimately to Cost of Goods Sold. This flow of costs parallels the physical flow: materials are put into process, and labor and overhead convert the materials into finished products, which are in turn sold.

Exhibit 10–4 provides data for an illustration of product costing and Exhibit 10–5 shows the statement of cost of goods manufactured and sold. This statement is a variant of the basic cost of sales statement you studied in Chapter 4. Notice that the statement shows the amounts of each factor (materials, labor, and overhead) incurred during the period as increases to work-in-process inventory. Figure 10–5 shows the flows of costs for the same illustration. Notice how the costs flow from their object classification (materials, direct labor) to Work-in-Process Inventory as the transformation of materials into product takes place. The costs then flow into Finished Goods Inventory. The debit to Finished Goods Inventory is Cost of Goods Manufactured as shown in the statement in Exhibit 10–5.

You already understand the calculation of cost of goods sold for a merchandiser. Notice that the calculation of cost of materials used in production and cost of goods manufactured parallels that familiar calculation. The debits to the account are added to the beginning balance, and the ending balance is subtracted to determine the amount credited (materials used in production or cost of goods manufactured). If you keep that general pattern in mind, you should have little problem with this statement.

Exhibit 10–5
Statement of Cost of Goods Manufactured and Sold

Beginning inventory of materials	$ 223,560	
Plus purchases	2,456,320	
Available for use	2,679,880	
Less ending materials	198,239	
Material used in production		$2,481,641
Direct labor		721,568
Factory overhead		4,532,897
Total manufacturing costs		7,736,106
Plus beginning work in process		143,287
Total costs in process		7,879,393
Less ending work in process		146,981
Cost of goods manufactured		7,732,412
Plus beginning finished goods		529,877
Cost of goods available for sale		8,262,289
Less ending finished goods		567,145
Cost of goods sold		$7,695,144

Figure 10–5
Flow of Costs

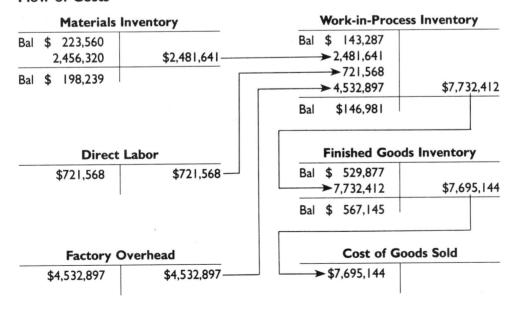

SUMMARY

Managerial accounting is concerned with the information needed to run an economic entity, be it a business or not-for-profit organization. Managers perform many tasks, having to do with planning, controlling, making decisions, and evaluating performance. Managerial accounting is essential for such tasks.

Managerial accounting requires classifying costs differently from the way that financial accounting does. In managerial accounting we classify costs according to the intended use of the information. Common classifications include those by behavior, by responsibility, by avoidability, and by product or period.

Manufacturing companies have more complicated inventory-costing problems than do merchandisers. The distinction between product costs and period costs is important in product costing.

Key Terms

avoidable cost	finished goods inventory
budget	indirect (common) cost
competence	integrity
controlling	manufacturing overhead
confidentiality	materials inventory
controllable cost	objectivity
cost behavior	performance report
cost driver	period cost
cost management	planning
cost of goods manufactured	product cost
direct cost	responsibility accounting
direct labor	scatter-diagram
direct materials	work-in-process inventory

DEMONSTRATION PROBLEM

Use the following information to prepare a statement of cost of goods manufactured and sold for November, 19X7, for Kryten Industries. All amounts are in thousands.

Material purchases for November	$287.5
Direct labor cost for November	256.5
Factory overhead for November	893.3
Cost of materials used in manufacturing	283.4

	November 1	November 30
Inventories:		
Materials	$ 98.5	$102.6
Work-in-process	123.9	98.3
Finished goods	153.3	134.6

Solution to Demonstration Problem

Kryten Industries
Statement of Cost of Goods Manufactured and Sold
November, 19X7

Beginning inventory of materials	$ 98.5	
Plus purchases	287.5	
Available for use	386.0	
Less ending materials	(102.6)	
Material used in production		$ 283.4
Direct labor		256.5
Factory overhead		893.3
Total manufacturing costs		1,433.2
Plus beginning work in process		123.9
Total costs in process		1,557.1
Less ending work in process		(98.3)
Cost of goods manufactured		1,458.8
Plus beginning finished goods		153.3
Cost of goods available for sale		1,612.1
Less ending finished goods		(134.6)
Cost of goods sold		$1,477.5

ASSIGNMENTS

10–1 Financial and Managerial Accounting

Describe the major similarities and differences of financial accounting and managerial accounting.

10–2 Planning and Control

Describe planning and control, and list a few activities of each.

10–3   Cost Estimation Methods

Describe cost estimation methods and their strengths and weaknesses.

10–4   Ethics

Walt Hansen, controller of TGH Industries, served on a committee charged with buying new data processing equipment. The cost was expected to exceed $8 million. CompuRama, one of the companies bidding for the business employed a sales engineer named Edward Jamal, who was a friend of Hansen's. On learning that TGH was considering buying its equipment, Jamal called Hansen and offered any help he might be able to give regarding the performance of the equipment. Partly based on conversations with Jamal, Hansen was impressed by Jamal's company's equipment and strongly supported buying it. The rest of the committee was unaware of the Hansen-Jamal friendship, and Hansen did not mention it because he recommended the equipment on the basis of its performance.

REQUIRED:

1. Has Hansen violated the IMA Standards? If so, how?
2. Suppose that Hansen disclosed his friendship with Jamal, TGH bought the equipment, and then Jamal took Hansen to Bermuda for a long weekend. How would that affect your answer to part 1.

10–5   Cost Classification—Behavior

Classify each cost listed below according to whether it is most likely to be fixed, variable, or mixed. If you believe the cost to be variable or mixed, state the measure of activity with which it should vary.

1. Wages of maintenance workers in office building.
2. Straight-line depreciation on factory equipment.
3. Wages of assembly line workers.
4. Travel expenses of salespeople.
5. Salaries of engineers in factory.
6. Units-of-production depreciation on factory equipment.
7. Advertising, where company policy is to spend 5% of sales on advertising.

10–6   Cost Classification—Direct or Indirect

Classify each cost listed below according to whether it is most likely to be direct or indirect to the Finishing Department of Argon Industries.

1. Wages of cleaning and maintenance workers in Argon's office building (separate from factory building).
2. Straight-line depreciation on factory equipment used in Finishing Department.

3. Wages of assembly line workers in Finishing Department.
4. Salaries of payroll clerks who process payroll for the entire factory.
5. Wages of maintenance workers in factory.
6. Units-of-production depreciation on factory equipment used in the Finishing Department.

10–7 Cost Classification—Period or Product

Classify each cost listed below according to whether it is a period cost or product cost for Martin Manufacturing Co. In some cases you might answer that the cost is part product, part period.

1. Wages of maintenance workers in office building.
2. Straight-line depreciation on factory equipment.
3. Wages of assembly line workers.
4. Salaries of payroll clerks who process payroll for the entire company.
5. Wages of maintenance workers in factory.
6. Costs of data processing, including all accounting for the entire company.

10–8 Cost Classification—Avoidability

UMN Industries manufactures and sells a wide variety of products. It is considering dropping its office-products line, which is about 20% of the business of one factory. Classify each cost listed below according to whether it is likely to be avoidable or unavoidable in a decision to drop the office-products line. If you think the cost might be partly avoidable, state your reasoning.

1. Wages of workers who spend all of their time making office products.
2. Salaries of salespeople who sell office products and other lines.
3. Straight-line depreciation on factory building.
4. Salaries of payroll clerks who process payroll for the entire factory where office products are made.
5. Wages of maintenance workers in factory making office products.

10–9 Cost Classification—Controllability

Classify each cost listed below according to whether it is most likely to be controllable by the manager of the Fabrication Department of Belton Manufacturing Company.

1. Wages of cleaning and maintenance workers in Belton's office building (separate from factory building).

2. Straight-line depreciation on factory equipment used in the Fabrication Department.

3. Wages of assembly line workers in the Fabrication Department.

4. Salaries of payroll clerks who process payroll for the entire factory.

5. Wages of maintenance workers in the factory, who work in all departments.

6. Units-of-production depreciation on factory equipment used in the Fabrication Department.

10–10   Cost Classification—Product versus Period

Classify each cost listed below according to whether it is most likely to be a product cost, a period cost, or a mix of the two for Carter Industries.

1. Wages of cleaning and maintenance workers in Carter's office building (separate from factory building).

2. Salary of the president of the company.

3. Wages of assembly line workers in the Fabrication Department.

4. Salaries of payroll clerks who process payroll for the factory.

5. Salaries of payroll clerks who process payroll for the selling and administrative functions.

6. Wages of maintenance workers in factory, who work in all departments.

7. Costs of the company's computer, which is used by nearly all departments.

8. Interest on debt used to finance building of factory.

10–11   Cost of Goods Manufactured

Use the following information to prepare a statement of cost of goods manufactured for Stone Inc. for April 19X6. All data are in thousands of dollars.

Material purchases for April	$ 750
Materials used in April	770
Direct labor cost for April	1,345
Factory overhead for April	2,567

	April 1	April 30
Inventories:		
Materials	$200	$180
Work-in-process	320	310

10–12 Cost of Goods Sold—Extension of Assignment 10–11

Use the following additional information about Stone, Inc. (in thousands of dollars) to determine cost of goods sold for April.

	April 1	April 30
Inventories of finished goods	$650	$690

10–13 Performance Report

Biggins Manufacturing employs managers who are in complete charge of product lines. The company prepares income statements for each product line that upper-level managers use to evaluate the managers of product lines. One such income statement for the Commercial Cleansers line for a recent month appears below, in thousands of dollars.

Income Statement
Commercial Cleansers

Sales		$2,526.8
Cost of sales		1,462.3
Gross profit		1,064.5
Other expenses:		
Travel	$ 76.5	
Advertising and promotion	498.3	
Office expenses	117.9	
Other expenses	121.4	814.1
Profit		$ 250.4

You have questioned the accountant who prepared this income statement and learned the following.

    a. Cost of sales includes $18.7 thousand in indirect costs allocated to the line.

    b. Advertising and promotion ordered by the manager of Commercial Cleansers totalled $409.1. The remainder is allocated to corporate advertising that does not mention specific products or lines.

    c. Other expenses are all indirect corporate costs allocated to products based on sales.

REQUIRED:

Prepare a new income statement using the principle of controllability.

10-14   Cost of Goods Manufactured and Sold

Use the following information to prepare a statement of cost of goods manufactured and sold for Ross Millworks for January 19X7. All data are in thousands of dollars.

Material purchases for January	$1,457.9
Direct labor cost for January	2,386.5
Factory overhead for January	5,687.3

	January 1	January 31
Inventories:		
Materials	$236.8	$221.9
Work-in-process	334.6	376.9
Finished goods	885.0	754.1

10-15   Scatter-Diagram

The following data relate to monthly machine hours and utility costs for the Placo Plant of WRM Industries.

Month	Machine Hours	Utility Costs
May	18,000	$26,500
June	16,000	24,500
July	22,000	29,300
August	21,000	28,600
September	25,000	31,900
October	17,000	25,400

REQUIRED:

Plot the data on a scatter-diagram and determine the fixed and variable components of utility cost.

10-16   Cost of Goods Manufactured and Sold

Use the following information to prepare a statement of cost of goods manufactured and sold for NoRo Manufacturing for July 19X7. All data are in thousands of dollars.

Material purchases for July	$?
Direct labor cost for July	3,256.5
Factory overhead for July	2,893.3
Cost of goods manufactured	7,836.7
Cost of materials used in manufacturing	1,589.7
Cost of goods sold	8,146.2

	July 1	July 31
Inventories:		
Materials	$224.5	$245.6
Work-in-process	445.9	?
Finished goods	?	887.6

10–17 Cost Analysis

Use the high-low method to determine the fixed and variable components of maintenance cost.

Machine Hours	Maintenance Cost
8,500	$34,500
10,200	38,750

10–18 Ethics

You have served as controller of Cleveland Foundry for eight months. The company has thrived, but the Environmental Protection Agency has informed the president that it believes Cleveland is guilty of several serious violations. The president has just told you and other senior officers. The news shakes everyone because the company could suffer greatly if the charges prove true, and they will be costly to fight, win or lose.

That evening, your retired father calls from Florida. After discussing the weather in Florida (good), in Cleveland (bad), the children (fine), and other family business, your father tells you that he just bought a large quantity of stock in Cleveland. "I figure that if they're smart enough to make you controller, they ought to be able to make some money for me."

REQUIRED:

What do you say to your father?

10–19 Cost of Goods Manufactured and Sold

Use the following information to prepare a statement of cost of goods manufactured and sold for WiltonWorks for August, 19X4. All data are in thousands of dollars.

Material used in August production	$378.9
Materials purchased in August	384.0
Direct labor cost for August	728.5
Factory overhead for August	927.3

	August 1	August 31
Inventories:		
Materials	$126.8	$131.9
Work-in-process	164.6	112.9
Finished goods	525.0	498.1

10-20   Cost Analysis

Use the high-low method to determine the fixed and variable components of utility cost.

Machine Hours	Utility Cost
8,500	$34,500
6,700	30,720
10,200	37,850
1,200	3,560
10,800	39,200

10-21   Avoidable Costs

Suppose you wish to spend the summer in your parents' house, but they
say you must pay rent based on the cost of your staying there. You
intend to take the normal advantages of living at home, eating there,
getting your laundry done, and so on.

REQUIRED:

1. How would you negotiate the rent?

2. How would you negotiate the rent from your parents' position?

10-22   DECISION CASE: RESPONSIBILITY ACCOUNTING

Managers of Kafka Products have been trying to isolate responsibility
for lines of business, which they had not done in the past. An assistant
controller prepared the following income statements for two major
product lines for a recent month, in thousands of dollars.

	Cleaners	Waxes
Revenues	$2,429.2	$2,391.2
Cost of sales:		
Materials	413.1	257.4
Direct labor	437.2	298.1
Manufacturing overhead	867.5	961.9
Total cost of sales	1,717.8	1,517.4
Gross profit	711.4	873.8
Selling and administrative expenses	349.2	287.3
Profit	$ 362.2	$ 586.5

The manager of Waxes was pleased at the results, which showed that her line earned over 60% more than Cleaners did, and on lower sales. Such a showing was important because the company was about to institute a bonus system that would reward managers based on the incomes of their lines. The controller, however, was not satisfied with these results and sought additional information, which is summarized below.

All material and labor costs are direct to the lines and are controllable, but some of the other costs shown for each line are not. About 40% of manufacturing overhead costs shown for Cleaners and 60% of the cost shown for Waxes is controllable by the two managers. The remaining amounts are not controllable by either manager. With selling and administrative expenses, about 30% of the amount shown for Cleaners and 50% of that shown for Waxes, are controllable by the respective managers.

REQUIRED:

Prepare an income statement for Kafka Products, by product line, using the principle of controllability. Comment on the results.

11

Product Costing

LEARNING OBJECTIVES

After studying Chapter 11, you should be able to:
1. Determine whether a company should use job-order, process, or standard costing.
2. Describe and diagram the flow of costs for a manufacturer.
3. Calculate costs using actual costing and normal costing.
4. Explain and apply activity-based costing.
5. Determine inventories and cost of sales using job-order, process, and backflush costing.
6. Distinguish between absorption costing and variable costing.

Chapter 10 introduced some of the terms of product costing, along with the statement of cost of goods manufactured and sold. This chapter continues the discussion. As you will recall, product costing is determining the unit costs of manufactured products, which are then used to assign costs to inventories and to cost of goods sold. Product costing therefore relates to the material from Chapter 4 and is a financial-accounting topic, for its main concerns have to do with published financial statements. However, there is a tendency to use information prepared for financial-accounting purposes inappropriately for internal managerial purposes—product costing is one such area. Many managers use information developed for product costing, or variations of that information, for pricing, analyzing profitability of products, and making various decisions about products or lines, such as whether to discontinue the manufacture of a product or product line. Such uses are often unwise.

Your previous study of cost behavior patterns will help in understanding and analyzing manufacturing costs. Product costing also affects human behavior, having important implications for control and performance evaluation.

MANUFACTURING COST FLOWS

As you know, merchandisers buy products that are ready for sale. Their product costs are limited to the purchase price and transportation or "other acquisition costs." Manufacturers, however, buy materials and components, then use labor and machinery to perform the various operations that result in finished products. In addition, manufacturers incur significant costs for support activities such as engineering, purchasing, personnel, accounting, and product design. Under GAAP, all of the costs required to manufacture products are treated as product costs, so it is necessary to include the costs of materials and components, of labor, and of manufacturing overhead—which is all manufacturing cost other than materials and labor. Selling and administrative expenses of manufacturers are expensed in the period incurred as *period costs,* a term familiar from earlier chapters.

Manufacturing costs are expensed when the product is sold (as cost of goods sold) and are called *product costs.* You have already studied the flow of product costs for a merchandiser. For a manufacturer, the flow is essentially the same, except that manufacturers have three types of inventory, and, as mentioned above, the cost of manufactured inventories includes materials, labor, and overhead costs. The three types of inventory are described below.

Figure 11–1
Flow of Costs

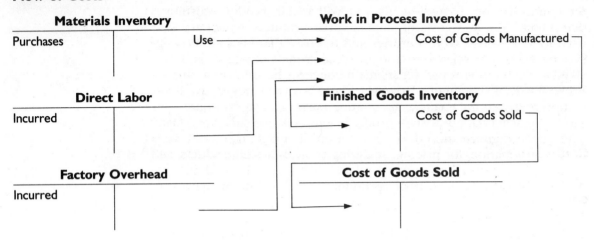

1. **Finished goods inventory** is the completed product that is ready for sale. This inventory is equivalent to merchandise in a merchandising concern.

2. **Work-in-process inventory** is partially finished units, such as partly assembled computers.

3. **Materials and components inventory** is the various materials (iron, glass, wood) and components (purchased switches, valves, handles) that are transformed into finished product. They have not yet been put into production. Here, again, there is no equivalent in a merchandising concern. For brevity, we shall sometimes use *materials* to refer to both materials and components.

The flow of product costs for a manufacturer is diagrammed in Figure 11–1, a refinement of Figure 10–5. The costs of materials and components are first recorded in the Materials account, then as they are used in production, their costs flow to the Work-in-Process Inventory account.[1] The cost of labor is first recorded in Direct Labor and then flows to Work-in-Process to reflect the work done on the product so far. Manufacturing overhead costs are recorded in Manufacturing Overhead, then flow to Work-in-Process because such items as supervision, power, and depreciation are critical in the manufacturing process. Thus, Work-in-Process is used to collect the costs of materials, labor,

Manufacturing costs flow through Work-in-Process Inventory.

[1] We capitalize the names of accounts and use lower case to refer to the things themselves.

and manufacturing overhead. As units of product are completed, their costs are transferred from Work-in-Process to Finished Goods. Finally, as units are sold their costs are transferred from Finished Goods to Cost of Goods Sold.

All manufacturing costs, both fixed and variable, become part of the cost of product. Manufacturing companies must use fixed costs in calculating per-unit product costs for financial reporting purposes and for some pricing decisions.

ABSORPTION COSTING

Absorption costing (or **full costing**), treats fixed manufacturing costs as product costs and requires calculating a fixed cost per unit. Absorption costing is required for financial reporting by GAAP, for income tax purposes, for regulatory reporting by public utilities, and for some government contracts. Manufacturers can use **direct costing** (or **variable costing**), for internal purposes. Variable costing does not use per-unit fixed costs. It treats fixed costs as period costs, expensing them as incurred, and treats only variable manufacturing costs as product costs. Variable costing is illustrated in the appendix to Chapter 12.

Absorption costing is required for financial reporting under GAAP. It is also used for internal managerial purposes by many managers despite its inconsistency with decision-making principles.

Inventories on the balance sheet and cost of goods sold on the income statement of manufacturers must include both variable and fixed manufacturing costs. This means that the behavioral classification of costs is not acceptable for external reporting. The accounting system must produce absorption costing information to satisfy these external requirements. In merchandising firms the only cost associated with a unit of product is a variable cost—the purchase cost of the unit.

Companies often use data required for external purposes for internal purposes, so managers are likely to encounter absorption costing reports. Managers who receive such reports must remember that per-unit costs include both variable and fixed manufacturing costs. As we know from the preceding chapter, total costs expressed as per-unit amounts can be misleading. Accordingly, managers in manufacturing firms must understand how the information was developed and, more importantly, how to interpret that information. Also, the determination of a product unit cost depends on the company's cost accumulation system.

MANUFACTURING METHODS AND PRODUCT COSTING

Product costing systems are influenced by the production process, of which there are four general types. The principles of product costing do not change from type to type, but the application of the principles does and the calculations do.

Process Costing

Some companies manufacture a single, homogeneous product in a more or less continuous process. Makers of sugar, bricks, bulk chemicals, and tomato juice are examples. Every unit of such products is essentially the same as every other. For these companies, the calculation of unit costs is relatively simple: divide total production costs by the number of units (pounds, gallons, etc.) produced. Such companies can use what is called **process costing.** Most such companies, however, use standard costing, which we cover in Chapter 14.

Job-Order Costing

At the other end of the spectrum from process costing are companies that rarely, if ever, make the same product twice. These are called *job-order companies* and they use **job-order costing.** An extreme case is a construction company, which never builds exactly the same bridge, office building, or house twice. A less extreme example is a printer, which might do 25 different jobs every day. A printer cannot calculate an average cost per job for a week when the jobs include, say, 25 sets of wedding invitations of different quantities, 2,000 business cards, and 75,000 football programs. Calculating an average cost by dividing total production costs for the period by total units produced accomplishes nothing because the units are so different. Managers of such companies are interested in the cost of each unit or batch because they will do the same *kind* of work again, even though not exactly the same work, and they want to analyze the profitability of, say, wedding invitations, and perhaps change prices.

Repetitive Manufacturing

Perhaps most common are **repetitive manufacturers** (or **mass producers**), which are hybrids, neither job-order nor process companies. They produce relatively standard products such as automobiles, but produce many different types of these products. Because they manufacture many products, they cannot use the simple process-costing formula given above. But because they make so many units, they cannot use job-order costing except at prohibitive recordkeeping costs. Consider an automobile manufacturer using ordinary job-order costing. It would have to keep track of the time spent to perform each operation on each car. The cost of keeping such records would be close to the cost of manufacturing the cars. Fortunately, these companies do not need to go to such extremes. They can use standard costing, which we discuss in Chapter 14.

ADVANCED MANUFACTURING

Many American companies are turning to **advanced manufacturing** techniques popularized by Japanese companies such as Toyota. There are many advanced methods and many terms to describe them, including *advanced manufacturing technologies, the new manufacturing environment, world-class manufacturing,* and *just-in-time manufacturing.* These modern manufacturing methods are a response to some serious problems of traditional, conventional manufacturing— problems involving quality, overproduction, and product design.

Problems with Traditional Manufacturing

American manufacturers dominated world markets after World War II and could sell everything they made. This favorable environment encouraged unwise practices. Quality of product was not as important as getting the product out the factory door, so companies made extra units, components, and parts "just in case" some turned out to be defective or the supply ran short. This practice caused high inventories of parts, components, goods in process, and finished product which were costly to store and finance. It is also costly to rework defective products.

Quality control during that time was a matter of inspecting after the product was finished, or perhaps at a few critical steps along the way. Thus a great deal of work was done on products that later had to be reworked or scrapped. Overproduction also led to sales at much lower than normal prices, such as to discount stores and outlets that buy manufacturers' overruns. Such sales can hurt sales at regular prices.

Efforts to sell as much product as possible led marketing to dominate manufacturing, with multitudes of products with special features being offered, such as the options available on American automobiles. Product design had only the customer in mind, with little concern for manufacturability. Many products proved extremely difficult to make with high quality at reasonable cost.

Proliferating products led to other difficulties. Multiproduct companies must change over from making one product to making another, often at considerable cost. The cost includes the wages of workers who set up for the change, which can occupy several hours. But the cost can also be much higher if changeovers result in lost production and therefore lost sales.

Advanced Manufacturing Techniques

Advanced manufacturing systems have common features.

Perhaps the most familiar of the new manufacturing methods is **just-in-time (JIT). Flexible manufacturing systems (FMS)** has been gaining popularity, as has **computer-integrated manufacturing (CIM).** All share some basic characteristics.

JIT is a philosophy of eliminating waste by sticking to the basics of efficiency and quality. An FMS is a manufacturing system where managers have reduced changeover costs to nominal amounts and so have made rapid changeovers possible. Some FMSs are so advanced that they manufacture single units instead of batches. An important advantage of FMSs is that they reduce greatly the response time between receiving a customer's order and filling it.

In CIM, computers control most operations. CIM encompasses FMS and is often idealized as the perfect manufacturing environment. There are few true CIM installations in service. JIT, FMS, and CIM share characteristics and it is not critical that you distinguish features of one from those of the other.

Eliminating Waste

Companies using JIT constantly strive to eliminate waste in all of its forms: materials, components, labor, and time. Toyota Motor Company developed JIT after World War II in Japan. Japan is a crowded country, and the Japanese do not tolerate waste. (The man generally credited with developing JIT, Taiichi Ohno, was an engineer with Toyota. He died in 1990 at age 78.) In JIT, there are two kinds of activities and costs: value-adding and non-value-adding. *Value-adding* activities include the manufacturing operations that change the product from a pile of materials and components into something useful. *Non- value-adding* activities and costs are waste. Moving semi-finished products from one work station to another does not add value to the product. Storing work-in-process between work stations is also non-value-adding.

Manufacturing Cells

Because moving semi-finished goods around the plant is non-value-adding, JIT companies use manufacturing *cells,* which do most, or all, of the work on a single product. These cells require less space than does

Figure 11–2
Conventional versus JIT Manufacturing

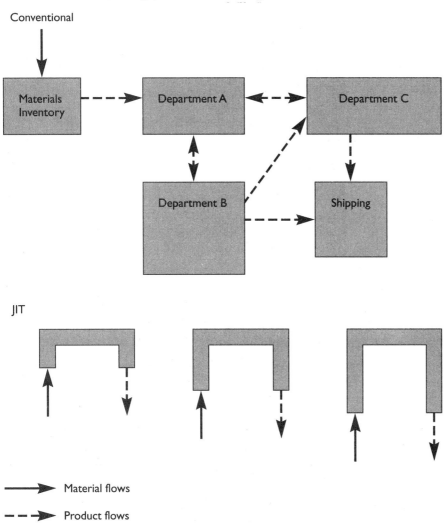

Conventional

JIT

→ Material flows

--→ Product flows

conventional manufacturing, as well as less movement of product. Figure 11–2 illustrates product flows in a conventional operation and in a JIT environment. The idea behind the conventional layout was to do the same kind of work in a single place, so that, for example, all drilling machinery was in the same area. In a cell structure, the idea is to do as much work as possible on the products in as small a space as possible, so that all of the machines needed for a particular product are together.

Workers in a cell structure must master several skills. Flexibility is important because workers must be able to shift from one kind of task (such as running a particular machine) to another to accommodate the needs of the moment. Workers in a JIT company enjoy much more responsibility than those in a conventional company. As a result, they are reported to have high morale and productivity. They work without close supervision. They perform most of their own machinery maintenance and do many other tasks that are left to specialists in conventional companies. Insight 11-1 describes how two such companies view their workers—quite differently from the way more conventional companies do.

Workers in a JIT system also inspect their own work; consequently, they rarely continue working on defective units. This practice greatly saves costs, because all work done on a defective unit is wasted. More important, the defective unit does not get to the customer. Warranty costs are one significant cost of defects, but the ill-will created by defective products is probably far and away the highest cost. Do you know people who will never again buy a particular make of automobile because they once bought a lemon?

INSIGHT 11-1
Decisions at Harley-Davidson

The vice-president and general manager of a maker of sophisticated telecommunications equipment, has described his company's experience this way: "Basically, what just-in-time does is tap that great, unmined resource—the intelligence of the manufacturing worker . . . we ask them to become more involved in making the process better." The company's attitude has benefited the workers. "They're more challenged." "They flourish in this environment."

Tom Peters, the popular writer who has chronicled some of the success stories of American business described Harley-Davidson, the motorcycle manufacturer as a great success story because of the same principle. Shop floor workers at Harley-Davidson routinely take on managerial roles. Peters related a conversation with a large young man in a torn T-shirt who mentioned that he was going to make a presentation to upper-level management for a new, very expensive piece of machinery. Peters was incredulous, but was assured that this was normal practice. The company gives workers a lot of responsibility and keeps them challenged by granting raises only when they master new jobs. The results are impressive: Harley-Davidson is probably the only company ever to ask the Federal government to remove restrictions on foreign competitors.

Reducing Lead Time

Lead time (or **cycle time**) is the entire time required to make and ship products—from the arrival of raw materials and purchased components to shipping the finished unit to the customer. JIT companies work hard to reduce lead time. Conventional factories can have lead times as high as three to six months, even though the time it actually takes to manufacture a product might be only a few days or even less. This is because such companies waste time by stocking large quantities of materials and components, making large batches of product, and interrupting production for rush orders. A component might sit in inventory for six weeks, then be used in a product that takes a month to go through production, then sit in finished goods inventory for another month before it is shipped to the customer. Keeping the component generates costs of insurance, personal property taxes, the risk of theft or deterioration, and the cost of the money tied up.

JIT companies attempt to reduce lead time until it equals manufacturing time. This ideal is impossible to achieve, but is a goal against which to measure progress. Some JIT companies have no loading docks. Suppliers' trucks drive into the plant and right up to the cell that needs the components. A cell might receive several deliveries a day. In a fully developed system, the cells turn materials and components into product the same day and ship the finished products that day or the next. Allen-Bradley is one U. S. company that is capable of doing just this.

Reducing lead time helps companies become more competitive.

Reducing lead time increases customer satisfaction, reduces costs (no storage space for inventory, no warehouses), and does away with the need to carry huge inventories of parts, work-in-process, and finished goods. In a conventional plant, problems with quality, interruptions, and other difficulties encourage managers to produce more components and finished products than are ordered. A manager who needs 20 components might order 25 "just in case" something goes wrong. This is sensible if quality is poor, but it leads to the undesirable results of high inventories and costs for storage, spoilage, financing, and handling.

Total Quality Control

All advanced manufacturers focus on **total quality control.** This means that they design quality into products at the very beginning. Then they also inspect work throughout the production process, rather than at the end. Advanced manufacturers work carefully with suppliers and drop those whose parts and components are not defect-free. Insight 11−2 describes how one company evaluates its vendors and what benefits it expects. Such practices have not been widespread until recent years.

Advanced manufacturers strive for continuous improvement in manufacturing operations. A worker who finds a defective component

INSIGHT 11–2
Evaluating Your Vendors

Copeland Electric, a subsidiary of Emerson Electric Co., evaluates vendors on ten factors. This list of ten was derived from a listing of all relevant factors by representatives from purchasing, engineering, quality assurance, materials managements, and accounting. Each vendor is given a numerical score on each factor. For instance, on the factor of delivery quality, a vendor delivering within one day of the date specified on the purchase order receives five points, while one delivering more than ten days early or five days late receives one point. Other factors are more qualitative, such as the factor of support, which is scored from one to five points based on the vendor's responsiveness to comments or problems. Other factors include dollar cost, quality costs, terms of sale (offering prompt payment discounts), and lead time. The program has increased vendor performance. Another benefit is that Copeland's managers have come to understand how vendors contribute to Copeland's success.

SOURCE: Michael A. Robinson and John E. Timmerman, "Vendor Analysis Supports JIT Manufacturing," *Management Accounting*, December 1987, 20–24. Copyright Institute of Management Accountants, 10 Paragon Drive, Montvale, N J 07645

can often shut down the entire operation until the cause of the defect is determined and cured. Such a drastic step is nevertheless practical, because a defective unit that gets all the way through production has wasted both time and materials. The unit must be reworked, at some cost, or scrapped. Quality and eliminating waste (including having low or no inventories) are related because inventory hides defective units. A company that makes large batches of components might not find a defective component until much later, when it is put into the product. Then it is too late to trace the defect back to the operation that needs corrective action. In a JIT operation defects are found immediately. Insight 11–3 shows that the benefits of JIT are not limited to manufacturing operations.

JIT Benefits Summarized

JIT companies produce better products at lower cost. High quality leads to customer acceptance—and increased sales. Short lead times get products to market much faster and this also increases sales. Many kinds of costs decline. Reducing defective products eliminates rework costs. Reducing inventories eliminates costs such as storage, insurance, and

INSIGHT 11–3
World Class Down on the Farm

Although the benefits of advanced, world-class techniques such as JIT are most obvious in manufacturing operations, they exist for nonmanufacturing operations as well. Peterson Ranch near Sacramento consists of two 3,000-acre production units. The ranch raises almonds, walnuts, and prunes. Of course, the ranch cannot manufacture its product just-in-time for delivery because it must wait for nature to take its course, but it does apply many other tenets of world-class manufacturing. The ranch emphasizes quality and maintains it by correct pruning, weed control, and eliminating foreign materials. Its products sell at premium prices because of their higher quality. The ranch employs people year-round, not seasonally as do some growers. This practice contributes to employee commitment and involvement. Detailed records of costs allow managers to spot areas for improvement. The ranch has identified 22 separate activities that relate to culture costs (all farming operations up to harvest).

SOURCE: Donald E. Keller and Paul Krause, " 'World Class' Down on the Farm," *Management Accounting*, May, 1990, 39–45. Copyright Institute of Management Accountants, 10 Paragon Drive, Montvale, N J 07645

financing. Continuous improvements in operations also reduce costs, as waste is reduced.

Morale of both workers and managers usually increases, because they have a bigger stake in the company's success, more responsibility, and more status; and all this usually increases productivity. Moreover, as we shall see later in this chapter, product costing in JIT companies (called backflushing) is simpler than it is for conventional manufacturers.

In summary, JIT is characterized by:

1. Small batches of production with low set-up time and cost.
2. Relatively stable production, avoiding large fluctuations.
3. Production that is pulled through, with components made as needed, not pushed through, with components made as convenient.
4. Multiskilled workers doing their own inspecting and much maintenance on machinery and equipment.
5. Constant searching for improvement and reduction of waste in materials, time, and effort.
6. Very low inventories, with zero inventory being an objective.

JOB-ORDER COSTING

A "job" can be a single unit (such as a building), a group of similar units (such as 500 wedding invitations), or a group of dissimilar units (such as a sofa, three chairs, and two tables). The critical point in job-order costing is that the company accounts for the job as a whole.

Because each job is different, job-order companies must keep track of the material costs and labor cost on each job and then apply manufacturing overhead to it. Tracing materials and labor to specific jobs is simple: workers keep track of time and materials they use on each job and report them on appropriate forms. Manufacturing overhead costs, however, cannot be so traced to specific jobs. Overhead costs are therefore applied to jobs indirectly, through the medium of an input activity such as direct labor hours or machine hours. The chosen activity is the one that drives overhead, either for the entire plant, for each department in the plant, or for similar types of overhead. Overhead application, which we discuss in detail shortly, requires determining an overhead rate per unit of the input activity, then using that rate to apply overhead to jobs. The rationale is that if, say, overhead is related to direct labor and a job requires 10 percent of the labor time for a month, that job should bear 10 percent of the month's overhead costs.

Selecting the cost driver is important in applying overhead.

One characteristic of job-order costing is that there is no need for a cost-flow assumption regarding jobs (there is for the use of materials). The reason is that job-order costing is a specific identification method in that costs are accumulated for each job. Exhibit 11–1 contains data for an illustration of job-order costing. Ecko Company manufactures large valves to customer specifications and uses machine hours to apply overhead. Workers filled out forms showing materials used on each job. They completed other forms showing their time as well as the machine time used for each job. These forms are the basis for determining the costs of materials and direct labor, and the numbers of machine hours given in the exhibit.

Actual Costing

One way to apply overhead costs to jobs is to calculate an overhead rate by dividing total overhead cost for the period by the total amount of the input factor used during the period, which is machine hours in our example. We then multiply this rate by the machine hours used on each job to determine the overhead for that job. This technique is called **actual costing.**

$$\text{Overhead Rate} = \frac{\text{Total Manufacturing Overhead}}{\text{Total Manufacturing Activity}}$$

Exhibit 11–1
Ecko Company Data for July

Total actual overhead costs			$80,000
Total machine hours			8,000

Job Number

Job Data	J-1	J-2	Total
Machine hours	6,000	2,000	8,000
Materials used	$44,000	$22,000	$66,000
Direct labor cost	$ 8,000	$ 2,000	$10,000

Budgeted (Planned) Data for Year

Machine hours	120,000
Overhead costs, $720,000 + ($3 per machine hour)	$1,080,000

In our example,

$$\text{Overhead Rate for July} = \$80,000/8,000$$
$$= \$10 \text{ per machine hour}$$

We can now determine the total costs of each job in July.

Job Number

	J-1	J-2
Overhead:		
6,000 hours × $10	$ 60,000	
2,000 hours × $10		$20,000
Materials	44,000	22,000
Direct labor	8,000	2,000
Total cost of job	$112,000	$44,000

Suppose that job J-1 was sold in July and that job J-2 was not finished at the end of July. The $112,000 cost of job J-1 appears in the July income statement as cost of goods sold. The $44,000 cost of job J-2 appears in the July 31 balance sheet as work-in-process inventory. Ecko's accountant will calculate a new overhead rate for August.

The T-accounts for Work-in-Process Inventory and Finished Goods Inventory appear as follows.

Work-in-Process Inventory

Materials	$ 66,000	
Labor	10,000	
Overhead	80,000	$112,000 to Finished Goods Inventory
	$156,000	$112,000
Ending Balance	$ 44,000	

Finished Goods Inventory

Job J-1	$112,000	$112,000 sale of J-1
Ending Balance	$ 0	

Problems of Actual Costing

Actual costing is very simple, but is rarely used. One reason is that you must wait until at least month-end to determine job costs. You might have to wait even longer because some invoices (utilities, for example) do not come in until the following month. Thus, you might not have even estimates of job costs until well after they have been produced and sold.

Perhaps more important, actual costing can give overhead rates that change considerably from month to month. These fluctuations in rates result from the fixed portion of total manufacturing overhead costs. There are two reasons for fluctuation. First, activity (machine hours in our example) is often different in different months. Many businesses are seasonal, and even most stable businesses have some high-activity and some low-activity months. Second, fixed overhead costs change from month to month. For example, heating costs are higher in winter. Remember that *fixed* does not mean "cannot change." It means that the cost does not change in response to changes in activity. So what if actual overhead rates fluctuate?

The problem with such fluctuations is that they can mislead managers using the data to analyze profitability or to set prices. Job-order companies often bid on jobs, so that pricing is very important. If they bid too low, they will be unprofitable; if too high, they will not get enough business.

Let us use an example to illustrate the point. Exhibit 11–1 shows that Ecko's budgeted variable overhead cost is $3 per machine hour and that its budgeted fixed overhead is $60,000 per month ($720,000/12). Suppose that in May its actual fixed overhead is $60,000, but in December, because of seasonal cost factors, it is $80,000. Ecko worked 12,000 machine hours in May and 5,000 in December, again because of seasonal factors. Under actual costing, the overhead rates for the two months are as follows.

	May	December
Total overhead costs:		
$60,000 + (12,000 × $3)	$96,000	
$80,000 + (5,000 × $3)		$95,000
Divided by machine hours	12,000	5,000
Overhead rate per machine hour	$ 8	$ 19

Suppose that Ecko does two similar jobs in May and December, each requiring 1,000 machine hours, $2,000 direct labor, and $11,000 in materials. The total costs of the jobs are as follows.

	May Job	December Job
Materials	$11,000	$11,000
Labor	2,000	2,000
Overhead, 1,000 × $8, 1,000 × $19	8,000	19,000
Total costs	$21,000	$32,000

Note that there is a significant difference between these costs. Suppose further that the selling price of each job was $33,000. A manager looking at the job done in December might erroneously conclude that it was just barely profitable. (Remember that the company also has selling and administrative expenses, so that its jobs must cover those costs as well as manufacturing costs.) The manager might also conclude that the May job was extremely profitable and might even think about reducing the price the next time a similar job comes in for bid. Most companies avoid this problem by using a technique called normal costing, discussed next.

Normal Costing

Under **normal costing,** the company uses the same overhead rate throughout the year. This rate is called a **predetermined overhead rate,** and is simply an overhead rate calculated in advance. It is based on expected, or budgeted, results, not on actual results, and is calculated at the beginning of the year.

$$\text{Predetermined Overhead Rate} = \frac{\text{Budgeted Manufacturing Overhead for Year}}{\text{Budgeted Production Activity for Year}}$$

Budgeted production activity (like actual activity in actual costing) can be expressed as direct labor hours, machine hours, or some other

Normal costing uses budgeted results.

measure that managers prefer. The difference between actual costing and normal costing is that normal costing uses budgeted results (costs and activities), while actual costing uses actual results.

Let us illustrate normal costing using the budgeted data from Exhibit 11−1. Total budgeted overhead for the year is $1,080,000, consisting of budgeted fixed costs of $720,000 and budgeted variable costs of $360,000 ($3 variable overhead per machine hour times 120,000 budgeted machine hours). The predetermined overhead rate is therefore $9 per machine hour ($1,080,000/120,000). We multiply this rate by the number of machine hours on each job to determine the overhead costs of the jobs.

	Job Number	
	J-1	J-2
Overhead:		
6,000 hours × $9	$ 54,000	
2,000 hours × $9		$18,000
Materials	44,000	22,000
Direct labor	8,000	2,000
Total cost of job	$106,000	$42,000

Notice that the material cost and direct labor cost are the same as they were under actual costing (see page 399). Only the overhead costs are different. Notice, too, that under actual costing, the entire $80,000 total actual cost ($60,000 + $20,000) was applied to the jobs. Under normal costing, only $72,000 ($54,000 + $18,000) was applied to jobs. It is rare that the total amount of overhead applied to all jobs during an accounting period will equal total actual overhead. It will happen only if total budgeted overhead equals total actual overhead and total actual hours equal total budgeted hours. (Offsetting differences could make the assignment come out even, but that is very unlikely.) The difference between actual overhead and applied overhead under normal costing is called **overapplied overhead** (if applied is greater than actual) or **underapplied overhead** (if actual is greater than applied, as is true in our example).

Which is right, actual or normal? We cannot answer this question, much as we cannot say that LIFO or FIFO is the "right" inventory cost-flow assumption. Normal costing was developed to minimize fluctuations in the overhead rate and to provide more timely cost data for products. If it helps managers to understand results better (which is a widespread belief), then it is "better" than actual costing.

Overapplied and Underapplied Overhead

What do we do with overapplied and underapplied overhead? There are several choices. One is to allocate it to Work-in-Process, Finished goods, and Cost of Goods Sold. This procedure in effect returns the company to actual costing and is used at year-end if overapplied or underapplied overhead is materially large. However, the most common method is to treat overapplied or underapplied overhead as an adjustment to cost of sales. Underapplied overhead increases cost of sales, overapplied overhead decreases it. Ecko has $8,000 of underapplied overhead ($80,000 actual overhead minus $72,000 applied overhead). Suppose that job J-1 was sold for $160,000, that J-2 was unfinished, and that selling and administrative expenses were $25,000. An income statement using actual costing appears below.

Sales	$160,000
Cost of sales (J-1, from page 399)	112,000
Gross profit	48,000
Selling and administrative expenses	25,000
Income	$ 23,000

Using normal costing, and showing underapplied overhead as an adjustment to cost of sales, we have the following.

Sales		$160,000
Normal cost of sales (J-1, from page 402)	$106,000	
Underapplied overhead	8,000	
Cost of sales		114,000
Gross profit		46,000
Selling and administrative expenses		25,000
Income		$ 21,000

Income is $2,000 less under normal costing than under actual costing. The difference relates to the differences in inventories. Job J-2 has a $44,000 cost under actual costing, $42,000 under normal costing.

What is the significance of overapplied or underapplied overhead? The predetermined overhead rate is based on both budgeted costs and budgeted production activity. Overapplied or underapplied overhead can result from actual costs being lower (a favorable variance) or higher (an unfavorable variance) than budgeted. Additionally, overapplied or underapplied overhead can result from a difference between actual activity and the activity used to calculate the predetermined overhead rate. The T-accounts for inventories appear below.

Work-in-Process Inventory

Materials	$ 66,000		
Labor	10,000		
Overhead	72,000	$106,000	to Finished Goods Inventory
	$148,000	$106,000	
Ending Balance	$ 42,000		

Finished Goods Inventory

Job J-1	$106,000	$106,000	sale of J-1
Ending Balance	$ 0		

Separate Overhead Rates and Activity-Based Costing

Activity-based costing uses several cost pools and drivers.

Our example used a single overhead rate for the entire factory. Most companies use different rates for different departments, called *departmental rates.* Some companies use one rate for overhead costs related to materials (such as purchasing, receiving, inspecting, storing, and insuring costs) and another rate for overhead costs related to labor or machine time. The use of separate rates is part of **activity-based costing (ABC)**. Companies using ABC identify the cost drivers for each overhead cost, or group of costs with the same driver. Such a group is called a **cost pool.** The company then applies overhead based on the rates associated with each driver, as the example below shows.

Separate rates are beneficial to many companies. In some companies, different input factors or activities influence overhead costs in different departments. Suppose TRM Industries has two major cost drivers—machine time and the number of parts each product requires. The use of separate rates does not create any conceptual problems. It simply means that we must apply overhead in more than one step. Data for TRM appear below.

	Part-related Overhead	Machine-related Overhead
Budgeted overhead costs	$500,000	$1,000,000
Activity:		
Number of parts	200,000	
Machine hours		100,000
Rates	$2.50/part	$10/MH

Suppose that job A-77 required 1,000 parts and 300 machine hours. Its cost is shown below, with labor and material costs assumed.

Job A-77

Material cost	$21,000
Direct labor cost	12,000
Overhead:	
Parts-related, 1,000 × $2.50	2,500
Machine-related, 300 × $10	3,000
Total cost	$38,500

ABC gives more accurate costs in the sense that the costs reflect the use of resources required for the job. Such costs can be especially helpful in such areas as evaluating the long-term profitability of a product or product line. It is also very helpful in cost management, as Insight 11−4 shows.

PROCESS COSTING

Companies that make a single product in a more or less continuous process can use **process costing,** which focuses on accumulating the costs to operate a process, or department, for a period of time, typically a month. Because all units are alike, calculating a cost per unit is appropriate. Recall that under job-order costing the point of focus is the job, not an individual unit, and that time periods are not particularly important. Like job-order companies, process-costing companies can use actual or normal costing.

Process costing concentrates on time periods and departments.

Process costing is relatively rare in practice. Most processing companies use standard costs, which obviates the need to perform some of the work we illustrate here. However, some of the concepts used in process costing are relevant to other techniques that you might encounter, so we therefore continue our discussion.

The general form of the unit-cost calculation follows.

$$\text{Unit Cost} = \frac{\text{Total Cost}}{\text{Equivalent Unit Production}}$$

Equivalent unit production (or just equivalent production) is a measure of work done. It represents the amounts of material, labor, and overhead expended on units of product. We cannot simply divide total costs by the number of units *finished* during a period because of work-

INSIGHT 11–4
Activity Costs

The Portables Group of Tektronix Company had been allocating overhead based on direct labor. Its engineers and managers had succeeded in reducing direct labor to less than 7% percent of total manufacturing cost. However, overhead costs were rising rapidly, so the overhead rate per direct labor hour was extremely high. Much of the rise in overhead was for costs such as purchasing, receiving, inspecting, storage, and recordkeeping. In fact, about 50% of overhead costs related to materials and components, not to labor. Because there was no overhead charge on these items, design engineers had no incentive to standardize and reduce the number of components, hence there was a proliferation of components.

The division began to allocate its material-related overhead based on both the number of component parts carried and their annual use. An example appears below. The division first determines the average cost per part, then uses the annual volume of the part to determine a cost per unit. This cost is allocated to each product that uses the part.

Total material-related overhead	$ 5,000,000
Total number of parts	6,250
Annual cost to carry part	$ 800
Cost per part:	
Part A, Annual Use of 20,000 units	$800/20,000 = $0.04
Part B, Annual Use of 500 units	$ 800/500 = $1.60

The allocations made it much more expensive to use a large number of components, and especially to introduce new ones. The costs encouraged engineers to reduce and standardize parts and the managers believe that the Group has achieved, and will continue to achieve, significant cost reductions.

SOURCE: John W. Jonez and Michael A. Wright "Material Burdening," *Management Accounting*, August 1987, 27–31.

in-process inventories. Work-in-process inventory contains units on which *some,* but not all work has been done, and we must recognize this work. So equivalent production must consider the degree of completion of in-process inventories. Suppose a company begins a month with no inventories, starts 12,000 units in process, finishes 10,000 units, and does 60% of the work on the other 2,000 that remain in process. It has done the *equivalent* of 11,200 units work (10,000 + [2,000 × 60%]).

Exhibit 11–2
Data for Example

	April	May
Units finished	10,000	12,000
Ending inventory of work-in-process	4,000	3,000
Percentage completed	40%	70%
Costs incurred	$29,000	$29,840

There are two cost-flow assumptions with process costing—weighted average and FIFO. We shall illustrate only the weighted average method here. Exhibit 11–2 contains data for our example. The calculation of unit cost, costs transferred to Finished Goods Inventory and ending inventory for April appear below.

Equivalent production:	
Units completed	10,000
Equivalent units in work-in-process, 4,000 × 40%	1,600
Equivalent production	11,600

$$\text{Unit Cost} = \$29,000/11,600$$
$$= \$2.50$$

The $2.50 is used to transfer costs to Finished Goods Inventory.

Finished Goods Inventory 10,000 × $2.50	$25,000	
Work-in-Process Inventory		$25,000

The T-account for Work-in-Process Inventory appears below.

Work-in-Process Inventory

Production Costs	$ 29,000	$25,000	to Finished Goods Inventory
Ending Balance	$ 4,000		

The ending balance is the cost of 1,600 *equivalent units,* $2.50 × 1,600.

For May, we have one change—a beginning inventory. Any weighted-average method, as you recall from Chapter 4, combines the cost of the beginning inventory with the costs incurred during the period. Here, too, we combine those costs, so that the calculations are as follows.

Equivalent production:	
Units completed	12,000
Equivalent units in work-in-process, 3,000 × 70%	2,100
Equivalent production	14,100

There is no need to consider the beginning inventory explicitly in calculating equivalent production because those units are included among the ones finished in May. That is, weighted-average equivalent production is calculated the same whether or not there is a beginning inventory.

The cost figure in the unit cost calculation is the sum of the beginning inventory and current period costs.

$$\text{Unit Cost} = (\$29,840 + \$4,000)/14,100$$

$$= \$2.40$$

The $2.40 is used to transfer costs to Finished Goods Inventory.

Finished Goods Inventory 12,000 × $2.40	$28,800	
Work-in-Process Inventory		$28,800

The ending inventory of work-in-process is $5,040, that is, $2.40 × 2,100 equivalent units. The T-account for Work-in-Process Inventory appears below.

Work-in-Process Inventory

Beginning Balance	$ 4,000		
Production Costs	29,840	$28,800	to Finished Goods Inventory
	33,840	28,800	
Ending Balance	$ 5,040		

Process costing is not always so straightforward. We have used only one percentage-of-completion figure, which assumes that units are equally complete with respect to materials, labor, and overhead. Usually, however, units in process have different completion percentages for materials and labor or machine time. In such cases, it is necessary to do the calculations separately. You must calculate equivalent production and unit costs for materials, for labor, and for overhead separately and make unit-cost calculations separately. Some assignments at the end of the chapter probe this complication. As a practical matter, labor and overhead are often treated together, and called *conversion costs.* For example, our illustrative company could have had 4,000 units 80% complete as to the material requirements, but only 40% complete as to conversion—labor and overhead. Highly automated processing companies might not classify any employees as direct laborers and might use machine time as the basis for estimating the percentage of completion for manufacturing overhead.

Other complications include lost or spoiled units and transfers from one department to another. You might study these and other finer points in later courses.

PRODUCT COSTING IN JIT COMPANIES

Companies using just-in-time (JIT) techniques fall into all three categories described earlier (job-order, process, repetitive), but tend toward repetitive or process manufacturing. Recall from our earlier discussion that JIT companies have very low inventories, if any at all. Such companies can use simpler costing techniques because the absence of inventories makes product costing a much less significant issue than it is for companies with large inventories. Many JIT companies use **backflush costing,** or just **backflushing.** It requires very few entries and is a less costly system to maintain than either job-order or process costing. Companies using backflushing often use a single account for materials and work-in-process because materials and components are delivered as needed and therefore do not sit in inventory. The account might be called **Raw-in-Process Inventory (RIP)** or **Raw and In-Process Inventory.** (There is also an account for finished goods.) The Raw-in-Process account receives all debits for production costs and is cleaned out (backflushed) at the end of the period to reflect production. The following example demonstrates the technique. There were no beginning inventories.

Materials and components purchased and put into process	$200,000
Labor and overhead costs incurred	240,000
Units completed	40,000
Units sold	35,000

There were no ending inventories of materials or in-process work. Material purchases are recorded in the following manner.

Raw-in-Process Inventory	$200,000	
Cash or Accounts Payable		$200,000

Because materials are put into process almost immediately, there is no need for separate accounts for materials and work-in-process.

Raw-in-Process Inventory	$240,000	
Cash, Accounts Payable, Accumulated		
Depreciation		$240,000
To record labor and overhead costs		

Where there is relatively little direct labor, there is no need for detailed labor reporting. These first two entries are made throughout the month as events (purchases of materials and components and incurrence of other manufacturing costs) require.

At month-end we compute the average cost of production as $11 ([$200,000 + $240,000]/40,000). Ending finished goods inventory of 5,000 units should then have $55,000 ($11 × 5,000) and cost of sales the remaining $385,000 ($11 × 35,000).

At the end of a period, or perhaps when units are sold, an entry such as the following is made.

Cost of Sales	$385,000	
Finished Goods Inventory	55,000	
Raw-in-Process Inventory		$440,000

After this entry is posted, RIP has a zero balance, reflecting no materials or in-process work on hand. This treatment is not the only possibility. Some companies charge all costs to Finished Goods Inventory as units are completed, then to Cost of Sales only at month-end.

SUMMARY

Product costing is determining costs of inventory and cost of goods sold for manufacturers. Manufacturing costs flow through work-in-process inventory to finished goods inventory to cost of goods sold.

Companies that rarely make the same product use job-order costing. They can use actual costing or normal costing, but normal costing is by far more common because it bases product costs on an expected annual average and avoids monthly fluctuations in overhead rates caused by seasonality. Using normal costing, the company applies overhead to jobs using a predetermined overhead rate. The rate is based on budgeted manufacturing overhead and budgeted activity of some input factor such as direct labor hours or machine hours. Normal costing nearly always shows a difference between actual overhead and applied

Predetermined = Budgeted man. overhead / Budgeted production act. (handwritten)

overhead. This difference is called underapplied or overapplied over-head and is usually shown as an adjustment to cost of goods sold in the income statement.

Process costing can be used by companies that manufacture the same product in a more or less continuous process. However, it is relatively rare because such companies can also use standard costing—a much better alternative for planning and control. JIT man-ufacturers can use backflush costing, which simplifies recordkeeping and is much less costly to maintain.

DEMONSTRATION PROBLEM

Arcon Machines uses job-order costing. It sets a plant-wide predeter-mined overhead rate using the following budgeted data:

Total Annual Factory Overhead = $240,000 + $2 × Direct Labor Hours

Annual budgeted direct labor hours are 60,000. In March the company had the following jobs in process. Actual factory overhead was $32,800 and selling and administrative expenses were $63,000.

	H-12	M-21	M-102
Materials used in March	$22,000	$40,000	$35,000
March direct labor cost	$13,000	$24,000	$15,000
Direct labor hours in March	1,300	2,400	1,500

Job H-12 was finished and sold for $150,000. The others were still in process at the end of March.

REQUIRED:

1. Calculate the predetermined overhead rate.
2. Determine the total cost of each job.
3. Determine the amount of overapplied or underapplied overhead.
4. Prepare an income statement assuming that the company treats misapplied overhead as an adjustment to cost of sales calculated using normal costing.

Solution to Demonstration Problem

1. The predetermined overhead rate is $6.

$$Rate = \frac{\$240,000 + 60,000 \times \$2}{60,000}$$

2.

	H-12	M-21	M-102
Materials used in March	$22,000	$40,000	$35,000
March direct labor cost	13,000	24,000	15,000
Applied overhead	7,800	14,400	9,000
Total costs	$42,800	$78,400	$59,000

3. Overhead applied is direct labor hours for each job multiplied by the $6 rate,

$6 × 1,300 = $7,800; $6 × 2,400 = $14,400; and $6 × 1,500 = $9,000.

Underapplied overhead:	
Actual overhead	$32,800
Applied ($7,800 + $14,400 + $9,000)	31,200
Underapplied overhead	$ 1,600

4.
Arcon Company
Income Statement—March

Sales		$150,000
Cost of sales, normal (H-12)	$42,800	
Underapplied overhead	1,600	
Cost of sales		44,400
Gross profit		105,600
Selling and administrative expenses		63,000
Income		$ 42,600

Key Terms

absorption (full) costing

activity-based costing (ABC)

actual costing

advanced manufacturing

backflushing

computer-integrated
    manufacturing (CIM)

cost pool

direct (variable) costing

equivalent unit production

flexible manufacturing system
    (FMS)

job-order costing

just-in-time manufacturing (JIT)

lead (cycle) time

normal costing

overhead application

predetermined overhead rate

process costing

repetitive manufacturing (mass
    producer)

total quality control

ASSIGNMENTS

11–1 Actual and Normal Costing
If a company begins and ends the year with no inventories, will its income be different depending on whether it uses actual costing or normal costing? Why or why not?

11–2 "Why Is It Called Normal?"
A friend of yours just asked you this question. He does not see why accountants calculate an overhead rate before the year begins and use it throughout the year. He says that each month's actual overhead cost ought to be applied to products.

REQUIRED:

Explain the idea of a predetermined overhead rate.

11–3 Activity-Based Costing
How does the use of several overhead rates differ from the use of a single rate? What advantages and disadvantages are there in using separate rates?

11–4 JIT and Conventional Manufacturing
Outline the major differences between JIT and conventional manufacturing and the advantages of JIT manufacturing over conventional methods.

11–5 Basic Actual Job-Order Costing
Belton Furniture uses actual job-order costing. It applies overhead based on direct labor hours. During July, Belton worked on two jobs.

	J-1	J-2
Material cost	$100,000	$200,000
Direct labor cost	$ 60,000	$ 90,000
Direct labor hours	8,000	12,000

20,000

Actual overhead was $220,000 in July.

REQUIRED:

1. Determine the overhead rate for July.
2. Determine the overhead to be applied to each of the two jobs.
3. Determine the total cost of each job.

11–6   Basic Normal Job-Order Costing—Extension of Assignment 11–5

Suppose that Belton changes to normal costing, applying overhead to jobs at a predetermined overhead rate of $10 per direct labor hour.

REQUIRED:

1. Determine the amount of overhead to be applied to each job.
2. Determine the total cost of each job.
3. Determine the amount of overapplied or underapplied overhead.

11–7   Job-Order Costing—Income Statements—Extension of Assignments 11–5 and 11–6

Belton sold job J-2 for $600,000. Job J-1 was not complete at the end of July. Selling and administrative expenses for July were $120,000.

REQUIRED:

1. Prepare an income statement for July using the results from Assignment 11–5.
2. Prepare an income statement for July using the results from Assignment 11–6. Show any misapplied overhead as an adjustment to normal cost of sales.
3. Determine the cost of work-in-process inventory for both costing methods.

11–8   Job-Order Costing—Machine Time

Typee Manufacturing operates a highly automated plant and applies overhead using machine hours. The predetermined overhead rate is based on 120,000 annual budgeted machine hours and $2,400,000 annual budgeted overhead. Typee experienced the following results in March, when it worked on two jobs.

	Job M-1	Job M-2
Material cost	$60,000	$130,000
Direct labor cost	$12,000	$ 15,000
Machine hours	4,000	7,000

Actual overhead was $218,000 in March.

REQUIRED:

1. Calculate the predetermined overhead rate.
2. Determine the amount of overhead to be applied to each job.
3. Determine the total cost of each job.
4. Determine the amount of overapplied or underapplied overhead for March.

11–9   Job-Order Costing—Income Statement

Lamson Manufacturing Company uses normal job-order costing. Its pre-determined overhead rate is based on 200,000 budgeted machine hours. Total manufacturing overhead is budgeted as:

$$\$800,000 + \$4 \times \text{Machine Hours}$$

Lamson began 19X5 with no inventories and had these results in 19X5.

	Total	Jobs Sold	Jobs in Ending Inventories
Material cost	$1,800,000	$1,600,000	$200,000
Direct labor cost	$ 900,000	$ 800,000	$100,000
Machine hours	175,000	155,000	20,000

Total sales were $6,000,000. Selling and administrative expenses were $1,850,000. Manufacturing overhead was $1,430,000.

REQUIRED:

1. Compute the predetermined overhead rate for 19X5.

2. Prepare an income statement for 19X5 with overapplied or under-applied overhead shown as an adjustment to normal cost of sales.

3. Determine the cost of the ending inventories.

11–10   Normal Job-Order Costing

Taylor Mills uses a predetermined overhead rate based on 100,000 monthly machine hours. Taylor budgets monthly manufacturing over-head budgeted using the formula:

$$\$380,000 + (\$2.60 \times \text{Machine Hours})$$

Taylor had the following results in September.

	Total	Jobs Sold	Work-in-Process	Finished Goods
Material cost	$1,010,000	$820,000	$100,000	$90,000
Direct labor cost	$ 630,000	$500,000	$ 70,000	$60,000
Machine hours	104,000	88,000	9,000	7,000

Actual overhead for the month was $710,000.

REQUIRED:

1. Compute the predetermined overhead rate based on machine hours.

2. Determine normal cost of goods sold for the month.

3. Determine the ending inventory of work-in-process.
4. Determine the ending inventory of finished goods.
5. Determine overapplied or underapplied overhead.

11-11   T-Accounts—Extension of Assignment 11-10

Prepare a T-account for Work-in-Process Inventory for the activity described in the previous assignment.

11-12   Predetermined Overhead Rates

Spalding Company uses a predetermined overhead rate based on machine hours. Spalding budgeted 40,000 machine hours and $360,000 in overhead costs for 19X6. The company actually worked 39,000 hours and incurred $357,000 overhead costs.

REQUIRED:

1. Compute the predetermined overhead rate for 19X6.
2. Determine the amount of overhead applied during 19X6.
3. Determine the amount of overapplied or underapplied overhead for 19X6.

11-13   Basic Job-Order Costing

Tucker Machining manufactures presses for the wine industry. Each press has some special features, so Tucker uses job-order costing. Tucker applies overhead at $15.00 per direct labor hour. During June the company worked on the following three jobs.

	J-11	J-12	J-13	Total
Direct labor hours	2,200	1,120	2,820	6,140
Direct labor cost	$21,600	$10,250	$30,870	$62,720
Material cost	$32,450	$18,360	$21,220	$72,030

Actual overhead was $89,330.

REQUIRED:

1. Determine the amount of overhead applied to each job.
2. Determine the total cost of each job.
3. Determine the amount of overapplied or underapplied overhead for June.

11-14   Basic Process Costing

CDE Company uses weighted-average process costing. The data below relate to July.

Beginning inventory	$2,100
Conversion costs incurred in July	$47,400
Units completed in July	30,000 units
Units in ending work-in-process, 60% complete	5,000 units

REQUIRED:

1. Determine equivalent production for July.
2. Determine the unit cost.
3. Determine the cost of the ending inventory of work-in-process.
4. Determine the cost of goods transferred to finished goods.
5. Prepare a T-account for Work-in-Process Inventory.

11–15 Basic Process Costing

The data below relate to the operations of Wharton Milling, Inc. for January.

Beginning inventory	$13,325
Units completed in March	80,000 units
Ending inventory, 40% complete	10,000 units

January production costs were $238,675.

REQUIRED:

1. Compute equivalent production.
2. Compute unit cost.
3. Compute the cost of the ending inventory.
4. Compute the cost of units finished and transferred to finished goods inventory.
5. Prepare a T-account for Work-in-Process Inventory.

11–16 Job-Order Costing for a Service Company

BMR, Inc. plans and carries out market research studies. The company uses a job-order costing system. One major cost component is direct cash costs such as travel and wages for interviewers. The other major cost components are professional salaries and overhead. During September BMR worked on the following jobs.

	Testosteronia	Barf-O-Matic	Liver Rama
Direct cash costs	$ 1,200	$ 9,800	$6,700
Professional salaries	$11,500	$22,800	$9,400

BMR applied overhead at $1.80 per dollar of professional salary. Actual overhead was $71,200.

REQUIRED:

1. Determine the overhead to be applied to each job.
2. Determine the total cost of each job.
3. Determine the amount of overapplied or underapplied overhead.

11–17   Process Costing—Two Factors

Chalmers Company manufactures water-proofing. Unit data for July follow.

Gallons completed in July	130,000
Gallons in ending inventory	24,000
Percentages complete:	
Materials	100%
Conversion costs	75%

Cost data appear below.

	Materials	**Conversion Costs**
Beginning inventory	$ 3,100	$ 9,300
Incurred during July	$29,240	$82,460

REQUIRED:

1. Compute equivalent production for (a) materials and (b) conversion costs.
2. Compute unit costs for each cost factor.
3. Determine the cost transferred to finished goods inventory.
4. Determine the ending inventory of work-in-process.
5. Prepare a T-account for Work-in-Process Inventory.

11–18   Job-Order Costing—Activity-Based Costing

Harmon Industries separates its overhead costs into two pools, one related to labor time, the other to the number of parts used in each product. The company uses these cost pools because a considerable amount of overhead cost relates to ordering, receiving, inspecting, storing, and keeping records on parts. Data appear below.

	Labor-related	**Part-related**
Total budgeted overhead	$1,200,000	$800,000
Total budgeted activity:		
Labor hours	150,000	
Number of parts		200,000

During October the company worked on two jobs.

	Job O-1	Job O-2
Material and part cost	$56,000	$44,000
Direct labor cost	$78,000	$84,000
Direct labor hours	7,000	8,000
Number of parts	11,000	9,000

Actual labor-related overhead was $110,000. Actual part-related overhead $76,000.

REQUIRED:

1. Calculate the predetermined overhead rate for each cost pool.
2. Determine the amount of overhead to be applied to each job and the total cost of each job.
3. Calculate the amount of overapplied or underapplied overhead for each cost pool.

11-19   Process Costing—Two Factors
The data below relate to April operations for NecHi Company, which manufactures lawn fertilizer.

Pounds completed in April	200,000 pounds
Ending inventory of work in process	30,000 pounds
Cost of materials used in production	$324,700
Conversion costs incurred	$657,800
Costs in beginning inventory:	
Materials	$ 31,800
Conversion costs	$ 39,800

Inventories were 100% complete for materials. The ending inventory was 60% complete for conversion costs.

REQUIRED:

1. Determine equivalent production for materials and for conversion costs.
2. Determine unit costs for materials and for conversion costs.
3. Determine the cost of the ending inventory of work-in-process and the cost transferred to finished goods inventory.

11-20   Backflush Costing
Calvin Industries uses just-in-time manufacturing and backflush costing. The company began September with no inventories, manufactured

10,000 units of product and sold 9,000. Calvin purchased and used materials and components costing $41,000 and spent $35,000 on labor and overhead.

REQUIRED:

1. Determine the cost per unit of product.
2. Determine the cost of the ending inventory of finished goods and cost of goods sold.

11–21   Backflush   Costing—Continuation   of   Assignment 11–20

REQUIRED:

Prepare journal entries and T-accounts to reflect Calvin's September activity.

11–22 DECISION CASE
OVERHEAD RATES

Taylor Industries uses a single, plant-wide overhead rate based on direct labor hours. Budgeted overhead is $4,000,000 and budgeted labor hours 200,000 for the coming year. The company worked on the following jobs in October.

	Job M-12	Job K-54
Material and part cost	$103,000	$82,000
Direct labor cost	$128,000	$47,000
Direct labor hours	13,000	5,000

REQUIRED:

1. Calculate the overhead rate per direct labor hour.
2. Determine the overhead cost to be applied to each job and the total cost of each job.

11–23 DECISION CASE
ACTIVITY-BASED COSTING—
CONTINUATION OF ASSIGNMENT 11–22

Some of Taylor's managers are not happy with the single overhead rate and asked the controller to separate overhead costs into three pools, one related to labor time, another to the number of parts used in each product, and another to the number of machine setups, each of which the managers believed to be an important cost driver. The controller developed the following data.

Activity	Annual Amount of Activity	Budgeted Annual Overhead Costs in Pool
Labor hours	200,000 hours	$1,600,000
Number of parts	25,000 parts	$1,000,000
Machine setups	20,000 setups	$1,400,000

The following additional information is available about the jobs worked on during October.

	Job M-12	Job K-54
Number of parts	1,000	4,000
Number of machine setups	200	500

REQUIRED:

1. Calculate the predetermined overhead rate for each cost pool, labor-related, part-related, and setup-related.

2. Determine the amount of overhead to be applied to each job and the total cost of each job.

3. Comment on the differences between the costs of the jobs here and in assignment 11−22.

CHAPTER

12

Cost-Volume-Profit Analysis and Short-Term Decision Making

LEARNING OBJECTIVES

After studying Chapter 12, you should be able to:
1. Explain the concept of contribution margin and its importance in planning.
2. Find the sales volume or selling price required to earn a target profit.
3. Describe and use the ideas of incremental revenues and costs in making short-term decisions.
4. Describe and use the ideas of sunk cost and opportunity cost in making short-term decisions.
5. Apply cost-volume-profit analysis and incremental revenue/cost principles to a variety of short-term decisions.

Managers continually plan and make decisions, many of which concern profit and the effects on profit of various proposed actions. For instance, how much will we increase profit if we increase unit sales by 10 percent? This chapter discusses one of the most fundamental principles of such planning and decision making: **cost-volume-profit (CVP) analysis.** The material in this chapter builds on Chapter 10, especially the behavioral classification of costs and the principle of avoidability of costs.

The principles discussed here are applicable not only to businesses but also to such not-for-profit entities as hospitals, colleges, charitable institutions, and government units. These principles are valid for personal decisions as well.

COST-VOLUME-PROFIT (CVP) ANALYSIS

Cost-volume-profit (CVP) analysis helps us answer two major types of questions: what if, and how? An example of the first type is, what will our profits be if sales are 10,000 units? If we sell an additional 5,000 units, what will the increase in profit be? If we lower our price by 10 percent and increase volume by 15 percent, what will our profits be? Examples of the second type of question relate to how we will meet our objectives: How many units must we sell to earn $200,000? What price must we charge to earn $50,000?

Cost Behavior and Contribution Margin

CVP analysis relies on the behavioral classification of costs. As we know from Chapter 10, costs are either fixed, or they vary with some activity. While that distinction is an oversimplification, it serves managers well in planning and decision-making. **Contribution margin per unit** is selling price per unit minus variable cost per unit. Think of it this way: of each unit sold, the revenue must first cover the variable cost, then what is left goes toward covering fixed costs and providing a profit. Contribution margin can also mean the difference between total sales and total variable costs.

Contribution margin is selling price less variable cost.

In CVP analysis, we prepare income statements differently from the way we do in financial accounting and as shown in Chapter 11. The income statement in Exhibit 12–1 is an example. The data for the income statement appear in the exhibit.

In CVP analysis we do not care what a cost *is* (salaries, depreciation), or is *for* (cost of goods sold, selling costs, administrative costs). We care only whether the cost is fixed or variable. While we could

---

Exhibit 12–1

RST Company
Operating Data and Income Statement

Data:

Unit sales	100,000
Selling price	$5
Variable cost	$3
Total fixed costs	$180,000

Income Statement

Sales (100,000 × $5)	$500,000
Variable costs (100,000 × $3)	300,000
Contribution margin (100,000 × $2)	200,000
Fixed costs	180,000
Income before taxes	$ 20,000

---

show the components of variable cost (purchase cost, commissions, freight) and fixed costs (salaries, rent, depreciation), it is not necessary. The formula below calculates income before taxes using the CVP model.

Profit = Unit Sales × (Selling Price − Unit Variable Cost) − Total Fixed Costs
   = Unit Sales × Contribution Margin − Total Fixed Costs

Note that this formula parallels the income statement. Unit sales times selling price is total sales and unit sales times variable cost is total variable cost. This format of the income statement is very helpful.

An important use of CVP analysis is to help managers predict how income will change if sales change. Suppose that the managers of RST Company want to predict income if unit sales rise by 10 percent. See if you can predict income before looking at the income statement below.

Sales (110,000 × $5)	$550,000
Variable costs (110,000 × $3)	330,000
Contribution margin (110,000 × $2)	220,000
Fixed costs	180,000
Income	$ 40,000

Income doubles, from $20,000 to $40,000, as sales rise by only 10 percent. This occurs because not all costs rise by 10 percent. Variable costs do, but fixed costs remain constant, leveraging income. You might also have noted that you could have simply calculated the new total contribution margin as $220,000 by multiplying the $2 per unit contribution margin by 110,000 units. You might even have seen that the increase in income is the additional $20,000 generated by the $2 unit contribution margin times the additional 10,000 units. These are important points. If fixed costs remain constant, income changes at the rate of contribution margin per unit times the change in unit sales. Thus, a drop in sales of 20,000 units will reduce income by $40,000 (20,000 × $2), down to zero.

CVP GRAPH AND RELEVANT RANGE

Figure 12–1 graphs the relationships. The revenue line shows total sales dollars at any volume and is simply the selling price per unit multiplied by unit volume. The vertical distance between total costs at any volume and fixed costs at that volume is total variable costs.

The lines on the graph extend to the vertical axis and far to the right. This is not usually reasonable because as the company moves outside its normal operating range, as measured here by sales, it probably finds costs behaving differently. In CVP analysis we assume that there is a range of volume over which we can use straight lines to represent total revenue and total cost. This range is called the **relevant range.** For instance, if the company shut down for a month, it would almost certainly turn out the lights, lay off some salaried employees, and take other steps that would reduce fixed costs. In other words, we really do not expect fixed costs to be the same regardless of volume. Rather, we expect them to be the same as we have planned within a reasonable operating range. Similarly, a manufacturing company operating at very low levels, or at very high levels, will probably have higher than normal variable costs per unit. At very low levels the company will be less efficient than at a normal operating volume, while at high levels it will likely have bottlenecks, will need to hire less skilled workers, and make other adjustments that would increase variable costs per unit.

Costs are not expected to behave the same outside the relevant range.

Future Orientation of CVP Analysis

CVP analysis deals with the future. We do not expect costs (variable or fixed) to stay the same month after month, or year after year. Inflation causes increases in both fixed and variable costs. Management can also influence costs, especially fixed costs. In fact, the term *fixed costs* is something of a misnomer. We do not expect these costs to be constant

Figure 12–1
CVP Graph (in thousands)

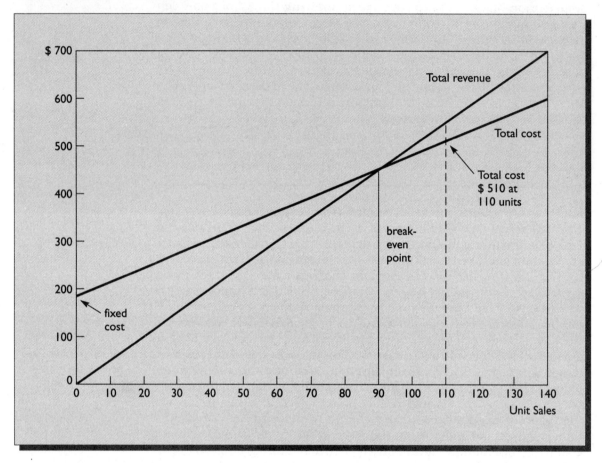

period to period or over wide ranges of volume. We call them fixed because they do not automatically change when volume changes. For instance, management can raise and lower salaries, advertising, travel, and other costs on very short notice. Such costs are often called *discretionary fixed costs*. In contrast, costs such as depreciation cannot be changed significantly at short notice and are called *committed fixed costs*. Generally, committed costs cannot be changed without changing the capacity of the company to operate. In doing CVP analysis, then, we assume that the managers have agreed on the level of discretionary costs. If they wish to change some of these costs, we must then simply change the numbers.

Some fixed costs can be changed quickly, others cannot.

Even though it is possible to reduce discretionary costs, it is not always wise. Cutting such costs as research and development, employee training, and quality control might benefit short-run profit performance, but only at the expense of the company's long-term health. For all of the reasons given above, some accountants prefer the term *nonvariable* to describe costs that we call *fixed.* There is no harm in using the term, but most people are accustomed to seeing *fixed.*

MEETING PROFIT TARGETS

We have just dealt with a typical "what if" question. Let us now turn to questions of what we must do to meet a target profit. Profit is the most common target, although targets can be expressed in terms of costs or sales.

Required Unit Sales

One commonly used target is **break-even,** the sales volume that produces neither a profit nor a loss. Of course, managers of businesses do not wish to break even, they want to show profits. But managers also want to know what they must do to break even. Managers of not-for-profit entities, which exist to provide services, not to earn profits, are also interested in what it takes to break even, since this is often their goal. For instance, the board of directors of a not-for-profit nursery school are interested in the number of children they must enroll to break even.

We shall illustrate two equivalent methods below, one using the contribution margin format of the income statement, the other using the formula for profit shown above. Look at the income statement in Exhibit 12−1 again. We want income to be zero, so, because total fixed costs are $180,000, we need total contribution margin of $180,000.

Contribution margin	$180,000
Fixed costs	180,000
Income	$ 0

How do we earn $180,000 in contribution margin? At a rate of $2 per unit, it takes 90,000 units ($180,000/$2) to achieve the target.

Sales (90,000 × $5)	$450,000
Variable costs (90,000 × $3)	270,000
Contribution margin (90,000 × $2)	180,000
Fixed costs	180,000
Income	$ 0

We can also solve the basic formula for unit sales. We add fixed costs to both sides and divide both sides by the quantity, selling price minus unit variable cost. The resulting formula below works for any target profit, but at the break-even point, profit is zero.

$$\text{Unit Sales} = \frac{\text{Fixed Costs} + \text{Profit}}{\text{Selling Price} - \text{Unit Variable Cost}}$$

The formula yields

$$\text{Unit Sales} = \frac{\$180,000 + \$0}{\$5 - \$3}$$
$$= 90,000$$

Of course, selling price minus unit variable cost is contribution margin per unit. But suppose we want to earn $50,000, not break even? Again, looking at the bottom of the income statement, we see the following.

Contribution margin	$230,000
Fixed costs	180,000
Income	$ 50,000

To earn $50,000 requires contribution margin of $230,000, which means 115,000 units at $2 each. We use the formula.

$$\text{Unit Sales} = \frac{\$180,000 + \$50,000}{\$2}$$
$$= \$230,000/\$2$$
$$= 115,000$$

The reason the two approaches illustrated here are equivalent is that they both require dividing total contribution margin by contribution margin per unit. They arrive at the same answer in different ways.

Setting Target Selling Prices

Many companies calculate **target selling prices,** prices that will yield **target profits.** (Of course, the company might decide to set other prices because of market conditions.) Suppose that the managers of RST want to earn $60,000 and they expect to sell 100,000 units. What price must they charge to meet the objective? Again, we can use the income statement approach or the formula. Starting with the formula, we solve for selling price as follows.

$$\text{Selling Price} = \frac{\text{Fixed Costs} + \text{Profit}}{\text{Unit Sales}} + \text{Unit Variable Cost}$$

That is, we now divide total required contribution margin by unit sales, which yields the required contribution margin per unit, to which we add unit variable cost to find the required price.

$$\text{Selling Price} = \frac{\$180,000 + \$60,000}{100,000} + \$3$$
$$= \$2.40 + \$3$$
$$= \$5.40$$

The $2.40 is the contribution margin per unit that 100,000 units must yield to earn $60,000 with fixed costs of $180,000. Using the income statement format gives the same result. We can now find total variable costs, because we know unit volume and variable cost per unit. Therefore, we can fill in the income statement as shown below.

Variable costs ($3 × 100,000)	300,000
Contribution margin	240,000
Fixed costs	180,000
Income	$ 60,000

Because we know total variable costs, we can tell that sales must be $540,000 ($300,000 variable costs plus $240,000 contribution margin). Sales of $540,000 divided by 100,000 units gives the $5.40 price.

The same principles can be used to find any unknown, but sales and selling price are the factors most likely to be unknown.

Contribution Margin Percentage

It is sometimes impossible to work with per-unit contribution margin because the company sells several products. The idea of a "unit" for a department store or supermarket makes little sense. In such cases we perform CVP analysis using the **contribution margin percentage,** which is simply contribution margin divided by sales. In effect, using the contribution margin percentage is making the "unit" a dollar of sales, instead of a physical unit. Managers in many companies are accustomed to thinking in dollar terms and therefore in percentage terms like this.

The contribution margin percentage expresses contribution margin per dollar of sales.

Even when a company's product lends itself to the "per unit" idea, we can choose to use the contribution margin percentage instead. In these cases, it is a matter of convenience whether we work with per-unit or percentage contribution margin. For RST Company, contribution margin is 40% ($2/$5), returning to the original data. We can substitute this percentage in the formula for calculating the unit volume required to earn a target profit, and find the answer in *sales dollars,* instead of in sales units.

$$\text{Sales Dollars} = \frac{\text{Fixed Costs} + \text{Profit}}{\text{Contribution Margin Percentage}}$$

For instance, we already know from the example above that to earn $50,000, RST must sell 115,000 units, or $575,000 ($5 × 115,000). Using the contribution margin percentage, we find the following.

$$\text{Sales} = \frac{\$180,000 + \$50,000}{40\%}$$
$$= \$575,000$$

When we use the contribution margin percentage, we are expressing volume in sales dollars instead of sales units. We can use other measures of volume as well. Service firms such as CPA firms, law firms, and consulting firms, use *chargeable hours* as the measure of volume. Some manufacturing companies use *percentage of capacity* as the measure. Other measures are possible depending on the characteristics of the business. For example, the Milwaukee Brewers baseball organization had a break-even point of 1.6 million paid admissions in 1989. The Brewers, like all major league teams, earn revenue from various sources, including television, concessions, and parking. The 1.6 million figure reflects all of these sources.

ASSUMPTIONS AND LIMITATIONS OF CVP ANALYSIS

We have already mentioned several conditions necessary for CVP analysis to be useful. First, the company must be operating within the relevant range. Second, it must be possible to graph both revenues and total costs as straight, rather than curved, lines. This second requirement means that selling price, per-unit variable cost, and total fixed costs must be constant throughout the relevant range. It also means that we can identify all costs as either fixed or as variable with sales. Two other assumptions are important as well.

CVP analysis requires several important assumptions.

First, CVP analysis assumes either (1) that the company sells only one product or (2) that the sales of each product are a constant percentage of total sales. Second, for *manufacturing companies only,* CVP requires that production equals sales. When production and sales are not equal, income predicted using CVP analysis will not equal income calculated using GAAP. This inequality results from rules of financial

INSIGHT 12–1
You Deserve a Break Today

Wise strategy sometimes dictates what appear to be unwise actions. McDonald's has always resisted dropping prices even when its competitors reduced theirs. In other words, its policy has been to refrain from engaging in price wars. But a few years ago, it was discounting its quarter-pound cheeseburger from $1.90 to $0.99, as well as reducing other prices, in a vigorous price war. CVP analysis would almost certainly have shown that action to be unwise. Suppose for the sake of analysis that the variable cost of the item is $0.60. A reduction in contribution margin from $1.30 ($1.90 − $0.60) to $0.39 ($0.99 − $0.60) requires that the company more than triple its sales to earn the same profit it had been earning. (Test yourself on this. Suppose the company is selling 1 million per day at $1.90. How many must it sell at $0.99 to earn the same total contribution margin if variable cost is $0.60? The answer is about 3.33 million.) Then why do it? McDonald's had some strategic reason, such as maintaining its market share in the expectation of keeping customers over the longer haul. At the time, growth in fast-food markets was slow and McDonald's managers probably thought they could weather a price war better than their competition could. Apparently, they were right.

"McDonald's Stoops to Conquer," *Business Week*, October 30, 1989, 120.

accounting and of tax law (we covered this issue briefly in Chapter 10). The appendix to the present chapter describes *variable costing,* a product costing method that overcomes the problem of CVP income not equaling GAAP income.

Despite the assumptions required, CVP analysis has real-world value because it is an effective planning tool. Managers apply CVP analysis to individual products, product lines, and other segments of a business as well as to the business as a whole. It is also important to bear in mind that the answers given by CVP analysis do not tell managers what to do. Managers take actions that appear to be, and often are, unprofitable for many reasons. Insight 12−1 describes how McDonald's departed from its usual practice of avoiding price wars.

SHORT-TERM DECISIONS

Short-term decisions are usually defined as those that are over with in less than a year. One year is an arbitrary cutoff, but it is in common use. It is better to say that short-term decisions are those in which the *time value of money,* a concept familiar from Chapter 7 is insignificant. (We cover decisions that do require considering the time value of money in Chapter 15.)

Quantitative analyses do not tell managers what they should do.

An important point about any analysis of decisions is that the quantitative information does not *tell* you what to do. Quantitative information or analysis is not a solution. The analysis only tells the decision maker the economic effects of proposed actions, provided the estimates are correct. Since all decision making relates to the future, it must deal with estimates, not facts. A manager might therefore choose not to take the course of action indicated by the quantitative analysis because he or she mistrusts the estimates.

Moreover, many decisions have important qualitative aspects that might induce a manager to select a course of action not recommended by the quantitative analysis. For instance, a manager might decide to make a component for a product even though the component can be bought cheaper on the outside. Some reasons could be a desire to continue employing the people who make the component, a belief that it is not in the long-term strategic interests to buy the component, a policy that the company will manufacture as much of its products as it possibly can, or a commitment to better quality control. Nonetheless, it is still wise to perform the quantitative analysis to see how much it would likely cost to adopt the second- or third-best action. While you might wish to control as much of the manufacture of your product as possible, at some point excessive cost might change your mind. Insight 12–2 describes how Fox Broadcasting faced just such a choice between increasing short-term profits and carrying out its long-term strategy.

Relevant Costs for Short-Term Decisions

For decision-making purposes we classify revenues and costs as relevant or irrelevant depending on whether they will differ depending on the courses of action we might take. Costs that we expect to differ are called **differential costs** or **incremental costs.** Revenues that we expect to differ are called **differential revenues** or **incremental revenues.** Two other important cost concepts are sunk cost and opportunity cost. As we will illustrate shortly, a **sunk cost** has already been incurred and therefore cannot differ depending on the action we take. Sunk costs are never relevant for decisions. An **opportunity cost** is the value of the next best alternative. Opportunity costs are relevant to decisions, but are not recorded in the accounts and are therefore sometimes overlooked. A familiar example of an opportunity cost is the salary that you could be earning if you were not in school. Perhaps the major cost of going to school is the opportunity cost of the lost income.

Relevant costs are incremental, avoidable, or differential.

INSIGHT 12–2
Sacrificing Short-Term Profits

Fox Broadcasting is an example of a company that has not permitted short-term profits to derail its strategic plan. In the face of a long-term drop-off in viewers among the major networks, Fox launched a number of new programs and ordered extra episodes of some popular shows such as "In Living Color" and "The Simpsons." Barry Diller, chair of the company, stated "Short-term results frankly have little to do with the upside potential." Fox spent freely to expand programming and start a news service. Diller also said, "We are being more aggressive this year in our expenses because we believe we will be a significant profit generator for the Fox Company." Some of Fox's managers had felt that the network was losing its vitality and was beginning to imitate the three major networks—a sure recipe for decline.

At the time Fox announced its actions, the three major networks were cutting back new programming and laying off employees, and Fox's advertising revenue was running $100 million less than it had been the previous year. Fox shared some of the risk by asking its 133 affiliated stations to pay for part of the package.

Greenville Piedmont, (South Carolina), July 22, 1991, from the *Los Angeles Times* wire service.

The already familiar tool of CVP analysis is also useful in analyzing short-term decisions. Let us illustrate all of these concepts with a simple, basic example. JMK Company has an overrun of production of one of its products. The cost to manufacture the excess units was $20,000. The company can sell the goods for $12,000. One manager says that it is foolish to sell for $12,000 something that cost $20,000. Is that manager correct? In answering this question, we should consider only the differential (relevant) revenues and costs, and we must consider the alternatives. If the company rejects the $12,000 offer, what will it do with the goods? If the answer is to dump them because there is no alternative use, then we can analyze the situation as follows.

	Sell	Dump
Incremental revenue	$12,000	$0
Incremental cost	0	0
Incremental profit	$12,000	$0

We call the revenues and costs in the above analysis *incremental,* but the term *differential* will do just as well. Either term means that these items will change according to the choices made. There are no incremental costs as the situation stands. But what of the $20,000 cost to make the goods? That cost is *sunk*: it has already been incurred and is the same no matter what we do with the goods.

Suppose now that the company could also modify the goods for a cost of $8,000 and sell them for $22,000. Is this option better than selling them as-is for $12,000? If we elect to modify the goods, then we give up the opportunity to sell them for $12,000, so the $12,000 is the *opportunity cost* of modifying the goods. We can incorporate this information into the analysis in several ways. The simplest is to proceed as we did above.

	Sell As Is	Sell After Modifying
Incremental revenue	$12,000	$22,000
Incremental cost	0	8,000
Incremental profit	$12,000	$14,000

The analysis shows that we earn $2,000 more by making the modifications. A term widely used to describe incremental costs is **avoidable cost.** The $8,000 cost to modify the goods is avoidable because the company does not have to incur it. It is incremental to the decision to modify the goods.

We can also analyze the situation using the opportunity cost concept directly, proceeding as follows.

Sell After Modifying

Incremental revenue		$22,000
Relevant costs:		
Incremental cost	$ 8,000	
Opportunity cost	12,000	
Total cost		20,000
Profit from modifying		$ 2,000

Notice that the $2,000 difference still holds. The advantage of the best alternative must always be the same, else you have made an error. This analysis of the incremental (differential) effects of the decision is representative of many types of short-term decisions. The variety of short-term decisions is virtually limitless, but the same principles of differential analysis always hold. We now apply these principles to a few common decisions.

Special Order Decision

Many companies manufacture goods for sale under their own name, while also making similar, or even identical, goods for sale under another name. Chain stores frequently buy from name-brand manufacturers and sell the goods under their own labels. Companies can use excess capacity and avoid laying off workers by taking special orders. One problem in analyzing all decisions is the tendency to use per-unit costs inappropriately. QPR Company expects the following results.

Sales (120,000 × $5)	$600,000
Variable costs (120,000 × $3)	360,000
Contribution margin (120,000 × $2)	240,000
Fixed costs	180,000
Income	$ 60,000

Suppose that a chain store approaches QPR to buy 10,000 units at $3.50. Selling these units to the chain will not affect sales at the regular price. A manager computes the unit cost to be $4.50, as follows.

Total variable cost	$360,000
Total fixed cost	180,000
Total cost	$540,000
Divided by unit volume	120,000
Unit cost	$4.50

The manager goes on to say that the company cannot sell goods for $3.50 that cost $4.50. Is he correct? Should QPR accept the order? We must look at the differential effects.

Increase in revenue (10,000 × $3.50)	$35,000
Increase in costs (10,000 × $3.00)	30,000
Increase in income	$ 5,000

Accepting the order increases income by $5,000 and is therefore wise. The fallacy of the unit cost calculation lies in the fixed costs. Fixed costs will not increase in total if the company makes another 10,000 units. Only the variable costs increase in this case. That is, the only relevant unit costs are the variable costs. The per-unit fixed cost is not differential.

Per unit fixed cost is an average, and averages are not always relevant. Note that the $4.50 average cost is $3.00 variable and $1.50 fixed

Per-unit fixed costs are misleading and should be avoided.

($180,000/120,000). If volume drops to 60,000 units, average fixed cost increases to $3.00 ($180,000/60,000). If volume increases to 150,000 units, average fixed cost is $1.20 ($180,000/150,000). The point is that fixed costs come in totals, not per-unit amounts. You cannot use a per-unit cost that has a fixed component to predict costs at another volume. Thus, the $4.50 unit cost is valid only at 120,000 units. At any other level of volume, unit cost will be something else. Most important, *unit fixed costs are never differential.* This is not to say that fixed costs cannot increase by managerial decision. In this special order example, we could have had some increase in fixed costs, because producing the additional 10,000 units might require hiring another supervisor.

One other point: Suppose that the managers believed that if they sold the 10,000 units to the chain, they would lose 2,000 units at the regular price. People who would otherwise buy from QPR's normal distributors would buy from the chain instead, or regular customers might resent seeing the product appear in discount stores. What would happen then? We have the same analysis as before, plus the effect of the lost sales.

Contribution margin from special order (10,000 × [$3.50 − $3.00])	$5,000
Lost contribution margin from lost regular sales (2,000 × $2)	4,000
Net gain	$1,000

We see that QPR now gains only $1,000, which its managers might believe is not worthwhile, so they might not accept the special order. Losing sales at the regular price is usually a possibility with special orders and managers must be alert to the effects.

Make or Buy Decision

Manufacturers continually decide whether to manufacture parts and components or to buy them from outside suppliers. There are many qualitative aspects to this decision, as well as difficult estimates. Questions include whether the outside supplier will be reliable, meet delivery schedules, and maintain quality. These and other questions will affect a particular decision. Quantitatively, a problem often arises because of the tendency to allocate fixed costs to the part or component. Suppose that Benson Company now makes a component. Another company offers to supply the component to Benson at a price of $9 per unit. Benson's controller prepares the following analysis of costs at a volume of 30,000 units, which is the estimated annual use of the component.

Materials at $2 per unit	$ 60,000
Direct labor at $3 per unit	90,000
Variable overhead at $2 per unit	60,000
Allocated fixed overhead (building depreciation, heat and light, etc.)	90,000
Total costs	$300,000

The cost to buy the component is $270,000 ($9 × 30,000), so at first glance buying appears desirable. However, the controller has included allocated fixed costs in the cost of making the component. These costs are not differential: they will be the same whether the company makes or buys the component. The names should suggest the nature of the costs. Building depreciation will not change so long as the company stays in the same building. Heating and lighting costs surely will not change materially unless buying the component means that part of the plant can be shut down. So the total differential cost of making the component is $210,000, which is a $60,000 savings over buying.

Why would the controller include non-differential fixed costs in the analysis? Many people believe that a full-cost calculation is necessary. They argue that looking only at variable costs is shortsighted because variable costs might be only a small part of total costs. The problem with this line of reasoning is that it ignores the context: the decision is, as we have stated it, a short-term one and therefore subject to periodic review. If Benson could use the space or equipment now devoted to making the component in a profitable way, that opportunity cost would be quite relevant. If some fixed costs would be reduced as a result of buying the component, they, too, would be relevant. But the allocated fixed costs are not relevant because they will not change as a result of the decision.

For example, suppose that Benson could use the space and equipment now devoted to the component to perform finishing operations on a product. These operations are now done in nearby rented space. The rent is $15,000 annually, and if Benson stopped making the component, it could save that amount. This new information brings the alternatives $15,000 closer.

Decision to Drop or Add a Segment

We used the term **segment** earlier in this book in connection with products or product lines. More generally, a segment is any activity of a company that a manager is analyzing. Thus, in addition to products and product lines, segments can be geographic areas, types of customers, or even specific time periods such as Mondays. An important point is that managers often have to decide whether to keep a segment or drop it. Should we close on Mondays? Continue selling to retailers or concentrate on wholesalers? Keep Golden Boy Shampoo or replace it? These are examples of questions related to dropping segments.

The basic rules of considering only differential items work here as well. The income statement shown below is for an average month for Argon Household Products. Argon's managers expect similar results in the future.

	Cleaners	Polishes	Disinfectants	Total
Sales	$5,600,000	$3,200,000	$2,100,000	$10,900,000
Variable costs	2,600,000	1,400,000	1,200,000	5,200,000
Contribution margin	3,000,000	1,800,000	900,000	5,700,000
Fixed costs	1,900,000	1,250,000	950,000	4,100,000
Profit (loss)	$1,100,000	$ 550,000	($ 50,000)	$ 1,600,000

One of Argon's managers looked at this report and decided that the disinfectant line should be dropped because it was losing money. That conclusion is correct only if the $950,000 fixed costs are avoidable. Argon will lose $900,000 in contribution margin if it drops disinfectants, so the question is how much it will save in fixed costs. Suppose that further analysis reveals that avoidable fixed costs associated with disinfectants are $300,000. Argon will lose $600,000 if it drops the line.

Lost contribution margin	$900,000
Saved fixed costs	300,000
Profit of disinfectants line	$600,000

The "profit" referred to above is the difference between Argon's income keeping disinfectants and dropping them. The $650,000 in unavoidable fixed costs (total of $950,000 less $300,000 avoidable) will continue whether or not the company sells disinfectants. In all likelihood, some of the fixed costs shown for each line are actually common to all lines, but are allocated to the lines. This practice is widespread, but is of doubtful value.

This is not to say that Argon should necessarily keep disinfectants. The disinfectant line might use space, machinery, or other resources that are in short supply. It might be that there is another, more profitable line that could replace disinfectants. Of course, if the new line could be added without replacing disinfectants, then the company could have both lines. But if disinfectants does use scarce resources, then replacing it with another line that could use the same space and machinery might be wise.

Managers know that carrying one product or line often helps to sell others. Shopping malls and department stores testify to the principle that many lines can benefit if stores carry products that people will come in to buy. The idea, of course, is that the people will stay and buy other products after they have found what they came for. Some companies follow a strategy of carrying a full line of products for this very reason even if some are unprofitable. In other words, they carry unprofitable products because they believe that it enhances overall profitability. Similarly, a company might provide a service that loses money but attracts customers. Such potential effects must be considered in decisions about dropping products or lines.

Qualitative considerations are important in decisions.

Decision on Using Scarce Resources

We mentioned the problem of scarce resources before. Many times companies are faced with shortages in labor, machinery, space, raw materials, or other critical input factors. In such cases the decision problem is how best to use the short supply of the factor.

Barnes Company makes two models of athletic shoes, one for running and one for cross-training. Barnes can sell all it can make of either model. Both models require processing on a special type of machinery. Barnes has only enough of these machines to get 2,000 hours of machine time per week. Data relating to the models appear below.

	Running	Cross-training
Selling price	$30	$25
Variable cost	18	10
Contribution margin	$12	$15
Number of shoes that can be made per machine hour	15	10

Fixed costs are the same whichever model is made. Which model should Barnes concentrate on, or does it matter? The cross-trainer has higher contribution margin, but it requires more machine time, the scarce resource. In cases where a resource is in short supply, the objective is to maximize the contribution margin per unit of the scarce resource. The following schedule illustrates the technique.

	Running	Cross-training
Contribution margin per unit	$ 12	$ 15
Multiplied by number of shoes that can be made per machine hour	15	10
Contribution margin per machine hour	$180	$150

Barnes should make only running shoes if it wishes to maximize its profit. We can also prove this conclusion by determining the total contribution margin that Barnes can earn making each model.

	Running	Cross-training
Contribution margin per unit	$ 12	$ 15
Total output per week:		
2,000 × 15	30,000	
2,000 × 10		20,000
Weekly contribution margin	$360,000	$300,000

This analysis verifies our previous conclusion. You can solve problems like this either by determining the contribution margin per unit of the scarce resource, or by finding the total contribution margin that the company can earn, as we just did.

A Word of Caution

We have presented analytical techniques for solving a variety of common problems. All methods stress CVP relationships and the determination of avoidable costs. It is critical, though, that managers understand what decision is being made so that they can determine what information is relevant. It is also very important to remember that in CVP analysis, as well as in decision making, you work with estimates, not certainties. The degree of uncertainty about estimates varies: managers might be fairly sure of selling prices, less sure of unit variable costs, and very uncertain about sales volumes. Uncertainty is a fact of economic life. There are ways of reducing uncertainty by obtaining more information, say, through test-marketing, but because planning deals with the future, we can never be sure.

SUMMARY

CVP analysis underlies a variety of analytical techniques used to plan operations. The principles of cost behavior and contribution margin are critical to applying CVP analysis. Managers use CVP analysis to predict income, to set prices, and to determine how much they must sell to earn a target profit. CVP analysis requires estimates about the future, as does decision making. The relevant range is an important concept, highlighting the point that CVP relationships are not valid from zero volume to 100 percent of capacity.

Short-term decision making is aided by an understanding of the principles of differential costs, sunk costs, and opportunity costs. The principles are the same for making all short-term decisions: the difficult part is determining how to apply those principles in a specific case. Typical short- term decisions include special orders, making or buying a component, dropping or adding segments, and using scarce resources.

DEMONSTRATION PROBLEM 12–1

Gates Company sells a single product for $20 per unit. It pays $14 per unit for the product. There are no other variable costs. Fixed costs are $120,000.

REQUIRED:

Do each of the following items independently.

1. Determine the break-even point in units and in dollars.
2. Determine the volume, both in units and in dollars, required to earn $40,000.
3. Gates's managers believe that they can sell 25,000 units. What selling price is needed to give a $40,000 monthly profit?

Solution to Demonstration Problem 12–1

1. 20,000 units, $400,000.

$$\frac{\$120,000}{(\$20 - \$14)} = 20,000$$

The $400,000 can be found either by multiplying 20,000 by $20 or, by using the contribution margin percentage of 30% ($6/$20),

$$\frac{\$120,000}{.30} = \$400,000$$

2. 26,667 units, $533,333

$$\frac{\$120,000 + \$40,000}{\$6} = 26,667$$

The $533,333 can be found by multiplying $20 by 26,667, or by using the 30% contribution margin percentage ($160,000/.30).

442 Chapter 12 Cost-Volume-Profit Analysis and Short-Term Decision Making

3. $20.40

$$\text{Price} = \frac{\$120{,}000 + \$40{,}000}{25{,}000} + \$14$$

$$= \$20.40$$

DEMONSTRATION PROBLEM 12–2

Craig Company makes two products. Data appear below.

	Product B	Product C
Sales	$400	$600
Variable costs	160	360
Contribution margin	240	240
Fixed costs	120	180
Income	$120	$ 60
Unit sales	40	120

REQUIRED:

Answer each of the following independently of the others unless told otherwise.

1. What will happen to income if the company drops product B and half of the fixed costs associated with product B are avoidable?

2. The variable cost of product C includes $0.60 for a part the company now buys from an outside supplier. Craig could manufacture the part itself for $0.35 variable cost plus $22 additional fixed costs. What is the advantage or disadvantage of making the part?

3. A chain store has offered to buy 10 units of product C at $4, well below the $5 regular price. Craig has plenty of capacity, and the sale to the chain should not result in lost regular sales. The sales manager is against the sale, saying that cost is $4.50, ($360 + $180)/120. What is the gain or loss on the order?

Solution to Demonstration Problem 12–2

1. Profit will fall by $180, which is the lost $240 contribution margin less the $60 saved fixed costs.

2. There is an $8 advantage to making the part.

Buy, 120 × $0.60	$72	
Make, 120 × $0.35	42	
Variable cost savings		$30
Additional fixed costs		22
Net advantage		$ 8

3. There is a gain of $10, 10 units at $1 contribution margin. Variable cost is $3 per unit, $360/120. The fixed costs are irrelevant because they will not change if the order is accepted.

APPENDIX—VARIABLE COSTING

The alternative income statement format we use in Chapter 12 reflects a product costing method that is an alternative to absorption costing. The chapter avoided the technical questions of product costing, however, which we will now consider in this appendix.

The alternative approach is **variable** or **direct costing,** which simply means that the cost of product excludes fixed manufacturing costs. Or, put another way, the cost of product includes only variable manufacturing costs. Thus, as discussed in this chapter, all fixed costs are expensed as incurred. While variable costing is not acceptable for financial reporting and tax purposes, it is helpful for planning and decision making. Variable costing presents information in CVP format and many managers prefer its use for internal purposes. Variable costing can be used by job order, processing, and repetitive manufacturers.

Let us look at an example. Data related to Aspen Industries' principal product appear below.

Unit variable manufacturing cost	$ 12
Annual fixed manufacturing costs	$ 800,000
Normal annual volume	100,000 units
Actual production	100,000 units
Sales, 90,000 units at $30	$2,700,000
Selling and administrative expenses	$ 300,000

There were no beginning inventories of this product. We first find the unit cost using absorption costing. Because there is only one product, we can set a normal cost per unit directly instead of first using an input factor such as direct labor hours. Under absorption costing, and using the normal volume to set a predetermined rate, we find that the cost per unit is $20, consisting of $12 variable and $8 fixed ($800,000/100,000). Under variable costing, the unit cost is the $12 variable cost. But what then happens to the $800,000 fixed manufacturing cost? It appears on the income statement as an expense, just as do selling and administrative expenses. An absorption costing income statement appears in Exhibit 12–2. A variable costing income statement is presented in Exhibit 12–3.

Absorption costing income is higher than variable costing income *in this case.* When production exceeds sales, absorption costing income will be higher than variable costing income, but when sales are higher than production, variable costing income will exceed absorption costing income. The source of the differences is the fixed costs in inventory.

Difference in incomes ($600,000 − $520,000)	$80,000
Difference in fixed costs in inventory, equals fixed	
costs in absorption costing inventory ($8 × 10,000)	$80,000

Exhibit 12–2
Aspen Industries
Income Statement (Absorption Costing)

Sales		$2,700,000
Cost of sales:		
Variable production costs ($12 × 100,000)	$1,200,000	
Fixed production costs	800,000	
Total	2,000,000	
Ending inventory ($20 × 10,000)	200,000	
Cost of sales		1,800,000
Gross margin		900,000
Selling and administrative expenses		300,000
Income		$ 600,000

Exhibit 12–3
Aspen Industries
Income Statement (Variable Costing)

Sales		$2,700,000
Cost of sales:		
Variable production costs ($12 × 100,000)	$1,200,000	
Ending inventory ($12 × 10,000)	120,000	
Cost of sales		1,080,000
Gross margin		1,620,000
Fixed production costs	800,000	
Selling and administrative expenses	300,000	1,100,000
Income		$ 520,000

If there are beginning inventories, the difference in incomes equals the change in fixed costs from the absorption costing beginning inventory to the absorption costing ending inventory.

Variable costing income statements allow managers to determine what is likely to happen to income if sales change. In our example, a 1,000 unit change in sales volume leads to an $18,000 increase in income (1,000 × [$30 − $12]). It is not possible to do such analyses with absorption costing income statements because income depends on production as well as on sales. The last point shows another advantage of variable costing: unlike absorption costing income, variable costing income is not affected by production. With absorption costing, it is possible that sales can rise significantly from one month to another while income falls, or vice versa. Because businesspeople think, rightly, that sales generate income, not production, such results are extremely confusing.

Key Terms

allocated cost

avoidable cost

break-even point

contribution margin

cost-volume-profit (CVP) analysis

differential revenues and costs

incremental revenues and costs

opportunity cost

relevant range

segment

sunk cost

target profit

target selling price

variable (direct) costing

ASSIGNMENTS

12–1 Airline Prices
The incremental cost to add a passenger to a scheduled airline flight is very small. Could an airline benefit by allowing people to show up at flight time and pay $15 to $20 to take a flight that normally costs $200, assuming that there is space available? Explain your answer.

12–2 Unit Costs
One day you observe a friend driving his new car around and around a parking lot. When you ask him why, he states that he wants to reduce the per-mile cost.

REQUIRED:

1. If your friend continues his behavior, will he reduce the per-mile cost of the car?

2. What advice might you give your friend?

12–3 Basic Income Statement

TRM Company expects the following results from one of its products.

Selling price	$100
Variable cost	$ 60
Fixed costs	$400,000
Sales	15,000 units

REQUIRED:

Prepare an income statement using the expected results above.

12–4   Basic CVP Analysis

Crampton Company makes a single product that it sells for $10. Unit variable cost is $4, and monthly fixed costs are $30,000.

REQUIRED:

1. What is the monthly break-even point in units? In dollars?
2. What monthly unit volume is needed to earn $12,000 per month?
3. Suppose the managers believe that they can sell 11,000 units per month. At what selling price will the company earn $12,000?
4. Suppose the company is selling 12,000 units at $10. The sales manager believes that spending an additional $3,000 on advertising and promotion will increase sales by 1,000 units per month. What will happen to monthly income if the proposal is adopted?

12–5   Foreign Business

Managers of Belmont Company have estimated the following for the coming year.

Selling price	$60
Variable costs per unit	$44
Total fixed costs	$940,000
Planned sales volume	70,000 units

REQUIRED:

Answer the following questions, considering each independently.

1. What is the break-even point in units?
2. The marketing manager wants to sell product in a foreign country where Belmont does not now do business. She will reduce the price (in the foreign country only) to $56 and do a $70,000 advertising campaign in the country. She expects to sell 15,000 units. There will also be additional variable costs for shipping and duties of $4 per unit. Will the venture be profitable?

12–6   Using Per-Unit Data

The controller of TAF, Inc. has given you the following *per-unit* analysis, based on a volume of 100,000 units.

Selling price		$20
Variable costs	$8	
Fixed costs	8	
Total costs		16
Profit		$ 4

REQUIRED:

Answer each of the following questions independently of the others.   *100,000*
                                                                          4
1. What total profit does TAF expect to earn?   *400,000*   *÷ 400,000*
2. What profit will TAF earn if it sells 110,000 units?
3. TAF's managers believe that it can sell 120,000 units. They have established a target profit of $450,000. What price per unit must TAF charge?

12–7 CVP Graph
Using the letters on the graph shown here, identify the following.
   a. Total costs
   b. Break-even point
   c. Total revenue
   d. Total variable costs
   e. Profit area
   f. Loss area
   g. Total fixed costs

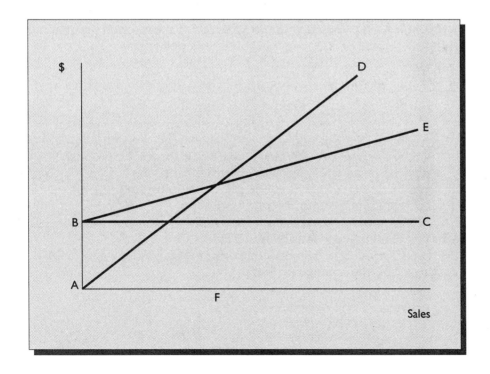

12–8   CVP Analysis for a Hospital

Grundy Memorial Hospital has been sending patients needing a partic-ular blood test to a nearby private clinic. Grundy sends the clinic about 200 patients per month. The clinic charges $40. Grundy's administrator has been considering ways for the hospital to perform the test. Doing so requires renting a machine for $2,000 per month and hiring a techni-cian for $2,400 per month. The variable cost is $8 per test.

REQUIRED:

1. If the hospital charges the same $40 fee that the clinic does, by how much will the hospital's monthly income increase or decrease?
2. What fee per test will allow the hospital to break even?

12–9   CVP for a Service Business

Microsource, Inc. develops accounting programs for medium-sized businesses. Most of its programs are developed to customer order and require considerable programming time and expertise. Microsource charges $50 per hour for programming time. Its managers have col-lected the following estimates for the coming year.

Total estimated chargeable hours	60,000
Total fixed costs, salaries, rent, etc.	$2,540,000

Microsource employs 30 full-time programmers at an average salary of $45,000, which is included in the $2,540,000 above. Each programmer should work about 2,000 chargeable hours per year.

REQUIRED:

1. If all estimates are met, what profit will Microsource earn?
2. What is the break-even point in chargeable hours?
3. Microsource's managers are considering an incentive plan for pro-grammers. They propose to pay, on average, a $5,000 base salary plus an average $20 per chargeable hour. Under the proposed plan: (a) what profit will Microsource earn for the year at 60,000 charge-able hours? (b) what is the break-even point? and (c) what prob-lems might arise with the proposed plan?

 ## 12–10   Sensitivity Analysis

Prestwick Division of Lundin Company makes luggage. The following data describe the average product.

Selling price	$300
Variable cost	$140
Monthly fixed costs	$8,000,000

REQUIRED:

Answer each of the following items independently.

1. Determine the break-even point in units.

2. Determine the break-even point, in units, supposing each of the following occur. Treat each independently; that is, use the original values above except for the item being changed.

   a. Unit variable costs increase by 10%.

   b. Selling price declines by 10%.

   c. Fixed costs increase by 10%.

12–11 Extending Store Hours

Bill Powers owns and runs the Office Center, which sells office supplies. He now stays open from 10 AM to 5 PM and is thinking about extending the hours till 8 PM. He believes that he will attract additional student business this way. Staying open will require paying an additional $400 per week to employees. Heat and light will increase another $20 per week. The Office Center is franchised, and Powers pays 8% of his revenues to the franchisor. It has a gross margin on sales of 37%.

REQUIRED:

1. Suppose Powers expects additional business of $1,500 per week. Should he extend the hours of operation?

2. How much additional business does Powers need to break even on the extra hours?

3. Suppose Powers stays open the extra time for several weeks and finds that sales during the 5 PM to 8 PM period average $2,000 per week. Does that mean that he made a good decision?

12–12 Converting an Income Statement to CVP Format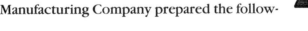

The controller of Halprin Manufacturing Company prepared the following income statement.

Halprin Manufacturing Company
Income Statement for March, 19X4

Sales (10,000 at $25)		$250,000
Cost of goods sold:		
Materials	$40,000	
Labor	65,000	
Overhead	80,000	185,000
Gross profit		65,000
Selling and administrative expenses		80,000
Loss		($ 15,000)

The controller gave you the following additional information. Materials and labor are variable costs, the overhead figure includes $50,000 fixed cost. Selling and administrative expenses include a 5% sales commission and the rest is fixed.

REQUIRED:

1. Prepare a new income statement using the contribution margin format.

2. Determine the break-even point in units.

3. Bud Halprin, the marketing manager, believes that sales could be increased by 3,000 units if an additional $15,000 were spent on advertising. His father, the president, says that average costs are now $26.50 ([$185,000 + $80,000]/10,000) and that adding to those costs is foolish. What do you think?

12–13   Product Selection—Machine Constraint

Garrison Company makes three products using a special machine that can be run only 200 hours per month.

	Regular	Deluxe	Luxury
Selling price	$12	$16	$21
Variable cost	7	8	10
Contribution margin	$ 5	$ 8	$11
Minutes of machine time required	6	10	15

Garrison can sell all it can produce of any product.

REQUIRED:

Determine which product Garrison should make.

12–14   CVP Analysis

BBD Inc., makes a variety of products. Data for one product appear below.

Selling price	$20
Variable cost	$12
Total fixed costs	$200,000

REQUIRED:

1. Determine the break-even point in units.

2. Determine the break-even point in dollars.

3. Determine the profit the company will earn selling 30,000 units.

4. The managers believe they can sell 30,000 units but want a profit of $70,000. Determine the price they must charge to meet the objective.

12–15 Pricing for a Day Care Center

First Community Church is considering a day care center for local children. The members of the board of the church are not looking to earn a profit on the center, but they do want it to break even or come very close. The center will be located in the basement of the church building. Members of the board have prepared the following estimates of expected costs to run the center.

Salaries, director and assistants	$36,600
Utilities	$ 2,800
Miscellaneous operating costs	$ 1,100
Supplies, paper, paint	$ 82 per child per year
Snacks, cookies, juice	$400 per child per year

With the staffing level envisioned in the cost estimates above, the center could accommodate 20 to 22 children.

REQUIRED:

1. Determine the monthly fee per child that will allow the center to break even if it has 20 children all year. You might find it simpler to solve for the annual fee and divide it by 12 months.

2. Suppose the board sets the monthly fee at $180. What is the break-even point in enrollment?

12–16 Special Order

Grant, Inc. expects to sell 350,000 saucepans in the coming year at $25. Per-unit manufacturing costs at that level of production are as follows.

Variable manufacturing costs	$9
Fixed manufacturing costs	$5

Early in the year, a representative of a chain store approached Grant with an offer to buy 28,000 pans at $11. Grant has plenty of capacity, and the sales manager believes there would be no effect on sales at the regular price.

REQUIRED:

1. Determine whether Grant should accept the order.

2. The sales manager now believes that Grant would likely lose sales of 8,000 saucepans at the regular price if it accepted the offer. Determine whether Grant should now accept the order.

12–17   Dropping a Segment

Tallman Clothing expects the following results for the coming year.

	Suits	Sportswear	Jeans	Total
Sales	$100,000	$150,000	$180,000	$430,000
Variable costs	45,000	60,000	60,000	165,000
Contribution margin	55,000	90,000	120,000	265,000
Fixed costs	80,000	50,000	60,000	190,000
Profit (loss)	($ 25,000)	$ 40,000	$ 60,000	$ 75,000

REQUIRED:

Answer each of the following questions independently.

1. Fixed costs are all allocated and unavoidable. What will happen to profit if Tallman drops suits?

2. Suppose now that $25,000 of the fixed costs shown for the suit segment are avoidable. What will happen to total profit if Tallman drops suits?

3. Suppose that the firm could avoid $25,000 in fixed costs by dropping suits (as in item 2). Additionally, the managers believe that if they did drop suits and increased the space available for the other lines, then sales of each of the other lines would rise by 20%. What will happen to Tallman's profit if it drops suits and all estimates prove correct?

12–18   Make or Buy

Bartell Company is introducing a new product. Its managers are trying to decide whether to make one of its components or to buy it from an outside supplier at $5 per unit. The company could make the part by using some machinery that has no other use and no resale value. The space that would be used to make the part also has no alternative use. An estimate of costs to make the part appears below.

Materials	$1.50
Direct labor	2.00
Variable manufacturing overhead	0.50
Fixed manufacturing overhead	2.50
Total cost	$6.50

The above estimate reflects anticipated volume of 20,000 units of the part. The fixed manufacturing overhead consists of depreciation on the machinery, and a share of the costs of the factory (heat, light, building depreciation, etc.) based on the floor space that manufacturing the part would occupy.

REQUIRED:

Determine whether Bartell should make or buy the part.

12–19 Variable Costing

CRD Company uses variable costing for internal reporting purposes. During 19X5, CRD had the following activity, after beginning the year with no inventories.

Units produced	100,000
Units sold ($10 selling price)	90,000
Variable manufacturing costs	$300,000
Fixed manufacturing costs	$400,000
Selling and administrative expenses, all fixed	$150,000

REQUIRED:

1. Determine the inventory cost per unit.
2. Prepare an income statement for 19X5 using variable costing.

12–20 Absorption Costing, Continuation of Assignment 12–19

Use the information in Assignment 12–19 to determine inventory cost per unit and prepare an income statement using absorption costing. Use production of 100,000 units to determine the unit fixed cost.

12–21 Relationships

Consider each situation below independently. You do not have to answer the questions in the order they are asked.

1. A company earned a $50,000 profit selling 100,000 units. Total contribution margin was $110,000, and variable costs were $5.40 per unit.

    a. What were fixed costs?

    b. What was the per unit selling price?

2. Variable costs were $12 per unit, selling price $20, fixed costs $100,000. The company had a profit of $30,000.

    a. What was total contribution margin?

    b. What were sales in units?

    c. What were sales in dollars?

3. A company increased its income from $20,000 to $26,000 when it increased sales from 40,000 to 50,000 units. The selling price was $1.70.

   a. What is unit contribution margin?

   b. What were unit variable costs?

   c. What were total fixed costs?

12–22   Sensitivity Analysis

Redan Division of Cothran Industries makes a number of office products. The following data describe the average product.

Selling price	$100
Variable cost	$35
Monthly fixed costs	$6,000,000
Monthly volume	150,000

REQUIRED:

Answer each of the following items independently.

1. Determine the monthly income Redan should earn.

2. Suppose that variable costs increase to $40 per unit while all other factors remain constant.

   a. What will monthly income be?

   b. How many units will Redan have to sell to earn the income you computed in part 1?

3. Variable costs are again $35, but the selling price is now $110.

   a. What will monthly income be?

   b. How many units will Redan have to sell to earn the income you computed in part 1?

4. Price and variable costs are again $100 and $35, but fixed costs are now $6,600,000.

   a. What will monthly income be?

   b. How many units will Redan have to sell to earn the income you computed in part 1?

12–23 DECISION CASE:
UNDERSTANDING CVP RELATIONSHIPS

Bob Cordett, manager of BassoHut, a franchise seafood store, cannot understand why his profit dropped so much from April to May. He shows you the income statements his accountant prepared and requests your help.

	April	May
Sales	$90,000	$75,000
Cost of sales	36,000	30,000
Gross profit	54,000	45,000
Operating expenses:		
Rent	3,200	3,200
Salaries and wages	29,500	26,500
Other	7,600	7,300
Total operating expenses	40,300	37,000
Income	$13,700	$ 8,000
Return on sales	15.2%	10.7%

Cordett tells you that salaries and wages includes his salary, those of the cooks, and wages to waiters. Cordett understood that income would decline when sales declined, but he expected to maintain the 15.2% return on sales from April.

REQUIRED:

1. Determine the fixed and variable components of each element of cost using the high-low method.

2. Prepare income statements using the contribution margin format for April and May.

3. Tell Cordett why the statements you prepared suit his needs better than the ones his accountant prepare.

13

Budgeting

LEARNING OBJECTIVES:

After studying Chapter 13, you will be able to:
1. Tell why organizations prepare budgets.
2. Identify the principal budgets that businesses prepare.
3. Prepare the basic set of budgets.
4. Discuss several behavioral problems of budgeting.

Virtually any organization—whether business, not-for-profit, or government—uses budgets to plan and control activities and spending. Budgets are the most explicit, sometimes the only, formal expressions of organizational objectives and the plans for achieving them. Budgeting has a significant human dimension: *people,* not numbers, plan and control. By following various budgeting practices, managers can affect behavior and performance, for both good and ill. Behavioral questions are thus often the most important factors in a company's budgeting process.

Budgets are crucial for both planning and control.

BUDGETS AND PLANNING

Budgets are formal plans that require managers to state clearly, in quantitative terms, both their objectives and the means to achieving them. Objectives (such as "earn $2 million profit on $15 million sales") guide managers' actions and expose them to rigorous questioning. For example, a production manager might question a sales manager's sales budget because of a lack of plant capacity. In this way and others, budgeting helps to coordinate the activities of different managers and allows them to spot problems early. Clear, quantitative statements also serve as benchmarks to measure progress.

Having formal plans makes it easier to respond to changes. For example, if sales appear to be stronger than expected, having the original budget should make it easier to determine how much additional production is needed and what that increase means for personnel requirements, space, and short-term financing.

Budgeting also helps reveal potential problems and plan their solutions. In preparing the budget, managers might see that the company needs a large, short-term bank loan. Knowing this well in advance should make it much easier to obtain the loan on favorable terms than if the cash shortage were not discovered until the bank balance dipped precariously low. Lenders are much more willing to lend to companies that show why and when they need money, and how they expect to repay it.

BUDGETS AND CONTROL

As stated earlier, budgets serve as benchmarks against which to measure progress and results. Comparing budgeted and actual results is one of the most basic steps in controlling operations. Differences between actual costs and budgeted costs are called *variances.* If costs are higher than budgeted, the responsible manager should explain why. Failing to meet a budget is not *necessarily* a sign of poor management, but it does require explanation. Managers usually want to investigate only significant variances. Small variances usually suggest that things are going about according to plan. The principle of *management by exception* states that managers should be concerned only about things that are *not* going according to plan.

Well-developed budgets also help managers to take corrective action if problems arise. The question "how are we doing?" can be answered only by reference to some objective or expectation. Most managers believe that budgeted performance is the best basis for judging actual performance. Using historical results to evaluate performance is unwise because there is no guarantee that historical performance is a high enough standard. Improvement is desirable, but, as an example, going from a grade of 44 on the first examination to a 51 on the next is hardly satisfactory.

Participation in budgeting often increases performance.

It is generally agreed that if all concerned managers accept a budget as reasonable and attainable, they will be more committed to achieving it. Such commitment is even higher when managers participate in developing budgets. Participating managers believe that they have some control over their destinies, and much research has shown that people who believe they exercise a reasonable amount of control over their performance are more satisfied and more productive than those who believe that others control their performance. Such **participative budgeting** is part of a trend to greater employee involvement in all phases of operations. Some companies use *quality circles,* where workers discuss ways to improve quality and some encourage workers to make suggestions for improving performance. Some involve employees extensively in developing budgets and other plans, and in determining how employees will be evaluated—all a part of what is often called *job enlargement.* Employee involvement was the cover story of a 1989 issue of *Business Week,* a sure sign that the idea has caught on in U. S. companies. We should say, however, that there are no panaceas; managers cannot achieve better performance simply by adopting modern managerial tools. Managers must commit to making these tools work. As Insight 13–1 explains, budgeting began in the public sector many centuries ago as a means of controlling spending. It still fulfills that purpose, but it is now a much broader management tool.

COMPREHENSIVE BUDGETS

A **comprehensive budget** is a set of financial statements and other schedules showing the budgeted results for a future period. (Budgeted

INSIGHT 13–1
Budgets in Olden Times

Government budgeting is much older than business budgeting and developed largely as taxation was democratized. Without democracy, kings and queens simply levied taxes to meet their fiscal needs and no one was in a position to question them. As taxation was vested in the English Parliament, however, kings and queens were no longer able to levy whatever taxes they chose. In the 18th century, Parliament required the sovereign to provide annual estimates of spending for the coming year. Parliament established various safeguards, including audits, to determine whether spending was as authorized.

The United States came to formal national budgets relatively late, largely because the federal government collected so little revenue for so long. From 1790 until 1900, average annual expenditures were $150 million. (That will get the federal government through about an hour today.) Today, in many government units below the federal level, it is illegal to overspend any budgeted item, such as overtime or telephone because the budget is a legal, binding document.

Michael Chatfield, *A History of Accounting Thought* (Hinsdale, IL: The Dryden Press, 1974): 189–193.

financial statements are also called *pro forma* statements, meaning "for the form.") A comprehensive budget includes an income statement, a balance sheet as of the end of the period, a cash flow statement, and production and purchases schedules, as well as other schedules, depending on the needs of the organization.

Budgeting encompasses CVP analysis but is also concerned with cash flow and the leads and lags between cash flow and accrual income. For instance, budgeting cash collections requires both predicting sales and estimating the pattern of cash collections (how much do we collect within 30 days? within 60 days?). Predicted cash collections combined with cash receipts from budgeted borrowing become a budget of cash receipts.

Comprehensive budgets include various components depending on the organization.

Comprehensive budgeting can be very complex: a change in a single figure can ripple through the whole set of budgets. For example, a change in budgeted sales for a month affects total costs, profit, cash receipts, purchases, cash flow, and the budgeted balance sheet.

Companies budget for specific periods. Most companies prepare annual budgets and usually break them down by month. Most companies also prepare long-term budgets, covering a period of three to five years. Figure 13–1 shows some of the interrelationships of the budgeting process.

FIGURE 13–1
Interrelationships of Budgeting Process

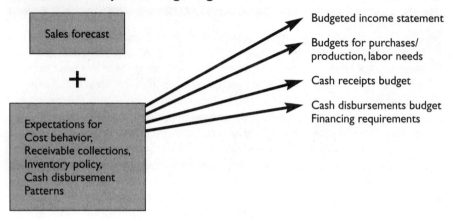

BUDGETING AND HUMAN BEHAVIOR

Behavioral aspects of budgeting are as important as the analytical aspects.

Budgeting is fraught with behavioral problems, both in the planning and control phases. Some of these problems are relatively straightforward, some quite subtle. They are perhaps the most important aspect of budgeting, for they influence the actions of managers and therefore the success of the organization. The principal problem is achieving **goal congruence,** which happens when managers, who will, like everyone else, work in their own best interests by attempting to achieve their own goals, also work in the organization's best interests. A lack of goal congruence handicaps the organization. One simple example: overemphasis on meeting cost budgets can result in managers taking unwise actions such as reducing expenditures for preventive maintenance or research and development. Although such reductions decrease short-term costs, they can have serious negative effects on longer-term results.

It is very difficult to design budgeting and performance evaluation programs that foster goal congruence. Much of the material that follows will be relevant to you no matter what your career. Virtually all managers prepare budgets and support their budget requests in discussions with their superiors. Similarly, most managers evaluate budgets of their subordinates. So most managers are on both ends of budgets.

Participative Budgeting

In some organizations budgets are imposed by upper levels of management. This is generally not good practice, as the persons responsible for achieving the budgets are not likely to feel committed to them. There is mounting evidence that persons who participate in setting levels of performance perform better than those who do not. People who participate in budgeting, therefore, tend to be more committed to meeting budgeted objectives than those who have budgets thrust upon them — **imposed budgets.** They *internalize* the objectives, and so do not require external pressure to achieve them.

Motivation

One continuing issue is the level at which budgets are set, how tight they are, and how much, or little, slack they allow. Some managers believe that budgets should be very tight to inspire very high performance and encourage very low costs. Others prefer to set budgets at reasonably attainable levels, usually called **currently attainable performance.** Advocates of tight budgets argue that very high objectives motivate people and that any slack in a budget encourages substandard performance. Managers with extremely high targets tend to become discouraged and lose any commitment they might have had. They might also act in ways that are detrimental in the long run, such as cutting preventive maintenance to reduce costs in the short-term, as described earlier. Extremely tight budgets are also useless for planning because they will almost certainly not be achieved. The effects on behavior of budgetary pressure are a common field of study. Insight 13−2 describes one such study.

Line Item Budgets

The problems associated with line budgeting characterize budgeting by not-for-profit entities, especially government units, but are also not unknown in business. *Line budgeting* means that a specific spending limit is imposed for each "line," which corresponds roughly to an account. An amount is authorized for such items as clerical salaries, travel, telephone, and equipment. These authorizations are sometimes exceedingly detailed and run to many pages. Line budgeting can harm the entity by taking flexibility away from managers. A manager cannot, for example, overspend on telephone costs even if she makes corresponding reductions in supplies, to keep total spending within the total authorization. Some flexibility permits managers to use their judgment in furthering the objectives of the organization, but strict line budgeting does not permit this.

Spend It or Lose It

Toward the end of the budget year, some managers scramble to be sure that they leave no money unspent, fearful that they must "use it or lose it." They do not want unspent allowances to be taken out of the next

INSIGHT 13–2
Meet the Budget, or Else!

Pressure to meet budgets is a fact of life for some managers. Achieving budgetary goals can become an end in itself wherein managers pay little attention to whether they are actually accomplishing the goals of the organization. Many studies have addressed this issue in attempting to determine how budgetary pressure affects the performance of managers. One study found that some managers who believed they were under budgetary pressure tended to show less initiative in problem solving. For example, they would curtail a desirable activity (say, employee training) if they were approaching their spending limits, rather than seek a more creative solution such as reducing expenditures for some other, less critical purpose. It was also found that managers who felt pressured had participated less in developing budgets. The pressured managers were more defensive than their peers who did not feel pressured. They tended to protect themselves with written explanations for not meeting budgets and written plans for corrective action.

Paul J. Carruth and Thurrell O. McClendon, "How Supervisors React to 'Meeting the Budget' Pressure," *Management Accounting*, November 1984, 50–54.

year's budget. For example, a manager who spends only $110,000 of his $120,000 travel budget might fear that he will have only $110,000 or less to spend next year. Such actions, unwise from the company's point of view, are quite common and are an excellent example of a lack of goal congruence.

Incremental Budgeting

Some budget practices cause serious managerial problems.

Under *incremental budgeting,* all departments receive the same increase or decrease, such as 5%, for each line item (such as 5% for salaries, 0% for equipment, 3% for travel). This approach ignores the output—the services that the unit provides—and it might build up slack in already inefficient departments, or cut back the operations of efficient departments. Incremental budgeting is often the result of unwillingness or inability to make judgments about the relative worth of activities. It perpetuates activities that could well be dropped and starves areas whose services are demanded at increasing rates. Incremental budgeting also fosters the "spend it or lose it" behavior mentioned above. Insight 13–3 tells how expanding budgets beyond simple estimates of cost can be used to identify profitable and unprofitable

INSIGHT 13–3
"Who's a Profitable Account? Who's Not?"

An example of the role of budgets in planning and in fixing responsibility is provided by JKL, Inc. an advertising agency. After growing rapidly, JKL began to show losses because it had failed to control costs and to evaluate the profitability of accounts. Each JKL manager must now set up budgets for the profitability of every new account. Since the account managers now feel responsible for profitability, they are motivated by and committed to that goal of profitability, not simply to achieving budgeted revenues or costs separately. As a result, JKL is growing profitably.

William B. Mills, "Drawing Up a Budgeting System for an Ad Agency," *Management Accounting*, December 1983, 46–51.

lines of business and to motivate managers to think in profit terms, not cost terms.

DEVELOPING BUDGETS

Virtually any business budget begins with the **sales budget.** (Budgets of other nonbusiness organizations usually begin with other sources of revenue such as dues, gifts, or grants.) Budgeted sales for a manufacturer determine budgeted production, and budgeted production in turn determines the anticipated needs for employees, material purchases, and other productive factors. The analysis is similar for merchandisers and service companies. The principal technical problem in budgeting is recognizing *leads* and *lags*. For example, revenue is recorded at the point of sale even if cash is not collected until much later. Cost of sales is also recognized at the point of sale, whether or not the company has paid the supplier.

SALES FORECASTING AND BUDGETING

Many companies can forecast sales by using the relationship between sales and some measure of economic activity. Sales of some products (e.g., cars, furniture, or appliances) often correlate closely with the

Sales forecasts are critical to budgeting.

overall economy as measured by Gross National Product, personal income, or other *economic indicator.* Sales of cement, lumber, and carpet are closely associated with building activity, sales of automobiles with interest rates (the lower the rates, the higher the sales), and so on. Such indicator methods are very effective if the company's sales are closely enough associated with another measure. Some companies' sales do not display any close associations, so they cannot use indicators.

Some companies forecast sales simply by projecting historical results into the future. If sales have been increasing at 8% per year, the company will forecast next year's sales as last year's sales plus 8%. Because the past is not necessarily a good guide to the future, this method has serious drawbacks. Managers projecting the past should consider factors that have changed from last year. For example, last year's sales could have been abnormally high because a major competitor experienced a strike and so was unable to meet demand.

Some companies use estimates of their salespeople and sales managers to forecast sales. Higher-level sales executives then use these individual forecasts, along with their own judgment, to develop the final forecast.

However a company forecasts sales, its managers must recognize that *they* can influence sales: a pessimistic forecast need not come true. Managers can investigate the effects of increasing advertising and promotion, decreasing the selling price, or adding more salespeople in order to change the forecast. Personal computer software can allow a manager to test many scenarios to see what might provide satisfactory results. Budgeting should be a *proactive* activity, one in which managers take action to prevent anticipated problems, not a passive, *reactive* one in which managers address problems only after they occur. Sales forecasts are essential to such an aggressive approach.

FLEXIBLE EXPENSE BUDGETING

A budget of major concern to any manager is the **expense budget.** Most managers are responsible for meeting a set of objectives within budgeted spending limits. Therefore, the way the budget is established is extremely important to the manager. There are two fundamental ways to set expense budgets, as flexible budgets or as static budgets. A **static expense budget** sets one particular level for spending. The level does not change if the workload changes, whether it goes up or down. In contrast, a **flexible expense budget** provides a spending allowance that depends on the activity the manager is responsible for. The more activity there is, the higher the **flexible budget allowance** goes, and vice versa. Flexible budgets are used extensively in manufacturing because activity is relatively easy to measure there. Activity is much more difficult to measure in administrative work.

Consider the following example. The cost of supplies in a manufacturing department follows this pattern.

$$\text{Supplies Cost} = \$12,000 + \$0.60 \times \text{Machine Hours}$$

This pattern of a mixed cost is familiar from Chapter 10. The formula also provides a flexible budget allowance for spending that depends on the number of machine hours the department operates. Suppose that the company budgets 10,000 machine hours. The budget would then call for $18,000 in supplies ($12,000 + $0.60 × 10,000). But that budget is not suitable for performance evaluation if the company actually works 11,000 machine hours (or 8,000, or any number other than 10,000). Because of the variable component of the budget, the flexible budget allowance should reflect the actual level of activity. A manager on a static budget is held to the $18,000 allowance and is therefore encouraged to keep machine hours down to keep the cost of supplies down. Holding down machine hours could reduce production and sales, another example of a lack of goal congruence.

Flexible budgets are adjusted to reflect actual activity.

Managers use budget formulas to develop a set of budget allowances based on various levels of activity, as shown in Exhibit 13–1. The figures for supplies come from the formula; the others are assumed. The total figures in the exhibit are the total budget allowances for the manager at the three levels of machine hours. The individual figures are the allowances for the associated costs at each level.

An alternative to establishing budgets for different levels of activity is simply to wait until the end of a period and then determine the flexible budget allowances after activity is known. This way managers

Exhibit 13–1
Department A
Budget Allowances

	10,000 hours	12,000 hours	14,000 hours
Supplies	$18,000	$19,200	$20,400
Fuel	9,000	9,500	10,000
Other costs (details omitted)	38,600	41,800	45,000
Totals	$65,600	$70,500	$75,400

Exhibit 13–2
Department A
Performance Report, April

Activity in machine hours   11,000

	Budget Allowance	Actual Cost	Variance
Supplies	$18,600	$18,300	$ 300
Fuel	9,250	9,450	(200)
Other costs (details omitted)	40,200	39,660	540
Totals	$68,050	$67,410	$ 640

can develop performance reports like the one in Exhibit 13–2. Such reports are used for evaluating the performance of the responsible managers. Various companies use the reports in various ways. Some tie bonuses to favorable variances, for example, while others provide bonuses to managers who meet budgets.

We show how to analyze variances in Chapter 14. Notice that the budget allowances conform to the patterns given earlier. Supplies are budgeted at $18,600 ($12,000 + $0.60 × 11,000) and the allowance for fuel is halfway between the amounts given above for 10,000 and 12,000 hours, as is the total budget allowance of $68,050.

Flexible budget allowances make it possible to evaluate performance based on activity. A manager who accomplishes more (makes more units, processes more transactions) should be expected to spend more. A static budget encourages managers to do as little as possible, because increasing activity increases costs, and they cannot meet the budget if it does not allow higher costs for higher activity. Static budgets are appropriate only for departments whose costs are all fixed, regardless of activity.

ILLUSTRATION OF A COMPREHENSIVE BUDGET

We illustrate the preparation of a comprehensive budget with Krell Stores, Inc. Krell's managers are developing its budgets for the first three months of 19X4. Exhibit 13–3 contains the basic data for the illustration. Exhibit 13–4 contains the solution, which was generated by a Lotus 1-2-3 template. Such a template allows the manager to make changes, say, in the cost of sales percentage, and quickly get the new

Exhibit 13–3
Krell Company Data

1. Sales budget: January $90,000, February $110,000, March $130,000, April $115,000, May $100,000
2. Cost of sales is 70% of sales.
3. Sales are collected as follows: 60% in the month of sale and 40% in the following month.
4. Fixed costs are $20,000 per month, including $4,000 depreciation.
5. Krell keeps inventory equal to budgeted sales requirements for the next two months.
6. Krell pays for purchases in the month after purchase.
7. The balance sheet as of December 31 appears below.

Balance Sheet as of December 31

Cash	$ 20,000	Payables	$ 76,000
Receivables	30,000		
Inventory	130,000	Common stock	220,000
Fixed assets	190,000	Retained earnings	74,000
Totals	$370,000		$370,000

results. Budgeting by hand can be very tedious even with a simplified case such as this illustration.

Budgeted Income Statement

The first operating budget is the *budgeted income statement,* shown in Exhibit 13–4. This type of statement should be familiar to you from Chapter 10 and requires no comment. Note that the statement is by month for the quarter. Some managers prepare only one statement for the quarter as a whole.

Purchases Budget

The **purchases budget** follows the budgeted income statement in Exhibit 13–4. This budget relies on a basic relationship you learned early in this book.

Cost of Sales = Beginning Inventory + Purchases − Ending Inventory

Rearranging this formula,

Purchases = Cost of Sales + Ending Inventory − Beginning Inventory

Exhibit 13–4
Krell Company Budgets

	January	February	March	Total
Budgeted Income Statements				
Sales	$ 90,000	$110,000	$130,000	$330,000
Cost of sales	63,000	77,000	91,000	231,000
Gross profit and contribution margin	27,000	33,000	39,000	99,000
Fixed costs	20,000	20,000	20,000	60,000
Profit	$ 7,000	$ 13,000	$ 19,000	$ 39,000
Purchases Budget				
Cost of sales	$ 63,000	$ 77,000	$ 91,000	$231,000
Desired ending inventory	168,000	171,500	150,500	150,500
Total requirements	231,000	248,500	241,500	381,500
Beginning inventory	130,000	168,000	171,500	130,000
Purchases	$101,000	$ 80,500	$ 70,000	$251,500
Cash Receipts Budget				
Current 60%	$ 54,000	$ 66,000	$ 78,000	$198,000
Prior 40%	30,000	36,000	44,000	110,000
Totals	$ 84,000	$102,000	$122,000	$308,000
Cash Disbursements Budget				
Prior month purchases	$ 76,000	$101,000	$ 80,500	$257,500
Cash fixed costs	16,000	16,000	16,000	48,000
Totals	$ 92,000	$117,000	$ 96,500	$305,500
Cash Budget				
Beginning balance	$ 20,000	$ 12,000	$ 10,000	$ 20,000
Receipts	84,000	102,000	122,000	308,000
Total available	104,000	114,000	132,000	328,000
Disbursements	92,000	117,000	96,500	305,500
Indicated balance	$ 12,000	($ 3,000)	$ 35,500	$ 22,500
Borrow (Repay)		13,000	(13,000)	
Ending balance	$ 12,000	$ 10,000	$ 22,500	$ 22,500

Continued

Are u Blind

Exhibit 13–4
Continued

Pro Forma Balance Sheet

Cash (cash budget)	$ 22,500	Payables	$ 70,000 (3)
Receivables (1)	52,000		
Inventory (purchases budget)	150,500	Common stock	220,000
Fixed assets (2)	178,000	Retained earnings	113,000 (4)
Totals	$403,000		$403,000

(1) 40% of March sales of $130,000.
(2) Original balance of $190,000 less three months depreciation at $4,000 per month.
(3) March purchases to be paid in April.
(4) Beginning balance of $74,000 plus $39,000 net income.

We use the January budget from Exhibit 13–4 in this rearranged formula.

$$\$101,000 = \$63,000 + \$168,000 - \$130,000$$

Please note carefully that all values in the purchases budget are costs, not selling prices. This point often causes confusion. If you stick to costs, you should have no problems.

Ending inventory is usually related to budgeted sales because a store stocks goods in anticipation of budgeted sales. Retail inventories are extremely high going into the Christmas selling season, and low coming out of the season. However, companies do not blindly stock up with goods, because there are significant costs to carrying inventory. The opportunity cost of the money tied up in inventory is very high. Storage costs such as insurance, personal property taxes (levied on assets other than real estate), spoilage, and the risk of obsolescence can also be significant. Inventory policy therefore aims for a balance between having too much—and, as a result, incurring costs such as those just mentioned—and carrying too little and thus suffering lost sales and profits.

Exhibit 13–3 states that Krell keeps inventory equal to budgeted sales requirements for the next two months (Item 5 in the exhibit). (Remember that values in the purchases budget are at cost.) *Budgeted sales requirements* are the physical amounts budgeted for sale in the next two months, so we express these amounts at cost, *not* at selling prices. Thus, ending inventory for January of $168,000 is cost of sales for February and March ($77,000 + $91,000), and similarly for all other months.

The total requirements row shows the amount needed to cover that month's sales plus the desired ending inventory. These requirements can be met from goods already on hand (beginning inventory) and from purchases. Of course, beginning inventory for any month is the previous month's ending inventory.

One final point: We might also prepare purchases or production budgets in units. If so, we would do the purchases budget in units, then multiply purchases in units by the purchase price to determine dollar purchases.

Cash Receipts Budget

The *cash receipts budget* is the first **financial budget**, one that deals with cash flow. It depends on the sales budget and the relationships of sales to cash collections from customers. Exhibit 13−2 states that 60% of sales are collected in the month of sale and 40% in the following month, with no bad debts. (If there were, say, 2% bad debts, then Krell would collect 38% of its sales in the month after sale.) Thus, February collections are $66,000 from February sales of $110,000 plus $36,000 from January sales of $90,000. Note that 60% of January sales of $90,000 are collected in January ($54,000) and 40% in February ($36,000). Cash receipts are typically not a serious analytical problem. Note that the cash receipts budget shows $30,000 collected in January from the prior month's sales; this amount is the accounts receivable amount from the beginning balance sheet.

Cash Disbursements Budget

Next is the *cash disbursements budget.* Krell's major cash disbursement is payments for purchases. Determining cash payments for purchases requires the purchases budget and information about the payment pattern. Exhibit 13−3 informs us that Krell pays for all its purchases in the month after purchase. Therefore, the January payment of $76,000 is for December purchases, which are reflected in accounts payable on the December 31, 19X3, balance sheet in Exhibit 13−3. After that, all amounts reflect the stated relationship. January purchases of $101,000 are paid for in February, and so on. The other cash disbursements for operating costs are lumped together. (If we had an item such as commissions paid in the month after they were earned, we would have to calculate them separately from expenses paid as incurred.) The last line in the cash disbursements budget, then, shows fixed operating costs, *net of depreciation.* It is very important that you recognize that depreciation is not a cash flow and is therefore excluded from the cash disbursements budget.

Cash Budget

We are now ready to prepare the **cash budget.** This is a simple matter of starting with the beginning balance, adding receipts from the cash receipts budget, subtracting disbursements from the cash disbursements budget, and determining the ending balance. The January cash budget begins with the December 31 cash balance on the balance sheet ($20,000), then adds cash receipts of $84,000 from the January cash budget, then subtracts the $92,000 January disbursements from the cash disbursements budget. The result, called the *indicated balance,* is cash the company would have if it did not borrow or repay a loan. No loan is needed in January, but you can see that at the end of February, Krell has a deficit, which prompts us to include a line for borrowing.

The amount borrowed must not only bring the cash balance to zero, but also provide Krell with cash to operate. Consequently, we have budgeted to borrow enough to bring the balance up to $10,000, an arbitrarily selected figure. At the end of March, Krell should be able to repay the entire loan. For simplicity, we ignored interest. Of course, budgeting for a loan does not necessarily mean that Krell can get a loan. If it cannot, it will have to scale back its purchases, and it will probably suffer reduced sales and profits as a result.

A few points about the cash budget are worth mentioning. Krell showed a profit every month (see the income statements in Exhibit 13–4), but still ran out of cash in February. Notice that cash receipts increase each month, but that there is a lag. Cash receipts never exceed sales during this budget period. (If Krell is going into its slow season, its receipts will start to exceed its sales as sales decline.) Companies can run out of cash while sales are rapidly increasing, because they pay cash to stock goods in advance of sales but collect cash after the sale. It is not enough to earn profits; companies must also be able to pay their bills.

The cash budget will be helpful to Krell's finance manager, who will have to seek the necessary loan. Bankers are much likelier to grant loans to applicants who have planned their needs and can show how they expect to repay the loan. Had Krell waited until the cash balance dipped to near zero before seeking a loan, it would probably have had to pay a higher interest rate, or might not even get the loan at all.

Had the cash budget shown steady, rapid increases in cash, Krell's managers would have been wise to think about investing some of the idle cash. Had the budget been extended to, say, 12 months, and a rapid increase been projected, the company could have planned to invest for at least that 12 month period and earned considerable interest. Alternatively, the company could have planned to pay off long-term debt (if it had any) or even bought back its own stock.

Budgeted Balance Sheet

A budgeted, or pro forma, balance sheet for March 31 also appears in Exhibit 13–4. This statement shows the managers how they will start off the next quarter—what assets and equities the company will have if all goes according to plan. The budgeted balance sheet also serves as an excellent check on the preparer's work. If it does not balance, there is probably an error in another budget. The statement also helps managers in controlling operations. They can compare actual and budgeted results to spot potential problems. For example, if inventory is much higher than budgeted, and actual sales approximate budgeted sales, there could be a serious problem. The company might be piling up goods it will have trouble selling. Similarly, high accounts receivable might reflect unwisely loosened credit terms that could lead to excessive bad debts and slowdowns in collecting sales. You should trace the numbers on the pro forma balance sheet back to their associated budgets or verify the calculations to make sure you understand where they come from.

SUMMARY

Budgets are the most formal statements of objectives in a firm. They coordinate the plans of many managers and many levels of management. Budgeting involves human behavior and some of its most important aspects have to do with its effects on behavior.

Budgeting for a business typically begins with a sales budget, the result of various methods of forecasting and determining how to influence sales. From there, it proceeds through budgeted income statements, budgets of purchases, cash receipts and disbursements, and a cash budget that shows whether borrowing or other financing will be needed. The final budget is usually the pro forma balance sheet, which shows how the company expects to wind up the budget period and start the next period.

APPENDIX—PRODUCTION AND PURCHASES BUDGET FOR MANUFACTURERS

Merchandisers budget purchases in accordance with inventory policies so that they will have enough goods to sell, but, they hope, not so many that the costs of carrying them will become excessive. A manufacturer must budget production in essentially the same way. Some manufacturers using flexible manufacturing systems need no inventories, but most manufacturers are not so fortunate and must carry enough finished goods to meet sales demands. Manufacturers must also carry enough inventories of raw materials and purchased components to meet production schedules. JIT (just-in-time) manufacturers, like those using flexible manufacturing, do not have significant inventories of materials and components, but they, again, are not the majority.

The **production budget** for a manufacturer is in the same form as a purchases budget for a merchandiser, except that it is typically done in units, not dollars. A separate budget of production costs is then prepared after the unit production budget. Manufacturers also prepare budgets for purchasing materials and components. These budgets are based, not on sales requirements, but on production requirements. This is reasonable because companies buy materials and components to *make* products. Production requirements are based on budgeted sales and finished goods inventory levels.

Suppose that Winfing Company, a manufacturer, wishes to keep an inventory of finished product equal to the budgeted sales needs for the following two months (much like the retailer in the earlier example). Winfing's managers have gathered the following budgeted data for 19X8.

1. Sales budget in units: January 10,000, February 12,000, March 13,000, April 15,000

2. Finished goods inventory is kept at budgeted sales for the next two months. Inventory at December 31 is 21,000 units.

3. Materials cost $8 per unit of product and are kept at 80% of the coming month's budgeted production requirements. Inventory at December 31 is $84,000.

Using this information, we can formulate a production budget through February.

Production Budget

	January	February	Total
Sales in units	10,000	12,000	22,000
Desired ending inventory*	25,000	28,000	28,000
Total requirements	35,000	40,000	50,000
Beginning inventory	21,000	25,000	21,000
Production	14,000	15,000	29,000

*January inventory of 25,000 units, is 12,000 for February plus 13,000 for March, February is 13,000 for March plus 15,000 for April.

We can now prepare the purchases budget for January.

Purchases Budget

Used in production*	$112,000
Desired ending inventory**	96,000
Total requirements	208,000
Beginning inventory	84,000
Purchases	$124,000

*14,000 × $8
**15,000 × 80% × $8

We see that the manufacturer's production/purchases budgets are more complicated than the merchandiser's purchase budget. Do note, however, that the manufacturer simply prepares one more budget than the merchandiser. There is no conceptual difference between the budgets used by the two types of business.

DEMONSTRATION PROBLEM

Use the data below to prepare a comprehensive budget for Morton Company for May and June. The budgets should include a budgeted income statement, budgets for cash receipts and disbursements, a cash budget, and a budgeted balance sheet as of June 30.

Morton Company Data

1. Sales budget: May $130,000, June $160,000, July $180,000, August $170,000.

2. Cost of sales is 60% of sales.

3. Sales are collected as follows: 70% in the month of sale and 30% in the following month.

4. Fixed costs are $25,000 per month, including $5,000 depreciation.

5. Morton keeps inventory equal to twice the budgeted sales requirements for the coming month.

6. Morton pays for its purchases in the month after purchase.

7. The balance sheet for April 30 appears below.

Morton Company
Balance Sheet as of April 30

Cash	$ 30,000	Payables	$ 98,000
Receivables	40,000		
Inventory	180,000	Common stock	500,000
Fixed assets	400,000	Retained earnings	52,000
Totals	$650,000		$650,000

Solution to Demonstration Problem

Morton Company Budgets

Budgeted Income Statements

	May	June	Total
Sales	$130,000	$160,000	$290,000
Cost of sales	78,000	96,000	174,000
Gross profit and contribution margin	52,000	64,000	116,000
Fixed costs	25,000	25,000	50,000
Profit	$ 27,000	$ 39,000	$ 66,000
Cash Receipts Budget			
Current, 70%	$ 91,000	$112,000	$203,000
Prior, 30%	40,000	39,000	79,000
Totals	$131,000	$151,000	$282,000
Purchases Budget			
Cost of sales	$ 78,000	$ 96,000	$174,000
Desired ending inventory*	192,000	216,000	216,000
Total requirements	270,000	312,000	390,000
Beginning inventory	180,000	192,000	180,000
Purchases	$ 90,000	$120,000	$210,000

*May, 2 × $96,000 = $192,000; June, 2 × $180,000 (July sales) × 60%

	May	June	Total
Cash Disbursements Budget			
Prior month purchases	$ 98,000	$ 90,000	$188,000
Cash fixed costs	20,000	20,000	40,000
Totals	$118,000	$110,000	$228,000
Cash Budget			
Beginning balance	$ 30,000	$ 43,000	$ 30,000
Receipts	131,000	151,000	282,000
Total available	161,000	194,000	312,000
Disbursements	118,000	110,000	228,000
Ending balance	$ 43,000	$ 84,000	$ 84,000

Pro Forma Balance Sheet

Cash (cash budget)	$ 84,000	Payables	$120,000 (3)
Receivables (1)	48,000		
Inventory (purchases budget)	216,000	Common stock	500,000
Fixed assets (2)	390,000	Retained earnings	118,000 (4)
Totals	$738,000		$738,000

(1) 30% of June sales of $160,000.
(2) Original balance of $400,000 less two months depreciation at $5,000 per month.
(3) June purchases to be paid in July.
(4) Beginning balance of $52,000 plus $66,000 net income.

Key Terms

cash budget

comprehensive budget

currently attainable
    performance

financial budget

flexible budget allowance

flexible expense budget

goal congruence

imposed budget

participative budgeting

production budget

purchases budget

sales budget

static expense budget

ASSIGNMENTS

13–1   Advantages of Budgeting

An acquaintance of yours has said that he sees no reason to budget because things change so fast in the real world that budgets serve no useful purpose. Answer this objection.

13–2   Budget Changes

Some organizations that receive an overall increase or decrease in their budgets over the past year of some percentage (say, 5%) then raise or lower the budgets of all departments by that same percentage. Does this practice make sense? Why or why not?

13–3   Cash Budgets

"A company that is earning a profit is also increasing its cash balance, so all that managers need to worry about is whether the company is profitable." Is this statement true? Why or why not?

13-4 Budgeting and Behavior
"Budgets are essentially mechanically developed plans that do not have to consider the responses of people." Is this statement true? Why or why not?

13-5 Income and Purchases Budgets

Kingston Sporting Goods has the following sales budget.

May	$120,000
June	$110,000

Cost of sales is 60%. Kingston tries to keep inventory equal to budgeted sales needs for the following month and began May with inventory of $60,000. Variable costs other than cost of sales are 10% of sales, and monthly fixed costs are $20,000, including $4,000 depreciation.

REQUIRED:
1. Prepare budgeted income statements for May and for June.
2. Prepare a purchases budget for May.

13-6 Cash Budget—Continuation of Assignment 13-5

Kingston collects 30% of its sales in the month of sale and 70% in the following month. April sales were $100,000. Kingston pays for its purchases in the month after purchase. Accounts payable for merchandise at the end of April were $55,000. Variable costs other than for cost of sales are paid as incurred, as are fixed costs requiring cash disbursement. The cash balance at the beginning of May is $15,000.

REQUIRED:
1. Prepare budgets of cash receipts and disbursements for May and for June.
2. Prepare cash budgets for May and for June.

13-7 Cash Budget
Vickrey Wholesale has the following budgets for sales and purchases for the first several months of 19X7.

Month	Sales Budget	Purchases Budget
January	$120,000	$ 85,000
February	140,000	100,000
March	150,000	110,000
April	170,000	115,000
May	180,000	120,000

Vickrey has fixed costs requiring cash of $35,000 per month. It collects 30% of its sales in the month of sale and 70% in the following month. It pays for 60% of its purchases in the month of purchase and 40% in the following month. Vickrey expects a cash balance of $20,000 at the end of January.

REQUIRED:

1. Prepare budgets of cash receipts and cash disbursements for February, March, and April.

2. Prepare cash budgets for February, March, and April.

13-8 Budgeted Income Statement and Purchases Budget

Calhoun Clothing has the following sales forecast for the first four months of 19X9.

January	$60,000
February	70,000
March	50,000
April	80,000

Cost of sales is 60% of sales. Fixed costs are $10,000 per month. Calhoun maintains inventory at 150% of the coming month's budgeted sales requirements and has $45,000 inventory at January 1.

REQUIRED:

1. Prepare a budgeted income statement for the first three months of 19X9 in total only, not by month.

2. Prepare a purchases budget for the first three months of 19X9 — both in total and by month.

13-9 Cash Budget—Continuation of Assignment 13-8

Calhoun pays for its purchases in the month after purchase. Accounts payable at December 31, 19X8, were $28,000. It collects 60% of its sales in the month of sale and 40% in the following month. Receivables at December 31, 19X8, to be collected in January, were $16,000. All of its fixed costs require cash disbursements and are paid as incurred. Its cash balance at December 31, 19X8, was $20,000.

REQUIRED:

1. Prepare a cash receipts budget for each of the first three months of 19X9 and for the quarter as a whole.

2. Prepare a cash disbursements budget for each of the first three months of 19X9 and for the quarter as a whole.

3. Prepare a cash budget for each of the first three months of 19X9 and for the quarter as a whole.

13–10   Pro Forma Balance Sheet—Continuation of Assignment 13–9

Calhoun's balance sheet at December 31, 19X8, appears below.

Assets		Equities	
Cash	$20,000	Accounts payable	$28,000
Receivables	16,000		
Inventory	45,000	Stockholders' equity	53,000
Totals	$81,000		$81,000

Calhoun leases its fixed assets.

Sales
Cost of Sales

REQUIRED:

Prepare a pro forma balance sheet as of March 31, 19X9.

13–11   Preparing Flexible Budgets

As a new assistant to the controller of HIJ Company, you must prepare a set of flexible budget allowances for overhead costs. You have the following data available.

Cost	Variable Amount per Machine Hour	Fixed Amount
Supplies	$0.50	$18,000
Repairs	0.12	5,800
Power	0.90	21,300
Depreciation	–	18,900

Supervision, the only other overhead item, is step-variable. It should be $7,000 at 10,000 machine hours and rise by $1,000 for each additional 1,000 machine hours.

REQUIRED:

Prepare a schedule showing the budgeted amount of each cost element, and of total budgeted overhead cost, at 10,000, 12,000, and 14,000 machine hours.

13–12   Flexible and Static Budgets

The supervisor of Department IIA of Crown Company has asked you about the report he just received. The production manager has questioned the supervisor about the use of manufacturing supplies, saying that he had exceeded the budget by $2,700 ($34,700 − $32,000). The monthly budget formula is as follows.

$$\text{Supplies Cost} = \$12,000 + (\$2.00 \times \text{Units Produced})$$

Department IIA was budgeted to produce 10,000 units in April, giving a budget allowance of $32,000. It actually produced 11,500 units and incurred $34,700 in supplies expense.

REQUIRED:

Tell the supervisor what he should say to the production manager.

13–13   Production Budget

Rudolph Office Products has the following sales budget for one of its paper glues, in cases: April 18,000, May 24,000, June 25,000. It keeps its inventory at twice the coming month's budgeted sales. At April 1, inventory is expected to be 41,000 cases.

REQUIRED:

Prepare production budgets for April and for May.

13–14   Cash Receipts Budget—Extension of Assignment 13–13

Rudolph charges a $100 selling price for its product and collects of 30% sales in the month of sale, and 70% in the following month.

REQUIRED:

Prepare cash receipts budgets for Rudolph for May and June.

13–15   Purchases Budget—Extension of Assignment 13–14

The manufacture of one case of Rudolph's glue requires 12 pounds of material that costs $2.50 per pound. Rudolph keeps its inventory of materials at 150% of the coming month's budgeted production requirements. At the beginning of April, Rudolph expects to have 540,000 pounds of material on hand bought for $2.50 per pound.

REQUIRED:

Prepare a materials purchases budget for April in (a) pounds and (b) dollars.

13–16   Budgeting for a CPA Firm

Jill Cram practices accounting in a mid-sized city. She employs two staff accountants and two clerks. Her monthly payroll is $8,700 per month. She also has other expenses, all fixed, of $4,800 per month for such items as rent, utilities, telephone, professional dues, and office supplies.

Cram's practice is seasonal, with January through April being very busy and the remaining eight months much less busy. Cram uses chargeable hours as her measure of volume, meaning hours worked on client business for which the clients are charged. She expects her two staff accountants to work an average of 150 chargeable hours each month during the eight slower months, and 200 hours each per month during the January—April busy season. Clerical personnel work about 600 chargeable hours each per year, and Cram works about 1,400. For both the clerical personnel and Cram, approximately 40% of their charged hours fall in the four-month busy season.

Cram charges $70 per hour for her time, $30 for the time of a staff accountant, and $15 for the time of clerical personnel.

REQUIRED:

Prepare a budget of revenues and expenses for the year. Separate the budgets for the periods of January through April and May through December.

13–17 Cash Receipts Budget

JTV Company has the following sales budget, in thousands of dollars.

	March	April	May
Budgeted sales	$1,100	$900	$1,600

JTV collects 30% of its sales in the month of sale, 40% in the first month after sale, and 28% in the second month after sale. The remaining 2% are bad debts. Sales in January were $1,600, in February $2,200.

REQUIRED:

Prepare a cash receipts budget for the March through May period, by month.

13–18 Quarterly Cash Budget

Kresswell Company expects the following results by quarters in 19X4 in thousands of dollars.

	1	2	3	4
Sales	$3,400	$4,100	$4,600	$3,600
Cash disbursements:				
Production costs	2,300	3,100	2,700	1,900
Selling and administrative	800	950	1,080	870
Purchases of fixed assets	800	500	400	200
Dividends	40	40	40	40

Accounts receivable at the end of a quarter are one-fourth of sales for the quarter. The beginning balance in accounts receivable is $600 thousand. Beginning cash is $120 thousand and the required minimum balance is $100 thousand. Any borrowings are made at the beginnings of quarters in which the need will occur, in $10 thousand multiples, and are repaid at the ends of quarters. Ignore interest.

REQUIRED:

1. Prepare a cash budget by quarters for the year.
2. What is the loan outstanding at the end of the year?
3. Can the firm be operating profitably in view of the heavy borrowing required?

13-19 Cash Budget for a Student

Gayle Lee is an English major at State University. Gayle wants a cash budget for the fall semester. Her parents have promised to help support her and want to know how much money she will need and when she will need it. She has collected the following information.

Cash at September 1	$1,100
Tuition, due early September	2,200
Room rent, due early September, for entire term	880
Textbook purchases, due mid-September	190

Gayle expects to spend $400 per month during the four months of the term for food and clothing. She also estimates expenditures for miscellaneous items at roughly $50 per month. She has a part-time job that pays $6 per hour and expects to work about 50 hours each month. She is not subject to income tax or social security tax. Finally, Gayle does not want her cash balance to go below $100 in case she has some emergency.

REQUIRED:

Prepare a cash budget for Gayle, showing how much support she will need from her parents each month.

13-20 One-Month Cash Budget

Lanford Department Store makes about 20% of its sales for cash. Credit sales are collected 20%, 30%, 50% in the month of sale, month after, and second month after sale, respectively. Cost of sales is 60% of selling prices. The store tries to maintain its inventory at twice the following month's budgeted sales. Lanford pays for two-thirds of its purchases in the month of purchase and one-third in the following month.

The general manager of the store has asked you to prepare a cash budget for August, and you have gathered the following data.

Sales:	
June (actual)	$260,000
July (actual)	300,000
August (budgeted)	340,000
September (budgeted)	330,000
Inventory at July 31	482,500
Cash at July 31	65,000
Accounts payable, merchandise, end of July	70,000

Selling and administrative expenses budgeted for August are $86,000 (including $14,000 depreciation). Lanford pays all cash expenses in the month incurred, except for purchases.

REQUIRED:

Prepare a cash budget for August.

13-21 DECISION CASE: BUDGETING FOR A NEW BUSINESS

Paul Lee is opening an electronics business in a new shopping center. He worked in several such stores as a student and is convinced that he can make a success of his own operation. He wants you to help him develop a financial plan to use to obtain a bank loan. He believes that the bank manager will be more receptive if he can present a careful analysis of his needs. Lee has collected the following data from a trade association's study of stores of the type and size he plans to open.

Average annual sales	$720,000
Average rent	$4,000 per month plus 5% of sales
Average gross profit	60% of sales
Average annual operating expenses (excluding rent and depreciation)	$240,000, paid as incurred

Inventory requirements are usually about a two-month supply. Lee also estimates that he will need $60,000 in equipment and fixtures, to be paid for in March. The equipment should have a useful life of ten years. He will sell for cash only and will get 30 days credit from his merchandise suppliers.

Lee expects to see rapid growth in sales for the first few months of operation and to reach the $60,000 monthly average ($720,000/12) in May. He projects sales of $40,000, $45,000, $50,000, and $55,000 the first four months.

REQUIRED:

1. Prepare a budgeted income statement for Lee's first year.

2. Prepare a schedule showing Lee's total financing requirements through April.

13–22 DECISION CASE: BUDGETING AND ETHICS

You are the assistant to Donna Grant, who is controller of the Power Fashions division of YuppyDales, Inc. Grant has asked you for assistance in developing next year's travel budget. She has told you the following:

> First, we have to make sure we spend this year's budget. We have $150,000 in the budget and have spent only $135,000, so I'll tell the General Manager of the division to send people somewhere, anywhere, before year-end. Then we'll ask for $190,000 next year and cite higher airline fares and hotel rates. Headquarters will cut that by 10% or so, but what they leave should give us some padding. They never even tell us how they arrive at the final budget allowances, so we have to be creative.

REQUIRED:

1. Why do you think Grant behaves as she does?

2. What recommendations might you make to the company regarding its budgeting practices?

3. Is Grant's behavior a violation of the Institute of Management Accountants Standards of Ethical Conduct? Why or why not?

14

Standard Costs— Control and Product Costing

LEARNING OBJECTIVES

After studying Chapter 14, you will be able to:
1. Describe how standard costs assist in planning and control.
2. Calculate the standard cost of a unit of product.
3. Calculate variances from standard and interpret those variances.

Chapter 10 briefly described the use of budgets in planning. Chapter 11 described job order and process costing methods of product costing. The current chapter ties together concepts of planning and control as discussed in Chapter 13 with related uses of standard costs. Standard costs are also used for product costing. Standard product costing is the method most widely used today. The **standard cost** of a unit of product is the cost that a company *should* incur to make a unit of product under efficient operations. A standard cost is therefore an expected cost—what the company should incur if operations go according to plan. Standard costs are used in budgeting and other planning and decision-making, such as deciding which products to emphasize and because they are used in budgets, standard costs serve as benchmarks to judge how well managers have controlled operations.

Standard costs bring many behavioral issues that we consider in setting performance standards and in using such standards for control and performance evaluation. Standard costs can also be used in non-manufacturing settings such as the service sector.

Thus, a unit of product typically has cost standards for materials, direct labor, variable overhead, and fixed overhead. The standard cost of any of these input factors (materials, labor, overhead) consists of two parts—a standard price, or rate for the factor (such as the price per yard of cotton fabric used to make shirts or the hourly rate paid to people who sew the shirts), and a standard quantity (the number of yards of cotton fabric that should be used to make a shirt or the number of minutes each sewing operation should take). Establishing standards requires careful study of production processes and is fraught with behavioral questions, which we consider later.

A standard cost is much like a budget for a unit of product. (In fact, managers use the term *budget* to describe the standard cost of manufacturing a quantity of product, say 20,000 units.) Standards are used in controlling operations and in evaluating performance of managers through the medium of **variances,** which are differences between actual results and budgeted, or standard, results. The variances we calculate later relate to the two components described above—price and quantity. We show how to calculate and evaluate variances throughout the chapter.

DEVELOPING STANDARD COSTS

Park Mills manufactures men's apparel. The company is about to begin manufacturing a new shirt. Park's industrial engineers have studied the cloth requirements for the shirt and examined the labor required for

cutting, sewing, and finishing. They have determined labor requirements if workers are producing at a reasonably high rate of efficiency,
but with allowances for fatigue and other factors that prevent achieving
100% efficiency.

In some companies the recommendations of such engineers are
adopted with little discussion and standard costs set on that basis. In
others, there is extensive negotiation or consultation with the employees who must meet the standard, and discussions with other managers,
such as the controller, before standards are adopted. Recall that participation is widely thought to be desirable in setting budget allowances.
Various managers have important interests in setting standards. Manufacturing managers will be held responsible for meeting the standards.
Engineers are evaluated partly on whether they can effect cost reductions. Both parties therefore want to protect their interests. Time and
motion studies might be used to provide guidance in setting labor time
standards. Of course, expected increases in material costs, wage rates,
and overhead rates have to be incorporated into the standards.

Suppose that all concerned managers have agreed on the following
standard quantities of materials and labor, along with the standard
prices of those inputs.

	Standard Quantity	× Standard Price	= Standard Cost
Material	1.5 yards of cloth	$ 4.00 per yard	$6.00
Direct labor	30 minutes	$10.00 per hour	$5.00

These standards are simplified. Shirts also have buttons, facing, and
perhaps elastic, or other materials, and in real life, several types of labor
are required, not just one. The principles, however, are valid regardless
of the number of different types of inputs. We now have standards for
materials and labor. All that remains is overhead. As other chapters have
discussed, overhead cost might be related to several production factors
such as labor time, machine time, or material use. You are also familiar
with the analysis necessary to separate overhead cost into fixed and
variable components. We need a standard overhead rate to use to apply
overhead to products, and the standard rate is calculated exactly as is
the predetermined overhead rate in Chapter 11. Suppose, then, that
Park's overhead is most closely related to labor time and is budgeted as:

$$\$2,400,000 + (\$2.00 \times \text{Direct Labor Hours})$$

The standard for *variable overhead* is simple to determine: because
one-half hour of labor is required, there should be $1.00 of variable
overhead for each shirt ($2.00 × 0.50 hours). Please note that both
variable and fixed overhead actually consist of many separate items

such as utilities, fringe benefits, supervision, depreciation, and the costs of support activities such as engineering, payroll, and accounting. For simplicity we do not enumerate these costs, but simply group them into the fixed and variable components.

Unlike the standard for variable overhead, the standard for *fixed overhead* cannot be found by looking only at budgeted cost. Calculating a fixed overhead standard requires that we select a level of activity, such as normal capacity or budgeted activity. You are already familiar with the use of budgeted activity in calculating a predetermined overhead rate using normal costing. *Normal activity* is the average activity expected over the next three to five years. It is therefore a longer-term concept than expected (budgeted) activity for the coming year. *Practical capacity* is the maximum level of activity the company can reasonably expect to sustain over a year. It is therefore less than the theoretical maximum the company could do, because it recognizes that no factory can operate full-blast all year long. Suppose Parks uses normal capacity of 600,000, giving a fixed overhead rate of $4.00 ($2,400,000/600,000). This calculation is similar to that done in Chapter 11 for a normal overhead rate. There is no difference in the calculations for normal and standard overhead rates, but there are differences in their uses. Exhibit 14–1 summarizes the information we have into a standard cost calculation. It also provides data on actual operations for October 19X5.

Standards for fixed overhead require decisions about activity.

VARIANCES

When we know unit production for a period, we can determine whether performance was up to standard by calculating *variances,* differences between planned (budgeted, or standard) and actual results. Let us note at the outset, though, that we cannot conclude that a particular manager did well or poorly simply by looking at variances. We shall revisit this point later.

Variances arise for many reasons, but the most common is simply the randomness of production operations. We really do not expect that the average time for making shirts will be *exactly* 0.50 hours month after month. Variances also occur because standards are sometimes incorrectly set. Inefficient or extra-efficient operations create variances. They also result from workers cutting corners or from managers buying cheaper, substandard materials.

Variances do not tell us the causes of differences between standard and actual cost. That is, they do not inform us as to the reason workers are performing above or below standard. However, we calculate variances to assist in identifying problems and to help fix responsibility.

Variances do not tell us that performance was good or bad.

Exhibit 14–1
Park Mills
Standard Cost

Materials, 1.5 yards at $4	$ 6.00
Direct labor, 0.50 hours at $10	5.00
Variable overhead, 0.50 hours at $2	1.00
Fixed overhead, 0.50 hours at $4	2.00
Total standard cost	$14.00

Fixed overhead based on $2,400,000 annual budgeted fixed overhead ($200,000 per month) and 600,000 direct labor hours at normal capacity.

Results for October 19X5

Shirts produced	90,000
Materials purchased	180,000 yards, $722,000
Materials used	139,000 yards
Direct labor	47,000 hours, $458,000
Variable overhead	$ 92,000
Fixed overhead	$196,000

Different managers are in charge of different operations, so identifying the responsibility of managers for variances is an important part of control.

You will see that variance analysis follows a pattern that makes intuitive sense. The key thought in variance analysis is to hold all factors constant but for the one under study. Because standard costs have only two components, standard rates or prices and standard quantities of inputs, we generally calculate only two variances, one for price or rate and one for quantity. One is related to differences between actual and standard prices or rates (e.g., paying workers more or less than the standard rate), the other relates to differences between the actual use and standard use of the input factor (e.g., use more or less material than standard allowed for the production achieved). Let us examine direct labor first.

Labor Variances

First, we can determine that making 90,000 shirts should have cost Park Mills $450,000 in direct labor (90,000 shirts × $5.00 or 45,000 hours × $10.00). This $450,000 is the *total standard cost* or *total budgeted direct labor cost* to make 90,000 shirts. Park actually spent $458,000, giving an $8,000 unfavorable variance. But this variance does not tell us the reasons for the difference. There are two possible reasons why Park spent more than standard. These reasons correspond to the calculation of a standard cost: the standard rate and the standard quantity. Accordingly, we break the total $8,000 variance into components related to the difference between the actual and standard rates of pay for laborers and the difference between the standard time and actual time used to produce the 90,000 shirts.

Direct Labor Rate Variance

The **direct labor rate variance** is the difference between the actual cost of direct labor ($458,000) and the cost that would have been incurred had the company paid the standard wage rate for the 47,000 hours actually worked (from Exhibit 14-1).

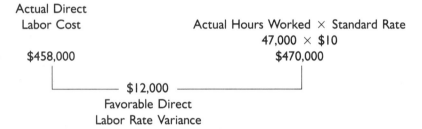

The variance is favorable because the amount spent, $458,000, is less than the amount that would have been spent for the 47,000 actual hours at the $10 standard rate. The actual rate was less than the standard rate. Note that we hold the amount of direct labor hours constant (at 47,000) and focus on the difference in wage rates. The actual hours times the standard rate is the *budget for the actual hours worked.*

Rate variances mean that actual rates differ from standard rates.

An alternative calculation method is to subtract the actual rate from the standard rate and multiply by the actual hours. The actual rate was $9.7447 ($458,000/47,000).

Labor Rate Variance = Difference in Rate × Actual Hours Worked
($10.00 − $9.7447) × 47,000 = $11,999 Favorable

The difference between this calculation and the preceding one that yielded $12,000 is from rounding the actual rate. Both calculation methods always give the same result, except for rounding.

What is the cause of this variance? The company might have shifted some lower paid workers to the $10-per-hour jobs and continued to pay these workers their old rates, or it might have hired new workers at less than the $10 standard rate.

Direct Labor Efficiency Variance

Efficiency variances mean that actual use differs from standard use.

The **direct labor efficiency variance** relates to the difference in the quantity of labor used, 47,000 hours instead of 45,000. The variance is the difference between the budget for actual hours worked (computed as $470,000 above in determining the labor rate variance) and the budget (standard cost) for the output achieved ($450,000 for 90,000 shirts). The analysis in Exhibit 14–2 shows both the labor efficiency and labor rate variances so that you can see the relationships.

For the efficiency variance, we hold the labor rate constant and concentrate on the difference between actual and standard hours. Note that we can also compute the standard cost for the 90,000 shirts by using the total standard hours allowed for 90,000 units and the standard wage rate.

$$\text{Total Standard Cost} = 90,000 \times 0.50 \times \$10 = \$450,000$$

The 45,000 (90,000 × 0.50) is called **standard hours allowed** and is commonly used to calculate variances. It is especially helpful when the company makes many products and is aggregating standard hours over many products. We can also use the same type of alternative calculation we used for the labor rate variance.

$$
\begin{aligned}
\text{Labor Efficiency Variance} &= \text{Change In Quantity} \times \text{Standard Rate} \\
&= (\text{Standard Hours} - \text{Actual Hours}) \times \text{Standard Rate} \\
&= (45,000 - 47,000) \times \$10 \\
&= -\$20,000 \text{ Unfavorable}
\end{aligned}
$$

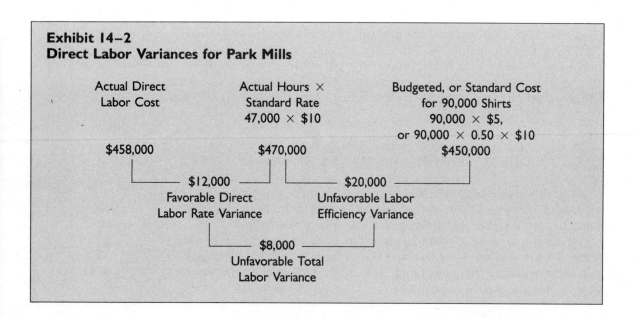

Exhibit 14–2
Direct Labor Variances for Park Mills

Actual Direct Labor Cost	Actual Hours × Standard Rate 47,000 × $10	Budgeted, or Standard Cost for 90,000 Shirts 90,000 × $5, or 90,000 × 0.50 × $10
$458,000	$470,000	$450,000

$12,000 Favorable Direct Labor Rate Variance

$20,000 Unfavorable Labor Efficiency Variance

$8,000 Unfavorable Total Labor Variance

Managers use various terms to refer to the two types of variances we have calculated (those related to rates and those related to quantities). Rate variances are sometimes called *price, budget, or spending* variances. Efficiency variances are sometimes called *use or quantity* variances. We calculate the two types of variances for several reasons. First, we want to know the sources of the total variance. Another reason is that the labor rate variance and labor efficiency variance are usually the responsibilities of different managers. In a large plant, the personnel manager is probably responsible for wage rates, while production supervisors are responsible for labor use. This point relates to our earlier comment about responsibility for variances. Still another reason is that there are differences in how managers can control variances. Managers can do very little about a labor rate variance caused by a tight labor market that makes it impossible to hire workers at the standard rate. But managers can probably do something about unfavorable efficiency variances that they determine to have been caused by poor supervision.

Variable Overhead Variances

The computations for *variable overhead variances* parallel those for direct labor. And when variable overhead is related to direct labor, as in this case, the computation uses the same basis—direct labor hours. Exhibit 14–3 shows the variable overhead calculations. When variable overhead is related to direct labor hours, the **variable overhead efficiency variance** results from using more or less *direct labor* than

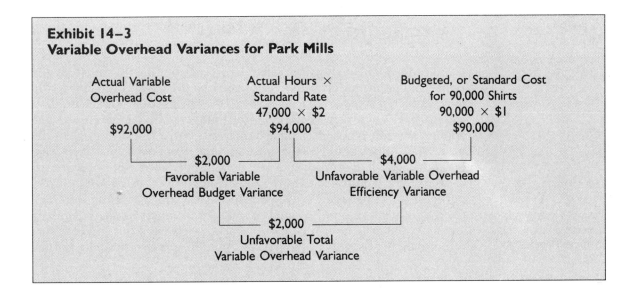

Exhibit 14–3
Variable Overhead Variances for Park Mills

Actual Variable Overhead Cost	Actual Hours × Standard Rate 47,000 × $2	Budgeted, or Standard Cost for 90,000 Shirts 90,000 × $1
$92,000	$94,000	$90,000

$2,000
Favorable Variable
Overhead Budget Variance

$4,000
Unfavorable Variable Overhead
Efficiency Variance

$2,000
Unfavorable Total
Variable Overhead Variance

standard, not more or less of a particular variable overhead item, such as power or supplies.

Notice that the variance that parallels the direct labor rate variance is called the **variable overhead budget variance** (or **spending variance**). This variable overhead variance, which is calculated in the same manner as the labor rate variance, is not *necessarily* caused by differences between actual and standard variable overhead rates, but can be caused by using more or less of a variable overhead item, such as cleaning rags or power. Thus, although the variable overhead variances are calculated like those for direct labor, their interpretations are not the same.

Fixed Overhead Variances

The calculation and interpretation of fixed overhead variances are different from the others discussed so far. There are two fixed overhead variances, the *budget variance* and the *volume variance*. The *budget variance* is simply the difference between actual fixed overhead and budgeted fixed overhead. Unlike budgeted variable overhead, budgeted fixed overhead does not depend on production, so the only calculation required for the **fixed overhead budget variance** is to subtract budgeted fixed overhead from actual fixed overhead. In our case, budgeted fixed overhead is $200,000 per month and actual fixed overhead is $196,000 (from Exhibit 14−1), giving a favorable budget variance of $4,000.

Fixed overhead variances differ from variable cost variances.

The **fixed overhead volume variance** (also called the **idle capacity variance, denominator variance,** or **volume variance**) is quite different. It is the difference between budgeted fixed overhead and applied fixed overhead. *Applied fixed overhead* is fixed overhead cost per unit multiplied by the number of units produced. Exhibit 14−4 shows the calculations.

We do not use the term "standard cost for 90,000 units" in the right-hand column because it is *not* the case that the company should have *incurred* fixed overhead of $180,000 in making 90,000 units. It should have incurred $200,000 —the budgeted fixed overhead. The applied amount is based on an arbitrary rate set at the beginning of the year. The $4-per-hour, $2-per-unit amount was based on $2,400,000 budgeted fixed overhead and 600,000 direct labor hours at normal capacity. But we do not expect to incur fixed overhead at a rate of $4 per hour or $2 per unit. We expect to incur $200,000 per month. The fixed overhead volume variance is calculated much like an efficiency variance. But it is not an efficiency variance. It does not indicate that performance was good or bad. Like misapplied overhead in normal

Volume variances do not indicate efficient or inefficient operation.

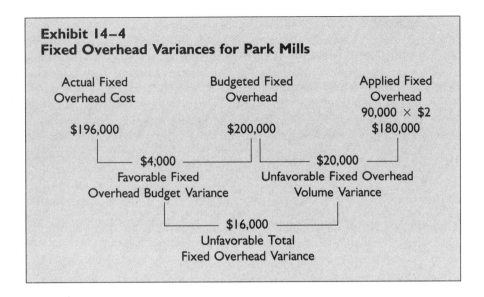

Exhibit 14–4
Fixed Overhead Variances for Park Mills

costing, the volume variance is simply the result of not working the same number of standard hours as the number used to calculate the standard fixed overhead rate. In our case, the standard rate of $4 per direct labor hour, calculated at the beginning of the year, was based on $2,400,000 budgeted fixed overhead and 600,000 direct labor hours at normal capacity. Expressed monthly, we have $200,000 and 50,000 hours (600,000/12). Thus, applied fixed overhead is as follows.

Applied Fixed Overhead = $200,000/50,000 hrs × (90,000 units × 0.50 hr/unit)
$$= \$4/hr \times 45,000 \text{ hrs}$$
$$= \$180,000$$

So the difference between the $200,000 budgeted and $180,000 applied overhead relates only to working 45,000 standard direct labor hours instead of 50,000. Had the fixed overhead rate been based on 45,000 monthly hours (540,000 annual hours), there would have been no volume variance. Had the fixed overhead rate been based on 500,000 annual hours (giving a rate of $4.80, [$2,400,000/500,000]), overhead would have been overapplied, yielding a favorable volume variance. So the volume variance has no economic significance. It indicates only that production was less than, or greater than, the level used to set the standard fixed overhead rate. It must be calculated to reconcile applied and actual fixed overhead (along with the budget variance).

Materials Variances

Material price variances are calculated at the time of purchase.

In one respect, materials differ from labor and overhead: they can be stored. With labor, it is "use it or lose it," but materials can be bought in one period, used in another. We therefore calculate the **material price variance** when we buy materials, and the **material use variance** when we use them. We cannot have a three column analysis as we did with labor and overhead. Rather, we must do each variance separately. The *material price variance* is the difference between the actual cost of purchasing materials and the budgeted (standard) cost of purchasing the actual quantity purchased. The *material use variance* is the difference between actual and standard use of materials multiplied by the standard price. Exhibit 14−5 shows the calculations.

We can also calculate both variances using the formulas. The actual price paid for materials was $4.0111 ($722,000/180,000).

$$\text{Material Price Variance} = \text{Difference in Price} \times \text{Actual Quantity Purchased}$$
$$= (\$4.00 - \$4.0111) \times 180,000 = -\$1,998 \text{ Unfavorable}$$

The difference is from rounding.

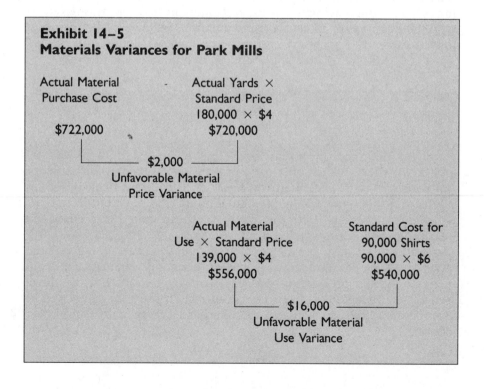

Exhibit 14−5
Materials Variances for Park Mills

Actual Material   -   Actual Yards ×
Purchase Cost   Standard Price
                                            180,000 × $4
        $722,000 $720,000
              └──────── $2,000 ────────┘
                    Unfavorable Material
                        Price Variance

                          Actual Material   Standard Cost for
                      Use × Standard Price   90,000 Shirts
                          139,000 × $4   90,000 × $6
                             $556,000 $540,000
                                   └──────── $16,000 ────────┘
                                        Unfavorable Material
                                            Use Variance

Material Use Variance = Difference in Quantity × Standard Price
= ([90,000 × 1.5] − 139,000) × \$4 = − \$16,000 Unfavorable

Different managers are almost always responsible for purchasing materials and using them in production. A purchasing manager is charged with buying materials of suitable quality at standard prices, while production supervisors are responsible for using materials.

Commonality of Variances

It might appear that there are eight different variances, but there are really only two variable cost variances—price and use. The forms of calculation for materials, direct labor, and variable overhead are the same. The calculations of price or spending variances concentrate on the difference between actual and standard costs arising because of price or rate differences. (The variable overhead spending variance is not interpreted the same as the others, but it is calculated the same.) The use or efficiency variances all focus on the difference between standard and actual costs arising because of differences in the amount of the input factor used. Exhibit 14−6 shows the relationships.

Fixed overhead variances are different from variable cost variances. The fixed overhead budget variance is simply the difference between actual and budgeted fixed cost. Budgeted fixed cost is the same at any level of production. The volume, idle capacity, or application variance

---

Exhibit 14−6
Variable Cost Variances

The following two equations are used to calculate all variances for all variable costs, that is, all variances for direct materials, direct labor, and variable overhead.

Use variance equation:
Use Variance = Difference in Quantity × Standard Price

Use variances may be called quantity, efficiency, or use variances.

Rate variance equation:
Rate Variance = Difference in Price × Actual Quantity

For materials, this variance is called a price variance.

is the difference between budgeted fixed overhead and applied fixed overhead. Applied fixed overhead is simply units produced multiplied by standard fixed overhead per unit—a calculation similar to that of standard variable costs.

USING VARIANCES TO EVALUATE PERFORMANCE

Variances can have many causes and are only the first step in control.

Calculating variances is only the first step in performance evaluation. As we said earlier, variances do not tell us their causes, nor who is responsible for them. Knowing that workers used more or less than the standard amount of materials does not explain *why* they did. One possible reason is inaccurate standards. The standards might be out of date, or they might reflect performance only under ideal conditions that can never be achieved.

Another reason that we cannot draw conclusions about performance directly from variances is that performance in one area is not necessarily independent of performance in another. A variance in one department might be caused by poor work done in a department that worked on the product earlier. For instance, the purchasing manager might have bought lower-quality materials, giving a favorable material price variance. But if the lower-quality materials are hard to use in production, the purchasing manager's action might increase both material use and labor time causing unfavorable material use, labor efficiency, and variable overhead efficiency variances in operating departments. Calculating a variance does not tell us why it occurred or which manager was responsible for it.

INVESTIGATING VARIANCES

One purpose of calculating variances is to decide whether to investigate them and, if necessary, take corrective action. But investigating every variance violates the cost/benefit principle, because some variances are caused by random factors, as we stated at the beginning of the chapter. The expected cost to investigate, and perhaps correct, a variance must, therefore, be less than the potential benefit to justify its undertaking. Consequently, managers usually establish cutoffs for investigating variances, such as $500 or 10% of total cost. In this way they aim to investigate only significant variances. Companies often use *control charts* for this purpose (see Figure 14–1). These charts usually

Figure 14–1
Control Chart

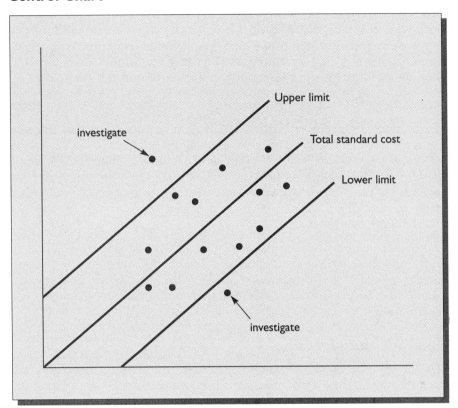

show past cost behavior patterns so that efforts will not be wasted investigating costs that normally show wide fluctuations. Not investigating such variances accords with the principle of management by exception.

Significant variances should be investigated whether they are favorable or unfavorable. Note that in Figure 14–1 there are indications to investigate both types. Some managers do not investigate favorable variances because favorable variances indicate that operations are more efficient than standard, but this is not good management. A favorable variance in one area might have unfavorable effects elsewhere, as we described might be the case with substandard materials. Also, favorable variances might result from harmful actions such as cutting corners or using lower-quality components. These actions could reduce the quality of the company's product, resulting in lost sales, lost profits, and a diminished reputation. Such actions are encouraged if unfavorable variances are punished, while favorable ones are rewarded. Additionally, failing to investigate large favorable variances allows poorly set standards (allowing too much labor time, for instance) to continue without correction. And finally, failing to investigate favorable variances may result in managers ignoring legitimate cost-cutting techniques discovered by line workers and having broader application within the company.

ESTABLISHING STANDARD COSTS

There are several ways to set standards. The most common are historical projections, engineering methods, manager judgment, and worker involvement.

Historical Projections

Companies can set standards simply by looking at previous actual results and making any obvious adjustments for changes in product design or manufacturing methods. Using the past to set performance standards can perpetuate inefficiencies, though, and few managers recommend it.

Engineering Methods

Engineers use various techniques to determine labor, machine, and material standards. They use time-and-motion studies to analyze the worker's motions required for each task. For example, a worker might reach into a box, pick out a part, inspect it, place it into an assembly, and put the completed assembly onto a moving belt. The engineer times each movement and develops a standard labor time for the whole operation. Engineers might also study the characteristics of the product and the materials or purchased components it uses to determine material use standards.

Engineers establish standards for some overhead costs as well, such as maintenance. They establish recommended cycles or intervals for performing various maintenance tasks and estimate their costs. For the most part, however, overhead standards are based on input factors such as labor time, machine time, or material content. Standards for overhead are more often developed using the methods illustrated in Chapter 10: high-low, scatter diagram, and regression analysis.

Managers' Estimates and Worker Involvement

Even if standards can be carefully engineered, most companies also use the judgment of their managers to establish standards. Managers who are close to the production process understand that some factors are difficult to capture in engineering analyses. Moreover, if managers who are responsible for meeting standards have some say in setting them, they are much more likely to commit themselves to achieving them. While the evidence is not conclusive, there is some ground for stating that performance is even further improved when managers involve their workers in setting standards. Some managers are uncomfortable involving their subordinate managers and workers in setting standards, fearing that the standards will be too loose, but evidence exists that most workers set reasonably tight standards for themselves.

Employee involvement is important in setting standards.

In other words, the general idea of increasing employee involvement in managerial decisions extends to setting standards. As mentioned earlier in this book, that *Business Week,* a popular weekly magazine, spent a good part of an issue on the subject of increasing worker involvement only a few years ago is evidence that this principle has been widely accepted.

STANDARD COSTS IN JIT COMPANIES

We illustrated backflushing, a product costing technique suitable for some JIT (just-in-time) manufacturers, in Chapter 11. Some JIT manufacturers do not use standard costs because of a belief that standards stifle improvement. They argue that people who are given standards to achieve consider the job done when they have met the standards, whereas a major principle of JIT is continual improvement, meaning that simply meeting standards is not enough. Some JIT companies do use standards, but continually raise them to stimulate improvement.

Even companies that do not use standards compare current period actual costs with prior period actual costs (or an average of the past several periods' costs) to see whether they are improving. Such comparisons are similar to variance calculations, with the prior period costs acting as the "standard."

Another reason that some JIT companies do not use standards is that standards relate to relatively small parts of operations, such as work centers or departments. Standards therefore distract from the JIT focus on the total operation and encourage *suboptimizing* behavior. We discussed this issue briefly earlier and used as an example the purchase of low-grade materials, which gives the purchasing manager a favorable variance while causing unfavorable variances in operating departments.

JIT companies use various measures in place of, or in addition to, standard costs. The following is a representative list.

Many JIT companies use other measures of performance than standards.

1. *Turnover of materials inventory, work-in-process inventory, and finished goods inventory.* These measures indicate how quickly the

company can manufacture and ship its products. You are familiar with the idea of inventory turnover for the stock of a merchandising company. These measures are often expressed as the days supply of inventory. For example, a company that operates with a four day supply of materials is, other things equal, doing better than one that requires a 12 day supply to keep its production lines running.

2. *Percentage of deliveries to customers made on-time.* This indicates how well the company is meeting its obligations to customers.

3. *Cycle time.* This is the total time it takes from receiving a customer order through making the product and shipping it to the customer. The closer this time comes to the manufacturing time, the less time the company is wasting. Time not spent making product is not *value-adding time.*

4. *Setup time.* This is the time it takes to change over from making one product to making another. In conventional companies, setups can take hours; in JIT companies they should be done in minutes.

5. *Quality measures.* There are many ways to assess and measure quality. Some common ways are the percentage of defective units, number of warranty claims or customer complaints, and number of units reworked.

These measures, and others, reflect the goals and objectives of JIT manufacturers, but they can also be used with good effect by conventional manufacturers.

STANDARD COSTS FOR PRODUCT COSTING

Standard costs are not just for planning and control. They can also serve as product costs. Chapter 11 illustrated actual costing and normal costing, job-order and process costing. Standard costing is an alternative to actual costing and normal costing. Standard costing means simply that inventories are valued at standard cost and variances appear on the income statement as expenses or negative expenses (if favorable).

Large and medium-sized manufacturing companies use standard costing much more than they use actual or normal costing. There are several reasons. First, standard costing integrates standard costs and variances into the company's accounts. Variances are calculated as a normal part of the accounting process, not *ad hoc*. In using standard costs, therefore, we achieve the objective of isolating variances as soon as possible, so that the information is available quickly, when it can be best used to take corrective action. Second, it is much simpler for repetitive manufacturers (mass producers of standard products) to use standard costs than to use actual or normal costs. Consider an automobile assembly plant that makes many models, including two-door, four-door, and station wagons, each with some combination of options such as air conditioning, power steering, and leather upholstery. So many different cars are made that the company cannot use process costing. Using the number of cars as the denominator of the unit cost calculation makes no sense because the cars are so different. But job-order costing is silly in such a plant. If workers filled out tags stating how long they took to put in the windshield, attach the door, or what-not, the cost of keeping records might approach the cost of making the car.

Standard costs work well here. The company uses them to value inventory, ignoring how much each individual car "actually" cost, because such information is not very helpful anyway. The company establishes standards for each model (two-door, four-door, etc.) and for each piece of optional equipment. A car in inventory can then be costed by determining its model and equipment. To determine total inventory, the company need only add the standard costs of each unit.

We illustrate standard costing using the example of Park Mills. Of course, to use standard costs for product costing, a company must make standard products. Many job order companies cannot use standard costs because they manufacture to customer order and so never make the same product twice. Standards are useless for such companies. But virtually any processing company or repetitive manufacturer, and some job order companies, can use standard costs for product costing. Insight 14-1 tells how using one JIT company greatly reduced the cost of paperwork.

INSIGHT 14-1
Cut the Journal Entries

One of the benefits of JIT, as Chapter 11 showed, is less recordkeeping. The experience of Hewlett-Packard (H-P) the electronics giant, provides a particularly vivid example. In one of its divisions, H-P eliminated much of its labor reporting after moving toward JIT and *saved 100,000 journal entries per month.** Other companies, too, are reporting the elimination of considerable amounts of records. Perhaps the most common example is the elimination of costly, elaborate, computer-based systems once used for tracking inventory. Because under JIT there should be minimal inventories, there is no need for such costly computerized systems to keep track of jobs.

*Rick Hunt, Linda Garrett, C. Mike Merz, "Direct Labor Not Always Relevant at H-P," *Management Accounting*, February 1985, 58–62.

JOURNAL ENTRIES

The journal entries required for Park's operations in October follow. These entries are not the only way that a company can account for standard costs, but are perhaps the most direct and straightforward. Let us assume that Park began the month with no inventories, sold 80,000 shirts for $20 each, and incurred selling and administrative expenses of $350,000.

1. Purchase of materials; record materials inventory at standard price of materials, isolating the material price variance.

Materials Inventory (180,000 × $4)	$720,000	
Material Price Variance	2,000	
Cash or Accounts Payable		$722,000

2. Record materials used at standard cost to Work-in-Process, actual use at standard price from Materials Inventory.

Work-in-Process (90,000 × 1.5 × $4)	$540,000	
Material Use Variance	16,000	
Materials Inventory (139,000 × $4)		$556,000

3. Record direct labor cost incurred, isolating the labor rate variance.

Direct Labor (47,000 × $10.00)	$470,000	
Direct Labor Rate Variance		$ 12,000
Cash		458,000

4. Record use of labor, clear out Direct Labor account and isolate efficiency variance.

Work-in-Process Inventory (90,000 × $5)	$450,000	
Direct Labor Efficiency Variance	20,000	
Direct Labor		$470,000

5. Record overhead costs incurred, overhead budget variances.

Variable Manufacturing Overhead (47,000 × $20)	$ 94,000	
Fixed Manufacturing Overhead (budgeted)	200,000	
Variable Overhead Budget Variance		$ 2,000
Fixed Overhead Budget Variance		4,000
Cash, Accrued Payables ($92,000 + $196,000)		288,000

6. Record application of variable overhead.

Work-in-Process Inventory (90,000 × $1)	$90,000	
Variable Overhead Efficiency Variance	4,000	
Variable Manufacturing Overhead		$94,000

7. Record application of fixed overhead.

Work-in-Process Inventory (90,000 × $2)	$180,000	
Fixed Overhead Volume Variance	20,000	
Fixed Manufacturing Overhead		$200,000

8. Record completion of 90,000 units, transfer standard cost to Finished Goods Inventory.

Finished Goods Inventory (90,000 × $14)	$1,260,000	
Work-in-Process Inventory		$1,260,000

9. Record sale of 80,000 shirts.

Cash or Accounts Receivable (80,000 × $20)	$1,600,000	
Sales		$1,600,000

10. Record cost of goods sold.

Cost of Goods Sold (80,000 × $14)	$1,120,000	
Finished Goods Inventory		$1,120,000

11. Record selling and administrative expenses.

Selling and Administrative Expenses	$350,000	
Cash, Payables		$350,000

At this point the inventory accounts appear as follows.

Work in Process Inventory

(2)	$ 540,000		
(4)	450,000		
(6)	90,000		
(7)	180,000	$1,260,000	(8)
	1,260,000	1,260,000	
Bal	$ 0		

Finished Goods Inventory

(8)	$1,260,000	$1,120,000	(10)
Bal	$ 140,000		

Materials Inventory

(1)	$720,000	$556,000	(2)
Bal	$164,000		

Notice that all inventory accounts contain the standard cost of the units therein. Materials Inventory shows $164,000, which is the 41,000 yards (180,000 − 139,000) at $4 per yard. Work-in-Process Inventory has a zero balance because no shirts are in process. Finished Goods Inventory shows $140,000, the standard cost of the 10,000 shirts on hand (90,000 produced − 80,000 sold). The variance accounts would in all likelihood appear on the income statement, as below, in summary form.

Park Mills
Income Statement for October, 19X5

Sales	$1,600,000
Standard cost of sales	1,120,000
Standard gross margin	480,000
Less variances	44,000
Actual gross margin	436,000
Selling and administrative expenses	350,000
Profit before taxes	$ 86,000

Comparison of Standard and Normal Costing

Normal costing and standard costing share some attributes, most notably the predetermined overhead rate. But the results under the two methods are not the same. Recall from Chapter 11 that under normal costing, overhead is applied based on *actual inputs.* Under standard costing, overhead is applied based on *standard inputs* (or on actual output, either 90,000 shirts or 45,000 standard hours in our example). Additionally, under standard costing, the material and labor components of cost are at standard, while under normal costing those components are at actual cost.

Let us see how the results differ for our example, as shown in Exhibit 14−7. The actual/normal cost of $14.417 is $0.417 above the standard cost. The ending inventory of finished goods is $4,170 higher than the standard cost, and cost of sales is higher. However, under standard costing, the variances are reported on the income statement,

---

Exhibit 14–7
Normal Costing for Park Mills

Normal Costing—Cost per Unit

Materials:

Materials per yard ($722,000/180,000)	$ 4.011
Times actual yards	139,000
Actual material cost	$ 557,530
Actual direct labor cost	458,000
Applied overhead ($6 × 47,000 direct labor hours)	282,000
Total normal cost	$1,297,530
Divided by 90,000 units equals unit cost	$14.417

Ending inventory of finished goods (10,000 × $14.417) = $144,170
Cost of goods sold (80,000 × $14.417) = $1,153,360
Underapplied overhead ($92,000 + $196,000 − $282,000) = $6,000

Income Statement for Park Mills

Sales	$1,600,000
Cost of sales	1,153,360
Normal gross margin	446,640
Underapplied overhead	6,000
Actual gross margin	440,640
Selling and administrative expenses	350,000
Profit before taxes	$ 90,640

---

reducing income. Thus, income is higher under normal costing in this illustration. Were the net variances favorable, standard costing income would have been higher.

SUMMARY

Standard costs are useful in planning and controlling operations, and in evaluating performance. The standard for each component of cost (material, labor, and overhead) is the standard price or rate multiplied by the standard quantity of the factor. Different managers are usually responsible for different types of variances, so variance calculation is a start to identifying responsibility.

There is a great deal of interdependence among managers: the performance of one often affects that of another. Consequently, an unfavorable variance does not necessarily indicate that performance was poor. Standard costs can also be used as product costs and have several advantages over actual and normal costs for that purpose.

DEMONSTRATION PROBLEM

Standard costs for one of Glenwood Mill's sweatshirts appear below.

Material, 2 pounds of yarn at $4 per pound	$ 8.00
Labor, 0.20 hours of labor at $9 per hour	1.80
Variable overhead, $8 per labor hour	1.60
Fixed overhead, $7 per labor hour	1.40
Total standard cost	$12.80

Standard fixed overhead is based on 18,000 standard hours and $126,000 budgeted fixed overhead per month. Actual results in March were as follows:

Production	100,000 sweatshirts
Materials purchased	190,000 pounds for $790,000
Materials used	202,000 pounds
Direct labor	21,000 hours, $180,100
Variable overhead	$166,500
Fixed overhead	$125,400

REQUIRED:

Compute all variances.

Solution to Demonstration Problem

Materials

Actual Cost	Budgeted Cost $4 × 190,000	
$790,000	$760,000	

$30,000 U
material price variance

	Budgeted Cost $4 × 202,000	Standard Cost $4 × 2 × 100,000
	$808,000	$800,000

$8,000 U
material use variance

Direct Labor

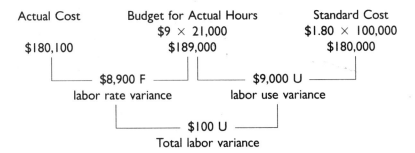

Actual Cost	Budget for Actual Hours $9 \times 21,000$	Standard Cost $1.80 \times 100,000$
$180,100	$189,000	$180,000

└───── $8,900 F ─────┘ └───── $9,000 U ─────┘
　　 labor rate variance　　　　　　 labor use variance

　　　　　　└───── $100 U ─────┘
　　　　　　　 Total labor variance

Variable Overhead

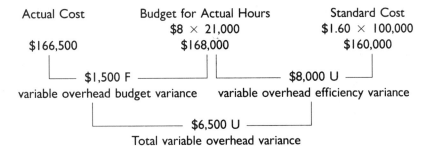

Actual Cost	Budget for Actual Hours $8 \times 21,000$	Standard Cost $1.60 \times 100,000$
$166,500	$168,000	$160,000

└───── $1,500 F ─────┘ └───── $8,000 U ─────┘
variable overhead budget variance　 variable overhead efficiency variance

　　　　　└───── $6,500 U ─────┘
　　　　 Total variable overhead variance

Fixed Overhead

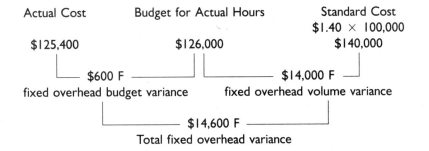

Actual Cost	Budget for Actual Hours	Standard Cost $1.40 \times 100,000$
$125,400	$126,000	$140,000

└───── $600 F ─────┘ └───── $14,000 F ─────┘
fixed overhead budget variance　　 fixed overhead volume variance

　　　　　└───── $14,600 F ─────┘
　　　　 Total fixed overhead variance

Key Terms

direct labor efficiency variance
direct labor rate variance
fixed overhead budget variance
fixed overhead volume variance
material price variance
material use variance

standard cost
variable overhead budget
　variance
variable overhead efficiency
　variance
variances

ASSIGNMENTS

14–1   Standard and Normal Costs
What differences are there between the normal costs you studied in Chapter 11 and standard costs?

14–2   Budget and Efficiency Variances
What is the difference between a budget variance and an efficiency variance for variable overhead?

14–3   Standards for Product Costing
"How can you use standard costs for product costs? Accounting is supposed to reflect what actually happens and that means actual costs. Aren't I right?" A classmate made the preceding statement. Tell him why he is wrong.

14–4   Effects of Events on Variances
For each of the following events, indicate what variance(s) might be affected and in which direction. The company does not change standards as these events occur.

1. Because of an increase in demand for its products, the company hires new, inexperienced workers to boost production.
2. The purchasing manager buys a large amount of material at a bargain price. The material is harder to work with than that usually bought.
3. Engineers redesign a major product so that it takes less labor time to manufacture.
4. The company acquires machinery that reduces labor time.

 ### 14–5   Comprehensive Variance Analysis
Cooper Kitchen Furniture makes various products. Standard costs for the Style 701 table follow.

Materials	44 feet of wood at $0.25 per foot
Direct labor	4 hours at $7 per hour
Variable overhead	$5 per direct labor hour
Fixed overhead	$6 per direct labor hour, based on $30,000 monthly budgeted fixed overhead and 5,000 monthly standard direct labor hours.

Cooper made 1,300 units of this style during February and had the following results.

Material purchases	58,000 feet at $0.22 $12,760
Material used	58,200 feet
Direct labor	4,950 hours at $7.10 $35,145
Variable overhead	$26,900
Fixed overhead	$29,700

REQUIRED:

Compute the standard cost of Style 701 and the variances for February.

14–6   Standard Costing—Extension of Assignment 14–5
Prepare journal entries to reflect Cooper's activity for February.

14–7   Standard Cost and Variance Relationships
Cormant Household Products has established the standard prices and quantities for a case of its floor wax.

Material	4 gallons at $2 per gallon
Direct labor	0.20 hours at $10 per hour
Variable overhead	$9 per direct labor hour

Cormant also has fixed overhead of $5,000,000 per year.

REQUIRED:

Fill in the blanks in the following items.

1. The standard cost per case of wax is
   a. For material _____
   b. For direct labor _____
   c. For variable overhead _____
2. At 70,000 hours of direct labor, total variable overhead cost should be _____ .
3. At 80,000 hours of direct labor, production should be _____ cases.
4. If 1,000,000 gallons of material are used, production should be _____ cases.
5. If Cormant uses 1,200,000 gallons of material, direct labor cost should be $ _____ .

14–8   Basic Standard Costs and Variances

Clegg Company manufactures elaborate birdbaths. Each requires 20 pounds of material and two labor hours. The standard price of materials is $2 per pound. The standard direct labor rate is $8 per hour and the standard variable overhead rate is $6 per direct labor hour. During November, Clegg manufactured 1,000 baths. It bought 25,000 pounds of material for $48,000 and used 21,000 pounds. Clegg paid direct laborers $15,800 for 1,900 hours and incurred $12,500 in variable overhead.

REQUIRED:

1. Determine the standard variable cost of a birdbath.

2. Determine all variable cost variances.

14–9   Basic Material Variances

Zimmer Company manufactures a product that requires 4 pounds of material that has a standard price of $5 per pound. During March, Zimmer bought 100,000 pounds of material for $496,000 and used 88,000 pounds to make 21,000 units of product.

REQUIRED:

Calculate the material price variance and material use variance.

14–10   Basic Labor and Variable Overhead Variances— Extension of Assignment 14–9

Zimmer Company's product requires 0.20 hours of direct labor. The standard wage rate is $12 per hour. Variable overhead is budgeted at $4 per direct labor hour. During March, Zimmer paid laborers $49,600 for 4,150 hours and incurred $15,700 variable overhead cost. Zimmer made 21,000 units of product.

REQUIRED:

Calculate the direct labor rate and efficiency variances and the variable overhead budget and efficiency variances.

14–11   Basic Variance Relationships, Materials

Fill in the blanks below.

Standard price per pound of material	$ _____
Standard use of material per unit of product	5 pounds
Units produced	_____
Pounds of material purchased	_____
Pounds of material used	108,000
Material use variance	_____
Amount paid for materials	$425,700
Material price variance	$2,300 Favorable
Standard material cost per unit of product	$20
Standard use of materials for output achieved	110,000

14-12 Variance Computations

Standard variable costs for one of Halsey Company's sweaters appear below.

Material, 2 pounds of yarn at $3 per pound	$ 6.00
Labor, 2 hours of labor at $6 per hour	12.00
Variable overhead, $3 per labor hour	6.00
Fixed overhead, $6 per labor hour	12.00
Total standard cost	$36.00

Fixed overhead is based on $14,400 budgeted fixed overhead and 2,400 standard direct labor hours. Actual results in March were as follows.

Production	1,000 sweaters
Materials purchased and used,	1,900 pounds for $5,900
Hours of labor worked	2,100 hours
Cost of labor	$12,100
Variable overhead incurred	$ 6,500
Fixed overhead incurred	$14,200

REQUIRED:

Compute all variances.

14-13 Comprehensive Variance Analysis

Mizno Company makes industrial cleaners. Standard costs for Sudsup appear below, along with actual results for March.

Materials, 3 pounds at $4 per pound	$12
Direct labor at $10 per hour	30
Variable overhead at $6 per DLH	18
Fixed overhead at $10 per DLH	30
Total standard cost	$90

Standard fixed overhead is based on $25,000 budgeted monthly fixed overhead and 2,500 monthly standard direct labor hours. Actual results for March follow.

1. Production was 1,200 units.
2. Material purchases were 3,200 pounds at $3.90 per pound.
3. The firm used 3,620 pounds of material in production.
4. Direct laborers worked 3,800 hours at $10.10, earning $38,380.
5. Variable overhead was $22,000.
6. Fixed overhead was $26,200.

REQUIRED:

Compute all variances.

14–14   Standard Product Costing—Extension of Assignment 14–13

Prepare journal entries to record Mizno's activity for March.

14–15   Variance Analysis in a Service Organization

Bartram Hospital performs various tests on blood, cells, and other physical materials. The hospital laboratory has developed standards for some of the common tests. Data appear below for blood tests.

Test	Standard Time, minutes
Cholesterol	11
Triglyceride	9
Blood sugar	6

During April, lab workers performed 2,000 cholesterol, 3,200 triglyceride, and 2,800 blood sugar tests. Workers spent 1,080 hours performing these tests. The standard wage rate is $12 per hour.

REQUIRED:

Determine the labor efficiency variance.

14–16   Variance Analysis

ReRex Company makes chemical cleaners. Data relating to the cost of a case of the product are given below. ReRex is highly automated and does not classify any employees as direct laborers. All manufacturing employees are considered indirect workers. Standard machine time is 30 minutes per case.

- Materials, 6 gallons at $1.50 per gallon
- Variable overhead, $10 per machine hour
- Fixed overhead, $15 per machine hour

Fixed overhead is based on $75,000 budgeted fixed overhead and 5,000 standard machine hours. In April ReRex produced 12,000 cases using 5,500 machine hours and incurred the following costs.

Materials (purchased and used)	73,500 gallons, $106,575
Variable overhead	$57,500
Fixed overhead	$72,400

REQUIRED:

Compute all variances.

14–17   Standard Costing—Extension of Assignment 14–16

Prepare journal entries for ReRex's activity in April.

14–18 Determining a Standard Cost

Le Bleu Parfum is considering a new perfume, to be called Empathy. A case of Empathy requires three gallons of enhanced water costing $0.20 per gallon and six ounces of essences of various animal glands costing $22 per ounce. Mixing, heating, and performing other operations requires 0.50 hours of vat time. Two workers tend each of the vats at all times. Workers earn $12 per hour, the variable overhead rate is $6 per vat-hour.

REQUIRED:

Determine the standard variable cost of a case of Empathy.

14–19 Variance Calculations—Continuation of Assignment 14–18

In June, Le Bleu produced 20,000 cases of Empathy. It used 58,000 gallons of enhanced water, 122,000 ounces of essences, and 9,900 vat-hours. Le Bleu bought 62,000 gallons of enhanced water at $0.205 per gallon and 130,000 ounces of essence at $21.50 per ounce. Direct laborers were paid $12.10 per hour for a total of 18,800 hours, variable overhead was $57,800.

REQUIRED:

Compute all variable cost variances.

14–20 DECISION CASE: PERFORMANCE MEASURES IN A JIT ENVIRONMENT

Baskin Company recently implemented JIT principles and its controller is having difficulty in analyzing performance. She has collected the following statistics and asks you to tell her how each could help evaluate performance in the two months.

	July	September
Average processing time, hours	41	36
Average cycle time, hours	76	64
Production, units	6,800	6,550
Maximum capacity, units	7,300	7,300
Defective units	82	77
Inventory of materials, days' supply	6	4
Inventory of work-in-process, days' supply	8	9
Inventory of finished goods, days' supply	3	2

REQUIRED:

Use the data above to describe where Baskin is improving and where it is not. You might wish to calculate some ratios using these raw numbers.

15

Capital Budgeting

LEARNING OBJECTIVES

After studying Chapter 15, you should be able to:
1. Distinguish between capital budgeting decisions and other decisions.
2. Explain why cash flows, instead of incomes, are used to make capital budgeting decisions.
3. Determine the net cash flows associated with an investment.
4. Determine the net present value and the internal rate of return of an investment, and tell whether the investment is desirable.
5. Explain why discounted cash flow techniques are superior to other commonly used techniques.

Like Chapter 7, this chapter uses the principles of the **time value of money.** If you need a review of that material, read Appendix B at the back of the book.

Chapter 12 presented short-term decisions, those that do not require considering the time value of money. **Capital budgeting** decisions involve large amounts of cash inflows and outflows over long periods, so they do require considering the time value of money. Examples of common capital budgeting decisions include whether to buy labor-saving machinery (like robots), whether to replace machinery that is still useful but technologically obsolete, whether to expand an existing factory or build a new one, and whether to increase output of an existing product or manufacture a new one.

The effects of such decisions usually last for several years, perhaps many years. Capital budgeting decisions usually require large outlays of cash, with returns in the form of cash inflows coming in over long periods of time. For that reason, capital budgeting decisions are often called *long-term decisions.* The principles of differential revenues and costs that we used with short-term decisions also apply to capital budgeting decisions. And, again, as with short-term decisions, capital budgeting decisions relate to the future, meaning that the information we use consists of estimates, not certainties.

Aside from the time value of money, there are two differences between short-term and capital budgeting decisions: we use *income* to evaluate short-term decisions, while we use *cash flows* to evaluate capital budgeting decisions. We also use income taxes in capital budgeting analyses, which we ignored in short-term decisions. We will explain these items shortly.

Capital budgeting decisions are usually riskier than short-term decisions and require much larger commitments of cash. One reason for their greater risk is that they are more difficult to reverse. A decision to concentrate advertising on one product, for example, can quickly be reversed if it does not work out. Building a factory to make a new product is not so easily reversed. An empty factory built to make a product that no one wanted to buy is a monument to a poor decision. For these reasons it is important that capital budgeting decisions use the best available information and analytical techniques. Insight 15−1 describes two capital budgeting decisions that could have had very serious financial effects on the companies.

Capital budgeting decisions are risky and costly.

CASH FLOWS

In Chapter 12, we used incremental revenues and incremental costs to determine whether to take a course of action. We did not mention cash

Cash flows are critical, not incomes.

INSIGHT 15–1
Cost of Smooth Shaving

The amounts involved in capital investment decisions can be extremely large, with many companies routinely committing amounts in the hundreds of millions. Gillette's Sensor razor is a good example. Gillette spent $125 million on a plant to make the razor, after spending $75 million on research and development. It was not finished: launching the product required $110 million in advertising for one year.* Gillette must sell a great many razors and blades to make that commitment pay off and if people do not like the razor, Gillette could lose a large proportion of its investment.

In another field, DuPont and Waste Management spent $25 million to build five plants to recycle plastic. The two companies hoped to be able to recycle 200 million tons per year by the mid-1990s. Such a decision is risky because there are no guarantees that the revenues from recycling will exceed the costs and allow the two companies to achieve a reasonable rate of return. Someone might invent a new plastic that cannot be recycled in those plants, or perhaps someone will come up with a substitute material for plastic. Government regulations are another factor that could hamstring the projects.**

*"How a $4 Razor Ends Up Costing $300 Million," *Business Week*, 29 January 1990, 62.
**"Recycling: The Newest Wrinkle in Waste Management's Bag," *Business Week*, 5 March 1990, 48.

flows, but we could have used cash flows just as easily as we used income, because all of the revenues and costs we considered there were also cash flows—or would be shortly. But consider the following example. Suppose that you can buy something today for $100,000 and sell it today for $105,000. You should do so because you will earn $5,000. Suppose, however, that you pay for the item today, but you will not be able to sell it for a year? You should not take this action, because $5,000 is not enough to compensate you for tying up your $100,000 for a year when you could buy U. S. government bonds and earn $7,000 to$8,000 or more. Yet an income statement will show a $5,000 profit regardless of when the cash is received. In capital budgeting decisions then, we are concerned with *when* cash goes out and comes back in, because of the opportunity cost of tying up our money.

The importance of using cash flows instead of income is most obvious with investments in depreciable assets. Annual depreciation, as you know from Chapters 5 and 6, is an allocation of the cost of an asset over its useful life. Depreciation does not require cash expenditure: the cash payment was made when the asset was bought.

However, depreciation *affects* cash flows. Depreciation is tax-deductible and therefore affects income taxes, which *are* a cash flow. Consequently, to determine cash flow, we must determine depreciation expense so that we can determine income taxes. In short-term decisions, any action that is desirable without considering income taxes is also desirable after taxes. This is because the tax effects of the typical short-term decisions we considered in Chapter 12 are typically a constant percentage of the pre-tax amounts. For example, with a 40% tax rate, an action that we expect to provide $10,000 pre-tax will provide $6,000 after tax, while one with a $15,000 pre-tax return will yield $9,000 after tax. So, the relative desirability of short-term decisions is not changed by introducing income taxes. But this is not necessarily true with capital budgeting decisions.

TIME VALUE OF MONEY AND COST OF CAPITAL

When there are significant delays between paying cash and receiving it, managers must consider the time value of money. They do so by determining whether the expected rate of return on an investment is high enough to justify making the investment. We use a cutoff rate, or target rate (discussed later), in making this analysis. The target rate should be **cost of capital,** which is the rate that the company must pay to attract investors to finance the company. Determining cost of capital is the province of managerial finance, but we will give a brief discussion here.

Cost of capital is the correct discount rate, but target rates are also used.

Companies obtain capital from debt and equity. The cost of the *debt capital* supplied by creditors is simply the effective interest rate on the debt, as discussed in Chapter 7. The cost of *equity capital* is more elusive, and for any given company the estimates of well-qualified analysts are likely to vary widely. The cost of equity capital is based on the return (dividends and capital gains) that investors expect. In a *very* simple situation we can approximate this cost by dividing the expected earnings by the market value of the stock (the inverse of the price-earnings ratio, as discussed fully in Chapter 19). Thus, if investors expect the company to earn $4 per share and the market price of the stock is $40 per share, the cost of equity capital is 10% ($4/$40).

Cost of capital is a weighted average of the costs of debt and equity capital. (The term *weighted-average cost of capital* is also used to describe cost of capital.) If a company has 40% debt and 60% equity, with costs of 10% for debt and 15% for equity, its cost of capital is 13%, calculated as follows (ignoring income taxes).

Component	Cost of Component	Percentage in Capital Structure	Weighted Average
Debt	10%	40%	4%
Equity	15%	60%	9%
Weighted average			13%

We can also think of cost of capital as the opportunity cost of money, for the company can always invest in itself by retiring its debt and repurchasing its shares. Cost of capital is therefore the minimum acceptable rate of return on investment and so is sometimes called the *cutoff rate of return.* Because cost of capital is so difficult to estimate, managers in many companies do not try to estimate it, but rather set a *target rate,* or *hurdle rate*—one that is considered high enough to provide satisfactory returns to the suppliers of capital.

CAPITAL BUDGETING TECHNIQUES

Several capital budgeting techniques use the time value of money and are conceptually correct: that is, they indicate correctly whether or not to make a particular investment. (Again, qualitative aspects or serious uncertainty might override the quantitative analysis. "Correctly" means only that the decision is economically sound given the available information.) These techniques are called **discounted cash flow (DCF)** techniques. We shall discuss and illustrate the two most commonly used. DCF techniques all use the time value of money: they discount cash flows associated with an investment. Additionally, we shall discuss and illustrate two non-DCF techniques that are unsound and can lead to poor decisions. They are, unfortunately, sometimes used in practice and it is therefore desirable that you understand them and their deficiencies.

Net Present Value (NPV)

Using the **net present value (NPV)** method, you discount all future cash flows back to their present value (as you do in finding a bond price, discussed in Chapter 7). If the present value of the inflows is greater than the investment, then the investment is desirable. If the present value of the inflows is less than the investment, then the investment is undesirable. If the present values are equal, the company is indifferent to the investment. This method is usually the most straightforward and the simplest to use.

Internal Rate of Return (IRR)

The other DCF technique that we shall take up is the **internal rate of return (IRR)** method. In applying this method, you find the rate of return that makes the present value of the cash inflows equal to the investment. That rate is the IRR. You then compare the IRR with the minimum acceptable rate, cost of capital or hurdle rate. If the IRR exceeds the latter rate, the investment is desirable. If the IRR is less than the hurdle rate, the investment is undesirable. If the two rates are equal, the company is indifferent.

Example (Machinery Investment)

Exhibit 15–1 shows data for an investment that QRS Company is considering. The investment is in machinery that will reduce labor costs for QRS's principal product. For the moment, we ignore income taxes in order to concentrate on the basics.

We see that the machinery will save $60,000 annually ($6 × 10,000) but QRS will spend $20,000 in cash fixed costs to operate it, giving a net cash saving of $40,000 annually. The question is whether that annual saving is worth the $120,000 investment. To answer this question, we shall first find the net present value (NPV) of the investment, then the IRR. To find the NPV, we find the *present value* of the future cash inflows, or, as in this case, the net reduction in cash outflows. We then subtract the $120,000 investment.

Exhibit 15–1
Data for Machinery Investment

Cost of machinery	$120,000
Useful life	10 years
Estimated salvage value	$0
Per-unit savings in labor cost	$6
Annual unit volume	10,000
Annual cash fixed operating costs	$ 20,000
Cost of capital	14%

Annual savings (10,000 × $6)	$ 60,000
Less cash fixed costs	20,000
Net cash flow	40,000
Present value factor for 14%, 10 years (Table 2, Appendix B)	5.216
Present value of future flows	$208,640
Less investment	120,000
Net present value	$ 88,640

The investment is very desirable, having a positive NPV because the present value of the future inflows is well in excess of the investment required. Again, using the NPV method, we accept investments with positive NPVs and reject those with negative NPVs. If the NPV is zero, we are indifferent. Of course, the foregoing assumes that there are no qualitative factors that might override the quantitative analysis.

We next analyze the investment using the IRR method in which we compare the IRR to the 14% cost of capital. (You might have already seen from your earlier study of bond prices that the IRR must be above 14% because discounting the future flows at 14% produced a positive NPV.) To find the IRR for an *annuity,* which is a stream of equal payments, we rely on the formula implicitly used above.

$$\text{Present Value of Flows} = \text{Annual Flow} \times \text{Present Value Factor}$$

The IRR is the **discount** (interest) **rate** that equates the present value of the flows with the investment. Thus, the present value of the flows must be $120,000. The flow is $40,000; therefore, we can find the present value factor by rearranging the formula.

$$\text{Present Value Factor} = \frac{\text{Investment}}{\text{Annual Flow}}$$
$$= \$120,000/\$40,000$$
$$= 3.0$$

We now know the factor and the period, 10 years. So we can look across Table 2 in Appendix B to find the closest factor. That factor is 3.092 in the 30% column. The IRR is therefore about 30%. Because 3.0 is less than 3.092, the IRR is a bit higher than 30%. If cash flows differ from year to year, finding the IRR is more time-consuming. However, financial calculators and electronic spreadsheets can do the computations quickly.

Relationship of NPV and IRR

The two DCF methods we have illustrated *always* give you the same decision—to accept or reject a given investment—provided that the discount rate used to determine the NPV is also the minimum acceptable rate used in conjunction with the IRR.[1] This is because, as stated before, if the NPV is positive, the IRR is greater than the discount rate; if the NPV is negative, the IRR is less than the discount rate; and if the NPV is zero, the two rates are equal.

NPV and IRR give the same decision (accept or reject) for an investment.

It is *very* important for you to remember that cash flows can come from any source. Instead of savings in labor cost, for instance, we could have had a new product that would yield a cash contribution margin of $60,000 annually with cash fixed costs of $20,000. The analysis would have been the same. *Any* cash inflow, or reduced cash outflow, is the same for capital budgeting purposes.

One more point: we did not specify how the investment is to be financed, whether with debt or equity. Should we use the interest rate on debt to discount cash flows if we will finance the investment with debt? No, we should use cost of capital to discount the flows no matter how we finance the project. *The method of financing is irrelevant to the capital budgeting decision.* The reason is that capital budgeting decisions are operating decisions—what should we do and how should we do it? Financing decisions are made in light of capital market conditions and are separate from specific operating decisions. A company must provide adequate returns to both creditors and stockholders. It could not survive if it tried to finance all of its investments with debt. The company would risk failure and it could not borrow additional money except at much higher interest rates. Its stockholders would sell their shares, driving down the price. Its returns would be too low to attract either creditors or stockholders.

Effects of Income Taxes on Net Cash Flow

Let us now modify our example to include income taxes at a 40% rate. The complicating factor here is that cash flows are now reduced by income taxes. The following pattern is appropriate under the new circumstances. We shall use straight-line depreciation on the investment in machinery.

Depreciation is relevant for calculating income taxes.

[1] There are some exceptions to this rule. Investments with alternating positive and negative cash flows can have more than one IRR, one or more of which could be lower than cost of capital.

	Tax	Cash Flow
Annual savings (10,000 × $6)	$60,000	$ 60,000
Less cash fixed costs	20,000	20,000
Pre-tax cash flow	40,000	40,000
Depreciation ($120,000/10)	12,000	
Increase in taxable income	28,000	
Increase in income taxes at 40%	11,200	11,200
Net cash flow		$ 28,800
Present value factor for 14%, 10 years (Table 2, Appendix B)		5.216
Present value of future flows		$150,221
Less investment		120,000
Net present value		$ 30,221

The investment is still desirable, because the NPV is still positive, but the margin has shrunk considerably. The higher income taxes are, the less attractive investments are.

Let us look at the differences between this analysis and the previous case. Here, we need to calculate the income tax effect on cash flows. Notice that depreciation does not show up in the cash flow column, only in the tax calculation. An alternative approach is to calculate the change in income after taxes, then add back depreciation to determine cash flow, as we did in preparing cash flow statements in Chapter 9.

Annual savings (10,000 × $6)	$ 60,000
Less cash fixed costs	20,000
Pre-tax cash flow	40,000
Depreciation ($120,000/10)	12,000
Increase in taxable income	28,000
Increase in income taxes at 40%	11,200
Increase in net income	16,800
Add back depreciation	12,000
Net cash flow	$ 28,800
Present value factor for 14%, 10 years (Table 2, Appendix B)	5.216
Present value of future flows	$150,221
Less investment	120,000
Net present value	$ 30,221

This approach is equivalent to the first. Use whichever suits you in a particular case.

It might be helpful to show one more approach to calculating cash flows that allows us to introduce a commonly used term, **depreciation tax shield.** In this approach, we look at the cash flows as consisting of two parts: (1) the operating flows, savings from the more efficient machinery, net of income taxes, and (2) the tax savings on the depreciation of the machinery.

Operating savings, pre-tax	$40,000	
Less income tax at 40%	16,000	
Net cash flow from operating savings		$24,000
Annual depreciation	$12,000	
Tax saving from depreciation at 40%		4,800
Net cash flow		$28,800

The $4,800 tax saving from depreciation is the tax shield, or depreciation tax shield. This approach is, again, equivalent to the first two. All three give exactly the same NPV. This last approach, however, focuses on the unique role of depreciation, and you might find it easier to work with than the first two.

Uneven Cash Flows

Our example included only equal cash flows. Few capital budgeting decisions are so computationally straightforward. It is much more likely that cash flows will differ from year to year, making it impossible to use the simple annuity factor to determine the present value of the future flows. There are many reasons. Most investments, especially those involving new products, do not start off at their maximum expected levels: they start low and build, then eventually decline. This means that revenues and cash expenses will also start low, build, and decline. Another reason is that depreciation *on the tax return* is rarely calculated using the straight-line method. Most companies use an accelerated depreciation method called the *Accelerated Cost Recovery System (ACRS).*[2] In most cases, ACRS uses declining-pattern depreciation, and it generally allows companies to depreciate assets over periods shorter than their useful economic lives. Uneven cash flows also result from salvage or recovery values of investments.

Salvage Values and Recoveries

Let us introduce a new example that differs from our previous example in two ways. First, the new investment has a $10,000 salvage value and

---

[2] Current tax law has modified the original ACRS schedules, and many people now use the term MACRS, for Modified Accelerated Cost Recovery System.

we also introduce a different type of investment, **working capital.** An investment in working capital is in accounts receivable and inventories, perhaps offset by increased accounts payable. A new product, as our example covers, usually will entail such investment to support the new sales. Customers will probably not all pay cash on delivery, so receivables will rise. The company will have to stock finished units of the new product and inventories of materials and components as well. Some of the investment in inventory might be offset by increases in accounts payable.

As you already know, if assets increase, so must equities. Investments in receivables and inventory represent differences between income statement items (sales, cost of sales) and cash flows. From Chapter 9 you know that a cash flow statement contains adjustments for changes in receivables, inventories, and payables (in fact, for all current assets and current liabilities except cash). So we must consider these changes in capital budgeting because they are cash flows. Data for our new example appear in Exhibit 15–2.

We must make a decision before we proceed. Tax law allows us to depreciate the entire cost of a depreciable asset over its useful life, not just its cost less salvage value. If we take that opportunity, we then will have a taxable gain of $10,000 when we sell the equipment. This is to our advantage because we get depreciation tax deductions earlier,

---

Exhibit 15–2
Data for New Product

Annual unit volume	15,000 in first year, 20,000 next three years
Selling price	$10
Unit variable cost	$ 4
Annual cash fixed operating costs	$40,000
Cost of equipment required to make new product	$100,000
Useful life	4 years
Estimated salvage value	$10,000
Increase in working capital: receivables and inventory less payables	$50,000
Tax rate	40%
Cost of capital	14%

The company uses straight-line depreciation.

which makes them more valuable. Therefore, we shall use this option and depreciate the whole $100,000, then pay tax on the gain at the end of year four.

The working capital investment differs from the investment in fixed assets in that the former has no tax effects. Taxes are paid based on revenues and expenses, not cash receipts and disbursements. Therefore, all we need to do with the investment in working capital is to treat it as an investment at time zero, and provide for its recovery at the end of the life of the project. In the last year of the life of the product, the receivables will be collected, inventories used up, and payables paid. Thus, working capital investments appear as outflows at the beginning of the period, inflows at the end.

Exhibit 15−3 shows the calculations. Note that most of them are already familiar. The only difference is that we have to make them for each year because of the varying flows. We use the "net income plus depreciation" method of calculating net cash flows because it is more convenient here.

The net present value is $36,400, so the investment is desirable. The working capital goes in as part of the investment at time zero, but is then recovered at the end of the useful life.

Working capital investment can be significant and so it must be considered.

It is hard to find the IRR on an investment with uneven cash flows by hand. Electronic spreadsheets and some hand-held calculators will do it, and trial-and-error methods will give close answers. In this case, because the NPV is a positive $36,400, the IRR must be greater than the 14% discount rate used to calculate the present values. We used a financial calculator to determine that the IRR is about 20%.

OTHER CAPITAL BUDGETING TECHNIQUES

Besides the DCF techniques, two others, though not theoretically sound are widely used and thus require some comment. Contrary to the argument sometimes made for them, these methods are not more "practical" than the NPV and IRR methods.

Payback

The **payback period** is the length of time it will take to recover the investment. An investment of $100,000 with annual net cash flows of $28,000 has a payback period of 3.57 ($100,000/$28,000) years. Payback does not consider profitability; it considers only the return *of* the investment, not the return *on* the investment. Nor does it consider the timing of the flows within the payback period, as we illustrate shortly.

Exhibit 15–3
NPV of Investment
Cash Inflows (thousands of dollars)

	Year 1	Year 2	Year 3	Year 4
Sales	$150	$200	$200	$200
Variable costs	60	80	80	80
Contribution margin	90	120	120	120
Cash fixed costs	40	40	40	40
Pre-tax cash flow	50	80	80	80
Depreciation	25	25	25	25
Income before taxes	25	55	55	55
Income taxes at 40%	10	22	22	22
Net income	15	33	33	33
Add back depreciation	25	25	25	25
Cash flow	$ 40	$ 58	$ 58	$ 58
Salvage value, net of tax				6*
Recovery of working capital				50
Net cash flow	$ 40	$ 58	$ 58	$114
Present value factors, Table 1	0.877	0.769	0.675	0.592
Present value of flows	$ 35.1	$ 44.6	$ 39.2	$ 67.5

Total present value	$186.4
Investment ($100 + $50)	150.0
Net present value	$ 36.4

*The calculation of the net cash flow from the salvage value is:

Salvage value	$10,000
Tax at 40%	4,000
Net cash	$ 6,000

Payback is inferior to DCF methods. Using the payback method, we compare the payback period with the maximum acceptable period; if the payback period is less than the maximum acceptable, we accept the investment, and vice versa. (The longer the payback period, the worse the investment.) Consider the following investments, both having initial investments of $100,000.

Cash Flows	Project A	Project B
Year 1	$80,000	$20,000
Year 2	20,000	80,000
Year 3	50,000	0

Both projects have two-year paybacks, but project A is surely better than project B. Whereas project B is undesirable at any discount rate (it only returns its original investment, with no profit), project A has an IRR of 26.8%, which is quite high. As we stated above, one disadvantage of payback is that it does not consider the timing of flows within the payback period, only the cumulative amount of flows to the payback period.

There are, however, some uses for payback. It provides a rough screen, because a long payback period usually means a bad investment. It also provides a way to evaluate risk. Other things equal, the longer it takes to get money back, the riskier the investment. An extremely short payback period, as described in Insight 15−2, indicates a good investment.

Payback has some uses, but is an inferior method.

Book Return on Investment (Book ROI)

The other non-DCF method has little to recommend it. The **book rate of return** or **book return on investment** (book ROI) is the return on investment ratio discussed in Chapter 19. Here, the calculation is as follows.

$$\text{Book ROI} = \frac{\text{Average Income}}{\text{Average Investment}}$$

Thus, the following project has a book ROI of 24%.

Year	Income
1	$30
2	40
3	20

The required investment is $250. Average income is $30 ($30 + $40 + $20)/3, and average investment is $125 ($250/2).

$$\text{Book ROI} = \frac{\$30}{\$125}$$
$$= 24\%$$

INSIGHT 15–2
When Payback Is All You Need

While payback should never be used exclusively for capital budgeting decisions, an extremely short payback usually indicates a wise investment. Any investment that will last more than a few years and pays back within one year is almost certainly desirable. The example below highlights not only a short payback, but also that increases in productivity can be found in all areas of an organization, not just in manufacturing.

A division of General Electric expected a *four-month* payback on a Pitney Bowes Star system. Four months is extraordinarily short and almost certainly means a high IRR and NPV if the life of the system is over a year. It is often difficult to compare the rates of shippers such as Federal Express, Airborne, United Parcel Service, and the U.S. Mail. The Star system finds the cheapest way to send a parcel. A clerk enters the destination and date by which delivery is to be made. Star then selects the carrier, writes out the forms for the carrier, and prints a mailing label. Without such a system, clerks decide whether to send the parcel by first-class mail, Federal Express, or whatever other choices are available. And clerks often send parcels much too expensively for the time they must arrive.*

*"Search for Tomorrow at Pitney Bowes," *Business Week*, 5 March 1990, 50.

The average investment in depreciable assets is the initial investment divided by 2, because by the end of the life of the project, the investment will be depreciated to zero, or close to zero. Book ROI does not consider cash flows, nor does it consider the timing of cash flows, so it is clearly inferior to DCF methods. If we were to use the method, we would compare the book ROI with a minimum acceptable figure. If the book ROI were higher, we would accept the investment, if lower we would reject it.

Some people argue that the DCF techniques are too sophisticated or require unreasonable assumptions. But the non-DCF methods require similar assumptions. The NPV and IRR methods require estimates of future cash flows. The payback method requires the same estimates, at least until the payback period is up. The book ROI method requires estimates of future net incomes. If you have those estimates, you can easily determine the associated cash flows. NPV requires an estimate of cost of capital, IRR a minimum acceptable rate. But the payback method requires a maximum acceptable payback period and the book ROI method a minimum acceptable book ROI. Thus, the non-DCF methods require about the same assumptions that the DCF methods do.

There is no reason to use book rate of return.

QUALITATIVE CONSIDERATIONS

As with short-term decisions, managers might cite qualitative factors in overriding capital budgeting decisions indicated by the quantitative analysis. They might reject a project with a positive NPV because company policy conflicts with the investment. For instance, Mercedes-Benz would almost surely not introduce a $10,000 automobile, because it would undermine the company's image and strategy of producing only high-quality, expensive automobiles. On the other side, a company might accept an investment with a negative NPV to bolster its reputation for technological prowess. It is still wise to evaluate decisions using discounted cash flows, because the economic cost of adhering to a policy might be extremely high and the managers should be aware of that cost. Insight 15−3 describes some investments that might never show adequate returns, but nonetheless might be extremely wise.

Qualitative aspects are especially important in capital budgeting decisions.

INSIGHT 15−3
Prestige Cars

Strategic considerations should play an important part in major capital investment decisions. Chrysler Corporation paid $25 million for Lamborghini, the famous maker of fast sports cars. It is unlikely that Chrysler will make high profits from the investment. However, the acquisition increased Chrysler's regular business in Europe by giving the company more credibility.*

Ford paid over $2.5 billion to buy Jaguar PLC and was then faced with the prospect of spending another $1 billion to expand capacity, add new models, and improve productivity of the troubled British luxury car maker. The reason given for Ford's costly acquisition was to "round out the top end of its lineup."**

In both of these cases, the companies might have had some other way to achieve their objectives. Ford might have introduced its own luxury line that could have competed with Jaguar and its competition. It might even have formed a new company to do so, as several Japanese companies have done, rather than bring out the car under its own nameplate. The point is that without understanding all of the motivation for a decision, we cannot say that it is good or bad.

*"The World's Fastest Car is Now a—Chrysler?," *Business Week,* 12 February 1990, 44.
**Richard A. Melcher, "Why Ford's European Cash Cow is Giving Less," *Business Week,* 27 November 1989, 134.

SUMMARY

Capital budgeting decisions involve cash inflows and outflows over periods longer than a year, often much longer. Such decisions are often risky and commit the company for long periods. We evaluate such decisions using two discounted cash flow methods: net present value and internal rate of return. Other methods, particularly payback and book ROI, are conceptually inferior and, contrary to the claims of some, not superior for practical reasons.

The relevance of depreciation in capital budgeting decisions is limited to its effect on income taxes. Depreciation is not a cash flow, but it does reduce taxes through the depreciation tax shield and therefore is relevant in determining net cash flows.

DEMONSTRATION PROBLEMS

Demonstration Problem 15–1
Answer the following items.

1. Stith invested $2,400 and received $1,000 per year for three years. What interest rate did she earn?
2. Roberts received $2,638 per year for five years as the result of an investment at 10%. How much did he invest?
3. James wants to invest $10,000 for 10 years. If he can earn 12% interest, what annual cash receipts can he obtain?
5. Jackson invested some money at a 10% interest rate and five years later received a single payment of $4,025. How much did she invest?

Solution to Demonstration Problem 15–1

1. About 12%, the present value factor is 2.4, $2,400/$1,000, which is closest to the factor for 12% for three years, 2.402.
2. Just about $10,000, $2,638 × 3.791.
3. About $1,770, $10,000/5.65.
4. Just about $2,500 ($4,025 × .621, the present value factor for 10% and 5 years).

DEMONSTRATION PROBLEM 15–2

Armstrong Industries is considering machinery that will save $9 in variable cost per unit of one of its best-selling products. The product sells 300,000 units per year. The machinery costs $6,000,000, has a five-year life with no salvage value expected, and will increase cash fixed operating costs by $500,000 per year. Armstrong uses straight-line depreciation. Cost of capital is 12% and the tax rate is 40%.

REQUIRED:

1. Determine the annual net cash flows after taxes.
2. Determine the NPV of the investment.
3. Determine the payback period of the investment.
4. Determine the IRR of the investment.

Solution to Demonstration Problem 15–2

1. $1,800,000

	Tax	Cash Flow
Annual savings (300,000 × $9)	$2,700,000	$2,700,000
Less cash fixed costs	500,000	500,000
Pre-tax cash flow	2,200,000	2,200,000
Depreciation ($6,000,000/5)	1,200,000	
Increase in taxable income	1,000,000	
Increase in income taxes at 40%	400,000	400,000
Net cash flow		$1,800,000

2. $489,000

Net cash flow, above	$1,800,000
Present value factor for 12%, 5 years	3.605
Present value of future flows	$6,489,000
Less investment	6,000,000
Net present value	$ 489,000

3. About 3.33 years, $6,000,000/$1,800,000.

4. About 15%. The factor being sought is 3.333 (the payback period), and the closest factor in the five-year row is in the 15% column.

Key Terms

book rate of return (book ROI)

capital budgeting

cost of capital

depreciation tax shield

discounted cash flows (DCF)

discount rate

internal rate of return (IRR)

net present value (NPV)

payback period

time value of money

working capital investment

ASSIGNMENTS

15–1   Effects of Interest Rates on Investment
Governments try to regulate economic activity in various ways. For example, the Federal Reserve Board influences interest rates. How does changing interest rates encourage or discourage investment?

15–2   Effects of Events on Capital Budgets
For each of the following items, indicate whether it would make your company more likely or less likely to make capital investments.

   a. Congress raises the income tax rate.

   b. One of your major competitors, which has become heavily burdened by debt, has declared bankruptcy.

   c. Wage rates in your industry will go up because of an industry-wide collective bargaining agreement.

   d. Congress lengthens the period over which you must depreciate assets for income tax purposes.

15–3   Discounting

Investment
annual CASh Flows

$\frac{30,000}{5000} = 6.00 = 14\%$ 14yR

   1. Find the approximate internal rate of return (IRR) for each of the following investments.

     a. Investment of $30,000 with annual cash flows of $5,000 for 14 years.

$\frac{90,000}{120,000} = .75$ Factor = .75   3 yR

     b. An investment of $90,000 with a single return of $120,000 at the end of three years.

   2. Find the NPVs of the following investments at a 12% discount rate.

30,000 x 5.650 - 120,000
169,500 - 120,000 =
49,500

     a. Annual flows of $30,000 for ten years are produced by an investment of $120,000.

8000 x 3.037 - 28,000 =
24,296 - 28,000 =
N = 3704 PVF - INV.

     b. An investment of $28,000 with annual flows of $8,000 for four years.

15–4   Basic Net Present Values — *USE TABLES A-1*

NCF x PVF - INV

Find the net present values of each of the following investments.

15,000 x 3.605 - 60,000
54,075 - 60,000 =
NPV -5,925 reject

   1. An investment of $60,000 produces annual net cash inflows of $15,000 for five years. The discount rate is 12%.

18,000 x 4.494 - 80,000
80,892 - 80,000 =
NPV 892 accept

   2. An investment of $80,000 produces annual net cash inflows of $18,000 for 10 years. The discount rate is 18%.

3. An investment of $60,000 produces annual net cash inflows of $20,000 for four years. The discount rate is 12%.

[handwritten: 20,000 × 3.037 - 69,000 / 60,740 - 60,000 = / NPV 740 accept]

15-5 Cash Flows

Winton Company expects to be able to sell 200,000 units of a new dot-matrix printer annually for the next four years. The selling price should be about $200, variable manufacturing cost about $70. To manufacture the printer, Winton will need equipment costing $20,000,000 and having a four-year life with no salvage value. The equipment will add $6,000,000 to cash fixed manufacturing costs. There will also be incremental selling expenses of $10,000,000 per year. Winton faces a 40% income tax rate.

REQUIRED:

Determine the annual net cash flow expected from the new printer, in millions of dollars.

15-6 NPV, Payback, and IRR—Extension of Assignment 15-5

Winton has a 14% cost of capital.

REQUIRED:

1. Determine the NPV.
2. Determine the payback period.
3. Determine the approximate IRR.
4. Determine the book rate of return.

[handwritten annotation table:]

15-5	Tax	CF
Annual Sales (200,000 × $200)	40,000,000	40,000,000
VC (200,000 × 70)	14,000,000	14,000,000
Cont. Margin	26,000,000	26,000,000
Cash Fixed cost	16,000,000	16,000,000
Pre-tax Cash flow	10,000,000	10,000,000
Depreciation 20,000,000/4	5,000,000	
Incr. in pretax inc.	5,000,000	
Income tax at 40%	2,000,000	
Net Cash flow		

[handwritten: AVG. INC / AVG. INV]

15-7 Basic Capital Budgeting Methods

Mizell Industries is considering an investment that will produce annual net cash flows of $200,000 after taxes for an investment of $800,000. The investment has a useful life of ten years.

REQUIRED:

1. Find the net present value of the investment using a 10% discount rate.
2. Find the payback period.
3. Find the approximate internal rate of return on the investment.

[handwritten: 200000 × 6.145 / 1,229,000 - 800,000 / 429,000 NPV]

[handwritten: 800000 / 200000 = 4 yrs]

[handwritten: 800,000 = 4·Factor 10 yrs / 200,000 / btwn 20% & 24% IRR]

15-8 NPV and IRR

Portland Millworks is considering equipment that promises to save $6,000 in cash operating costs per year. The equipment will cost $16,800. Its estimated useful life is four years. It will have no salvage value. Ignore taxes.

[handwritten: 6000 × 3.170 - 16,800 / 19,020 - 16,800 / 2220 NPV]

[handwritten: 16,800 / 6,000 = 2.8 / IRR = 16%]

REQUIRED:

1. Compute the NPV if the minimum desired rate of return is 10%.
2. Determine the IRR.

15–9 Time Value of Money   — Table A I

Answer the following questions.

1. Jack received $6,440 from an investment made five years ago at an interest rate of 10%. How much did he invest?
2. An investment of $2,000 returned a single payment of $5,400. The interest rate was 18%. How many years elapsed between the investment and the return?
3. A person received seven annual payments of $1,000 from an investment. The interest rate was 12%. What was the amount of the investment?
4. A $20,000 investment made today will provide a 10% return. The returns will be paid in equal amounts over five years. What is the amount of the annual payment?

15–10 Cost Savings

Wilson Sportswear currently makes about 200,000 pairs of Superlux jeans per year at a variable cost of $11.50. Wilson can buy equipment for $400,000 that will reduce unit variable cost to $9.25, while increasing cash fixed costs by $200,000. The equipment will have no salvage value at the end of its four-year life and will be depreciated using the straight-line method. Wilson has a 12% cost of capital. Ignore taxes.

REQUIRED:

Determine the NPV of the investment.

15–11 Income Taxes—Continuation of Assignment 15–10

Redo assignment 15–10 assuming that Wilson has a 40% income tax rate.

15–12 NPV and IRR

Grone, Inc., can reduce its annual cash operating costs by $20,000 by spending $60,000 for equipment that has a five-year life and no salvage value. Grone uses straight-line depreciation. Cost of capital is 14%. Ignore taxes.

REQUIRED:

1. Determine the NPV of the investment.
2. Determine the approximate IRR.

15–13 Income Taxes—Continuation of Assignment 15–12

Redo assignment 15–12 assuming that Grone has a 40% income tax rate.

15–14 Capital Budgeting for a Hospital

Plandome General Hospital does not do X-rays, but sends patients to a clinic a few miles away. The hospital can acquire an X-ray machine for $120,000. The machine should last for ten years and have no salvage value. Estimated revenue is $85,000 per year, and estimated annual cash costs are $63,000. The hospital uses an 8% discount rate for its capital budgeting decisions and is not subject to income taxes.

REQUIRED:

Determine the NPV, payback period, and IRR.

15–15 New Product—Working Capital

Martin Furniture has the following data related to a proposed new cabinet for its office furniture line.

Annual unit volume	250,000
Selling price	$60
Unit variable cost	$25
Annual cash fixed costs	$4,500,000

Making the cabinet requires $6,000,000 in equipment that has a three-year life with no salvage value. Cost of capital is 12%, the income tax rate is 40%, and straight-line depreciation will be used. There will also be additional accounts receivable of about $3,500,000 and additional inventories of $1,200,000.

REQUIRED:

Determine the NPV of the investment. Use thousands of dollars.

15–16 Retirement Options

Jill Barber retires soon. Her employer has a pension plan that offers an annuity of $40,000 per year beginning the day of retirement and ending at death. Jill could live on $40,000 per year but much prefers to spend $50,000 per year and live better. The plan also offers a lump-sum settlement of $350,000 to be paid the day of retirement. Barber believes that she could earn a 10% return investing the lump-sum payment. She has no relatives and does not care whether she leaves an estate.

If Barber chooses the lump-sum payment, she will take $50,000 to live on the first year of retirement and invest the rest. She will then draw $50,000 at the beginning of every year until the money runs out.

REQUIRED:

Determine how long Barber can keep spending $50,000 per year.

15–17 Comparison of Methods

Broadway Inc. has the following investment opportunities in labor-saving machinery.

	Machine A	Machine B
Cost	$140,000	$140,000
Cash Inflows:		
Year 1	70,000	70,000
Year 2	70,000	20,000
Year 3	0	90,000
Year 4	40,000	40,000

Broadway's cost of capital is 16%. Ignore income taxes.

REQUIRED:

1. Determine the payback period for each investment.

2. Determine the NPV of each investment.

3. Suppose that Broadway can accept only one, or neither, of the investments. Which should it accept, if either?

15–18 Donation to a Charity

Jack Billingsley is a wealthy man who recently suffered a heart attack. Because of the excellent care he received at Madison Memorial Hospital, he has decided to give it a substantial donation. He is considering two ways to make the gift. One is to give $10 million today, the other is to give $1.6 million per year for 10 years.

Billingsley uses a 9% discount factor in making decisions that involve cash flows over an extended period. The hospital does not have a formal method of evaluating such alternatives. Dr. Sym, the administrator of the hospital, believes that 8% is a reasonable discount rate because that is the cost of borrowing.

REQUIRED:

1. Determine which alternative is better for the hospital.

2. Determine which alternative is better for Billingsley.

3. How much does Billingsley have to give per year to have a $10 million present value?

4. How much does the hospital have to receive per year to have a $10 million present value?

15–19 Comparison of Methods

Benson Inc. has the following investment opportunities in machinery that will allow it to increase production and sales.

	Preston 380	Moornam 560
Cost	$300,000	$300,000
Cash Inflows:		
Year 1	50,000	160,000
Year 2	100,000	160,000
Year 3	100,000	60,000
Year 4	170,000	20,000
Total cash inflows	$420,000	$400,000
Average income	$ 30,000	$ 25,000

Benson's cost of capital is 16%. Ignore income taxes.

REQUIRED:

1. Determine the book rate of return on average investment for each opportunity.

2. Determine the NPV of each investment.

3. Suppose that Benson can accept only one, or neither, of the investments. Which should it accept, if either?

15–20 Investing in JIT

Morgan Industries is moving toward just-in-time manufacturing, but some of its upper-level managers are skeptical about the returns that JIT can provide. The controller has estimated that the company could save $2 million annually for ten years if it invested $12 million in new equipment and plant rearrangement, all of which would be depreciated over ten years using the straight-line method. Inventories would also fall from the current $8 million to about $0.5 million. The company would have to buy new equipment at the end of ten years. However, it would not see an increase in inventory at that time. Morgan faces a 40% income tax rate and a 10% cost of capital.

REQUIRED:

Determine the NPV of the investment.

15–21 DECISION CASE:
WORKING CAPITAL INVESTMENT

The managers of Trapnell Automotive Enterprises want to introduce a new wax. They anticipate volume of 500,000 cans annually for the next five years at $8 each. They expect variable costs of $3 per unit and annual cash fixed costs $1,400,000. The wax requires machinery costing $1,500,000 with a five-year life and no salvage value. Trapnell uses straight-line depreciation. Additionally, accounts receivable will increase about $600,000, inventories about $400,000. These amounts will be returned in full at the end of the five years. The tax rate is 40% and cost of capital is 16%.

REQUIRED:

Determine the NPV of the investment.

15–22 DECISION CASE: EXPANDING PRODUCTION

Managers of Burnside Manufacturing Company have been considering an expansion of productive capacity for some time. Demand for its major products regularly outstrips its ability to produce. The managers have been reluctant to embark on an expensive expansion program without reasonable assurance of profitability.

The production manager has determined that he could produce another 100,000 units annually with new equipment that costs $900,000. The marketing manager believes the additional units could easily be sold. The equipment has a four-year life with no salvage value, will add $200,000 to annual cash fixed operating costs, and will be depreciated using the straight-line method. The additional 100,000 units will have an average contribution margin of $6. Cost of capital is 10% and the tax rate is 40%.

REQUIRED:

Determine whether Burnside should acquire the equipment.

affiliated companies - parent & it subsidiary

consolidated financial comp. - financial statement of a parent comp. combined with its subsidiary

horizontal integration - Involves the combination of comp. w.tin the same industry

vertical integration - The combination of a company with its suppliers of customers.

goodwill - Any excess of the price paid for net assets over their fair market value,

joint venture - A temporary joining of two (or more) companies to undertake a project.

minority interest - The equity of shareholders owning less than 50% of a company's stock when a parent corporation own more than 50%.

parent - A company that owns a majority of the stock of another company.

tender offer - An offer to buy stock at a specified price, usually in an attempt to take control of a company

pooling of interests - Stock of the acquiring company is exchanged for substantially all the voting common stock of the acquired company.

External auditor - An independent contractor.

internal auditor - Reports to the board of Directors

adverse opinion - Auditors believes that the financial statements are not presented fairly.

qualified opinion - contain the phrase "except for"

unqualified opinion - Auditors believes financial statements are "fair" presentations.

analytical procedures - Test relationships among financial and nonfinancial items to identify specific risks.

scope - What was covered by the audit as what was not

internal control - Any policy, proceaure, or management action that provides assurance that company objectives will meet

separation of duties - principal that states that a storeroom clerk should not issue supplies & maintain the record of supplies on hand.

independence - Gained by having the audit department report to the board of directors.

16

Responsibility Accounting

LEARNING OBJECTIVES

After studying Chapter 16, you should be able to:
1. Describe and understand the concepts underlying decentralization and the various responsibility centers.
2. Prepare performance reports that reflect the principle of controllability.
3. Discuss reasons for allocating and for not allocating common costs.
4. Describe and calculate measures of performance for profit centers.
5. Discuss reasons for reporting income and investment in various ways on performance reports.
6. Analyze decisions that involve intracompany transfers and evaluate transfer prices.

In this chapter our attention turns to performance evaluation, which requires a *responsibility accounting system,* that is, one in which accounting information is reported to assist managers in controlling their operations and evaluating their subordinates. We treat behavioral questions here because responsibility accounting systems often encourage particular kinds of behavior, some good and some bad. Cost allocation, which we have discussed in earlier chapters, is again a major topic.

RESPONSIBILITY CENTERS

A *responsibility center* is an area under the control of a manager—for example, a department; a group of departments; or a product, product line, or geographical area. However, because the actions of one manager can affect the performance of others, it can be difficult to isolate responsibility. Poorly manufactured goods are difficult for even the best sales managers to sell. A fine production manager cannot meet cost budgets in the face of constantly changing production schedules brought on by poor sales planning. It is possible, nonetheless, to measure performance by judicious assignment of responsibilities and careful selection of criteria for evaluation.

Responsibility centers are critical to performance evaluation.

There are four principal kinds of responsibility centers: revenue centers, cost centers, profit centers, and investment centers.

Revenue Centers

A **revenue center** generates revenues, but incurs little or no cost. In hospitals, revenue centers include surgery, medical services, operating room, and obstetrics. Marketing departments are often treated as revenue centers. Salespeople or sales districts might be treated as revenue centers (or as profit centers as we discuss below) if they generate little expense.

Cost Centers

Cost centers generate costs, not revenues. Their managers are responsible only for costs. Chapter 14 on standard costs describes the basic ways of evaluating cost centers. Some cost centers are small, such as work stations in a plant; some are extremely large, such as an entire factory.

Profit Centers and Investment Centers

A **profit center** generates both revenues and costs, from which we can calculate some sort of profit. (We might stop at contribution margin, or might include direct fixed costs. We might also include allocated indirect costs.) Managers of profit centers are responsible for both revenues and costs.

A manager of an **investment center** is responsible for revenues, costs, and investment in assets. Here, we can calculate some kind of *return on investment.* In both profit and investment centers, a critical question is the extent to which the managers *control* the components. Thus, even a center that has investment might be treated as a profit center if its manager cannot control the amount of investment.

There are relatively few profit centers in the strict sense: it is usually necessary to have *some* investment to generate revenues. In practice, though, managers often use the term *profit center* to refer to both profit centers and investment centers. Most modern companies use profit and investment centers extensively.

RESPONSIBILITY REPORTING

Responsibility accounting is behavioral. As Chapter 13 stated, **goal congruence** is critical in budgeting; it is also critical in performance evaluation, as discussed in this chapter. Managers must be motivated to work toward the organization's goal as well as their own goals. The selection of criteria or measures for evaluation is important here. For instance, salespeople whose evaluations depend only on unit sales have no incentive to try to sell the most profitable products, only those they can sell in the highest quantities. The system used for performance evaluation must therefore use criteria for evaluation that managers can control and that will encourage managers to work in the company's best interests.

Without doubt, performance measurement criteria influence managers' actions. Indeed, it is frequently argued that criteria emphasizing production over quality has been an important factor in making U.S. businesses less competitive than Japanese and others. Similarly, a preoccupation with short-term results has been cited as motivating managers to take actions not in the organization's long-term interests. Examples include reducing expenditures for such long-term investments as research and development, employee training, and automation.

Controllability of costs is the best indication of relevance.

It is also essential that managers believe that the system fairly reflects performance and that they have reasonable control over the factors that will be evaluated—for example, costs. Reports on managerial performance should include costs controllable by the manager. All costs are controllable by some manager, if only the chief executive officer.

Reports for Cost Centers

Exhibit 16–1 shows a hierarchy of reports. The reports show the direct, controllable costs associated with each level. Note that the total

Exhibit 16–1
Sample Monthly Reports for Cost Centers
(in thousands of dollars)

Report to Supervisor of Drilling Cell

	Budget	Over (Under)
Materials	$13.3	$ 1.1
Direct labor	26.4	(2.2)
Other controllable costs	16.6	1.8
Totals	$56.3	$ 0.7

Report to Manager of Machining Department

	Budget	Over (Under)
Drilling cell	$ 56.3	$ 0.7
Other cells	436.8	6.0
Total costs of cells	493.1	6.7
General department costs:		
Indirect labor	22.4	0.9
Janitorial	7.3	(0.2)
Power	11.6	0.2
Total department costs	$534.4	$ 7.6

Report to Manager of Charlotte Plant

	Budget	Over (Under)
Machining department	$ 534.4	$ 7.6
Other departments	3,265.2	12.3
Total department costs	3,799.6	19.9
General plant costs:		
Building security	25.3	0.3
Factory accounting	87.8	1.3
Other	44.7	(0.7)
Total plant costs	$3,957.4	$20.8

cost assigned to every manager above the first level is greater than the sum of the costs reported to his or her subordinates. Each department manager is responsible for all costs of the work cells under the supervisors as well as for costs that she controls, but that supervisors do not control. These costs are indirect labor, janitorial, and power. Similarly, the plant manager is responsible for more costs than are the departmental managers. These include engineering, building security, and factory accounting. We shortly discuss the wisdom of allocating these **common,** or **indirect,** costs to lower levels. In this exhibit we show for each manager only the costs that that manager can control.

COST ALLOCATION IN RESPONSIBILITY ACCOUNTING

Some responsibility centers provide services to others and are called **service centers** or **service departments.** Examples of service departments are engineering, payroll, legal, accounting, and data processing. Maintaining internal service departments is cheaper than having each department do its own, say, payroll. Internal service departments are also helpful in controlling the quality of service or dealing with sensitive issues, such as a legal department does.

Responsibility centers that work on products, called **operating departments,** benefit from the work done by service centers. Accordingly, many accountants argue that they should pay for the services. Payment is typically in the form of allocations of indirect costs; that is, allocating the costs of service centers to operating departments. We have seen in several chapters that allocating indirect costs is unwise in planning and in making decisions. But many accountants believe that it can be helpful in control and performance evaluation. Some of their principal reasons follow.

Reasons for Allocating Indirect Costs

One reason for allocating indirect costs, already mentioned, is that service departments benefit users and therefore the users should have to pay for the services. Another commonly cited reason is that managers of operating departments should be reminded that their direct costs are not the company's only costs, and that they must be held responsible for significant indirect costs as well.

Cost allocation is a behavioral issue.

The most compelling reasons for allocating indirect costs, however, are behavioral. Some argue that allocating indirect costs encourages managers to use services wisely. Managers might use too much service if it is free. This creates strains on the service centers' capacities and increases their costs. Consider a company that has a WATS line, which allows employees to make unlimited telephone calls on one number for a flat monthly fee. There is no incremental cost for a specific call, so some would argue that the using departments should not pay for the service. However, if there is no charge, people will probably overuse the service, creating bottlenecks and eventually requiring additional lines, thus increasing costs. A related reason for allocating costs is that it encourages operating managers to pressure service department managers to control service costs. The communications manager seeking another WATS line, for instance, would need the support of the operating managers who are to pay for it.

Reasons for not Allocating Costs

The principal arguments against allocating service department costs are also behavioral. One major argument is that the costs of service centers, being indirect to operating departments, are not controllable by the operating managers. Therefore, allocating such costs violates the principle of controllability with potentially serious consequences. Managers who are allocated costs they do not control are likely to distrust the responsibility accounting system and try to outwit it. Operating managers might also underuse the service if the charges are too high.

Another important reason is related to making decisions. The allocated service department costs are not likely to be incremental to decisions, but can appear so because of the allocation method. For instance, if a service cost is allocated as a percentage of sales, an operating manager will consider it to be a variable cost—if sales rise, so does the allocation. But if, as is likely, the cost is not incremental to the company, then a manager including it in a decision analysis could come to the wrong conclusion. The extent to which allocations are important depends on the company. As Insight 16–1 shows, JIT companies are likely to have less common cost and therefore less need for allocation. The amount of centrally performed service is an important factor in determining how much allocation will be done.

Cost Allocation Bases

Costs are allocated on some basis—some measure of activity or use of the service. Personnel department costs are usually allocated on the number of employees in the using departments; occupancy costs such as building depreciation, property taxes, and security, on the basis of square footage occupied by the departments.

The allocation basis should ideally reflect cause-and-effect. Users should be charged the costs that their use creates. While this is often possible for variable costs, it is usually not possible for fixed indirect costs. For fixed costs, perhaps the best that can be achieved is to use a basis that reflects the benefits the user receives. For example, it is quite

INSIGHT 16–1
Eliminating Allocation Problems

In JIT companies, the allocation question is less severe than it is in conventional manufacturers. As you recall, JIT companies use manufacturing cells where workers concentrate on a single product or related group of products. Workers also do many of the tasks done by support personnel in conventional companies. Some costs, such as those associated with moving products about in the factory, disappear in a JIT environment. Other costs, such as maintenance, supplies, supervision, depreciation, and other manufacturing support items become direct to cells and hence to products and lines. In fact, the product or line is the relevant center in a JIT company, rather than the department, as is true in conventional manufacturers. These costs are indirect to products and lines for conventional manufacturers.

Eliminating the need for allocations makes it possible to determine the cost of a product more accurately. Obviously, the more the costs that can be traced directly to a product, the more confidence you have that you have captured the cost.

appropriate to allocate heating expense based on the space each department occupies.

Because it is often difficult to find bases as described here, many companies allocate at least some costs on an arbitrary basis such as sales. Such a basis does not reflect causality or benefits, but rather only the "ability to bear" the allocation. Fortunately, such costs are often not large. Examples include the salary of the president of the company and charitable contributions. Costs of this type might also be allocated based on assets. And it is possible to allocate some costs while leaving others unallocated.

Cost Allocation Methods

After the basis for allocating each cost is selected, there remains the question which costs are to be allocated. Three choices are (1) allocate actual costs based on actual use, (2) allocate budgeted costs using dual rates, and (3) allocate through transfer prices. These are not the only choices, but are sufficient for our purposes.

Allocating Actual Costs Based on Actual Use

Allocating actual costs is not a good idea, as we shall see. It is reasonable to allocate variable costs based on actual use of a service because use drives variable cost. It is not wise, however, to allocate fixed costs based on the operating centers' actual use. Consider the following example. A copying department has monthly fixed costs of $100,000. The schedule below shows the number of copies made by Department A and by all other departments lumped together.

	Department A	All Other Departments	Total Use
Month 1	10,000	90,000	100,000
Month 2	10,000	40,000	50,000

Department A would receive allocations of $10,000 (10% of use, so 10% of cost) in month 1, $20,000 in month 2 (20% of use). But Department A made the same number of copies in both months. Thus, using actual use to allocate fixed indirect costs has the drawback that a manager's allocation depends not only on what he uses, but also on what the other departments use. This is not a good situation, as each manager will try to use the service only when other departments are also using it—probably creating bottlenecks.

Additionally, the method is unsound because it allocates actual costs and therefore passes the inefficiencies (or efficiencies, if actual costs are less than budgeted costs) of the service department on to the operating departments. It is better to allocate budgeted costs, if possible.

Allocating Budgeted Costs Using Dual Rates

Perhaps the most widely made recommendations are, first, to allocate budgeted or standard costs, not actual costs, and second to avoid using actual use to allocate fixed costs. One method is to allocate budgeted variable costs based on use (because total variable costs change as use changes) and budgeted fixed costs based on long-term expected use. The term *dual rates* describes this method, because the two types of cost are allocated differently.

This method overcomes the problems associated with allocating fixed costs based on use, because the amount of fixed cost to be allocated is a lump sum determined before the year begins. The idea supporting this approach is that fixed costs are incurred to provide the capacity to serve, and the decisions that determined the size (capacity) of the Maintenance Department were based, at least in part, on estimates made earlier by the managers of the operating departments. The argument is that if the manager of the Assembly Department has requested some amount of capacity, he or she should pay for it. Allocating variable costs based on actual use and fixed costs based on expected long-term use is also called the *dual method.*

In our example above, suppose that Department A is expected to use 15% of the service over the long term. Its monthly allocation of the

$100,000 fixed costs would then be $15,000 (15% × $100,000) regardless of its use, and importantly, regardless of other departments' use. If there were variable costs in the service department, these would still be allocated on actual use. This charge based on use will encourage managers not to overuse or underuse the service.

Allocating through Transfer Prices

Some companies turn service centers into **artificial profit centers,** which deal entirely within the company and charge prices for their services. These intracompany prices are called **transfer prices.** They often reflect market prices for the services, which the operating departments would have to pay to obtain the services from an outside company. In many cases, however, market prices are not available, so cost-based prices are used.

Transfer prices are an alternative to cost allocation.

There are several advantages to using transfer prices instead of allocations. One is that the service centers are forced to be efficient and to offer services of acceptable quality, else they will not "earn" enough revenues from selling their services to cover their costs. In some companies, users can buy the service outside the company if they do not like the transfer price. This imposes a market discipline on the service center. If a service department consistently loses money, the company might decide to shut it down and obtain the service elsewhere. Another advantage is that upper management can also raise (lower) transfer prices to discourage (encourage) use of any particular service. The benefits of artificial profit centers to one large company are outlined in Insight 16–2.

Allocations and Decisions

Chapter 12 showed that allocated costs are not helpful for short-term decisions. However, allocations can reflect long-term costs of activities. Accountants use activity-based costing, described in Chapter 11, in evaluating lines of product or other segments in much the same ways we have discussed earlier. The professional literature is full of reports of companies that have cut products or increased prices in response to allocations showing that the products were not contributing to the long-term welfare of the company.

EVALUATING PROFIT AND INVESTMENT CENTERS

We come now to the evaluation of profit centers and investment centers. We shall use the term *division,* because many profit/investment centers are divisions of companies. Divisions are usually **decentral-**

INSIGHT 16–2
Everyone in Business

Weyerhauser, the huge, integrated paper company, uses artificial profit centers extensively and believes that they contribute to cost control and higher profits. The company requires that all service departments charge back their costs to users. The service departments can also sell to outsiders, while the internal users can go outside for the services, or take them over themselves. Managers are free to deal with whomever they please. The system has generated much entreprenurial activity by service department managers. The Information Systems Department has even advertised for business from outsiders.

One benefit of the system is that managers better understand the costs of the services they use. They now understand how changing their operations will affect those costs because they know how they are charged for the service. For instance, the Financial Services Department charges a flat amount for processing each salaried employee. Thus, users considering increasing the number of salaried personnel know what the cost will be. Another important benefit is that service providers now must respond to their "customers," rather than do what they wish. A service department that does a poor job or does not respond to the needs of the users will not survive.

SOURCE: H. Thomas Johnson and Dennis A. Loewe, "How Weyerhauser Controls Overhead Costs," *Management Accounting*, August 1987, 20–26.

ized, with decision-making authority spread throughout the company and managers of investment centers having authority similar to that of company presidents. Companies use two principal measures to evaluate divisions. There are also interesting problems when divisions within a company do business with one another—a very common situation.

The principles used in developing performance reports for cost centers apply also to profit and investment centers. Controllability is the principal concern, and the arguments we have described about allocating common costs relate also to profit/investment centers. Exhibit 16–2 shows sample reports for profit centers—product lines in this case. These reports show actual results only for the current month and year-to-date, a common format. Some reports will also show budgeted figures or differences between budgeted and actual results. Other segments are possible, such as geographic areas (districts, regions, countries). Note the similarities to the reports in Exhibit 16–1, with some costs not being allocated to some centers. The term **product margin** refers to contribution margin less fixed costs direct to the

Exhibit 16–2
Sample Monthly Reports for Profit Centers
(thousands of dollars)

Report to Product Manager—Luv Shampoo

	Year-to-date	Month
Sales	$217.3	$33.2
Variable costs	98.2	8.5
Contribution margin	119.1	24.7
Direct fixed costs	76.4	15.4
Product margin	$ 42.7	$ 9.3

Report to Manager of Hair-Care Products

Product margins:	Year-to-date	Month
Luv Shampoo	$ 42.7	$ 9.3
Beauty Mousse	112.3	23.5
Carefree Coloring	104.2	22.9
Total product margins	259.2	55.7
Costs direct to Hair Care line	15.6	4.5
Product line margin	$243.6	$51.2

Report to Manager of Cosmetics

Product line margins:	Year-to-date	Month
Hair Care	$243.6	$ 51.2
Deodorants	335.6	66.9
Skin Care	416.5	98.2
Total product line margins	995.7	216.3
Costs direct to Cosmetics	35.6	8.4
Product line margin	$960.1	$207.9

product or product line. These costs are considered controllable by the managers to whom they are allocated. An example of a cost controllable by the cosmetics line manager, but not by the hair-care line manager, is travel expenses of salespeople who sell all products in all lines.

Advantages of Decentralization

Decentralization allows the managers who are closest to the situation to make decisions. This is an advantage because they have better informa-tion than managers at central headquarters and can respond quickly to changes in the environment. If the manager of a supermarket had to go to his district manager every time he wanted to change the price of lettuce, it would take too long for decisions to be made. (The district manager might have 20 store managers, each requesting decisions on 100 matters every day.)

Many accountants and other managers believe that decentralization also has the advantage of increasing motivation. Behavioral scientists have concluded that people with broad responsibilities are more interested in their work and perform it better than those with narrower responsibilities. The term *job enlargement* describes the assigning of broader responsibilities to people at any level—managerial or factory floor—that has become a popular practice in today's business world as well as in not-for-profit organizations. Recall our discussion of JIT manufacturers, where workers take on much greater responsibility than they had in the past. Of course, conventional companies also use employee involvement to increase productivity.

It is also easier to evaluate performance of managers in a decentralized organization. If different managers are responsible for production and sales, for example, poor sales performance could be the fault of either manager. The product might be substandard or the salesforce might be unskilled. But if a single manager is in charge of a profit center, that manager is answerable for the entire operation.

Disadvantages of Decentralization

The major problem with decentralization is that managers striving to work for the best for their units might make decisions that hurt the firm. Again, the issue is goal congruence. There are two principal areas where dysfunctional consequences can arise. One is in the selection of performance evaluation measures and methods. The other is in transfer prices. We will consider these in turn.

MEASURES OF PERFORMANCE

The measures that we discuss here help corporate managers evaluate *operations*—cost centers, profit/investment centers—but they do not necessarily say anything about how well the managers are performing. For example, investment centers in rapidly growing industries, such as leisure products, should be more profitable than those in mature, stable industries such as food. A poor manager might show good results, a good manager poor results, because of their industries. Recognizing this problem, corporate managers usually evaluate managers based on budgets. The budgets should reflect the prospects of each division and represent good, but attainable performance. Thus, if the measures we discuss here are to be used to evaluate managers as well as operations, they must be very carefully interpreted.

Return on Investment (ROI)

ROI is the most common measure of performance.

Profit is an incomplete measure of performance for investment centers because it fails to consider the investment required to generate it. The most widely used measure is **return on investment (ROI),** the ratio of income to investment. Of course, for profit centers, profit is as far as we can go.

$$\text{ROI} = \frac{\text{Divisional Income}}{\text{Divisional Investment}}$$

In evaluating investment centers, we are concerned with operating results, so we usually exclude interest expense, income taxes (which depend on financing as well as on operations), and long-term debt from the calculations. Most companies, then, define *divisional income* as income before interest and income taxes, or *operating income.* The problems with allocations of indirect costs that we discussed in connection with cost centers also arise with profit and investment centers. That is, should corporate costs be allocated to investment centers? The same arguments that applied to cost centers apply to profit and investment centers.

Companies also define *investment* in various ways. Perhaps the most common definition is current assets plus plant assets. This excludes goodwill and other intangible assets controlled by the company as a whole. Often investment is defined to include current liabilities under the manager's control, such as trade payables and accruals. Long-term debt is almost never included. The rationale for subtracting some liabilities (which of course raises ROI because it reduces investment) is that current liabilities are operating-related. Payables and accruals arise because of the level of operations and are therefore reasonably included. Some dispute this position and exclude current liabilities from the calculation of investment. There are also several terms used as synonyms for ROI. Among the most common are ROCE (return on capital employed), ROA (return on assets), and ROAE (return on assets employed).

The ROI formula given earlier can be analyzed into separate elements that assist managers in evaluating performance.

$$\text{ROI} = \frac{\text{Income}}{\text{Sales}} \times \frac{\text{Sales}}{\text{Investment}}$$
$$= \text{Margin} \times \text{Turnover}$$

The margin-times-turnover format allows managers to examine the components of ROI. The first factor, income/sales, is the *return on sales (ROS)* ratio, often termed *profit margin* or simply **margin.** The second term, sales/investment, is called *asset turnover* (or *investment turnover,* or just **turnover**).

The expanded equation yields exactly the same ROI as the simpler income/investment equation, because *sales* is in the numerator of one factor and the denominator of the other and thus cancels out. A couple of points are worth mentioning. First, an increase in sales, other factors constant, does not improve ROI, because sales cancels out. Margin falls, while turnover rises. Only a change in income or investment can change ROI. Of course, if sales increase and income does also (a likely outcome), then ROI will increase, unless investment increases enough to cancel out the increase in income.

Looking at the two factors in ROI can help managers to understand performance and analyze strategies. Consider the two divisions described below, both parts of the same company. They both earn the same ROI, but in different ways. All data are in millions.

	Luxury Goods Division	**X-Mart Division**
Sales	$60	$100
Income	$12	$8
Investment	$60	$40
Margin	20%	8%
Turnover	I time	2.5 times
ROI	20%	20%

The Luxury Goods Division has a high margin, but low turnover, while the reverse is true for the X-Mart Division. Discount operations rely on high turnover because they earn low margins. Thus, turnover is critical to that division. The Luxury Goods Division stocks more product and holds it longer, increasing its investment. It probably also has more expensive fixtures and is in high-rent locations. Its resultant low turnover means that it must maintain high margins to be successful.

Although ROI is the most common measure of divisional performance, it suffers from some defects, as we shall see shortly. Some managers prefer an alternative measure called residual income (RI).

Residual Income

Residual income is total profit less a minimum required return. The minimum required return is the minimum required *rate* of return multiplied by investment. That is,

$$RI = \text{Income} - (\text{Minimum Required ROI} \times \text{Investment})$$

Suppose a company earns $300,000, has investment of $800,000, and the minimum required ROI is 20%. RI is as follows.

Income	$300,000
Minimum required return ($800,000 × 20%)	160,000
RI	$140,000

The idea is that the minimum required return ($160,000 here) is the amount needed to "repay" the investors who provided the $800,000 that the company invested in the investment center. The minimum required rate of return is therefore at least equal to the cost of capital, as described in Chapter 15.

Residual income overcomes some problems with ROI.

Some believe that RI has an important advantage over ROI as a measure of divisional performance because it better highlights the worth of a division to the company. Suppose that Division X earns $400,000 income on an investment of $2,000,000, an ROI of 20%, while Division Y earns $1,500,000 on an investment of $10,000,000, an ROI of 15%. Suppose the required ROI is 10%. The RIs are as follows.

	Division X	**Division Y**
Income	$400,000	$1,500,000
Minimum required:		
$2,000,000 × 10%	200,000	
$10,000,000 × 10%		1,000,000
RI	$200,000	$ 500,000

Division Y provides more RI, so is returning a higher amount over the amount required to carry its investment. In this sense, Division Y is more valuable to the company.

Another advantage of RI stems from a potential problem with ROI. Using ROI to evaluate managers can encourage them to reject investments that are desirable from the standpoint of the company and accept undesirable ones. Suppose a division manager expects income of $250,000 on investment of $1,000,000 (ROI of 25%). She can invest an additional $200,000 and earn an additional $40,000. ROI would then be 24.17% ($290,000/$1,200,000). If the manager were evaluated on ROI, she would not accept the investment. But if the company's minimum required ROI were 15% (or any rate below 20%), the company would be better off with the investment. If the divisional manager were evaluated on RI, she would make the investment.

	Do Not Make Investment	**Make Investment**
Income	$250,000	$290,000
Minimum required:		
$1,000,000 × 15%	150,000	
$1,200,000 × 15%	_____	180,000
RI	$100,000	$110,000

Using ROI to measure performance encourages managers to make investments with ROIs greater than that currently earned, whether high or low. Using RI encourages managers to invest when the expected ROI is higher than the desired return. Using RI thus fosters goal congruence, while using ROI does not necessarily do so.

Measuring Income and Investment

There are many issues in measuring the components of ROI and RI, most beyond the scope of this book. One continuing issue is whether income and investment should be measured in accordance with the principle of controllability, with few or no allocations of corporate expenses or corporate assets. Some accountants take this position. Others, relying on arguments presented earlier, believe that judicious use of allocations can encourage desirable behavior. Some companies use one measure to evaluate divisions, another to evaluate their managers.

Income and Cash Flow

While the vast majority of companies use some form of income to calculate ROI and RI, some prefer to use cash flow. Cash flow does not suffer from the effects of arbitrary allocations such as depreciation, and it represents the amount that the division can return to the company. The company cannot invest income; it must have cash to invest. Using cash flow to measure performance also encourages managers to keep down investment. For instance, a manager will be more concerned about rising inventories if she is evaluated on cash flow rather than income.

Fixed Asset Valuation

Most companies use net book value—cost less accumulated depreciation—to value fixed assets. DuPont and others use gross cost, not subtracting accumulated depreciation. One argument for gross cost is that assets should be maintained in good condition, and therefore managers should not be relieved of the responsibility of earning a satisfac-

tory return on the total initial investment. Remember that accumulated depreciation lowers total assets and therefore raises ROI and RI.
Gross cost also overcomes the objection that managers with older
plants gain an advantage because of the low book value of their plants.
ROI and RI based on net book value *should* increase as plants grow
older. Some accountants prefer replacement costs over historical costs
(gross or net) because replacement costs represent today's required
investment for the same facilities and put all managers on the same
basis.

Valuation and definition are problems no matter what measure is used.

Multinational companies have the additional problem that fluctuations in the value of currency make it difficult to evaluate performance
of an overseas operations. For instance, if the value of the dollar falls
against the British pound (that is, a pound becomes worth more dollars), a Britain-based division will show higher profits in dollars simply
because of the fall in the dollar's value, which may not have anything to
do with the skill of the British manager. An example of how currency
values affect companies appears in Insight 16–3.

INSIGHT 16–3
In One Currency, Out Another

Some companies and divisions routinely do business in several currencies. Some
even earn revenue in one currency and pay expenses in another. The Toronto
Blue Jays baseball team collects its admissions in Canadian dollars, but pays its
players in U.S. dollars. (It collects some revenues in U.S. dollars and pays some
expenses in Canadian dollars.) What happens to the team if the U.S. dollar rises
against the Canadian dollar, that is, if it takes fewer U.S. dollars to buy a Canadian
dollar and more Canadian dollars to buy a U.S. dollar? Will the team be better
or worse off?

The team will be worse off. Suppose the U.S. dollar can buy 1.25 Canadian
dollars, or equivalently, that the Canadian dollar can buy 80 U.S. cents. Suppose
further that the team pays 800,000 U.S. dollars in salaries. The team takes its
Canadian dollars to a bank and exchanges them for U.S. dollars. To buy 800,000
U.S. dollars requires 1,000,000 Canadian dollars (800,000 × 1.25). If the exchange rate goes to 1.40 Canadian dollars per U.S. dollar, the team must use
1,120,000 Canadian dollars to meet its payroll. Of course, the Canadian dollar
could also strengthen against the U.S. dollar, making the team better off. As
this example shows, performance evaluation can be greatly complicated by
exchange rate fluctuations.

TRANSFER PRICES

We introduced transfer prices earlier in connection with service centers. Many investment centers (and profit centers) also deal with others in the same company. An integrated oil company such as Exxon might have a drilling division that sells to its sister transportation division (ship or pipeline), that in turn sells to a sister refinery, that finally sells to the retail division. These transactions require transfer prices. And transfer prices are especially important to investment centers because they affect the income of both the buying and selling divisions, *but not the income of the company as a whole.* Each intracompany sale generates revenue to one division and cost to the other, so the sale cancels out. Nonetheless, transfer prices are important in evaluating the performance of the investment centers and therefore divisional managers are concerned about them.

Transfer pricing policies are usually set by corporate management. They range from cost-plus to market prices to negotiated prices (meaning that individual managers work out their own prices). Market-based prices are sometimes best, from the company's standpoint, but sometimes not. The following example shows why.

Transfer pricing significantly affects divisions and their managers.

Transfers and Decisions

The following income statement relates to Division A's expected operations for the year. Division A sells the same product to outsiders and to its sister Division B.

	To Division B	To Outsiders
Sales, 2,000 × $12	$24,000	
20,000 × $12		$240,000
Variable costs at $4	8,000	80,000
Contribution margin	16,000	160,000
Fixed costs, all common, allocated on basis of relative sales	6,000	60,000
Profit	$10,000	$100,000

Division B has found an outside supplier willing to sell it 2,000 units per year at $9 each. Division B's manager tells Division A's manager that he will go outside for the 2,000 units unless Division A reduces the price to $9. What happens now depends on Division A's manager. Suppose that Division A refuses to meet the $9 price. Division B will buy from the outside supplier. Is this good for the company and for the divisions? It depends on whether Division A is operating at capacity. More exactly, it depends on whether Divison A could sell another 2,000 units to outsiders. If Division A could sell all 2,000 units it now supplies Division B to outsiders, then everyone is better off, or no worse off, if Division B buys outside. This is because Division B saves $6,000 buying outside (2,000×[$12 − $9]) and Division A simply shifts its 2,000 units to outsiders, maintaining its profit.

If the selling division is operating at capacity, then the $12 market transfer price gives the correct signal to the buying division. Division A will not sell the units to Division B for less than $12 because it can sell them to outsiders for $12. Division B would prefer to pay $9 over $12, so it will go outside.

Now suppose that Division A is not at capacity and could not increase its outside sales if it lost Division B's business. The company would lose, then, $10,000 if Division B went outside.

Cost to buy outside, 2,000 × $9	$18,000
Cost to make inside, 2,000 × $4	8,000
Advantage to making	$10,000

What about Division A? The manager of Division A should now be willing to meet the $9 price. Comparative income statements show the advantage to be $10,000, which is simply the contribution margin that Division A could earn selling the 2,000 for $9, with $4 variable cost. It is the same $10,000 by which the company benefits. Division B saves its $6,000 whether it buys outside or from Division A because it now pays $9 instead of $12.

	Meet $9 Price	Do Not Meet Price
Sales, 2,000 × $9	$ 18,000	$ 0
20,000 × $12	240,000	240,000
Total sales	258,000	240,000
Variable costs, 22,000 × $4	88,000	
Variable costs, 20,000 × $4		80,000
Contribution margin	170,000	160,000
Fixed costs	66,000	66,000
Profit	$104,000	$ 94,000

This example is a make-or-buy decision, as discussed in Chapter 12. That there are two divisions is irrelevant to the company as a whole, but is quite relevant to the individual division managers whose performance is affected by their profits. If the managers use information wisely and understand cost behavior, they should reach the correct decisions. It is also worth noting that Division A faces a special-order problem, as also discussed in Chapter 12.

Multinational companies have special problems with transfer prices. Different income tax rates prevail among different countries so that companies are motivated to shift income from high-tax to low-tax countries. Companies with divisions that operate in different countries can accomplish tax-reduction by raising transfer prices if the selling division is in a lower-tax country than the buying division, and lowering prices if the seller is in a higher-tax country. The idea is to shift the profit to the division in the lower-tax country. Of course, there are serious ethical questions in such shifting, as well as legal questions. And at least one divisional manager is going to be hurt, so performance evaluation becomes more difficult. The practice of setting transfer prices to increase overall company profits is extremely complicated, and other factors enter the decisions.

Transfer pricing is a difficult topic, engaging the attention of many managers over long periods. A great deal is written about it in the accounting and general business literature because it is a pervasive problem in business and in other segmented organizations.

SUMMARY

Responsibility accounting is a critical element in evaluating the performance of segments and their managers. The principle of controllability is important, as is the encouragement of desirable behavior. Cost allocations can be effective in promoting desired behavior, but must be used with care lest they encourage dysfunctional behavior.

Return on investment (ROI) is the most commonly used measure of performance for investment centers. Residual income (RI) is also popular. Using either measure, or both, requires careful defining and calculating of income and investment. These measures are usually based on the principle of controllability.

Sales made within the company require transfer prices, which are a very thorny problem. Transfer prices might encourage managers to take unwise (from the company's view) actions. In contrast, managers who understand their cost structures and are free to take or leave business with sister divisions are likely to make decisions in both the company's and their own best interests.

DEMONSTRATION PROBLEM

Cannon Industries operates several divisions. Budgeted results for Burke Division appear below. The minimum required ROI is 20%.

Sales, 100,000 units at $10	$1,000,000
Variable costs, 100,000 at $4	400,000
Contribution margin	600,000
Fixed costs	200,000
Income	$ 400,000
Investment	$1,200,000

REQUIRED:

1. Determine ROI.
2. Determine RI.
3. The manager of the division has the opportunity to invest another $300,000 and expects annual income to increase by $66,000. Would the manager be likely to accept the investment if the basis for evaluation were ROI? What if RI were the basis?
4. Burke's $4 variable cost includes $1.20 for a component it now buys from Colman Division of Cannon Industries. Burke has the opportunity to buy the component from an outside supplier for $0.90. Burke's manager has told Colman's manager that he will buy from the outsider unless Colman reduces its price to $0.90. Colman Division's budgeted income statement appears below, prior to the information from Burke.

Sales to outsiders at $1.50	$150,000
Sales to Burke Division at $1.20	120,000
Total sales	270,000
Variable costs at $0.70	140,000
Contribution margin	130,000
Fixed costs	60,000
Income	$ 70,000

If Colman loses Burke's business, it cannot save any fixed costs, nor can it increase outside sales. Should Colman refuse to meet the outsider's $0.90 price? Show why or why not.

Solution to Demonstration Problem

1. 33.3%, $400,000/$1,200,000
2. $160,000, $400,000 − 20% × $1,200,000
3. A manager evaluated on ROI would not accept the investment, which yields 22% ($66,000/$300,000), less than the 33.3% now earned. If RI were the basis, the manager would accept the investment because it would increase RI by $6,000 ($66,000 − 20% × $300,000).
4. Colman will lose $20,000 by refusing to meet the $0.90 price. The critical point to remember is that Colman can no longer earn $70,000. It will therefore lose contribution at $0.20 per unit ($0.90 − $0.70) for 100,000 units, or $20,000. The following income statements prove the result.

	Reduce Price	Refuse to Reduce Price
Sales to outsiders at $1.50	$150,000	$150,000
Sales to Burke Division at $0.90	90,000	0
Total sales	240,000	150,000
Variable costs at $0.70	140,000	70,000
Contribution margin	100,000	80,000
Fixed costs	60,000	60,000
Income	$ 40,000	$ 20,000

The better result is the $40,000 profit. Colman will then lose $0.30 revenue per unit ($1.20 − $0.90), reducing profit by $30,000 from the original $70,000. However, losing the business is worse.

Key Terms

artificial profit center

common (indirect) costs

cost allocation

cost center

decentralization

goal congruence

investment center

margin

operating department

profit center

profit margin

service department

residual income (RI)

return on investment (ROI)

revenue center

transfer price

turnover (of assets or investment)

ASSIGNMENTS

16–1   Alternative Allocation Bases

The following data refer to the three departments of ABC Company.

[Handwritten left margin: $ROI = \dfrac{INC}{Sales} \times \dfrac{Sales}{INV}$]

	A	B	C
Sales	$400,000	$200,000	$400,000
Square feet of space occupied	5,000	10,000	5,000

Total costs to be allocated are $100,000.

REQUIRED:

Allocate the costs to the departments on the bases of (a) sales dollars and (b) square feet of space occupied.

16–2   Basic ROI and RI

Moro Division of Layton Industries expects the following results for the coming year. All dollar amounts are in millions.

[Handwritten left margin:
Sales 32.0
VC (12.8) (32 × 40%)
—————
CM 19.2
FC (12.5)
—————
INCOME 6.7
① ROI = INC/Sales × Sales/INV = 6.7/22.5 = .297
② ROI Required 15%
Income 6.700
Reqd. ROI 3.375 (15% × 22.5)
Residual Inc 3.325]*

Sales	$32.0
Fixed costs	$12.5
Variable costs	40% of sales
Investment	$22.5

REQUIRED:

1. Determine the ROI that Moro will earn.
2. What will Moro's RI be if the minimum required ROI is 15%?

16–3   ROI, RI, and Decisions

Jimson Division expects to earn $1.2 million on an investment of $4.0 million, without considering any of the following information. A chain store has offered to buy 200 thousand units of one of Jimson's products at $10 each. Variable cost is $7 per unit, and the division would have to incur additional fixed costs of $400 thousand to fill the order. Jimson would also have increased investment of $1 million for receivables and inventories.

REQUIRED:

1. Determine Jimson's ROI before the special order.
2. Determine Jimson's ROI after the special order. If Jimson's manager is evaluated on ROI, will she accept the order?

[Handwritten left margin: 1.2/4.0]

3. Suppose that the minimum required ROI is 15%. Determine Jimson's RI (a) before the special order and (b) after the special order. Will the manager accept the order if she is evaluated on RI?

16–4   Basic Performance Reports

Building Products Division of OPN, Inc. has several product lines. Data for January, 19X3 appear below, in thousands of dollars. Several lines are combined in the data for "All Other Building Products Lines."

	Roofing Products Line	All Other Building Products Lines
Sales	$335.6	$1,268.9
Variable costs	112.5	542.3
Fixed costs	83.2	489.2

All variable costs are direct to the lines and controllable. Of the fixed costs shown, about $40.2 thousand are direct to Roofing Products, $378.2 are direct to "Other Lines." The remaining fixed costs were allocated to the lines and relate to the entire division.

REQUIRED:

Prepare performance reports for the Roofing Products Line and for All Other Building Products Lines, as well as for the division as a whole using the format of Exhibit 16–2.

16–5   Transfer Prices and Goal Congruence

Borlant Company has set transfer prices for many of its service departments. The charge for typing and proofreading is $11 per hour, based on total budgeted hours and total budgeted costs for the central stenographic pool. Budgeted costs for the pool are about 90% fixed. An outside stenographic service has given the manager of the Marketing Research department a price of $10 per hour for similar services. The task will require about 800 hours. The manager of Marketing Research informs the manager of the stenographic pool of the outside price and is told to take it if she so wishes. The manager of the stenographic pool will not reduce his price.

REQUIRED:

Comment on the position taken by the manager of the stenographic pool. Make a recommendation.

16–6   ROI and RI in Investment Decisions

The manager of TriCo Division of Exten, Inc., has developed the following investment opportunities. Investment in the division without considering any of these opportunities is $10,000,000 and profits are $2,500,000.

[handwritten: ① Current 2500,000/1,000,000 = 25%]

Investment Opportunity	Amount of Investment	Annual Profit
A	$ 500,000	$ 70,000
B	700,000	200,000
C	1,000,000	230,000
D	1,100,000	290,000
E	1,200,000	216,000

[handwritten left of table:
A. 70,000/500,000 = 14%
B. 200,000/70,000 = 28.6%
C. 230,000/1,000,000 = 23%
D. 29000/1,10000 = 26.4%
E. 21600/120,000 = 18%
Highest ROI > 25%
Income - Required % = RI]

REQUIRED:

1. Assuming the division manager wishes to maximize ROI, (a) which projects will he select, and (b) what ROI will he earn?

2. Assuming the manager now wishes to maximize RI, which projects will he select and what RI will he earn if the minimum desired ROI is (a) 15% and (b) 20%.

3. Which policy (maximizing ROI or maximizing RI) is usually better for the company?

16-7   Basic Transfer Pricing

Ti-Sol Division of Quorat Industries has been buying 100,000 units of a component from an outside supplier at $1.10 each. Grant Division of Quorat manufactures the component as well. The manager of Ti-Sol recently asked the manager of Grant whether he would be interested in supplying the component, and at what price. Grant Division expects the following results in the coming year, without considering sales to Ti-Sol.

Sales, 2,000,000 at $1.50	$3,000,000
Variable costs at $0.60	1,200,000
Contribution margin	1,800,000
Fixed costs	1,000,000
Profit	$ 800,000

[handwritten: profit .20 x 100,000 + 800,000   Current]

Grant can produce 2,500,000 units per year.

REQUIRED:

1. Suppose that Grant sells the component to Ti-Sol at $0.80 each. What will Grant Division's income be?

2. By how much, and in what direction, will income for Quorat Industries change if Grant supplies the component to Ti-Sol?

3. Repeat items 1 and 2 assuming that Grant can produce only 2,000,000 units.

[handwritten notes, bottom left:
Sales 820,000 (80-.60)
VC 1,200,000
CM -380,000
Sales before 110,000 (100,00 x 1.10)
after (60,000) (100000 x .60)
50,000
Sales 2,930,000
VC 1,200,000
CM 1,730,000
FC 1,000,000
Income 730,000]

[handwritten: Ti-Sol will save 50,000]

[handwritten: company decreases by 940,000]

16-8 Basic Allocation Methods

Z-Mart Stores has three profit centers and one service center, a central data processing department. The information below relates to operations in 19X6.

	Hardware	Household Goods	Clothing
Percentage of central purchasing services used in current year	20%	40%	40%
Expected percentage of long-term use of central purchasing services	30%	30%	40%

Budgeted central purchasing costs were $600,000 fixed and $300,000 variable. Actual fixed costs were $620,000, and actual variable costs were $290,000.

REQUIRED:

1. Allocate the actual central purchasing costs to the profit centers based on actual use of the services.

2. Allocate the budgeted variable central purchasing costs to the profit centers based on actual use of the services and the budgeted fixed costs based on expected long-term use.

3. Which of the two methods do you prefer? Why?

16-9 Transfer Pricing

Clarkson Division of Dempsey Industries manufactures furniture. Data on chair Style 504 appear below.

Selling price		$700
Variable costs:		
Fabric	$110	
Other variable costs	280	
Total variable costs		390
Contribution margin		$310
Expected volume		2,000 units

Clarkson buys the fabric from an outside supplier. The manager of Clarkson learns that Midland Division of Dempsey makes a fabric that would meet his requirements. Midland sells the fabric to outside customers for $140. Variable cost to Midland is $60. The manager of Clarkson offers to buy the fabric from Midland at $80.

[Handwritten margin notes:]

EXCESS capacity
2000 @ $80
SP to outsiders $140   to Clarkson 80
VL   (60)   (60)
CM   80   20

a. 2000 × 20 = 40,000 increase
b. 2000 × (110-80) = 6000 increase
c. 200 × (110-60) = 100,000 increase
② No additional capacity
a. 2000 (140-80) = 120,000 dec.
b. 2000 (110-80) = 60,000 inc
c. 2000 × 80 = 160,000 dec.
   2000 × (110-60) = 100,000 inc

$ROI = \frac{Inc}{Sales} \times \frac{Sales}{Inv}$

(1.) $\frac{500}{2,000} \times \frac{2000}{2,500}$

.25 × 0.8 =
.2

.26 × .80 = 20.8%

① 3,0,000,000 × 2 = 60,000,000 Sales
6,000,000 + 3,000,000 = 9,000,000 profit

② $\frac{10,000,000}{60,000,000}$ = 16.67%

REQUIRED:

1. Midland has plenty of capacity to serve its outside customers and meet Clarkson's needs. If Clarkson bought 2,000 units of the fabric from Midland at the $80 price:

   a. What will happen to Midland's income?

   b. What will happen to Clarkson Division's income?

   c. What will happen to Dempsey Industries' income?

2. Redo item 1 assuming that Midland has no excess capacity and would lose outside sales if it supplied Clarkson.

16–10 Components of ROI

The following data refer to the three divisions of Multico, Inc.

	Big Division	Gigantic Division	Enormous Division
Sales	$2,000	$3,000	$5,000
Profit	500	300	300
Investment	2,500	2,000	1,500

REQUIRED:

Do each item independently of the others.

1. Use the margin times turnover formula to compute ROI for each division.

2. Suppose that each division could increase its margin by one percentage point, holding total sales the same as above. Compute ROI for each division, and comment on the differences between the results here and those in item 1.

3. Suppose that each division could increase its turnover by 0.50 times (not 50%) by lowering its investment while holding total sales the same as above. Compute ROI for each division, and comment on the differences between the results here and those in item 1. Remember to use the original margins from item 1.

16–11 Basic RI Relationships

Swart Division had RI of $3 million, investment of $30 million, and asset turnover of 2. The minimum required ROI was 20%.

REQUIRED:

Do each independently.

1. Determine Swart's sales, profit, and ROS.

2. Determine the ROS that Swart needs to raise its RI by $1 million, holding sales and investment constant.

(handwritten) ③ 9,000,000 - 20% x 24,000,000 = 4,200,000

3. Suppose that Swart could increase its asset turnover to 2.5 times by reducing investment, holding sales and income constant at $60 million and $9 million, respectively. What RI will it earn?

16–12 Appropriate Transfer Price

Silicon Division of CRS Industries makes an electronic component that it now sells only to outside companies. The Instrumentation Products Division of CRS is bringing out a new device that requires a sophisticated chip. Silicon sells the chip for $28 and incurs variable costs of $8. The Instrumentation Products Division can acquire a suitable chip from outside the company for $22. Silicon is not operating at capacity.

REQUIRED:

1. Determine the advantage to CRS Industries as a whole for the Instrumentation Products Division to buy the chip from Silicon, as opposed to buying it outside.
2. What is the least that Silicon would accept for the chip?
3. What is the most that Instrumentation would pay Silicon for the chip?
4. How would your answers to each of the preceding items change if Silicon were working at capacity?

16–13 ROI Relationships

Proctor Division of NNG Industries had sales of $30 million, ROI of 30%, and asset turnover of 3 times.

(handwritten) ROI = Inc/Sales x Sale/Inv
30% = x/30Mil x 3
x = 3 mil
Sales/Inv = 3
30Mil/x = 3
x = 10 mil

REQUIRED:

(handwritten) 10 mil   3 mil   10%

1. Determine Proctor's (a) investment, (b) profit, (c) ROS.
2. Suppose that Proctor could increase its asset turnover to 4 by reducing its investment, with sales and income remaining constant. What would its ROI be? *(handwritten)* ROI = 10% x 4 = 40%
3. Referring back to the original turnover of 3 and margin of 10%, what would ROI be if Proctor could increase its margin by one percentage point, without changing sales or investment. *(handwritten)* ROI = ROS x Turnover; 33% = 11% x 3

16–14 Adequacy of Performance Measure

The sales manager of Bjork Company is evaluated on total sales and receives a bonus for exceeding the sales budget. Data for 19X3 are shown below, in thousands.

	\multicolumn{4}{c}{Product}
	A	B	C	Total
Sales budget	$100	$300	$600	$1,000
Variable costs	75	150	180	405
Contribution margin	$ 25	$150	$420	$ 595

Actual sales for 19X3 follow.

	Product			
	A	B	C	Total
	$500	$400	$200	$1,100

Actual prices equaled budgeted prices, and variable costs were in-curred as budgeted (per unit).

REQUIRED:

1. Did the sales manager perform well?
2. What suggestions can you offer regarding performance measures?

16–15 Performance Reporting and Allocations

Carolina Furniture, an outlet store, allocates indirect costs to its two departments based on sales. The income statement for 19X5 appears below.

	Indoor Furniture	Patio Furniture	Total
Sales	$400,000	$400,000	$800,000
Direct costs	180,000	180,000	360,000
Controllable profit	220,000	220,000	440,000
Indirect costs	180,000	180,000	360,000
Income	$ 40,000	$ 40,000	$ 80,000

In 19X6 the Indoor Department increased its prices, and its sales increased to $500,000, while those of the Patio Department remained at $400,000. Direct costs of each department were again $180,000, and total indirect costs were again $360,000.

REQUIRED:

1. Prepare a departmental income statement for 19X6 allocating indirect costs based on sales.
2. Comment on the results. Are they logical? Did the manager of Patio Furniture do a better job in 19X6 than in 19X5?

16–16 Responsibility for Factory Costs

The object classification of a cost (wages, rent, shipping, salaries, etc.) does not necessarily tell you whether it is the responsibility of a particular manager. For each of the costs listed below, indicate whether it is likely to be the responsibility of each of the following: (a) supervisor (b) department manager, and (c) plant manager.

1. Wages of direct laborers
2. Rent on production equipment
3. Wages of maintenance workers who work in only one department

4. Electricity for machinery
5. Cost of materials
6. Property taxes on plant building
7. Costs of processing factory payroll

16–17 Performance Report

Midland Toolworks has six operating departments, each with a manager responsible for materials, direct and indirect labor, supplies, small tools, and equipment maintenance. The department managers are not responsible for any other costs or for buying equipment. The manager of the Grinding Department received the following performance report last month. The costs of building occupancy have been allocated to the department.

	Budget	Actual	Over (Under)
Materials	$ 41,700	$ 40,800	($ 900)
Direct labor	47,200	47,500	300
Indirect labor	23,950	24,720	770
Supplies	16,100	15,950	(150)
Small tools	14,200	14,340	140
Equipment depreciation	22,800	22,800	0
Equipment maintenance	15,700	14,950	(750)
Building depreciation	12,200	12,200	0
Building maintenance	2,980	3,080	100
Property taxes	7,760	7,770	10
Total	$204,590	$204,110	($ 480)

REQUIRED:

Prepare a new performance report that shows only the costs for which the manager of the Grinding Department is responsible.

16–18 Performance Report for a Cost Center

Bart Stanley manages the Foundry Department of Norcom Industries. He recently received the following performance report.

Monthly Cost Report—Foundry Department
May, 19X9

Materials	$ 22,800
Direct labor	48,800
Indirect labor	3,380
Power	28,875
Other	25,600
Total	$129,455

The report contained a note from Stanley's supervisor stating that power cost was higher than in previous months and requesting an explanation. Power cost is mixed, with the variable portion mostly controllable by the department managers. However, the fixed component relates to factory-wide activities and is not controllable at the departmental level. The amounts shown are allocations based on the department's use of the services each month. The Foundry Department used 97,500 kilowatt-hours of power in May. Budgeted monthly cost of power is:

$$\text{Power Cost} = \$130,000 + \$0.11 \text{ per Kilowatt-hour}$$

The Foundry Department is expected to use about 10% of the total power over the long-term. Of the "Other" costs, about $7,350 are controllable at the department level and the rest are allocated. All other costs on the report are controllable by the department manager.

REQUIRED:

Prepare a new performance report for the Foundry Department showing the controllable costs and noncontrollable costs separately. Include fixed power cost in the controllable portion based on the department's long-term use of the services.

16–19   Evaluating Compensation Plans

Rickman Company sells a variety of paper products. It pays its salespeople a base salary plus a commission of 10% on gross sales. The following data relate to two of the company's salespeople for 19X6.

	William Waters	Carolyn Bates
Gross sales	$250,000	$180,000
Commissions	25,000	18,000
Sales returns and allowances	18,500	9,000
Bad debts	9,500	2,300
Cost of goods sold (all variable)	131,000	66,000
Travel, entertainment, other direct expenses	18,600	17,500

REQUIRED:

1. Which salesperson contributed more to company profit? Prepare a performance report showing each salesperson's contribution to profit.

2. What changes, if any, do you recommend in the compensation method?

16–20   Allocations and Decisions

Cramer Company is a distributor that handles many product lines, each under the control of a manager who is evaluated partly on profit. The expenses charged to each line are the direct costs of the line plus a corporate charge of 15% of sales that covers indirect costs, such as salaries of the corporate staff, interest on debt, and service functions (data processing, legal, accounting, personnel, etc.). These costs are virtually all fixed. The corporate controller estimated that the 15% charge would cover all indirect expenses at total company-wide sales of $60 million for the coming year.

The manager of one line can sell 10,000 units to a chain store at $50 each. Per-unit variable costs are $43, ignoring the 15% charge. There are no incremental fixed costs associated with the order, and there is sufficient capacity to make the additional units.

REQUIRED:

1. With performance based on product-line profit, will the manager accept the order? Why or why not?
2. Is it in the company's best interests for the manager to accept the order? Why or why not?

16–21   Cost Allocations and Performance Measurement

Edwards Company allocates indirect costs to its three product lines. Each line is the responsibility of a manager whose performance is based on ROI. Income statements for a typical month are as follows, in thousands of dollars.

	A	B	C	Total
Sales	$1,200	$800	$400	$2,400
Variable costs	720	400	170	1,290
Contribution margin	480	400	230	1,110
Indirect costs, allocated	450	300	150	900
Income	$ 30	$100	$ 80	$ 210

The manager of line A believes that if he reduces his price from $10 per unit to $9 per unit, sales will rise from 120,000 to 170,000 units. Unit variable costs will remain the same. Sales of the other lines will not be affected.

REQUIRED:

1. Determine whether the price decrease will benefit the company.
2. Prepare a new set of income statements based on the manager's estimates. Reallocate the indirect costs based on the new dollar sales figures. Is it in the manager's best interest to reduce the price? Comment on the company's method of allocating indirect costs.

16–22 DECISION CASE:
ASSIGNING RESPONSIBILITY

The controller of Arden Company charges the sales departments with overtime premium paid to factory workers when a sales manager requests an order that requires overtime. (Overtime premium is the difference between the wage rate paid when workers are on overtime and their regular rate.) There are ten sales managers responsible for the ten product lines. During March, budgeted production was 100,000 units; capacity production, without overtime, is 110,000 units. Early in March, four of the sales managers each put in rush orders for an additional 5,000 units (20,000 total additional units). All of the units require the same labor time.

   The production manager scheduled the extra 5,000 units of products A and B during regular working hours and the extra production of C and D after normal closing time, when overtime rates were paid. Total overtime premium was $100,000 for the 20,000 additional units.

REQUIRED:

State how you would charge each of the four sales managers with overtime premium and how much.

16–23 DECISION CASE:
INCURRED COSTS AND PERFORMANCE

Hammer Petroleum operates a refinery in the midwestern United States. The company employs about 200 people who drive trucks that deliver home-heating oil. The drivers are paid $14 per hour. In the summer there are no heating oil deliveries, and the drivers work in the refinery, since it needs additional workers in the summer. Jobs in the refinery usually pay $9 per hour, but the drivers receive their $14 wage. The refinery manager is charged with the $14 wage when the drivers work in the refinery. The manager in charge of fuel-oil distribution bears no charge for the drivers during the summer. Although the refinery manager does not object to employing the drivers during the summer, he is not happy about being charged $14 when he can hire students and other temporary employees for $9.

REQUIRED:

Discuss the issues involved, and make a recommendation about the charges for the drivers' wages during the summer.

17

Business Combinations: Acquisitions and Consolidated Financial Statements

LEARNING OBJECTIVES

After studying Chapter 17, you should be able to:
1. Understand how business combinations come about.
2. Describe the primary methods of accounting for business combinations.
3. Understand the role that the accountant plays in the acquisition of one company by another.
4. Explain the concept of consolidated financial statements.
5. Prepare a consolidated balance sheet and income statement.

Mergers and **acquisitions** are in the news. Almost daily we read or hear of some company acquired by another. But this is not a new phenomenon. For a long time now, the financial statements of most large companies have been combinations of the financial statements of several companies. Companies combine for various reasons, including efficiency, diversification, as a defense against takeovers, and to procure tax advantages. **Horizontal integration** involves the combination of companies within the same industries. Many banks have greatly increased in size through such acquisitions. NCNB Corporation acquired First Republic Bank in Texas. (Exhibit 17–1 shows the impact of this acquisition on the earnings of NCNB.) Then two years after rejecting an offer from NCNB, Citizens & Southern Corporation merged with Sovran Financial Corporation to create C&S/Sovran Corporation, a giant bank with $50 billion in assets. In 1991 NCNB acquired C&S/Sovran Corporation, creating Nation's Bank, the third largest bank in the United States. Additional examples of horizontal integration are given in Insights 17–1 and 17–2.

Vertical integration involves the combination of a company with its suppliers or customers. Sometimes companies acquire only portions of other companies. For example, Sonoco Products, an international packaging company, acquired a plant from Boise Cascade. Thus, a com-

---

Exhibit 17–1
Acquisition of First Republic Bank of Texas by NCNB Corporation

NCNB Corporation and Subsidiaries
Management's Discussion and Analysis
First Quarter 1990 Compared to First Quarter 1989
(An excerpt from NCNB First Quarter Report 1990, *page 11)*
Net income for the first quarter of 1990 was $140.062 million, compared to $75.790 million in first quarter of 1989. . . . Primary earnings per share, after dividends on preferred shares, were $.33 for the three months ended March 31, 1990, compared to $.82 for the same period of 1989. Fully diluted earnings per common share were $1.28 for the first quarter of 1990, compared to $.80 for the same interval of 1989.

A principal factor in the increase in net income from 1989 to 1990 was the full benefit of the earnings of NCNB Texas (formerly First Republic Bank) and the utilization by the corporation of the tax benefits of NCNB Texas. NCNB Corporation completed its acquisition of NCNB Texas effective August 1, 1989, and has elected to consolidate the results of NCNB Texas retroactively to January 1, 1989.

INSIGHT 17–1
Beatrice: One Company with Many Parts

Beatrice Foods is an example of a company that achieved phenomenal growth by acquiring other companies. By the mid-1980s Beatrice had acquired more than 400 companies and become the largest food company in the United States. At its peak, Beatrice employed over 100,000 people, had sales approaching $13 billion, and was ranked twenty-sixth in the *Fortune 500*. Brand names owned by Beatrice included Tropicana, Orville Reddenbacher, La Choy, Dannon, Swiss Miss, Meadow Gold, Milk Duds, Hunts, Wesson, Sunbeam, Country Hearth, Peter Pan, Manwich, Butterball, Sizzlean, and many others. However, all the detachable components of Beatrice made the company an ideal target for a leveraged buyout. To acquire Beatrice stock, the Wall Street firm of Kohlberg Kravis Roberts borrowed $8 billion. To pay back the loan, KKR separated and sold the Beatrice-owned companies. The acquisition was begun in 1986, and the sale of the component companies was completed in 1990. The sales proceeds exceeded the purchase price by $9 billion. (Kraft succeeded Beatrice as the nation's largest food company, only to be acquired by Phillip Morris in 1988.)

Interestingly, Beatrice International was sold in 1988 for $985 million to the TLC Group headed by Reginald Lewis, and became the largest black-owned company in the United States.*

*Milton Moskowitz, Robert Levering, and Michael Katz, "Beatrice," *Everybody's Business* (New York: Doubleday, 1990), 24–25.

pany can grow by acquisition in several ways. In this chapter we examine all types of acquisitions and their effects on financial statements.

TYPES OF ACQUISITIONS

The basic types of acquisitions are described in the following paragraphs. As we study acquisitions, we must be careful to distinguish between those transactions resulting in the acquisition of the assets (or net assets) of a company for cash and those resulting from purchases or exchanges of stock.

Asset Purchase

A purchase of assets might be limited to specifically identified assets (specific inventories, receivables, and equipment), might include all the

INSIGHT 17-2
The Pac-Man Defense

In the early video game PAC-man, players manipulate the PAC-man, a mostly defenseless creature chased by demons that seek to catch and swallow it. From time to time, however, the PAC-man quarry stops its flight, becomes aggressive, and turns the tables by pursuing and swallowing the demons. Hence the term *PAC-man defense,* in which a company that is the target of a takeover attempt, avoids the takeover by becoming suddenly aggressive and turning the tables by acquiring the would-be acquirer.

Consider the example of American Brands, Inc., which with sales of over $7 billion, is the third largest liquor manufacturer and the fifth largest cigarette manufacturer in the United States. E-II Holdings was a company composed primarily of companies acquired when Beatrice Foods was broken up and sold. When E-II Holdings targeted American Brands for a takeover, American Brands successfully used the PAC-man defense: it suddenly became aggressive and turned the tables by swallowing the would-be acquirer for $2.7 billion.*

*Milton Moskowitz, Robert Levering, and Michael Katz, "American Brands, Inc.," *Everybody's Business* (New York: Doubleday, 1990), 320–321.

assets of one operation in a multi-operation company (the entire Carthage Company mill), or might consist of all the assets of a company (all Mobile Milling Company assets). When assets are purchased, they are placed on the books of the acquiring company at acquisition cost and cash (or a liability) is credited. Asset purchases have been discussed in earlier chapters.

Net Asset Purchase

In a net asset purchase, the company purchases the assets of a business or business segment and also assumes the related liabilities. If Acme Company acquires all the assets of Baker Company and also assumes Baker's liabilities, Baker will cease to exist as a separate entity.

A company might purchase the assets of a business and also assume its liabilities.

Accounts Receivable	$100,000	
Inventory	200,000	
Equipment	700,000	
Note Payable		$100,000
Mortgage Payable		400,000
Cash		500,000

Stock Purchase

In a stock purchase, a company acquires all or part interest in another company by purchasing its stock. Here the acquiring company can negotiate with the management of the other company or can make a public **tender offer** directly to the stockholders of the company to be acquired—that is, an offer to buy stock at a specified price and thus take control of the company. When a company acquires 5% of another company in a takeover, the acquiring company must make certain disclosures to the Securities and Exchange Commission, the target company, and the stockholders. Exhibit 17–2 is an example of an unsolicited takeover offer extracted from the 1989 annual report of Pennwalt Corporation.

If Acme Company acquired Baker Company by purchasing Baker's outstanding stock, the entry on the books of the acquiring company would be as follows.

Investment in Baker Company	$500,000	
Cash		$500,000

After a stock purchase acquisition, the acquired company still continues as a separate entity.

Following a stock purchase acquisition, the acquired company (Baker) continues as a separate entity, but one now controlled by the acquiring company (Acme). Accounting under the purchase method is fully explained later in the chapter.

Other Combinations

Sometimes two companies merge through a **pooling of interests**, where stock of the acquiring company is exchanged for substantially all

---

Exhibit 17–2
Pennwalt Corporation
Unsolicited Takeover Offer
(extracted from the 1989 annual report of Pennwalt Corporation)

NOTES TO THE CONSOLIDATED FINANCIAL STATEMENTS
17 (In Part): Commitments and Contingencies

On December 13, 1988 Centaur Partners initiated an unsolicited $100 per share offer for the outstanding shares of the Company. On February 14, 1989, this offer was raised to $110 per share. At this time, the Company is unable to predict the outcome of this offer, or the impact that this or any other offer, or related development, may have on the future results or financial condition of the company.

the voting common stock of the acquired company. For financial reporting, the accounts of both companies are simply added together at book value following a pooling of interests. Assets are added to assets, liabilities to liabilities, and equities to equities. The accounts are not restated to market value, as is the case with the purchase method. We will not illustrate the accounting treatment of a pooling of interests.[1]

Another type of business combination is the **joint venture,** a temporary joining of two (or more) companies to undertake a specific project. The companies do not combine financial statements. Insight 17–3 contains *The Wall Street Journal's* definition of many terms currently in the merger news.

THE ACCOUNTANT'S ROLE IN ACQUISITIONS

Accountants are frequently involved in acquisitions as advisors and as auditors to confirm the existence and value of assets. Thus, accountants can be valuable to management before, during, and after the acquisition.

Before the Acquisition

Asset and net asset acquisitions may be negotiated based on book values. For example, in an asset acquisition, a price might be set at the book value of all the inventories, plant, property, and equipment of the Carthage Company mill plus $1,000,000. When managers negotiate prices based on book value, accountants might be consulted about the wording of the contract. To be clear, a contract should specify that book values must be determined using generally accepted accounting principles (GAAP). When there is a choice among GAAP, as between LIFO and FIFO inventory methods, management must understand how the alternative methods affect the purchase price. More frequently, the acquiring company will ask for permission to conduct a preacquisition audit to determine that assets and liabilities are properly recorded. Before acquisition, an audit by accountants and an inspection of assets by consultants can provide crucial guidance in establishing a purchase price.

The acquiring company may conduct a preacquisition audit.

[1] Our discussion focuses on the purchase method because this method is by far the most common form of business combination. The 1989 edition of *Accounting Trends and Techniques,* surveying the annual reports of 600 industrial and merchandising corporations, disclosed the following information regarding the forms of business combination.

	1988	1987	1986	1985
Pooling of Interests	14	21	22	24
Purchase Method	216	194	239	200

During the Acquisition

When there is no preacquisition audit, the contract might provide a period of time prior to the settlement date during which the purchaser is allowed to adjust the price based upon adjustments to the book value of particular assets conveyed. In the Carthage Company mill example, the contract might state that the value of inventories is subject to audit

INSIGHT 17–3
Words of Wall Street

- *Arbitrager*—A person who endeavors to profit from offsetting long and short security positions or from a disparity in market prices on different markets. Although the term can be used of private individuals, it generally refers to broker–dealers or their employees who conduct the arbitrage operations.

- *Baby Bond*—A bond with a face value of less than the usual $1,000. Common face values of baby bonds are $100 and $500.

- *Crown Jewel Defense*—A management strategy to thwart a hostile takeover by agreeing to sell to a third party the company's most valuable asset, or assets (its "crown jewel") in order to make the company less attractive to the raider. Such a defense will bring stockholder suits if the asset is sold for less than its fair market value.

- *Feemail*—Disparaging slang for the legal fees charged by attorneys to settle stockholder suits that attempt to bar management from ransoming shares held by prospective corporate raiders.

- *Floating an Issue*—Industry jargon for the issuance and public distribution of a new issue of securities. For example, "LMN is floating an issue of convertible debentures."

- *Golden Parachute*—One uses a parachute in the event of an air disaster to descend to the ground safely. Similarly, when a company anticipates a takeover or other financial adversity that may "ground" present executives, the executives vote themselves termination or other retirement benefits that will—no matter what the fortunes of the company—provide them a safe passage to financial security.

- *Greenmail*—Slang term used in conjunction with takeover bids, tender offers, or unfriendly proxy flights. The concept is similar to blackmail. Greenmail involves the purchase of a significant block of stock for one of two purposes: either to sell the block to a corporate raider, or to tender it to the company for a premium price. Because the sale of the block to a raider would threaten the continuity of management, management feels impelled to buy the shares at a premium, rather than have the shares sold to an unfriendly corporate raider.

- *Insider*—A person who (1) controls a corporation, (2) owns 10% or more of a company's stock, or (3) has inside information. The term is used most often of the directors and elected officers of a corporation.

continued

INSIGHT 17–3
Continued

- *Junk Bond*—Bonds with a credit rating of BB or lower. Such bonds have speculative overtones.

- *Penny Stocks*—Wall Street expression for relatively low-priced, highly speculative securities. Although the term implies securities priced at less than $1 per share, it is not limited to such shares. Many member firms have special margin maintenance requirements for such shares and often limit purchases of such shares to unsolicited orders by clients.

- *Poison Pill*—A corporate finance tactic to defend against unfriendly takeovers in which the "poison pill" is generally an issue of convertible preferred stock distributed as a stock dividend to current stockholders. The preferred stock is convertible into a number of common shares equal to or greater than the present number of outstanding shares. However, because of dividend adjustments, there is little incentive to convert unless there is a takeover. The takeover attempt, therefore, becomes its own "poison" because it will vastly increase the price that will have to be paid for the company.

- *Raider*—Anyone who tries to buy control of a company's stock in oder to install new management. Federal law places restrictions on raiders if they become control persons—that is, holders of 10% or more of a company's outstanding stock. The term is not generally used of the purchaser who is buying stock as an investment.

- *Red Herring*—A preliminary prospectus whose name arises from the caveat, printed in red along the left border of the cover, warning the reader that the document does not contain all of the information about the issue and that some of the information may be changed before the final prospectus is issued.

- *Scorched Earth Tactic*—A corporate defense tactic whereby an unwilling takeover target discourages bidders by selling off assets or by entering into long-term contractual commitments to make itself less attractive to the buyer.

- *Tombstone*—The newspaper advertisement of a public distribution of securities. The advertisement, which may be made before or after the fact, is basically a public–relations event for the underwriting syndicate. It is called a tombstone because the announcement is factual and refers the reader to the prospectus, the offering circular, or the official statement for details of the issue.

- *White Knight*—A person or corporation who saves a corporation from an unfriendly takeover by, in turn, taking over the corporation.

and adjustment, but the value of equipment is not. In such case, auditors will inspect inventories for obsolete or nonexistent goods. They will confirm allowances for reducing inventories to the lower of cost or market. Auditors will examine all book values that can be adjusted. The adjustment period is usually very short, so auditors will direct their attention to asset values that can be adjusted and will confine their work to searching for overstatements that can be adjusted to reduce the purchase price. Understatements (assets with book value less than market value) are of no concern at this point.

After the Acquisition

When a company acquires the assets or net assets of another, the operations of the acquired entity (a single plant, for example) will generally be merged with the operations of the acquiring company. In this case, once the acquisition is complete, accountants will begin consolidating the different bookkeeping systems. Even if operations and accounting systems are not to be combined (as is usually the case in a stock investment or pooling of interests), management might want a complete audit of the entity acquired, with attention to efficiency and effectiveness, rather than simply the fairness of financial statements. Even when a complete audit is not undertaken, accountants can be of assistance in evaluating the effectiveness of duplicate functions and management groups that will be combined and reduced. Insight 17−4 tells how accountants assisted in one acquisition.

CONSOLIDATED FINANCIAL STATEMENTS

When one company owns more than 50% of the stock of another, the company has a controlling interest.

When a company invests in the stock of another company, the balance sheet classification depends on the length of time that management intends to hold the stock. When management intends to hold the stock for more than one year, the stock is shown on the balance sheet as a noncurrent asset, Investments. The investor (acquiring) company, like any shareholder, is able to participate in the management of the investee (acquired) company. When a company owns more than 50% of the outstanding stock of another company, the investor company, referred to as the **parent,** is said to have a controlling interest in the investee company, referred to as the **subsidiary.** When a company (the parent) owns a majority of the stock of another company (the subsidiary), the companies are, for all practical purposes, combined, and the financial statements of the two companies are consolidated and shown as if the two companies were one **economic entity.** The process of combining the companies is called **consolidation.** The financial statements of a parent company combined with its subsidiary are called **consolidated financial statements.** The parent and its subsidiary (or subsidiaries) are referred to as **affiliated** companies.

An economic entity, as we explained in Chapter 1, is an activity for which separate accounting records can be created. The parent and its subsidiary are each economic entities for which separate account-

INSIGHT 17–4
Accountants Save Money in Acquisitions

Managers of a Denver company saved almost $2 million by involving the company's internal auditors in the acquisition of a large manufacturer. The purchase price negotiated by management was based on a percentage of the net sales of the manufacturer, plus a multiple of its earnings. The acquiring company's accountants were able to significantly reduce the purchase price in two ways.

First, on examining the manufacturer's accounting records, the auditors found that a large maintenance expense in the previous year that had significant future benefit should actually have been treated as an asset (an addition to equipment) and depreciated over its useful life. When this was done, the additional depreciation expense reduced the manufacturer's earnings and, hence, the cost of acquiring the company. This one discovery reduced the acquisition price by $1,500,000.

Additionally, unrealistically long lives had been used to calculate depreciation on other equipment. Shorter lives resulted in more annual depreciation expense. Here again, additional depreciation expense reduced both the net income of the manufacturer and the cost of the acquisition.

How to Save Millions, E. Theodore Keys, Jr. ed., (Altamonte Springs, FL: Institute of Internal Auditors, 1988), 71–72.

ing records are kept and for which separate financial statements are issued. But because of the common control (stockholders control the parent and, through the parent, also control the subsidiary), the combined companies can also be treated as a single economic entity. Stockholders, creditors and others must see the financial statements of the combined entity if they are to understand the relationship between the companies and its economic implications.[2] The requirement that affiliated companies publish consolidated financial statements reflects the concept of **substance over form**: the affiliated companies, are, in substance, one economic entity, regardless of their separate legal forms. Virtually all large companies issue consolidated statements.[3]

Affiliated companies are in substance one economic entity.

We illustrate consolidated statements using the financial statements of a parent, Broom, Inc., and its subsidiary, Lite Touch Industries. Suppose

[2] Each company in an affiliated group (parent or subsidiary) may issue separate company financial statements for regulatory agencies or for special purposes such as obtaining financing or credit from suppliers.

[3] Of the 600 industrial and merchandising companies cited in the 1989 edition of *Accounting Trends and Techniques,* only 10 companies did not publish consolidated financial statements for 1988.

Broom buys 100% of the stock of Lite Touch for the book value of its owners' equity ($30,000 of common stock plus retained earnings of $10,000). We assume that the book value and fair value of Broom's owners' equity are equal. The balance sheet equation for Lite Touch is shown below.

Assets = Liabilities + Owners' Equity
$100,000 = $60,000   + $40,000

The entry for the purchase of Lite Touch stock is as follows:

| Investment in Lite Touch | $40,000 | |
| Cash | | $40,000 |

What has Broom purchased? Since the fair market value and the book value of the Lite Touch owners' equity are $40,000, Broom has purchased these property rights. (You will remember from Chapter 1 that owners' equity means owners' property rights. It is useful here to think of the owners' equity amount as the amount of owners' property rights.) If Broom shows the stock simply as an investment of $40,000, the true nature of the relationship is not disclosed, for Broom now owns every asset that Lite Touch owns and owes every debt that Lite Touch owes. If Broom is to properly disclose its ownership of Lite Touch, it must show every asset owned and debt owed by Lite Touch. The balance sheet equation of Broom before the purchase of the Lite Touch stock follows.

Assets = Liabilities + Owners' Equity
$500,000 = $300,000 + $200,000

Total assets for Broom are the same before and after the investment in Lite Touch. (Investment in Lite Touch is debited, but Cash is credited.)
    When Broom prepares consolidated financial statements, Broom must remove the $40,000 investment in Lite Touch and replace it with the individual assets and liabilities of Lite Touch. Note that the total owners' equity of Broom is not changed by the consolidation.

	Assets	=	Liabilities	+	Owners' Equity
Broom before consolidation	$500,000	=	$300,000	+	$200,000
Less investment in Lite Touch	(40,000)				
Plus the assets and liabilities of Lite Touch	100,000		60,000		
B consolidated balance sheet	$560,000	=	$360,000	+	$200,000

Exhibit 17–3
Simple Consolidation

	Broom (Parent)	Lite Touch (Subsidiary)	Eliminating Entries	Consolidated Statements
Assets				
Cash	$ 60,000	$ 10,000		$ 70,000
Inventory	30,000	15,000		45,000
Receivables	70,000	25,000		95,000
Property (net)	300,000	50,000		350,000
Investment—Lite Touch	40,000	-	(40,000)	
Total assets	$500,000	$100,000		$560,000
Liabilities				
Payables	$100,000	30,000		130,000
Mortgage note	20C,000	30,000		230,000
Total liabilities	$300,000	60,000		360,000
Owners' Equity				
Common stock	150,000	30,000	(30,000)	150,000
Retained earnings	50,000	10,000	(10,000)	50,000
Total owners' equity	200,000	40,000		200,000
Total equities	$500,000	$100,000		$560,000

The consolidation of the individual accounts of Broom and Lite Touch is shown in Exhibit 17–3. Eliminating entries enclosed in parentheses are reductions. The eliminating entry that removes the $40,000 investment from the balance sheet of Broom also removes the owners' equity from the balance sheet of Lite Touch. In consolidation, the net assets of Lite Touch are added to those of Broom, resulting in consolidated net assets of $200,000 ($560,000 − $360,000), the same as Broom's net assets before consolidation, that is $200,000, or $500,000 − $300,000 above. This entry is shown in the "Eliminating Entries" column in Exhibit 17–3.

One eliminating entry removes the investment account from the parent's balance sheet and the owners' equity accounts from the subsidiary's balance sheet.

Common Stock	$30,000	
Retained Earnings	10,000	
Investment in Lite Touch		$40,000

Several conditions make the preparation of consolidated financial statements more complicated. First, remember that acquiring more than 50% of the voting stock enables the parent to control the operations of its subsidiary and requires the preparation of consolidated statements. When a parent owns more than 50% but less than 100%, **minority shareholders** own the remainder and their **minority interest** must be shown in the consolidated financial statements. Second, the net assets of a company might be purchased at a cost greater than its book value. When this happens, the carrying values of the assets are increased to reflect their fair market value. Any excess of the price paid for net assets over their fair market value is called **goodwill.** Goodwill is an intangible asset and is amortized to expense over a period not to exceed 40 years.

Any excess of the price paid by the parent over the fair market value of the subsidiary's net assets is called goodwill.

Finally, the parent might have borrowed (lent) money from (to) its subsidiary that has not yet been repaid at the date the consolidated financial statements are prepared. Also, the company might have had sales transactions with its subsidiary during the course of the year. Since these transactions do not represent business activity with entities outside the firm (the subsidiary is part of the parent), their effects must be eliminated when consolidated statements are prepared. If these transactions are not eliminated, assets, liabilities, revenues, and expenses of the combined company will all be overstated.

To illustrate, suppose that Broom purchased 80% of Lite Touch common stock (and, hence, 80% of Lite Touch owners' equity or net assets) for $42,000, which is $10,000 more than the fair market value of the Lite Touch net assets ($40,000 total book value x 80% = $32,000). For simplicity, we assume the fair market value of Lite Touch assets equals their book value. Suppose further that Broom owes Lite Touch $5,000 at the balance sheet date. The entry for the investment is as follows:

Investment in Lite Touch	$42,000	
Cash		$42,000

Remember, the $42,000 represents an 80% investment in Lite Touch. The reconciliation of the price paid and the net assets (value) received is as follows:

Lite Touch owners' equity	$40,000
Percentage acquired	× .80
Value Acquired	32,000
Plus Excess	10,000
Investment in Lite Touch	$42,000

Again, when Broom wishes to prepare consolidated financial statements, it must remove the Investment in Lite Touch account and replace it with the individual assets and liabilities of Lite Touch. Since Broom owns only 80% of Lite Touch stock (or net assets), the $42,000 investment may be eliminated against only 80% of the Lite Touch owners' equity. When the investment is eliminated against 80% of Lite Touch owners' equity, the $10,000 excess over fair market value (here equal to book value) must be allocated and debited to goodwill.

Common Stock	$30,000	
Retained Earnings	10,000	
Goodwill ($42,000 − $32,000)	10,000	
Investment in Lite Touch		$42,000
Minority Interest		8,000

The $5,000 loan must also be removed from both the receivables and payable of the affiliated companies. The eliminating entry is:

Payables	$ 5,000	
Receivables		$ 5,000

The $6,000 in the Common Stock account ($30,000 − $24,000), and the $2,000 in Retained Earnings account ($10,000 − $8,000) that remain after eliminating the Broom investment are shown as an $8,000 minority interest in the consolidated financial statements. This minority interest is the interest of the other (outside) stockholders in the stock (and hence the net assets) of Lite Touch. The minority interest and all the combining entries are shown in Exhibit 17−4.

When a sale has taken place between a parent and a subsidiary, all effects of the sale must be removed. Sales between a parent and its subsidiary are similar to a mother who buys cookies baked by her preteen son. The son has received $5. Has the family income risen by $5? Of course not. Family income rises only when the cookies are sold to someone outside the family. Returning to our original example, suppose Broom buys from its 100% owned subsidiary, Lite Touch, merchandise for $20,000 that had cost $12,000. Broom has not sold the inventory to another company outside the consolidated "family" at the balance sheet date. Lite Touch has recorded revenue of $20,000, cost of goods sold of $12,000, and profit of $8,000. Has the income of the consolidated entity (parent and subsidiary) risen? Of course not. Consolidated income rises only when the inventory is sold (by parent or subsidiary) to a company outside the consolidated "family."

To eliminate the effects of the sale between Lite Touch and Broom the following workpaper entries simply reverse the effects of the orig-

Exhibit 17–4
Consolidation with Complications

	Broom (Parent)	Lite Touch (Subsidiary)	Eliminating Entries	Consolidated Statements
Assets				
Cash	$ 58,000	$ 10,000		$ 68,000
Inventory	30,000	15,000		45,000
Receivables	70,000	25,000	(5,000)	90,000
Property (net)	300,000	50,000		350,000
Investment—Lite Touch	42,000	-	(42,000)	
Goodwill			10,000	10,000
Total assets	$500,000	$100,000		$563,000
Liabilities				
Payables	$100,000	30,000	(5,000)	$125,000
Mortgage note	200,000	30,000		230,000
Total liabilities	300,000	60,000		355,000
Owners' Equity				
Common stock	150,000	30,000	(30,000)	150,000
Retained earnings	50,000	10,000	(10,000)	50,000
Minority interest			8,000	8,000
Total owners' equity	200,000	40,000		208,000
Total Equities	$500,000	$100,000		$563,000

inal transactions. Visualize the original entries made on the books of Lite Touch and Broom:

Lite Touch

Cash	$20,000	
Revenues		$20,000
Cost of Goods Sold	12,000	
Inventory		12,000

Broom

Inventory	$20,000	
Cash		$20,000

To remove the merchandise at its intercompany sales price from Broom's inventory and the intercompany revenue from Lite Touch's income statement, we make the following entry.

Revenues	$20,000	
Inventory		$20,000

To place the merchandise back in inventory at its original cost and remove the intercompany cost of goods sold from Lite Touch's income statement, we make the following entry.

Inventory	$12,000	
Cost of Goods Sold		$12,000

The cash account does not have to be adjusted, since the debit on the books of Lite Touch and the credit on the books of Broom offset each other, resulting in a cash balance that is correct for the consolidated entity.

Exhibit 17–5 shows the effect of this intercompany sale on the consolidated income statement and balance sheet. This exhibit uses the beginning balance sheets from Exhibit 17–3 and illustrates the workpaper eliminations that must be made in consolidating financial statements.

SUMMARY

Mergers and acquisitions occur in several ways. A company may acquire all or a portion of another company, or two companies may decide to combine and continue as one. Acquisitions may take the form of horizontal or vertical integration. They may prevent a takeover. Also, a company might purchase only specific assets or all of the assets of another company.

The most popular method used to account for the acquisition of the net assets of a company is called the purchase method. Using this method, one company acquires the net assets of another by paying cash or other assets to the acquired company. Also, a company might acquire control over the net assets of another company by purchasing the stock of another company. In the pooling of interests method, both companies exchange shares of stock and continue as one entity.

Accountants can assist management before, during and after an acquisition. Before acquisition, accountants might assist with a preacqui-

Exhibit 17–5
Consolidation with Intercompany Sales
(Parent Owns 100% of Subsidiary Stock)

	Broom (Parent)	Lite Touch (Subsidiary)	Eliminating Entries	Consolidated Statements
Income Statement				
Sales	$100,000	$ 30,000	($20,000)	$110,000
Cost of goods sold	70,000	20,000	(12,000)	78,000
Gross profit	30,000	10,000	(8,000)	32,000
Other expenses	20,000	6,000		26,000
Net income	$ 10,000	$ 4,000	($8,000)*	$ 6,000
Balance Sheet				
Assets				
Cash	$ 60,000	$ 10,000		$ 70,000
Inventory	30,000	15,000	(20,000)	
			12,000	37,000
Receivables	70,000	25,000		95,000
Property (net)	300,000	50,000		350,000
Investment—Lite Touch	40,000	-	(40,000)	
Total assets	$500,000	$100,000	($48,000)	$552,000
Liabilities				
Payables	$100,000	30,000		130,000
Mortgage note	200,000	30,000		230,000
Total liabilities	300,000	60,000		360,000
Owners' Equity				
Common stock	150,000	30,000	(30,000)	150,000
Retained earnings	50,000	10,000	(10,000)	
			(8,000)*	42,000
Total owners' equity	200,000	40,000	(48,000)	192,000
Total equities	$500,000	$100,000	($48,000)	$552,000

*The $8,000 reduction in combined earnings results in an $8,000 reduction in combined retained earnings. Both effects are shown in this example.

sition audit to determine the proper asset and liability values in order to aid management in establishing a purchase price. When a preacquisition audit is not conducted, accountants might be called upon to examine purchased assets for possible adjustment of the purchase price. The acquired company might also be initially audited by accountants, and accountants prepare the consolidated financial statements as well.

A company that acquires more than 50% of the outstanding voting stock of an acquired company is called the parent company. The acquired company is called the subsidiary. In this case the financial statements of the companies are consolidated. The companies' financial statements are consolidated because the company is really one economic entity. This form of presentation is consistent with the concept of substance over form, that is, the financial statements of the companies are presented as if they were one company, regardless of their legal form.

A company that has an investment of over 50% of the voting stock of another company carries that investment in an account called Investment in Subsidiary (normally using the subsidiary's name). When consolidated financial statements are prepared, the parent company removes the Investment in Subsidiary account and replaces it with the subsidiary's individual assets and liabilities, which are added to those of the parent. The eliminating entry that removes the Investment account from the parent's balance sheet also removes the owners' equity accounts from the subsidiary's balance sheet to avoid double counting. When the parent owns more than 50% of the voting stock but less than 100%, minority shareholders own the remainder, and their minority interest is shown as a reduction in arriving at consolidated net income. The minority interest in the consolidated net assets is shown as a separate component of consolidated owners' equity. If the net assets of an acquired company are purchased at an amount greater than their book value, the carrying values of those assets are increased to reflect fair market value. Any remaining excess is called goodwill and amortized to expense over a period not to exceed 40 years. Finally, intercompany payables, receivables, and sales must be eliminated in preparing the consolidated balance sheet and the income statement.

DEMONSTRATION PROBLEM

Irish Company purchased 100% of the outstanding stock of Dutch Company for 100% of the book value of the Dutch Company owners' equity. During the year, Dutch sold merchandise costing $8,000 to Irish for $10,000. Income statement and balance sheet amounts for the two companies, shown below, include a $5,000 account payable from Irish to Dutch.

	Irish (parent)	Dutch (subsidiary)
Income Statement		
Sales	$ 50,000	$25,000
Cost of sales	30,000	15,000
Gross profit	20,000	10,000
Other expenses	15,000	6,000
Net income	$ 5,000	$ 4,000
Balance Sheet		
Assets		
Current assets	$ 30,000	$20,000
Property (net)	125,000	70,000
Investment in Dutch	25,000	–
Total assets	$180,000	$90,000
Liabilities		
Current liabilities	$ 20,000	$15,000
Bonds payable	100,000	50,000
Total liabilities	$120,000	$65,000
Owners' Equity		
Common stock	$ 40,000	$10,000
Retained earnings	20,000	15,000
Total owners' equity	60,000	25,000
Total equities	$180,000	$90,000

REQUIRED:

Prepare a worksheet showing the eliminating entries and the consolidated income statement and balance sheet amounts.

Solution to Demonstration Problem

The solution requires the steps shown in the combining schedule below. (The steps need not be done in the order listed.) Notice that each step shows equal debits and credits.

1. The $10,000 sale and related cost of goods sold ($8,000) and net income ($2,000) are eliminated when the two income statements are combined.

2. The inventory is removed from the current assets of Dutch (where it is carried at its intercompany cost of $10,000) and placed in the current assets of the combined company at its original cost of $8,000. The $2,000 difference is a reduction in the combined retained earnings.
3. The $5,000 intercompany debt is removed from both current assets and current liabilities.
4. The investment in Dutch is eliminated against the Dutch common stock and retained earnings.

	Irish (parent)	Dutch (subsidiary)	Eliminating Entries	Consolidated Statement
Income Statement				
Sales	$ 50,000	$25,000	($10,000)	$ 65,000
Cost of sales	30,000	15,000	(8,000)	37,000
Gross profit	20,000	10,000	(2,000)	28,000
Other expenses	15,000	6,000		21,000
Net income	$ 5,000	$ 4,000	($ 2,000)*	$ 7,000
Balance Sheet:				
Assets				
Current assets	$ 30,000	$20,000	(5,000)	$ 43,000
			(10,000)	
			8,000	
Property (net)	125,000	70,000		195,000
Investment in Dutch	25,000	–	(25,000)	
Total assets	$180,000	$90,000	($32,000)	$238,000
Liabilities				
Current liabilities	$ 20,000	15,000	(5,000)	$ 30,000
Bonds payable	100,000	50,000		150,000
Total liabilities	$120,000	65,000		$180,000
Owners' Equity				
Common Stock	$ 40,000	10,000	(10,000)	$ 40,000
Retained earnings	20,000	15,000	(15,000)	18,000
			(2,000)*	
Total owners' equity	60,000	25,000	(27,000)	58,000
Total equities	$180,000	$90,000	($32,000)	$238,000

*The $2,000 reduction in combined earnings results in a $2,000 reduction in combined retained earnings.

Key Terms

acquisition

affiliate

consolidated financial
    statements

consolidation

economic entity

goodwill

horizontal integration

joint venture

merger

minority interest

minority shareholders

parent

pooling of interests method

purchase method

subsidiary

substance over form

tender offer

vertical integration

ASSIGNMENTS

17–1 Growing by Acquisition

Acquisitions occur in several ways. A company may acquire all or part of another company, or two companies may combine and continue as one.

REQUIRED:

1. Describe the different types of acquisitions a company might make, and explain what a merger and a joint venture are.

2. Which of the different types of acquisitions could be considered a merger?

17–2 After the Acquisition

XYZ Corporation merges with ABC Company in a pooling of interests. Both companies manufacture and sell tires for recreational vehicles. Both companies sell in the Midwest, although XYZ has its sales headquarters, including market research, in Chicago, and ABC is located in Kansas City. Both companies have internal audit staffs, technical service centers, and product-development programs. Mark Lewis, president of the new, combined company, believes the company must "trim down" to get "lean and mean" if profit goals are to be achieved. He has ordered the accountants to begin combining the accounting systems of the two companies.

REQUIRED:

In what other ways might Mark Lewis use the accountants to make the merger successful?

17–3 Using Accountants in Acquisitions

Behlow Brassworks is considering acquiring the net assets of the Napa Valley division of a major competitor. Contract negotiations have just begun.

REQUIRED:

How can Behlow Brassworks get the most benefit from its accountants during the acquisition?

17–4 Net Asset Purchase

Brown Company buys the inventories, plant, property, and equipment, and assumes the debt of the Apple Company's Decatur plant. The purchase contract is for the assets at net book value plus $500,000. The $500,000 is deemed to be the difference between the fair market value and book value of plant, property, and equipment. The book value of the inventories is $400,000 and the book value of the plant, property, and equipment is $2,100,000. There is a $800,000 mortgage on the plant. Brown believes the fair market value of the inventory acquired is equal to its book value.

REQUIRED:

1. What are the potential problems in a contract to purchase based on the book value of assets?
2. How might management have used the accountants in negotiating the asset acquisition?
3. Make the journal entry for Brown Company's asset acquisition.

17–5 Stock Purchase Acquisition

Dalton Company acquired Jones Company by purchasing 100% of Jones's outstanding common stock for $300,000. Following the stock purchase, Jones continued to operate as a separate entity, owned and controlled by Dalton.

REQUIRED:

Make the journal entry to record Dalton's investment in Jones stock.

17–6 Consolidated Balance Sheets Using the Balance Sheet Equation

Parent Company buys 100% of the stock of Subsidiary Company for the book value of its owners' equity (common stock plus retained earnings). The balance sheet totals for both companies immediately before the stock purchase are shown below.

	Assets	=	Liabilities	+	Owners' Equity
Parent Company	$700,000	=	$400,000	+	$300,000
Subsidiary Company	$200,000	=	$150,000	+	$ 50,000

REQUIRED:

1. Make the journal entry for the Parent Company investment in Subsidiary Company stock.
2. What are the balance sheet totals of Parent Company immediately after the stock purchase? Of Subsidiary Company?
3. Prepare a schedule showing the balance sheet totals for Parent Company that would appear in the consolidated statements.
4. If Parent Company had common stock of $200,000 and retained earnings of $100,000 before the consolidation, construct the owners' equity section of the consolidated balance sheet.

17–7   Minority Interest Using the Balance Sheet Equation

Parent Company buys 90% of the stock of Subsidiary Company for 90% of the book value of its owners' equity (common stock plus retained earnings). The balance sheet totals for both companies immediately before the stock purchase are shown below.

	Assets	=	Liabilities	+	Owners' Equity
Parent Company	$700,000	=	$400,000	+	$300,000
Subsidiary Company	$200,000	=	$150,000	+	$ 50,000

The owners' equity accounts of Parent and Subsidiary were composed of:

	Parent	Subsidiary
Common stock	$200,000	$25,000
Retained earnings	100,000	25,000

REQUIRED:

1. Make the journal entry for the Parent Company investment in Subsidiary Company stock.
2. Prepare a schedule showing the balance sheet totals for Parent Company that would appear in the consolidated statements.
3. Show the account balances in the owners equity section of the consolidated balance sheet.

17–8   Goodwill Using the Balance Sheet Equation

Parent Company buys 100% of the stock of Subsidiary Company for the book value of its owners' equity (common stock plus retained earnings) plus $10,000. The fair market value of the Subsidiary assets is equal to their book value. The balance sheet totals for both companies immediately before the stock purchase are shown below.

	Assets	=	Liabilities	+	Owners' Equity
Parent Company	$700,000	=	$400,000	+	$300,000
Subsidiary Company	$200,000	=	$150,000	+	$ 50,000

REQUIRED:

1. Make the journal entry for the Parent Company investment in Subsidiary Company stock.

2. Prepare a schedule showing the balance sheet totals for Parent Company that would appear in the consolidated statements.

3. How would the $10,000 paid above the fair market value of the Subsidiary Company net assets be shown in the consolidated financial statements?

17–9 Preparing Simple Consolidated Statements, 100% Stock Purchased

Apple Company purchased 100% of the outstanding stock of Peach Company for the book value of the Peach Company owners' equity. Balance sheet amounts for the two companies are shown below.

	Apple (parent)	Peach (subsidiary)
Assets		
Current assets	$ 50,000	$ 30,000
Property (net)	600,000	100,000
Investment in Peach	60,000	–
Total assets	$710,000	$130,000
Liabilities		
Current liabilities	$160,000	$ 20,000
Mortgage note	300,000	50,000
Total liabilities	460,000	70,000
Owners' Equity		
Common stock	200,000	40,000
Retained earnings	50,000	20,000
Total owners' equity	250,000	60,000
Total equities	$710,000	$130,000

REQUIRED:

1. Give the journal entry for the investment in Peach.
2. Prepare a worksheet showing the eliminating entries and the consolidated balance sheet amounts.

 17–10   Minority Interest In Consolidated Statements

Apple Company purchases 80% of Peach Company common stock for an amount equal to 80% of the book value of the common stock. Balance sheet amounts for the two companies appear below.

	Apple (Parent)	Peach (Subsidiary)
Assets		
Current assets	$ 62,000	$ 30,000
Property (net)	600,000	100,000
Investment in Peach	48,000	–
Total assets	$710,000	$130,000
Liabilities		
Current liabilities	$160,000	$ 20,000
Mortgage note	300,000	50,000
Total liabilities	460,000	70,000
Owners' Equity		
Common stock	200,000	40,000
Retained earnings	50,000	20,000
Total owners' equity	250,000	60,000
Total equities	$710,000	$130,000

REQUIRED:

1. Give the journal entry for the investment in Peach.
2. Prepare a worksheet showing the combining entries and the consolidated balance sheet amounts, including minority interest.

17–11   Goodwill in Consolidated Statements, 100% Stock Purchased

Apple Company purchased 100% of the outstanding stock of Peach Company for $15,000 over the book value of the Peach Company owners' equity. Balance sheet amounts for the two companies are shown below.

	Apple (Parent)	Peach (Subsidiary)
Assets		
Current assets	$ 35,000	$ 30,000
Property (net)	600,000	100,000
Investment in Peach	75,000	–
Total assets	$710,000	$130,000
Liabilities		
Current liabilities	$160,000	$ 20,000
Mortgage note	300,000	50,000
Total liabilities	460,000	70,000
Owners' Equity		
Common stock	200,000	40,000
Retained earnings	50,000	20,000
Total owners' equity	250,000	60,000
Total equities	$710,000	$130,000

REQUIRED:

1. Give the journal entry for the investment in Peach.
2. Prepare a worksheet showing the eliminating entries and the consolidated balance sheet amounts.

17–12 Goodwill in Consolidated Statements, 90% Stock Purchased

Apple Company purchased 90% of the outstanding stock of Peach Company for $5,000 over the book value of 90% the book value of the Peach Company owners' equity. Balance sheet amounts for the two companies are shown below.

	Apple (Parent)	Peach (Subsidiary)
Assets		
Current Assets	$ 51,000	$ 30,000
Property (net)	600,000	100,000
Investment in Peach	59,000	–
Total Assets	$710,000	$130,000

	Apple (Parent)	Peach (Subsidiary)
Liabilities		
Current liabilities	$160,000	$ 20,000
Mortgage note	300,000	50,000
Total liabilities	460,000	70,000
Owners' Equity		
Common stock	200,000	40,000
Retained earnings	50,000	20,000
Total owners' equity	$250,000	$ 60,000
Total equities	$710,000	$130,000

REQUIRED:

1. Give the journal entry for the investment in Peach.
2. Prepare a worksheet showing the eliminating entries and the consolidated balance sheet amounts.

17–13   Consolidation with Intercompany Debt, 80% Ownership

Apple Company purchased 80% of the outstanding stock of Peach Company for 80% of the book value of the Peach Company owners' equity. Balance sheet amounts for the two companies, shown below, include a $15,000 one month note payable from Apple to Peach.

	Apple (Parent)	Peach (Subsidiary)
Assets		
Current assets	$ 62,000	$ 30,000
Property (net)	600,000	100,000
Investment in Peach	48,000	–
Total assets	$710,000	$130,000
Liabilities		
Current liabilities	$160,000	$ 20,000
Mortgage note	300,000	50,000
Total liabilities	460,000	70,000
Owners' Equity		
Common stock	200,000	40,000
Retained earnings	50,000	20,000
Total owners' equity	$250,000	$ 60,000
Total equities	$710,000	$130,000

REQUIRED:

1. Give the journal entry for the investment in Peach.

2. Prepare a worksheet showing the eliminating entries and the consolidated balance sheet amounts.

17–14 Consolidated Income Statements with Intercompany Sales

Apple Company owns 100% of the Peach Company common stock. During the year, Apple sold merchandise costing $10,000 to Peach for $15,000. Peach sold half the merchandise purchased from Apple to Pear Company for $9,000. The income statement amounts for both Apple and Peach follow.

	Apple (parent)	Peach (subsidiary)
Income Statement		
Sales	$150,000	$50,000
Cost of Sales	75,000	40,000
Gross Profit	75,000	10,000
Other Expenses	60,000	3,000
Net Income	$ 15,000	$ 7,000

REQUIRED:

What is the effect of the sale to Pear Company on the consolidated income statements?

17–15 Consolidated Statements, Intercompany Debt and Sales

Apple Company purchased 100% of the outstanding stock of Peach Company for 100% of the book value of the Peach Company owners' equity. During the year, Peach sold merchandise costing $9,000 to Apple for $14,000. Balance sheet amounts for the two companies, shown below, include an $11,000 account payable from Apple to Peach.

Income Statement:

	Apple (parent)	Peach (subsidiary)
Sales	$150,000	$50,000
Cost of Sales	75,000	40,000
Gross Profit	75,000	10,000
Other Expenses	60,000	3,000
Net Income	$ 15,000	$ 7,000

	Apple (parent)	Peach (subsidiary)
Balance Sheet:		
Assets		
Current assets	$ 50,000	$ 30,000
Property (net)	600,000	100,000
Investment in Peach	60,000	–
Total assets	$710,000	$130,000
Liabilities		
Current liabilities	$160,000	$ 20,000
Mortgage note	300,000	50,000
Total liabilities	460,000	70,000
Owners' Equity		
Common stock	200,000	40,000
Retained earnings	50,000	20,000
Total owners' equity	250,000	60,000
Total equities	$710,000	$130,000

REQUIRED:

Prepare a worksheet showing the combining entries and the consolidated income statement and balance sheet amounts.

17–16   Wal-Mart Acquisitions

Study the Wal-Mart annual report.

REQUIRED:

1. Does Wal-Mart publish consolidated financial statements?

2. Did Wal-Mart have any acquisition activity in 1990? (Hint: Read the notes to the financial statements and/or the letter to shareholders.)

3. What does Note 1 say about Wal-Mart's accounting policies regarding consolidations?

17–17 DECISION CASE:
AUDITING DURING THE ACQUISITION

Jan Mellon is the auditor in charge of an audit team assigned to confirm the existence of the assets acquired in a net asset purchase of a bottling plant by the Drink Lite Company.

"We have thirty days to confirm the book value of the inventories here," Jan explained. "During that time, the purchase contract allows management to change the purchase price to reflect discrepancies we find. So ignore understatements. And ignore assets other than inventory."

"Gee," Timothy observed, "this is my first acquisition audit, but it seems that the value of equipment here is much greater than the value of inventory on hand. Shouldn't we look at that first? And why only overstatements? Couldn't there also be errors and omissions that cause understatements as well? It seems strange to ignore this possibility."

REQUIRED:

Respond to Timothy.

17–18 DECISION CASE:
CONSOLIDATED STATEMENTS

Jackie Peters is confused. "I can see," Jackie puzzled, "that if one company buys a plant or a division of another company, those assets become part of the purchasing company and should be shown in the financial statements just like any other assets. But when a company buys stock of another company— even all the stock of another company — it is the stock that the investing company owns, not the individual assets. I can't see how consolidated statements do anything but confuse the stockholders."

REQUIRED:

Explain to Jackie why consolidated financial statements are useful to stockholders. Include an explanation of "substance over form."

17–19 DECISION CASE:
NET ASSET PURCHASE

Clarkston Company buys all the receivables, inventories, plant, property, and equipment of the Milldale Company's Fall River plant for cash. The purchase contract is for the net assets at book value, per GAAP, plus $400,000. The book value of raw material inventory and parts and supplies inventory can be adjusted for obsolete, damaged, or nonexistent goods for two months following the signing of the purchase contract. No other book values can be adjusted, except as necessary to bring them in conformity with GAAP. The amount paid above book value is due to the fair market value of plant and equipment. All other assets are thought to have fair market values equal to their book values. The purchase price is to be split among the assets acquired in proportion to their fair market values. Clarkston will assume the mortgage on the Fall River plant. The net assets of the Milldale Company's Fall River plant are shown below.

Asset	Book Value
Receivables	$150,000
Inventories:	
Raw materials	100,000
Parts and supplies	70,000
Finished goods	100,000
Plant and equipment	800,000
Land	400,000
Long-term debt	500,000

REQUIRED:

During the two months after the purchase contract, the inventory of parts and supplies is found to be overstated by $20,000. Construct a schedule adjusting the accounts of the Fall River plant to fair market value, and make the journal entry for the acquisition.

18

Auditors, Audit Reports, and Internal Control

LEARNING OBJECTIVES

After studying Chapter 18, you should be able to:
1. Understand what auditors do, and distinguish between the objectives of internal and external auditors.
2. Discuss the objectives of internal controls.
3. Describe several internal controls and how they assist the auditor.
4. Tell how auditors use sampling and analytical procedures.
5. Discuss the components in an annual report and the types of opinions external auditors give.
6. Discuss the elements in an internal auditor's report.

Annual reports examined by an independent Certified Public Accountant (CPA) make it possible for investors and creditors to decide whether to buy stock in or issue credit to a company they have never seen, managed by people they have never met. Internal auditors, reporting to the Board of Directors, issue reports that help managers run operations more efficiently and effectively. All auditors rely on internal controls in making their examinations. This chapter discusses the roles of internal and external auditors, the reports they issue, and the internal controls on which they rely.

INTERNAL AND EXTERNAL AUDITORS

The original definition of the noun *auditor* was one who listens, or one who hears, and an early *audit* was called a "hearing" of the accounts. The traditional role of the auditor, in examining records or accounts to check their accuracy, is expanding, and today they are often expected to check the results of business activities in all areas. There are two types of auditors, internal and external. Their functions are discussed below and summarized in Exhibit 18–1.

External Auditors

The function of an **external auditor** is to express an opinion on published company financial statements. The **auditor's opinion,** or **audit opinion,** provides assurance to stockholders, creditors, and other financial statement users outside the company that the financial statements fairly present the company's financial position and results of operations in accordance with generally accepted accounting principles (GAAP). Decisions to buy or sell shares of stock are usually based to a great extent on the information in a company's financial statements. Managers of financial institutions use financial statements in making loan decisions, and other companies might use the same information in deciding whether to do business with a company. All readers need the assurance of fair presentation in compliance with GAAP provided by the external auditor. The external audit report is discussed later in the chapter.

External auditors express an opinion on published financial statements.

The external auditor is an independent contractor and is not an employee of the company that is audited. The audit firm is selected by the board of directors and is responsible to the board and to third-party users of financial statements—that is, users outside the company. External auditors must be licensed as **Certified Public Accountants (CPAs)** by the states in which they practice. An accountant earns the

Exhibit 18–1
Comparison of Internal and External Auditor Functions

Attribute	Internal Auditor	External Auditor
Certification	CIA	CPA
Certification required?	No	Yes
Responsible to third parties?	No	Yes
Independent of the auditee?	Yes	Yes
Reports to	Top management and the board	Stockholders
Reports on fairness of financial statements	No	Yes
Reports on compliance with rules and policies	Yes	Yes
Reports on efficiency and effectiveness of operations	Yes	Sometimes
Report contains an audit opinion	Sometimes	Yes

CPA designation by passing a rigorous examination given by the American Institute of Certified Public Accountants and by satisfying the experience requirements of the licensing state.

Internal Auditors

Internal auditors are employees of the company.

Unlike CPAs, **internal auditors** are employees of the company. They are responsible to management and the board of directors and not to third-party users of financial statements. Internal auditors are not required to be licensed, but many are certified by the Institute of Internal Auditors (IIA), an international organization headquartered in Orlando, Florida. An accountant earns the **Certified Internal Auditor (CIA)** designation by passing a rigorous examination and meeting the experience requirement of the Institute. CIA is an international designation recognized in countries around the world. Internal auditors might also be CPAs or have other credentials as evidence of competence, particularly in data processing.

An internal auditor examines business activities and creates reports to assist management in achieving efficient, effective, goal-directed operations. For example, an internal auditor might check scrap procedures to see that all materials scrapped are unsuitable for use, and that scrap is sorted (aluminum, steel, cardboard) into separate containers so that the company can obtain the best prices. Or the auditor might examine the purchasing department to see if bid procedures are being followed and approved vendors used. The kinds of things internal auditors do are described in Insight 18–1. Sometimes an internal audit report includes an opinion on the activities audited, but frequently it does not. The structure of an internal audit report is discussed later in the chapter.

INDEPENDENCE

In order for audit report users to rely on the auditor's work, all auditors (internal and external) must be **independent** of the entity or activity that they audit. An auditor who reported, for example, on the effectiveness of his own boss (who controls the auditor's raises), or on the financial statements of a company that the auditor's spouse managed, could hardly be expected to be free of bias. The codes of ethics for both internal and external auditors are discussed in Insight 18–2.

All auditors must be independent of the entity or activity they audit.

Independence is protected for external auditors by having them report only to stockholders and the board of directors and by insisting that the auditors be free of any relationship with the auditee that could even appear to compromise independence. A CPA cannot own stock in or make a loan to the auditee, cannot accept gifts from the auditee, and cannot have a relative who has a financial or managerial relationship with the auditee.

Because internal auditors are employees of the company, they cannot be independent in the same way that a CPA is independent. Nonetheless, while the internal auditor cannot be independent of the company as a whole, he or she can be independent of the entities and activities that are audited. This independence is achieved by having the internal audit department report directly to top management, or, better still, to the board of directors. Frequently, only the audit committee of the board of directors has the authority to dismiss the director of the internal audit department. In this way the internal auditors are protected from pressures that might be exerted by a powerful auditee (such as the head of an operating department), and the auditee knows that the auditor, representing the board, has a powerful position within the company.

INSIGHT 18–1
What Do Internal Auditors Do?

The following two episodes are examples of how internal auditors increase efficiency and effectiveness of operations to increase company profits.

$5,000 Switch Engine Savings

An auditor's review of railroad shipping costs at a chemical plant revealed that over $10,000 per year was spent for in-plant railroad car switching and spotting. A switch engine was being leased full time, and a substantial number of spotting charges were being paid the railroad for service within the plant.

Analysis of switch engine use, however, showed that it was used only six months a year—on one seasonal product. The auditor presented this information to the plant manager with a recommendation to negotiate a shorter lease period and use the engine to reduce the level of switching service being provided by the railroad. The plant manager's ready acceptance of this recommendation reduced these costs by at least $5,000 per year.

The Case of the Scrap That Wasn't

Getting out into the plant to see what lies behind the numbers may reveal opportunities for savings. The auditor, in this case, in reviewing the control over sales of scrap cable, found that most of the "scrap" could be used productively.

The company made cable connectors, which are lengths of cable varying from 5 to 200 feet, with plugs attached at each end. The auditor observed that cable at the end of a reel, which was shorter than the length of the connectors being run, was being scrapped. For example, if 200-foot connectors were being run, any length less than 200 feet left on the end of the reel was scrapped.

The auditor recommended that the cable ends be used to produce connectors of shorter lengths. This suggestion resulted in annual savings of $40,000.

How to Save Millions, E. Theodore Keys, Jr., ed. (Altamonte Springs, FL: Institute of Internal Auditors, 1988), 9, 41.

INSIGHT 18–2
Auditor Ethics

Investors and other members of the public rely heavily on the assurances given by auditors. This reliance is justified in part because both internal auditors and public accountants are members of professions governed by codes of conduct. All Certified Internal Auditors (CIAs) and members of the Institute of Internal Auditors are expected to adhere to the Institute's Code of Ethics. Certified Public Accountants (CPAs) must abide by the Principles of Professional Conduct published by the American Institute of Certified Public Accountants.

Both codes require auditors to be moral, professionally competent, and to exercise good professional judgment in discharging their duties. Both groups must strive to improve their proficiency and the quality of the service they provide. Because internal auditors work inside the company and often have access to sensitive data, their code stresses loyalty and confidentiality. The code for public accountants stresses serving the public interest and fulfilling the public's trust.

Both codes require auditors to be independent of the activity audited, both in fact and appearance. The appearance of impropriety or a lack of independence damages the worth of the auditor's report. The auditor's work must warrant reliance to be valuable. The public is well served by the rigid ethical standards to which auditors must adhere.

WHAT AUDITORS DO

Auditors can be concerned with five facets of business operation:

1. The reliability and integrity of information.
2. The extent of management's compliance with company policies, plans, and procedures, and government laws, and regulations.
3. How well assets are safeguarded.
4. The effectiveness and efficiency of operations.
5. The extent to which established objectives and goals are accomplished.

External auditors are primarily concerned with items 1 and 3. Internal auditors are concerned with all five, but especially with items 4 and 5.

An auditor seeking to determine the reliability of accounting information or the effectiveness of an operation could check every transaction or operating activity. In modern businesses, however, this is not practical. Between audits, businesses may accumulate millions of separate transactions or operating activities. As a result, the auditor looks for ways to report on a large volume of aggregated activities without checking each individual activity. This may be accomplished in two ways: (1) studying the account characteristics and (2) sampling the accounts audited.

The auditor can reduce the work required to audit a collection of many accounts by spending more time on accounts that are judged to have a high likelihood of misstatement and less (or no) time on those judged to have a low likelihood of misstatement. The auditor may judge the likelihood of misstatement based on past experience, the type of account, the internal controls in each of the account areas, and the results of analytical procedures (discussed below) applied to the accounts included in the audit. For example, an auditor will probably spend more time auditing accounts receivable than fixed assets. There are many transactions—charges and payments—to customer accounts receivable, and, hence, many opportunities for misstatement. There are, generally, few fixed asset transactions and thus few opportunities for misstatement there.

Analytical Procedures

Analytical procedures identify risks by detecting unusual or unexpected relationships.

Analytical procedures test relationships among financial and nonfinancial items. They identify specific risks by detecting unusual or unexpected relationships in aggregated data. If, for instance, sales supplies expense increased from 5% of sales in prior years to 15% this year, the auditor would probably examine this account in greater detail than if the expense remained the same percentage. The sudden increase might indicate errors or fraud in the accounting for sales supplies.

Audit Samples

Having selected the accounts to be audited, the auditor does not examine every transaction. Instead, he or she checks only a judgmental or statistically determined **sample** of the transactions. For instance, an auditor wishing to check the accuracy of an accounts receivable balance composed of thousands of individual accounts would test a sample of 200 or so accounts and from the results of the test of the sample, draw a conclusion about the population of all accounts receivable. If there were no material errors in the sample, the auditor would usually conclude that the balance in accounts receivable was reasonable. The size of the sample is determined by several factors, including the internal controls the company has established over these accounts.

INTERNAL CONTROL

In Chapter 3 we viewed internal control only as a tool for safeguarding cash. But in both account examinations and sampling, **internal control** is a factor in determining the extent of audit testing. In this chapter we are concerned with internal control as it affects the extent of audit testing. From this viewpoint, internal control is any policy, procedure, or management action that provides assurance that company objectives will be met. There are five objectives of internal control, corresponding to the five areas of business activity with which auditors are concerned.

All auditors rely on internal controls.

These objectives are to ensure:

1. The reliability and integrity of information.
2. Management's compliance with policies, plans, procedures, laws, and regulations.
3. The safeguarding of assets.
4. The effectiveness and efficiency of operations.
5. The accomplishment of established objectives and goals.

Again, external auditors are primarily concerned with objectives 1 and 3; internal auditors with all five but especially objectives 4 and 5.

To understand the importance of internal controls, you should try to visualize the extent to which each control ensures compliance with company policies. Many forms of internal control are possible; this chapter presents only a few.

Prenumbered Documents

Many documents are used either to record important information or to authorize certain activities. A purchase requisition lists the items requested by a user department and the date they were requested. An approved purchase order authorizes the purchase of the items requested on the requisition. Other documents have value in and of themselves. Cents-off coupons on soap, for example, will be redeemed at face value from the grocer by the soap manufacturer. Gift certificates may be accepted by all restaurants in a national chain. All documents that management wishes to control should be **prenumbered** so that management can require that employees account for all in their possession.

The absentee owner of a new pizza restaurant franchise was concerned about low sales. She had hired a skilled manager, and the restaurant appeared busy, yet recorded sales were significantly below those achieved by other franchisees. An audit of prenumbered order pad pages disclosed many missing pages—all from the order pads of one waitress. The waitress was supposed to take each order slip, which served also as the bill, with the customer's payment to the cash register for processing. Instead, on some of the large orders each evening, she pocketed both the payment and the order. Auditing the prenumbered order pad pages—placing the pages in numerical sequence—brought the theft to light.

Separation of Duties

The principle of **separation of duties** is based on the presumption that acts requiring *collusion*—two people conspiring to conceal an error or commit a fraud—are less likely to occur than those that can be committed by one person acting alone. Accordingly, one person should not be allowed to both receive customer payments and maintain the balances in customer accounts. If both duties are assigned to the same person, a criminal activity called *lapping* might occur. Suppose John's job includes both receiving customer payments and maintaining the balances in customer accounts. When a payment of $500 is received from ABC Company, John takes the money. He does not credit the ABC account receivable for the $500 payment. The next day, John receives a $500 payment from XYZ Ltd. He credits the $500 received from XYZ Ltd. to the ABC Company account. Now the ABC account is correct and the XYZ account is short. The next day, when a payment is received from DND Corporation, that payment is used to cover the shortage in the XYZ account. And so on. No account is ever short more than one day, because John "laps" the payments, and John has successfully removed $500 from the system. If John is responsible for a large number of accounts, he can, by lapping the payments for more and more accounts, steal a great deal of money.

Lapping is a criminal activity.

Even an employee who does not steal might conceal errors and consequently misstate an account balance in an effort to avoid a reprimand or dismissal. Mary is a storeroom clerk who both issues supplies and maintains the accounting record of the supplies on hand in the storeroom. When an inventory count reveals a discrepancy between the storeroom records and the actual supplies on hand, she is tempted to misstate the records and make the count agree with the records.

When incompatible duties are not separated, auditors must do more checking to be assured that account balances are not materially misstated. An auditor examining the records maintained by either John or Mary will have to examine a larger sample of the records—perhaps all of them—to be certain that fraud or errors have not caused the account to be misstated. In contrast, if assets (cash or supplies) are handled by one person and the accounting records are maintained by another, intentional misstatement of the accounts requires collusion and is less likely to occur. In such cases, the auditor can be satisfied of the accuracy of the account balances with much less testing.

Other incompatible functions are ordering and receiving materials, or issuing checks and reconciling the bank balance. In the first instance, the employee can create a bogus order, indicate receipt when no goods were received, and cause a payment to be made to a fictitious supplier, himself. In the second, an employee can issue a check to a fictitious payee (again himself) and conceal the check when it is returned with the bank statement.

Small companies must often be creative to separate incompatible functions. For example, payments mailed to the company can be opened by any employee who makes a list of the amounts received. Payments received can then be safely given to another person responsible for posting to customer accounts. At the end of the day, the total receipts deposited in the bank must be the same as the total on the list prepared by the mail opener.

Incompatible functions can be separated even for a night clerk working alone in a market. The night clerk receives money and records the sale on the cash register. How can the functions be separated with only one person? Easy. The customer acts as the second person. Have you not seen signs that say "Ask for your receipt"? Those signs attempt to ensure the customer's involvement. Customers, in general, expect their purchase to be entered in the cash register and they want a receipt listing the items purchased. The expectations of the customer force the clerk to ring up the sale. When the sale is rung up, a record is created inside the cash register, inaccessible to the clerk. The accounting (the inaccessible record) and the custody of the cash are separated.

Mandatory Vacations

Many fraudulent schemes require constant attention by the perpetrator. In our illustration of lapping, John must constantly monitor and redirect customer payments to avoid being caught. In many cases, managers and other employees are shocked to learn of fraud committed by a fellow worker. "Why, John was such a devoted employee!" they might exclaim. "He had not missed a day's work in ten years. He would not take a vacation and he would come in sick with the flu—and once even the afternoon following surgery! So selfless and devoted!" Why would John never miss work? He could not miss work and let someone else do his job without risking exposure.

Many fraudulent schemes require constant attention.

Mandatory vacations—two weeks, taken all at once—allow someone new to perform each job. Unusual or fraudulent activities cannot be sustained. Assets are protected, and the auditor can be more confident about correctness of the account balances.

Limited Access

Many companies require cards or badges for access to the plant or offices. Such limited access is often based on the "need to know" or "need to go." A computer center typically limits access to data, as well as to the physical facilities, through some type of user authentication as follows:

1. *Something you know*—a password or encryption (coding) of data.
2. *Something you have*—a token or a smart card imprinted with your access code (as at a bank electronic teller machine).
3. *Something you are*—the retina of your eye or your finger or hand prints.
4. *Somewhere you are*—dial-back security, in which the computer must be able to dial you back at an approved location, in order to foil hackers who attempt to access a system using a modem.

Most companies now process their transactions by computer. A company must have internal controls to protect its computer records and to enable auditors to confirm, with confidence, the existence of assets or the validity of management representations in financial statements or operating reports. Controls benefit not only management but also employees in that (1) temptations to steal or conceal (manipulate the records) are removed, and (2) employees are protected from unfair suspicion and criticism when irregularities are discovered. Insight 18–3 offers a look at the problems auditors have in modern manufacturing environments where traditional controls are often not in place.

ANNUAL REPORTS AND THE AUDIT OPINION

An auditor renders an opinion on statements prepared by management.

An independent auditor performs an audit to express an opinion on the financial statements' fairness of presentation and compliance with GAAP. Financial statements are part of a company's annual report. Other parts include representations of management, supplementary tables, and the notes to the financial statements. *All* of the annual report is prepared by managers and their accountants. *None* of it is prepared by the independent auditor. This is an important point: the auditor renders an opinion on the financial statements that are solely the responsibility of management. This part of the chapter discusses the annual report and the audit opinion rendered by the external auditor. The last part of the chapter discusses audit reports issued by internal auditors.

INSIGHT 18–3
JIT Complicates the Auditors' Job

Part of the JIT approach to production involves a reduction in paperwork. Long-term orders are placed with suppliers who deliver many small shipments "just in time" to be used. These shipments are often delivered directly to the using department, rather than to a central receiving dock for distribution. Because the shipments are received ready to be used—car seats may be delivered on racks already in the same order as the cars in which they will be installed, for example—there may be no traditional receiving reports. Payments to suppliers may be made according to the supplier's delivery schedule rather than after the accounting department receives proof that goods were received. Inside the company, production cells often pass work-in-process from operation to operation without the move tickets common to older manufacturing processes.

To auditors, documentation is evidence that internal controls are functioning and can be relied on. When there is little documentation, auditors may feel that they must perform additional tests before relying on accounting and production records. Auditors in a JIT environment are having to learn to rely on new controls, other than documents, to avoid unnecessary testing. Completed units, for example, are evidence that the components necessary to produce those units were received. Likewise, a production line that is operating on schedule is evidence that suppliers are meeting delivery schedules.

An annual report is designed to satisfy many different users with many different information needs. Stockholders, potential stockholders, creditors, potential creditors, economists, financial analysts, suppliers, and customers all use published annual reports. To meet the needs of this diverse audience, the contents of an annual report are structured by both convention and legal requirements. Financial statements must conform to reporting standards established by the Financial Accounting Standards Board (FASB), the Securities and Exchange Commission (SEC), and various committees of the American Institute of Certified Public Accountants (AICPA).

Financial statement users might find the reporting requirements of these diverse groups to be a mixed blessing. Because financial statement presentation is very structured, it does not precisely meet the needs of any one group. Each user finds something lacking. But because of the high degree of structure and the involvement of the CPA, financial statement users are able to rely on the fair presentation of the information they receive. We can examine the financial statements of a company in Florida or in Alaska, and decide to buy stock or extend credit on that basis even though we do not know any of the managers and have never seen the company's factory or offices.

A large company might spend a million dollars to have a CPA firm audit its financial statements, and half that amount again to have the assembled annual report published and distributed. If you examine an annual report, you will notice that the financial statements are the dull, drab pages with columns of numbers in the rear. The rest of the annual report, in contrast, is often quite beautiful! You might find full-color illustrations and photographs of the company's offices or products.

Management's Presentation

Management information is in the glossy, front part of the annual report. It typically consists of three sections:

1. Annual Report Highlights
2. Letter to Shareholders
3. Review of Operations

The *Annual Report Highlights* is generally the first section in the annual report and contains highlights of the company's operations, or financial statements, or stock performance—or whatever else management deems important enough to discuss. Frequently the highlights section includes graphs or tables that display the trends management wishes to emphasize. The highlights almost always give good news. Generally, this section also contains the company's sales, profits, and earnings per share for several years.

The *Letter to Shareholders* commonly begins: "I am pleased to report (or inform or otherwise convey)..." or "Last year was an exceptional year, because...." The letter is from the president or from both the president and the chairman of the board, whose photographs usually accompany the letter. Frequently the letter compares the current year with prior years but, just as often, it dwells on things hoped for in the future rather than things achieved in the past.

The *Review of Operations* is usually the largest component in the annual report. Most of the photographs and artwork are in this section. Still, it might also offer valuable information about the company's products or the areas of operation the company is stressing for the future.

Financial Statements

The financial statements are the heart of the annual report. They consist of a balance sheet, income statement, statement of cash flows, and the accompanying notes, tables, auditor's opinion, and management's discussion and analysis.

Notes

The notes to the financial statements are an integral part of them and often are as informative as the statements themselves. There are two types of notes: (1) major accounting policies, and (2) additional disclosures, such as purchase commitments, noncurrent liabilities (interest rates and due dates), inventory components, and employee pension provisions.

The notes help the reader understand the financial statements.

Note 1 is always a summary of the accounting policies used by the company. This book describes alternative methods of accounting for inventories and depreciation, and for estimating bad debts. Different methods of accounting can cause large differences in the financial statements, so it is important to know which ones the company used.

Supplementary Tables

A number of supplementary tables may be prepared as part of the financial statements:

1. *Reporting by segments*—The FASB requires companies that meet certain criteria report business activity by segment, such as by product line, major customer, or geographic segment so that investors can assess the risk of the different kinds of operations.

2. *Financial reporting and changing prices*—Companies are encouraged (but not required) to show the effect of inflation on financial statements for the last five years so that investors can evaluate the company's performance and financial position in constant dollars.

3. *Five-year summary of financial data*—Companies are required by the SEC to show income statement data (including earnings per share and other significant ratios) for at least five years in their Form 10-K so that investors can study trends in operating results. Many companies include this information in their annual reports.

4. *Two-year quarterly data*—Quarterly information on income, dividends, and stock prices is helpful to investors, especially for companies with seasonal operations. This information is required in Form 10-K by the SEC.

Management's Discussion and Analysis

The section containing management's discussion and analysis is required by the SEC and is part of the financial statements. Here, management discusses summarized income statement and balance sheet data for the past three years (and longer if necessary to keep the summary from being misleading). Management is required to discuss all developments affecting four areas of operations.

1. *Results of operations*—Operating and nonoperating income-generating activities.
2. *Capital resources*—The acquisition and financing of fixed assets.
3. *Liquidity*—The availability of cash from operations and credit arrangements.
4. *Other*—Any material events or uncertainties known to management that would cause the reported information not to be indicative of future operating results or financial condition.

Auditor's Opinion

Published annual reports are audited by an independent CPA, who expresses an opinion on the financial statements prepared by management in a short report addressed to the stockholders and board of directors.

An auditor may give three types of audit opinion.

The auditor may give three types of audit opinion or may *disclaim* meaning he or she expresses no opinion at all. An auditor disclaims an opinion when he is unable to satisfy himself that the financial statements are presented fairly. The three types of audit opinion follow.

1. **Unqualified** or **clean opinion**—The auditor believes the financial statements are "fair" presentations of the company's financial position, results of operations, and cash flows for the year in conformity with GAAP.
2. **Qualified opinion**—The auditor takes exception to "fair presentation" and points out to the financial statement user the particular area which the auditor believes is not presented fairly in accordance with GAAP. Qualified opinions contain the phrase "except for." The auditor normally issues this type opinion when (a) there has been an isolated departure from GAAP, or (b) the auditee has restricted the scope of the auditor's examination (i.e., the auditor can give an opinion on the statements "except for" that portion not examined). In a qualified or "except for" opinion, the auditor believes that the remainder of the statements are "presented fairly."
3. **Adverse opinion**—The auditor believes that the financial statements are *not* "presented fairly." An adverse opinion states the factors that led the auditor to decide that the financial statements are not "presented fairly." An adverse opinion is rendered when a departure from GAAP is so pervasive as to make the financial state-

ments misleading. An adverse opinion differs from a disclaimer in that a disclaimer arises only from a lack of knowledge by the auditor as to whether the financial statements are fairly presented.

The auditors' report on the 1990 financial statements of Boise Cascade in Exhibit 18–2 is an unqualified audit report. Note that since the financial statements are not prepared by the auditors, the first paragraph of the audit opinion points out that management, not the auditors, is responsible for the financial statements.

The second paragraph of the audit report tells what an audit is. The auditor *tests* the accounting records and supporting documents to form an opinion on the fairness of the financial statements. The auditor does not check every transaction that occurred during the year and cannot *know* that the statements are fair presentations of company activities. The auditor uses **generally accepted auditing standards (GAAS)** promulgated by the AICPA as guidance in performing audit tests.

The third paragraph contains the auditor's opinion and states that the financial statements conform to GAAP, which, as you know, are all

---

Exhibit 18–2
Example of Unqualified Audit Report

Report of Independent Public Accountants

To the Shareholders of Boise Cascade Corporation:

We have audited the accompanying balance sheets of Boise Cascade Corporation (a Delaware corporation) and subsidiaries as of December 31, 1990, 1989 and 1988, and the related statements of income, shareholders' equity, and cash flows for the years then ended. These financial statements are the responsibility of the Company's management. Our responsibility is to express an opinion on these financial statements based on our audits.

We conducted our audits in accordance with generally accepted auditing standards. Those standards require that we plan and perform the audit to obtain reasonable assurance about whether the financial statements are free of material misstatement. An audit includes examining, on a test basis, evidence supporting the amounts and disclosures in the financial statements. An audit also includes assessing the accounting principles used and significant estimates made by management, as well as evaluating the overall financial statement presentation. We believe that our audits provide a reasonable basis for our opinion.

In our opinion, the financial statements referred to above present fairly, in all material respects, the financial position of Boise Cascade Corporation and subsidiaries as of December 31, 1990, 1989 and 1988, and the results of their operations and their cash flows for the years then ended in conformity with generally accepted accounting principles.

Boise, Idaho
February 1, 1991

Arthur Andersen & Co.

the rules, standards, and procedures promulgated by the AICPA, FASB, SEC, and other authoritative bodies to guide accountants and auditors in their work.

INTERNATIONAL ACCOUNTING AND AUDITING

There are only a dozen major international accounting firms. Their offices are located primarily in North America and Europe. There have, however, been several attempts to standardize accounting worldwide, and there are approximately ten standard setting bodies that participate in issuing pronouncements on international accounting issues. The International Accounting Standards Committee issues international standards that can be used by all countries. The European Economic Community issues financial reporting standards to be used by member countries. Interestingly, the United States has the world's most extensive financial statement disclosure requirements, due primarily to the influence and regulations of the Securities and Exchange Commission.

Harmonization of international accounting standards has not worked.

The current view of international accounting is that different economies, cultures, and tax laws make standardization impossible. Countries and international standard setting bodies are striving instead to achieve a *harmonization* that will make the financial statements of different countries comparable to one another. Because countries are increasingly in international competition for markets and capital, self interest is likely to promote comparability in financial reporting far more effectively than the efforts of the international standard-setting bodies.

The United States appears to see itself as a member of a world community, as evidenced by the Foreign Corrupt Practices Act (FCPA), passed in 1977. (The FCPA is discussed in Insight 18–4.) Still, not all companies—or analysts—see ethics in the same way. Insights 18–5 and 18–6 discuss corporate ethics and the influence of the audit committee on corporate ethics.

REPORTS OF INTERNAL AUDITORS

Because internal auditors do not submit reports to readers outside the company, their reports follow no standard form. Each **internal audit** is tailored to the individual situation. The primary purpose of an internal auditor's report, however, is always the same: to communicate the auditor's findings and make recommendations. The Standards of the

INSIGHT 18–4
The Foreign Corrupt Practices Act

The Foreign Corrupt Practices Act of 1977 has had great impact on businesses and auditors in the United States. The act deals with two issues: (1) bribery of foreign officials, and (2) maintaining internal controls.

Legal scholars have noted that this act is unique in that it makes it illegal to bribe someone else's government—and penalizes the person giving the bribe, rather than the person accepting. The Foreign Corrupt Practices Act introduced an era in which the Western condemnation of bribery spread worldwide. (This does not imply that bribery does not still exist, however!)

Equally important for investors, the act requires that companies maintain effective systems of internal control. Prior to the act, managers decided what controls they wished to have; if a control system was annoying or expensive, they were free to eliminate it. Often, as a result, the absence of controls brought on risks that were borne by the company's investors, not its managers. The Foreign Corrupt Practices Act removes decisions about internal control from the discretion of management and makes all companies subject to the reporting requirements of the SEC meet its requirements.

Institute of Internal Auditors (IIA) recommend that a report contain the following elements.

1. *Purpose.* The auditor should state the **purpose** or reason for the audit, such as to determine the level of compliance with company policies on scrap disposal, or to examine the efficiency and effectiveness of the market research department.

2. *Scope.* The auditor should state the **scope** of the audit, or what was covered and what was not. The auditor might explain, for instance, that the audit examined compliance with the company policies for disposing of scrap generated by operations, but did not include an examination of the appropriateness of the quantity of scrap produced.

3. *Audit results.* The auditor should tell what was found. For instance, personnel are complying with scrap disposal policies at the Norwich plant but are selling scrap metal without competitive bids at the Middleton plant.

4. *Recommendations.* The report of a deficiency should be accompanied by a recommended course of action. Perhaps the auditor recommends that personnel at the Middleton plant be monitored for compliance with company policy on scrap disposal, or that respon-

INSIGHT 18–5
Rating Corporate Conscience: Don't Call for Phillip Morris

Despite the stigma society increasingly places on smoking, the cigarette business is still booming. Although smoking is decreasing in the United States, it is increasing in the Third World. Twenty years ago, for example, 70% of the men in the United States smoked. Today, less than 29% of all people in the United States smoke. In China, by contrast, smoking has increased steadily over the same period, until now 80% of the Chinese men smoke.*

Phillip Morris is the world's largest cigarette manufacturer and Marlboro (a Phillip Morris brand) is the world's best selling cigarette. Phillip Morris is an exceedingly profitable company. In the United States, Phillip Morris maintains its profits in a shrinking market by increasing its market share and raising prices. To accomplish this, the company spends more on advertising (for all its products) than any other company in the United States. In 1990 Phillip Morris won 42% of the United States cigarette market; worldwide, its market share was 6%. Tobacco products provide less than 50% of total sales dollars, but 60% of profits.

Phillip Morris has long been a leader in supporting the arts and organizations for women and minorities. It has also been in the forefront of companies employing and promoting minorities. Despite this, the authors of *Everybody's Business* cite the lung cancer deaths linked to cigarette smoking and give Phillip Morris a zero rating for corporate conscience. How does the public view Phillip Morris? The value of an investment in Phillip Morris' stock increased thirteen-fold during the 1980s.**

*"A Chinese Lesson," University of California at Berkeley Wellness Letter, May 1991, 2–3.
**Milton Moskowitz, Robert Levering, and Michael Katz, *Everybody's Business* (New York: Doubleday, 1990), 315.

sibility for scrap disposal at the Middleton plant be given to the purchasing department.

5. *Opinions and conclusions, where appropriate.* Although many internal auditors avoid drawing conclusions or giving an opinion on the entity or activity they audit, management's first question of the auditor is likely to be, "Well, what do you think?" Internal audit opinions are the auditor's evaluation of the effects of any deficiencies found, such as: "Compliance with scrap disposal policies at the Middleton plant is inadequate. Failure to obtain competitive bids on scrap might cause the Middleton plant to lose significant revenues by accepting lower prices on the scrap metal generated by operations."

INSIGHT 18–6
Corporate Ethics and the Audit Committee

An audit committee is ideally composed of three to seven outside members of a company's board of directors. Outside board members do not work for the company in any capacity. The New York Stock Exchange began, in 1978, requiring all its listed companies to have audit committees. In 1987 the National Committee on Fraudulent Financial Reporting strongly urged all companies to have audit committees. As a result, over 80% of all publically traded companies now have audit committees.

The growth in audit committees is an encouraging sign—perhaps, some analysts speculate, the phenomenon is a backlash brought about by the business scandals of the previous decades. The audit committee handles all relations with both external and internal auditors. It gives assurance that any problem discovered by an auditor will receive a full hearing; auditors who find improprieties (as they did in the S&L and other scandals) now have someone powerful who cares. In fact, audit committees do more than care. All members of a company's board of directors are responsible for exercising sound business judgment, and are legally liable for their actions if they do not. As a result, they are eager to be informed.

Typical of audit committee responsibilities are the following.

■ Approve the appointment or removal of the Internal Auditor.

■ Review and approve the Audit Division Charter, each year's internal audit plan, staffing needs and budget requirements.

■ Review and investigate all significant findings and recommendations noted by the Internal Audit Division and the independent Certified Public Accountants.

■ Report to the Board of Directors summarizing the activities of the committee.

■ Recommend the appointment of the independent Certified Public Accountants.

SUMMARY

The traditional role of the auditor has been to examine records and accounts to check their accuracy. However, the role is expanding, and auditors are more and more responsible not only for checking the accuracy of accounting records, but for checking the results of business activities in all areas. External auditors express opinions on financial statements included in company annual reports read by a broad, varied audience. Internal auditors examine and report to the company on the efficiency and effectiveness of all areas of its operations. Internal control encompasses all the measures management has put in place to ensure that company objectives are met. All auditors vary their level of testing depending on the effectiveness of a company's system of internal control.

Key Terms

adverse opinion

analytical procedures

annual report

audit opinion

Certified Public Accountant (CPA)

Certified Internal Auditor (CIA)

external auditor

financial statements

generally accepted accounting principles (GAAP)

generally accepted auditing standards (GAAS)

independence

internal auditor

internal control

internal audit

limited access

mandatory vacations

prenumbered documents

purpose

qualified opinion

sample

scope

separation of duties

unqualified opinion

ASSIGNMENTS

18–1   Two Types of Auditors

Ned is graduating from Midwestern College. He would like to be an auditor, but he is confused. Big City Trust Company employs almost 100 auditors, yet the local CPA firm has told Ned that they audit the bank.

REQUIRED:

Explain to Ned what internal and external auditors do and why Big City Trust needs both internal and external auditors?

18–2   Independence

Susan Walker is a CIA employed by Master Machine Works. She audits the operations of the different manufacturing and sales sites. Charlie Falls is a CPA with his own practice. "How can you be independent in your audits," Charlie asks Susan over lunch one day. "You work for the folks you audit. You've got to know your job is on the line if you say too many negative things."

"Why, Charlie," Susan responds, "it's you I worry about. You don't even have a job; you just have clients. If you lost a big client, you could lose your Jag. How can you be independent enough to give anything other than a clean opinion?"

REQUIRED:

1. Why is independence important for an auditor?
2. How do internal and external auditors maintain their independence?

18-3   CPA versus CIA

"Wow, Man!" Billy said. "I thought auditors were CPAs and that the CIA was a group of James Bond type government spies." Billy's Mom laughed. "Well, your uncle Joe is a CIA, but he works for Texas Oil and carries a briefcase instead of a gun. But he does have a neat car."

REQUIRED:

What is a CPA? A CIA? Compare these two types of auditors.

18-4   What Auditors Do

Dave Burk, manager of purchasing for the Gary branch, was nervous. The auditors were due to examine the purchasing department next week. "They're just a bunch of nitpicking snoops. They'll try to find some little something to hang me with, and there will go my bonus . . ."

REQUIRED:

Are auditors just nitpicking snoops? Discuss the concerns of auditors in modern business.

18-5   Internal Control and the Customer

Molly Fair is a waitress at the Far West Family Saloon. She serves soda schooners saloon style to tired Tucson tourists. The customers sit at tables. Molly takes orders and carries the soda schooners to tables on her tray. On hot days, hundreds of tourists visit the saloon. A large sign on the wall says: "Your Order Free If There Is A Red Star On Your Cash Register Receipt."

REQUIRED:

How does the sign serve as an element of internal control?

18-6   Sampling

"Oh, rats!" cried Brenda Nelson, manager of accounts receivable. "The darned auditors are coming. I bet they'll take forever. There are over 5,000 individual customer accounts." Brenda pecked at her calculator.

"Why, at ten minutes per account, that's 833 hours, or—Great Scott!—almost twenty-one weeks."

REQUIRED:

Explain how an auditor might examine accounts receivable in less time than Brenda expects.

18–7   Analytical Procedures

The gross margin percentage and accounts receivable turnover of Mercy Hospital Supply Company are given below.

	19X3	19X2	19X1
Gross margin percentage	32%	37%	45%
Accounts receivable turnover	8.0	8.5	8.1

REQUIRED:

How might an auditor planning the tests for an examination of Mercy's financial records and operations view these trends?

18–8   Internal Control

The primary objective of internal control is to prevent fraud by employees. If there is no employee fraud, the company is either lucky, or internal controls are working.

REQUIRED:

1. Evaluate the statement above.

2. List and describe the four types of internal control measures discussed in the text.

18–9   Annual Report Users

An annual report is designed to satisfy many different users with many different information needs. Stockholders, potential stockholders, creditors, potential creditors, economists, financial analysts, suppliers, and customers all use published annual reports.

REQUIRED:

1. How do accountants prepare reports that will satisfy all users? Who sets the standards for these reports?

2. Why might some financial statement users find structured, standardized financial statements a mixed blessing?

18–10   Financial Statements and Certified Public Accountants

Identify each of the following statements as true or false.

1. The CPA prepares the financial statements included in the annual report.

2. Management's part of the annual report typically consists of three sections, Annual Report Highlights, Letter to Shareholders, and Review of Operations.

18–11 Reporting Requirements

The text describes the reporting requirements to which financial statement preparers must adhere as being, at times, a "mixed blessing."

REQUIRED:

Comment on this statement.

18–12 Annual Reports

The auditor is primarily concerned with the financial statements, their accompanying notes, and the schedules and other excerpts from the financial statements. The rest of the annual report is controlled by management.

REQUIRED:

List the annual report components other than the financial statements and notes.

18–13 Auditor's Opinion

The audit report expresses an opinion on the financial statements prepared by management.

REQUIRED:

1. To whom is the audit report addressed?
2. What types of opinion might the auditor give?

18–14 Preparing the Audit Report

John is cynical. "I don't see why anyone would feel better just knowing the auditors gave some company's financial statements an unqualified opinion," he snorted. "After all, it was the auditors who prepared the statements—what do folks expect them to say?"

"Yeh!" C. J. agreed. "And they're not fooling me. A company has thousands of transactions; the auditors couldn't check everything, even if they wanted to."

REQUIRED:

1. Comment on John's statement.
2. Comment on the support offered by C. J.

18–15 The Audit Opinion

Each paragraph in an unqualified audit opinion has a specific purpose.

REQUIRED:

Discuss the content of each paragraph of an unqualified audit opinion.

18–16   Reports of Internal Auditors

Lea Chong, manager of the boxing plant, has just received the internal auditors' report of their recent audit. Lea is puzzled. "I have worked for three different companies and in each, the internal auditors have used a different report format. That doesn't seem right to me."

REQUIRED:

1. Why is there no standard form for an internal auditor's report?
2. Describe the general content of an internal audit report.

18–17   Separation of Incompatible Functions and Accounts Receivable

Jackie Harris is the customer account executive at Baldwin Books, a wholesaler of craft and hobby books. Jackie has a great deal of customer contact. She receives both new book orders and payments on customer accounts. Often, because the customers are small, Jackie will receive both the customer's payment on account and its new book order in the same envelope. Jackie records the payment in the customer's account and approves the new order. Often customers phone Jackie to discuss their accounts and orders. The customers like dealing with Jackie, and Mrs. B. K. Baldwin, president of the company, is proud of the customer service Jackie gives as account executive.

REQUIRED:

Evaluate the internal control problems and benefits of Jackie's job. Include a discussion of lapping.

18–18   Wal-Mart Internal Auditors

Wal-Mart has retail stores located across the United States.

REQUIRED:

Do you think Wal-Mart has internal auditors? If so, what might they do to improve company profitability?

18–19   Wal-Mart Annual Report

Answer the following questions using the information contained in the Wal-Mart annual report.

1. What does the Letter to Stockholders say about Sam's Clubs? What officers signed the Letter to Stockholders?
2. What is the pattern of dividends per share since 1982?
3. What percentage increases in sales are disclosed in Management's Discussion and Analysis?

4. Referring to the notes to the financial statements, what debt is due in 2020?

5. Read the Statement of Responsibility. Who is responsible for the financial statements? What has been done about corporate ethics?

6. What office did the late Sam M. Walton hold?

18–20 DECISION CASE:
SELECTING ACCOUNTS TO TEST

Jordan and Edwards, Certified Public Accountants, are auditing the financial statements of Green Bay Fish Company. Selected account balances (in thousands) for the last three years follow.

	19X3	19X2	19X1
Sales	$12,000	$13,200	$12,000
Trade receivables	1,200	1,100	1,000
Trade payables	2,300	1,400	500
Supplies expense	34	32	33
Advertising	987	2,560	1,900
Equipment (net)	35,000	38,000	41,000

REQUIRED:

Use analytical procedures to suggest accounts for detailed testing by Jordan and Edwards in the audit of Green Bay Fish Company. Where appropriate, comment on the type of account and, hence, the risk involved.

18–21 DECISION CASE:
INTERNAL CONTROL IN A SMALL BUSINESS

You are an auditor assigned to audit a small movie theater, The Bargain Movie House. The owner/manager of the theater, Jewel Williams, has recorded $120,000 in ticket and concession sales revenues. Three teenagers from the local high school are employed at the theater. One collects ticket money and admits patrons to the theater, tearing a ticket in half and giving a stub to each person admitted. The money is kept in a cigar box with the unused tickets. No one ever checks the stubs once they are given to the customer. The second teen sells candy, popcorn and soda. The cash from soda sales is kept in the cash drawer of an inoperable cash register. The third teen sweeps up, helps Jewel Williams in the projection booth, and serves as a backup in case someone does not come to work. Ms. Williams counts the cash each night and records a single amount in her ledger as "Ticket and Concession Sales."

REQUIRED:

Discuss any weaknesses in internal control you find at The Bargain Movie House and describe how they might be corrected.

CHAPTER

19

Analyzing Financial Statements

LEARNING OBJECTIVES

After studying Chapter 19, you should be able to:
1. Understand the importance of financial statement analysis to managers, creditors, and stockholders.
2. Use horizontal analysis to examine financial statement changes from period to period.
3. Use vertical analysis to examine the relationship among items in financial statements for a single period.
4. Use ratios to compare account relationships in a particular company to accepted benchmarks or performance norms.
5. Discuss how financial leverage can work to increase or decrease a company's return on its owners' equity.
6. Understand how the text of the annual report supplements the financial statements and assists in analyzing a company's position and potential.
7. Understand the disclosure of discontinued operations, extraordinary items, and accounting changes.

Earlier chapters have pointed out how ratios help managers and others determine whether a company is performing well in a specific area, such as collecting its accounts receivable within a reasonable time. Financial statements as a whole serve many other users, both inside and outside a company. This chapter completes our discussions and illustrations of techniques that financial analysts and others use to judge the health and earning power of a company. Financial analysts make decisions, or assist others in making decisions, such as whether to buy, sell, or hold stocks and bonds, whether to make short-term loans, and whether to extend trade credit. Some analysts work for brokerage firms, providing information that the firm uses to advise its clients. Other analysts sell their investment advice. Individual investors also perform financial analyses. The balance sheet, the income statement, and the statement of cash flows provide much of the information needed for making these investment decisions.

We approach this chapter on financial statements, then, not from the preparer's point of view, but from the user's. Accordingly, this chapter addresses analysis by investors and creditors. Managers within the company also use these techniques.

INVESTMENT DECISIONS

Many entities make investment decisions. Banks make short-term loans, insurance companies buy and sell bonds, mutual funds and private investors buy and sell stocks and bonds. Labor unions analyze financial statements to determine whether proposed wage increases are justified. Financial analysts must therefore tailor their analyses to the particular kinds of decisions their clients make. To this end, analysts sometimes recast financial statements to highlight concerns. For example, an analyst might adjust the statements to reflect price level changes. Or she might eliminate intangible assets from the balance sheet.

The analysis needed depends on the decision to be made.

The principal purpose of financial analysis is to form judgments about the future—will the company be able to repay a six-month bank loan, a ten-year bond? Will its income grow? Is the dividend payment likely to rise? Is the market price of the stock too high, too low? As you know, amounts in financial statements depend on expectations. The allowance for doubtful accounts is an example. The useful lives of assets are another. For the most part, however, the analyst works with historical information and assumes, unless there is other information to the contrary, that historical trends will continue.

A company might be hurt by some event that it cannot control. A competitor could bring out a much improved product, a strike might result in lost markets, or a major product could become obsolete. Analysts watch for developments that indicate that the future will differ from the past. And because good management is critical to success, one of the major questions that the analyst seeks to answer is whether the managers are running the company efficiently and effectively.

The analysis considers both quantitative and qualitative information.

As you can see, financial statement analysis focuses not only on financial and quantitative information, but on nonfinancial and qualitative information as well. Other sources of information that assist in financial statement analysis are the financial press (for example, *The Wall Street Journal*), reports to the Securities and Exchange Commission, and business service publications (such as *Value Line,* and *Dun & Bradstreet*). One problem caused by the mass of data available to analysts is discussed in Insight 19−1.

Our focus here is on financial and quantitative information in the company's financial statements. We will apply analytical tools and techniques to the financial statements to examine significant relationships as well as trends. These analytical tools and techniques fall into three groups: horizontal analysis, vertical analysis, and ratio analysis.

HORIZONTAL ANALYSIS

Horizontal analysis examines changes from period to period.

Horizontal analysis deals with the changes in accounting numbers from period to period. This analysis addresses such questions as the following: Are sales, gross profit, expenses, and net income increasing or decreasing over time? What was the change in sales from last year? Has cash increased or decreased over the last two years? Sometimes the dollar change from one period to the next period in a particular account is not sufficient by itself to allow an informed decision regarding that account. Use of the percentage change in the account may enhance the user's understanding of the change in the account under analysis.

Comparative financial statements present a company's financial statements for two or more successive periods. Two steps are necessary to perform the analysis. First, compute the dollar amount of the change from the base year, the year against which you are making the comparison. Second, divide the dollar amount of the change by the base year amount. Exhibits 19−1 and 19−2, which contain the comparative financial statements for Jensen Company for 19X0 and 19X1, help illustrate horizontal analysis.

Exhibit 19−1 indicates that net sales increased by 18.6% during 19X1, with cost of goods sold increasing by 19.7%. These increases resulted in a gross profit increase of 16.7%. Selling and general expenses increased while administrative expenses decreased. It appears

INSIGHT 19–1
Using Data in Analysis

Investors face an almost endless quantity of data available for inclusion in their analysis. Not all data is useful, however, and investors may be distracted and mislead by inaccurate and incomplete data. Still, investors tend to use all the data they are given. *Money* magazine illustrated this point with the following question:*

The Huns under Attila invaded Europe and penetrated deeply into what is now France, where they were defeated and forced to turn eastward. Answer these two questions:

1. Did these events occur before or after the year A.D. 812? (Note: The number 812 was chosen arbitrarily by adding 400 to the last three digits of a randomly picked *Money* staffer's phone number.)

2. In what year did Attila's defeat occur?

The first question only serves to supply the random date (812) and explain its origin. Answers to the first question are irrelevant. But answers to the second question tell a great deal about the way people use data. When the random number supplied was high (1400 or so), people guessed high. When the random number was low (500 or so), people guessed low. The average of the responses to the high numbers was 988. The average of the responses to the low numbers was 629. This phenomenon is called anchoring. The number given in the question tends to "anchor" people's guess as to the date of Attila's defeat—even though they know the number is random and meaningless. People asked this question do not clearly think, "When was Attila defeated?". Instead, they think, "How far before or after A.D. 812 was Attila defeated?" The same thing often occurs in business. If a plant is for sale for $500,000, that asking price may anchor the prospective buyer's offer.

(Note: Attila was defeated in A.D. 451.)

*For a full discussion of the phenomenon discussed here, see Clint Willis, "The Ten Mistakes to Avoid with Your Money," *Money*, June 1990, 85–86.

from the analysis that the 34% increase in net income was attributable to the combination of the increase in gross profit and a lesser increase in expenses.

An examination of Exhibit 19–2 reveals that the company's current assets and current liabilities fell slightly in 19X1. Additionally, long-term liabilities were reduced by almost 20%. The company also ex-

Exhibit 19–1
Jensen Company
Comparative Statements of Income and Retained Earnings
For the Years Ended December 31, 19X0 and 19X1

	19X1	19X0	Increase (Decrease) 19X1 over 19X0 Amount	Percent
Net sales	$990,000	$835,000	$155,000	18.6
Cost of goods sold	620,000	518,000	102,000	19.7
Gross profit	370,000	317,000	53,000	16.7
Operating expenses:				
Selling	117,000	96,000	21,000	21.9
Administrative	62,000	67,000	(5,000)	(7.5)
General	89,000	77,000	12,000	15.6
Total operating expenses:	268,000	240,000	28,000	11.7
Income from operations	102,000	77,000	25,000	32.5
Other expenses (net)	4,000	2,000	2,000	100.0
Income before income taxes	98,000	75,000	23,000	30.7
Income tax expense	35,000	28,000	7,000	25.0
Net income	$ 63,000	$ 47,000	$ 16,000	34.0
Retained earnings, January 1	183,000	160,000	23,000	14.4
	246,000	207,000	39,000	18.8
Less dividends paid	30,000	24,000	6,000	25.0
Retained earnings, December 31	$216,000	$183,000	$ 33,000	18.0

panded by purchasing property, plant, and equipment. More than likely, the funds used for expansion were obtained through equity financing, since the Common Stock and Paid-in Capital in Excess of Par Value accounts increased during 19X1.

Note that the largest percentage increase was for prepaid expenses (100%), but its absolute dollar amount is not significant. The analyst should keep in mind that percentage changes must be viewed from the perspective of the item's relative significance to the company's financial statements as a whole. Prepaid expenses are only $6,000. On the other hand, the percentage increase in property, plant, and equipment is only 5.9%. However, these are the company's most significant assets, because they are used in producing goods.

Exhibit 19–2
Jensen Company
Comparative Balance Sheets
December 31, 19X0 and 19X1

			Increase (Decrease) 19X1 over 19X0	
Assets	**19X1**	**19X0**	**Amount**	**Percent**
Current assets:				
Cash	$ 32,000	$ 38,000	$ (6,000)	(15.8)
Accounts receivable (net)	123,000	153,000	(30,000)	(19.6)
Inventories	94,000	81,000	13,000	16.0
Prepaid expenses	6,000	3,000	3,000	100.0
Total current assets	255,000	275,000	(20,000)	(7.3)
Property, plant, and equipment (net)	615,000	581,000	34,000	5.9
Intangible assets (net)	10,000	13,000	(3,000)	(23.1)
Total assets	$880,000	$869,000	$ 11,000	1.3
Liabilities and Stockholders' Equity				
Current liabilities:				
Accounts payable	$ 63,000	$ 71,000	$ (8,000)	(11.3)
Notes payable	30,000	33,000	(3,000)	(9.1)
Accrued liabilities	26,000	21,000	5,000	23.8
Total current liabilities	119,000	125,000	(6,000)	(4.8)
Long-term liabilities:				
Notes payable, 8% due 2002	200,000	250,000	(50,000)	(20.0)
Total liabilities	319,000	375,000	(56,000)	(14.9)
Stockholders' equity:				
Common stock, $5 par value	295,000	280,000	15,000	5.4
Paid-in capital in excess of par	50,000	31,000	19,000	61.3
Retained earnings	216,000	183,000	33,000	18.0
Total stockholders' equity	561,000	494,000	67,000	13.6
Total liabilities & stockholders' equity	$880,000	$869,000	$ 11,000	1.3

Trend Analysis

An analyst who has comparative financial statements for more than two periods can perform **trend analysis,** a type of horizontal analysis in which a base year is selected and comparisons made to it. Trend analysis is useful in comparing financial statements over several time periods because they (1) disclose changes occurring over time and (2) provide information as to the direction in which a company is moving. For example, investors and creditors are generally interested in and pleased to see an increasing trend in sales, gross profit, and net income. On the other hand, percentages indicating a decreasing trend in these items would not be favorable.

Exhibit 19–3 is a five-year summary of selected financial data from the 1988 annual report of Esselte Business Systems, Inc.

We can compute trend percentages for the data in Exhibit 19–3 by using 1984 as the base year. Trend percentages for the years 1985 through 1988 follow.

	1988	1987	1986	1985	1984
Net sales	230%	204%	159%	114%	100%
Income from operations	197	182	148	115	100
Interest expense, net	224	189	136	94	100
Income before extraordinary					
credit	210	201	160	117	100
Extraordinary credit	–	40	42	83	100
Net income	196	191	153	115	100

Exhibit 19–3
Five-Year Summary of Selected Financial Data
Esselte Business Systems Inc.

Selected Consolidated Financial Data (excerpt)

Year Ended December 31

Income Statement Data (amounts in thousands)	1988	1987	1986	1985	1984
Net sales	$1,401,183	$1,242,408	$972,832	$695,509	$610,161
Income from operations	136,507	126,081	102,868	79,434	69,309
Interest expense, net	26,483	22,356	16,013	11,053	11,809
Income before extraordinary					
credit	58,939	56,534	45,043	32,815	28,105
Extraordinary credit	–	776	811	1,588	1,923
Net income	58,939	57,310	45,854	34,403	30,028

Esselte's net sales and net income have steadily and significantly increased since 1984. Obviously the company is doing quite well and is growing, with net sales and net income doubling over the five year period. This is good news for Esselte's stockholders.

Trend analysis can be used for any financial statement item, and is not necessarily confined to income statement items. Again, even though a percentage change in an item might appear to be significant, the change should be viewed in the context of its relationship to other financial statement items and also in terms of absolute dollars.

VERTICAL ANALYSIS

While horizontal analysis deals with the dollar and percentage change in financial statement items over time, **vertical analysis** focuses on the relationships in a single period's financial statements. Exhibit 19−4 illustrates the development of percentage figures. The percentages appearing beside the income statement amounts were computed by dividing those amounts by the net sales figure for that year. Vertical analysis of the income statement presents each item on the income statement as a percentage of net sales. In this manner the items all sum to 100%. The percentage of each financial statement item is an indication of the relative importance of that item in determining net income.

Vertical analysis examines relationships within the statements.

Vertical analysis of the 19X0 and 19X1 comparative income statements from Exhibit 19−4 indicates that the gross profit decreased slightly from 19X0 and net income rose by almost 1%. This was accomplished partly by reducing operating expenses. You can also see that the change in net income as a percentage of sales (also called return on sales), was modest even though Jensen had a large dollar increase in sales of $155,000.

Analysts and managers examine percentages of various expenses to sales to compare the company with a norm, such as the average value for an industry. Some industry associations publish such norms as ratios.

In Exhibit 19−5, presenting the 19X0 and 19X1 comparative balance sheets of Jensen Company, each item is presented as a percentage of total assets or total liabilities and stockholders' equity. The comparative balance sheets for 19X0 and 19X1 reveal that current assets were a smaller percentage of total assets in 19X1 than in 19X0. However, this is not a problem, because the company had a smaller percentage of current liabilities relative to total liabilities and stockholders' equity in 19X1 than in 19X0. Additionally, the company reduced its percentage of long-term notes payable in 19X1. Total stockholders' equity increased from 56.8% of total liabilities and stockholders' equity to 63.7%. This was caused by the issuance of additional common stock

Exhibit 19–4
Jensen Company
Comparative Statements of Income and Retained Earnings
For the Years Ended December 31, 19X0 and 19X1

	19X1	19X0	19X1 Percent	19X0 Percent
Net sales	$990,000	$835,000	100.0%	100.0%
Cost of goods sold	620,000	518,000	62.6	62.0
Gross profit	370,000	317,000	37.4	38.0
Operating expenses:				
Selling	117,000	96,000	11.8	11.5
Administrative	62,000	67,000	6.3	8.0
General	89,000	77,000	9.0	9.2
Total operating expenses:	268,000	240,000	27.1	28.7
Income from operations	102,000	77,000	10.3	9.2
Other expenses (net)	4,000	2,000	0.4	0.2
Income before income taxes	98,000	75,000	9.9	9.0
Income tax expense	35,000	28,000	3.5	3.4
Net income	$ 63,000	$ 47,000	6.4%	5.6%

and the increase in retained earnings due to an excess of net income over dividends paid.

Common-Size Financial Statements

A form of vertical analysis is to present financial statements that show only percentages—**common-size financial statements.** All figures on a common-size balance sheet are expressed as percentages of total assets or total liabilities and stockholders' equity. Similarly, on a common-size income statement, the items are expressed as percentages of net sales.

Common-size statements can give the reader a better feel for the relationship between a particular item and sales (on the income statement), or between the item and total assets or total liabilities and stockholders' equity (on the balance sheet). These statements can also be compared to industry averages to assess a company's standing in its industry and line of business. The use of common-size financial statements allows comparisons among companies of different sizes. That is,

Exhibit 19–5
Jensen Company
Comparative Balance Sheets
December 31, 19X0 and 19X1

Assets	19X1	19X0	19X1 Percent	19X0 Percent
Current assets:				
Cash	$ 32,000	$ 38,000	3.6%	4.4%
Accounts receivable, net	123,000	153,000	14.0	17.6
Inventories	94,000	81,000	10.7	9.3
Prepaid expenses	6,000	3,000	0.7	0.3
Total current assets	255,000	275,000	29.0	31.6
Property, plant, and equipment (net)	615,000	581,000	69.9	66.9
Intangible assets (net)	10,000	13,000	1.1	1.5
Total assets	$880,000	$869,000	100.0%	100.0%
Liabilities and Stockholders' Equity				
Current liabilities:				
Accounts payable	$ 63,000	$ 71,000	7.2%	8.2%
Notes payable	30,000	33,000	3.4	3.8
Accrued liabilities	26,000	21,000	3.0	2.4
Total current liabilities	119,000	125,000	13.6	14.4
Long-term liabilities:				
Notes payable, 8% due 2002	200,000	250,000	22.7	28.8
Total liabilities	319,000	375,000	36.3	43.2
Stockholders' equity:				
Common stock, $5 par value	295,000	280,000	33.5	32.2
Paid-in capital in excess of par	50,000	31,000	5.7	3.6
Retained earnings	216,000	183,000	24.5	21.0
Total stockholders' equity	561,000	494,000	63.7	56.8
Total liabilities & stockholders' equity	$880,000	$869,000	100.0%	100.0%

it may be difficult to make a comparison of the financial statements of General Motors Corporation (GMC) and Chrysler Corporation because GMC is so much larger. However, the financial statements of each company could be modified to common-size financial statements to facilitate the analysis. In this manner, changes in the relative size of the components will be apparent—changes that could be missed if only the absolute dollar amounts were examined. For example, although sales might have increased from one period to the next, a reader might not notice that gross margin had decreased or that selling expenses increased as a percent of sales. Common-size statements highlight both of these changes.

TECHNIQUES OF RATIO ANALYSIS

Although there are many aspects to financial analysis, the calculation and interpretation of financial ratios is one of the most prominent. Analysts compare ratios for a particular company to *benchmarks,* or norms. Ratios in and of themselves tell you very little. When compared to norms, their informational value greatly increases. Common benchmarks are average ratios for the industry the company operates in, values that the analyst considers good or bad, and values for the same company in previous years. There are four areas of interest to investors that correspond to the kinds of decisions they make: liquidity, activity, solvency, and profitability. They form the basis for classifying ratios. **Liquidity** is the ability to meet short-term liabilities, **activity** refers to how efficiently a firm is utilizing its assets, and **solvency** to its ability to meet long-term obligations. **Profitability** is the company's capacity to generate profits.

As we begin our discussion of financial analysis, two important points should be made. First, computing ratios is only a starting point in analyzing a company. Ratios do not give you answers, but they do provide signs, or clues to what might be expected. Second, ratios often give conflicting signals. For instance, the more cash a company has, the better it is able to pay its debts. But having lots of cash is not good, because cash earns little or no return and the company would have higher profits if it invested the cash wisely. This type of seeming paradox crops up throughout financial statement analysis.

Areas of Interest

We said earlier that investors make various types of financial decisions. Creditors whose loans are of relatively short duration (under six months, perhaps a year), care about the company's current condition and near-term prospects. Banks and vendors are examples of such creditors. They want to know the likelihood that a company will be able to pay its obligations in the near future. Banks also make longer-term loans, as do insurance companies and pension funds. Mutual funds and individual investors buy bonds. These investors are making relatively long-term commitments, one year and up, perhaps to 30 years. Such investors are concerned much more with the company's long-term solvency than with its short-term outlook. (They are, of course, also concerned with the short term, because the company cannot reach long-term goals without surviving the short term.) Long-term creditors are interested in financial stability, overall financial strength, and earnings prospects. Their analytical task is usually more difficult than that of the short-term investor.

Stockholders have the most difficult analytical task. A company can pay its short-term debt, repay its bonds and other long-term loans with interest, and still not earn enough to justify the purchase of its common stock. Stockholders are concerned with profitability, earnings, dividends, and increases in the market price of a company's shares, as well as with liquidity and solvency.

Illustrative Financial Statements

We shall use the comparative financial statements and additional financial information about Jensen Company for 19X0 and 19X1 shown in Exhibits 19−6 and 19−7. (These are the same financial statements introduced as Exhibits 19−1 and 19−2.) We have prepared common-size financial statements for Jensen Company. They can help us spot trends and to compare one company to another, or to benchmark values. Again, we stress that ratios by themselves tell you little: only in comparison to preestablished criteria do they allow analysts to make judgments.

The income statement has at least three important ratios. One is the **gross profit ratio,** gross profit divided by net sales, the second is the **operating ratio,** income before interest and taxes divided by net sales,[1] and the third is **return on sales (ROS),** net income divided by net sales. These ratios for Jensen Company in 19X1 are 37.4%, 11.5%, and 6.4%, respectively. The gross profit ratio decreased slightly in 19X1 over 19X0, but ROS increased.

Income statement ratios are primarily concerned with profitability and provide clues to efficiency, that is, how well the company's managers were able to turn each dollar in sales into gross profit, operating profit, and net income. Analysts can draw various conclusions depend-

---

[1] The operating ratio can also be defined as operating income divided by net sales. Operating income equals net income plus interest expense plus income tax expense. In the example, Jensen Company had 19X1 net income of $63,000, interest expense of $16,000 ($200,000 long-term debt × 8%), and income tax expense of $35,000. Therefore, its operating ratio for 1991 is calculated as follows.

$$\frac{\$63,000 + \$16,000 + \$35,000}{\$990,000} = \frac{\$114,000}{\$990,000} = 11.5\%$$

Exhibit 19–6
Jensen Company
Comparative Balance Sheets
December 31, 19X0 and 19X1

Assets	19X1	19X0	19X1 Percent	19X0 Percent
Current assets:				
Cash	$ 32,000	$ 38,000	3.6%	4.4%
Accounts receivable, net	123,000	153,000	14.0	17.6
Inventories	94,000	81,000	10.7	9.3
Prepaid expenses	6,000	3,000	0.7	0.3
Total current assets	255,000	275,000	29.0	31.6
Property, plant, and equipment (net)	615,000	581,000	69.9	66.9
Intangible assets (net)	10,000	13,000	1.1	1.5
Total assets	$880,000	$869,000	100.0%	100.0%
Liabilities and Stockholders' Equity				
Current liabilities:				
Accounts payable	$ 63,000	$ 71,000	7.2%	8.2%
Notes payable	30,000	33,000	3.4	3.8
Accrued liabilities	26,000	21,000	3.0	2.4
Total current liabilities	119,000	125,000	13.6	14.4
Long-term liabilities:				
Notes payable, 8% due 2002	200,000	250,000	22.7	28.8
Total liabilities	319,000	375,000	36.3	43.2
Stockholders' equity:				
Common stock, $5 par value	295,000	280,000	33.5	32.2
Paid-in capital in excess of par	50,000	31,000	5.7	3.6
Retained earnings	216,000	183,000	24.5	21.0
Total stockholders' equity	561,000	494,000	63.7	56.8
Total liabilities & stockholders' equity	$880,000	$869,000	100.0%	100.0%

ing on the results. For example, if the gross profit ratio is high (compared to a norm), while the operating ratio is low, the analyst might conclude that the company is using a high-price, high-promotion strategy. A high gross profit ratio indicates either higher selling prices or lower cost of goods sold. A low operating ratio (with a high gross profit

Exhibit 19–7
Jensen Company
Comparative Statements of Income and Retained Earnings
For the Years Ended December 31, 19X0 and 19X1

	19X1	19X0	19X1 Percent	19X0 Percent
Net sales	$990,000	$835,000	100.0%	100.0%
Cost of goods sold	620,000	518,000	62.6	62.0
Gross profit	370,000	317,000	37.4	38.0
Operating expenses:				
Selling	117,000	96,000	11.8	11.5
Administrative	62,000	67,000	6.3	8.0
General	89,000	77,000	9.0	9.2
Total operating expenses:	268,000	240,000	27.1	28.7
Income from operations	102,000	77,000	10.3	9.2
Other expenses (net)	4,000	2,000	0.4	0.2
Income before income taxes	98,000	75,000	9.9	9.0
Income tax expense	35,000	28,000	3.5	3.4
Net income	$ 63,000	$ 47,000	6.4%	5.6%

Other information: Dividends declared and paid were $30,000 in 19X1, $24,000 in 19X0. Operating expenses include depreciation of $50,000 in 19X1 and $35,000 in 19X0. Operating expenses also include interest expense of $16,000 in 19X1 and $20,000 in 19X0. The company had 56,000 shares outstanding at the end of 19X0 and 59,000 at the end of 19X1. Its stock had a market value of $18 per share and $27 per share at the end of 19X0 and 19X1, respectively.

ratio) indicates relatively high operating expenses such as advertising and promotion. Other explanations are possible, and the analyst will do a good deal more work before reaching a conclusion.

Balance sheet ratios are, by themselves, usually less important than income statement ratios. One use is to spot trends in particular asset and liability categories. For example, suppose that inventories are becoming higher relative to receivables and cash. This could be an indication that the company is holding slow-moving goods and might have to reduce prices greatly to sell the inventory and stay competitive. We now proceed to considering the three major areas of interest in ratio analysis.

Income statement ratios are usually more important than balance sheet ratios.

Liquidity

High liquidity is manifested by relatively high current assets compared to current liabilities, and also by a high proportion of current assets in cash and receivables (as opposed to inventory or prepaid expenses).

Working Capital

As you know, **working capital** is the difference between current assets and current liabilities. It is a crude measure of liquidity. Jensen Company had the following amounts of working capital at the ends of 19X1 and 19X0.

	19X1	19X0
Current assets	$255,000	$275,000
Current liabilities	119,000	125,000
Working capital	$136,000	$150,000

The decrease in working capital is not necessarily a sign of decreased liquidity. Working capital is a dollar amount, not a ratio, and it is difficult to evaluate dollar amounts by themselves. Better measures of liquidity include the current ratio and quick ratio (discussed next). Because different cost flow assumptions (such as LIFO or FIFO), result in differing inventory amounts on the balance sheet, intercompany comparisons of working capital and liquidity might not be valid. This changes the focus to that of ratio trend analysis for each company rather than direct comparisons among companies. The use of different inventory cost flow assumptions also affects intercompany comparisons of the current ratio.

Current Ratio

The **current ratio,** current assets divided by current liabilities, is probably the most fundamental liquidity ratio. Because it is a ratio, it can be used to compare companies of different sizes or the same company at different balance sheet dates.

Jensen Company's current ratios are:

$$19X1: \frac{\$255,000}{\$119,000} = 2.14$$

$$19X0: \frac{\$275,000}{\$125,000} = 2.20$$

We can say that, on the basis of the current ratio, Jensen *seemed* to be less liquid at the end of 19X1. There is a major problem with the

current ratio (and others), called the **composition problem,** meaning
that the use of a total, such as total current assets (or current liabilities)
might obscure information about individual components. The current
ratio does not tell us how soon current assets are likely to be converted
into cash. Nor does it tell us how soon the current liabilities must be
paid. The analyst can look at the common-size balance sheet to see the
extent to which current assets are composed of relatively liquid items,
such as cash and receivables, and can also use current activity ratios
that we discuss shortly.

Generally, the higher the current ratio is, the better. Some representative current ratios reported in recent annual reports follow: Nike,
Inc., 3.07 to 1, Fedders Corporation 2.5 to 1, Georgia-Pacific Corporation 1.9 to 1, National Intergroup, Inc., 1.8 to 1, Schering-Plough
Corporation 1.4 to 1, Harris Corporation 1.2 to 1, and Gannett Company, Inc., 1.3 to 1.

What should the current ratio be? Some analysts use a rule of thumb *The current and quick*
of 2.0 to 1. However, we cannot give a definite answer because the ratio *ratios measure liquidity.*
needs to be interpreted relative to the industry norm, or as part of a
trend, and needs to be evaluated in light of its components.

Quick Ratio (Acid-test Ratio)

The **quick ratio,** or *acid-test ratio*, is quick assets divided by current
liabilities. Quick assets are cash, temporary investments, and accounts
receivable: or, current assets less inventory and prepayments. The
quick ratio is a more stringent test of liquidity (the "acid test") than the
current ratio since it indicates whether a company could extinguish its
current liabilities if they came due shortly. Quick assets are near-cash,
and most will probably be available to pay current liabilities within a
fairly short time.

$$\text{Quick Ratio} = \frac{\text{Cash} + \text{Temporary Investments} + \text{Receivables}}{\text{Current Liabilities}}$$

Jensen's quick ratios are as follows.

$$\text{19X1:} \frac{\$32,000 + \$123,000}{\$119,000} = 1.30$$

$$\text{19X0:} \frac{\$38,000 + \$153,000}{\$125,000} = 1.53$$

Jensen's liquidity seems to have decreased because its quick ratio
decreased. We could say that the firm is not in a better position to meet
current liabilities at the end of 19X1 because the ratio of its most liquid

assets to its current liabilities decreased. We would still like to know how soon its current liabilities have to be paid and how rapidly the firm can expect to turn its receivables and inventory into cash. The payment schedules for current liabilities cannot be determined simply by the examination of financial statements, but we can gain insight into the liquidity of receivables and inventory. In examining the balance sheet of Jensen Company for 19X0 and 19X1 (Exhibit 19–6), we can see that the cause of the decrease in the ratio is the decrease in accounts receivable and the increase in inventory in 19X1. The increase in inventory means that Jensen may have a more difficult time paying off debts in 19X2 than in 19X1, because the company must first sell its inventory and convert it to cash before paying its debts.

Current Asset Activity Ratios

Current asset activity ratios tell us how quickly cash will be received.

The current ratio and the quick ratio tell us about coverage of current liabilities by current or quick assets. They do not tell us how soon our current assets or quick assets will be converted into cash, that is, how liquid are the current assets. Obviously cash is already cash, and temporary investments can usually be converted at very short notice. However, receivables and inventories might take some time to convert. The next two ratios, and their variations, tell us about how quickly receivables and inventory will be turned into cash. In general, activity ratios take the following form:

$$\text{Activity Ratio} = \frac{\text{Best Measure of Asset Activity}}{\text{Asset}}$$

Accounts Receivable Turnover

Accounts receivable turnover measures how rapidly receivables are collected, or turned over. The ratio is sales divided by average net accounts receivable.

$$\text{Accounts Receivable Turnover} = \frac{\text{Net Sales}}{\text{Average Net Accounts Receivables}}$$

The numerator should be net *credit* sales because cash sales do not generate accounts receivable. However, in most cases the analyst does not know credit sales and so uses total net sales. Average net accounts receivable is usually the beginning balance plus the ending balance, divided by 2. Some analysts use the end-of-year figure only, instead of the average. This is largely a matter of preference. One problem that arises in using averages or year-end balances is that the balances might not be representative of the year. The year-end balance could be especially high or low and give misleading results. (Recall that last year's ending balance is this year's beginning balance, so if the ending balance is not representative, neither is the beginning balance.) One answer is to calculate a monthly average, but the analyst probably does not have monthly data. An analyst who knows of such a problem will put less reliance on the calculated turnover.

The ratio reveals the number of times during the year that the average accounts receivable balance was converted into cash. In general, the higher the turnover is, the better. A high turnover means that receivables are collected rapidly. Reducing the amount of sales dollars tied up in accounts receivable results in more dollars being available for other purposes. However, a high turnover ratio might also indicate that the company's credit policies are too strict, which could harm sales and reduce profitability. The accounts receivable turnover ratio for Jensen Company for 19X1 follows.

$$\frac{\$990,000}{(\$153,000 + \$123,000)/2} = 7.17$$

The numerator is the net sales figure from the income statement in Exhibit 19−7, and the denominator is the accounts receivable figures from the balance sheets in Exhibit 19−6.

Some analysts do not use receivable turnover, but instead use a related ratio called **days' sales in accounts receivable** to assess the efficiency of accounts receivable management. This figure represents the average age of ending accounts receivable and is calculated as follows.

$$\text{Days' Sales in Accounts Receivable} = \frac{\text{Ending Accounts Receivable}}{\text{Average Daily Sales}}$$

Average daily sales is simply annual net sales divided by 365 (again, net credit sales should be used). This ratio also suffers from the problem that the ending balance might not be representative of the year. Moreover, the calculation assumes that daily sales in the recent past were the same as average daily sales.

Jensen Company has average daily sales of $2,712 ($990,000/365) for 19X1 and $2,288 ($835,000/365) for 19X0. Hence, days' sales in accounts receivable are:

$$19X1: \frac{\$123,000}{\$2,712} = 45 \text{ days}$$

$$19X0: \frac{\$153,000}{\$2,288} = 67 \text{ days}$$

On average, Jensen's accounts receivable were 67 days old at the end of 19X0 and 45 days old at the end of 19X1. The collection period has decreased considerably in one year, perhaps due to tightening credit policies. When evaluating the efficiency of managing accounts receivable, remember that the numbers (whether a single day's sales or the number of days' sales in accounts receivable) for one period do not tell us everything. The trend is also of considerable interest.

Other things equal, the faster customers pay, the better. An increase in days' sales in accounts receivables (or a decrease in turnover) suggests that the firm is becoming less efficient in collecting its accounts. But there are always trade-offs; if the firm loses sales because of tight credit policies, the advantage of faster collection might be more than offset by the loss of profits because of lower total sales.

Inventory Turnover

We use similar analyses with inventories. **Inventory turnover** is extremely important, because the quicker the inventory is sold, the quicker the company converts its investment to cash. Inventory turnover is calculated as follows:

$$\text{Inventory Turnover} = \frac{\text{Cost of Goods Sold}}{\text{Average Inventory}}$$

Again, average inventory is usually the beginning balance plus the ending balance divided by 2. Some analysts use the year-end balance instead of the average. The same problem of representativeness applies here as with accounts receivable. The year-end balance might not be indicative of the average balance. In the absence of monthly data, the analyst must not rely heavily on the calculated turnover.

Inventory turnover is important because investment in inventory is expensive. Among the costs of holding inventory are personal property taxes, insurance, pilferage, obsolescence, and probably most important, interest on the funds tied up in inventory. It is partly because of such costs that manufacturers in the United States have begun to adopt the just-in-time (JIT) inventory method that Japanese companies pioneered. A JIT system minimizes inventory, which therefore maximizes turnover. Not all companies can reduce their inventories drastically, however. For a retailer, low inventory will probably lead to lost current and future sales as frustrated customers tell their friends that the store's selection is poor.

Jensen Company's inventory turnover for 19X1 is about 7 times, calculated as follows.

$$\frac{\$620,000}{(\$81,000 + \$94,000)/2} = 7.1$$

This ratio measures the efficiency with which the firm moves its inventory. Other things equal, the higher the turnover, the better.[2] Inventory turnover is a critical measure for businesses such as discount stores and food stores. These businesses have low profit margins and need rapid turnover to earn satisfactory returns. In contrast, companies that have high profit margins, such as jewelers, can be profitable with low turnovers.

Inventory turnover has a counterpart, **days' sales in inventory.** This ratio is calculated as follows.

$$\text{Days' Sales in Inventory} = \frac{\text{Ending Inventory}}{\text{Average Daily Cost of Goods Sold}}$$

Average daily cost of goods sold is simply cost of goods sold for the year divided by 365. For Jensen this figure is $1,699 ($620,000/365) for 19X1 and $1,419 ($518,000/365) for 19X0. The days' sales in inventory are as follows:

$$\textbf{19X1:} \ \frac{\$94,000}{\$1,699} = 55.3 \text{ days}$$

$$\textbf{19X0:} \ \frac{\$81,000}{\$1,419} = 57.1 \text{ days}$$

The decline in days' sales in inventory could indicate a deliberate change in inventory policy, or perhaps just a temporary reduction of inventory because of heavier than expected sales near the end of the year. Because inventory turnover rates vary widely and are related to a company's profit margin, the analyst should compare the rate to industry norms as well as the trend of the ratio over time.

Implications of Turnover

The importance of turnover as it relates to accounts receivable and inventory cannot be overemphasized. The "operating cycle wheel" in Figure 19–1 helps illustrate this importance. The wheel rotates clockwise. As each rotation (turn) is made, cost of goods sold, operating expenses, income taxes, and dividends are paid, profits are earned, and cash is generated. It should be obvious from the figure that the more times the operating cycle wheel turns in a period, the greater the profit earned and the higher the cash flow. To make the wheel spin faster (and

---

[2] High turnover can also mean that the company is experiencing stockouts by not maintaining enough inventory. Therefore, a company seeks to maintain a turnover ratio that balances carrying costs and stockouts. This trade-off results in the most profitable turnover rate, not necessarily the highest rate.

Figure 19–1
Operating Cycle Wheel

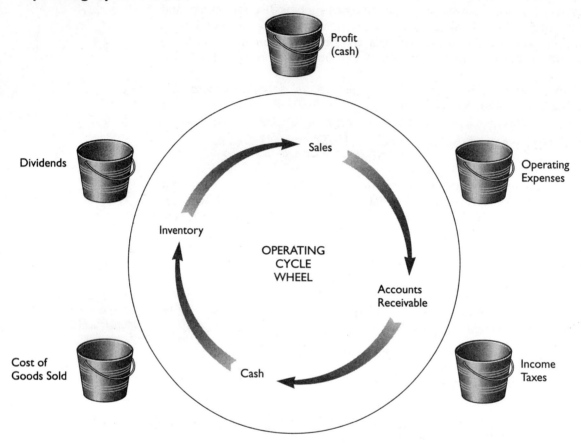

earn more) in a period, accounts receivable must be collected as rapidly as possible to make funds available for other purposes so that the company will not need to seek short-term loans to pay for current operations. Similarly, by keeping inventory levels at a minimum (relative to sales) through increased turnover, a company minimizes inventory financing requirements and (as we will show later) increases return on investment.

Turnover can be too high or too low.

Several points should be made however. First, remember that collecting accounts receivable rapidly might result from a too-strict credit policy and lead to lost sales. A company should consider its sales level and seek to maintain a turnover ratio consistent with an effective credit policy, rather than simply trying to maximize turnover. Second, while minimizing inventory levels might increase the turnover ratio, a company runs the risk of stockouts and delays in delivery resulting in lost sales. This means that a company should not seek to obtain the highest inventory turnover ratio but instead strive to maintain the most profitable ratio given a desired sales level and considering the associated costs of carrying inventory and stockouts.

Profitability

Profitability can be measured in dollars (net income) or by ratios. Most common measures of profitability are variations of **return on investment (ROI)**, a group of ratios having the general form

$$\text{Return on Investment} = \frac{\text{Income}}{\text{Investment}}$$

Most measures in the group relate an income statement component (such as income from operations or net income), to a balance sheet component (such as stockholders' equity). Stockholders and potential stockholders are interested in the return they can expect from their investment. As Chapter 16 discussed, managers in the firm are concerned with earning satisfactory returns on the investments they control. As a practical matter, then, different users define income and investment differently when measuring the same basic relationship.

Income and investment can be defined in different ways.

Return on Assets

One profitability ratio is **return on assets (ROA),** which measures **operating efficiency** and is especially applicable to divisions or other investment centers. It indicates how well managers have used the assets under their control to generate income. The most common calculation of the ratio follows.

$$\text{Return on Assets} = \frac{\text{Income Before Interest and Taxes}}{\text{Average Total Assets}}$$

For Jensen Company, ROA was 13.0% for 19X1, calculated as follows.

$$\frac{\$98,000 + \$16,000}{(\$869,000 + \$880,000)/2} = 13.0\%$$

We use *income before interest and income taxes,* which is the same as *net income plus interest and income taxes* ($63,000 + $16,000 + $35,000 = $114,000). The ratio is concerned with operations. Interest and income taxes depend greatly on how the company *finances* assets, so we exclude them. Others disagree; some add back interest but not taxes, while others use other variations. Arguments support several measures of the numerator and denominator in the ROA calculation. Your choice depends partly on your own personal preference.

The most common measure of average total assets is the sum of the beginning and ending balance sheet amounts divided by 2. Significant month-to-month fluctuations are less likely with total assets than with current assets such as receivables and inventory, but it is better to use monthly data if total assets do fluctuate significantly. Average total assets is used in the calculation, because income—the numerator—is earned continuously throughout the year. Regardless, some analysts use end-of-year assets in the denominator, some use beginning-of-year amounts, and still others use total assets minus current liabilities. Analysts who subtract current liabilities argue that they provide "automatic, stable" sources of financing and that they actually relate to operations.

Comparisons of different firms are hindered by the use of different inventory cost flow assumptions, depreciation methods, and estimated asset service lives.

Return on Common Equity (ROE)[3]

Common stockholders care about the return on *their* investment. That return depends not only on profitable operations, but also on the amount of debt and preferred stock in the capital structure. Jensen has no preferred stock.

Return on common equity (ROE) is computed as follows.

$$\text{Return on Common Equity} = \frac{\text{Net Income}}{\text{Average Common Stockholders' Equity}}$$

For a company with no preferred stock, average common stockholders' equity is simply the sum of the beginning and ending amounts of stockholders' equity divided by 2. If the company does have preferred stock, the analyst must subtract preferred dividends from net income in the numerator, and the amount of total stockholders' equity attributable to preferred stock from total stockholders' equity in the denominator to obtain common stockholders' equity.[4] ROE for Jensen Company in 19X1 is almost 12%.

$$\frac{\$63,000}{(\$494,000 + \$561,000)/2} = 11.9\%$$

---

[3] Return on common equity was discussed in Chapter 8.
[4] There are several ways of determining the amount of total stockholders' equity attributable to preferred stock. The best method, where possible, is to use the *call value* of preferred stock. Call value, discussed in Chapter 8, is the amount that the firm would have to pay to retire the preferred stock, and it is usually more than par value. Par value could be used for preferred stocks that have no call value.

Creditors receive interest, a fixed amount, and do not receive anything beyond interest if the company is profitable. Companies can therefore increase ROE by using debt, provided that ROA is greater than the interest rate it pays to creditors. Using debt (or preferred stock) to increase ROE is called **leverage** or **trading on the equity.** Leverage increases risk as it also provides the potential for greater return.

Effects of Leverage

Leverage is related to debt and the **debt ratio.** The higher the ratio is, the higher the leverage. Suppose a company requires $500,000 in total assets and expects to earn an 18% ROA, or $90,000 annually before interest and income taxes. The tax rate is 40%. The company has three financing alternatives: (1) all common stock; (2) $200,000 common stock and $300,000 in 7% bonds (giving interest expense of $21,000); and (3) $200,000 in common stock and $300,000 in 8% preferred stock (requiring dividends of $24,000). Condensed income statements under the three alternatives follow.

Leverage can increase the return on owners' equity.

	All Common Stock	Debt and Common Stock	Preferred and Common Stock
Income before interest and taxes	$ 90,000	$ 90,000	$ 90,000
Interest expense at 7%	-0-	(21,000)	-0-
Income before taxes	90,000	69,000	90,000
Income taxes at 40%	(36,000)	(27,600)	(36,000)
Net income	$ 54,000	$ 41,400	$ 54,000
Less preferred stock dividends	-0-	-0-	(24,000)
Earnings available for common	$ 54,000	$ 41,400	$ 30,000
Divided by common equity	$500,000	$200,000	$200,000
Equals return on common equity	10.8%	20.7%	15.0%

The plans that include debt or preferred stock result in lower earnings available for common equity, but in higher ROEs than the company can achieve if it uses all common stock. You can see that the use of debt or preferred stock at a rate (7% for debt and 8% for preferred stock) lower than ROA ($90,000/$500,000 = 18%), increases ROE. The favorable leverage results from the interest expense and the dividend payments being fixed. Additionally, because interest is tax deductible, its after-tax cost is only 4.2% [7% × (1 − .40)]. For this reason, many companies prefer to finance using debt rather than preferred stock. Remember though, that if income before interest and taxes declines, the company must still make interest payments, while it pays preferred dividends at the discretion of the board of directors. (Of course, there are cumulative preferred stocks whose dividends in arrears must be paid before common stockholders receive any dividends.)

Summarizing, we can generalize that if a company can earn a higher return than the interest rate it must pay to acquire the funds, then the company's stockholders will earn a greater return on their investment (ROE) than if they had provided all of the funds.

When earnings are low, leverage decreases the return on owners' equity.

Unfortunately, leverage can work in the opposite direction. That is, while it benefits common stockholders when earnings are high, it can penalize them when earnings are low. If our example company earns only $30,000 before interest and taxes, the effects of leverage will have the following results.

	All Common Stock	Debt and Common Stock	Preferred and Common Stock
Income before interest and taxes	$ 30,000	$ 30,000	$ 30,000
Interest expense at 7%	-0-	(21,000)	-0-
Income before taxes	30,000	9,000	30,000
Income taxes at 40%	(12,000)	(3,600)	(12,000)
Net income	$ 18,000	$ 5,400	$ 18,000
Less preferred stock dividends	-0-	-0-	(24,000)
Earnings available for common stock	$ 18,000	$ 5,400	($ 6,000)
Divided by common equity invested	$500,000	$200,000	$ 200,000
Equals return on common equity	3.6%	2.7%	Negative

ROA ($30,000/$500,000 = 6%) is lower than the cost of borrowing of 7% and the 8% cost of preferred stock dividends, and so ROE is very poor under all three plans, though highest when there is all common stock. Because of the risk associated with leverage, only companies with relatively stable revenues and expenses, such as public utilities, should use high leverage. Leverage is especially risky in cyclical businesses such as automobiles, where income can fluctuate significantly. If a heavily leveraged company had several unprofitable years, it could be forced into bankruptcy.

Some observers describe the 1980s as being filled with "takeover madness." Many of these takeovers were structured as **leveraged buyouts (LBOs).** In a leveraged buyout, a small group of investors acquires a target company. The transaction is structured so that a very large amount of debt and a small amount of stock is used. The debt is to be paid with funds generated by the acquired company's operations and/or the sale of its assets. Many LBOs used high-yield, high-risk bonds. These unsecured **junk bonds** were of low quality because of the risk associated with the payment of principal at the bond's maturity date. The debt burden may put pressure on the company's cash flow as well as its debt ratios, making additional financing difficult. The financial press described many instances where companies defaulted on their debt payments after a leveraged buyout. See Insight 19–2 for a discussion of junk bonds.

Earnings per Share

Most investors do not buy entire companies, but rather some number of shares and so care about per-share data. **Earnings per share (EPS)** is the most widely reported statistic in the financial press and in recommendations by investment services. In the absence of complicating factors, EPS is calculated as follows.

EPS is the most widely used ratio.

$$\text{Earnings per Share} = \frac{\text{Net Income Available for Common Stockholders}}{\text{Weighted-Average Common Shares Outstanding}}$$

(Complicating factors relating to earnings per share are discussed in the appendix to this chapter.) Preferred stock dividends are subtracted from net income in arriving at earnings available to common stockholders, because preferred stockholders have first claim to dividends. The weighted-average number of common shares outstanding is the best measure of the shares outstanding throughout the period. Exhibit 19–7 indicates that Jensen Company had 56,000 shares outstanding at the end of 19X0 and 59,000 shares at the end of 19X1. Jensen's EPS figures are

$$19X0: \frac{\$47,000 - \$0}{56,000 \text{ shares}} = \$0.84$$

$$19X1: \frac{\$63,000 - \$0}{59,000 \text{ shares}} = \$1.07$$

EPS in 19X1 was $0.23 higher than in 19X0. This is a 27% growth rate, which can be calculated as follows:

$$\text{Growth Rate of EPS} = \frac{\text{EPS Current Year} - \text{EPS Prior Year}}{\text{EPS Prior Year}}$$

For Jensen Company, therefore, the calculation is as shown.

$$\frac{\$1.07 - \$.84}{\$.84} = 27.4\%$$

The growth rate of EPS is useful because, in general, the higher the growth rate the investing public expects from a firm, the more it will be

INSIGHT 19–2
Junk Bonds—High Yield, High Risk

Junk bonds are generally issued in three types of situations. First, they are issued by companies that are in weak financial condition, usually indicated by being heavily in debt. The second situation is where a company is undergoing a financial restructuring, such as occurs in an LBO. Finally, junk bonds are issued by emerging growth companies who normally have inadequate cash flows. Because these companies lack a favorable credit history, they are a riskier investment, prohibiting them from being able to issue bonds at a lower interest rate. Interest rates on junk bonds typically are at least 10% and sometimes over 20%.

The problems relating to junk bonds stem from the fact that most have provisions relating to automatic interest escalators, which normally take one of three forms:

1. Interest rate resets. In this case, the company must increase the interest rate if, by a certain date, the company's bonds are not trading at face value or slightly above face value. The purpose of raising the interest rate is to boost the price of the bond back up to face value. In June of 1990, Western Union Corporation's 16.5% bonds were trading at 92, or $92 for each $100 face value bond. So the company increased the rate it paid to 19.25%, resulting in a $7 million increase in interest expense per year. Western Union warned its investors that it might inevitably file for bankruptcy protection if it could not get relief from its creditors. RJR Nabisco, Inc., the largest leveraged buyout in history, also has interest reset provisions relating to its junk bonds.

2. Deferred payment instruments. These instruments force the investors to wait about five years to receive any cash. In the interim period, investors receive more paper (bonds). When the interest payments start, investors are holding more bonds than they paid for and so they receive larger interest payments. These instruments are also called paid-in-kind (PIK) bonds, and were discussed in Insight 7–2 in Chapter 7.

3. Zero coupon bonds. Investors normally purchase these bonds at a deep discount such as 34% or 40% from face value and do not collect interest until maturity or for several years. Companies such as Interco Inc., (a St. Louis consumer products company) and Southland Corporation (parent company of 7-Eleven stores) are examples of companies who have zero coupon bonds whose interest payments are postponed for the first five years. Zero coupon bonds were discussed in Insight 7–1 in Chapter 7.

Source: "The Junk-Bond Time Bombs Could Go Off," *Business Week*, 9 April 1990, 68–70.

INSIGHT 19–3
What Should Be the Price of a Company's Stock?

Financial statement analysis is frequently used to determine the worth of a company's stock. But this is a judgment difficult to make. Robert Heilbroner, an economist writing for *The New Yorker,* notes that the stock market is composed of many different buyers and sellers, all concerned about the outcomes of their own transactions. These investors act according to whatever particular information each can collect and in the light of their individual expectations about the future. As a result, the level of stock prices reflects the collective judgment of many, many different individuals—it is a collective judgment that considers more information than any one individual could ever hope to possess, or even consider in a decision model due to the complexity of it all. This notion—that the collective market "knows" more than any one investor ever could—is called the *efficient market hypothesis.*

As a result of the dynamic interactions of many investors, no analyst can ever *know* what the correct price of a company's stock should be, because the correct price depends on what people (including the analyst) think it should be. To predict the movement of stock prices, then, it is as important to understand mass psychology as financial statement analysis. The investor must buy stock, not of the most attractive company as determined by financial statement analysis, but of the company *other* investors will select, those investors making their selections from their own points of view.*

*For an expanded discussion of economic predictions, see Robert Heilbroner, "Reflections (Economic Predictions)," *The New Yorker,* 8 July 1991, 70–77.

willing to pay for the common stock. Growth rates should be viewed over a number of years, though, rather than for a single year, because growth must be sustained for it to be significant. One theory on how the market price of a stock is determined is discussed in Insight 19–3.

Price-Earnings Ratio

The **price-earnings (PE) ratio** is the market price of a share of common stock divided by its EPS (earnings per share).

$$\text{Price-Earnings Ratio} = \frac{\text{Market Price per Share}}{\text{Earnings per Share}}$$

This ratio is an important factor in decisions to buy, hold, or sell shares of stock and is reported in *The Wall Street Journal* and other financial papers. It represents the amount an investor pays to buy a dollar of earnings. High-growth companies usually have high PE ratios, while low-growth, stable, or declining firms have low ones. Exhibit 19–7 states that Jensen Company's common stock sold at $18 per share at the end of 19X0 and $27 at the end of 19X1. The PE ratios are as follows.

$$\textbf{19X0: } \frac{\$18.00}{\$.84} = 21.4$$

$$\textbf{19X1: } \frac{\$27.00}{\$1.07} = 25.2$$

The PE ratio increased from 19X0 to 19X1, indicating investors' willingness to pay more for each dollar of earnings. The increase in the PE ratio could have happened because the company's prospects were more highly regarded or because PE ratios in general increased because of expectations of a better economic climate.

Stockholders benefit from both dividends and growth.

The return that common stockholders receive on their investment has two components: (1) dividends and (2) increases in share prices. If investors expect that earnings and dividends will increase, then generally they are willing to pay more for that share of stock. The PE ratio focuses on both factors. To illustrate, if the market price of Lee Company stock is $50 and the market price of Bee Company stock is $30, one might conclude that Lee Company stock is worth more and perhaps that the company is doing better than Bee Company. However, if the EPS figures for Lee Company and Bee Company are $6.50 and $1.95, respectively, we see that the PE ratios are as follows.

$$\textbf{Lee Company: } \frac{\$50.00}{\$6.50} = 7.7$$

$$\textbf{Bee Company: } \frac{\$30.00}{\$1.95} = 15.4$$

Stockholder expectations regarding growth in earnings and dividends are apparently higher for Bee than for Lee Company. Investors are willing to pay much more for a given amount of the earnings of Bee Company than of Lee Company.

Dividend Yield and Payout Ratio

Investors receive dividends and, they hope, increases in the market value of their shares. The **dividend yield** is a measure of the percentage of market value that is paid annually in dividends and is calculated as follows:

$$\text{Dividend Yield} = \frac{\text{Dividend per Share}}{\text{Market Price per Share}}$$

Jensen Company declared and paid dividends of $24,000 in 19X0 and $30,000 in 19X1 on 56,000 and 59,000 shares, respectively. This resulted in dividends per share of $0.43 and $0.51 for 19X0 and 19X1, respectively. With the share prices of $18 and $27 at the ends of 19X0 and 19X1, dividend yields are as follows.

$$19X0: \frac{\$.43}{\$18.00} = 2.39\%$$

$$19X1: \frac{\$.51}{\$27.00} = 1.89\%$$

Investors compare dividend yields to other investment opportunities. They will usually accept lower yields from companies that plow back earnings. The expectation is that reinvestment will lead to increased earnings and dividends in the future. Investors who favor high-growth companies are not looking for dividends as much as for increases in the market price of the common stock. Because such increases may or may not occur, investing in high-growth companies is generally riskier than investing in companies that pay relatively high, stable dividends.

High-growth companies can be risky.

The **dividend payout ratio** is the ratio of dividends per share to earnings per share. For Jensen Company the payout ratio in 19X1 was 48% ($0.51/$1.07) and in 19X0 was 51% ($0.43/$0.84). Again, companies with high growth rates usually have relatively low dividend yields and payout ratios because they are investing cash that could be used for dividends.

Most companies try to have a stable dividend payment, as opposed to one that fluctuates with earnings. For this reason, the dividend amount, and not the payout ratio, is the principal consideration of dividend policy.

Solvency

Solvency relates to long-term safety, to whether the company will be able to pay its long-term liabilities. Long-term creditors and stockholders are alike interested in solvency. Long-term creditors are interested in receiving interest payments and repayment of principal. Stockholders are concerned because the company cannot pay dividends, nor can its share price increase, if it fails to survive.

Debt Ratio

The **debt ratio** is a very simple and very common measure of solvency.

$$\text{Debt Ratio} = \frac{\text{Total Liabilities}}{\text{Total Assets}}$$

This ratio measures the percentage of debt in the capital structure. Like other ratios, it has several variations. Some prefer the **debt-to-equity ratio,** total liabilities divided by stockholders' equity. Some like the ratio of long-term liabilities to total assets or of long-term liabilities to fixed assets. All versions attempt to get at the debt burden: is the company too highly leveraged? The higher the debt ratio is, the riskier the company. As we noted earlier, companies in some industries can safely take on very high percentages of debt, while companies in other industries must keep the debt ratio low.

Jensen's debt ratios for 19X0 and 19X1 are as follows.

$$19X0: \frac{\$375,000}{\$869,000} = 43\%$$

$$19X1: \frac{\$319,000}{\$880,000} = 36\%$$

The debt ratio decreased from 19X0 to 19X1. This means that a larger proportion of the assets are financed by the owners than by the creditors. Reducing the ratio lessens the pressure of the continuing principal and interest payments. Also, if the company attempts to borrow additional funds, the interest rate charged by a lender might be lower because of the relatively low debt ratio. However, decreasing the ratio also reduces leverage and therefore can reduce ROE.

Times Interest Earned

The debt ratio indicates the impact of debt on the balance sheet of the company. We can obtain additional information by calculating the burden that interest expense places on the company. **Times interest earned,** or interest coverage, measures the extent to which operations cover interest expense. The higher the ratio is, the more likely the firm will be able to continue meeting the interest payments.

$$\text{Times Interest Earned} = \frac{\text{Income Before Interest and Taxes}}{\text{Interest Expense}}$$

Income before interest and taxes is, of course, operating income. Jensen Company had interest coverage of 4.75 times in 19X0 and 7.13 times in 19X1.

$$19X0: \frac{\$95,000}{\$20,000} = 4.75$$

$$19X1: \frac{\$114,000}{\$16,000} = 7.13$$

We use operating income in the ratio because interest is tax-deductible. A variation is to approximate cash flow in the numerator by also adding back depreciation.

Cash Flow Ratios

Cash flow ratios can be used to examine a company's solvency. These are the ratios that are used to assess a company's cash flow. Because the cash flow statement has only recently become a required statement, these ratios are relatively new. Three ratios proposed by Brandt, et al. appear useful.[5]

Cash flow ratios are useful in analyzing solvency.

$$\text{Overall Cash Flow Ratio} = \frac{\text{Cash Flow from Operations}}{\text{Financing} + \text{Investing Cash Outflows}}$$

$$\text{Cash Return on Sales} = \frac{\text{Cash Flow from Operations}}{\text{Sales}}$$

$$\text{Cash Flow to Net Income} = \frac{\text{Cash Flow from Operations}}{\text{Net Income}}$$

The *overall cash flow ratio* measures the extent to which internally generated cash flow from operations supplies the cash required for investing and financing activities. *Cash return on sales* is a measure similar to the traditional return on sales (i.e., net income/sales). This ratio and the *cash flow to net income* ratio help analysts determine if the company's ability to generate sales and earnings is matched by appropriate cash flows. Cash flow ratios were not calculated for Jensen Company because a statement of cash flows was not presented. These ratios were also discussed in Chapter 9.

Exhibit 19–8 provides a table summarizing the ratios from our discussion.

ADDITIONAL DISCLOSURES

The annual report contains more than just the financial statements of a company. Supplemental schedules and other information appear after the financial statements. This section of the annual report is the **notes to the financial statements.** Included in this section are such disclosures as the summary of significant accounting policies followed by the

[5] For a discussion of the ratios cited in the chapter, plus other ratios that can be used to analyze cash flows, see Lloyd Brandt, Jr., Joseph R. Danos, and J. Herman Brasseaux, "Financial Statement Analysis: Benefits and Pitfalls" (Part Two), *The Practical Accountant,* June 1989, 69–78.

Exhibit 19–8 Summary of Ratios and Analytical Measurements

Liquidity

1. Working Capital = Current Assets − Current Liabilities

2. Current Ratio = $\dfrac{\text{Current Assets}}{\text{Current Liabilities}}$

3. Quick Ratio = $\dfrac{\text{Cash + Temporary Investments + Receivables}}{\text{Current Liabilities}}$

Activity

4. Accounts Receivable Turnover = $\dfrac{\text{Net Sales}}{\text{Average Net Accounts Receivables}}$

5. Days' Sales in Accounts Receivable = $\dfrac{\text{Ending Accounts Receivable}}{\text{Average Daily Sales}}$

6. Inventory Turnover = $\dfrac{\text{Cost of Goods Sold}}{\text{Average Inventory}}$

7. Days' Sales in Inventory = $\dfrac{\text{Ending Inventory}}{\text{Average Daily Cost of Goods Sold}}$

Profitability

8. Return on Investment = $\dfrac{\text{Income}}{\text{Investment}}$

9. Return on Assets = $\dfrac{\text{Income Before Interest and Taxes}}{\text{Average Total Assets}}$

10. Return on Common Equity = $\dfrac{\text{Net Income}}{\text{Average Common Stockholders' Equity}}$

11. Earnings per Share = $\dfrac{\text{Net Income Available for Common Stockholders}}{\text{Weighted-Average Common Shares Outstanding}}$

12. Growth Rate of EPS = $\dfrac{\text{EPS Current Year − EPS Prior Year}}{\text{EPS Prior Year}}$

13. Price-Earnings Ratio = $\dfrac{\text{Market Price per Share}}{\text{Earnings per Share}}$

14. Dividend Yield = $\dfrac{\text{Dividend per Share}}{\text{Market Price per Share}}$

15. Dividend Payout Ratio = $\dfrac{\text{Dividend per Share}}{\text{Earnings per Share}}$

Solvency

16. Debt Ratio = $\dfrac{\text{Total Liabilities}}{\text{Total Assets}}$

17. Debt-to-Equity Ratio = $\dfrac{\text{Total Liabilities}}{\text{Total Stockholders' Equity}}$

18. Times Interest Earned = $\dfrac{\text{Income Before Interest and Taxes, or Operating Income}}{\text{Interest Expense}}$

Cash Flow

19. Overall Cash Flow Ratio = $\dfrac{\text{Cash Flow from Operations}}{\text{Financing + Investing Cash Outflows}}$

20. Cash Return on Sales = $\dfrac{\text{Cash Flow from Operations}}{\text{Sales}}$

21. Cash Flow to Net Income = $\dfrac{\text{Cash Flow from Operations}}{\text{Net Income}}$

GP% or ratio = $\dfrac{CM}{\text{Sales}}$

Operational ratio = $\dfrac{IBIT}{\text{Sales}}$

ROS = $\dfrac{\text{NET INCOME}}{\text{Sales}}$

company (for example, inventory and depreciation methods); categories of inventory and plant and equipment; maturities and interest rates of long-term debt; profit-sharing and pension information; litigation the company is involved in; and research and development expenditures. Analysts use the information appearing in the notes to help explain their findings using other types of financial statement analysis.

Some annual reports include **management's discussion and analysis** of the company's financial condition and results of operations. This discussion includes summarized income statement and balance sheet data for at least each of the last three years. It includes specific information on the company's financial condition, results of operations, liquidity, capital resources, and any material events or uncertainties that could cause the currently reported information not to be indicative of future operating results or financial condition. Exhibits 19–9 and 19–10 present Note 1 and management's discussion and analysis of operations for Boise Cascade. Insight 19–4 examines one case where analysts failed to read beyond the numbers.

Analysts must read beyond the numbers.

INSIGHT 19–4
Reading Beyond the Numbers

"Analysts are wonderful at crunching numbers, but the job also entails making judgments—seeing the puzzle's basic shape in spite of its missing pieces." This quote is taken from an article on the failure of analysts to foresee a 40% drop in the price of the stock of Columbia Gas System, Inc..* Only one analyst, Joseph Egan at Pforzheimer & Company, recognized Columbia's problem and advised clients to sell their Columbia stock before the price fell.

How did Mr. Egan detect what other analysts missed? He read beyond the numbers in the financial statements. When Egan studied Columbia's first-quarter report, he found that Columbia had "take-or-pay" purchase contracts for gas and that gas prices had fallen significantly since the contracts were signed. The contracts obligated Columbia to pay prices that were 59% higher than the current market price. As gas prices fell, Columbia was squeezed between a falling selling price and a rigid (and high) purchase price. The potential loss from Columbia's purchase contracts caused Columbia's banks to suspend credit. The fall of Columbia's stock left analysts shaking their heads. But not Mr. Egan. He read beyond the numbers.

*This material is from Roger Lowenstein, "Columbia Gas: How Analysts Blew the Call," *The Wall Street Journal*, 8 July 1991, C1 and C8.

Exhibit 19–9
Note I to the Financial Statements, Boise Cascade Corporation

1. Summary of Significant Accounting Policies

■ **Consolidation.**   The financial statements include the accounts of the Company and all subsidiaries after elimination of intercompany balances and transactions.

■ **Other Income (Expense).**   "Other income (expense), net" on the Statements of Income includes equity in earnings and losses of joint ventures, gains and losses on the sale and disposition of property, and other miscellaneous income and expense items. In 1990, a $12,000,000 reserve was established for the anticipated cost of streamlining administrative functions and consolidating the Company's coated and uncoated white paper businesses. In 1989, the Company recorded a modest gain from the sale of its Specialty Paperboard Division.

■ **Foreign Currency Translation.**   Foreign exchange gains and losses reported on the Statements of Income arise primarily from activities of the Company's Canadian subsidiaries. The Company has entered into forward contracts to purchase 100,000,000 Canadian dollars at various dates in 1992. Gains or losses in the market value of the forward contracts are recorded as they are incurred. These gains or losses significantly offset gains or losses arising from translation of the Canadian subsidiaries' net liabilities. Translation adjustments for other foreign subsidiaries were insignificant and have been included in "Retained earnings" on the Balance Sheets.

■ **Net Income Per Common Share.**   Net income per common share was determined by dividing net income, as adjusted below, by applicable shares outstanding.

	Year Ended December 31		
	1990	1989	1988
	(expressed in thousands)		
Net income as reported	$ 75,270	$ 267,580	$ 289,120
Preferred dividends	(13,791)	(6,943)	(2,333)
Primary income	61,479	260,637	286,787
Assumed conversions:			
Preferred dividends eliminated	13,791	6,943	2,333
Interest on 7% debentures eliminated	4,443	4,467	2,992
Supplemental ESOP contribution	(5,566)	(4,571)	—
Fully diluted income	$ 74,147	$ 267,476	$ 292,112
Average number of common shares			
Primary	38,014	42,100	45,232
Fully diluted	45,673	46,943	47,481

The computation of fully diluted income per share for the year ended December 31, 1990, was antidilutive; therefore, the amounts reported for primary and fully diluted earnings are the same.

Primary income excludes preferred dividends, net of a tax benefit on the Company's Series D ESOP (employee stock ownership plan) preferred stock, which was issued in July 1989. To determine fully diluted income, dividends and interest, net of any applicable taxes, have been added back to primary income to reflect assumed conversions. Fully diluted income was reduced by the amount of additional after-tax contributions that the Company would be required to make to its ESOP if the Series D ESOP preferred shares were converted to common stock. Primary average shares include common shares outstanding and common stock equivalents attributable to outstanding stock options. In addition to common and common equivalent shares, fully diluted average shares include common shares that would be issuable upon conversion of the Company's convertible securities (see Notes 3 and 6).

■ **Cash and Short-Term Investments.**   Short-term investments consist of investments that have a maturity of three months or less. At December 31, 1990, $9,712,000 of cash and short-term investments of a wholly owned insurance subsidiary was committed for use in maintaining statutory liquidity requirements of that subsidiary.

Exhibit 19-9
Continued

■ **Inventory Valuation.** The Company uses the last-in, first-out (LIFO) method of inventory valuation for raw materials and finished goods inventories at substantially all of its domestic wood products and paper manufacturing facilities. All other inventories are valued at the lower of cost or market, with cost based on the average or first-in, first-out (FIFO) valuation method. Manufactured inventories include costs for materials, labor, and factory overhead. The cost of inventories, valued at the lower of average cost or market, exceeded the LIFO inventory valuation by $52,608,000 in 1990, $58,618,000 in 1989, and $42,583,000 in 1988.

Inventories include the following:

	December 31		
	1990	1989	1988
	(expressed in thousands)		
Finished goods and work in process	$ 261,312	$ 235,627	$ 221,516
Logs	45,502	39,516	35,675
Other raw materials and supplies	178,158	149,296	141,558
	$ 484,972	$ 424,439	$ 398,749

■ **Property.** Property and equipment are recorded at cost. Cost includes expenditures for major improvements and replacements and the net amount of interest cost associated with significant capital additions. Primarily due to expansion and modernization projects at pulp and paper mills in International Falls, Minnesota, and Rumford, Maine, capitalized interest for 1990 increased to $35,533,000. Capitalized interest was $15,981,000 in 1989 and $3,238,000 in 1988. Substantially all of the Company's paper and wood products manufacturing facilities determine depreciation by the units-of-production method, and other operations use the straight-line method. Operations which use composite depreciation methods include gains and losses from partial sales and retirements in accumulated depreciation. Gains and losses at other operations are included in income as they occur. Estimated service lives of principal items of property and equipment range from 3 to 40 years.

Cost of company timber harvested and amortization of logging roads are determined on the basis of the annual amount of timber cut in relation to the total amount of recoverable timber. Timber and timberlands are stated at cost, less the accumulated total of timber previously harvested.

A portion of the Company's wood requirements are acquired from public and private sources. Except for deposits required pursuant to wood supply contracts, no amounts are recorded until such time as the Company becomes liable for the timber. At December 31, 1990, based on average prices at the time, the unrecorded amount of those contracts was estimated to be approximately $160,000,000.

■ **Start-Up Costs.** Preoperating costs incurred during the construction and start-up of major new manufacturing facilities are capitalized and amortized over periods ranging from 5 to 15 years.

The unamortized balance of start-up costs, included in "Other assets" on the Balance Sheets, is as follows:

	December 31		
	1990	1989	1988
	(expressed in thousands)		
Balance at beginning of the year	$ 32,406	$ 32,630	$ 37,747
Capitalized [1]	22,054	3,778	—
Amortized	(4,000)	(4,002)	(4,035)
Attributable to facility sold	—	—	(1,082)
Balance at end of the year	$ 50,460	$ 32,406	$ 32,630

[1] Capitalized start-up costs shown are attributable to the expansion and modernization project at the pulp and paper mill in International Falls, Minnesota.

Exhibit 19–9
Continued

■ **Research and Development Costs.** Research and development costs are expensed as incurred. During 1990, 1989, and 1988, research and development expenses were $11,430,000, $11,143,000, and $9,485,000.

■ **Other Events.** During 1988, a nine-week strike at 15 of the Company's Northwest wood products facilities resulted in approximately 86 million square feet of lost plywood production and 99 million board feet of lost lumber production.

Exhibit 19–10
Example of Management's Discussion and Analysis of Operations
Boise Cascade Corporation

The following discussion and analysis of operations for 1989, compared with 1988 and 1987, should be read in conjunction with the "Income From Operations" and "Financial Condition" sections on pages 12 and 13 of this annual report and with the financial information on pages 14 through 29.

Boise Cascade reported net income of $268 million in 1989, compared with net income of $289 million in 1988 and $183 million in 1987. Fully diluted earnings per share were $5.70 in 1989, compared with $6.15 in 1988 and $3.64 in 1987.

Operating income for our paper and paper products segment in 1989 was $405 million, down from a record $517 million in 1988. Operating income for this segment in 1987 was $326 million. Paper-segment earnings declined through 1989, reflecting weak prices for our uncoated white papers, newsprint, and coated paper grades. Those declines reflected softening orders, as customers went through major inventory adjustments. Prices also weakened, as markets for those paper grades began to anticipate or absorb new capacity. In addition, our Northwest pulp and paper mills experienced a sharp increase in the cost of wood chips. The increase was attributable to restrictions on the harvest of timber from public lands in the Northwest, combined with a strong export market for logs and chips.

In 1988, markets for our uncoated free sheet papers were strong, with steadily improving performance. That improvement began during the second half of 1987, following some weakness during the first half of the year. Coated paper markets were robust in 1988, with demand outpacing supply. The dramatic improvement in coated paper markets began in 1987, following a period of overcapacity that had existed since 1985. Newsprint began 1988 with a price increase, following a year of strengthening prices in 1987. As 1988 progressed, some market discounting took place in anticipation of new capacity. Markets for containerboard were strong during the three-year period ending in 1989, but our corrugated container business experienced difficulty passing on the higher cost of containerboard in the form of increased box prices. During the second quarter of 1989, the Company sold its Specialty Paperboard Division for a small gain.

Boise Cascade's office products segment added to its record performance in 1989. Sales volume exceeded $1 billion for the first time, an increase of 17 percent over that of 1988, after 1988 sales volume had exceeded that of 1987 by 18 percent. Operating income for 1989 was $67 million, compared with $62 million in 1988 and $48 million in 1987. Growth in income during 1989 lagged growth in sales primarily because of start-up costs associated with two new facilities.

Operating income for our building products segment in 1989 was $107 million, compared with $54 million in strike-affected 1988 and $96 million in 1987. The 1989 performance was due to a combination of factors, including the efficiency of the Company's wood products facilities, vigorous rebuilding activity after Hurricane Hugo and the California earthquake, and strong pricing for many wood products and residual chips caused by constraints on timber supply. The positive effect of higher prices was partially offset by delivered-log costs that were about 9 percent above those of 1988.

The lower operating income reported in 1988 resulted from somewhat weaker markets for building products, an increase in the cost of raw materials, and an industrywide labor dispute in the Northwest that affected production at 15 of our wood products facilities for nine weeks. The Company lost production of approximately 86 million square feet of plywood and 99 million board feet of lumber as a result of that strike. In addition, the Company sold three wood products manufacturing facilities in 1988 that had combined annual production capacity of about 295 million square feet of plywood and 46 million board feet of lumber.

Results for 1987 were attributable to a combination of restructuring and cost-containment efforts over the previous several years, capital investments, and strong lumber and plywood prices. During 1987, we sold our 20 remaining retail building distribution centers.

OTHER EARNINGS DISCLOSURES

Investors and creditors pay close attention to income statements because income statements assist in evaluating performance and in predicting future cash flows that result in dividends. In arriving at the net income figure on the income statement, the management of a company normally separates revenues and expenses into operating and nonoperating components. Although financial statement users are interested in total net income, they generally focus on income from operations, because that component is usually more significant and continuous than income from nonoperating activities such as dividend revenue from stock owned and interest expense on bonds.

In addition to nonoperating revenues and expenses, certain other components of net income are shown separately. The purpose of presenting these items separately is to bring them to the attention of the reader. These other separate components are discontinued operations, extraordinary items, and changes in accounting principles, each of which will be discussed. Additionally, an earnings per share figure is normally computed and presented on the face of the income statement. Exhibit 19–11 is the income statement from the 1988 annual report of Valero Energy Corporation, Inc. Notice that the company has reported a loss from discontinued operations, an extraordinary item, and an accounting change.

Discontinued Operations

A company may sell or abandon a segment of its operations, resulting in **discontinued operations,** a very common event in business.[6] Valero Petroleum, in Exhibit 19–11, reported $31.8 million of income from continuing operations in 1987. Notice the amount of reported income taxes from operations by Valero. The income taxes are from continuing operations of segments of the company that will be in existence in the next fiscal year. Valero Energy Corporation shows a net loss from discontinued operations of $14.3 million in 1987. That year, the company discontinued operations of a wholly-owned subsidiary that processed oil and gas.

Valero's income statement section dealing with the discontinued operations is divided into two components: (1) the income or loss from the segment's operations until the date of disposal and (2) the gain or loss from the disposal of the segment. This form of presentation is

---

[6] In fact, *Accounting Trends & Techniques* reports that of 600 industrial and merchandising companies surveyed in 1988, 83 companies discontinued the operation of a business segment.

Exhibit 19–11
Valero Energy Corporation Earnings Disclosures

CONSOLIDATED STATEMENTS OF INCOME
(Thousands of Dollars, Except Per Share Amounts)

	Year Ended December 31,		
	1988	1987	1986
OPERATING REVENUES	$ 770,635	$ 628,529	$ 651,332
COSTS AND EXPENSES:			
Cost of sales	596,778	570,904	658,090
Operating expenses	101,392	81,620	27,540
Depreciation expense	33,749	33,271	33,028
Total	731,919	685,795	718,658
OPERATING INCOME (LOSS)	38,716	(57,266)	(67,326)
EQUITY IN EARNINGS OF VALERO NATURAL GAS PARTNERS, L.P. AND PREDECESSOR OPERATIONS	15,227	40,586	85,291
GAIN ON DISPOSITION OF ASSETS	—	84,503	—
OTHER INCOME (EXPENSE), NET	3,853	251	(976)
INTEREST AND DEBT EXPENSE:			
Incurred	(23,683)	(45,349)	(90,071)
Capitalized	262	555	162
INCOME (LOSS) FROM CONTINUING OPERATIONS BEFORE FEDERAL INCOME TAXES	34,375	23,280	(72,920)
FEDERAL INCOME TAX EXPENSE (BENEFIT)	3,800	(8,584)	(33,913)
INCOME (LOSS) FROM CONTINUING OPERATIONS	30,575	31,864	(39,007)
DISCONTINUED OPERATIONS:			
(Loss) from discontinued operations (net of income tax benefit)	—	(1,717)	(53,148)
(Loss) on disposal of discontinued operations (net of income tax benefit)	—	(12,611)	(7,733)
	—	(14,328)	(60,881)
INCOME (LOSS) BEFORE EXTRAORDINARY ITEM AND CUMULATIVE EFFECT OF ACCOUNTING CHANGE	30,575	17,536	(99,888)
EXTRAORDINARY ITEM-(loss) on early extinguishment of debt (net of income tax benefit)	—	(11,627)	—
CUMULATIVE EFFECT ON PRIOR YEARS (TO DECEMBER 31, 1986) OF CHANGE IN METHOD OF ACCOUNTING FOR INCOME TAXES	—	7,000	—
NET INCOME (LOSS)	30,575	12,909	(99,888)
Less: Preferred and Serial Preference Stock dividend requirements	16,537	11,371	9,451
NET INCOME (LOSS) APPLICABLE TO COMMON STOCK	$ 14,038	$ 1,538	$(109,339)
EARNINGS (LOSS) PER SHARE OF COMMON STOCK:			
Continuing operations	$ .54	$ .80	$ (1.93)
Discontinued operations	—	(.56)	(2.43)
Extraordinary item	—	(.45)	—
Cumulative effect of accounting change	—	.27	—
Total	$ .54	$ .06	$ (4.36)
DIVIDENDS DECLARED PER SHARE OF COMMON STOCK	$ —	$ —	$ —

required because the company operated the segment for a portion of the year. The income or loss from discontinued operation and the gain or loss on disposal are each reported net of income taxes.

Extraordinary Items

An **extraordinary item** is one that is material in amount, unusual and infrequent in occurrence, and not expected to recur in the normal course of business. The item is presented separately, rather than as a component of income from operations, to put the reader on notice that it is indeed extraordinary and that because of it, the comparability of the current period's financial statements with those of prior periods is affected. Examples of extraordinary items include gains or losses from fire, flood, earthquake, or the expropriation of a company's assets by a foreign government.

Such events are company-specific in that the qualities of unusualness and infrequency must be viewed from the perspective of the reporting company. In other words, management must assess whether the event is unusual and infrequent given the character of a company's business and its geographic location. For example, a loss by a company in Chicago, Illinois, due to an earthquake would normally be classified as an extraordinary item. However, an earthquake loss in southern California most likely would not, because earthquakes are recurring events in that part of the country. A natural disaster could result in losses for a company, but hurricane losses in southern Florida are not extraordinary items, because hurricanes in that environment are expected and are a cost of doing business. These two criteria thus limit the events that are reported as extraordinary items on the income statement.

Extraordinary items are reported net of their tax effects as a separate component of net income. There is a subtotal identifying net income before extraordinary items and another (after the items) identifying net income including extraordinary items. This form of presentation alerts the reader to the fact that although the item is included in the computation of net income, it does not result from normal operations, and is unlikely to occur in the foreseeable future.

Accounting Changes

A company may change from one generally accepted accounting principle to another. Examples of such **accounting changes** include a change from the FIFO method of costing inventories to the LIFO method or a change from the sum-of-the-years'-digits depreciation method to the straight-line method. Accounting changes are always disclosed in the notes to the financial statements, because they affect the comparability of a company's financial statements after the change to those of prior periods. Additionally, for most types of accounting changes, the effect on the earnings of prior years (called a *cumulative effect*) of adopting a new accounting principle is also disclosed as a separate item following extraordinary items (if any), in the income statement.

To illustrate the computation of the cumulative effect, assume that in 19X3 a company changed its depreciation method on its machinery from the double-declining balance method to the straight-line method of depreciation. The machinery originally cost $250,000 when purchased in 19X1, had an estimated useful life of five years, and no salvage value. Following is the calculation of the cumulative effect and the reporting of that effect in the financial statements in the year of the change.

Year	Double-Declining Balance Depreciation	Straight-Line Depreciation	Excess of Double-Declining Depreciation over Straight-Line
19X1	$100,000	$50,000	$50,000
19X2	60,000	50,000	10,000
			$60,000

Note that the excess or cumulative effect relates to the period starting with the purchase date of the asset and ending at the beginning of the current year. The new principle, in this case straight-line depreciation, is used in the current year's income statement. The cumulative effect of the change on prior years' earnings is interpreted this way: had straight-line depreciation been used instead of double-declining balance in 19X1 and 19X2, net income would have been $60,000 greater (ignoring income taxes) for that period of time.

If the tax rate is 30%, the following income statement presentation is made.

Income from operations before the cumulative effect of change in accounting principle	$340,000
Cumulative effect on prior years' income of a change from double-declining balance depreciation to the straight-line depreciation method (less tax effect of $18,000)	42,000
Net income	$382,000

Exhibit 19–12 presents the disclosure relating to an accounting change resulting from a change of the costs included in inventories for National Intergroup, Inc.

Exhibit 19–12
National Intergroup, Inc.
Disclosure of Accounting Change

National Intergroup, Inc. and Subsidiaries

(Thousands of Dollars Except for Per Share Amounts)

	For The Years Ended		
	March 31,		December 31,
	1988	1987	1985
Net Sales and Other Revenue	**$3,355,293**	$4,473,674	$2,066,238
Operating Costs			
Cost of products sold	**3,044,951**	4,148,096	1,992,450
Selling, general and administrative expenses	**212,857**	217,313	72,903
Depreciation and amortization	**49,187**	60,245	24,830
	3,306,995	4,425,654	2,090,183
	48,298	48,020	(23,945)
Unusual Items			
Provision for sale of Luxembourg facility	**(24,000)**	—	—
Loss on trading contracts and purchase commitments	**—**	—	(5,209)
	(24,000)	—	(5,209)
Operating income (loss) from continuing operations	**24,298**	48,020	(29,154)
Financing Costs			
Interest income	**22,338**	16,101	36,810
Interest expense	**89,087**	90,197	54,010
	66,749	74,096	17,200
Loss from continuing operations before provision for income taxes, minority interests, equity in earnings (losses) of affiliates, extraordinary items and cumulative effect of change in accounting principle	**(42,451)**	(26,076)	(46,354)
Income Tax Provision	**2,760**	2,007	709
Loss from continuing operations before minority interests, equity in earnings (losses) of affiliates, extraordinary items and cumulative effect of change in accounting principle	**(45,211)**	(28,083)	(47,063)
Minority Interests	**—**	—	(123)
Equity in Earnings (Losses) of Affiliates			
National Steel Corporation	**30,861**	(13,050)	(44,218)
Permian Partners, L.P.	**(8,426)**	—	—
	22,435	(13,050)	(44,218)
Loss from continuing operations before extraordinary items and cumulative effect of change in accounting principle	**(22,776)**	(41,133)	(91,158)
Discontinued Operations			
Income (loss) from discontinued operations (Less applicable income taxes of $302 in 1985)	**(1,121)**	(3,824)	62,123
(Loss) gain on disposal of discontinued operations	**(745)**	—	13,805
	(1,866)	(3,824)	75,928
Loss before extraordinary items and cumulative effect of change in accounting principle	**(24,642)**	(44,957)	(15,230)
Extraordinary Items	**92**		
Cumulative Effect on Prior Years (to March 31, 1987) of Change in Method of Accounting for Certain Overhead Costs in Inventory	**2,655**	—	—
Net Loss	**$ (21,895)**	$ (44,957)	$ (15,230)
Per Share of Common Stock			
Loss from continuing operations before extraordinary items and cumulative effect of change in accounting principle	**$ (1.31)**	$ (2.28)	$ (4.99)
Discontinued operations	**(.09)**	(.18)	3.55
Extraordinary items	**.01**	—	—
Cumulative effect on prior years (to March 31, 1987) of change in method of accounting for certain overhead costs in inventory	**.12**	—	—
Net Loss	**$ (1.27)**	$ (2.46)	$ (1.44)
Pro Forma Amounts Assuming Accounting Change is Applied Retroactively			
Loss before extraordinary items	**$ (24,642)**	$ (45,653)	$ (14,260)
Loss per share of common stock before extraordinary items	**$ (1.40)**	$ (2.49)	$ (1.39)
Net loss	**$ (24,550)**	$ (45,653)	$ (14,260)
Net loss per share of common stock	**$ (1.39)**	$ (2.49)	$ (1.39)

See notes to consolidated financial statements.

SUMMARY

Financial statement analysis using horizontal, vertical, and ratio analysis assists users in making investment decisions. But the results of these tools cannot be viewed in a vacuum. They are only one source of information. Analysts are concerned with trends in the financial statement items as well as with particular ratios. Horizontal analysis studies changes in amounts and percentages in comparative financial statements. One form of horizontal analysis is trend analysis, where changes in key figures are viewed across several time periods.

Vertical analysis examines the relationship of individual financial statement items. Financial statement components are expressed as percentages. Vertical analysis of the income statement, using sales as 100%, indicates the percentage of sales relating to such items as cost of goods sold, gross margin, operating expenses, and net income. Similarly, vertical analysis of the balance sheet shows each item or key figure as a percentage of total assets or equities. A type of vertical analysis is the preparation of common-size financial statements, where each item on the financial statements is expressed as a percentage.

Ratio analysis can be classified into three major types: liquidity, profitability, and solvency. Which ratios to use and which to emphasize depend on the type of decision to be made. Short-term creditors are concerned primarily with liquidity. Long-term creditors are more concerned with solvency. Common stockholders are most concerned with profitability.

Ratio analysis must be used with care. Ratios provide information only in the context of a comparison. They can be interpreted only in comparison with past ratios of the same company, with ratios of other companies in the same industry, or with some predetermined norm. The reader should realize that different accounting methods such as LIFO and FIFO, or sum-of-the-years'-digits depreciation and straight-line depreciation, can cause similar firms to show quite different ratios.

The income statement may contain the effects of discontinued operations, extraordinary items, or accounting changes. These items are separately disclosed, net of their income tax effects. The purpose of separate disclosure is to highlight the impact of these items on net income and to isolate the effect from income from continuing operations.

APPENDIX—EARNINGS PER SHARE

Earnings per share (EPS), sometimes referred to as *net income per share of outstanding stock*, is presented as a separate item at the bottom of the income statement. Earnings per share is the single most widely used financial ratio. This information is frequently cited in the financial press and readers of financial statements depend heavily on it to assess company performance. Because of the importance attached to the earnings per share figure, the Accounting Principles Board (APB) decided that this information should be computed and reported in the financial statements of all companies. APB Opinion No. 15 deals with the computation of EPS figures for companies. The calculation is often quite complex. For example, although Opinion No. 15 contains detailed instructions for computing EPS, a separate official interpretation of Opinion No. 15 (over 100 pages long), was issued by the Board to assist accountants in understanding the pronouncement.

Our purpose here is not to explain the detailed computations, but to focus on the basic calculation of EPS and the purpose of the ratio. Some discussion of Opinion No. 15 is necessary for a proper understanding of the EPS figure.

EPS is the income per share available to the common stockholders and, in its simplest form, is net income divided by the number of common shares outstanding.

$$\text{EPS} = \frac{\text{Net Income Available to Common Shareholders}}{\text{Number of Shares of Common Stock Outstanding}}$$

This formula is valid, however, only for a company with a capital structure that (1) contains only common stock and (2) has an unchanging number of shares of stock during the period.

What happens if the company has preferred stockholders? In this situation, some of the company's net income must be paid in dividends to preferred stockholders. In calculating earnings per share of common stock, one treats the dividend payments on preferred stock as conceptually similar to interest on debt and subtracts them from net income in arriving at income available to common stockholders. Also, if the company issues or reacquires shares of common stock during the period, there is no single number of shares outstanding, and the weighted-average number of shares outstanding must be used in the denominator. The equation thus becomes

$$\text{EPS} = \frac{\text{Net Income} - \text{Preferred Dividends}}{\text{Weighted-Average Number of Common Shares Outstanding}}$$

To illustrate the computation of EPS when preferred stock is present and there are changes in the number of common shares outstanding, assume that Hooks Company has net income of $58,000 and paid preferred stock dividends of $16,000 during 19X0. On January 1,

19X0, the company had 10,000 shares of common stock outstanding, and also issued an additional 12,000 shares on October 1, 19X0. The company's year-end is December 31. Income available to the common stockholders is $42,000 ($58,000 less dividends of $16,000), and the weighted-average number of common shares outstanding is computed as follows.

Shares Outstanding		**Weighted Average**
10,000 for 12 months	$10,000 \times \dfrac{12 \text{ months}}{12 \text{ months}} =$	10,000
12,000 issued on October 1	$12,000 \times \dfrac{3 \text{ months}}{12 \text{ months}} =$	3,000
		13,000

Weighted-average number of common shares outstanding

$$\text{EPS} = \frac{\text{Net Income} - \text{Preferred Dividends}}{\text{Weighted-Average Number of Common Shares Outstanding}}$$

$$\text{EPS} = \frac{\$42,000}{13,000 \text{ shares}}$$

$$\text{EPS} = \$3.23$$

Thus far, our example assumed a simple capital structure, meaning that the company does not have any debt or equity securities that have the potential to dilute or reduce EPS. Convertible bonds and convertible preferred stock are examples of items that have a potentially dilutive effect on EPS. Convertible bonds and preferred stock are potentially dilutive when conversion of the bonds or preferred stock into common stock would (1) increase the denominator by increasing the number of common shares outstanding and (2) increase the numerator by eliminating payments of interest or preferred stock dividends. Convertible bonds and preferred stock *are* dilutive when conversion of the bonds or preferred stock into common stock would result in a decrease in earnings per share. Investors are very interested in the reduction in EPS that might be caused by potentially dilutive securities. Potentially dilutive securities change a simple capital structure to a complex capital structure.

Stock options and warrants can also increase the denominator, because they give the holder the right to purchase a given number of shares at a specified price. In this instance, the company is committed to issue additional shares of common stock if and when the holders of options and warrants choose to exercise their conversion privilege.

Stock options and warrants do not affect the numerator of the EPS formula.

Accountants calculate two measures of earnings per share. The first is called primary earnings per share and includes the effects of any potentially dilutive securities that are *reasonably expected* to be converted into common stock (called common stock equivalents). The second measure of earnings per share is called fully diluted earnings per share and involves the calculation of a hypothetical figure that includes the effects of converting all potentially dilutive securities. Fully diluted earnings per share is normally less than primary earnings per share. Essentially, it is a worst-case scenario in that it assumes that all potentially dilutive securities will be converted. Details of these calculations are beyond the scope of this text. We give only a simple example of the effect of dilutive securities.

Assume Bartlet Company has earnings of $120,000 and 20,000 weighted-average shares of common stock outstanding. Bartlet also has 5,000 shares of preferred stock that can be converted into an equal number of common shares. The preferred stock pays a $4 dividend per share. The preferred stock is a common stock equivalent because conditions in the stock market make it likely that the preferred stock will be converted.

If the preferred stock were not convertible, EPS would be as follows.

$$EPS = \frac{\text{Net Income} - \text{Preferred Dividends}}{\text{Weighted-Average Number of Common Shares Outstanding}}$$

$$= \frac{\$120,000 - \$20,000}{20,000 \text{ shares}}$$

$$= \$5.00$$

The presence of the preferred stock removes consideration of the preferred stock dividends from the numerator and adds 5,000 shares of common stock to the denominator. (That would be the effect of converting the preferred stock to common stock.)

$$\text{Primary EPS} = \frac{\$120,000}{(20,000 + 5,000)}$$

$$= \$4.80$$

The preferred stock is dilutive because it lowers primary EPS from $5 to $4.80.

Bartlet also has bonds outstanding that can be converted into 6,000 shares of common stock. The bonds are not common stock equivalents because market conditions do not make it likely that the bonds will be converted. Interest on the bonds is $4,000 per year and would not be paid if the bonds were converted. To calculate the fully diluted EPS, you must add back the bond interest to net income, and the additional 6,000 shares on stock must be added to the denominator. (That would be the effect of converting the bonds to common stock.)

$$\text{Fully Diluted EPS} = \frac{(\$120,000 + \$4,000)}{(20,000 + 5,000 + 6,000)}$$

$$= \$4.00$$

The bonds are dilutive because conversion would lower EPS from $4.80 to $4.00.

PRESENTATION OF EARNINGS PER SHARE

If extraordinary items, accounting changes, and gains or losses from discontinued operations are included in net income for the period, separate EPS figures are presented for income from continuing operations, discontinued operations, extraordinary items, accounting changes, and net income. Refer back to Exhibit 19–11 and see how the Valero Energy Corporation presented its EPS figures in its 1988 annual report.

DEMONSTRATION PROBLEM 19–1

Perform a horizontal and vertical analysis of comparative financial statements for the Boise Cascade Corporation for the year ended December 31, 1990.

Solution to Demonstration Problem 19–1
Recall that horizontal analysis involves two steps:

1. Calculate the dollar amount of the change from the base year (in this case 1989) to the current year.
2. Divide the amount of the change by the base year (1989) amount.

Comparative Balance Sheet—Horizontal Analysis

Boise Cascade Corporation
Comparative Balance Sheet
December 31, 1990 and 1989
(expressed in thousands)

	1990	1989	Increase (Decrease) Amount	Percent
Assets				
Current:				
Cash and cash items	$ 19,781	$ 19,715	$ 66	0.3 %
Short-term investments	6,165	5,526	639	11.6
Receivables (net)	412,558	421,568	(9,010)	(2.1)
Inventories	484,972	424,439	60,533	14.3
Deferred income tax				
benefits	55,115	48,716	6,399	13.1
Other	18,992	12,353	6,639	53.7
	997,583	932,317	65,266	7.0
Property:				
Property and equipment	4,881,672	4,211,786	669,886	15.9
Accumulated depreciation	(1,726,794)	(1,583,210)	143,584	9.1
	3,154,878	2,628,576	526,302	20.0
Timber, timberlands, and				
and timber deposits	391,985	388,294	3,691	1.0
	3,546,863	3,016,870	529,993	17.6
Other assets	240,324	193,438	46,886	24.2
Total assets	$ 4,784,770	$ 4,142,625	$642,145	15.5
Liabilities and Shareholders' Equity				
Current:				
Notes payable	$ 40,000	$ -0-	40,000	–*
Current portion of				
long-term debt	136,731	30,390	106,341	350.0
Income taxes payable	140	4,273	(4,133)	(96.7)
Accounts payable	344,384	391,542	(47,158)	(12.0)
Accrued liabilities:				
Compensation & benefits	99,530	114,082	(14,552)	(12.8)
Interest payable	38,460	40,071	(1,611)	(4.0)
Other	99,127	97,866	1,261	1.3
	758,372	678,224	80,148	11.8

	1990	1989	Increase (Decrease) Amount	Increase (Decrease) Percent
Debt:				
Long-term debt, less current portion	1,648,826	1,204,978	443,848	36.8
Guarantee of 8.5% ESOP debt	285,678	292,581	(6,903)	2.4
Deferred income taxes	394,162	307,111	87,051	28.3
Other long-term liabilities	122,201	84,431	37,770	44.7
	2,450,867	1,889,101	561,766	29.7
Shareholders' equity:				
Preferred stock	302,807	303,518	(711)	0.2
Deferred ESOP benefit	(285,678)	(292,581)	6,903	2.4
Common stock	94,871	94,866	5	0.0
Retained earnings	1,463,531	1,469,497	(5,966)	0.4
Total stockholders' equity	1,575,531	1,575,300	231	0.0
Total liabilities and stockholders' equity	$4,784,770	$4,142,625	$642,145	15.5

*Mathematically, you cannot calculate a percentage change if the base year is zero.

Horizontal analysis of the balance sheet indicates that while total assets increased by 15% over 1989, short-term debt grew by approximately 12% and long-term debt by 30%. These are not good signs; however, they must be viewed in the context of Boise Cascade's industry performance. In 1990 there was a downturn in the paper industry and a slowing of the U.S. economy.

Comparative Income Statement—Horizontal Analysis

Boise Cascade Corporation
Comparative Income Statement
December 31, 1990 and 1989
(expressed in thousands)

	1990	1989	Increase (Decrease) Amount	Percent
Revenues				
Sales	$4,185,920	$4,338,030	$(152,110)	(3.5)%
Other income (expense)	(1,360)	15,020	(16,380)	109.1
Costs and expenses				
Materials, labor and other operating expenses	3,318,350	3,218,120	100,230	3.1
Depreciation and cost of company timber harvested	212,890	202,060	10,830	5.4
Selling & administrative expenses	419,430	406,400	13,030	3.2
	3,950,670	3,826,580	124,090	3.2
Income from operations	233,890	526,470	(292,580)	(55.6)
Interest expense	(116,620)	(95,810)	20,810	21.7
Interest income	3,610	6,370	(2,760)	(43.3)
Foreign exchange gain (loss)	520	(160)	680	425.0
	(112,490)	(89,600)	22,890	25.5
Income before income taxes	121,400	436,870	(315,470)	(72.2)
Income tax provision	46,130	169,290	(123,160)	(72.8)
Net income	$ 75,270	$ 267,580	$(192,310)	(71.9)

Horizontal analysis of the income statement indicates that sales decreased by 3.5% in 1990 and costs and expenses increased by 3.2% resulting in a decrease in income from operations of 55.6%. The cyclical downturn in the paper industry resulted in a drop in net income of 71.9%.

Comparative Balance Sheet—Vertical Analysis
Vertical analysis of the balance sheet shows the relationship between (1) each asset account and total assets, and (2) each liability and stockholders' equity account and total liabilities and stockholders' equity. In each case total assets and stockholders' equity are 100% and each account is expressed as a percentage of 100%.

Boise Cascade Corporation
Comparative Balance Sheet
December 31, 1990 and 1989
(expressed in thousands)

Assets	Amount	Percent	Amount	Percent
Current:				
Cash and cash items	$ 19,781	0.4%	$ 19,715	0.5%
Short-term investments	6,165	0.1	5,526	0.1
Receivables (net)	412,558	8.6	421,568	10.2
Inventories	484,972	10.1	424,439	10.2
Deferred income tax benefits	55,115	1.2	48,716	1.2
Other	18,992	0.4	12,353	0.3
	997,583	20.8	932,317	22.5
Property:				
Property and equipment	4,881,672		4,211,786	
Accumulated depreciation	(1,726,794)		(1,583,210)	
	3,154,878	65.9	2,628,576	63.4
Timber, timberlands, and				
timber deposits	391,985	8.2	388,294	9.4
	3,546,863	74.1	3,016,870	72.8
Other assets	240,324	5.1	193,438	4.7
Total assets	$ 4,784,770	100.0%	$ 4,142,625	100.0%

Liabilities and Shareholders' Equity

Current:				
Notes payable	$ 40,000	0.8%	$ -0-	0.0%
Current portion of long-term				
debt	136,731	2.9	30,390	0.7
Income taxes payable	140	0.0	4,273	0.1
Accounts payable	344,384	7.2	391,542	9.5
Accrued liabilities:				
Compensation & benefits	99,530	2.1	114,082	2.8
Interest payable	38,460	0.8	40,071	0.9
Other	99,127	2.1	97,866	2.4
	758,372	15.9	678,224	16.4
Debt:				
Long-term debt, less current				
portion	1,648,826	34.5	1,204,978	29.1
Guarantee of 8.5% ESOP debt	285,678	6.0	292,581	7.1
Deferred income taxes	394,162	8.2	307,111	7.4
Other long-term liabilities	122,201	2.5	84,431	2.0
	2,450,867	51.2	1,889,101	45.6

Shareholders' equity:				
Preferred stock	302,807	6.3	303,518	7.3
Deferred ESOP benefit	(285,678)	(6.0)	(292,581)	(7.1)
Common stock	94,871	2.0	94,866	2.3
Retained earnings	1,463,531	30.6	1,469,497	35.5
Total stockholders' equity	1,575,531	32.9	1,575,300	38.0
Total liabilities and stockholders' equity	$4,784,770	100.0%	$4,142,625	100.0%

Our analysis indicates that current assets fell slightly in 1990 while plant assets increased. Boise Cascade was able to somewhat reduce its short-term debt but its long-term debt increased. Total stockholders' equity was down from 1989, due mostly to a decrease in retained earnings from a lower net income in 1990 than 1989.

Comparative Income Statement—Vertical Analysis

Vertical analysis of the income statement shows the relationship of each item on the income statement to sales which is 100%.

Boise Cascade Corporation
Comparative Income Statement
December 31, 1990 and 1989
(expressed in thousands)

	1990		1989	
	Amount	Percent	Amount	Percent
Revenues:				
Sales	$4,185,920	100.0%	$4,338,030	100.0%
Other income (expense)	(1,360)	0.0	15,020	0.3
Costs and expenses:				
Materials, labor, and other operating expenses	3,318,350	79.3	3,218,120	74.2
Depreciation and cost of company timber harvested	212,890	5.1	202,060	4.6
Selling & administrative expenses	419,430	10.0	406,400	9.4
	3,950,670	94.4	3,826,580	88.2
Income from operations:	233,890	5.6	526,470	12.1
Interest expense	(116,620)	(2.8)	(95,810)	(2.2)
Interest income	3,610	0.1	6,370	0.1
Foreign exchange gain (loss)	520	0.0	(160)	0.0
	(112,490)	(2.7)	(89,600)	(2.1)

	1990		1989	
	Amount	**Percent**	**Amount**	**Percent**
Income before income taxes	121,400	2.9	436,870	10.0
Income tax provision	46,130	1.1	169,290	3.9
Net income	$ 75,270	1.8%	$267,580	6.1%

Increased expenses and a reduction in sales resulted in a significant decline in net income in 1990.

DEMONSTRATION PROBLEM 19–2

This problem requires you to review the ratios that were introduced in previous chapters. If necessary, reread discussions of the importance of each ratio in the text.

The current ratio is a liquidity ratio and measures the relationship between current assets and current liabilities.

$$\text{Current Ratio} = \frac{\text{Current Assets}}{\text{Current Liabilities}}$$

The current ratio for Boise Cascade in 1990 was $\frac{\$997,583}{\$758,372} =$ 1.32:1

Another liquidity ratio is the quick ratio.

$$\text{Quick Ratio} = \frac{\text{Cash + Short-Term Investments + Receivables}}{\text{Current Liabilities}}$$

For Boise Cascade, the quick ratio for 1990 is

$$\frac{\$19,781 + \$6,165 + \$412,558}{\$758,372} = .58:1$$

In general, firms attempt to maintain a current ratio of 2:1 and a quick ratio of 1:1.

Two turnover ratios relating to fixed assets are the fixed asset turnover ratio and the total asset turnover ratio. These ratios measure the relationship between fixed and total assets and sales. They are used in assessing managements' ability to employ the investment in those assets effectively.

The fixed asset turnover ratio is calculated as

$$\frac{\text{Sales}}{\text{Average Fixed Assets}}$$

In 1990 the ratio is computed as

$$\frac{\$4,185,920}{(\$3,546,863 + \$3,016,870)/2} = 1.28{:}1$$

The total asset turnover ratio is calculated as

$$\frac{\text{Sales}}{\text{Average Total Assets}}$$

For 1990 the ratio is computed as

$$\frac{\$4,185,920}{(\$4,784,770 + \$4,142,625)/2} = .94{:}1$$

The price-earnings ratio and the dividend payout ratio are examples of profitability ratios that related earnings to the price of a company's stock or the dividend paid by the company.

$$\text{Price-Earnings Ratio} = \frac{\text{Common Stock Market Price}}{\text{Earnings per Common Share}}$$

$$\text{Dividend Payout Ratio} = \frac{\text{Dividend per Common Share}}{\text{Earnings per Common Share}}$$

The ratios for 1990 for Boise Cascade are calculated as

$$\text{Price-Earnings Ratio} = \frac{\$26.00}{\$1.62} = 16.1{:}1$$

$$\text{Dividend Payout Ratio} = \frac{\$1.52}{\$1.62} = .94$$

The cash flow ratios for Boise Cascade are

$$\text{Overall Cash Flow Ratio} = \frac{\text{Cash Flow from Operations}}{\text{Financing} + \text{Investing Cash Outflows}}$$

$$= \frac{\$251,886}{[\$518,544 + (\$769,725)]} = 1.00$$

$$\text{Cash Return on Sales} = \frac{\text{Cash Flow from Operations}}{\text{Sales}}$$

$$= \frac{\$251,886}{\$4,185,920} = .06$$

$$\text{Cash Flow to Net Income} = \frac{\text{Cash Flow from Operations}}{\text{Net Income}}$$

$$= \frac{\$251,886}{\$75,270} = 3.35$$

Boise Cascade's cash flow from operations is slightly more than cash needed for investing and financing. Cash provided by operations is over 3 ⅓ times net income, but only 6 cents in cash flows from each sales dollar.

The inventory and accounts receivable turnovers for Boise Cascade are

$$\text{Inventory Turnover} = \frac{\text{Cost of Goods Sold}}{\text{Average Inventory}}$$

$$= \frac{\$3,318,350}{[(\$484,972+\$424,439)/2]} = 7.3 \text{ times}$$

Days' sales in inventory is 53 days, calculated as follows.

$$\text{Average Daily Cost of Goods Sold} = \frac{\text{Cost of Goods Sold}}{365} = \frac{\$3,381,350}{365} = \$9,091$$

$$\text{Days' Sales in Inventory} = \frac{\text{Ending Inventory}}{\text{Average Daily Cost of Goods Sold}} = \frac{\$484,972}{\$9,091} = 53 \text{ days}$$

$$\text{Receivable Turnover} = \frac{\text{Sales}}{\text{Average Accounts Receivable}} = \frac{\$4,185,920}{[(\$412,558+\$421,568)/2]} = 10 \text{ times}$$

Average turnover period for accounts receivable is 36 days, calculated as follows.

$$\text{Average Daily Sales} = \frac{\text{Sales}}{365} = \frac{\$4,185,920}{365} = \$11,468$$

$$\text{Days' Sales in Accounts Receivable} = \frac{\text{Ending Accounts Receivable}}{\text{Average Daily Sales}}$$

$$= \frac{\$412,558}{\$11,468} = 36 \text{ days}$$

The more common ratios used to evaluate a company's solvency or overall debt and equity position are shown below with calculations of the same measures for Boise Cascade for 1990. We have used total debt where debt is specified. Some analysts prefer to use only noncurrent debt.

$$\text{Times Interest Earned} = \frac{\text{Earnings Before Interest and Taxes*}}{\text{Interest Expense}}$$

$$= \frac{\$75{,}270 + \$46{,}130 + \$116{,}620}{\$116{,}620} = 2.04 \text{ times}$$

$$\text{Debt to Total Assets} = \frac{\text{Total Debt}}{\text{Total Assets}}$$

$$= \frac{\$758{,}352 + \$2{,}450{,}867}{\$4{,}784{,}770} = .67$$

$$\text{Debt to Stockholders' Equity} = \frac{\text{Debt}}{\text{Total Stockholders' Equity}}$$

*Often calculated by adding interest and taxes to net income.

1990: $\dfrac{\$758{,}372 + \$2{,}450{,}867}{\$1{,}575{,}531} = 2.04$ **1989:** $\dfrac{\$678{,}224 + \$1{,}889{,}101}{\$1{,}575{,}300} = 1.63$

The debt to equity ratio increased from 1989 to 1990 for Boise Cascade. The increase reflected additional borrowing by the company, which was required to fund its capital expenditure program in a year when earnings were down. Capital expenditures were at a record high in 1990.

Key Terms

accounting changes

common-size financial statements

comparative financial statements

composition problem

discontinued operations

earnings per share (EPS)

extraordinary items

horizontal analysis

junk bonds

leverage

leveraged buyout (LBO)

liquidity

management's discussion and analysis

operating efficiency

profitability

solvency

trading on the equity

trend analysis

vertical analysis

working capital

SALES - EXPENSES = NI

ASSIGNMENTS

19–1   Different Interests

Carol approves business loans for City Trust Bank. "I analyze financial statements and other data to determine if a company is a good loan prospect," she explains to Fred.

"Wow," Fred exclaims. "I guess you get all the good stock tips."

"Actually, no," Carol explains. "Not all good loan customers are good investment prospects."

REQUIRED:

Discuss Carol's remark.

19–2   Income Statement Ratios

The following data are available for Apex Company.

Sales	$120,000,000
Cost of goods sold	80,000,000
Selling and administrative	30,000,000
Interest	2,000,000
Income taxes	4,000,000
Net income	4,000,000

REQUIRED:

1. Calculate the following income statement ratios:
   a. Gross profit ratio
   b. Operating ratio
   c. Return on sales
2. How are these ratios interpreted?

19–3   Liquidity Ratios

Clown Town Products has the following current accounts.

Current Assets

	19X4	19X5
Cash	$20,000	$25,000
Accounts receivable	39,000	55,000
Inventory	40,000	45,000
Prepaids	10,000	5,000

130,000 —

Current Liabilities

Accounts payable	$35,000	$30,000
Notes payable	10,000	-0-

REQUIRED:

1. Calculate the following liquidity measures for Clown Town as of the end of 19X5.

   a. Working capital

   b. Current ratio

   c. Quick (Acid-test) ratio

2. How should these measures be interpreted? (Refer specifically to the rule of thumb for the current ratio.)

19–4 Current Asset Activity Ratios

JC Williams Retail Stores has the following selected account balances for 19XX.

Income statement accounts:	
Sales	$300,000
Cost of goods sold	150,000
Balance sheet accounts:	
Accounts receivable	$ 50,000
Inventory	40,000

The following are industry standards that JC Williams' managers believe are appropriate standards.

Accounts receivable turnover ratio	5
Number of days' sales in accounts receivable	72
Inventory turnover ratio	4
Number of days' sales in inventory	90

JC Williams' managers are proud of the receivables measures but want to improve the inventory measures. "We want to be the best," J. C. Williams announced.

REQUIRED:

1. Calculate the following activity measures for JC Williams.

   a. Accounts receivable turnover ratio

   b. Number of days' sales in accounts receivable

   c. Inventory turnover ratio

   d. Number of days' sales in inventory

2. How should these measures be interpreted? Refer specifically to the industry standards and to management's feelings.

19–5   Profitability Ratios

ABC Company has net income of $40,000. Interest and taxes totaled $60,000. The following summary totals are taken from ABC's balance sheet. ABC has no preferred stock.

Average total assets	$800,000
Average total liabilities (including long-term debt)	440,000

REQUIRED:

1. Calculate the following for ABC.
   a. Return on assets
   b. Return on common equity
2. ABC pays 13% interest on its long-term debt. Is ABC using leverage effectively?

19–6   Stock Profitability Ratios

The following selected information is taken from the financial statements of Dad's Place, Inc. Dad's average market price at the end of the fourth quarter was $20.00

Shares of stock outstanding (all year):	
common	100,000
preferred	-0-
Earnings	$200,000
Dividends	90,000

REQUIRED:

1. Calculate the following:
   a. Earnings per share
   b. Price-earnings ratio
   c. Dividend yield
   d. Payout ratio
2. What do each of these measures tell us?

19–7   Solvency Ratios

Adam Hat Company had total assets of $3,500,000 and stockholders' equity of $1,500,000. The weighted average interest rate on debt was 11%. Adam Hat earned $840,000 and paid taxes of $90,000.

REQUIRED:

Calculate the following ratios. Explain the meaning of each.

1. Debt ratio
2. Times interest earned

19-8 Cash Flow Ratios

Garr Company had $40,000 in cash on January 1. During the year Garr used $60,000 in cash repaying a long term debt and invested $30,000. Operating activities provided $70,000, net income was $42,000, and sales were $280,000.

REQUIRED:

1. Calculate the cash flow ratios below:
   a. Overall cash flow ratio
   b. Cash return on sales
   c. Cash flow to net income
2. Evaluate the cash flows of Garr.

19-9 Financial Statement Analysis and Auditors

Analytical procedures help auditors look for unexpected relationships or trends in data. Auditors then devise tests to determine the cause of the unexpected relationship or trend.

REQUIRED:

Describe how financial statement analysis techniques help auditors.

19-10 Analytical Procedures

Jan Jones is auditing the Cleveland division of Wholeheart Animal Foods. Selected account balances (in thousands) for the Cleveland division for the last three years follow.

Account / Year	19X3	19X2	19X1
Sales	$ 55,000	$ 65,500	$ 60,000
Cost of goods sold	30,600	36,200	33,000
Trade receivables	17,200	16,000	15,000
Inventories	11,000	13,300	11,800
Sales commissions	1,650	3,275	3,000
Utilities	5,000	5,500	3,800
Equipment (net)	175,000	180,000	156,000
Accounts payable	5,000	3,300	2,600
Supplies expense	2,300	2,620	2,300
Advertising	10,700	5,350	7,800

REQUIRED:

Use analytical procedures to examine the relationships and trends in the Cleveland division's accounts. What areas should Jan Jones examine closely?

19–11   Horizontal Analysis of the Balance Sheet

Prepare a horizontal analysis of the balance sheet for the Ennis Company for the years 19X1 and 19X2.

Ennis Company
Comparative Balance Sheets
December 31, 19X1 and 19X2

	19X2	19X1
Assets		
Current assets	$ 23,000	$ 34,000
Property, plant, and equipment (net)	162,000	185,000
Intangible assets (net)	15,000	11,000
Other assets	57,000	62,000
Total assets	$257,000	$292,000
Liabilities and Stockholders' Equity		
Current liabilities	$ 35,000	$ 27,000
Long-term liabilities	98,000	87,000
Common stock	50,000	45,000
Paid-in capital in excess of par	10,000	8,000
Retained earnings	64,000	125,000
Total liabilities and stockholders' equity	$257,000	$292,000

19–12   Trend Analysis

Compute trend percentages using 19X5 as the base year for Monida Company based on the following selected financial data:

	19X9	19X8	19X7	19X6	19X5
Summary of Operations:					
Net sales	$98,152	$85,804	$78,077	$74,027	$72,686
Gross profit	24,022	20,855	17,617	16,379	17,315
Interest expense	394	160	216	296	379
Provision for income taxes	3,884	3,947	2,947	2,599	3,652
Net earnings	5,593	4,079	3,636	3,205	5,534

REQUIRED:

What conclusions can you draw from your analysis?

19–13   Vertical Analysis

Using the information provided in the comparative statements of income, perform a vertical analysis for Bitterroot Corporation.

Bitterroot Corporation
Comparative Statements of Income
For the Years Ended December 31, 19X1 and 19X2

	19X2	19X1
Net sales	$452,000	$397,000
Cost of goods sold	265,000	223,000
Gross profit	187,000	174,000
Operating expenses:		
Selling	52,000	64,000
Administrative	22,000	24,000
General	37,000	31,000
Total operating expenses	111,000	119,000
Income from operations	76,000	55,000
Other expenses	7,000	5,000
Income before income taxes	69,000	50,000
Income tax expense	21,000	15,000
Net income	$ 48,000	$ 35,000

19–14   Common-Size Balance Sheet—Continuation of Assignment 19–11

Use the data from Assignment 19–11. Prepare a common-size balance sheet for Ennis Company for the years 19X1 and 19X2.

19–15   Wal-Mart Stores, Inc. Income Statement Ratios

Use the Wal-Mart financial statements to determine the following income statement ratios for 1991.

1. Gross profit ratio
2. Operating ratio
3. Return on sales

19–16   Wal-Mart Stores, Inc. Liquidity Measures

Use the Wal-Mart financial statements to calculate the following liquidity measures for 1991.

1. Working capital
2. Current ratio
3. Quick (Acid-test) ratio

19–17 Wal-Mart Stores, Inc. Current Asset Activity Ratios

Use the Wal-Mart financial statements to calculate the following activity ratios for 1991.

1. Accounts receivable turnover ratio
2. Number of days' sales in accounts receivable
3. Inventory turnover ratio
4. Number of days' sales in inventory

19–18 Wal-Mart Stores, Inc. Profitability Ratios

Use the Wal-Mart financial statements to calculate the following profitability ratios for 1991. Where a year-end market value is needed, use the average of the high and low market prices for the last quarter.

1. Return on assets
2. Return on common equity
3. Price-earnings ratio
4. Dividend yield
5. Payout ratio

19–19 Wal-Mart Stores, Inc. Solvency and Cash Flow Ratios

Use the Wal-Mart financial statements to calculate the following solvency and cash flow ratios for 1991.

1. Debt ratio
2. Times interest earned ratio
3. Overall cash flow ratio
4. Cash return on sales
5. Cash flow to net income

19–20 Wal-Mart Stores, Inc. Horizontal Analysis

Use the Wal-Mart financial statements to prepare a horizontal analysis of the Wal-Mart income statements for 1990 and 1991.

19–21 Wal-Mart Stores, Inc. Vertical Analysis

Use the Wal-Mart financial statements to prepare a vertical analysis of the Wal-Mart income statements for 1990 and 1991.

19–22   Wal-Mart Stores, Inc. Common-Size Income Statement

Use the Wal-Mart financial statements to prepare comparative common-size income statements for Wal-Mart for 1990 and 1991.

19–23   Format of an Income Statement

Shown below is data relating to the operations of French Company during 19X2:

Net sales	$7,800,000
Selling expenses	2,300,000
Administrative expenses	1,500,000
Income tax expense from operations	706,000
Cumulative effect of a change in account principle (increase in net income, net of applicable income taxes)	90,000
Loss on disposal of discontinued segment (net of applicable income taxes benefits)	575,080
Extraordinary gain (net of applicable income taxes)	257,900
Loss from operations of discontinued segment (net of applicable income tax benefits)	3,137,600
General expenses	890,000
Cash dividends declared	350,000
Prior period adjustment (net of applicable income taxes)	(76,000)

REQUIRED:

Prepare a condensed income statement for 19X2 for the French Company.

19–24   Calculation of Earnings Per Share With Complicating Factors

Assume Feltham Corporation has earnings of $120,000 for the year 19X2. The company started the year with 10,000 shares of common stock outstanding. On April 1, the company sold an additional 12,000 shares and on October 1 another 3,000 shares were sold. Feltham also has 3,000 shares of preferred stock that can be converted for an equal number of common shares. The preferred stock pays a $2.00 dividend per share. The preferred stock is a common stock equivalent because conditions in the stock market make it likely that the preferred stock will be converted. The company also has bonds outstanding that can be converted into 6,500 shares of common stock. The bonds are not common stock equivalents because market conditions do not make it likely that the bonds will be converted. Interest on the bonds is $5,000 per year and would not be paid if the bonds were converted.

REQUIRED:

Calculate both primary and fully diluted earnings per share for the Feltham Corporation for the year ended December 31, 19X2.

19–25 DECISION CASE:
FINANCIAL STATEMENT RELATIONSHIPS

You have been requested to draft a balance sheet for Sage Company at December 31, 19X1 based on the following selected information. The company's total stockholders' equity amounts to $2,000,000 and consists of 200,000 shares of $4 par value stock (sold at par) and retained earnings. The company has a quick (acid-test) ratio of 1.025 to 1 and a ratio of current liabilities to total stockholders' equity of 1 to 1. There is no long-term debt. Net income for the year was $900,000 with a return on sales ratio of 10%. The inventory turnover ratio was 5 times and the gross profit ratio was 25%. Additionally, days' sales in accounts receivable were 38 days (using a 360-day year), and all sales were made on account. Property, plant, and equipment were recorded net of accumulated depreciation and totaled $600,000 at December 31, 19X1.

REQUIRED:

Draft a balance sheet for the Sage Company at December 31, 19X1.

19–26 DECISION CASE:
RATIOS IN FINANCIAL STATEMENT ANALYSIS

The consolidated financial statements and selected financial data of Texas Instruments Incorporated and Subsidiaries for the years 1989 and 1988 are presented below. Using this information calculate the following for 1989:

1. Income statement ratios
    -   a. Gross profit ratio
    -   b. Operating ratio
    -   c. Return on sales

2. Liquidity
    -   a. Working capital
    -   b. Current ratio
    -   c. Quick (Acid-test) ratio

3. Current asset activity ratios
    -   a. Accounts receivable turnover ratio
    -   b. Number of days' sales in accounts receivable

    c. Inventory turnover ratio

    d. Number of days' sales in inventory

4. Profitability ratios

    a. Return on assets

    b. Return on common equity

    c. Price-earnings ratio (where a year-end market value is needed, use the average of the high and low market prices for the last quarter)

    d. Dividend yield (where a year-end market value is needed, use the average of the high and low market prices for the end of the last quarter)

    e. Payout ratio

5. Solvency ratios

    a. Debt ratio

    b. Times interest earned ratio

    c. Overall cash flow ratio

Consolidated Financial Statements
Texas Instruments Incorporated and Subsidiaries
(In millions of dollars, except per-share amounts.)

Income	For the years ended December 31		
	1989	1988	1987
Net revenues	$6,521.9	$6,446.9	$5,816.2
Operating costs and expenses:			
Cost of revenues	5,089.7	4,835.4	4,409.6
General, administrative and marketing	1,044.7	1,017.1	908.8
Employees' pension and profit sharing plans	68.1	92.1	85.4
Total	6,202.5	5,944.6	5,403.8
Profit from operations	319.4	502.3	412.4
Other income (expense) net	59.0	47.5	10.0
Interest on loans	23.6	33.4	20.7
Income before provision for income taxes	354.8	516.4	401.7
Provision for income taxes	63.1	150.1	80.3
Net income	$ 291.7	$ 366.3	$ 321.4
Net income, less dividends accrued on preferred stock	$ 252.8	$ 335.8	$ 301.2
Earnings per common and common equivalent share	$ 3.04	$ 4.05	$ 3.74

Balance Sheet	December 31	
	1989	1988
Assets		
Current assets:		
Cash and cash equivalents	$ 418.2	$ 541.3
Short-term investments	219.2	239.1
Accounts receivable, less allowance for losses of $41.7 in 1989 and $49.0 in 1988	942.9	942.1
Inventories (net of progress billings)	806.4	769.7
Prepaid expenses	59.7	56.4
Total current assets	2,446.4	2,548.6
Property, plant and equipment at cost	3,641.1	3,073.7
Less accumulated depreciation	(1,511.4)	(1,347.6)
Property, plant and equipment (net)	2,129.7	1,726.1
Other assets	228.3	152.8
Total assets	$4,804.4	$4,427.5
Liabilities and Stockholders' Equity		
Current liabilities:		
Loans payable and current portion long-term debt	$ 42.7	$ 22.9
Accounts payable and accrued expenses	1,210.7	1,091.0
Income taxes payable	24.4	39.0
Accrued pension and profit sharing contributions	7.5	28.9
Dividends payable	17.5	17.6
Total current liabilities	1,302.8	1,199.4
Long-term debt	617.5	623.8
Accrued pension costs	128.9	115.2
Deferred credits and other liabilities	270.3	245.5
Stockholders' equity:		
Preferred stock, $25 par value. Authorized—10,000,000 shares. Market auction preferred (stated at liquidation value). Shares issued and outstanding: 1989 and 1988—3,000	300.0	300.0
Convertible money market preferred (stated at liquidation value). Shares issued and outstanding: 1989 and 1988—2,208	220.8	220.8
Participating cumulative preferred. None issued	—	—
Common stock, $1 par value. Authorized—300,000,000 shares. Shares issued: 1989—81,606,649; 1988—80,746,272	81.6	80.8
Paid-in capital	483.1	437.1
Retained earnings	1,403.9	1,209.4
Less treasury common stock at cost. Shares: 1989—102,754; 1988—100,182	(4.5)	(4.5)
Total stockholders' equity	2,484.9	2,243.6
Total liabilities and stockholders' equity	$4,804.4	$4,427.5

See accompanying notes.

Consolidated Financial Statements
Texas Instruments Incorporated and Subsidiaries
(In millions of dollars, except per-share amounts.)

	For the years ended December 31		
Cash Flows	1989	1988	1987
Cash flows from operating activities:			
Net income..	$ 291.7	$ 366.3	$ 321.4
Depreciation......................................	453.7	389.8	380.1
Net currency exchange losses	11.6	2.0	10.9
(Increase) decrease in working capital (excluding cash and cash equivalents, short-term investments, loans payable and current portion long-term debt, and dividends payable):			
Accounts receivable	(27.0)	(117.1)	(143.6)
Inventories	(36.7)	(31.0)	(129.2)
Prepaid expenses	(4.9)	(5.3)	(14.1)
Accounts payable and accrued expenses	163.1	42.3	37.4
Income taxes payable	(8.9)	8.0	2.8
Accrued pension and profit sharing contributions	(21.1)	(30.8)	54.9
Other	(23.0)	77.5	(58.0)
Net cash provided by operating activities	798.5	701.7	462.6
Cash flows from investing activities:			
Additions to property, plant and equipment	(862.5)	(656.1)	(464.3)
Additions to short-term investments	(44.8)	(476.8)	(662.3)
Proceeds from short-term investments	75.5	478.2	428.8
Net cash used in investing activities	(831.8)	(654.7)	(697.8)
Cash flows from financing activities:			
Dividends paid on common and preferred stock	(97.3)	(87.2)	(72.8)
Issuance of preferred stock, net proceeds...................	—	—	221.3
Sales and other common stock transactions	46.8	80.1	58.0
Additions to loans payable.............................	33.7	17.6	24.7
Payments on loans payable.............................	(22.2)	(50.3)	(48.0)
Additions to long-term debt............................	152.2	150.7	301.3
Payments on long-term debt............................	(158.9)	(10.4)	(8.6)
Other	(37.1)	(23.9)	(31.1)
Net cash provided by (used in) financing activities	(82.8)	76.6	444.8
Effect of exchange rate changes on cash	(7.0)	(4.2)	4.9
Net increase (decrease) in cash and cash equivalents	(123.1)	119.4	214.5
Cash and cash equivalents at beginning of year	541.3	421.9	207.4
Cash and cash equivalents at end of year	$ 418.2	$ 541.3	$ 421.9

See accompanying notes.

Inflation

Within the limits of generally accepted accounting principles, the company believes its financial statements tend to reasonably match current levels of costs with revenues of the period, except for depreciation. To the extent current costs of fixed assets exceed historical costs, depreciation on an inflation-adjusted basis would be greater than historical cost depreciation.

Common Stock Prices and Dividends

TI common stock is listed on the New York Stock Exchange and traded principally in that market. The table below shows the high and low prices of TI common stock on the composite tape as reported by *The Wall Street Journal* and the dividends paid per common share for each quarter during the past two years.

	Quarter			
	1st	2nd	3rd	4th
Stock prices:				
1989 High	$ 44.75	$ 46.75	$ 42.00	$ 39.50
Low	37.13	38.00	37.25	28.13
1988 High	60.00	54.50	49.75	42.38
Low	41.50	42.00	37.50	34.50
Dividends paid:				
1989	$ .18	$ .18	$ .18	$ .18
1988	.18	.18	.18	.18

Quarterly Financial Data

1989	Millions of Dollars, Except Per-share Amounts			
	1st	2nd	3rd	4th
Net revenues	$1,596.9	$1,630.0	$1,570.7	$1,724.4
Profit from operations	101.5	135.4	68.0	14.4
Income before provision for income taxes	110.5	138.6	78.9	26.9
Net income	84.6	106.1	65.0	35.9
Earnings per common and common equivalent share	$ .90	$ 1.14	$ .67	$ .33

1988	Millions of Dollars, Except Per-share Amounts			
	1st	2nd	3rd	4th
Net revenues	$1,530.7	$1,583.3	$1,600.1	$1,732.8
Profit from operations	107.8	128.4	128.3	137.9
Income before provision for income taxes	124.6	124.4	130.0	137.4
Net income	85.5	91.8	93.7	95.3
Earnings per common and common equivalent share	$ .95	$ 1.02	$ 1.03	$ 1.04

Net revenues in the first, second, third and fourth quarters of 1989 included royalty revenue of $36 million, $66 million, $32 million and $31 million. Net revenues in the first, second, third and fourth quarters of 1988 included royalty revenue of $63 million, $25 million, $23 million and $41 million.

Earnings per common and common equivalent share are based on average common and common equivalent shares outstanding (81,485,050 and 84,192,965 for the fourth quarters of 1989 and 1988) and "net income, less dividends accrued on preferred stock" ($26.6 million and $86.3 million for the fourth quarters of 1989 and 1988). In computing per-share earnings, "net income, less dividends accrued on preferred stock" is increased for dividends and interest, net of tax and profit sharing effect, ($1.3 million for the fourth quarter of 1988) on the convertible preferred stock and convertible debentures considered dilutive common stock equivalents.

APPENDIX A—ANNUAL REPORTS

1990 Annual Report
Boise Cascade Corporation

The effects of the national economic downturn did not spare your Company last year, as the paper industry, which has always been cyclical, felt the full force of downward business pressures. As a result, our net income and earnings per share were down significantly from the record and near-record levels of 1988 and 1989.

Midway through the year, however, we updated our strategy and embarked upon a substantive five-point plan — our Blueprint for the '90s — to position the Company to achieve materially higher earnings and cash flow over the next five years. This plan aims to build on the progress we made in the 1980s, when we focused on our core businesses, modernized and expanded many of our paper operations, became a low-cost producer of wood products, expanded our office products facilities, expanded our wood chip production, and maintained our dividend and a prudent debt-to-equity ratio.

BOISE CASCADE'S PERFORMANCE IN 1990

The paper industry downturn affected some companies more than others. Boise Cascade has been particularly hard hit because the paper grades that make up the bulk of our product line are the ones that have been hurt by a tem-

ESSAGE TO SHAREHOLDERS

porary excess of industry capacity. This has resulted in weaker prices for these grades. For example, the annualized effect of a $50-per-ton price decline in just one grade of paper can knock 60¢ per share off the Company's earnings.

Other factors affecting the Company's performance in 1990 were slow growth in the U.S. economy and weakness in the markets for many of our products. In addition, our paper operations were affected by disruptions and associated costs, as a number of major capital projects were completed and some subsequent start-ups went less smoothly than we had hoped. Pacific Northwest wood costs remained high in response to the efforts of preservationist groups to reduce the amount of public timber available for harvest in the region. And our interest expense increased as a result of our record capital investment.

■ PAPER AND PAPER PRODUCTS. Income for this segment was down in 1990, reflecting weaker prices for many of the grades we manufacture, combined with the effects of the previously mentioned operating disruptions related to capital projects. Weak pulp and paper prices were the clearest indicator of the downside of the cycle for this business. The operating problems we experienced in 1990 were most significant at our mills in International Falls, Minnesota, and Rumford, Maine, where we had been carrying out major expansion and modernization projects. These projects were essentially complete by the end of the year, and as a result, we believe the disruptions are largely behind us. Our new uncoated white paper machine in International Falls, in particular, had a very good start-up in December and promises to be a big contributor to future earnings.

■ OFFICE PRODUCTS. Operating income for this segment was also down somewhat in 1990, as the growth in sales volume slowed from the teens to single digits. The slowing growth in sales volume reflected a general weakening of the economy and increased competition on the wholesale side of this business. Slower sales growth and increased competition resulted in downward pressure on prices and margins in this business.

■ BUILDING PRODUCTS. Operating income for this segment was markedly lower in 1990 than in the prior year. The decline was due to a combination of factors, including sluggish demand and a corresponding eight-year low in housing starts which reflected the weakening economy, lower prices for most of the wood products we make, and high delivered-log costs in the Pacific Northwest in response to the efforts of preservationist groups to reduce the amount of public timber available for harvest in the region.

OUR FINANCIAL POSITION

Due to the decline in earnings, our cash flow in 1990 was below that of 1989 but was still a healthy $252 million.

The Company's annual common stock dividend rate remained at $1.52 in 1990. We have always placed a high importance on maintaining the dividend, even during downturns in the business cycle. And, in fact, we held our dividend during the tough times of the early 1980s, when some of our competitors eliminated or reduced theirs.

We invested a record $824 million in 1990 to improve, modernize, and expand our facilities. To fund the year's capital program, we supplemented the cash generated by operations with borrowing. That borrowing contributed to an increase in our debt level in 1990, compared with that of 1989.

OUR BLUEPRINT FOR THE '90s

That's a brief summary of our performance during the-past year. But 1990 is history. Now, I'd like to tell you how our Blueprint for the '90s will improve our performance over the next five years. Essentially, the Blueprint states that the Company will:

■ Focus on white papers, meaning the business and printing papers that have the best growth potential of the various major grades and, therefore, offer the greatest potential returns. At the same time, we will reduce our relative position in newsprint.

■ Continue to invest capital in our paper mills that are or have the potential to be world-class.

■ Reduce our pulp and paper presence in the Pacific Northwest because of high wood chip costs there while focusing our growth in other regions of North America.

■ Continue to grow in our office products distribution business, especially in the fast-growing consumer side of the business, through which we sell directly to large businesses.

■ Continue to invest in and benefit from the integrative value of our building products business.

I'm confident that this plan will help us become a stronger and more focused Company, and I'm also excited about how we're carrying out this plan. We're learning to better draw on the skills and ideas of our employees through the use of Total Quality processes, which incorporate the principles of continuous improvement and employee involvement in everything we do. They are an essential element of our plan to improve the Company's competitive position by becoming the preferred supplier to each of our customers.

OUTLOOK

I believe we're taking appropriate steps to increase the Company's earnings over the next five years. We expect the operating environment for most of our businesses to remain tough in 1991, as the U.S. economy continues its recessionary behavior. Add to that a continuing squeeze on our margins resulting from weak prices for paper, wood, and office products; increased interest expense; and continued escalation of Northwest wood costs, and you have an indication that our earnings performance in 1991 — especially in the first half of the year — may not yet show the improvement we're confident is coming.

I say we're confident that improvement is coming because of the steps we *took* in the decade of the 1980s to sharpen our focus and because of the steps we *are taking* in connection with our Blueprint for the '90s. Moreover, in 1991, we expect to begin to see the benefit from the $2 billion investment we've made in our facilities since the beginning of 1988 — especially in our paper facilities. We know the business cycle will eventually rebound, bringing the return of stronger paper markets. And, as I mentioned earlier, we believe the operating problems associated with our record capital investment program are largely behind us. We believe the market for office products will remain healthy, although perhaps not as robust as in past years. And we think the market for wood products will begin to show some improvement in the second half of 1991. We'll also continue to manage our capital investment — reduced to about $300 million in 1991 — with an eye toward maintaining a prudent balance sheet.

So, while 1991 may be a difficult year, we're moving briskly ahead with the steps that will make significant improvements in our long-term value to shareholders.

John B. Fery
Chairman of the Board
Chief Executive Officer

It makes perfect sense if you want to grow in the paper business to focus on those grades that have the greatest projected growth in demand and that offer the greatest potential returns. And that's what we're doing by focusing our efforts on white papers. Although the markets for coated and uncoated white papers were weak in 1990, these grades of paper — copier papers, business forms, printing papers, envelope papers, and the paper used in magazines and catalogs — are forecast to have the highest growth rates among the major grades in the 1990s. Demand for each of them is expected to grow one to three percentage points faster than growth in the gross national product.

Boise Cascade is already taking steps to meet that demand. In December of 1990, we started up a new uncoated white paper machine at our mill in International Falls, Minnesota. That machine, part of a multimillion-dollar modernization and expansion project at the mill, will uitmately add 30 percent to the Company's uncoated white paper capacity — or about 300,000 tons a year.

In addition, we hope to begin construction of a new coated paper machine at our mill in Rumford, Maine, in 1992.

OBJECTIVE 1 **FOCUS OUR GROWTH IN WHITE PAPERS**

On top of the large modernization program that we completed there in 1990, the new machine will increase the Company's annual coated paper capacity by almost 80 percent — or about 320,000 tons a year. The exact timing of that new machine will be determined by available cash flow, as well as by market conditions.

We also have the potential to add capacity at several of our other mills that produce business and printing papers. At the same time, we intend to maintain our presence in containerboard and corrugated boxes because of our competitive cost position and the close integration of those two businesses.

The flip side of the coin is our plan to reduce our position in grades that we have chosen not to focus on — carbonless paper, for example, a market we have decided to exit. To that end, we announced in September 1990 that we had reached an agreement in principle to sell our one carbonless paper mill in Vancouver, Washington — a sale that was still pending at year-end. In addition, over time, we plan to reduce our relative position in newsprint and limit new investments in this grade, because it does not have the same growth prospects that white papers have. In that regard, we are seeking a joint venture partner for our mill in West Tacoma, Washington, a facility in which we plan to install a deinking/newsprint recycling plant.

We define world-class status as, among other things, the ability to compete globally by having high quality and a low cost structure. And that's exactly the direction in which we're headed with our pulp and paper mills and the $725 million in capital investment we made in our pulp and paper operations in 1990.

Some of our facilities are already there. Our mill in DeRidder. Louisiana, for instance, is in the lowest 10 percent of the industry in terms of cost for producing newsprint. The DeRidder mill is also a model of what we can achieve when we combine smart capital investment with high levels of employee involvement — a combination that's essential to reaching world-class status. DeRidder is a good example of how a world-class facility can be highly successful, even though its product lines — newsprint and containerboard — are slower-growth grades.

In December 1990, we started up our new world-class uncoated white paper machine in International Falls. Our mill in Rumford is moving steadily toward world-class status with the completion in 1990 of two machine rebuilds. a cogeneration project. and a pulp mill modernization. And our mill in Fort Frances, Ontario, is already a low-cost, high-quality producer of uncoated groundwood papers.

OBJECTIVE 2

CONTINUE TO INVEST CAPITAL TO ACHIEVE WORLD-CLASS STATUS IN OUR PULP AND PAPER MILLS

A number of other mills in our system have the potential to become world-class facilities, and they are on a plan to reach that potential. Because of a variety of constraints, some of our mills do not have the potential to attain world-class status. For those facilities, we are investigating alternate directions, including sale or joint venture.

W hen we first announced our Blueprint for the '90s in the summer of 1990, many observers may have jumped to the wrong conclusion. In fact, we are not pulling out of the Pacific Northwest. We have a concentration of wood products manufacturing facilities in the Northwest supported by over a million acres of timberland. And we intend to continue as a competitive factor in the wood products business in that region. What we did say, however, was that we would *reduce our Northwest pulp and paper presence while we expand elsewhere in North America*. Examples of our expansion are cited on the previous pages.

The reason for this geographical shift in our paper business is obvious. The cost of wood chips, the raw material for our paper mills, has risen dramatically in the Northwest over the past few years — as a result of anticipated shrinkage in the availability of fiber in the area and continued demand from export markets. The cost of wood in the region today is significantly higher than it is in other regions of the country. We expect these costs to remain high, as

| OBJECTIVE | 3 | REDUCE OUR PULP AND PAPER PRESENCE IN THE PACIFIC NORTHWEST |

an increasing amount of public timber in the Northwest is withdrawn from commercial harvest because of environmental pressures. That has been a concern for us and for our customers, because until 1990, we purchased about 50 percent of our wood chips in the Northwest on the open market.

We've reacted to the high cost of wood chips by focusing our growth plans outside the region. We've also taken steps to reduce our dependence on open-market chip purchases for our Northwest paper mills. One way to reduce that dependence is simply to improve our ability to generate our own chips.

We did that in 1990 by purchasing a facility in northeast Oregon that chips whole logs not suited to the manufacture of solid wood products. That facility has contributed to reducing our reliance on purchased wood chips in the Pacific Northwest to 40 percent. We are also planning a hardwood plantation near our pulp and paper mill in Wallula, Washington, which will eventually supply about one-third of that mill's chip needs.

In the final analysis, though, our growth emphasis in paper in the 1990s will be elsewhere in North America.

The office products business is a real gem for Boise Cascade, providing steady growth in sales and operating income. In 1990, our office products business provided 25 percent of the Company's sales and about 20 percent of our operating income. And in 1990, that operating income represented a 21 percent return on capital investment. An added plus: The capital requirements of this business are modest, compared with those of our paper business, and thus, our growth in office products doesn't tax our ability to allocate capital.

Boise Cascade is among the largest and best distributors of office supplies in the country. We sell wholesale to office supply dealers and directly to large customers (which we call the consumer channel), such as corporations and government offices. We've kept this business competitive by investing in innovative computer systems that track orders, manage inventories, and expedite billing. We also have some of the best people in the business — people who know how to consistently meet customer expectations.

It's not hard to see why we expect continued success in this business. The prospects are particularly good in our strong consumer channel, which we see growing at a rate better than the growth in the gross national product.

OBJECTIVE 4 — CONTINUE TO GROW IN OUR OFFICE PRODUCTS BUSINESS

The overall market for office products cooled in 1990, as the economy slowed and pricing pressure increased because of stepped-up competition, particularly on the wholesale side of the business. However, looking ahead, we believe we're ready to compete effectively in what remains a healthy market. Typical of our growth plans are two major relocations that were completed in 1990. Our facilities that serve the Cincinnati and Philadelphia markets moved into much larger buildings so that they can carry more inventory, process orders faster, and serve more customers. These moves should begin to contribute to profits in 1991.

The rationale for this objective is simple. We are among the most efficient producers and distributors of wood products in North America today. And we intend to maintain that position.

Located in the Pacific Northwest and in the South, our wood products manufacturing facilities produce primarily lumber, plywood, veneer, and particleboard. And our wholesale building materials distribution centers make sure that these and other products reach our customers as efficiently as possible.

We have invested more than $400 million in the last ten years to lower the operating costs of our wood products manufacturing facilities. Our manufacturing costs in the Pacific Northwest, for example, are 25 to 30 percent below the region's average as reported by Resource Information Systems, Inc. (RISI). That low cost structure couldn't reverse the tough market conditions we saw in 1990 — high log costs, weak prices, and depressed housing starts. But it certainly helped us get through the year in better shape than would otherwise have been the case.

OBJECTIVE 5

CONTINUE TO INVEST IN OUR BUILDING PRODUCTS BUSINESS

We intend to continue investing in this business to make even further improvements in our cost structure and the quality of our products. We're also excited about our entry into value-added wood products. Specifically, in the third quarter of 1990, we started up a new $25 million facility in Medford, Oregon, to manufacture laminated veneer lumber (LVL) and wooden I-beams. LVL is a high-strength lumber product made from glued and pressed plywood veneers. It is being used more and more in residential and other construction and should be a good earnings contributor in the 1990s.

Supporting our investment in the building products business are the Company's timberlands. We can supply about a third of the needs of our wood products operations in the Pacific Northwest. In that region, we supplement our own significant timberland base by purchasing public and private timber. And even though an increasing amount of public timber in the region is being withdrawn from commercial harvest due to pressure from preservationist groups, we're confident that our low-cost wood products facilities will compete effectively with anyone in that area for the public and private wood available in the 1990s.

The people of Boise Cascade are the essential element for successful implementation of the Company's Blueprint for the '90s. Recognizing that, the Company expanded its efforts in the area of Total Quality during the year to draw fully on the knowledge and expertise of those people.

At Boise Cascade, we define Total Quality as a way of managing characterized by:

- A focus on the customer in order to earn and retain the status of preferred supplier.
- A focus on involving people in quality improvement.
- A focus on continuous improvement of all of our processes, which will result in improvements in our products and services.

Just as 1990 marked the beginning of the decade, the use of Total Quality processes marks the beginning of a new era for Boise Cascade — a new era in the way in which Boise Cascade makes decisions, the way in which it manages people and processes, the way in which it forms partnerships with employees, customers, and suppliers and, yes, the way in which it operates efficiently and profitably.

TOTAL QUALITY — DRAWING ON THE EXPERTISE OF OUR PEOPLE TO MAKE THE BLUEPRINT A REALITY

Some divisions of the Company have been benefiting from Total Quality processes for several years and, during that time, have received preferred supplier designations from a number of major customers.

Boise Cascade Chairman of the Board and Chief Executive Officer John Fery has said, "The Total Quality process is critical to strengthening our competitive position." In that regard, this process is really the *framework* within which the Company will execute the five strategic objectives that compose the Blueprint for the '90s.

As discussed in the preceding pages, the Company's 1990 earnings were below our expectations. And 1991 is expected to be a very difficult year. So what's the strategy described in our Blueprint for the '90s going to do for us in the longer-term future?

By following this strategy in the context of our Total Quality process, we expect the Company's earnings and cash flow to increase materially over the next five years. And we plan to continue our long-standing cash dividend policy of paying out about 30 percent of earnings, on average over time.

True, 1990 and 1991 are a tough period for Boise Cascade. But stronger paper and wood products markets *will* return. And the steps we've outlined in our Blueprint for the '90s will position us *and* our shareholders to realize the benefits of those improved markets.

To accomplish our objectives, we will invest our capital judiciously. Some of that capital will be generated through the sale or joint venture of nonstrategic assets, as mentioned earlier in this report.

We're well on our way to becoming an even stronger, more focused company . . . a company that's finding new ways to draw on the skills and ideas of its people . . . a company that's making measurable progress in improving the quality of our products and services . . . a company that's adding capacity in the right areas . . . a company that's continuing to lower its cost structure . . . in short, a company that will continue to make significant improvements in its long-term value to customers, employees, shareholders, and the communities in which we operate.

THE END RESULT — WE WILL MATERIALLY INCREASE OUR EARNINGS OVER THE NEXT FIVE YEARS

FINANCIAL INFORMATION

Contents

Financial Review

■ Income From Operations.

Boise Cascade reported net income of $75 million in 1990, compared with net income of $268 million in 1989. Fully diluted earnings per share were $1.62 in 1990, compared with $5.70 in 1989.

The decline in the Company's income was due largely to four factors: a cyclical downturn in the paper business characterized by a period during which industry capacity in certain pulp and paper grades exceeded demand, markets that weakened as growth in the U.S. economy slowed, paper mill operating disruptions and costs associated with our record capital program, and high wood costs in the Pacific Northwest combined with decreasing product prices. Also contributing to the decline in the Company's income was an increase in interest expense associated with the high level of capital investment.

Operating income for our paper and paper products segment in 1990 was $187 million, down from $405 million in 1989. The decline was due to weaker prices for many of the grades of pulp and paper that we manufacture, combined with the effects of operating problems and costs associated with major capital expansion and modernization projects at a number of mills. Paper-segment sales volume remained relatively flat, compared with that of 1989.

Paper-segment earnings declined throughout most of the year, reflecting progressive weakening in two of our major grades — containerboard and market pulp. Prices for coated papers were somewhat weaker than year-ago levels for the first nine months of 1990 and then declined further in the fourth quarter. The softness in pulp and paper prices was due to the industry's temporary overcapacity in some grades, combined with flat or sluggish demand. In addition, our corrugated container business continued to experience tight margins, as box prices decreased along

with containerboard prices. The market for our uncoated white papers began the year with prices significantly below the 1989 average price level, but prices firmed as the year progressed. On average, prices for newsprint in the first half of 1990 were also below those of the same period in 1989. However, prices began to improve in the second half of the year, as the market reacted to a constraint on supply caused primarily by strikes of some industry producers. Prices were also buoyed by the margin pressure experienced by some North American producers.

In addition to softness in prices, several of our paper manufacturing facilities experienced operating disruptions and associated costs in connection with capital projects during the year. Those issues were most significant at our mills in International Falls, Minnesota, and Rumford, Maine, where we had been carrying out major expansion and modernization projects. These projects were essentially complete by the end of 1990, and as a result, we believe these capital-related operating difficulties are behind us.

In connection with the Company's strategic objectives for our paper business, we announced our intent to sell our Vancouver, Washington, paper mill and to seek a joint venture partner for our paper mill in West Tacoma, Washington. Neither transaction had been completed at year-end. On December 31, we sold corrugated container plants in LaPorte, Indiana, and Milford, Connecticut, that do not fit our long-term strategic objectives for this business.

Operating income for Boise Cascade's office products segment in 1990 was $58 million, compared with $67 million in 1989. Sales volume continued to grow in 1990, compared with that of 1989, but at a slower rate. The slowing growth in sales volume reflected a general weakening of the economy and increased competition

on the wholesale side of this business, especially in the last three quarters, which resulted in downward pressure on prices and margins in this business.

Operating income for the Company's building products segment in 1990 was $42 million, compared with $107 million in 1989. The decrease was due to a combination of factors, including lower prices for the wood products we manufacture, high delivered-log costs in the Pacific Northwest where most of our facilities are located, and sluggish demand and a corresponding eight-year low in housing starts, reflecting a weakening economy.

■ Financial Condition.

In 1990, operations provided $252 million in cash, compared with $495 million in 1989. The working capital ratio was 1.32:1 at the end of 1990, compared with 1.37:1 at the end of 1989.

On December 31, 1990, the Company's long-term debt-to-equity ratio was 1.23:1, compared with .95:1 at the end of 1989. The increase in the debt-to-equity ratio reflects additional borrowing required to fund our aggressive capital program in a year when earnings were down. We should also note that our debt-to-equity ratio includes the guarantee by the Company of the debt incurred by the trustee of our leveraged employee stock ownership plan (ESOP). While that guarantee has a negative impact on our debt-to-equity ratio, it has virtually no effect on our cash flow coverage ratios or on other measures of our financial strength.

The Company maintains a shelf registration for debt securities with the Securities and Exchange Commission (SEC). During 1990, the Company issued public debt under this registration totaling $424 million. In March, we issued $100 million of 9.9 percent notes due in 2000 at 99.45 percent of face value. In June, we issued $125 million of 9.85 percent notes due in 2002

	Common Stock Prices						Common Stock Dividends		
	1990		1989		1988		1990	1989	1988
Quarter	High	Low	High	Low	High	Low	Paid Per Share		
First	$46¼	$35⅜	$43½	$39¾	$50	$36	$.38	$.35	$.30
Second	40⅜	33¾	46½	42¼	49	40⅝	.38	.35	.30
Third	38⅛	24¼	48	42⅝	47⅜	41	.38	.35	.30
Fourth	27⅝	19¾	45⅛	40¼	45¾	39¼	.38	.35	.30

The Company's common stock is traded principally on the New York Stock Exchange.

at 100 percent of face value. In December, we issued $120 million of 10.125 percent notes due in 1997 at 99.692 percent of face value. And in the second half of 1990, we issued medium-term notes totaling $79 million. The medium-term notes range in maturity from three to ten years.

In January of 1990, the Company redeemed $50 million of 12 percent notes due in 1992.

In December 1990, we filed a new shelf registration with the SEC for $400 million. After incorporating the remaining $26 million of an existing shelf registration, the new filing provided us with the capacity to issue new public debt of $426 million. The timing and terms for issuing this debt will depend on our financing needs and market conditions.

In addition, the Company maintains a committed revolving credit agreement of $750 million with a group of banks. The revolving loan period expires in 1994, and at that time, the Company has the option of converting the agreement to a three-year term loan. As of December 31, 1990, we had no borrowings outstanding under this agreement.

The Company also maintains a commercial paper program of up to $300 million in order to provide additional financing flexibility. The amount of commercial paper outstanding under this program is supported by a portion of the revolving credit agreement described in the preceding paragraph. On December 31, 1990, our outstanding commercial paper totaled $161 million.

Additional information about the Company's credit agreements and debt is contained in Note 3 accompanying the financial statements.

■ **Capital Investment.** Capital investment in 1990 was $824 million, compared with $723 million in 1989. Of the 1990 capital program, approximately $725 million was invested in a variety of projects in the Company's paper and paper products segment. The largest single portion of 1990 expenditures in the paper business — $284 million — went to the final stage of the expansion and modernization project at our uncoated white paper mill in International Falls. The centerpiece of that project — a new, world-class paper machine — came on line in December

and will ultimately increase the mill's uncoated white paper production capacity from 205,000 to 505,000 tons a year.

Another $79 million of our 1990 capital investment went toward the expansion and modernization project at our coated paper mill in Rumford. Included in that project were the rebuilds of two coated paper machines and a pulp mill modernization.

The Company's capital investment in 1991 is expected to be about $300 million. The 1991 capital budget will be allocated to cost-saving, modernization, maintenance, environmental, and safety projects. We have deferred until 1992 any spending for a planned new coated paper machine at our Rumford mill.

■ **Dividends.** In 1990, Boise Cascade's quarterly cash dividend rate was 38¢ per common share. As we have said previously, our objective is to pay out, on average over time, approximately 30 percent of earnings in the form of a cash dividend.

■ **Return on Shareholders' Equity.** Our return on average shareholders' equity was 4.7 percent in 1990, compared with 16.2 percent in 1989.

■ **Income Taxes and Postretirement Benefits Other Than Pensions.** The Financial Accounting Standards Board (FASB) is in the process of revising a standard that requires a change in the way deferred taxes are calculated. The deadline for adopting the standard has been tentatively scheduled for 1993, and we expect to adopt the proposed

standard at that time with a one-time adjustment. Based on information that is currently available, we anticipate that adoption will have a favorable impact on net income.

The FASB has also issued a standard that applies to postretirement benefits other than pensions. Among other things, that standard will require the Company to accrue the cost of its share of retiree medical benefits. Currently, those costs are recorded at the time the benefits are provided. The FASB requires companies to adopt the standard by 1993.

The Company has the choice of recording the benefit obligation as a one-time adjustment at the time the standard is adopted or on a prospective basis over a period that cannot exceed 20 years. The Company has not yet determined what the financial impact will be, which of these methods it will use, or when the standard will be adopted.

■ **Employee Stock Ownership Plan.** The Company maintains a leveraged employee stock ownership plan (ESOP) for U.S. salaried employees. The ESOP was established in 1989 with 6.7 million shares of convertible preferred stock. (Each share of the preferred stock is convertible to .80357 share of common stock.) The shares in the ESOP are being allocated to salaried employees over the next 14 years as part of an existing retirement savings plan for those employees. A portion of the ESOP stock allocated to salaried employees is intended to help offset the Company's planned annual reductions in its subsidy of retiree medical costs for those employees.

1990 Capital Investment by Business

	Expansion	Quality/ Efficiency [1]	Timber and Timberlands	Replacement, Environmental, and Other	Total
		(expressed in millions)			
Paper and paper products	$427	$ 93	$—	$205	$725
Office products	24	10	—	5	39
Building products	11	12	—	12	35
Timber and timberlands	—	—	14	—	14
Other	2	1	—	8	11
Total	$464	$116	$14	$230	$824

[1] Quality and efficiency projects include quality improvements, modernization, energy, and cost-saving projects.

Balance Sheets
Boise Cascade Corporation and Subsidiaries

Assets	December 31		
	1990	1989	1988
	(expressed in thousands)		
Current			
Cash and cash items (Note 1)	$ 19,781	$ 19,715	$ 12,103
Short-term investments at cost, which approximates market (Note 1)	6,165	5,526	11,157
	25,946	25,241	23,260
Receivables, less allowances of $4,315,000, $3,800,000, and $3,405,000	412,558	421,568	393,371
Inventories (Note 1)	484,972	424,439	398,749
Deferred income tax benefits	55,115	48,716	40,404
Other	18,992	12,353	10,819
	997,583	932,317	866,603
Property (Note 1)			
Property and equipment	4,881,672	4,211,786	3,649,164
Accumulated depreciation	(1,726,794)	(1,583,210)	(1,473,079)
	3,154,878	2,628,576	2,176,085
Timber, timberlands, and timber deposits	391,985	388,294	389,201
	3,546,863	3,016,870	2,565,286
Other assets (Note 1)	240,324	193,438	178,354
Total assets	$4,784,770	$4,142,625	$3,610,243

Liabilities and Shareholders' Equity	December 31		
	1990	1989	1988
	(expressed in thousands)		

Current

Notes payable	$ 40,000	$ —	$ —
Current portion of long-term debt	136,731	30,390	73,320
Income taxes payable	140	4,273	4,558
Accounts payable	344,384	391,542	354,827
Accrued liabilities			
Compensation and benefits	99,530	114,082	111,508
Interest payable	38,460	40,071	37,194
Other	99,127	97,866	99,208
	758,372	678,224	680,615

Debt (Note 3)

Long-term debt, less current portion	1,648,826	1,204,978	925,112
Guarantee of 8.5% ESOP debt	285,678	292,581	—
	1,934,504	1,497,559	925,112

Other

Deferred income taxes (Note 2)	394,162	307,111	250,126
Other long-term liabilities	122,201	84,431	76,818
	516,363	391,542	326,944

Commitments and contingent liabilities (Notes 1, 2, 5, and 8)

Shareholders' equity (Note 6)

Preferred stock – no par value; 10,000,000 shares authorized;			
Series D ESOP: 6,729,039 and 6,744,840 shares outstanding			
in 1990 and 1989	302,807	303,518	—
Deferred ESOP benefit	(285,678)	(292,581)	—
Common stock – $2.50 par value; 200,000,000 shares authorized;			
37,948,511, 37,946,255, and 44,921,814 shares outstanding	94,871	94,866	112,305
Additional paid-in capital	—	—	203,277
Retained earnings (Notes 1 and 3)	1,463,531	1,469,497	1,361,990
Total shareholders' equity	1,575,531	1,575,300	1,677,572
Total liabilities and shareholders' equity	$4,784,770	$4,142,625	$3,610,243
Book value per common share	$ 41.07	$ 41.23	$ 37.34

The accompanying notes are an integral part of these Financial Statements.

Statements of Income
Boise Cascade Corporation and Subsidiaries

	Year Ended December 31		
	1990	1989	1988
	(expressed in thousands)		
Revenues			
Sales	**$4,185,920**	$4,338,030	$4,094,630
Other income (expense), net (Note 1)	**(1,360)**	15,020	4,710
	4,184,560	4,353,050	4,099,340
Costs and expenses			
Materials, labor, and other operating expenses	**3,318,350**	3,218,120	2,974,370
Depreciation and cost of company timber harvested	**212,890**	202,060	187,600
Selling and administrative expenses	**419,430**	406,400	362,480
	3,950,670	3,826,580	3,524,450
Income from operations	**233,890**	526,470	574,890
Interest expense	**(116,620)**	(95,810)	(100,460)
Interest income	**3,610**	6,370	3,540
Foreign exchange gain (loss)	**520**	(160)	(90)
	(112,490)	(89,600)	(97,010)
Income before income taxes	**121,400**	436,870	477,880
Income tax provision (Note 2)	**46,130**	169,290	188,760
Net income	**$ 75,270**	$ 267,580	$ 289,120
Net income per common share (Note 1)			
Primary	**$1.62**	$6.19	$6.34
Fully diluted	**$1.62**	$5.70	$6.15

The accompanying notes are an integral part of these Financial Statements.

Statements of Cash Flows

Boise Cascade Corporation and Subsidiaries

| | Year Ended December 31 | | |
	1990	1989	1988
	(expressed in thousands)		
Cash provided by (used for) operations			
Net income	**$ 75,270**	$267,580	$289,120
Items in income not using cash			
Depreciation and cost of company timber harvested	**212,890**	202,060	187,600
Deferred income tax provision	**54,446**	36,026	47,561
Amortization and other	**6,779**	6,095	11,005
Receivables	**36,947**	(28,057)	(33,873)
Inventories	**(63,822)**	(43,550)	(27,393)
Accounts payable and accrued liabilities	**(60,525)**	50,876	119,635
Current and deferred income taxes	**(7,065)**	9,234	(22,062)
Other	**(3,034)**	(5,222)	(665)
Cash provided by operations	**251,886**	495,042	570,928
Cash provided by (used for) financing			
Cash dividends paid			
Common stock	**(57,671)**	(60,774)	(54,866)
Preferred stock	**(22,348)**	(11,192)	(3,500)
	(80,019)	(71,966)	(58,366)
Notes payable	**40,000**	—	(31,000)
Additions to long-term debt	**649,917**	304,923	99,737
Payments of long-term debt	**(91,978)**	(75,063)	(195,545)
Purchases of common stock (Note 6)	**(158)**	(316,476)	(12,753)
Issuance of preferred stock (Note 6)	**—**	303,541	—
Other	**782**	1,805	(64)
Cash provided by (used for) financing	**518,544**	146,764	(197,991)
Cash provided by (used for) investment			
Expenditures for property and equipment	**(744,020)**	(693,771)	(424,258)
Expenditures for timber and timberlands	**(13,681)**	(5,158)	(6,055)
Sales of operating assets (Note 1)	**14,359**	66,428	71,608
Other	**(26,383)**	(7,324)	(12,630)
Cash used for investment	**(769,725)**	(639,825)	(371,335)
Increase in cash and short-term investments	**705**	1,981	1,602
Balance at beginning of the year	**25,241**	23,260	21,658
Balance at end of the year	**$ 25,946**	$ 25,241	$ 23,260

The accompanying notes are an integral part of these Financial Statements.

Statements of Shareholders' Equity
Boise Cascade Corporation and Subsidiaries

		For the Years Ended December 31, 1988, 1989, and 1990					
Common Shares Outstanding	Notes 1, 3, 5, and 6	Total Share-holders' Equity	Preferred Stock	Deferred ESOP Benefit	Common Stock	Additional Paid-in Capital	Retained Earnings
		(expressed in thousands)					
45,119,809	Balance at December 31, 1987	$ 1,559,496	$ 97,147	$ —	$ 112,799	$ 211,587	$ 1,137,963
	Net income	289,120					289,120
	Exchange of Series C preferred stock	(95,112)	(95,112)				
	Cash dividends declared						
	Common stock	(56,231)					(56,231)
	Preferred stock	(1,750)					(1,750)
	Redemption of common stock rights	(4,492)					(4,492)
92,871	Stock options exercised	3,531			232	3,299	
(338,379)	Treasury stock cancellations	(14,630)			(846)	(13,784)	
47,513	Other	(2,360)	(2,035)		120	2,175	(2,620)
44,921,814	Balance at December 31, 1988	1,677,572	—	—	112,305	203,277	1,361,990
	Net income	267,580					267,580
	Cash dividends declared						
	Common stock	(59,469)					(59,469)
	Preferred stock	(11,192)					(11,192)
168,227	Stock options exercised	6,596			420	2,829	3,347
(7,136,469)	Treasury stock cancellations	(316,841)			(17,841)	(206,315)	(92,685)
	Employee stock ownership plan (ESOP)	8,541	303,541	(295,000)			
(7,317)	Other	2,513	(23)	2,419	(18)	209	(74)
37,946,255	Balance at December 31, 1989	1,575,300	303,518	(292,581)	94,866	—	1,469,497
	Net income	**75,270**					**75,270**
	Cash dividends declared						
	Common stock	**(57,715)**					**(57,715)**
	Preferred stock	**(22,348)**					**(22,348)**
7,583	Stock options exercised	**288**			**18**		**270**
(5,332)	Treasury stock cancellations	**(181)**			**(13)**		**(168)**
5	Other	**4,917**	**(711)**	**6,903**			**(1,275)**
37,948,511	Balance at December 31, 1990	**$ 1,575,531**	**$ 302,807**	**$ (285,678)**	**$ 94,871**	**$ —**	**$ 1,463,531**

The accompanying notes are an integral part of these Financial Statements.

Notes to Financial Statements
Boise Cascade Corporation and Subsidiaries

1. Summary of Significant Accounting Policies

■ **Consolidation.** The financial statements include the accounts of the Company and all subsidiaries after elimination of intercompany balances and transactions.

■ **Other Income (Expense).** "Other income (expense), net" on the Statements of Income includes equity in earnings and losses of joint ventures, gains and losses on the sale and disposition of property, and other miscellaneous income and expense items. In 1990, a $12,000,000 reserve was established for the anticipated cost of streamlining administrative functions and consolidating the Company's coated and uncoated white paper businesses. In 1989, the Company recorded a modest gain from the sale of its Specialty Paperboard Division.

■ **Foreign Currency Translation.** Foreign exchange gains and losses reported on the Statements of Income arise primarily from activities of the Company's Canadian subsidiaries. The Company has entered into forward contracts to purchase 100,000,000 Canadian dollars at various dates in 1992. Gains or losses in the market value of the forward contracts are recorded as they are incurred. These gains or losses significantly offset gains or losses arising from translation of the Canadian subsidiaries' net liabilities. Translation adjustments for other foreign subsidiaries were insignificant and have been included in "Retained earnings" on the Balance Sheets.

■ **Net Income Per Common Share.** Net income per common share was determined by dividing net income, as adjusted below, by applicable shares outstanding.

	Year Ended December 31		
	1990	1989	1988
	(expressed in thousands)		
Net income as reported	$ 75,270	$ 267,580	$ 289,120
Preferred dividends	(13,791)	(6,943)	(2,333)
Primary income	61,479	260,637	286,787
Assumed conversions:			
Preferred dividends eliminated	13,791	6,943	2,333
Interest on 7% debentures eliminated	4,443	4,467	2,992
Supplemental ESOP contribution	(5,566)	(4,571)	—
Fully diluted income	$ 74,147	$ 267,476	$ 292,112
Average number of common shares			
Primary	38,014	42,100	45,232
Fully diluted	45,673	46,943	47,481

The computation of fully diluted income per share for the year ended December 31, 1990, was antidilutive; therefore, the amounts reported for primary and fully diluted earnings are the same.

Primary income excludes preferred dividends, net of a tax benefit on the Company's Series D ESOP (employee stock ownership plan) preferred stock, which was issued in July 1989. To determine fully diluted income, dividends and interest, net of any applicable taxes, have been added back to primary income to reflect assumed conversions. Fully diluted income was reduced by the amount of additional after-tax contributions that the Company would be required to make to its ESOP if the Series D ESOP preferred shares were converted to common stock. Primary average shares include common shares outstanding and common stock equivalents attributable to outstanding stock options. In addition to common and common equivalent shares, fully diluted average shares include common shares that would be issuable upon conversion of the Company's convertible securities (see Notes 3 and 6).

■ **Cash and Short-Term Investments.** Short-term investments consist of investments that have a maturity of three months or less. At December 31, 1990, $9,712,000 of cash and short-term investments of a wholly owned insurance subsidiary was committed for use in maintaining statutory liquidity requirements of that subsidiary.

Notes to Financial Statements
Boise Cascade Corporation and Subsidiaries

■ **Inventory Valuation.** The Company uses the last-in, first-out (LIFO) method of inventory valuation for raw materials and finished goods inventories at substantially all of its domestic wood products and paper manufacturing facilities. All other inventories are valued at the lower of cost or market, with cost based on the average or first-in, first-out (FIFO) valuation method. Manufactured inventories include costs for materials, labor, and factory overhead. The cost of inventories, valued at the lower of average cost or market, exceeded the LIFO inventory valuation by $52,608,000 in 1990, $58,618,000 in 1989, and $42,583,000 in 1988.

Inventories include the following:

	December 31		
	1990	1989	1988
	(expressed in thousands)		
Finished goods and work in process	$ 261,312	$ 235,627	$ 221,516
Logs	45,502	39,516	35,675
Other raw materials and supplies	178,158	149,296	141,558
	$ 484,972	$ 424,439	$ 398,749

■ **Property.** Property and equipment are recorded at cost. Cost includes expenditures for major improvements and replacements and the net amount of interest cost associated with significant capital additions. Primarily due to expansion and modernization projects at pulp and paper mills in International Falls, Minnesota, and Rumford, Maine, capitalized interest for 1990 increased to $35,533,000. Capitalized interest was $15,981,000 in 1989 and $3,238,000 in 1988. Substantially all of the Company's paper and wood products manufacturing facilities determine depreciation by the units-of-production method, and other operations use the straight-line method. Operations which use composite depreciation methods include gains and losses from partial sales and retirements in accumulated depreciation. Gains and losses at other operations are included in income as they occur. Estimated service lives of principal items of property and equipment range from 3 to 40 years.

Cost of company timber harvested and amortization of logging roads are determined on the basis of the annual amount of timber cut in relation to the total amount of recoverable timber. Timber and timberlands are stated at cost, less the accumulated total of timber previously harvested.

A portion of the Company's wood requirements are acquired from public and private sources. Except for deposits required pursuant to wood supply contracts, no amounts are recorded until such time as the Company becomes liable for the timber. At December 31, 1990, based on average prices at the time, the unrecorded amount of those contracts was estimated to be approximately $160,000,000.

■ **Start-Up Costs.** Preoperating costs incurred during the construction and start-up of major new manufacturing facilities are capitalized and amortized over periods ranging from 5 to 15 years.

The unamortized balance of start-up costs, included in "Other assets" on the Balance Sheets, is as follows:

	December 31		
	1990	1989	1988
	(expressed in thousands)		
Balance at beginning of the year	$ 32,406	$ 32,630	$ 37,747
Capitalized [1]	22,054	3,778	—
Amortized	(4,000)	(4,002)	(4,035)
Attributable to facility sold	—	—	(1,082)
Balance at end of the year	$ 50,460	$ 32,406	$ 32,630

[1] Capitalized start-up costs shown are attributable to the expansion and modernization project at the pulp and paper mill in International Falls, Minnesota.

■ **Research and Development Costs.** Research and development costs are expensed as incurred. During 1990, 1989, and 1988, research and development expenses were $11,430,000, $11,143,000, and $9,485,000.

■ **Other Events.** During 1988, a nine-week strike at 15 of the Company's Northwest wood products facilities resulted in approximately 86 million square feet of lost plywood production and 99 million board feet of lost lumber production.

2. Income Taxes

The Company provides income taxes for all items included on the Statements of Income, regardless of when such items are reported for tax purposes or when the taxes are actually paid. The Financial Accounting Standards Board is in the process of revising a standard on accounting for income taxes that, when implemented, would require a change in the way the Company computes deferred taxes (see page 13 for additional information).

The income tax provision includes the following:

	Year Ended December 31		
	1990	1989	1988
	(expressed in thousands)		
Current income tax provision (refund)			
Federal	$ (15,982)	$ 91,458	$ 79,716
State	773	16,914	15,363
Foreign	6,893	24,892	46,120
	(8,316)	133,264	141,199
Deferred income tax provision			
Federal	43,229	27,942	41,525
State	4,533	5,150	3,330
Foreign	6,684	2,934	2,706
	54,446	36,026	47,561
Total income tax provision	$ 46,130	$ 169,290	$ 188,760

During 1990, the Company received income tax refunds, net of cash payments, of $4,366,000, compared with cash payments for income taxes, net of refunds received, of $124,441,000 in 1989 and $163,960,000 in 1988.

A reconciliation of the theoretical tax provision, assuming all income had been taxed at the statutory U.S. federal income tax rate, and the Company's actual tax provision is as follows:

	Year Ended December 31					
	1990		1989		1988	
	Amount	% of Pretax Income	Amount	% of Pretax Income	Amount	% of Pretax Income
	(expressed in thousands, except percentages)					
Theoretical tax provision	$ 41,274	34.0%	$ 148,535	34.0%	$ 162,479	34.0%
Increases (decreases) in taxes resulting from						
State tax provision	3,502	2.9	14,563	3.3	12,337	2.6
Foreign income taxed at more than theoretical rate	2,342	1.9	5,298	1.2	15,667	3.3
Other	(988)	(.8)	894	.3	(1,723)	(.4)
Actual tax provision	$ 46,130	38.0%	$ 169,290	38.8%	$ 188,760	39.5%

Notes to Financial Statements
Boise Cascade Corporation and Subsidiaries

The deferred income tax provision results from timing differences in recognition of revenue and expense for tax and financial reporting purposes. The nature of these differences and the tax effect of each are as follows:

	Year Ended December 31		
	1990	1989	1988
	(expressed in thousands)		
Book depreciation less than tax depreciation	$ 52,325	$ 37,834	$ 24,712
Expenses deferred for book purposes	6,293	—	—
Investment and other tax credits used	—	—	19,631
Other	(4,172)	(1,808)	3,218
Deferred income tax provision	$ 54,446	$ 36,026	$ 47,561

The Company had alternative minimum tax credits for tax purposes of $12,716,000 available at December 31, 1990, that may be carried forward indefinitely to be utilized in years in which the regular tax payable exceeds the minimum tax payable.

At December 31, 1990, certain foreign subsidiaries of the Company had $255,000,000 of undistributed earnings. U.S. income taxes, net of allowable foreign income tax credits, have been provided on $15,000,000 of the undistributed earnings. No U.S. tax has been provided on $240,000,000 of undistributed earnings of Canadian subsidiaries that have been indefinitely reinvested in Canada.

Pretax income from domestic and foreign sources is as follows:

	Year Ended December 31		
	1990	1989	1988
	(expressed in thousands)		
Domestic	$ 79,140	$ 364,780	$ 375,140
Foreign	42,260	72,090	102,740
Pretax income	$ 121,400	$ 436,870	$ 477,880

The Company's federal income tax returns have been examined through 1985, and 1986 and 1987 tax returns are currently under review. Certain deficiencies have been proposed, but the amount of the deficiencies, if any, that may result upon settlement of these years cannot be determined at this time. The Company believes that it has adequately provided for any such deficiencies and that settlements will not have a material adverse effect on the Company's financial condition.

3. Debt

At December 31, 1990, the Company had an unsecured revolving credit agreement that permitted it to borrow up to $750,000,000, of which $161,390,000 of borrowing rights had been allocated by the Company to support outstanding commercial paper. During 1990, a $110,000,000 unsecured revolving credit agreement was completed for one of the Company's Canadian subsidiaries that permitted borrowing in either U.S. or Canadian dollars. Amounts drawn under this revolver are guaranteed by the Company and are consolidated with borrowings of the Company for reporting purposes. On December 31, 1990, borrowings of US$50,000,000 were outstanding under the Canadian revolver. In addition, the Company had entered into an "interest rate swap," resulting in an effective fixed interest rate of 8.9% with respect to that borrowing. The difference between the variable and fixed interest rates is accrued as either a payable or receivable as interest rates change during the life of the swap agreement. The Company will resume payments of interest based on one of the pricing formulas available under the credit agreement upon termination of the swap agreement.

The revolving credit agreements provide the Company with a choice of several pricing formulas. At December 31, 1990, the effective interest rates would have ranged from 7.6% to 10.3% for borrowings in U.S. dollars and from 11.2% to 12.6% for borrowings in Canadian dollars. Commitment fees are required on the unused portion of the credits. The revolving period on the $750,000,000 lending commitment expires in May 1994, and any borrowings outstanding at that time are payable in quarterly installments ending in May 1997. The revolving period on the $110,000,000 lending commitment expires in May 1995, and any amounts outstanding at that time are payable in quarterly installments ending in June 1996. Compensating balances are not required.

In December 1990, the Company filed a new shelf registration with the Securities and Exchange Commission for additional debt securities. After incorporating the remaining $26,000,000 from a prior shelf registration, the Company had $426,000,000 of shelf capacity for new publicly registered debt.

In 1989, the Company guaranteed debt used to fund an employee stock ownership plan that is part of the Savings and Supplemental Retirement Plan for the Company's U.S. salaried employees (see Note 5). The Company has recorded the debt on its Balance Sheets, along with an offset in the shareholders' equity section that is entitled "Deferred ESOP benefit." The Company has guaranteed certain tax indemnities on the ESOP debt, and the interest rate on the guaranteed debt is subject to adjustment for events that are described in the loan agreement.

The Company may redeem all or part of the 7% unsecured convertible subordinated debentures at specified amounts that decline to $50 par value per debenture on May 1, 1996. Sinking fund payments are required after May 1, 1996. Each debenture is convertible into 1.1415 shares of the Company's common stock.

Long-term debt, most of which is unsecured, consists of the following:

	December 31		
	1990	1989	1988
	(expressed in thousands)		
7.75% notes, due in 1991	$ 100,000	$ 99,966	$ 99,863
11.875% notes, due in 1993, net of unamortized discount of $161,000 [1]	99,839	99,760	99,681
13.125% notes, due in 1994, callable in 1991	58,145	58,145	58,145
8.375% notes, due in 1994, callable in 1992, net of unamortized discount of $118,000 [1]	99,882	99,810	99,737
10.25% notes, due in 1996, callable in 1993	100,000	100,000	100,000
10.125% notes, due in 1997, net of unamortized discount of $306,000 [1] [2]	99,694	—	—
9.625% notes, due in 1998, callable in 1995, net of unamortized discount of $260,000 [1]	99,740	99,683	99,626
9.9% notes, due in 2000, net of unamortized discount of $506,000 [1]	99,494	—	—
9.875% notes, due in 2001, callable in 1999	100,000	100,000	—
9.85% notes, due in 2002	125,000	—	—
9.45% debentures, due in 2009, net of unamortized discount of $424,000 [1]	149,576	149,554	—
7% convertible subordinated debentures, due in 2016, net of unamortized discount of $1,862,000 [1]	96,026	95,677	95,328
Medium-term notes, Series A, with interest rates averaging 9.5% in 1990, due in varying amounts through 2000	79,000	—	—
Notes payable and other indebtedness, with interest rates averaging 8.9%, 10.7%, and 11%, due in varying amounts annually through 2012	69,528	58,508	114,410
Revenue bonds, with interest rates averaging 7.9%, 7.8%, and 7.7%, due in varying amounts annually through 2014, net of unamortized discount of $2,222,000 [1]	166,149	141,201	142,995
American & Foreign Power Company Inc. 5% debentures, due in 2030, net of unamortized discount of $2,055,000 [1]	32,510	35,144	38,647
Commercial paper, with interest rates averaging 8.2% in 1990 and 9.4% in 1989, net of unamortized discount of $416,000 [1]	160,974	47,920	—
Revolving credit borrowings, with interest rates averaging 8.2% in 1990	50,000	—	—
12% notes, due in 1992, called in 1990	—	50,000	50,000
	1,785,557	1,235,368	998,432
Less current portion	136,731	30,390	73,320
	1,648,826	1,204,978	925,112
Guarantee of 8.5% ESOP debt, due in installments through 2004	285,678	292,581	—
	$1,934,504	$1,497,559	$ 925,112

[1] The amount of net unamortized discount disclosed applies to long-term debt outstanding at December 31, 1990.

[2] In January 1991, the Company drew an additional $20,000,000 of 10.125% notes pursuant to a delayed delivery contract.

Notes to Financial Statements
Boise Cascade Corporation and Subsidiaries

The scheduled payments of long-term debt are $136,731,000 in 1991, $49,022,000 in 1992, $159,964,000 in 1993, $159,741,000 in 1994, and $25,757,000 in 1995. Cash payments for interest, net of interest capitalized, were $118,231,000 in 1990, $92,928,000 in 1989, and $93,012,000 in 1988.

The Company's loan agreements contain covenants and restrictions, none of which are expected to affect its operations significantly. At December 31, 1990, $275,814,000 of retained earnings was available for dividends.

4. Leases

Lease obligations for which the Company assumes substantially all property rights and risks of ownership are capitalized. All other leases are treated as operating leases. Rental expenses for operating leases, net of sublease rentals, were $24,699,000 in 1990, $24,903,000 in 1989, and $26,823,000 in 1988.

The Company has various operating leases with remaining terms of more than one year. These leases have minimum lease payment requirements, net of sublease rentals, of $10,875,000 for 1991, $7,402,000 for 1992, $5,580,000 for 1993, $4,907,000 for 1994, and $3,980,000 for 1995, with total payments thereafter of $121,702,000.

Substantially all lease agreements have fixed payment terms based upon the lapse of time. Certain lease agreements provide the Company with the option to purchase the leased property. Additionally, certain lease agreements contain renewal options ranging up to 15 years, with fixed payment terms similar to those in the original lease agreements.

5. Retirement and Benefit Plans

Substantially all of the Company's employees are covered by pension plans. The plans are primarily noncontributory, defined benefit plans. The pension benefit for salaried employees is based primarily on years of service and the highest five-year average compensation, and the benefit for hourly employees is generally based on a fixed amount per year of service. The Company's contributions to its pension plans vary from year to year, but the Company has made at least the minimum contribution required by law in each year. The assets of the pension plans are invested primarily in common stocks, fixed-income securities, and cash and cash equivalents.

The assumptions used by the Company's actuaries in the calculations of pension expense and plan obligations are estimates of factors that will determine, among other things, the amount and timing of future benefit payments. On January 1, 1990, the asset return assumption was increased to 10% from the 8.5% used previously, and the salary escalation was decreased to 6.5% from 7%. The discount rate assumption was 8.5% at December 31, 1990 and 1989, and 9% at December 31, 1988. Certain other assumption changes made in the normal course during 1990 had an offsetting effect to the asset return and salary escalation assumption changes.

The components of pension expense are as follows:

	Year Ended December 31		
	1990	1989	1988
	(expressed in thousands)		
Benefits earned by employees	$ 18,979	$ 15,828	$ 14,657
Interest cost on projected benefit obligation	66,277	59,819	55,478
(Earnings) losses from plan assets	16,743	(133,336)	(83,220)
Assumed earnings from plan assets (more) less than actual earnings or losses	(90,790)	74,716	28,089
Amortization of unrecognized net initial asset	(12,675)	(12,679)	(12,604)
Amortization of net experience gains and losses from prior periods	4,711	536	829
Amortization of unrecognized prior service costs	2,462	2,064	1,718
Company-sponsored plans [1]	5,707	6,948	4,947
Multiemployer pension plans	636	773	834
Total pension expense	$ 6,343	$ 7,721	$ 5,781

[1] The Company anticipates that it will contribute $6,992,000 to the pension plans it sponsors for the 1990 plan year. The contributions for the 1989 and 1988 plan years were $7,350,000 and $6,320,000.

The following table, which includes only Company-sponsored plans, compares the pension obligation with assets available to meet that obligation:

	Plans With Assets in Excess of the Accumulated Benefit Obligation			Plans With an Accumulated Benefit Obligation in Excess of Assets		
	December 31			December 31		
	1990	1989	1988	1990	1989	1988
			(expressed in millions)			
Accumulated benefit obligation						
Vested	$(482.2)	$(532.0)	$(468.3)	$(281.0)	$(156.0)	$(143.6)
Nonvested	(2.5)	(2.4)	(2.1)	(2.9)	(2.6)	(2.6)
Provision for salary escalation	(87.5)	(85.2)	(74.0)	(1.9)	(2.8)	(3.0)
Projected benefit obligation	(572.2)	(619.6)	(544.4)	(285.8)	(161.4)	(149.2)
Plan assets at fair market value	564.6	710.2	621.7	212.3	118.0	104.0
Net plan assets (obligation)	$ (7.6)	$ 90.6	$ 77.3	$ (73.5)	$ (43.4)	$ (45.2)

The following table reconciles the net plan assets (obligation) to the prepayment (obligation) recorded on the Company's Balance Sheets:

	Plans With Assets in Excess of the Accumulated Benefit Obligation			Plans With an Accumulated Benefit Obligation in Excess of Assets		
	December 31			December 31		
	1990	1989	1988	1990	1989	1988
			(expressed in millions)			
Net plan assets (obligation)	$ (7.6)	$ 90.6	$ 77.3	$ (73.5)	$ (43.4)	$ (45.2)
Remainder of unrecognized initial (asset) obligation [1]	(59.4)	(85.4)	(97.9)	(11.1)	2.2	2.6
Other unrecognized items [2]	92.5	10.8	31.0	49.4	10.5	13.6
Adjustment to record minimum liability	—	—	—	(38.2)	(13.5)	(15.3)
Net recorded prepayment (obligation)	$ 25.5	$ 16.0	$ 10.4	$ (73.4)	$ (44.2)	$ (44.3)

[1] The unrecognized initial (asset) obligation calculated at January 1, 1986, is being amortized over a weighted average of 11 years.

[2] "Other unrecognized items" reflects changes in actuarial assumptions, net changes in prior service costs, and net experience gains and losses since January 1, 1986.

The Company and its retired employees currently share in the cost of providing retiree medical benefits. The portion of benefits paid by the Company on behalf of U.S. salaried employees retiring after December 31, 1989, is expected to decrease over time, with the result that the Company will eventually cease to share in the cost of providing medical benefits for retiring U.S. salaried employees. The type of benefit provided and the extent of coverage vary based on employee classification, date of retirement, location, and other factors. In general, the Company's share of the cost of retiree medical benefits is recorded at the time the benefits are provided. Costs incurred by the Company during 1990 were $8,545,000, compared with $7,621,000 in 1989 and $6,994,000 in 1988. In December 1990, the Financial Accounting Standards Board issued Statement No. 106, "Employers' Accounting for Postretirement Benefits Other Than Pensions." The new statement will require the Company to accrue retiree medical costs (see page 13 for additional information).

The Company sponsors savings and supplemental retirement programs for its U.S. salaried employees, certain of its employees subject to collective bargaining agreements beginning in mid-1989, and certain nonunion hourly employees beginning in mid-1988. In mid-1989, the plan for salaried employees was amended to provide for an employee stock ownership plan. Under that plan, the Company's Series D ESOP convertible preferred stock (see Note 6) is allocated to eligible participants in annual installments through 2004 as principal and interest payments are made on the ESOP debt guaranteed by the Company. Total expense for these plans, which was recorded in accordance with the consensus reached by the Emerging Issues Task Force of the Financial Accounting Standards Board, was $9,759,000 in 1990, compared with $11,462,000 in 1989 and $6,359,000 in 1988.

Notes to Financial Statements
Boise Cascade Corporation and Subsidiaries

6. Shareholders' Equity

■ **Preferred Stock.**   At December 31, 1990, 6,729,039 shares of 7.375% Series D ESOP convertible preferred stock were outstanding. This stock was sold to the trustee of the Company's Savings and Supplemental Retirement Plan for the Company's U.S. salaried employees in July 1989 (see Note 5). Each ESOP preferred share is entitled to one vote, bears an annual cumulative dividend of $3.31875, is convertible at any time by the trustee to .80357 share of common stock, and has a preference of $45 in liquidation. The ESOP preferred shares may not be redeemed for less than the liquidation preference.

In May 1988, substantially all of the Company's $3.50 Series C convertible exchangeable preferred stock was exchanged for 7% convertible subordinated debentures due in 2016 (see Note 3).

The remaining authorized but unissued preferred shares may be issued with such voting rights, dividend rates, conversion privileges, sinking fund requirements, and redemption prices as the board of directors may determine, without action by the shareholders.

■ **Common Stock.**   At December 31, 1990, there were 37,948,511 common shares outstanding. Of the unissued shares, a total of 62,097,891 shares were reserved for the following: 50,023,201 shares for the common share rights discussed below, 5,407,253 shares for conversion of the Series D ESOP preferred shares, 4,432,658 shares for issuance under the 1984 Key Executive Stock Option Plan, and 2,234,779 shares for conversion of the 7% convertible subordinated debentures.

In December 1988, the Company redeemed the rights which had been issued under a shareholder rights plan adopted in January 1986. One right was attached to each share of the Company's common stock, and the redemption price was 10¢ per right.

Pursuant to the shareholder rights plan adopted in December 1988 and as amended in September 1990, holders of common stock received a distribution of one right for each common share held. The rights become exercisable ten days after a person or group acquires 15% of the Company's outstanding voting securities or ten business days after a person or group commences or announces an intention to commence a tender or exchange offer that could result in the acquisition of 15% of these securities. If a person acquires 15% or more of the Company's outstanding voting securities, on the tenth day thereafter, unless this time period is extended by the board of directors, each right would, subject to certain adjustments and alternatives, entitle the rightholder to purchase common stock of the Company or the acquiring company having a market value of twice the $175 exercise price of the right (except that the acquiring person or group and other related holders would not be able to purchase common stock of the Company on these terms). The rights are nonvoting, may be redeemed by the Company at a price of 1¢ per right at any time prior to the tenth day after an individual or group acquires 15% of the Company's voting stock, unless extended, and expire in 1998. Additional details are set forth in the Amended and Restated Rights Agreement filed with the Securities and Exchange Commission on September 26, 1990.

The 1984 Key Executive Stock Option Plan provides for the granting of options to purchase shares of the Company's common stock. Stock appreciation rights may be substituted for some of these options at the time the options are exercised. The stock appreciation rights provide that the difference between the option price and the price of the Company's common stock on the date of exercise be distributed in cash in lieu of shares of common stock.

Additional information relating to the option plan is as follows:

	Year Ended December 31		
	1990	1989	1988
Balance at beginning of the year	1,957,656	1,709,889	1,888,654
Options granted [1]	924,700	439,600	—
Options exercised	(7,583)	(168,227)	(92,871)
Stock appreciation rights exercised	—	(6,333)	(51,832)
Options canceled	(68,271)	(17,273)	(34,062)
Balance at end of the year	2,806,502[2]	1,957,656	1,709,889
Price range of: Options and rights exercised	$28 – $38	$23 – $47	$24 – $38
Options outstanding	$23 – $47	$23 – $47	$23 – $47

[1] The option price is equal to the fair market value of the Company's common stock on the date the options were granted.

[2] At December 31, 1990, options for 1,883,502 shares were exercisable, and 659,447 stock appreciation rights were outstanding.

During 1990, the Company purchased 4,591 shares of its common stock under a program approved by the board of directors and, at December 31, 1990, was authorized to purchase up to 5,435,894 additional shares. In 1989, 7,127,136 shares were purchased, including 6,822,008 shares that were purchased with proceeds received from the sale of the Series D ESOP preferred stock. In 1988, 295,049 shares were purchased.

7. Segment Information

Boise Cascade Corporation is an integrated forest products company headquartered in Boise, Idaho, with operations located primarily in the United States and Canada. The Company manufactures and distributes paper and paper products, office products, and building products and owns and manages timberland to support these operations.

No single customer accounts for 10% of consolidated trade sales. Operations in geographic areas other than the United States and Canada and export sales to foreign unaffiliated customers are immaterial. During 1990, the Company's Canadian paper operations made sales of $20,117,000 to Company paper operations in the U.S., and similar sales in 1989 and 1988 were $27,335,000 and $21,676,000.

■ **Summary of Significant Segment Accounting Policies.** Intersegment sales are recorded primarily at market prices. Corporate assets are primarily cash and short-term investments, deferred income tax benefits, prepaid expenses, certain receivables, and property and equipment.

The Company's segments exclude timber-related assets and capital expenditures, because any allocation of these assets would be arbitrary. Company timber harvested is included in segment results at cost.

Notes to Financial Statements
Boise Cascade Corporation and Subsidiaries

An analysis of the Company's operations by segment and by geographic area is as follows: [1]

	Sales			Operating Income [2]	Depreciation and Cost of Company Timber Harvested	Capital Expend- itures [3]	Assets
	Trade	Inter- segment	Total				
Year Ended December 31, 1990			(expressed in thousands)				
Paper and paper products							
United States	$1,869,325	$121,919	$1,991,244	$131,525	$130,809	$601,129	$2,767,240
Canada	338,102	3	338,105	55,483	23,961	66,790	440,308
	2,207,427	121,922	2,329,349	187,008	154,770	667,919	3,207,548
Office products	1,076,973	2,355	1,079,328	57,609	16,299	32,461	409,874
Building products	889,211	49,300	938,511	41,977	30,696	31,923	377,629
Other operations	12,309	49,867	62,176	8,451	7,459	9,884	115,867
Total	4,185,920	223,444	4,409,364	295,045	209,224	742,187	4,110,918
Intersegment eliminations	—	(223,444)	(223,444)	(69)	—	—	(19,251)
Timber, timberlands, and timber deposits	—	—	—	—	—	13,681	391,985
Corporate and other	—	—	—	(58,509)	3,666	1,833	301,118
Consolidated totals	$4,185,920	$ —	$4,185,920	$236,467	$212,890	$757,701	$4,784,770
Year Ended December 31, 1989							
Paper and paper products							
United States	$2,045,416	$111,045	$2,156,461	$312,574	$129,090	$509,600	$2,261,624
Canada	334,957	2	334,959	92,360	21,794	76,075	393,724
	2,380,373	111,047	2,491,420	404,934	150,884	585,675	2,655,348
Office products	1,011,894	1,747	1,013,641	66,672	13,627	29,399	390,266
Building products	935,885	56,863	992,748	107,182	28,383	53,852	379,068
Other operations	9,878	47,420	57,298	5,650	5,658	22,882	114,466
Total	4,338,030	217,077	4,555,107	584,438	198,552	691,808	3,539,148
Intersegment eliminations	—	(217,077)	(217,077)	341	—	—	(22,670)
Timber, timberlands, and timber deposits	—	—	—	—	—	5,158	388,294
Corporate and other	—	—	—	(56,758)	3,508	1,963	237,853
Consolidated totals	$4,338,030	$ —	$4,338,030	$528,021	$202,060	$698,929	$4,142,625
Year Ended December 31, 1988							
Paper and paper products							
United States	$2,054,366	$ 93,205	$2,147,571	$391,470	$121,473	$283,774	$1,929,062
Canada	351,710	33	351,743	125,954	22,484	48,337	335,568
	2,406,076	93,238	2,499,314	517,424	143,957	332,111	2,264,630
Office products	868,596	1,295	869,891	62,141	10,192	41,214	338,082
Building products	809,334	31,478	840,812	54,216	25,080	43,498	333,725
Other operations	10,624	44,390	55,014	4,218	5,051	6,034	100,349
Total	4,094,630	170,401	4,265,031	637,999	184,280	422,857	3,036,786
Intersegment eliminations	—	(170,401)	(170,401)	(1,176)	—	—	(17,320)
Timber, timberlands, and timber deposits	—	—	—	—	—	6,055	389,201
Corporate and other	—	—	—	(59,659)	3,320	1,401	201,576
Consolidated totals	$4,094,630	$ —	$4,094,630	$577,164	$187,600	$430,313	$3,610,243

[1] Operations are located primarily in the U.S. except as noted.

[2] Operating income includes interest income allocated to the Company's segments in the amounts of $2,577,000 for 1990, $1,551,000 for 1989, and $2,274,000 for 1988.

[3] Capital expenditures shown are exclusive of estimated related working capital requirements, lease commitments, and other expenditures of $66,256,000 in 1990, $23,872,000 in 1989, and $21,498,000 in 1988.

8. Litigation and Legal Matters

In 1980, the Federal Trade Commission initiated an action before a Federal Trade Commission administrative law judge alleging that the Company had purchased some office products for resale by the Company's office products business at net prices below the prices available to its dealer competitors and contrary to the Robinson-Patman Act and the Federal Trade Commission Act. In February 1986, the Federal Trade Commission issued a cease and desist order against the alleged improper practices. In January 1988, the United States Court of Appeals for the District of Columbia Circuit reversed the Federal Trade Commission ruling, concluding that the Commission had failed to establish that the Company's purchasing practices caused any adverse effect on competition in the office products industry. The case was sent back to the Federal Trade Commission. On November 1, 1990, the Commission reissued the 1986 cease and desist order based on a finding that the disputed purchasing practices may have caused injury to competition. The Company has filed an appeal of the Commission's latest decision with the U.S. Circuit Court of Appeals. The Company cannot predict what the outcome of the appeal will be, but the Company believes that its purchasing practices are lawful.

The Company is involved in other litigation and administrative proceedings primarily arising in the normal course of its business. In the opinion of management, the Company's recovery, if any, or the Company's liability, if any, under any pending litigation or administrative proceeding, including that described in the preceding paragraph, would not materially affect its financial condition or operations.

Report of Independent Public Accountants

To the Shareholders of Boise Cascade Corporation:

We have audited the accompanying balance sheets of Boise Cascade Corporation (a Delaware corporation) and subsidiaries as of December 31, 1990, 1989 and 1988, and the related statements of income, shareholders' equity, and cash flows for the years then ended. These financial statements are the responsibility of the Company's management. Our responsibility is to express an opinion on these financial statements based on our audits.

We conducted our audits in accordance with generally accepted auditing standards. Those standards require that we plan and perform the audit to obtain reasonable assurance about whether the financial statements are free of material misstatement. An audit includes examining, on a test basis, evidence supporting the amounts and disclosures in the financial statements. An audit also includes assessing the accounting principles used and significant estimates made by management, as well as evaluating the overall financial statement presentation. We believe that our audits provide a reasonable basis for our opinion.

In our opinion, the financial statements referred to above present fairly, in all material respects, the financial position of Boise Cascade Corporation and subsidiaries as of December 31, 1990, 1989 and 1988, and the results of their operations and their cash flows for the years then ended in conformity with generally accepted accounting principles.

Boise, Idaho
February 1, 1991

Arthur Andersen & Co.

Report of Management

The management of Boise Cascade Corporation is primarily responsible for the information and representations contained in this annual report. The financial statements and related notes were prepared in conformity with generally accepted accounting principles appropriate in the circumstances. In preparing the financial statements, management has, when necessary, made judgments and estimates based on currently available information.

Management maintains a comprehensive system of internal controls based on written policies and procedures and the careful selection and training of employees. The system is designed to provide reasonable assurance that assets are safeguarded against loss or unauthorized use and that transactions are executed in accordance with management's authorization. The concept of reasonable assurance is based on recognition that the cost of a particular accounting control should not exceed the benefit expected to be derived.

The Company's Internal Audit staff monitors the Company's financial reporting system and the related internal accounting controls, which are also tested by Arthur Andersen & Co., Boise Cascade's independent public accountants.

The Audit Committee of the board of directors, which is composed solely of outside directors, meets periodically with management, representatives of the Company's Internal Audit Department, and Arthur Andersen & Co. representatives to assure that each group is carrying out its responsibilities. The Internal Audit staff and the independent public accountants have access to the Audit Committee, without the presence of management, to discuss the results of their examinations, the adequacy of internal accounting controls, and the quality of financial reporting.

Quarterly Results of Operations

Quarter	Net Sales			Gross Profit			Net Income			Primary and Fully Diluted Net Income Per Common Share					
	1990	1989	1988	1990	1989	1988	1990	1989	1988[1]	1990[2]		1989		1988	
						(expressed in millions, except per-common-share amounts)									
First	$1,066	$1,099	$1,016	$178	$248	$229	$ 33	$ 78	$ 69	$ .79	$ .73	$1.74	$1.68	$1.47	$1.44
Second	1,051	1,092	1,007	161	237	231	23	75	72	.52	.50	1.68	1.62	1.59	1.54
Third	1,054	1,081	1,037	152	227	234	14	63	72	.27	.27	1.49	1.30	1.58	1.53
Fourth	1,015	1,066	1,035	164	206	239	5	52	76	.04	.04	1.28	1.10	1.70	1.64
	$4,186	$4,338	$4,095	$655	$918	$933	$ 75	$268	$289	$1.62	$1.62	$6.19	$5.70	$6.34	$6.15

[1] A nine-week strike at 15 of the Company's Northwest wood products facilities began in late June and ended in mid-August 1988. The strike resulted in approximately 86 million square feet of lost plywood production and 99 million board feet of lost lumber production.

[2] The computation of fully diluted net income per common share for the third and fourth quarters and the year ended December 31, 1990, was antidilutive; therefore, the amounts reported for primary and fully diluted earnings are the same. In addition, the total of fully diluted net income per share for the four quarters will not equal the $1.62 fully diluted earnings per share reported for 1990.

Discussion and Analysis of Operations

The following discussion and analysis of operations for 1989, compared with 1988 and 1987, should be read in conjunction with the "Income From Operations" and "Financial Condition" sections on pages 12 and 13 of this annual report and with the financial information on pages 14 through 29.

Boise Cascade reported net income of $268 million in 1989, compared with net income of $289 million in 1988 and $183 million in 1987. Fully diluted earnings per share were $5.70 in 1989, compared with $6.15 in 1988 and $3.64 in 1987.

Operating income for our paper and paper products segment in 1989 was $405 million, down from a record $517 million in 1988. Operating income for this segment in 1987 was $326 million. Paper-segment earnings declined through 1989, reflecting weak prices for our uncoated white papers, newsprint, and coated paper grades. Those declines reflected softening orders, as customers went through major inventory adjustments. Prices also weakened, as markets for those paper grades began to anticipate or absorb new capacity. In addition, our Northwest pulp and paper mills experienced a sharp increase in the cost of wood chips. The increase was attributable to restrictions on the harvest of timber from public lands in the Northwest, combined with a strong export market for logs and chips.

In 1988, markets for our uncoated free sheet papers were strong, with steadily improving performance. That improvement began during the second half of 1987, following some weakness during the first half of the year. Coated paper markets were robust in 1988, with demand outpacing supply. The dramatic improvement in coated paper markets began in 1987, following a period of overcapacity that had existed since 1985. Newsprint began 1988 with a price increase, following a year of strengthening prices in 1987. As 1988 progressed, some market discounting took place in anticipation of new capacity. Markets for containerboard were strong during the three-year period ending in 1989, but our corrugated container business experienced difficulty passing on the higher cost of containerboard in the form of increased box prices. During the second quarter of 1989, the Company sold its Specialty Paperboard Division for a small gain.

Boise Cascade's office products segment added to its record performance in 1989. Sales volume exceeded $1 billion for the first time, an increase of 17 percent over that of 1988, after 1988 sales volume had exceeded that of 1987 by 18 percent. Operating income for 1989 was $67 million, compared with $62 million in 1988 and $48 million in 1987. Growth in income during 1989 lagged growth in sales primarily because of start-up costs associated with two new facilities.

Operating income for our building products segment in 1989 was $107 million, compared with $54 million in strike-affected 1988 and $96 million in 1987. The 1989 performance was due to a combination of factors, including the efficiency of the Company's wood products facilities, vigorous rebuilding activity after Hurricane Hugo and the California earthquake, and strong pricing for many wood products and residual chips caused by constraints on timber supply. The positive effect of higher prices was partially offset by delivered-log costs that were about 9 percent above those of 1988.

The lower operating income reported in 1988 resulted from somewhat weaker markets for building products, an increase in the cost of raw materials, and an industrywide labor dispute in the Northwest that affected production at 15 of our wood products facilities for nine weeks. The Company lost production of approximately 86 million square feet of plywood and 99 million board feet of lumber as a result of that strike. In addition, the Company sold three wood products manufacturing facilities in 1988 that had combined annual production capacity of about 295 million square feet of plywood and 46 million board feet of lumber.

Results for 1987 were attributable to a combination of restructuring and cost-containment efforts over the previous several years, capital investments, and strong lumber and plywood prices. During 1987, we sold our 20 remaining retail building distribution centers.

STATISTICAL INFORMATION

Contents

Financial Review
Boise Cascade Corporation and Subsidiaries

Eleven-Year Comparison	Year Ended December 31										
	1990	1989	1988	1987	1986	1985	1984	1983	1982	1981	1980
	(expressed in millions, except per-common-share amounts)										
Sales by Segment											
Paper and paper products ..	**$2,329**	$2,491	$2,499	$2,156	$1,853	$1,874	$1,660	$1,412	$1,314	$1,405	$1,256
Office products	**1,079**	1,014	870	735	676	651	584	468	406	399	347
Building products	**939**	993	841	1,030	986	957	1,278	1,268	921	1,084	1,250
Other operations	**62**	57	55	56	356	388	460	450	418	390	344
	4,409	4,555	4,265	3,977	3,871	3,870	3,982	3,598	3,059	3,278	3,197
Intersegment eliminations ...	**(223)**	(217)	(170)	(156)	(131)	(133)	(165)	(147)	(147)	(171)	(178)
Trade sales	**$4,186**	$4,338	$4,095	$3,821	$3,740	$3,737	$3,817	$3,451	$2,912	$3,107	$3,019
Income by Segment											
Paper and paper products ..	**$ 187**	$ 405	$ 517	$ 326	$ 197	$ 209	$ 258	$ 129	$ 103	$ 224	$ 178
Office products	**58**	67	62	48	47	37	37	26	21	19	21
Building products	**42**	107	54	96	86	41	(102)	15	(52)	(23)	12
Other operations	**8**	5	5	5	13	26	17	37	36	33	32
	295	584	638	475	343	313	210	207	108	253	243
Corporate administration and other	**(58)**	(56)	(61)	(50)	(59)	(49)	(55)	(55)	(47)	(39)	(37)
Segment income from operations	**237**	528	577	425	284	264	155	152	61	214	206
Less: interest income allocated to segments ...	**(3)**	(2)	(2)	(3)	(3)	(4)	(3)	(3)	(3)	(5)	(3)
Income from operations	**234**	526	575	422	281	260	152	149	58	209	203
Interest expense	**(117)**	(96)	(101)	(105)	(114)	(114)	(79)	(71)	(84)	(82)	(49)
Interest income and other	**4**	7	4	1	5	12	11	10	22	58	7
	(113)	(89)	(97)	(104)	(109)	(102)	(68)	(61)	(62)	(24)	(42)
Income (loss) before income taxes and extraordinary items	**121**	437	478	318	172	158	84	88	(4)	185	161
Income tax provision (benefit)	**46**	169	189	135	70	54	14	28	(11)	65	26
Income before extraordinary items	**75**	268	289	183	102	104	70	60	7	120	135
Extraordinary items, net of taxes	**—**	—	—	—	—	—	—	—	—	—	13
Net income	**$ 75**	$ 268	$ 289	$ 183	$ 102	$ 104	$ 70	$ 60	$ 7	$ 120	$ 148
Net income per common share [1]											
Primary	**$ 1.62**	$ 6.19	$ 6.34	$ 3.70	$ 1.99	$ 2.07	$ 1.34	$ 1.14	$ .16	$ 2.70	$ 3.05
Fully diluted	**1.62[2]**	5.70	6.15	3.64	1.98	2.06	1.33	1.14	.16	2.68	3.02

[1] Before an extraordinary gain of 28¢ per primary and fully diluted share in 1980.

[2] Primary and fully diluted amounts are the same because the computation of fully diluted net income per common share was antidilutive.

Eleven-Year Comparison

	December 31										
	1990	**1989**	**1988**	**1987**	**1986**	**1985**	**1984**	**1983**	**1982**	**1981**	**1980**
	(expressed in millions)										
Balance Sheets											
Assets											
Cash and short-term investments	$ **26**	$ 25	$ 23	$ 22	$ 35	$ 38	$ 74	$ 73	$ 35	$ 44	$ 38
Receivables, net	**413**	422	393	359	360	314	356	339	270	269	292
Inventories	**485**	424	399	374	392	378	468	443	384	424	392
Other current assets	**74**	61	52	70	74	59	74	81	33	30	52
	998	932	867	825	861	789	972	936	722	767	774
Property and equipment	**4,882**	4,212	3,649	3,316	3,386	3,043	2,950	2,399	2,288	2,238	2,154
Accumulated depreciation	**(1,727)**	(1,583)	(1,473)	(1,357)	(1,318)	(1,173)	(1,124)	(1,003)	(877)	(813)	(716)
	3,155	2,629	2,176	1,959	2,068	1,870	1,826	1,396	1,411	1,425	1,438
Timber, timberlands, and timber deposits	**392**	388	389	405	414	423	435	280	286	315	306
Other assets	**240**	194	178	186	191	186	177	226	244	233	170
	$4,785	$4,143	$3,610	$3,375	$3,534	$3,268	$3,410	$2,838	$2,663	$2,740	$2,688
Liabilities and Shareholders' Equity											
Notes payable	$ **40**	$ —	$ —	$ 31	$ —	$ 20	$ 53	$ 9	$ 19	$ —	$ 1
Current portion of long-term debt	**137**	30	73	47	51	33	26	76	34	23	25
Income taxes payable	**—**	4	5	9	4	15	19	7	1	20	26
Accounts payable and accrued liabilities	**581**	644	603	476	493	477	595	482	362	388	385
	758	678	681	563	548	545	693	574	416	431	437
Long-term debt, less current portion	**1,649**	1,205	925	938	1,154	1,026	1,057	607	752	779	805
Guarantee of 8.5% ESOP debt	**286**	293	—	—	—	—	—	—	—	—	—
Deferred income taxes	**394**	307	250	235	171	150	140	165	107	107	104
Other long-term liabilities	**122**	85	76	79	86	97	102	93	86	80	69
Shareholders' equity	**1,576**	1,575	1,678	1,560	1,575	1,450	1,418	1,399	1,302	1,343	1,273
	$4,785	$4,143	$3,610	$3,375	$3,534	$3,268	$3,410	$2,838	$2,663	$2,740	$2,688

	Year Ended December 31										
Sales Dollar Uses											
Materials and other expenses	$ **.66**	$ .62	$ .60	$ .61	$ .63	$ .63	$ .66	$ .64	$ .65	$ .61	$ .61
Employee compensation and benefits	**.21**	.19	.19	.20	.21	.22	.22	.23	.24	.23	.24
Energy	**.05**	.04	.05	.05	.06	.06	.06	.06	.07	.06	.06
Depreciation and cost of company timber harvested	**.05**	.05	.04	.05	.05	.05	.04	.04	.04	.04	.04
Income taxes	**.01**	.04	.05	.04	.02	.01	—	.01	—	.02	.01
Earnings	**.02**	.06	.07	.05	.03	.03	.02	.02	—	.04	.04
Total	**$1.00**	$1.00	$1.00	$1.00	$1.00	$1.00	$1.00	$1.00	$1.00	$1.00	$1.00

Financial Review
Boise Cascade Corporation and Subsidiaries

Eleven-Year Comparison	Year Ended December 31										
	1990	1989	1988	1987	1986	1985	1984	1983	1982	1981	1980
	(expressed in millions)										
Statements of Cash Flows											
Cash provided by (used for) operations											
Net income	$ 75	$268	$289	$183	$102	$104	$ 70	$ 60	$ 7	$120	$135
Depreciation and cost of company timber harvested	213	202	188	186	191	176	147	152	131	134	122
Deferred income tax provision (benefit)	54	36	47	59	36	29	(14)	15	(10)	21	(15)
Amortization and other	7	6	11	10	11	10	47	17	12	7	1
Receivables	37	(28)	(34)	(33)	(38)	11	(18)	(69)	(1)	23	(28)
Inventories	(64)	(44)	(27)	(40)	(3)	38	(8)	(58)	40	(32)	(14)
Accounts payable and accrued liabilities	(60)	51	120	18	6	(111)	108	120	(27)	3	17
Current and deferred income taxes	(7)	9	(22)	8	(44)	(5)	6	4	(11)	(6)	13
Other	(3)	(5)	(1)	—	—	(33)	2	(2)	(1)	3	(1)
	252	495	571	391	261	219	340	239	140	273	230
Cash provided by (used for) financing											
Cash dividends paid	(80)	(72)	(58)	(62)	(61)	(62)	(61)	(58)	(51)	(50)	(45)
Notes payable	40	—	(31)	31	(20)	(33)	44	(10)	19	(1)	(24)
Additions to (payments of) long-term debt, net	558	230	(96)	(214)	146	(21)	298	(104)	(16)	(27)	229
Purchases of common stock	—	(317)	(13)	(154)	(12)	(13)	(28)	—	—	—	—
Issuance of preferred stock	—	304	—	—	97	—	—	97	—	—	—
Issuance of common stock	—	—	—	—	—	—	38	—	—	—	—
Other	1	2	—	12	5	—	—	—	—	—	—
	519	147	(198)	(387)	155	(129)	291	(75)	(48)	(78)	160
Cash provided by (used for) investment											
Expenditures for property and equipment	(744)	(694)	(424)	(229)	(251)	(330)	(414)	(142)	(123)	(141)	(311)
Expenditures for timber and timberlands	(14)	(5)	(6)	(9)	(6)	(7)	(16)	(4)	(3)	(9)	(87)
Sales of operating assets ...	14	66	71	221	—	196	—	—	—	—	—
Purchases of facilities	—	—	—	—	(161)	—	(195)	—	—	—	—
Other	(26)	(7)	(13)	—	(1)	15	(5)	20	25	(39)	4
	(770)	(640)	(372)	(17)	(419)	(126)	(630)	(126)	(101)	(189)	(394)
Increase (decrease) in cash and short-term investments	$ 1	$ 2	$ 1	$ (13)	$ (3)	$ (36)	$ 1	$ 38	$ (9)	$ 6	$ (4)

Summary Information

Eleven-Year Comparison	Year Ended December 31										
	1990	1989	1988	1987	1986	1985	1984	1983	1982	1981	1980

Financial Information

Shareholders' equity per common share [1]	$41.07	$41.23	$37.34	$32.41	$30.34	$29.90	$28.92	$29.10	$29.15	$30.09	$28.55
Return on sales [2]	1.8%	6.2%	7.1%	4.8%	2.7%	2.8%	1.8%	1.7%	0.3%	3.9%	4.5%
Return on shareholders' equity [2]	4.7%	16.2%	18.1%	11.6%	6.7%	7.2%	4.9%	4.3%	0.6%	9.2%	11.1%
Return on total capital [2]	3.9%	10.2%	12.2%	8.4%	5.6%	5.9%	4.6%	4.2%	2.2%	7.0%	7.6%
Current ratio	1.32:1	1.37:1	1.27:1	1.47:1	1.57:1	1.45:1	1.40:1	1.63:1	1.74:1	1.78:1	1.77:1
Debt to equity	1.23:1	.95:1	.55:1	.60:1	.73:1	.71:1	.75:1	.43:1	.58:1	.58:1	.63:1
Debt to total capitalization	55.1%	48.7%	35.5%	37.6%	42.3%	41.4%	42.7%	30.3%	36.6%	36.7%	38.7%
Investment turnover	1.09	1.35	1.42	1.33	1.30	1.36	1.60	1.51	1.25	1.35	1.44
Earnings before interest, taxes, and depreciation (in millions)	$ 451	$ 735	$ 767	$ 609	$ 478	$ 448	$ 310	$ 311	$ 211	$ 401	$ 345
Capital expenditures (in millions) [3]	$ 824	$ 723	$ 452	$ 259	$ 441	$ 350	$ 651	$ 160	$ 151	$ 237	$ 432
Year-end annualized common dividend rate	$ 1.52	$ 1.52	$ 1.40	$ 1.20	$ 1.14	$ 1.14	$ 1.14	$ 1.14	$ 1.14	$ 1.14	$ 1.05

Other Information

Number of employees	19,810	19,539	19,835	20,244	23,333	22,960	27,594	28,708	27,239	29,600	32,330
Number of common shares (in thousands)											
Outstanding at year-end	37,949	37,946	44,922	45,120	48,572	45,106	45,517	44,568	44,491	44,440	44,378
Average primary	38,014	42,100	45,232	47,546	47,715	45,389	44,455	44,522	44,459	44,417	44,364
Average fully diluted	45,673	46,943	47,481	50,219	48,051	45,581	44,657	44,794	44,706	44,848	44,785
Fee timber (thousands of acres)	2,839	2,837	2,894	3,135	3,124	3,150	3,198	3,240	3,268	3,302	3,135
Effective tax rate	38.0%	38.8%	39.5%	42.5%	41.0%	34.0%	17.4%	31.6%	N/M	35.0%	15.7%
Common stock price range											
High	$46.25	$48.00	$50.00	$52.12	$38.92	$30.60	$27.00	$28.42	$24.15	$28.95	$25.50
Low	19.75	39.75	36.00	28.80	26.70	22.35	19.50	20.70	11.85	16.95	16.20
Close	26.00	44.38	41.25	40.80	35.85	28.20	24.37	26.25	23.40	20.55	20.47

[1] Shareholders' equity per common share is calculated by dividing the total of common stock, additional paid-in capital, if applicable, and retained earnings by common shares outstanding at year-end.

[2] Before an extraordinary gain in 1980.

[3] Including property and equipment, timber and timberlands, estimated related working capital requirements, lease commitments, and other items.

Paper and Paper Products

Financial Data by Segment	Year Ended December 31										
	1990	1989	1988	1987	1986	1985	1984	1983	1982	1981	1980
	(expressed in millions)										
Revenues											
Trade sales	$2,207	$2,380	$2,406	$2,074	$1,792	$1,816	$1,631	$1,389	$1,295	$1,388	$1,244
Intersegment sales	122	111	93	82	61	58	29	23	19	17	12
Other income (expense), net	2	12	10	5	(2)	19	17	1	5	4	3
	2,331	2,503	2,509	2,161	1,851	1,893	1,677	1,413	1,319	1,409	1,259
Costs and expenses											
Materials, labor, and other operating expenses	1,903	1,856	1,757	1,616	1,452	1,499	1,268	1,135	1,082	1,055	962
Depreciation and cost of company timber harvested	155	151	144	137	131	116	89	96	83	84	71
Selling and administrative expenses	86	91	91	82	71	69	62	53	51	46	48
	2,144	2,098	1,992	1,835	1,654	1,684	1,419	1,284	1,216	1,185	1,081
Segment income from operations [1]	$ 187	$ 405	$ 517	$ 326	$ 197	$ 209	$ 258	$ 129	$ 103	$ 224	$ 178
Identifiable assets	$3,208	$2,655	$2,265	$2,041	$1,976	$1,776	$1,732	$1,303	$1,287	$1,330	$1,308
Capital expenditures											
Property and equipment	$ 668	$ 586	$ 332	$ 168	$ 286	$ 237	$ 343	$ 82	$ 57	$ 83	$ 248
Estimated related working capital requirements, leases, and other	57	16	14	19	24	11	14	(2)	10	51	20
	$ 725	$ 602	$ 346	$ 187	$ 310	$ 248	$ 357	$ 80	$ 67	$ 134	$ 268

[1] Income from operations is before corporate administrative costs, interest expense, corporate interest income, foreign exchange gains and losses, and income taxes.

Selected Paper Products Prices [1]

	(average annual net selling prices per short ton)										
Uncoated free sheet papers	$815	$873	$821	$712	$651	$628	$707	$633	$641	$672	$617
Newsprint	442	452	482	420	373	405	391	366	404	394	350
Containerboard	350	368	368	326	262	249	293	239	258	286	253
Coated papers	798	817	793	645	699	762	710	601	609	507	613

[1] Net selling price equals gross invoice price to the mills less trade discounts and freight costs. The above prices represent the average annual net selling prices for all products sold within the reported categories.

Percentage of Total Company Sales

Year	%
80	39
81	43
82	43
83	39
84	42
85	48
86	48
87	54
88	59
89	55
90	53

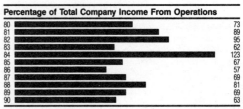

Percentage of Total Company Income From Operations

Year	%
80	73
81	89
82	95
83	62
84	123
85	67
86	57
87	69
88	81
89	69
90	63

Paper Locations and 1990 Production Statistics [1]	Annual Practical Capacity	Number of Machines	Production
	(tons)		(tons)
10 Pulp and Paper Mills			
Jackson, Alabama			
Market pulp	135,000	1	129,196
Uncoated free sheet papers	90,000	1	88,193
DeRidder, Louisiana			
Containerboard	435,000	1	424,042
Newsprint	395,000	2	396,237
Rumford, Maine			
Coated papers	415,000	4	370,572
Uncoated free sheet papers	110,000 [2]	5	89,360
Market pulp	—	—	19,759
International Falls, Minnesota			
Uncoated free sheet papers	355,000 [3]	4	205,584
St. Helens, Oregon			
Uncoated free sheet papers	220,000	3	210,090
Steilacoom (West Tacoma), Washington			
Newsprint	195,000	2	188,283
Vancouver, Washington [4]			
Uncoated free sheet papers	110,000	3	59,025
Carbonless paper	—	—	43,833
Wallula, Washington			
Uncoated free sheet papers	190,000	1	181,403
Market pulp	120,000	1	132,725
Containerboard	110,000	1	107,486
Fort Frances, Ontario, Canada			
Uncoated groundwood papers	280,000	3	272,324
Market pulp	120,000	1	109,580
Kenora, Ontario, Canada			
Newsprint	340,000 [5]	3	287,757
Uncoated groundwood papers	—	—	42,561
Total [6]	3,620,000	36	3,358,010
Operating rate during the year [6]			96%

Annual Practical Capacity by Product
At December 31, 1990 [6]

Uncoated free sheet papers	1,075,000
Newsprint	930,000
Containerboard	545,000
Coated papers	415,000
Market pulp	375,000
Uncoated groundwood papers	280,000
Total	3,620,000

[1] Not listed is a converting plant in Salem, Oregon.

[2] A portion of uncoated free sheet paper capacity may be used to produce market pulp.

[3] Annual practical capacity at December 31, 1990, includes 150,000 tons of 1991 production attributable to a new uncoated free sheet paper machine that commenced operations in December 1990. Eventual annual capacity of the new machine is expected to be 300,000 tons.

[4] In 1990, the Company reached an agreement in principle to sell its mill in Vancouver, Washington. The sale was pending at year-end.

[5] A portion of newsprint capacity may be used to produce uncoated groundwood papers.

[6] Production, practical capacity, and operating rate include intercompany transactions.

Paper and Paper Products

Paper Sales Volumes

	1990	1989	1988	1987	1986	1985	1984	1983	1982	1981	1980
					(thousands of tons)						
Uncoated free sheet papers	**891**	835	834	841	787	809	759	770	720	814	794
Newsprint	**873**	859	830	821	812	733	755	697	641	757	593
Containerboard	**529**	536	517	483	456	442	412	406	365	497	555
Coated papers	**365**	389	380	375	346	353	363	342	291	231	196
Uncoated groundwood papers	**314**	305	316	295	277	228	258	254	240	235	232
Market pulp	**307**	286	310	320	204	228	326	262	204	272	209
Other [1]	**43**	91	143	144	140	133	134	111	70	75	68
	3,322	3,301	3,330	3,279	3,022	2,926	3,007	2,842	2,531	2,881	2,647

[1] Includes specialty paperboard and carbonless paper. The Company sold its specialty paperboard mills in June 1989.

Corrugated Container 1990 Production Statistics

	Domestic 19 Plants	European Joint Venture 3 Plants
	(millions of square feet)	
Total production	7,097	1,776
Operating rate during the year	85%	98%
Practical capacity at year-end	7,259	2,007

Corrugated Container Locations

Domestic [1]
Athens, Alabama [2]
Huntsville, Alabama
West Memphis, Arkansas
Golden, Colorado
Burley, Idaho
Nampa, Idaho
Lincoln, Illinois

Indianapolis, Indiana
Louisville, Kentucky
St. Paul, Minnesota
Sparks, Nevada [2]
Lumberton, North Carolina
Newton, North Carolina
Salem, Oregon
Greeneville, Tennessee [2]

Memphis, Tennessee [2]
Salt Lake City, Utah [2]
Spokane, Washington [2]
Wallula, Washington
European Joint Venture
Kalsdorf, Austria
Vienna-Liesing, Austria
Ansbach, Germany

[1] In December 1990, the Company sold its plants in Milford, Connecticut, and LaPorte, Indiana.

[2] These plants manufacture corrugated containers from corrugated sheets obtained from other plants.

Corrugated Container Sales Volumes

	1990	1989	1988	1987	1986	1985	1984	1983	1982	1981	1980
					(millions of square feet)						
Domestic	**7,087**	7,091	7,310	7,304	7,010	6,545	5,485	5,267	4,868	5,293	5,855
European joint venture	**1,776**	1,588	1,544	1,487	1,565	1,638	1,490	1,365	1,435	1,601	1,065
	8,863	8,679	8,854	8,791	8,575	8,183	6,975	6,632	6,303	6,894	6,920

Office Products

Financial Data by Segment	Year Ended December 31										
	1990	1989	1988	1987	1986	1985	1984	1983	1982	1981	1980
					(expressed in millions)						
Revenues											
Trade sales	**$1,077**	$1,012	$ 869	$ 734	$ 675	$ 650	$ 583	$ 467	$ 405	$ 398	$ 346
Intersegment sales	**2**	2	1	1	1	1	1	1	1	1	1
Other income, net	**1**	—	—	—	2	—	1	—	—	—	—
	1,080	1,014	870	735	678	651	585	468	406	399	347
Costs and expenses											
Materials, labor, and other operating expenses	**759**	708	610	521	481	468	422	343	295	293	249
Depreciation	**16**	14	10	9	8	8	5	3	3	2	2
Selling and administrative expenses	**247**	225	188	157	142	138	121	96	87	85	75
	1,022	947	808	687	631	614	548	442	385	380	326
Segment income from operations [1]	**$ 58**	$ 67	$ 62	$ 48	$ 47	$ 37	$ 37	$ 26	$ 21	$ 19	$ 21
Identifiable assets	**$ 410**	$ 390	$ 338	$ 265	$ 232	$ 220	$ 195	$ 152	$ 119	$ 119	$ 108
Capital expenditures											
Property and equipment	**$ 32**	$ 29	$ 41	$ 14	$ 28	$ 15	$ 30	$ 4	$ 6	$ 9	$ 2
Estimated related working capital requirements, leases, and other	**7**	9	10	4	5	4	13	5	4	7	3
	$ 39	$ 38	$ 51	$ 18	$ 33	$ 19	$ 43	$ 9	$ 10	$ 16	$ 5

[1] Income from operations is before corporate administrative costs, interest expense, corporate interest income, foreign exchange gains and losses, and income taxes.

Office Products Market Areas (Physical Location)

34 Distribution Centers

Phoenix, Arizona
Tucson, Arizona
Los Angeles (Rancho Dominguez), California
San Francisco (Menlo Park), California
Denver, Colorado
Hartford (Naugatuck), Connecticut
Baltimore/Washington, D.C. (Jessup, Maryland)
Jacksonville, Florida
Miami (Hialeah), Florida

Tampa, Florida
Atlanta (Smyrna), Georgia
Hilo, Hawaii
Honolulu, Hawaii
Kahului, Hawaii
Lihue, Hawaii
Chicago (Itasca), Illinois
Indianapolis, Indiana
Boston (Billerica), Massachusetts
Detroit (Warren), Michigan
Minneapolis-St. Paul (Brooklyn Park), Minnesota

Kansas City, Missouri
New York (Moonachie, New Jersey)
Charlotte, North Carolina
Cincinnati, Ohio
Cleveland (Valley View), Ohio
Columbus, Ohio
Portland, Oregon
Philadelphia (Bristol), Pennsylvania
Nashville, Tennessee
Dallas (Garland), Texas
Houston, Texas

Salt Lake City, Utah
Seattle (Kent), Washington
Milwaukee, Wisconsin

1 Minidistribution Center
Pittsburgh, Pennsylvania

5 Retail Outlets [1]
Hopaco —
Aiea, Hawaii
Honolulu, Hawaii (2 outlets)
Kahului, Hawaii
Kaneohe, Hawaii

[1] During 1990, the Company closed one retail outlet in Honolulu, Hawaii, and an outlet in Hilo, Hawaii.

Percentage of Total Company Sales

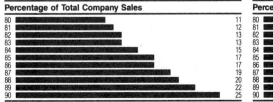

80	11
81	12
82	13
83	13
84	15
85	17
86	17
87	19
88	20
89	22
90	25

Percentage of Total Company Income From Operations

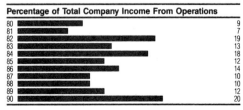

80	9
81	7
82	19
83	13
84	18
85	12
86	14
87	10
88	10
89	12
90	20

Building Products

Financial Data by Segment	Year Ended December 31										
	1990	1989	1988	1987	1986	1985	1984	1983	1982	1981	1980
					(expressed in millions)						
Revenues											
Trade sales	$ 889	$ 936	$ 809	$1,002	$ 959	$ 928	$1,192	$1,194	$ 840	$ 976	$1,128
Intersegment sales	50	57	32	28	27	29	86	74	81	108	122
Other income (expense), net	3	1	1	4	6	23	7	(1)	11	3	(3)
	942	994	842	1,034	992	980	1,285	1,267	932	1,087	1,247
Costs and expenses											
Materials, labor, and other operating expenses	833	825	731	855	821	837	1,135	1,085	837	956	1,066
Depreciation and cost of company timber harvested	31	28	25	32	32	34	38	38	31	33	34
Selling and administrative expenses	36	34	32	51	53	68	126	129	116	121	135
Provision for restructuring operations	—	—	—	—	—	—	88	—	—	—	—
	900	887	788	938	906	939	1,387	1,252	984	1,110	1,235
Segment income (loss) from operations [1]	$ 42	$ 107	$ 54	$ 96	$ 86	$ 41	$ (102)	$ 15	$ (52)	$ (23)	$ 12
Identifiable assets	$ 378	$ 379	$ 334	$ 360	$ 384	$ 388	$ 538	$ 560	$ 524	$ 536	$ 567
Capital expenditures											
Property and equipment	$ 32	$ 54	$ 44	$ 37	$ 25	$ 35	$ 71	$ 27	$ 33	$ 36	$ 46
Estimated related working capital requirements, leases, and other	3	—	(1)	—	—	(2)	(3)	3	5	6	3
	$ 35	$ 54	$ 43	$ 37	$ 25	$ 33	$ 68	$ 30	$ 38	$ 42	$ 49

[1] Income (loss) from operations is before corporate administrative costs, interest expense, corporate interest income, foreign exchange gains and losses, and income taxes.

Selected Wood Products Prices [1]

	1990	1989	1988	1987	1986	1985	1984	1983	1982	1981	1980
				(average annual net selling prices per thousand board/square feet)							
Lumber	$328	$348	$335	$347	$310	$274	$288	$296	$229	$252	$265
Plywood (3/8″ basis)	166	178	155	157	159	156	160	160	145	160	165

[1] Net selling price equals gross invoice price to the mills less trade discounts and freight costs. The above prices represent the average annual net selling prices for all products sold within the reported categories.

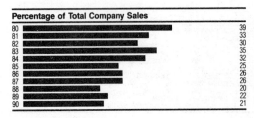

Percentage of Total Company Sales

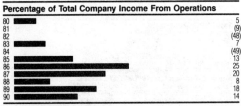

Percentage of Total Company Income From Operations

Wood Products Locations and 1990 Production Statistics [1]	Sawmills		Plywood and Veneer Mills		Particle-board
	Number	Production	Number	Production	
				(3/8" basis)	(3/4" basis)
		(millions of board feet)		(millions of square feet)	
Mill Locations by Area					
Northwest					
Cascade, Idaho	1	67			
Council, Idaho	1	33			
Emmett, Idaho			1	180	
Horseshoe Bend, Idaho	1	66			
Elgin, Oregon	1	81	1	153	
Independence, Oregon			1	(v)	
Joseph, Oregon	1	38			
La Grande, Oregon	1	50			179
Medford, Oregon	1	60	1	326	
St. Helens, Oregon			1	(v)	
White City, Oregon [2]	1	55	2	(v-1 mill) 136	
Willamina, Oregon			1	(v)	
Goldendale, Washington [3]	1	—			
Kettle Falls, Washington	2	76	1	193	
Yakima, Washington	1	120	1	144	
Central Canada					
Kenora, Ontario, Canada [3]	1	—			
South					
Jackson, Alabama	1	48			
Fisher, Louisiana	1	89			
Florien, Louisiana			1	297	
Oakdale, Louisiana			1	258	
Total	15	783	12	1,687	179
Operating rate during the year		84%		96%	97%
Practical capacity at year-end		933		1,775	185

[v] Represents veneer mills only.

[1] Not listed is a wood beam plant in Emmett, Idaho.

[2] The laminated veneer lumber plant in White City, Oregon, was in a start-up phase at the end of 1990.

[3] Effective January 1, 1990, the Company curtailed operation of its sawmill in Goldendale, Washington, due to a shortage of logs in central Washington. The sawmill in Kenora, Ontario, was temporarily shut down at the end of January 1988 due to poor market conditions and had not recommenced operations by year-end 1990.

Building Products Sales Volumes

	1990	1989	1988	1987	1986	1985	1984	1983	1982	1981	1980
					(millions)						
Plywood (square feet)	**1,682**	1,679	1,590	1,878	1,772	1,616	1,442	1,381	889	1,027	1,256
Lumber (board feet)	**782**	815	798	911	843	795	825	833	650	676	670
Particleboard (square feet)	**179**	188	166	180	181	183	175	159	115	115	108
Building materials distribution (sales dollars)	**$289**	$279	$225	$330	$350	$417	$709	$731	$513	$547	$552

Building Materials Distribution Locations

Phoenix, Arizona	Idaho Falls, Idaho	Spokane, Washington
Denver, Colorado	Billings, Montana	Woodinville, Washington
Boise, Idaho	Salt Lake City, Utah	Yakima, Washington

Facility Locations and Timberlands
Boise Cascade Corporation and Subsidiaries

Timberlands
indicated
by shading

Other facilities in:
Austria
Hawaii
Germany

● Paper   ○ Corrugated Container   ■ Office Products   □ Wood Products   ▲ Building Materials Distribution

Timber Resources

	Northwest	Midwest-Central Canada	New England	South	Total
	December 31, 1990				
	(thousands of acres)				
Fee	1,349	316	673	501	2,839
Leases and contracts	12	—	—	296	308
Canadian government licenses	—	3,038	—	—	3,038
Total	1,361	3,354	673	797	6,185 (1)
Approximate percentage of total fiber requirements available from: (2)					
Owned and controlled timber resources	24%	91%	88%	31%	43%
Residuals from processed purchased logs	13	—	—	9	8
Total	37%	91%	88%	40%	51%

(1) On December 31, 1990, the Company's inventory of merchantable sawtimber was approximately 10 billion board feet, and its inventory of pulpwood was approximately 66.1 million cords.

(2) Assumes harvesting of Company-owned and controlled timber resources on a sustained timber yield basis and operation of the Company's paper and wood products manufacturing facilities at practical capacity. Percentages shown represent weighted average consumption on a cubic volume basis. Approximately 64% of the wood chips consumed by the Company's Northwest pulp and paper mills in 1990 were obtained from Company sources.

Products and Distribution Businesses

Products

Paper

Business papers Xerographic, xerographic colors, bond, laser, 25% cotton laser, ion deposition, and recycled xerographic

Printing papers Offset and opaque offset

Publication papers Groundwood printing papers and #3, #4, and #5 coated-two-side papers for gravure and web offset printing

Converting papers Envelope, tablet, coated-one-side (C1S) label, coated-one-side (C1S) release, and recycled envelope

Forms papers Form bond, magnetic ink character recognition (MICR), optical character recognition (OCR), tag, ledger, form backing, safety paper, 3800 and xerographic, and recycled form bond

Newsprint

Linerboard and corrugating medium

Market pulp Northern bleached softwood, Southern softwood, and Southern hardwood kraft pulp

Corrugated Containers

Conventional and custom-designed containers for packing produce, processed food, and manufactured products; retail point-of-purchase displays; inner pack; containers featuring high-quality graphics and label laminations; bulk containers for liquids and solid materials; E-flute; and a wide array of specialty corrugated products

Wood

Lumber Softwood lumber from various domestic species

Plywood Structural plywood products in various grades for construction applications and sanded plywood

Particleboard Industrial, underlayment, cut-to-size, shelving, and stepping

Specialties Cut stock, finger-jointed lumber, laminated beams and decking, and laminated veneer lumber for beams and I-joists

Distribution Businesses

Building Materials

Lumber, plywood, particleboard, engineered wood products (I-beams, laminated veneer lumber, and laminated beams), fiberboard siding, roofing, gypsum board, insulation, ceiling tile, paneling, molding, windows, doors, builders' hardware, and metal products (nails, drywall screws, wire, rebar, flashing, and vents)

Office Products

Office and computer supplies, office and computer furniture, and xerographic paper

Board of Directors

Anne L. Armstrong, Armstrong, Texas; former United States Ambassador to Great Britain and counselor to the President of the United States (1) (3)

Robert E. Coleman, former chairman of the board and chief executive officer, Riegel Textile Corporation, Greenville, South Carolina (2) (4)

William S. Cook, former chairman of the board and chief executive officer, Union Pacific Corporation, New York, New York (1) (4)

John B. Fery, chairman of the board and chief executive officer, Boise Cascade Corporation, Boise, Idaho (1) (4)

Robert K. Jaedicke, former dean and currently a professor, Graduate School of Business, Stanford University, Stanford, California (1) (2)

*__James A. McClure__, McCall, Idaho; former United States Senator from Idaho; president, McClure, Gerard & Neuenschwander, Inc., Washington, D.C. (2)

Michael B. Morris, former president – petroleum operations, Conoco Inc., Houston, Texas (2) (3)

Paul J. Phoenix, chairman of the board and chief executive officer, Dofasco Inc., Hamilton, Ontario, Canada (2) (4)

A. William Reynolds, chairman of the board and chief executive officer, GenCorp Inc., Fairlawn, Ohio (3) (4)

Frank A. Shrontz, chairman of the board and chief executive officer, The Boeing Company, Seattle, Washington (2)

Edson W. Spencer, former chairman of the board and chief executive officer, Honeywell Inc., Minneapolis, Minnesota (2) (3)

Robert H. Waterman, Jr., president, The Waterman Group, Inc., and chairman of the board, Waterman & Miller, Inc., San Francisco, California (3) (4)

*Elected since last Annual Report.

1. **Member of Executive Committee, John B. Fery, chairman.** When necessary between regularly scheduled board meetings, the Executive Committee has the authority to exercise most of the powers and authority of the full board in management of the business and affairs of the Company.

2. **Member of Audit Committee, Robert K. Jaedicke, chairman.** The Audit Committee meets periodically with management, the Company's Internal Audit staff, and representatives of the Company's independent public accounting firm to assure that each group is carrying out its responsibilities. The committee reviews the scope of internal and external audit activities and the results of the annual audit and recommends a firm of independent auditors each year.

3. **Member of Nominating Committee, Anne L. Armstrong, chairman.** The Nominating Committee reviews nominations for election as directors and makes recommendations to the board.

4. **Member of Human Resources Committee, William S. Cook, chairman.** The Human Resources Committee works with the Company's management in the review of human resources programs and compensation.

Executive Officers

John B. Fery
Chairman of the Board
and Chief Executive Officer

Peter G. Danis Jr.
Executive Vice President
Office Products,
Building Products,
Corrugated Containers,
and Transportation and
Procurement

George J. Harad
Executive Vice President
Paper

John E. Clute
Senior Vice President
Human Resources
and General Counsel

Rex L. Dorman
Senior Vice President
and Chief Financial Officer

E. Thomas Edquist
Senior Vice President
and General Manager
Office Products

John A. Haase
Senior Vice President
Paper Technical
Resources

Alice E. Hennessey
Senior Vice President
Corporate Relations
and Corporate Secretary

Terry R. Lock
Senior Vice President
Marketing and Sales
White Paper

Richard B. Parrish
Senior Vice President
and General Manager
Timber and Wood
Products

N. David Spence
Senior Vice President
Manufacturing
White Paper

John H. Wasserlein
Senior Vice President
and General Manager
Publishing and
Packaging Paper

J. Randolph Ayre
Vice President
Legal

J. Ray Barbee
Vice President and
General Sales Manager
White Paper

Stanley R. Bell
Vice President and
General Manager
Building Materials
Distribution

John C. Bender
Vice President and
General Sales Manager
Timber and Wood
Products

Alex P. Bormann
Vice President
Paper Engineering

Ronald L. Clark
Vice President and
General Manager
Corrugated Containers

Theodore Crumley
Vice President
and Controller

A. Ben Groce
Vice President
Maine Operations
White Paper

J. Michael Gwartney
Vice President
Human Resources

Irving Littman
Vice President
and Treasurer

Carol B. Moerdyk
Vice President
Corporate Planning
and Development

D. Ray Ryden
Vice President
Transportation and
Procurement

Donald F. Smith
Vice President
Timberland Resources

Jerry P. Soderberg
Vice President and
General Sales Manager
Publishing and
Packaging Paper

J. Kirk Sullivan
Vice President
Governmental and
Environmental Affairs

Wal-Mart
1991 Annual Report

Financial Highlights

(Dollar amounts in thousands except per share data)

January 31,	1991	1990
Net sales	$32,601,594	$25,810,656
Net income	1,291,024	1,075,900
Net income per share	1.14	.95*
Working capital	2,424,361	1,867,301
Current ratio	1.6	1.7
Shareholders' equity	5,365,524	3,965,561
Common stock outstanding at year end	1,142,281,964	1,132,270,208*

Stores in operation at year end:		
Wal-Mart Stores	1,573	1,402
Sam's Clubs	148	123

MARKET PRICE OF COMMON STOCK
Fiscal years ended January 31,

Quarter	1991 High	1991 Low	1990* High	1990* Low
April 30	$25.63*	$20.31*	$18.19	$15.69
July 31	36.13*	24.88*	21.63	17.19
October 31	30.63	25.00	22.00	18.50
January 31	33.00	26.75	23.69	20.00

DIVIDENDS PAID PER SHARE OF COMMON STOCK
Fiscal years ended January 31,

1991 Quarterly		1990* Quarterly	
April 9	$.035*	April 10	$.0275
July 6	.035	July 7	.0275
October 4	.035	October 4	.0275
January 2	.035	January 2	.0275

Adjusted to reflect the two-for-one stock split on July 6, 1990.

Net Sales
(Billions of Dollars)

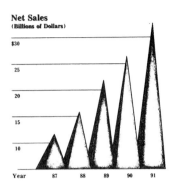

Net Income Per Share
(Dollars)

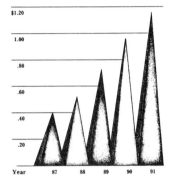

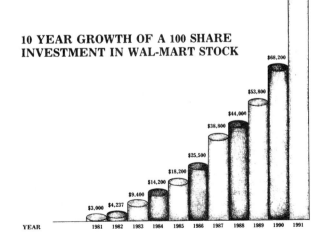

10 YEAR GROWTH OF A 100 SHARE INVESTMENT IN WAL-MART STOCK

Assumes holding of 3,200 shares of Wal-Mart stock as of January 31, 1991 (100 original shares purchased on January 31, 1981, adjusted to reflect five subsequent stock splits).

Fellow Shareholder:

A new decade. A new era for Wal-Mart; an era in which we plan to grow to a truly nationwide retailer, and should we continue to perform, our sales and earnings will also grow beyond where most could have envisioned at the dawn of the 80's. We are happy to report that our Associates have achieved a record-setting fiscal year ending January 31, 1991 in both sales of $32.602 billion and earnings of $1.291 billion. We are proud of all 328,000 Wal-Mart and Sam's Associates for their hard work and dedication to quality and customer service -- once again, our people have made the difference.

★ **FINANCIAL HIGHLIGHTS**

° We increased our sales 26 percent to $32.602 billion from $25.811 billion. Comparable stores and clubs, those units which were open at least twelve months as of January 31, 1990, increased sales by 10 percent. This was our ninth year of double digit comparable sales gains in the past ten years. Sales productivity per comparable gross square foot of total discount store space grew to $263, from $250 last year and $194 just five years ago.

° Net income increased 20 percent to $1.291 billion, equivalent to $1.14 per share fully diluted, compared with $1.076 billion or $0.95 per share last year.

° Return on shareholders' equity was 32.6 percent, our 16th consecutive year of 30 percent or greater return. Shareholders' equity grew $1.400 billion to $5.366 billion, up 35.3 percent from last year's $3.966 billion.

° Among other financial highlights in 1990, was the Board of Directors' approval of an increase in Common Stock dividends to 14 cents per share compared with 11 cents per share last year, an increase of 27.3 percent. In addition, as a result of our strong performance, broad acceptance in the financial markets, and the Board's confidence in the Company's future, the Board authorized a two-for-one stock split on July 6, 1990, in the form ot a 100 percent stock dividend. In July, 1990 the Company sold $500 million of 9.10% notes due July 15, 2000. The proceeds from the sales of these notes were used primarily for retail and distribution capacity expansion.

★**OPERATIONAL HIGHLIGHTS**

° Wal-Mart stores expanded its trade territory to 34 states with our first entries in California (10), Nevada (3), North Dakota (5), Pennsylvania (3), South Dakota (7) and Utah (5). Our focus on "exceeding our customers' expectations" with wider aisles and significantly more customer space moved ahead with our new stores averaging almost 100,000 square feet. Total retail square footage in Wal-Mart stores grew to 111 million, an increase of 19.4 percent from last year.

° Sam's Clubs opened 25 new clubs; four were the 130,000 prototype facilities which provide the necessary space to incorporate fresh departments of produce, meat and bakery. Sam's ended the year with five clubs that incorporate the fresh concepts. Sam's sales increased to $6.6 billion -- an average of $44 million per club, up 36 percent from sales of $4.8 billion or $39 million per club one year ago. Our Sam's Associates have continued to exceed all of our expectations, adopting "HEATKTE" (high expectations are the key to everything) as their strategic rallying cry.

° Transportation and Distribution managed challenging growth while improving service rates this past year. Our square footage of distribution capacity grew from 11.8 million to 14.6 million, a 23.7 percent increase. New centers, each exceeding 1 million square-feet, were opened in Seymour, Indiana (March), Searcy, Arkansas (May) and Loveland, Colorado (September). Also, a new special-purpose shoe facility was opened in Ft. Smith, Arkansas. These great Associates delivered over 315,000 trailer-loads of merchandise, driving in excess of 190 million miles to bring to our customers the merchandise they wanted, when they wanted it, and at an expense level we believe to be unparalleled in our industry. Our distribution Associates are empowered, motivated and equipped with state-of-the-art systems and conveyors to raise productivity to new heights.

★ **STRATEGIC HIGHLIGHTS**

° On December 10, 1990, the acquisition of the McLane Company, Inc., was completed. McLane is a provider of retail and grocery distribution services currently supplying approximately 26,000 retail customers. McLane's national distribution system of 14 centers in 11 states provides over 12,500 types of grocery and non-grocery products, including perishable, non-perishable and general merchandise items.

° Effective February 2, 1991, Sam's Clubs merged the 28 wholesale clubs of The Wholesale Club, Inc. of Indianapolis, Indiana into its operations. These new partners have 28 units located in six states in the midwest, all of which will be fully integrated with Sam's in calendar year 1991.

° "The Wal-Mart Way," a phrase often employed to summarize our unconventional approach to business and the determination of our Associates, has taken on new meaning to capture our commitment to "Total Quality," which is essential to our future success. We stepped outside our retailing world to examine the best-managed companies in the United States in an effort to determine the fundamentals of their success and to "benchmark" our own performances, thereby challenging ourselves to ongoing improvement. We believe Total Quality is our vehicle for proliferating the very best things we do while incorporating the new ideas our people have that will assure our future. "Total Quality - it's a journey not a destination."

° In November 1990, we announced to our vendor-partners, "Retail Link", an aggressive step to further our partnership relations by moving beyond electronic data sharing. We desire to provide our vendors the quality of information concerning sales trends and inventory levels to facilitate genuine partnering in our mutual goal to serve our customers. The actual systems capitalize on existing bar code and satellite communications capacities to bring our suppliers closer to our individual stores.

° "People development, not just a good 'program' for any growing company but a must to secure our future," is how Suzanne Allford, Vice President of our People Division began her recent announcement of our new decentralized approach to improve our retail management development. We believe that our store and club managers are our best teachers and instructors. Corporately, it's our job to provide them with the very best tools and facilities. Our belief that this can only be done using practical hands-on methods led us to move our retail management seminars from our home office out to ten of our distribution centers, near to the stores and clubs, to expose our management team to the heart of our distribution network.

° We announced our agreement with Conoco Inc. to sell our nine convenience store gasoline retail outlets in January, 1991. Our experiment with these facilities was very successful and provided us with a great laboratory to learn even more about retailing. Upon completion in the first quarter, this disposition will permit us to focus additional attention on the Sam's and Wal-Mart portions of our business.

° Our customers are concerned about the quality of our land, air and water and we believe they want the opportunity to make a personal difference. We have joined hands with our vendors and Associates to provide that opportunity through improved packaging and product development, home office recycling efforts, store-located recycling collection bins, and by sponsoring local community efforts to clean highways of litter, plant trees, and heighten awareness. Wal-Mart has made a commitment to the environment.

Thank you for your confidence in the Associates of Wal-Mart.

David D. Glass
President and
Chief Executive Officer

Donald G. Soderquist
Vice Chairman and
Chief Operating Officer

Wal-Mart and Sam's ...

⭐ Home Office and 3 Distribution Centers

· Wal-Mart Store

■ Distribution Center

▲ Sam's Club

★ Hypermart ★ USA

◆ McLane Distribution Center

1573
Wal-Mart stores

Alabama	73
Arizona	20
Arkansas	77
California	10
Colorado	29
Florida	113
Georgia	79
Illinois	80
Indiana	49
Iowa	37
Kansas	41
Kentucky	64
Louisiana	74
Michigan	9
Minnesota	9
Mississippi	56
Missouri	105
Nebraska	14
Nevada	3
New Mexico	19
North Carolina	58
North Dakota	5
Ohio	28
Oklahoma	80
Pennsylvania	3
South Carolina	47
South Dakota	7
Tennessee	85
Texas	230
Utah	5
Virginia	18
West Virginia	6
Wisconsin	33
Wyoming	7

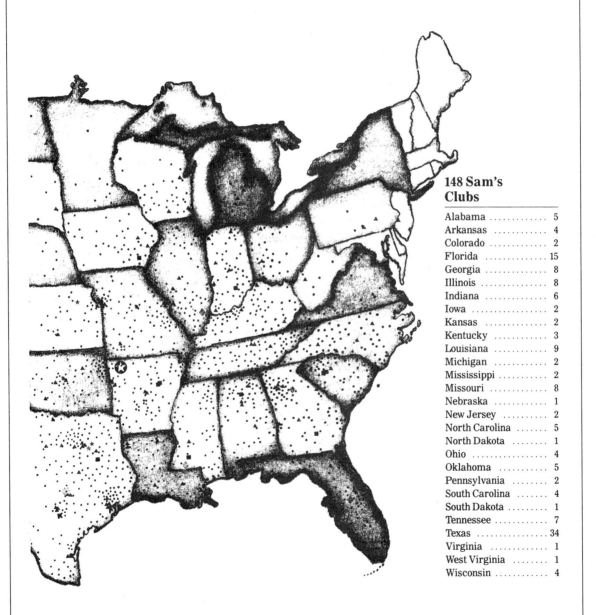

35 States and Growing

Fiscal Year Ended January 31, 1991

148 Sam's Clubs

Alabama	5
Arkansas	4
Colorado	2
Florida	15
Georgia	8
Illinois	8
Indiana	6
Iowa	2
Kansas	2
Kentucky	3
Louisiana	9
Michigan	2
Mississippi	2
Missouri	8
Nebraska	1
New Jersey	2
North Carolina	5
North Dakota	1
Ohio	4
Oklahoma	5
Pennsylvania	2
South Carolina	4
South Dakota	1
Tennessee	7
Texas	34
Virginia	1
West Virginia	1
Wisconsin	4

Ten-Year Financial Summary

Wal-Mart Stores, Inc. and Subsidiaries

(Dollar amounts in thousands except per share data)	1991	1990
EARNINGS		
Net sales	$32,601,594	$25,810,656
Net sales increase	26%	25%
Comparative store sales increases	10%	11%
Licensed department rentals and other income-net	261,814	174,644
Cost of sales	25,499,834	20,070,034
Operating, selling and general and administrative expenses	5,152,178	4,069,695
Interest costs:		
Debt	42,716	20,346
Capital leases	125,920	117,725
Taxes on income	751,736	631,600
Net income	1,291,024	1,075,900
Per share of common stock:*		
Net income	1.14	.95
Dividends	.14	.11
FINANCIAL POSITION		
Current assets	$ 6,414,775	$ 4,712,616
Inventories at replacement cost	6,207,852	4,750,619
Less LIFO reserve	399,436	322,546
Inventories at LIFO cost	5,808,416	4,428,073
Net property, plant, equipment and capital leases	4,712,039	3,430,059
Total assets	11,388,915	8,198,484
Current liabilities	3,990,414	2,845,315
Long-term debt	740,254	185,152
Long-term obligations under capital leases	1,158,621	1,087,403
Preferred stock with mandatory redemption provisions	—	—
Shareholders' equity	5,365,524	3,965,561
FINANCIAL RATIOS		
Current ratio	1.6	1.7
Inventories/working capital	2.4	2.4
Return on assets**	15.7%	16.9%
Return on shareholders' equity**	32.6%	35.8%
Other year-end data:		
Number of Wal-Mart stores	1,573	1,402
Number of Sam's Clubs	148	123
Average Wal-Mart store size	70,700	66,400
Number of associates	328,000	271,000
Number of shareholders	122,414	79,929

*All per share data have been adjusted to reflect the two-for-one stock split on July 6, 1990.

**On beginning of year balances.

1989	1988	1987	1986	1985	1984	1983	1982
$20,649,001	$15,959,255	$11,909,076	$ 8,451,489	$ 6,400,861	$ 4,666,909	$ 3,376,252	$ 2,444,997
29%	34%	41%	32%	37%	38%	38%	49%
12%	11%	13%	9%	15%	15%	11%	15%
136,867	104,783	84,623	55,127	52,167	36,031	22,435	17,650
16,056,856	12,281,744	9,053,219	6,361,271	4,722,440	3,418,025	2,458,235	1,787,496
3,267,864	2,599,367	2,007,645	1,485,210	1,181,455	892,887	677,029	495,010
36,286	25,262	10,442	1,903	5,207	4,935	20,297	16,053
99,395	88,995	76,367	54,640	42,506	29,946	18,570	15,351
488,246	441,027	395,940	276,119	230,653	160,903	100,416	65,943
837,221	627,643	450,086	327,473	270,767	196,244	124,140	82,794
.74	.55	.40	.29	.24	.17	.11	.08
.08	.06	.0425	.035	.0263	.0175	.0113	.0082
$ 3,630,987	$ 2,905,145	$ 2,353,271	$ 1,784,275	$ 1,303,254	$ 1,005,567	$ 720,537	$ 589,161
3,642,696	2,854,556	2,184,847	1,528,349	1,227,264	857,155	658,949	578,088
291,329	202,796	153,875	140,181	123,339	121,760	103,247	87,515
3,351,367	2,651,760	2,030,972	1,388,168	1,103,925	735,395	555,702	490,573
2,661,954	2,144,852	1,676,282	1,303,450	870,309	628,151	457,509	333,026
6,359,668	5,131,809	4,049,092	3,103,645	2,205,229	1,652,254	1,187,448	937,513
2,065,909	1,743,763	1,340,291	992,683	688,968	502,763	347,318	339,961
184,439	185,672	179,234	180,682	41,237	40,866	106,465	104,581
1,009,046	866,972	764,128	595,205	449,886	339,930	222,610	154,196
—	—	—	4,902	5,874	6,411	6,861	7,438
3,007,909	2,257,267	1,690,493	1,277,659	984,672	737,503	488,109	323,942
1.8	1.7	1.8	1.8	1.9	2.0	2.1	1.7
2.1	2.3	2.0	1.8	1.8	1.5	1.5	2.0
16.3%	15.5%	14.5%	14.8%	16.4%	16.5%	13.2%	14.0%
37.1%	37.1%	35.2%	33.3%	36.7%	40.2%	38.3%	33.3%
1,259	1,114	980	859	745	642	551	491
105	84	49	23	11	3		
63,500	61,500	59,000	57,000	55,000	53,000	50,000	49,000
223,000	183,000	141,000	104,000	81,000	62,000	46,000	41,000
80,270	79,777	32,896	21,828	14,799	14,172	4,855	2,698

Management's Discussion and Analysis

RESULTS OF OPERATIONS

Sales for the three fiscal years ended January 31, 1991, and the respective total and comparable store percentage increases over the prior year were as follows:

Fiscal year ended January 31,	Sales	Total company increases	Comparable stores increases
1991	$32,601,594,000	26%	10%
1990	25,810,656,000	25	11
1989	20,649,001,000	29	12

Sales increases were primarily due to the productivity of comparable stores, the contribution of new stores (176 Wal-Mart stores - five were closed - and 25 Sam's units in fiscal 1991, 145 Wal-Mart stores - two were closed - and 18 Sam's units in fiscal 1990 and 145 Wal-Mart stores and 21 Sam's units in fiscal 1989), and inflation of approximately three percent.

The Sam's units contributed the following sales for the periods indicated:

Fiscal year ended January 31,	Sales
1991	$6,578,595,000
1990	4,840,870,000
1989	3,828,683,000

Cost of sales as a percentage of sales increased .5% in fiscal 1991 as compared with fiscal 1990, and remained constant in fiscal 1990 as compared with fiscal 1989. The increase was due to the cost of sales in the Sam's units, which is significantly higher than in the balance of the Company (due to lower markon on purchases), the continuation of reduced initial markons supporting emphasis in the Wal-Mart stores on everyday low prices, and LIFO costs being higher in 1991 as a percentage of sales compared with fiscal 1990.

Operating, selling and general and administrative expenses as a percentage of sales remained constant in fiscal 1991 as compared with fiscal 1990, and decreased .1% in fiscal 1990 as compared with fiscal 1989. The decrease in fiscal 1990 was due to reduced payroll and payroll-related benefits and taxes.

Interest costs as a percentage of sales remained constant in fiscal 1991 as compared with fiscal 1990, and decreased .1% in fiscal 1990 as compared with fiscal 1989. See NOTE 2 of Notes to Consolidated Financial Statements for additional information on interest and debt.

The effective tax rate was 36.8% in fiscal 1991, 37.0% in fiscal 1990 and 36.8% in fiscal 1989. See NOTE 4 of Notes to Consolidated Financial Statements for additional information on taxes.

In December 1990, Wal-Mart acquired all the outstanding common stock of McLane Company, Inc. and in February 1991, acquired all the outstanding common stock of The Wholesale Club, Inc. Because both of these entities, as a percentage of sales, have lower gross profit margins (due to lower markons on purchases), and lower expense and net profit ratios than Wal-Mart's historical ratios, Wal-Mart's consolidated ratios will be affected in the future. See NOTE 8 of Notes to Consolidated Financial Statements for additional information pertaining to the acquisitions.

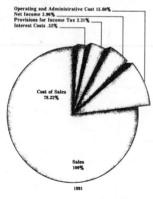
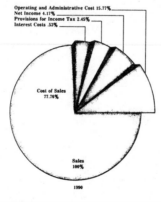
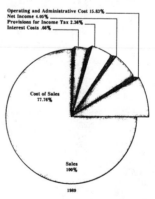

LIQUIDITY AND CAPITAL RESOURCES

Fiscal 1991

Cash provided from current operations was a record $1,295,885,000 in fiscal 1991. These funds combined with long-term borrowings of $500,306,000 and issuance of commercial paper of $395,179,000 were used to finance capital expenditures of $1,388,298,000 (excluding leased properties) for fixtures, equipment, and leasehold improvements, to pay dividends, to provide general working capital and to finance the building of 72 Wal-Mart stores and 25 Sam's Clubs, the acquisition and funding of the operations of McLane Company, Inc., completion of construction for three distribution centers and partial construction of three distribution centers. Real estate developers provided financing to build 49 additional Wal-Mart stores, and 55 Wal-Mart stores were financed with sale/leaseback transactions.

The Company maintains $945,000,000 in lines of credit to support the short-term borrowing and commercial paper, of which $549,821,000 was available at January 31, 1991, sufficient to finance the seasonal buildups in merchandise inventories and interim financing requirements for store properties developed under sale/leaseback arrangements.

For fiscal 1992, the Company's expansion program includes 150 to 160 Wal-Mart stores, 35 Sam's Clubs, and two Supercenter stores. Total capital expenditures planned for fiscal 1992 are approximately $2,400,000,000. This includes 62 Wal-Mart stores, 35 Sam's Clubs, fixture additions, equipment, acquisitions of land and construction of stores and clubs to be opened in subsequent fiscal years, completion of three distribution centers scheduled to open the last half of fiscal 1992 and home office renovations. These expenditures will be financed primarily with internally generated funds and the issuance of long-term debt. The remaining expansion program will be funded with leases from developers and sale/leaseback arrangements.

In the first quarter of fiscal 1992, the Company issued ten year notes totalling $750,000,000. These notes become due in 2001 and bear interest of $8^5/8\%$. The Company is considering the issuance of long-term debt totalling $250,000,000 in the second or third quarter of fiscal 1992. Proceeds from these issues will be used to support the Company's expansion program and general working capital needs.

The Company's debt (including obligations under capital leases)-to-equity ratio increased to .36:1 at the end of fiscal 1991 as compared with .33:1 at the end of the preceding year.

In view of the Company's significant liquid assets, its consistent ability to generate cash flows from operations and the availability of external financing, the Company foresees no difficulty in providing financing necessary to fund its expansion programs and working capital needs for the foreseeable future.

Statement of Financial Accounting Standard No. 96 "Accounting for Income Taxes" was issued in December, 1987. The statement will be effective for the Company's fiscal year ended January 31, 1993. The statement requires deferred income taxes to be recorded using the liability method and when applied will not have a material effect on the Company's financial statements.

Return on shareholders' equity is a measure of the Company's effectiveness in the use of its resources. It measures the relationship of net income to beginning of the year shareholders' equity. The Company's returns on shareholders' equity for the three years ended January 31, 1991, 1990 and 1989 were 32.6%, 35.8% and 37.1%, respectively.

Dividends for fiscal 1992 have been increased to 17 cents per share from 14 cents per share, payable quarterly at 4.25 cents per share.

Fiscal 1990

Cash provided from operating activities was $866,817,000. The Company had access to $905,000,000 in lines of credit to support short-term borrowing and the issuance of commercial paper.

Payments for purchase of property, plant and equipment totaled $954,602,000, excluding leased store properties, and were financed with internally generated funds. The debt-to-equity ratio decreased to .33:1 in fiscal 1990 from .40:1 in fiscal 1989.

Consolidated Statements of Income

Wal-Mart Stores, Inc. and Subsidiaries

(Amounts in thousands except per share data)	Fiscal year ended January 31,		
	1991	1990	1989
Revenues:			
Net sales	$32,601,594	$25,810,656	$20,649,001
Rentals from licensed departments	22,362	16,685	12,961
Other income-net	239,452	157,959	123,906
	32,863,408	25,985,300	20,785,868
Costs and expenses:			
Cost of sales	25,499,834	20,070,034	16,056,856
Operating, selling and general and administrative expenses	5,152,178	4,069,695	3,267,864
Interest costs:			
Debt	42,716	20,346	36,286
Capital leases	125,920	117,725	99,395
	30,820,648	24,277,800	19,460,401
Income before income taxes	2,042,760	1,707,500	1,325,467
Provision for federal and state income taxes:			
Current	737,020	608,912	474,016
Deferred	14,716	22,688	14,230
	751,736	631,600	488,246
Net income	$ 1,291,024	$ 1,075,900	$ 837,221
Net income per share	$ 1.14	$ .95*	$ .74*

Adjusted to reflect the two-for-one stock split on July 6, 1990.

See accompanying notes.

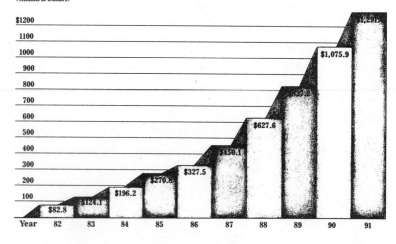

Net Income
(Millions of Dollars)

Consolidated Balance Sheets

Wal-Mart Stores, Inc. and Subsidiaries

(Amounts in thousands)	January 31,	
	1991	1990
ASSETS		
Current assets:		
Cash and cash equivalents	$ 13,014	$ 12,790
Receivables	305,070	155,811
Recoverable costs from sale/leaseback	239,867	78,727
Inventories:		
At replacement cost	6,207,852	4,750,619
Less LIFO reserve	399,436	322,546
LIFO	5,808,416	4,428,073
Prepaid expenses	48,408	37,215
TOTAL CURRENT ASSETS	6,414,775	4,712,616
Property, plant and equipment, at cost:		
Land	833,344	463,110
Buildings and improvements	1,764,155	1,227,519
Fixtures and equipment	2,037,476	1,441,752
Transportation equipment	63,237	57,215
	4,698,212	3,189,596
Less accumulated depreciation	974,060	711,763
Net property, plant and equipment	3,724,152	2,477,833
Property under capital leases	1,298,452	1,212,169
Less accumulated amortization	310,565	259,943
Net property under capital leases	987,887	952,226
Other assets and deferred charges	262,101	55,809
Total assets	$ 11,388,915	$ 8,198,484
LIABILITIES AND SHAREHOLDERS' EQUITY		
Current liabilities:		
Commercial paper	$ 395,179	$ 184,774
Accounts payable	2,651,315	1,826,720
Accrued liabilities:		
Salaries	189,535	157,216
Other	539,020	473,677
Accrued federal and state income taxes	184,512	179,049
Long-term debt due within one year	6,394	1,581
Obligations under capital leases due within one year	24,459	22,298
TOTAL CURRENT LIABILITIES	3,990,414	2,845,315
Long-term debt	740,254	185,152
Long-term obligations under capital leases	1,158,621	1,087,403
Deferred income taxes	134,102	115,053
Shareholders' equity:		
Common stock (shares outstanding, 1,142,282 in 1991 and 566,135 in 1990)	114,228	56,614
Capital in excess of par value	415,586	180,465
Retained earnings	4,835,710	3,728,482
TOTAL SHAREHOLDERS' EQUITY	5,365,524	3,965,561
Total liabilities and shareholders' equity	$ 11,388,915	$ 8,198,484

See accompanying notes.

Consolidated Statements of Shareholders' Equity

Wal-Mart Stores, Inc. and Subsidiaries

(Amounts in thousands except per share data)	Number of shares	Common stock	Capital in excess of par value	Retained earnings	Total
Balance - January 31, 1988	565,112	$ 56,511	$ 170,440	$2,030,316	$2,257,267
Net income				837,221	837,221
Cash dividends ($.08* per share)				(90,464)	(90,464)
Exercise of stock options	609	61	2,974		3,035
Tax benefit from stock options			4,778		4,778
Other	(130)	(13)	(3,915)		(3,928)
Balance - January 31, 1989	565,591	56,559	174,277	2,777,073	3,007,909
Net income				1,075,900	1,075,900
Cash dividends ($.11* per share)				(124,491)	(124,491)
Exercise of stock options	679	68	3,876		3,944
Tax benefit from stock options			7,000		7,000
Other	(135)	(13)	(4,688)		(4,701)
Balance - January 31, 1990	566,135	56,614	180,465	3,728,482	3,965,561
Net income				1,291,024	1,291,024
Cash dividends ($.14* per share)				(158,889)	(158,889)
Exercise of stock options	156	15	1,327		1,342
Other	(34)	(4)	(1,626)		(1,630)
Two-for-one stock split	566,257	56,625	(56,625)		
Exercise of stock options	506	51	2,427		2,478
Shares issued for McLane acquisition	10,366	1,037	273,659		274,696
Tax benefit from stock options			6,075		6,075
Purchase of stock	(1,000)	(100)	(819)	(24,907)	(25,826)
Walton Enterprises, Inc. stock exchange			14,000		14,000
Other	(104)	(10)	(3,297)		(3,307)
Balance - January 31, 1991	1,142,282	$ 114,228	$ 415,586	$4,835,710	$5,365,524

Cash dividends per share on stock prior to July 6, 1990, have been adjusted to reflect the two-for-one stock split on that date.

See accompanying notes.

Percentage of Return on Shareholders' Equity

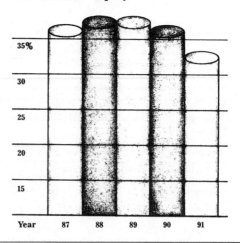

Consolidated Statements of Cash Flows

Wal-Mart Stores, Inc. and Subsidiaries

(Amounts in thousands)	Fiscal year ended January 31,		
	1991	1990	1989
Cash flows from operating activities:			
Net income	$ 1,291,024	$ 1,075,900	$ 837,221
Adjustments to reconcile net income to			
net cash provided by operating activities:			
Depreciation and amortization	346,614	269,406	213,629
Loss from sale of assets	3,378	5,039	1,073
Increase in accounts receivable	(58,324)	(29,173)	(30,710)
Increase in inventories	(1,087,520)	(1,076,706)	(699,607)
Decrease (increase) in prepaid expenses	11,823	(11,439)	(6,561)
Increase in accounts payable	689,435	436,990	289,769
Increase in accrued liabilities	84,739	174,112	114,954
Increase in deferred income tax	14,716	22,688	14,230
Net cash provided by operating activities	1,295,885	866,817	733,998
Cash flows from investing activities:			
Payments for property, plant and equipment	(1,388,298)	(954,602)	(592,756)
Recoverable sale/leaseback expenditures	(235,894)	(131,464)	(204,262)
Sale/leaseback arrangements			
and other property sales	91,000	184,900	246,797
Decrease in other assets	7,058	7,375	9,087
Net cash used in investing activities	(1,526,134)	(893,791)	(541,134)
Cash flows from financing activities:			
Increase (decrease) in commercial paper	30,405	165,774	(85,382)
Proceeds from issuance of long-term debt	500,306	4,763	1,624
Proceeds from Walton Enterprises, Inc. stock exchange	14,000	-	-
Exercise of stock options	4,958	243	3,885
Payments for purchase of common stock	(25,826)	-	-
Dividends paid	(158,889)	(124,491)	(90,464)
Payment of long-term debt	(109,304)	(4,159)	(3,213)
Payment of capital lease obligation	(25,177)	(20,919)	(18,086)
Net cash provided by (used in) financing activities	230,473	27,211	(191,636)
Net increase in cash and cash equivalents	224	237	1,228
Cash and cash equivalents at beginning of year	12,790	12,553	11,325
Cash and cash equivalents at end of year	$ 13,014	$ 12,790	$ 12,553
Supplemental disclosure of cash flow information:			
Income tax paid	$ 721,036	$ 551,021	$ 473,631
Interest paid	166,134	136,762	134,048
Capital lease obligations incurred	100,972	104,122	164,845
McLane Company, Inc. liabilities at acquisition date	513,000	-	-

See accompanying notes.

Notes to Consolidated Financial Statements

Wal-Mart Stores, Inc. and Subsidiaries

Note 1 Summary of significant accounting policies

Segment information—The Company and its subsidiaries are principally engaged in the operation of mass merchandising stores in a 35-state region. No single customer accounts for a significant portion of its consolidated sales.

Consolidation—The consolidated financial statements include the accounts of all subsidiaries.

Cash and cash equivalents—The Company considers all highly liquid investments with a maturity of three months or less when purchased, to be "cash equivalents."

Inventories—Inventories are stated principally at cost (last-in, first-out), which is not in excess of market, using the retail method for inventories in stores.

Pre-opening costs—Costs associated with the opening of new stores are expensed during the first full month of operations. The costs are carried as prepaid expenses prior to the store opening.

Recoverable costs from sale/leaseback—All costs of acquisition and construction of properties for which the Company has a commitment for sale/leaseback are accumulated in current assets until properties are sold.

Interest during construction—In order that interest costs properly reflect only that portion relating to current operations, interest on borrowed funds during the construction of property, plant and equipment is capitalized. Interest costs capitalized (excluding amounts related to properties developed under sale/leaseback arrangements) are $25,688,000, $16,688,000 and $8,801,000 in 1991, 1990 and 1989, respectively.

Depreciation—Depreciation for financial statement purposes is provided on the straight-line method over the estimated useful lives of the various assets. For income tax purposes, accelerated methods are used with recognition of deferred income taxes for the resulting timing differences.

Operating, selling and general and administrative expenses—Buying, warehousing and occupancy costs are included in operating, selling and general and administrative expenses.

Income taxes—Deferred income taxes are provided on timing differences between financial statement and taxable income.

Net income per share—Net income per share is based on the weighted average outstanding common shares and stock options reduced by shares assumed to have been purchased from such options under the treasury stock method.

Stock options—Proceeds from the sale of common stock issued under the stock option plans and related tax benefits which accrue to the Company are accounted for as capital transactions, and no charges or credits are made to income in connection with the plans.

Note 2 Notes payable and long-term debt

Information on short-term borrowings and interest rates follows:

	Fiscal years ended January 31,		
	1991	1990	1989
Maximum amount outstanding at month-end	$761,244,000	$846,600,000	$698,888,000
Average daily short-term borrowings	$345,452,000	$239,482,000	$321,370,000
Weighted average interest rate	8.2%	8.8%	7.7%

At January 31, 1991, the Company had committed lines of credit with ten banks to support short-term borrowings and commercial paper in an aggregate of $400,000,000. In addition, the Company had uncommitted facilities to support master participating agreements totalling $545,000,000. Short-term borrowings under these lines of credit bear interest at or below the prime rate.

Long-term debt at January 31 consists of:

		1991	1990
$9^1/_{10}$%	Notes due July 2000	$500,000,000	$ —
$10^7/_8$%	Debentures due August 2000	100,000,000	100,000,000
$8^1/_3$-$14^1/_8$%	Mortgage notes due 1991 through 2020	66,914,000	28,957,000
	Tax-exempt mortgage obligations, at an average rate of 7.9% due 1991 through 2014	32,395,000	15,705,000
$8^1/_2$%	Participating Mortgage Certificates II due 2005	22,924,000	23,303,000
9%	Participating Mortgage Certificates due 2005	14,615,000	14,762,000
	Other	3,406,000	2,425,000
		$740,254,000	$185,152,000

Long-term debt of $136,847,000 is collateralized by property with an aggregate carrying value of approximately $207,158,000.

Annual maturities on long-term debt during the next five years are:

Fiscal years ending January 31,	Annual maturity
1992	$ 6,394,000
1993	9,159,000
1994	7,756,000
1995	9,164,000
1996	6,130,000

Under the terms of the $9^1/_{10}$% Notes and $10^7/_8$% Debentures, the Company has agreed to observe certain covenants. Among these are provisions relating to amounts of additional secured debt and long-term leases.

The agreements relating to the Participating Mortgage Certificates contain provisions for contingent additional interest to be payable based on the sales performance of the Wal-Mart stores collateralized by the issues.

Note 3 Defined contribution plan

The Company maintains a profit sharing plan under which most full and many part-time associates become participants following one year of employment with the Company. Annual contributions, based on the profitability of the Company, are made at the sole discretion of the Company. Contributions were $98,327,000 in 1991, $90,447,000 in 1990, and $77,067,000 in 1989.

Note 4 Income taxes

Reconciliations of the statutory federal income tax rate to the effective tax rate, as a percent of pre-tax financial income, are as follows:

	1991	1990	1989
Statutory tax rate	34.0%	34.0%	34.0%
State income taxes	3.0	3.0	3.0
Other	(.2)	—	(.2)
Effective tax rate	36.8%	37.0%	36.8%

Deferred tax expense results from timing differences in the recognition of revenue and expense for tax and financial reporting purposes with respect to the following:

	1991	1990	1989
Depreciation	$ 44,144,000	$ 49,345,000	$ 30,632,000
Capital leases	(10,948,000)	(10,661,000)	(7,741,000)
Other	(18,480,000)	(15,996,000)	(8,661,000)
	$ 14,716,000	$ 22,688,000	$ 14,230,000

Note 5 Preferred and common stock

The Company has 100 million shares of $.10 preferred stock authorized but unissued.

There are 1.3 billion shares of $.10 par value common stock authorized, with 1,142,281,964 shares of common stock issued and outstanding at January 31, 1991, and 566,135,104 shares issued and outstanding at January 31, 1990. On May 31, 1990, the Board of Directors authorized a two-for-one stock split effected in the form of a 100% stock dividend paid on July 6, 1990. The common stock is listed on the New York Stock Exchange and the Pacific Stock Exchange, and at January 31, 1991, there were 122,414 shareholders of record.

At January 31, 1991, 8,363,521 shares of common stock were reserved for issuance under stock option plans. The options granted under the stock option plans expire 10 years from date of grant and may be exercised in nine annual installments. Further information concerning the options is as follows:

	Shares	Option price (market price at date of grant) Per share	Total
Shares under option			
January 31, 1990	7,103,402	$ .97-21.31	$ 96,215,999
Options granted	1,440,554	20.50-29.00	40,750,955
Options canceled	(260,918)	4.80-27.00	(4,663,722)
Options exercised	(818,056)	.97-21.31	(3,820,491)
January 31, 1991 (1,575,987 shares exercisable)	7,464,982	$ 1.16-29.00	$ 128,482,741
Shares available for option			
January 31, 1990	2,088,476		
January 31, 1991	898,539		

Note 6 Licensed department sales

The sales of licensed departments as reported by licensees are $140,893,000, $111,147,000 and $101,346,000 for 1991, 1990 and 1989, respectively.

Note 7 Long-term lease obligations

The Company and certain of its subsidiaries have long-term leases for stores and equipment. Rentals (including for certain leases amounts applicable to taxes, insurance, maintenance, other operating expenses and contingent rentals) under all operating leases were $267,455,000 in 1991, $233,390,000 in 1990 and $194,684,000 in 1989.

Aggregate minimum annual rentals at January 31, 1991, under noncancelable leases are as follows:

Fiscal years	Operating leases	Capital leases
1992	$ 228,006,000	$ 155,206,000
1993	231,551,000	156,406,000
1994	220,734,000	156,511,000
1995	212,670,000	156,195,000
1996	203,396,000	156,507,000
Thereafter	2,471,868,000	2,106,407,000
Total minimum rentals	$3,568,225,000	2,887,232,000
Less estimated executory costs		36,132,000
Net minimum lease payments		2,851,100,000
Less imputed interest at rates ranging from 8.5% to 14.0%		1,668,020,000
Present value of net minimum lease payments		$ 1,183,080,000

Certain of the leases provide for contingent additional rentals based on percentage of sales. Such additional rentals amounted to $23,204,000 in 1991, $22,128,000 in 1990 and $19,590,000 in 1989.

Substantially all of the store leases have renewal options for additional terms from five to 25 years at the same or lower minimum rentals.

The Company has entered into lease commitments for land and buildings for 69 future locations. The lease commitments with real estate developers or through sale/leaseback arrangements provide for minimum rentals for 20 to 25 years, excluding renewal options, which if consummated based on current cost estimates will approximate $26,228,000 annually over the lease terms.

Note 8 Acquisitions

On December 10, 1990, the Company acquired all of the outstanding common stock of McLane Company, Inc. (McLane). For its most recent fiscal year, McLane had sales of approximately $2,894,939,000, which included $596,217,000 in sales to the Company. This transaction was accounted for as a purchase and the results of operations of McLane since the date of its acquisition have been included in the results of operation of the Company. Pro forma results of operation are not presented for 1991 or 1990 due to insignificant differences from the historical results presented.

Effective February 2, 1991, the Company acquired 28 wholesale clubs in a purchase transaction of all the outstanding common stock of The Wholesale Club, Inc. For its most recent fiscal year, The Wholesale Club, Inc. had sales of $725,944,000.

Note 9 Quarterly financial data (unaudited)

Summarized consolidated quarterly financial data for 1991 and 1990 is as follows:

	Quarters ended			
1991	April 30,	July 31,	October 31,	January 31,
Net sales	$6,768,195,000	$7,543,510,000	$7,930,951,000	$10,358,938,000
Cost of sales	5,276,954,000	5,906,145,000	6,196,905,000	8,119,830,000
Net income	253,443,000	272,931,000	282,807,000	481,843,000
Net income per share	$.22*	$.24	$.25	$.42
1990				
Net sales	$5,373,260,000	$6,046,413,000	$6,283,497,000	$ 8,107,486,000
Cost of sales	4,171,610,000	4,728,606,000	4,881,263,000	6,288,555,000
Net income	198,289,000	219,048,000	232,701,000	425,862,000
Net income per share*	$.18	$.19	$.20	$.38

* Per share data prior to quarter ending July 31, 1990 have been adjusted to reflect the two-for-one stock split on July 6, 1990.

Net income for the quarter ended January 31, 1990 was increased $24,626,000 ($.02 per share) due to adjustment of the estimated inflation rate and other factors used to compute LIFO inventory cost for the first three quarters to the actual data for the year.

Report of Independent Auditors

The Board of Directors and Shareholders
Wal-Mart Stores, Inc.

We have audited the accompanying consolidated balance sheets of Wal-Mart Stores, Inc., and Subsidiaries as of January 31, 1991 and 1990, and the related consolidated statements of income, shareholders' equity, and cash flows for each of the three years in the period ended January 31, 1991. These financial statements are the responsibility of the Company's management. Our responsibility is to express an opinion on these financial statements based on our audits.

We conducted our audits in accordance with generally accepted auditing standards. Those standards require that we plan and perform the audit to obtain reasonable assurance about whether the financial statements are free of material misstatement. An audit includes examining, on a test basis, evidence supporting the amounts and disclosures in the financial statements. An audit also includes assessing the accounting principles used and significant estimates made by management, as well as evaluating the overall financial statement presentation. We believe that our audits provide a reasonable basis for our opinion.

In our opinion, the financial statements referred to above present fairly, in all material respects, the consolidated financial position of Wal-Mart Stores, Inc., and Subsidiaries at January 31, 1991 and 1990, and their consolidated results of operations and cash flows for each of the three years in the period ended January 31, 1991, in conformity with generally accepted accounting principles.

Ernst & Young

Ernst & Young

Tulsa, Oklahoma
March 26, 1991

Responsibility for Financial Statements

The financial statements and information of Wal-Mart Stores, Inc. and Subsidiaries presented in this Report have been prepared by management which has responsibility for their integrity and objectivity. These financial statements have been prepared in conformity with generally accepted accounting principles, applying certain estimates and judgments based upon currently available information and management's view of current conditions and circumstances. The services of certain specialists, both from within the Company and from outside the Company, have been utilized in making such estimates and judgments.

Management has developed and maintains a system of accounting and controls, including an extensive internal audit program, designed to provide reasonable assurance that the Company's assets are protected from improper use and that accounting records

provide a reliable basis for the preparation of financial statements. This system is continually reviewed, improved and modified in response to changing business conditions and operations and to recommendations made by the independent auditors and the internal auditors. Management believes that the accounting and control systems provide reasonable assurance that assets are safeguarded and financial information is reliable.

The Company has adopted a Statement of Responsibility which is intended to guide our management in the continued observance of high ethical standards of honesty, integrity and fairness in the conduct of the business and in accordance with the law. Compliance with the guidelines and standards is continuously reviewed and is acknowledged in writing by all management associates.

The Board of Directors, through the activities of its Audit Committee consisting solely of outside Directors, participates in the process of reporting financial information. The duties of the Committee include keeping informed of the financial condition of the Company and reviewing its financial policies and procedures, its internal accounting controls and the objectivity of its financial reporting. Both the Company's independent auditors and the internal auditors have free access to the Audit Committee and the Board of Directors and meet with the Committee periodically, with and without management present.

Paul R. Carter
Executive Vice President and
Chief Financial Officer

Corporate Information

Registrar and Transfer Agent
Boatmen's Trust Company
510 Locust Street
Post Office Box 14768
St. Louis, Missouri 63178

Trustee
$9^1/10\%$ Notes:
Harris Trust and Savings Bank
111 West Monroe Street
Chicago, Illinois 60690

$10^7/8\%$ Debentures:
Bankers Trust Company
4 Albany Street
Ninth Floor
New York, New York 10015

Independent Auditors
Ernst & Young
4300 One Williams Center
Tulsa, Oklahoma 74172

Listings
New York Stock Exchange
Stock Symbol: WMT

Pacific Stock Exchange
Stock Symbol: WMT

Annual Meeting
Our Annual Meeting of Shareholders will be held on Friday, June 7, 1991, at 10:00 a.m. in Barnhill Arena on the University of Arkansas campus, Fayetteville, Arkansas. You are cordially invited to attend. A proxy statement, including a request for proxies will be mailed to shareholders in early May, 1991.

Investors' Inquiries
Form 10-K Report
A copy of the Company's Annual Report on Form 10-K for the fiscal year ended January 31, 1991, as filed with the Securities and Exchange Commission, may be obtained without charge by writing to:
    Bette Hendrix
    Assistant Secretary
    Wal-Mart Stores, Inc.
    Bentonville, Arkansas 72716

Board of Directors

David R. Banks	Chairman of the Board, President, and Chief Executive Officer Beverly Enterprises
Paul R. Carter	Executive Vice President and Chief Financial Officer, Wal-Mart Stores, Inc.
Hillary Rodham Clinton	Partner, Rose Law Firm, P.A.
John A. Cooper, Jr.	Chairman of the Board, Cooper Communities, Inc.
Robert H. Dedman	Chairman of the Board, Club Corporation International
David D. Glass	President and Chief Executive Officer, Wal-Mart Stores, Inc.
F. Kenneth Iverson	Chairman of the Board and Chief Executive Officer, Nucor Corporation
A. L. Johnson	Vice Chairman, Wal-Mart Stores, Inc., Chief Executive Officer, Sam's Clubs, Division of Wal-Mart Stores, Inc.
James H. Jones	Chairman of the Board and Chief Executive Officer, Jameson Pharmaceutical Corp.
Robert Kahn	President, Robert Kahn and Associates Wal-Mart Stores, Inc. Consultant
R. Drayton McLane, Jr.	Vice Chairman, Wal-Mart Stores, Inc. President and Chief Executive Officer McLane Company, Inc., a wholly owned subsidiary of Wal-Mart Stores, Inc.
Jack Shewmaker	Vice Chairman, Retired, Wal-Mart Stores, Inc. Consultant
Donald G. Soderquist	Vice Chairman and Chief Operating Officer, Wal-Mart Stores, Inc.
John E. Tate	Executive Vice President, Retired, Wal-Mart Stores, Inc. Consultant
James L. Walton	Senior Vice President, Wal-Mart Stores, Inc.
Sam M. Walton	Chairman of the Board, Wal-Mart Stores, Inc.
S. Robson Walton	Vice Chairman, Wal-Mart Stores, Inc.

Committees Of The Board

Executive Committee
Paul R. Carter
David D. Glass
A.L. Johnson
R. Drayton McLane, Jr.
Donald G. Soderquist
James L. Walton
Sam M. Walton
S. Robson Walton

Audit Committee
F. Kenneth Iverson
James H. Jones
Robert Kahn

Stock Option Committee
David D. Glass
Donald G. Soderquist
S. Robson Walton

**Special
Stock Option Committee**
John A. Cooper, Jr.
F. Kenneth Iverson
James H. Jones

APPENDIX B—TIME VALUE OF MONEY

State lotteries that advertise million dollar payoffs typically pay these amounts over 20 years or so. The sweepstakes that various publishers send also speak of millions, but also to be paid over some future period. Would you prefer getting $1 million today, or $50,000 per year for 20 years (which adds up to $1 million)? Ignoring some potentially tricky tax matters, you should prefer the $1 million today. A dollar received today is worth more than a dollar to be received in the future. This is because even if you will not need the money until some time in the future, you can take the dollar you get today and invest it so that you will have more than a dollar in the future. (If you invested $1 million today, you could earn $70,000 to $90,000 income per year forever, with relatively low risk, which is better than $50,000 per year for 20 years.) This point sums up the important principle of the *time value of money*, which is basic to many areas of accounting, including pricing bonds and making investment decisions such as acquiring machinery for a factory. The time value of money is important any time you receive or pay cash at some future date.

PRESENT VALUE

The usual way that we consider the time value of money is to calculate *present values* or to *discount* future cash flows back to the present. The concept of present value is related to that of *compound interest*, which is earning interest on interest as well as on principal. Perhaps the easiest way to understand present values is to start with *future values* and analyze a decision in that way. Suppose that you have the choice of receiving $1,000 today or $1,500 at the end of five years. Suppose the interest rate you could earn on the $1,000 to be received today is 10%. If you invest $1,000 in a savings account at 10% interest compounded annually, the balance in the account, the future value, after five years is $1,611.

Year	Principal at Beginning of Year	Interest at 10%	Principal at End of Year
	(a)	(b)	(a + b)
1	$1,000	$1,000 × 10% = $100	$1,100
2	$1,100	$1,100 × 10% = $110	$1,210
3	$1,210	$1,210 × 10% = $121	$1,331
4	$1,331	$1,331 × 10% = $133	$1,464
5	$1,464	$1,464 × 10% = $147	$1,611

This schedule tells us that we are better off taking $1,000 today than $1,500 in five years, *at a 10% rate of interest.* We could have considerably more than $1,500 by investing the $1,000 today.

We could also have found the future value using the formula,

$$FV = (1 + i)^n$$

where *FV* is future value of $1, i = the interest rate, and n = the number of periods. We then multiply the amount by the future value of $1. In our example, $FV = (1.10)^5 = 1.6105$ (round to 1.611), so multiplying by $1,000 gives $1,611. The future value of $1,000 is $1,611 at the end of five years. *Therefore, the present value of $1,611 to be received in five years is $1,000.* The relationship between present and future values is reciprocal. Table A shows present value factors for single payments. These factors are based on the formula,

$$PV = 1/(1 + i)^n$$

which is the reciprocal of the future value formula.

Many calculators and computer programs include future and present value functions. Table A (page 780) shows that the present value factor for five periods at 10% is .621, which is 1/1.611 (rounded). Multiplying $1,611 by 0.621 results in a present value of $1,000 (rounded). So we could also make the decision (accept the $1,000 today) by finding the present value of the $1,500 to be received in five years.

$$PV = \$5,000 \times 0.621 = \$931.50$$

The $931.50 is less than $1,000, again indicating that $1,000 today is worth more than $1,500 to be received in five years.

Present Value of Annuity

An *annuity* is a stream of equal payments. Bonds typically pay interest every six months, long-term leases require annual payments, and some investments yield the same flow every year. We can find the present value of an annuity by finding the present value of each payment and adding the present values together, but there is an easier way. Table B (page 781) shows present value factors for annuities of $1. The factors are, except for some rounding, the cumulative sums of the factors in Table A. Look at the factor for 12% and three years in Table B, 2.402. It is the sum of the factors for one, two, and three periods in Table A (.893 + .797 + .712 = 2.402).

Extending our previous example, suppose we wish to know whether we should accept a lump sum of $3,500 today, or a $1,000 annuity for five years, with payments to be received at the ends of the years. The interest rate is 8%. Using the present value factors from Table A, we can calculate the following.

Payments	1	2	3	4	5

Present
Value
$ 926 = _____ $1,000 × .926
    857 = _____ $1,000 × .857
    794 = _____ $1,000 × .794
    735 = _____ $1,000 × .735
    681 = _____ $1,000 × .681
$3,993

Because the present value of the receipts is greater than the lump sum, we should opt to receive the annuity rather than the lump sum.

There is an easier approach to finding the present value of an annuity. Table B gives factors for present values of annuities of $1. Using the present value factor from Table B gives the same result we obtained before.

$$\$1,000 \times 3.993 = \$3,993$$

It is usually more convenient to use the table, especially when there are many payments. Any pattern of payments can be handled as a set of single payments. It is easier if the payments are the same, so that we can use the annuity factors.

Determining a Mortgage Payment

In determining the present value of a mortgage payment, we can use the relationship used above to find the present value of an annuity.

Periodic Payment × Annuity Factor = Present Value
$1,000   ×   3.993   = $3,993

If, for example, the mortgage is for $300,000 for five years at 8%, the present value in the equation above is the amount borrowed

($300,000), the factor is the annuity factor for a five-period annuity at 8% (3.993), and we solve for the periodic payment.

$$\text{Periodic Payment} \times \text{Annuity Factor} = \text{Present Value}$$
$$\text{Periodic Payment} \times \quad 3.993 \quad = \quad \$300,000$$
$$\text{Periodic Payment} = \frac{\$300,000}{3.993} = \$75,131.48$$

The annual mortgage payment is thus $75,131.48. This mortgage ($300,000 for five years at 8%) is the mortgage amortized in the Chapter 7 Demonstration Problem.

Finding Interest Rates

Many times you need to find the interest rate, or discount rate, that a particular pattern of cash receipts and payments yields. Computers are especially helpful here because they can do complex calculations very quickly. We shall be content with finding rates for simple cases, using the present value tables.

Interest Rate for Single Payment

Suppose you could have $1,920 at the end of five years by investing $1,000 today. What is the interest rate? Remember that we find the present value of a single payment by

$$PV = \text{Payment} \times \text{Factor from Table A}$$

Here we know the present value ($1,000) and the payment ($1,920), but not the factor. Rearranging the formula, we have

$$\text{Factor} = \frac{PV}{\text{Payment}}$$
$$= \frac{\$1,000}{\$1,920}$$
$$= .521$$

We know that .521 is the factor for five periods and an unknown interest rate. We can therefore look through Table A in the 5-year row and find the closest factor. At 14% we find .519, which is close enough. We can say, then, that the interest rate is a bit less than 14% because .521 is greater than .519. Notice that as we go across the row, the factors get smaller, so we know that a higher factor means a lower rate.

Interest Rate for an Annuity

Suppose now that you could earn $1,000 per year for 10 years by investing $4,830 today. What is the interest rate? Again, the present value calculation is

$$PV = \text{Annuity} \times \text{Factor from Table B}$$

We again know the annuity and its present value, so the factor is

$$\text{Factor} = \frac{PV}{\text{Annuity}} = \frac{\$4,830}{\$1,000} = 4.83$$

Searching the 10-year row, we find 4.833 in the 16% column, so we know that the investment has an interest rate a bit higher than 16%.

Periods Other Than Years

In many cases the period that we are interested in is less than a year. You have seen advertisements for savings certificates stating that they earn, say, 8.5% to yield 8.88%. The higher yield is caused by compounding more than once a year. Suppose that a savings certificate earns 10% but is compounded semiannually. That means it earns 5% each six-month period, and the compounding will raise the return over 10%. The following schedule shows the effect of more frequent compounding.

Period	Principal at Beginning of Period	Interest at 5%	Principal at End of Period
	(a)	(b)	(a + b)
1	$1,000.00	$1,000.00 × 5% = $50.00	$1,050.00
2	$1,050.00	$1,050.00 × 5% = $52.50	$1,102.50
3	$1,102.50	$1,102.50 × 5% = $55.12	$1,157.62
4	$1,157.62	$1,157.62 × 5% = $57.88	$1,215.50

Thus, after two years (four six-month periods), $1,000 at 5% per six-month period gives $1,215.50, which is more than you would have if you invested at 10% compounded annually. In our first example, the investment of $1,000 at 10% grew to $1,210 at the end of two years. The difference here is not great, but it can become significant with large amounts of money invested over long periods.

Using present value tables requires an additional step when compounding is more frequent. The present value of $1,215.50 at 10% for two years is $1,004.00 ($1,215.50 × 0.826 from Table A), not $1,000.

What we must do to adjust for the more frequent compounding is to use the 5% interest rate and four periods, not 10% and two periods. Thus, using Table A, we have $PV = \$1,215.50 \times 0.823 = \$1,000.36$, which differs from $1,000.00 because of rounding. When you deal with periods shorter than a year, you divide the interest rate by the number of compoundings (usually two) and multiply the number of periods by the number of compoundings. Thus, you should think of Tables A and B as giving factors for *periods,* not necessarily for years.

DEMONSTRATION PROBLEMS

Go through the next few problems carefully to be sure you understand the principles.

1. You want to accumulate $100,000 by the end of ten years to begin your own business. (a) How much must you invest today at 10% to achieve your objective? (b) How much must you invest today at 10% compounded semiannually (5% per six-month period)?

2. You have the opportunity to make an investment that will yield $10,000 per year for ten years. The investment costs $61,000. At a 12% interest rate, should you make the investment? What is the approximate interest rate on the investment?

3. An investment should return $10,000 per year for four years and $30,000 at the end of the fifth year. What is the most you would be willing to pay for this investment if your discount rate is 12%?

4. What is the interest rate on a $10,000 investment that returns $25,000 at the end of five years?

Solutions to Demonstration Problems

1. This problem requires finding the present value of $100,000 due at the end of 10 years.

    a. Using Table A, we have $100,000 × 0.386 = $38,600. You need to invest $38,600 today at 10% to have $100,000 in 10 years.

    b. Again, we use Table A, but we use 5% and 20 periods to get $100,000 × 0.377 = $37,700. You need to invest less when compounding is semiannual than when it is annual, at the same annual interest rate.

2. This problem requires finding the present value of an annuity and comparing it to the $61,000 investment. Using Table B, we have *PV* = $10,000 × 5.65 = $56,500. The present value of $10,000 per year for 10 years is $56,500. That is the most you should be willing to pay for the $10,000 annuity. Therefore, you should not pay $61,000 to make this investment. The interest rate is less than 12% because the present value of the inflows is less than the investment. The factor is $61,000/$10,000 = 6.100. The closest factor in the 10-year row is 6.145 for 10%. The rate is therefore a bit greater than 10%.

3. This problem has two parts. We solve it the long way shown below, then take advantage of the pattern that there is a $10,000 five-year annuity plus an extra $20,000 at the end of year five.

Year	Amount	PV Factor	PV
1	$10,000	.893	$ 8,930
2	10,000	.797	7,970
3	10,000	.712	7,120
4	10,000	.636	6,360
5	30,000	.567	17,010
Total			$47,390

The easiest way to handle such a pattern is to find the present value of a five-year annuity of $10,000 and the present value of $20,000 at the end of five years.

$$PV = (\$10,000 \times 3.605) + (\$20,000 \times .567) = \$47,390$$

We could also do a four-year annuity of $10,000 plus a single payment of $30,000. PV = ($10,000 × 3.037) + ($30,000 × .567) = $47,380
The difference occurs from rounding.

4. This is a single payment.

$$PV\ factor = \frac{\$10,000}{\$25,000} = .400$$

The closest factor in the 5-year row is .402, the factor for 20%. The rate is therefore a bit less than 20%.

Table A
Present Value of $1

Time period

	8%	10%	12%	14%	15%	16%	17%	18%	20%	22%	24%	28%	30%
1	0.926	0.909	0.893	0.877	0.870	0.862	0.855	0.847	0.833	0.820	0.806	0.781	0.769
2	0.857	0.826	0.797	0.769	0.756	0.743	0.731	0.718	0.694	0.672	0.650	0.610	0.592
3	0.794	0.751	0.712	0.675	0.658	0.641	0.624	0.609	0.579	0.551	0.524	0.477	0.455
4	0.735	0.683	0.636	0.592	0.572	0.552	0.534	0.516	0.482	0.451	0.423	0.373	0.350
5	0.681	0.621	0.567	0.519	0.497	0.476	0.456	0.437	0.402	0.370	0.341	0.291	0.269
6	0.630	0.564	0.507	0.456	0.432	0.410	0.390	0.370	0.335	0.303	0.275	0.227	0.207
7	0.583	0.513	0.452	0.400	0.376	0.354	0.333	0.314	0.279	0.249	0.222	0.178	0.159
8	0.540	0.467	0.404	0.351	0.327	0.305	0.285	0.266	0.233	0.204	0.179	0.139	0.123
9	0.500	0.424	0.361	0.308	0.284	0.263	0.243	0.225	0.194	0.167	0.144	0.108	0.094
10	0.463	0.386	0.322	0.270	0.247	0.227	0.208	0.191	0.162	0.137	0.116	0.085	0.073
11	0.429	0.350	0.287	0.237	0.215	0.195	0.178	0.162	0.135	0.112	0.094	0.066	0.056
12	0.397	0.319	0.257	0.208	0.187	0.168	0.152	0.137	0.112	0.092	0.076	0.052	0.043
13	0.368	0.290	0.229	0.182	0.163	0.145	0.130	0.116	0.093	0.075	0.061	0.040	0.033
14	0.340	0.263	0.205	0.160	0.141	0.125	0.111	0.099	0.078	0.062	0.049	0.032	0.025
15	0.315	0.239	0.183	0.140	0.123	0.108	0.095	0.084	0.065	0.051	0.040	0.025	0.020
16	0.292	0.218	0.163	0.123	0.107	0.093	0.081	0.071	0.054	0.042	0.032	0.019	0.015
17	0.270	0.198	0.146	0.108	0.093	0.080	0.069	0.060	0.045	0.034	0.026	0.015	0.012
18	0.250	0.180	0.130	0.095	0.081	0.069	0.059	0.051	0.038	0.028	0.021	0.012	0.009
19	0.232	0.164	0.116	0.083	0.070	0.060	0.051	0.043	0.031	0.023	0.017	0.009	0.007
20	0.215	0.149	0.104	0.073	0.061	0.051	0.043	0.037	0.026	0.019	0.014	0.007	0.005
25	0.146	0.092	0.059	0.038	0.030	0.024	0.020	0.016	0.010	0.007	0.005	0.002	0.001
30	0.099	0.057	0.033	0.020	0.015	0.012	0.009	0.007	0.004	0.003	0.002	0.001	0.000

Table B
Present Value of $1 Annuity

	8%	10%	12%	14%	15%	16%	17%	18%	20%	22%	24%	28%	30%
1	0.926	0.909	0.893	0.877	0.870	0.862	0.855	0.847	0.833	0.820	0.806	0.781	0.769
2	1.783	1.736	1.690	1.647	1.626	1.605	1.585	1.566	1.528	1.492	1.457	1.392	1.361
3	2.577	2.487	2.402	2.322	2.283	2.246	2.210	2.174	2.106	2.042	1.981	1.868	1.816
4	3.312	3.170	3.037	2.914	2.855	2.798	2.743	2.690	2.589	2.494	2.404	2.241	2.166
5	3.993	3.791	3.605	3.433	3.352	3.274	3.199	3.127	2.991	2.864	2.745	2.532	2.436
6	4.623	4.355	4.111	3.889	3.784	3.685	3.589	3.498	3.326	3.167	3.020	2.759	2.643
7	5.206	4.868	4.564	4.288	4.160	4.039	3.922	3.812	3.605	3.416	3.242	2.937	2.802
8	5.747	5.335	4.968	4.639	4.487	4.344	4.207	4.078	3.837	3.619	3.421	3.076	2.925
9	6.247	5.759	5.328	4.946	4.772	4.607	4.451	4.303	4.031	3.786	3.566	3.184	3.019
10	6.710	6.145	5.650	5.216	5.019	4.833	4.659	4.494	4.192	3.923	3.682	3.269	3.092
11	7.139	6.495	5.938	5.453	5.234	5.029	4.836	4.656	4.327	4.035	3.776	3.335	3.147
12	7.536	6.814	6.194	5.660	5.421	5.197	4.988	4.793	4.439	4.127	3.851	3.387	3.190
13	7.904	7.103	6.424	5.842	5.583	5.342	5.118	4.910	4.533	4.203	3.912	3.427	3.223
14	8.244	7.367	6.628	6.002	5.724	5.468	5.229	5.008	4.611	4.265	3.962	3.459	3.249
15	8.559	7.606	6.811	6.142	5.847	5.575	5.324	5.092	4.675	4.315	4.001	3.483	3.268
16	8.851	7.824	6.974	6.265	5.954	5.668	5.405	5.162	4.730	4.357	4.033	3.503	3.283
17	9.122	8.022	7.120	6.373	6.047	5.749	5.475	5.222	4.775	4.391	4.059	3.518	3.295
18	9.372	8.201	7.250	6.467	6.128	5.818	5.534	5.273	4.812	4.419	4.080	3.529	3.304
19	9.604	8.365	7.366	6.550	6.198	5.877	5.584	5.316	4.843	4.442	4.097	3.539	3.311
20	9.818	8.514	7.469	6.623	6.259	5.929	5.628	5.353	4.870	4.460	4.110	3.546	3.316
25	10.675	9.077	7.843	6.873	6.464	6.097	5.766	5.467	4.948	4.514	4.147	3.564	3.329
30	11.258	9.427	8.055	7.003	6.566	6.177	5.829	5.517	4.979	4.534	4.160	3.569	3.332

INDEX

disposal of plant assets, 199–204
dividend payout ratio, 665
dividend yield, 664–665
dividend-payout ratio, 305–307
dividends, 24, 285–292
  declaration date, 288
  payment date, 288
  record date, 288
  stock dividends, 289–292
  stock splits, 293
donated assets, 167
double declining balance depreciation, 174–175
double-entry accounting, 9
drop or add a segment, 437–439
dual rate allocation, 549–550

earnings disclosures and statement analysis, 673–678
earnings per share, 661–663
economic entity, 21, 584
effective interest rate, 244
effective interest rate amortization, bonds, 250–251
entity concept, 8
equity securities, unrealized losses, 305
equivalent production, 405–409
ethics of managerial accountants, 358–359
ex-dividend, 288
expense budget, 464
expenses, 15
external auditor, 609
  and internal auditor, 610
  duties, 613–614
  independence, 611
extraordinary items, 675

FIFO, 140–143
financial statement analysis, 636–678
financial statement disclosure in statement analysis, 667–672
Financial Accounting Standards Board (FASB), 7
financing activities, 327
finished goods, 373–375, 388–389, 403, 408, 410
first-in, first out, see FIFO
fixed and variable costs, 362–363
fixed asset turnover, 220
fixed overhead applied, 494–495
fixed overhead variances, 494–495
flexible budget, 464–466
flow of costs, 373–377

foreign currency adjustment in owners' equity, 303–305
formulas
  accounts receivable turnover, 668
  annual depreciation expense, 171
  book ROI, 529
  cash flow to net income, 668
  cash return on sales, 668
  cost-volume-profit analysis, 424, 428, 430
  current ratio, 668
  days' sales in accounts receivable, 668
  days' sales in inventory, 668
  debt ratio, 668
  debt-to-equity ratio, 668
  direct labor variances, 492
  dividend payout ratio, 668
  dividend yield, 668
  earnings per share, 688
  fixed overhead variances, 495
  growth rate of EPS, 668
  inventory turnover, 668
  materials variances, 496
  overall cash flow ratio, 668
  overhead rate, 398
  per unit depletion, 207
  predetermined rate, 401
  present value factor, 522
  present value of flows, 522
  price-earnings ratio, 668
  purchases budget, 467
  quick ratio, 668
  residual income, 555
  return on assets, 668
  return on common equity, 668
  return on investment, 668
  ROI, 544
  sum-of-the-years'-digits, 174
  times interest earned, 668
  total cost, 363
  unit cost, 405
  variable cost variances, 497
  variable overhead variances, 493
  working capital, 668
franchises, 211
freight-in, 129
full costing, see absorption costing
future value, 240

GAAP, see generally accepted accounting principles
gains and losses, 328–330
general journal, 62
general purpose financial statements, 7
generally accepted accounting principles (GAAP), 6

going concern principle, 12
goodwill, 213–217, 588–589
gross margin inventory method, 145
gross price inventory method, 136–138
gross profit ratio, 647–649
group depreciation, 175–176

hedging, 255
high-low method, 365–366
horizontal analysis, 638–641
hurdle rate, 520

impairment of plant assets, 205
imposed budgets, 461
improvements to land, 165
inadequacy of productive assets, 169
income statement, 14
incremental budgeting, 462–463
indirect method of cash from operations, 322–334
installment method of revenue recognition, 100
intangibles, 209–219
interest computation formula, 97
internal auditor
  and external auditor, 610
  auditing standards (GAAS), 624
  Certified Internal Auditor (CIA), 610–611
  duties, 613–614
  independence, 611
  reports, 624–627
internal control, 78–80, 83–84, 615–618
  lapping, 616
  limited access, 618
  mandatory vacations, 617
  prenumbered documents, 615–616
  separation of duties, 616–617
internal rate of return, (IRR), 521–523
international
  accounting and auditing, 624
  aspects of managerial accounting, 359
  debt denominated in foreign currency, 253–255
  foreign currency adjustment in owners' equity, 303–305
  restrictions on LIFO, 142–143
inventoriable costs, see product cost
inventory, 126–149
  estimating methods, 144–147
  FIFO, 140–143
  LIFO, 141–143